SIXTH EDITION

Reading Strategies and Practices

A Compendium

Robert J. Tierney
University of British Columbia

John E. Readence
University of Nevada, Las Vegas

Boston ▪ New York ▪ San Francisco
Mexico City ▪ Montreal ▪ Toronto ▪ London ▪ Madrid ▪ Munich ▪ Paris
Hong Kong ▪ Singapore ▪ Tokyo ▪ Cape Town ▪ Sydney

Senior Editor: *Aurora Martínez Ramos*
Series Editorial Assistant: *Erin Beatty*
Executive Marketing Manager: *Amy Cronin Jordan*
Editorial-Production Service: *Omegatype Typography, Inc.*
Manufacturing Buyer: *Andrew Turso*
Composition and Prepress Buyer: *Linda Cox*
Cover Administrator: *Kristina Mose Libon*
Electronic Composition: *Omegatype Typography, Inc.*

For related titles and support materials, visit our online catalog at www.ablongman.com.

Between the time Website information is gathered and published, some sites may have closed. Also, the transcription of URLs can result in typographical errors. The publisher would appreciate notification where these errors occur so that they may be corrected in subsequent editions.

Library of Congress Cataloging-in-Publication Data

Tierney, Robert J.
Reading strategies and practices : a compendium / Robert J. Tierney, John E. Readence.—6th ed.
p. cm.
Includes bibliographical references and index.
ISBN 0-205-38639-3
1. Reading. 2. Reading comprehension. I. Readence, John, E. II. Title.

LB1050.T57 2005

2004040113

Printed in the United States of America

10 9 8 7 6 5 4 3 2 1 09 08 07 06 05 04

Contents

Preface

This new edition of *Reading Strategies and Practices: A Compendium* represents a significant improvement over the earlier editions. Some of the changes that were made include the following:

- Overviews relating strategies and practices to developments in the field, including policy matters
- Addition of new strategies and practices
- Revision of existing descriptions of strategies, especially the cautions and comments for each strategy
- Updated lists of references
- Addition of several new strategies and deletion of some others within existing units
- Discussion of each strategy in terms of current research findings that addresses their utility and in terms of recommendations from major research syntheses.

This book is a compendium of strategies; it is not a description of a single approach, nor is it intended to be eclectic. The inclusion of a strategy should not be perceived as our endorsement of that strategy. There are some strategies that we view as problematic; there are others about which we disagree.

We appreciate those of you who have used the book, especially those colleagues who gave us feedback for this revision. We hope you will find this new edition even more useful than its predecessors. Ideally, the book will stimulate reflection, discussion, evaluation, and intelligent use of instructional procedures. We especially want it to fill a void by being a ready reference for teachers and prospective teachers who want a clear, overall perspective of instructional procedures and who approach their teaching with a view to experimentation and decision making. The first five editions were used in numerous courses at the undergraduate and graduate level for such purposes; the new edition should have similar utility. We also recommend the book to administrators and others concerned with reading improvement—including parents.

Finally, we would like to thank several individuals who helped with the book. We would like to acknowledge our colleagues' contributions. We thank Ruth Allman for her assistance with library research. We greatly appreciate the support of Aurora Martínez with Allyn and Bacon, and of Omegatype Typography, Inc.

Allyn and Bacon thanks the reviewers of this edition, who provided many helpful comments: Terri L. Brandvold, Idaho State University; Deborah E. Doty, Northern Kentucky University; Shelly Hong Xu, California State University, Long Beach; Lilian McEnery, University of Houston–Clear Lake; and Glenda Jo Pennington, Ohio Valley College.

How to Use This Book

Intended Purposes

The purpose of this book is to afford the reader an active role in examining and evaluating instructional techniques. We do not expect readers to become familiar with all of the strategies or practices presented in the text, nor do we even advocate reading the text from cover to cover. Rather, we recommend reading it selectively and reflectively. Readers should select the units and strategies they wish to review and evaluate.

How Is This Book Organized?

For organizational purposes, the text is divided into 14 units. Within each unit we delineate our intent and provide recommendations as well as cautions for using various strategies and practices. The 14 units under which the strategies and practices have been classified are as follows:

Unit 1: Lesson Frameworks for Literacy Support
Unit 2: Holistic, Whole-Language, Learner-Centered, and Literature-Based Approaches
Unit 3: Developing Literacies through Language Experience, Shared Reading, and Use of Multiple Representations
Unit 4: Intervention Programs for At-Risk Readers
Unit 5: Phonics and Word Identification
Unit 6: Oral Reading
Unit 7: Comprehension Development and Thinking Critically
Unit 8: Meaning Vocabulary
Unit 9: Responding to Reading as Writers and Genre Study
Unit 10: Response to Literature and Drama
Unit 11: Discussion and Cooperative Learning
Unit 12: Content Area Literacy

Unit 13: Studying

Unit 14: Assessment Strategies for Classrooms, Teachers, and Students

Some readers may disagree with the separation of teaching strategies and practices into these particular strands. This breakdown is intended as one viable method of organization; it is not suggested as a divinely inspired division of reading or curriculum.

The 14 units of this text describe more than 85 strategies and practices. As an aid to examining and evaluating these techniques, each unit provides the reader with an overview and a consistent organizational pattern. The following section describes how these aids might be used.

Unit Overview

At the beginning of each unit, an overview provides an introduction to the various strategies and practices presented in that section. This overview serves three essential purposes:

1. Since only selected strategies have been included within the various units, the overview provides information on the rationale for selecting strategies.

2. Since several strategies could be classified into more than one unit, the overview provides information on the basis for the present classification.

3. The overview provides the reader with a brief orientation, which enables purposeful reading of each section and thus facilitates the evaluation, comparison, and intelligent selection of strategies and practices or their adaptations.

Strategies and Practices

In detailing the major features of the various strategies and practices, the discussion of each adopts the following framework:

Purpose
Rationale
Intended Audience
Description of the Procedures
Cautions and Comments

Users of this book should realize that the description of the procedures should not displace their exploration of the primary sources, as these primary sources have fuller descriptions and include details, suggestions, and cautions (including the voices of the developers and others) that we are not able to include in this volume.

About the Authors

Robert J. Tierney is Dean of the Faculty of Education at the University of British Columbia. He received his Ph.D. from the University of Georgia and has been a member of the faculty at the Ohio State University, the University of Illinois, Harvard University, and the University of Arizona. A teacher, consultant, and researcher in both the United States and Australia, Dr. Tierney has written books and numerous articles dealing with theory, research, and practice on literacy, literacy education, and assessment.

John E. Readence received his M.A. at the Ohio State University and his Ph.D. in reading education from Arizona State University. A teacher at both the public school and college levels and a consultant for numerous school districts, Dr. Readence has published many articles and textbooks in the education field. He has held positions at Kansas State University, the University of Georgia, and Louisiana State University, among others, and currently serves as Professor of Education at the University of Nevada, Las Vegas. He is the past editor of *Reading Research Quarterly.* His current instructional and research interests focus on teachers' thought processes and literacy acquisition, K–12.

UNIT 1

Lesson Frameworks for Literacy Support

UNIT OVERVIEW

In most classrooms, teachers approach reading instruction and content area learning (e.g., social studies and science) with a general framework within which students are guided through a range of activities. The present unit describes seven frameworks that have been labeled *lesson frameworks for reader support.* The first framework, Guided Reading, was developed in conjunction with the exploration of the Reading Recovery within the context of regular classrooms in which students are engaged in reading carefully leveled trade books. The second framework, Four Blocks, engages students in four sets of reading-writing activities tied to either trade books or anthologized selections. Two of the strategies (Directed Reading Activity and Directed Reading-Thinking Activity) are used primarily with short selections included in anthologies such as those mostly associated with basal or basic reading programs. The strategy Scaffolded Reading Experience is used primarily with content area textbook material. Direct Instruction is an approach to teaching reading based on a model of teaching that has its roots in behavioristic orientation to student engagement as well as a careful analysis of the component skills needed by individual readers. Finally, New Basics and Rich Literacy Tasks represent an important precursor for advent of literacy programs designed to prepare students for the multiple literacies that already exist in the day-to-day experiences of students as they enlist digitally based technologies and other text forms in a multilayered and multimedia world.

Each of these frameworks represents a combination of practices that reflects what the proponents of these practices view as likely to support literacy development. Over the last few years, discussions of these core programs have increased as notions of evidence-based practice are being debated alongside of the realization that equating these models with the notion of a single best approach is problematic. Indeed, whereas most literacy education researchers are adamant that the notion of a single best approach to literacy is wrongheaded to meet different students' needs, many literacy educators would suggest that there are some elements in common across more effective versus less effective reading approaches tied to evaluations of evidence-based practices. In turn, they would suggest that the frameworks such as those included in this unit offer a way of organizing literacy instruction so that some of these elements are included. In accordance with these notions, the International Reading Association (2002) has a position statement on evidence-based practices that queries notions of "best" programs at the same time that it suggests what it deems to be evidence-based practices:

> Time and again, research has confirmed that regardless of the quality of a program, resource, or strategy, it is the teacher and learning situation that make the difference (Bond and Dykstra, 1967/1997). This evidence underscores the need to join practices grounded in sound and rigorous research with well-prepared and skillful teachers. . . .
>
> In its simplest form, *evidence-based reading instruction* means that a particular program or collection of instructional practices has a record of success. That is, there is reliable, trustworthy, and valid evidence to suggest that when the program is used with a particular group of children, the children can be expected to make adequate gains in reading achievement. . . . In addition to evaluating the quality of the data by which programs or practices are judged, teachers also must ask if the children in their classroom closely resemble the children from whom the evidence was collected. . . . [I]f the answer to all of these questions is yes, then teachers might conclude that there is a good fit and that their children might be expected to make similar achievement gains with the same program or practice. If, however, the answer to some or all of our questions is no, then it is difficult to predict whether similar results might be achieved.
>
> The quest to find the "best programs" for teaching reading has a long and quite unsuccessful history. . . .
>
> Current critical and comprehensive research reviews . . . indicate widespread agreement among literacy experts concerning the particular literacy practices and experiences in which effective teachers routinely engage children. . . .
>
> - Teach reading for authentic meaning making literacy experience
> - Use high-quality literature
> - Integrate comprehensive word study/phonics program into reading/writing instruction
> - Use multiple texts that link and expand concepts
> - Balance teacher- and student-led discussions
> - Build a whole-class community that emphasizes important concepts and builds background knowledge
> - Work with students in small groups while other students read and write about what they have read
> - Give students plenty of time to read in class
> - Give students direct instruction in decoding and comprehension
> - Use a variety of assessment techniques to inform instruction
>
> The challenge that confronts teachers and administrators is the need to view the evidence that they read through the lens of their particular school and classroom setting. (International Reading Association, 2002, 232–236)

Comments by other educational professionals reflect similar sentiments. For example, Taylor, Pressley, and Pearson (2002), in their comprehensive review and studies of effective schools, stress the need for caution in importing findings from one setting to another setting, but they do suggest that the more effective settings have certain characteristics. In so doing, they stress that the *how* may be more important than the *what*. Included in the elements that they identify is a balanced approach that includes a mix of reading materials, support for reading, directed and independent learning opportunities, and grouping patterns as well as effort for sustained engagement of students in reading and teachers on literacy improvement through coaching, use of assessment sources, parental engagement, and professional development and mentoring. The frameworks selected for inclusion in this text constitute a subset only. Other units within the compendium describe pratices that could be viewed as affording lesson frameworks for reading and writing. Indeed, it is difficult to distinguish the goals and intended scope of the present practices from the frameworks offered in several others—especially Unit 2 (Holistic, Whole-Language, Learner-Centered, and Literature-Based Approaches) as well as selected practices described in other units.

Guided Reading. Developed by Irene Fountas and Gay Su Pinnell, Guided Reading is a means of engaging students in meaningful reading of extended texts in conjunction with developing problem-solving abilities with the support of teacher guidance and other students.

Four Blocks (Cunningham, Hall, and Defee, 1991, 1998). Designed to meet the needs of students reading at multiple reading levels, Four Blocks is a framework for beginning reading instruction that uses a combination of major instructional approaches to reading: guided reading, self-selected reading, working with words, and writing.

Directed Reading Activity (DRA). Over the years, the Directed Reading Activity has probably been the most widely used framework for a "total" reading lesson. In many ways, it has served as the basis for many of the lessons that have been developed to accompany basal reading selections. Five basic steps constitute a DRA. These steps purport to provide the structure for the improvement of a wide spectrum of reading skills—the most important of which is comprehension. This strategy, which may be applied to reading selections that vary in both length and readability, is suggested for use with students at all grade levels.

Directed Reading-Thinking Activity (DR-TA). Assuming that critical reading performance requires the reader to become skilled at determining purposes for reading, the Directed Reading-Thinking Activity emphasizes that the reader declares his or her own purposes for reading. Like the DRA, the Directed Reading-Thinking Activity may be applied to reading selections that vary in both length and readability, and it is suggested for use with students at all grade levels.

Scaffolded Reading Experience (SRE). The Scaffolded Reading Experience was developed by Graves and Graves (1994) as a framework to assist students in successfully understanding, learning from, and enjoying a text selection. The SRE is designed as a set of prereading, during reading, and postreading activities that teachers fit to the students and the texts.

Direct Instruction (DI). Direct Instruction represents a teacher-directed approach to reading instruction using curriculum design tenets involving carefully sequenced and detailed teaching objectives emanating from an analysis of the necessary component skills.

New Basics/Rich Literacy Tasks. New Basics/Rich Literacy Tasks represent the efforts of the Queensland Department of Education with the guidance of Allan Luke and other scholars in developing a curriculum to adapt literacy programs to meet the needs of diverse communities as they engage with and prepare for the multiple literacies that move us beyond print-based literacies.

As the different frameworks are reviewed, we would stress the important role of the teacher in all of these frameworks. As Duffy and Hoffman (2002) noted:

> Classrooms and schools . . . are multilayered and vary from context to context. One size does not fit all. So when we impose the seductively simple idea of implementing "research-based" correlates, we see only superficial improvements in teaching and only get gains in low-level literacy skills.
>
> Creating substantial forms of instructional effectiveness and substantive forms of literacy achievement requires that we examine the deeper structures guiding teachers' and school leaders' enactment of teaching. This enacting is not a simple matter of technical competence with observed correlates of effectiveness. Rather, the best teachers weave a variety of teaching activities together in an infinitely complex and dynamic response to the flow of classroom life, and the best school leaders weave school conditions together in an infinitely complex response to life in schools. It is more like orchestration than a straightforward implementation. (p. 376)

REFERENCES

Cunningham, P. M., D. P. Hall, and M. Defee. 1991. Non-ability-grouped multilevel instruction: A year in a first grade classroom. *The Reading Teacher* 44: 566–571.

———. 1998. Non-ablility-grouped, multilevel instruction: Eight years later. *The Reading Teacher* 51: 652–664.

Duffy, G., and J. V. Hoffman. 2002. Beating the odds in literacy education: Not the "betting on" but the "bettering of" schools and teachers. In B. Taylor, M. Pressley, and P. D. Pearson (Eds.), *Teaching reading: Effective schools, accomplished teachers.* Mahwah, NJ: Erlbaum, 375–387.

Graves, M. F., and B. B. Graves. 1994. *Scaffolding reading experiences: Designs for student success.* Norwood, MA: Christopher-Gordon.

International Reading Association. 2002. *Evidence-based reading instruction: Putting the National Reading Panel report into practice.* Newark, DE: Author, 232–236.

Stahl, S. A., and D. A. Hayes (Eds.). 1997. *Instructional models in reading.* Mahwah, NJ: Erlbaum, 59–84.

Taylor, B., M. Pressley, and P. D. Pearson. 2002. Research-supported characteristics of teachers and schools that promote teaching achievement. In B. Taylor, M. Pressley, P. D. Pearson (Eds.), *Teaching reading. Effective schools, accomplished teachers.* Mahwah, NJ: Erlbaum, 361–373.

Guided Reading

Purpose

Guided Reading was developed by Irene Fountas and Gay Su Pinnell (1996) as a means of engaging students in meaningful reading of extended texts in conjunction with developing problem-solving abilities with the support of teacher guidance and other students.

Rationale

The framework provides for the guided reading and development of strategies in conjunction with the careful selection and placement of students in groups. While it appears to be the cornerstone of a reading program (especially in terms of developing a student's ability to strategically read for meaning), Guided Reading is viewed as one component of a literacy program that incorporates other whole class, individual, and group activities such as reading aloud, shared reading, interactive writing, independent reading and writing, and so on. As Fountas and Pinnell (1996) state:

> it is the heart of a balanced reading program. (p. 1)
>
> . . . Guided reading is a context in which a teacher supports each reader's development of effective strategies for processing novel texts at increasingly challenging levels of difficulty. (p. 2)

The Guided Reading framework places an emphasis on the following:

1. The importance of teacher mediation and peer support in the development of reading for meaning, especially the problem-solving strategies which undergird independent reading.

2. The importance of careful placement of students to ensure that they have the opportunity by reading material at an appropriate level whereby they are challenged, but not to the point of frustration.

3. The vigilance of teachers as they observe and place students in groups with other students and select texts for students to read, including practice with and extension of their problem-solving strategies.

4. Opportunities for students to be engaged in the use and expansion of skills and strategies as they read extended text.

As Fountas and Pinnell state:

- It gives children the opportunity to develop as individual readers while participating in a socially supported activity.
- It gives teachers the opportunity to observe as they process new texts.
- It gives individual readers the opportunity to develop the reading strategies so that they can read increasingly difficult texts independently.
- It gives children enjoyable, successful experiences in reading for meaning.
- It develops the abilities needed for independent reading.
- It helps children learn how to introduce texts to themselves. (1996, 1–2)

Many of the elements of Guided reading have as their source, practices first developed by Marie Clay and extended in the United States especially in conjunction with attempts to develop whole class practices compatible with the learning and teaching principles of Reading Recovery. The framework draws heavily from the Early Literacy Learning Initiative (ELLI), which was developed by a team of teacher educators (Irene Fountas, Gay Su Pinnell, Diane DeFord, Carol Lyons, Billie Askew, Mary Fried, Rosemary Estice, Andrea McCarrier, and others).

The Ohio State University Early Literacy Learning Initiative includes Guided Reading as one of several elements that purport to constitute a balanced literacy program:

1. Reading aloud (whole class or small group) a selected body of children's literature having certain features which lend themselves to several rereadings intended to develop students' enjoyment and opportunities to model reading for different purposes as well as knowledge of language and books.

2. Shared reading.

3. Guided Reading (details to follow).

4. Independent reading (alone or with partners)—reading a range of material including some from a collection at their level.

5. Shared writing where teachers and students work together to compose messages with teachers sometimes acting as scribes.

6. Interactive writing where teachers and students engage in a group writing experience not unlike a language experience or dictated story approach.

7. Guided writing or writing workshop where teachers engage students in process writing including conferencing as well as mini-lessons.

8. Independent writing where students engage in writing their own stories, informational pieces, labels, and so on.

Intended Audience

Guided Reading is intended for use with students in the first three or four grades of school but can be adapted for use with older students.

Description of the Procedures

After careful observation of children, the teacher places together a group of children for a mediated reading experience where they will each read the same text which is carefully selected to be appropriately challenging. The goal is to have a group who uses similar processes and can handle material at a similar level of difficulty with some teacher support. The teacher briefly introduces the text to the small group and provides incidental support to selected students as children read the text and then return to the text for discussion of strategy development. The steps in Guided Reading are

1. Teacher preparation and selection of material
2. Introduction to the selection
3. Students' reading of the text with teacher observation and incidental support
4. Conversation and discussion of story including rereading, revisiting, and extending the text.
5. Teacher assessment and follow-up
6. Managing Guided Reading in conjunction with other elements of a classroom literacy program

1. Teacher Preparation and Selection of Material. Fountas and Pinnell stress the importance of identifying material that will challenge, but not overchallenge, the students. They suggest as a rule that the student should be able to read (with teacher support and an introduction) about 90 percent of the words accurately. At the same time, the teachers need to avoid selecting texts that are so easy that students will have no opportunity to build strategies. If words are unknown, are they likely to be accessible via the students' use of strategies such as word analysis and prediction strategies? And, does the text offer a few opportunities to problem-solve? To this end, they discuss the possibility of using some of the leveling of books used in conjunction with the books that serve as a resource for Reading Recovery. In addition, they stress the importance of the material being interesting and consideration for other features such as length, layout, cohesiveness, and so on.

2. Introduction to the Selection. While suggesting that more challenging books may need more of an introduction, they support the adage of Clay, Holdaway, and others that teachers need to be careful to avoid an overly elongated introduction. In essence, they strive for an introduction that is lively, creates interest, and readies the child, but does not give too many things away. In terms of introduction to concepts, words, or language patterns, they suggest briefly dealing with those that are deemed critical and unlikely to be understood without some introduction. In other words, the selection of the text and introduction are intended to propel the students' engagement in reading the selection successfully, including their enlistment of strategies to solve problems and read for meaning. It is likely that different selections and different occasions will call for doing different activities to prompt the students' engagement prior to reading. Hopefully, introductions will engage students in a preliminary conversation about the story as it prompts expectations, raises questions, and highlights/foreshadows certain information or concepts.

3. Students' Reading of the Text with Teacher Observation and Incidental Support. During the students' reading of the texts, teachers are observing and noting students' behaviors—especially problem-solving. It is as if the teacher's role is to listen in, take notes, and plan for follow-up. In those situations when students may need immediate help, then the goal is to provide them guidance which engages their use and reflection on the strategies they can and do use. The students are expected to read the whole text or a portion to themselves either quietly or silently. They may request help in problem-solving

4. Conversation and Discussion of Story Including Rereading, Revisiting, and Extending the Text. Following the reading of the text, the students are engaged in a combination of conversations/discussion of what they have read as well as opportunities to discuss and explore their problem-solving. The goal is to engage the students in talk about their recall and personal responses, including predictions and questions. Rereading of a selection (either as a group, with partners, or independently) may take place to afford an opportunity for students to revisit the story and increase their fluency as well as revisit or expand upon their problem-solving. Teachers are encouraged to return to the text for one or two teaching opportunities such as finding evidence or discussing various kinds of problem-solving. Occasionally, students are encouraged to extend the text through further discussion, writing, or drama.

5. Teacher Assessment and Follow-Up. Fountas and Pinnell stress that the ultimate test is whether Guided Reading, together with other reading experiences, responds to the students' growth as readers, including their ability to handle a range of increasingly difficult text as a vehicle for learning. In addition, students should be showing evidence of developing strategic behaviors associated with the notion of a self-improving or self-extending system (e.g., self-monitoring, searching, and self-correcting). They emphasize the need for teachers to maintain careful observations and to do frequent incidental and systemic checks of students' progress—including enlisting the use of running records as well as teacher-prepared checklists by which to note the students' strategy usage, signs of faltering or fluency, and so on.

6. Managing Guided Reading in Conjunction with Other Elements of a Classroom Literacy Program. While Guided Reading may be the cornerstone, it is not intended to be the sole element of a literacy program. Students are expected to be engaged in several other activities that may complement or accompany Guided Reading activities. Teachers would expect to work with different groups on Guided Reading as well as establish a range of other activities that they would support differentially over the week. Some activities may engage the students in independent work; others might involve cooperative groups or partnerships. The Fountas and Pinnell text details how teachers might provide different kinds of support in conjunction with these various activities, including ways they might be interconnected through common themes or as follow-up.

Cautions and Comments

Since its inception, Guided Reading has received a great deal of attention from practitioners, school district personnel, and the originators themselves. In turn, they have provided further resources, refinement, and research, as well as project evaluation information. Guided Reading together with its counterpart, the Literacy Collaborative (www.lcosu.org), has been shown to be more successful than other schoolwide programs including basals driven by Direct Instruction and other models or Success for All. The resources address a wide range of needs of teachers in different settings, and the approach includes many of the elements associated with past studies of effective schools (IRA, 2002; Taylor, Pressley, and Pearson, 2002). The reference list includes a number of articles representative of the professional engagement of educators in exploration of its use. Further examples can be reviewed by pursuing web searches of the procedure (e.g., www.mcps.k12.md.us/curriculum/english/guided_rdg.html).

While Guided Reading might not have been the target of detailed comparative studies, the framework clearly represents a concerted multiyear attempt to pull together research, theory, and the thinking and best practices of countless teachers and teacher educators who are engaged and have been engaged in successful work with students. The developers acknowledge their debt to others, including Marie Clay, whose work has been a key antecedent to these efforts, as well as collaborators such as many other developers connected with their related Reading Recovery efforts, and the Ohio State ELLI. We can rest assured that the framework has emerged and has been refined and revised, and revised again, and will undergo further revision, we suspect, as they learn from and with others who use the framework.

Guided Reading would appear to have antecedents and connections to several other strategies and frameworks. For example, Guided Reading varies the teacher's level of support in some ways consistent with notions of teacher support discussed in conjunction with the Explicit Teaching of Reading Comprehension (see Unit 7). While Guided Reading suggests more varied and flexible levels of teacher support, both draw heavily from the same notion of the gradual release of responsibility of teacher support in their suggestions for how strategic reading develops. In other ways, Guided Reading complements and overlaps with the suggestions emanating from strategies such as the Directed Reading Activity, Shared Book Experience, and Language-Experience Approach (see Units 1 and 3).

Guided reading is a strategy that demands a teacher be willing to engage in thoughtful observation of children as well as in careful consideration of materials and constant rethinking of the grouping of children. The use of running records as well as other forms of observing and notetaking are highlighted as important complements to teacher decision-making and planning.

The question of ability grouping is admittedly one of the thorniest issues for Guided Reading. The authors discuss at great length the disadvantages of maintaining ability groups and make a case for the dynamic placement of students—shifting students to other groups as they are able to meet the demands of different selections. However, one might question whether or not students will be frequently moved and if the apparent stagnation that occurs as a result of ability grouping will occur. Certainly, they suggest a range of other activities that might serve to counteract the impact of stagnant ability grouping.

Teachers using Guided Reading will need to have access to and knowledge of reading materials carefully leveled and organized to support the selection of material to meet the needs of students. While the authors and others affiliated with Reading Recovery or its offshoots (e.g., ELLI) might have access to an extensive library of materials from which to select, we suspect that many teachers are going to need to add resources and access to such material.

Guided Reading offers teachers an organization and principles, together with examples, to assist teachers in developing what might be considered a comprehensive approach to the reading-writing curriculum. While the framework is not prepackaged, it may appear to lock teachers into an organizational scheme which may have only the look of developing strategic readers and writers. To be successful, teachers will need to be constantly researching and refining their teaching and assessment strategies as they adjust, adapt, expand, and improve their reading-writing programs to meet the needs of their students.

REFERENCES

Antonacci, P. A. 2000. Reading in the zone of proximal development: Mediating literacy development in beginner readers through guided reading. *Reading Horizons* 41(1): 19–34. Compares and demonstrates a traditional basal approach with a guided reading approach.

Blachowicz, C., and D. Ogle. 2001. *Reading comprehension: Strategies for independent learners.* New York: Guilford Press. Provides a thoughtful discussion and suggestions for the use of a range of strategies.

Button, K., M. J. Johnson, and P. Furgerson. 1996. Interactive writing in a primary classroom. *The Reading Teacher* 49(6): 446–454. Details the use of interactive writing in conjunction with The Ohio State University Early Literacy Learning Initiative (ELLI).

Byrd, D., and P. Westfall. 2000. *Guided Reading coaching tool.* Portland, ME: Stenhouse. Offers examples of materials that can support Guided Reading lessons and assessments.

Fawson, P. C., and D. R. Reutzel. 2000. But I only have a basal: Implementing Guided Reading in the early grades. *The Reading Teacher* 54(1): 84–114. Describes a way to use basal readers as an integral part of a Guided Reading program/leveled text.

Fountas, I. C., and G. S. Pinnell. 1996. *Guided reading: Good first teaching for all children.* Portsmouth, NH: Heinemann. Provides a comprehensive introduction to Guided Reading with a host of support materials including classroom management plans, leveled book lists, examples of check lists, and observational schedules.

———. 1999. *Matching books to readers: Using leveled books in guided reading, K–3.* Portsmouth, NH: Heinemann. Provides detailed procedures for leveling books, putting together and using these books in classrooms in conjunction with running records, and so on.

Hoyt, L., M. E. Mooney, and B. Parkes (Eds.). 2003. *Exploring information texts: From theory to practice.* Portsmouth, NH: Heinemann. Edited text that includes discussions on Guided Reading.

International Reading Association. 2002. *Evidence-based reading instruction: Putting the National Reading panel report into practice.* Newark, DE: Author, 232–236. Discusses the elements that undergird effective reading programs.

Malik, S. (1999). Guided Reading and writing: Learning how. *Perspectives in Education and Deafness* 17(5): 26. Addresses the use of writing in conjunction with Guided Reading.

Morrow, L. M., M. Collucci, and A. Radzin. 2002. Staff development for early literacy teachers: Changing to Guided Reading. *Dimensions of Early Childhood* 30(4): 5–9.

Opitz, M. F., and M. P. Ford. 2001. *Reaching readers: Innovative and flexible strategies for Guided Reading*. Portsmouth, NH: Heinemann.

Pinnell, G. S., and I. C. Fountas. 1998. *Word matters: Teaching phonics and spelling in the reading/writing classroom.* Portsmouth, NH: Heinemann. Provides details of dealing with teaching phonics and spelling in conjunction with Guided Reading.

Rog, L. J. 2003. *Guided Reading basics.* Portland, ME: Stenhouse. Provides a practical guide for implementing Guided Reading lessons for students at different levels—emergent, early, developmental, and fluent.

Skidmore D., M. Perez-Parent, and S. Arnfield. 2003. Teacher-pupil dialogue in the Guided Reading session. *Reading* 37(2): 47–53. Reflections on an examination of teacher–student interations during Guided Reading.

Sowell, D. J. 2003. Strategy strips for self-reliant readers. *The Reading Teacher* 56: 530–532. Describes a technique using reading strategy strips with small guided reading groups.

Tancock, S. M. 1994. A literacy lesson framework for children with reading problems. *The Reading Teacher* 48: 130–140. Describes a literacy lesson (similar to Guided Reading) for students with reading difficulties.

Taylor, B., M. Pressley, and P. D. Pearson. 2002. Research-supported characteristics of teachers and schools that promote teaching achievement. In B. Taylor, M. Pressley, P. D. Pearson (Eds.), *Teaching reading: Effective schools, accomplished teachers.* Mahwah, NJ: Erlbaum, 361–373. Discusses the research on effective schools and teachers as a basis for suggesting key elements for an effective reading program.

Vilaume, S. K., and E. G. Brabham. 2001. Guided Reading: Who is in the driver's seat? *The Reading Teacher* 55(3): 260–263. Discusses the teacher and student roles in Guided Reading.

Weaver, B. M. 2000. *Leveling Books, K–6: Matching readers to text.* Newark, DE: International Reading Association. Explains the importance of leveling, reviews leveling systems, and provides a step-by-step leveling procedure for grades K–6.

Whitehead, D. 1994. Teaching literacy and learning strategies through a Modified Guided Silent Reading procedure. *Journal of Reading* 38: 24–30. Compares the use in New Zealand classes of two variations of the Guided Silent Reading procedure: GSR and MGSR. The MGSR is intended to shift more control to students.

———. 2002. "The story means more to me now": Teaching thinking through Guided Reading. *Reading Literacy and Language* 36(1): 33–37. Discusses the engagement of students' comprehension in conjunction with Guided Reading.

Four Blocks

Purpose

Four Blocks (Cunningham, Hall, and Defee, 1991, 1998) is a framework for beginning reading instruction designed to meet the needs of students reading at multiple reading levels by using a combination of major instructional approaches to reading.

Rationale

Cunningham et al. designed Four Blocks to accomplish two goals: (1) meeting the needs of students encompassing a wide range of entering literacy levels without putting them in ability groupings, and (2) finding a way to combine the major approaches to beginning reading instruction. It was their thinking that teachers attempt to meet the needs of poor readers by putting them in the *low* reading group and slowing down the pace of instruction. However, the evidence on doing this is not very promising. Generally, students placed in the low reading group remain in that grouping throughout their elementary school years and almost never learn to read and write at the appropriate grade-level standards (Allington, 1983).

Additionally, Cunningham et al. were concerned with the way various approaches to reading instruction wax and wane in their popularity. When they published their original description of Four Blocks (Cunningham et al., 1991), literature-based instruction was popular. At this point in time that approach is falling into disfavor, and phonics approaches are becoming popular. It was their thinking that there is no one best method of teaching reading since it belies what we know about how students learn; that is, students do not learn in the same way or at the same rate. Individual differences are a reality; therefore, to teach all students the same way, with the same method, is nonsensical. To avoid this, they recommended a combination of approaches to reading instruction. To meet their stated goals Cunningham et al. developed Four Blocks, a framework for beginning reading instruction that was both multilevel and multimethod.

Intended Audience

Since Four Blocks is a framework for beginning reading and writing instruction, it is appropriate for the early grades and has been implemented specifically in grades 1–3.

Description of the Procedures

In this framework, reading and writing time is divided fairly evenly among four different approaches to instruction, that is, the 2½ hours of reading and writing instruction is divided into four blocks of 30–40 minutes each. The four blocks are: (1) guided reading, (2) self-selected reading, (3) working with words, and (4) writing. Before describing each of these blocks, it should be mentioned that when providing instruction, teachers try to integrate them. They are not necessarily treated as discrete entities; rather, teachers try to make connections among the blocks. Most often, this is done by taking a theme approach to teaching. The kinds of materials about which students read and write and the words with which students work can be connected via a theme.

1. Guided Reading. Originally Cunningham et al. called this the basal block. Recently, teachers have augmented, or replaced, the basal with other materials. The guided reading block is now carried out with the class basal, basals from previously adopted series, multiple copies of trade books, and various combinations of these materials. The purpose of the guided reading block is to expose students to a wide variety of literature, teach them comprehension strategies, and teach them how to read in materials that become progressively more difficult.

In the beginning of the first grade most of the guided reading time involves the reading of predictable books, read in some format of shared reading (e.g., echo, choral; see Unit 6). Comprehension activities involve having the students take on roles and become the characters of a book as the rest of the students read along. Little book versions of Big Books are read and reread with partners, in small groups, and individually. As the year progresses shared reading continues as part of guided reading, but other books—not predictable or Big—are added. Emphasis begins to switch from reading together to reading alone or with a partner. Teachers also begin to change how they present a book. Instead of always reading a book to children, teachers can change their focus to the pictures, having students name the objects in the pictures or make predictions based on them. They might also point out some important but difficult words that students will have to read. After students read the text, they reconvene as a large group to discuss the book, sometimes reading it as a whole class. Comprehension strategies are taught and practiced; predictions about the books are checked. Another reading of the book might have students act out the various parts or be accompanied by a writing activity, done individually or in pairs.

Cunningham et al. suggest it is difficult to make the guided reading block multilevel, as any selection students read as a group might be too easy for some and too difficult for others. Because the other three blocks involve materials above grade level, Cunningham et al. are not concerned about students who find guided reading books too easy. Instead, they concentrate their efforts on struggling readers by adapting instruction. Teachers begin this by selecting two selections weekly, one on grade level and the other easier. Each book is read multiple times, with different purposes and in different formats. The repeated readings enable almost all students to reach fluency by the time the last reading occurs. Those students who still need help can be supported by a partner who is taught to help the poorer reader deal with the selection. In addition, teachers can also meet with small groups of students who need help as long as the groups remain flexible and change members.

2. Self-Selected Reading. Self-selected reading is also known as individualized reading or readers' workshop (see Unit 2). Under whatever name used, self-selected reading allows students to choose what they want to read and what parts of it to which they wish to respond. Teachers hold individual conferences with students, and opportunities are provided to share with others what they are reading. This block includes a teacher read-aloud using a wide range of literature. Students also read on their own from the books teachers have gathered. The classroom library endeavors to have as great a range of levels and types of books as possible. As students read, teachers have conferences and make anecdotal records of a number of students daily. The block concludes with one to two students sharing what they are reading.

Self-selected reading is, by definition, multilevel. Students' choices of books are only limited by their availability and how willing and able students are to read from them. Advanced readers are steered toward books that will be challenging to them. For those students having difficulties selecting a book to read, Cunningham et al. recommend: (a) helping students determine when a book is right and when it is not, (b) suggesting they read books already read aloud by the teacher, (c) encouraging reading with a friend and rereading books they enjoy, (d) making a number of informational picture books available, and (e) setting up programs in which they can read to younger students while practicing with easy books and having a real purpose for doing so. Finally, with early first graders, Cunningham et al. suggest teaching them that there are three ways to read a book. First, they can *pretend read* a book by telling the story of a familiar book. Second, they can *picture read* from a real book and talk about all the objects depicted in the pictures. Third, they can read by *reading the words.* Of course, teachers need to model these ways to read for students early in the school year.

3. Working with Words. In the working-with-words block students learn to read and spell high-frequency words and learn the visual and sound patterns of words to allow them to decode and spell many other words. This block has a number of suggested activities: (a) word wall, (b) rounding up the rhymes, (c) making words, and (d) guess the covered word.

a. Word wall. The word wall is a collection of high-frequency words displayed alphabetically by the first letter. Cunningham et al. suggest that these words be written on colored paper with heavy black markers. Five new words are added weekly until 110–120 words are displayed. Students spend the first 10 minutes of this block reviewing the word wall words; practice entails looking and saying the old and new words, writing the words on paper, clapping or snapping the letters, and self-correcting the words with the teacher, if necessary. After word wall practice, the remaining 15–25 minutes of this block are used to do activities to help students decode and spell. The word wall is a multilevel activity, as some students are still learning to read these high-frequency words. Those who can already read them are learning to spell them.

b. Rounding up the rhymes. This activity is actually a follow-up to the guided reading of a selection or a book the teacher has shared with the students at the beginning of self-selected reading. After the book has been read one to two times for meaning and enjoyment, it may be revisited during the working-with-words block to draw students' attention to the rhyming words. As the book is read this time, students are encouraged to point out the words that rhyme. These words are written down on index cards and placed in a pocket chart. Next, students are reminded that words that rhyme usually have the same spelling pattern; they are asked to examine the words they've selected to identify, by underlining, those words that end the same. Those without the same visual pattern would be discarded. For instance, *fed* and *said* would be discarded while *lead* and *dead* would be kept for further examination. This activity concludes with a transfer step in which students are asked to read and spell new words based upon their growing knowledge of rhymes and spelling patterns. Students are told that many times words are encountered as they read that are new to them, but they can use the rhymes and spelling patterns they already know to help them read and spell the words. Using our previous example, r*ead* or h*ead* might be written by the teacher for student exploration.

Rounding up the rhymes is multilevel, as some students are still developing their phonemic awareness skills while others are practicing their initial letter substitution. More advanced readers are working on the strategy of using known words to decode and spell unknown words that rhyme.

c. Making words. Making words was designed by Cunningham and Cunningham (1992) as an active, hands-on activity in which students learn how to look for the patterns in words and how changing a letter can change the whole word. Students are given the letters from a 6- to 8-letter word chosen by the teacher for its relation to an activity students are doing in an another block; for example, the letters from the word *animals* would be given in random order to students for this activity. The activity begins by making 2-letter words from the letters and proceeds on to build 3-, 4-, and 5-letter words until the final word can be figured out. Words made are then sorted and read by a number of patterns: beginning sounds, endings, and rhymes. Sorted for rhymes, students might generate *main* and *slain* or *an* and *man.* Students can then follow the same procedure as specified in rounding up the rhymes and conclude with a transfer step, reading and spelling out words that might be encountered in students' reading. In this case, transfer words might be *stain* or *span.*

Making words is a multilevel activity, as it begins with short words and progresses to longer, more difficult words, with the final challenge being to use all the letters to make up the secret word. In this activity even those students with limited literacy ability can make the little words and can sort words into patterns. In this way they can read and spell new words based upon the visual patterns they can say and spell.

d. Guess the covered word. The purpose of this activity is to provide practice for students in cross-checking meaning with letter-sound information. Cunningham et al. suggest that in this activity four to five sentences are written on the board, each with a word covered by two sticky notes; the length of the sticky notes needs to be adjusted to avoid providing word length clues to students. Students are asked to guess what the covered word is and explain their guess; teachers need to point out that there may be many possibilities to fit the context of the sentence. Next, the teacher takes off the first sticky note which has covered all the letters up to the vowel; guesses which do not conform to the revealed visual pattern are eliminated. New guesses which fit both the context and the visual pattern are now made. When new guesses cease to be offered, the entire word is revealed and discussed. For those students who need it, this activity provides a review of beginning letter sounds; for more advanced students, it helps solidify the strategy of combining meaning, beginning letters, and word length as clues to the identification of unknown words.

4. Writing. The writing block is conducted as a writers' workshop (see Unit 2) and begins with a 10-minute period in which the teacher models the writing process. With an overhead projector or a large piece of chart paper, the teacher writes and thinks aloud about what to write and how to write it, keying in a few items a day. The teacher models using the word wall and invents the spelling of a few big words. The teacher also makes a few deliberate mistakes; when the writing is done or the next day, the students help the teacher edit the piece.

The next part of this block is a focus on students' own writing. Each student may be at a different point in their writing—some finishing a piece or starting a new one and others editing or illustrating. While students write, the teacher holds a conference with some individuals and helps them get their pieces ready to publish. Publication time occurs after three to five drafts of a piece; the student chooses one on which to put the finishing touches. Spelling errors are fixed and mechanics are cleared up; Cunningham et al. point out how important this is as they want students' published writing to be easily read by others. The block ends with Author's Chair (see Unit 9), where several students share their writing.

The writing block can be multilevel if teachers allow students to choose their own topic, accept first-draft writing at whatever level the students happen to be, and allow them as many days as needed to finish their pieces. In this way all students can succeed. Additionally, Cunningham et al. suggest that teacher modeling of writing and the publishing conferences allow for further multilevel activities. The teacher modeling lessons can contribute to making writing multilevel by focusing in on different facets of the writing process, different topics, and/or different lengths of writing. Teachers can individualize their teaching in the publishing conferences; the conferences provide the opportunity for the *teachable moment,* as both advanced and struggling writers can be moved forward in their individual writing needs. Finally, it should be pointed out that when students write, some of them are actually working on becoming better writers. For others, writing provides the vehicle for them to figure out reading.

Cautions and Comments

As Cunningham et al. set out to do with Four Blocks, they have developed a framework which incorporates the major approaches to reading (e.g., basals, phonics, literature-based instruction) without moving students into ability groups. Additionally, they have shown how each block can be made multilevel. In Cunningham et al. (1998) they provide data on the successful implementation of this framework. Specifically, they provide longitudinal data from the original Four Blocks school as well as new data from a suburban school district and one rural school as evidence that this framework is effective in teaching both struggling and advanced students to read and write and/or improve upon their overall reading and writing. Additionally, they report that if extra support is needed for struggling readers beyond the four blocks of instruction, the framework seems very compatible with special reading programs including Reading Recovery (see Unit 4). Perhaps the success of Four Blocks can be attributable to the fact that each teacher who tries it will find at least some part of it to be familiar; since it is not a totally novel approach, it allows teachers an anchor as they implement the framework. Cunningham et al. insist that each Four Blocks' classroom must be built upon giving each block its allotted time. Beyond that, they believe teachers should have wide latitude in doing instruction in ways they and the students find most effective and satisfying. While they offer general support for the approach, their explorations fail to delve into the problems that they have incurred or the extent to which students' overall achievements correlate with becoming more strategic and self-motivated literacy inquirers.

As the Four Blocks program has been explored in a variety of different school settings, Cunningham and her colleagues have developed an expanding range of web-based support material (www.wfu.edu/~cunningh/fourblocks) including research and evaluation information as well as other resources to guide district personnel, professional development personnel, and teachers in the use of the framework.

REFERENCES

Allington, R. L. 1983. The reading instruction provided readers of differing reading ability. *The Elementary School Journal* 83: 549–559. Study showing poor readers are not given the opportunities necessary to learn to read better.

Cunningham, P. M., and J. W. Cunningham. 1992. Making words: Enhancing the invented spelling-decoding connection. *The Reading Teacher* 46: 106–115. A description of the making words strategy.

Cunningham, P., and D. Hall. 2001. Guided reading, self-selected reading, working with words, writing: The Four Blocks in classrooms that work. Available at www.wfu.edu~cunningh/fourblocks.

Cunningham, P. M., D. P. Hall, and M. Defee. 1991. Nonability-grouped, multilevel instruction: A year in a first grade classroom. *The Reading Teacher* 44: 566–571. Original description of Four Blocks.

Cunningham, P. M., D. P. Hall, and M. Defee. 1998. Nonability-grouped, multilevel instruction: Eight years later. *The Reading Teacher* 51: 652–664. Update of Four Blocks, with research results.

Directed Reading Activity

Purpose

The purpose of the Directed Reading Activity (DRA) (Betts, 1946) is to: (1) give teachers a basic format from which to provide systematic instruction on a group basis; (2) improve students' word recognition and comprehension skills; (3) successfully guide students through a reading selection; and (4) engage students in reading text (Blanton and Moorman, 1990).

Rationale

DRA is a structured strategy used by classroom teachers as a comprehensive means to provide reading instruction to children through a reading selection and was once used as the basis for developing teaching guidelines for basal reader selections. Indeed, Betts (1946) compiled the guidelines that various authors of basal readers generally recommended for teaching reading. Betts described a plan to follow when there was general agreement among the authors:

> First, the group should be prepared, oriented, or made ready, for the reading of a story or selection. Second, the first reading should be guided silent reading. Third, word-recognition skills and comprehension should be developed during the silent reading. Fourth, the reading—silent or oral, depending upon the needs of the pupil—should be done for purposes different from those served by the first, or silent, reading. Fifth, the follow-up on the "reading lesson" should be differentiated in terms of pupil needs. (p. 492)

Intended Audience

The DRA is normally associated with basal reader instruction in the elementary grades, but the teacher may adapt it for any reading selection. For example, Shepherd (1973) has illustrated the use of DRA with content area textbooks from the middle school level through high school.

Description of the Procedures

Although there may be minor differences as to what constitutes the DRA, it usually contains the following components, all of which the teacher may modify to fit a student's needs:

1. Readiness
2. Directed silent reading
3. Comprehension check and discussion
4. Oral rereading
5. Follow-up activities

Stage 1: Readiness. The readiness, or preparation, stage of the DRA involves getting students ready to enter the story by relating the story selection to their past experiences, developing their interest in reading it, and setting their purposes for reading. Four components comprise the readiness stage of the DRA.

a. Develop concept background. Here it is suggested that the teacher connect the new concepts that the students will be exposed to in the reading selection with their previous experiences or readings. Any misconceptions or hazy understandings by the students are expected to be clarified before they read the story.

The teacher may build background through various means, including discussions centering around the story title and illustrations in the selection, personal experiences of the students related to the story content, films, pictures, maps, or other audiovisual displays.

b. Create interest. Starting with the notion that children must be interested or motivated to read a selection in order to maximize their comprehension and enjoyment of its contents, the teacher attempts also to create interest in the early stages. The mechanical side of the selection alone, its title and the various illustrations, many times may serve to arouse students' interest; however, the teacher may also have to keep creating enthusiasm for students to read the story effectively. In some cases developing conceptual background (the previously discussed section) may suffice. If not, the teacher may choose to read a short, introductory portion of the selection in hopes of inspiring the students to want to read the rest. At other times, the teacher may wish to use multimedia material and/or experiences to stimulate interest.

c. Introduce new vocabulary. Here the teacher's task is to prepare students for any words they will encounter that are outside the students' reading vocabularies and word recognition abilities. To emphasize word meanings and not just word pronunciations, the teacher may introduce new vocabulary in context, both orally and visually. For example, the teacher might first use the word *orally* in a sentence, followed by a visual presentation on the chalkboard using meaningful phrases or sentences. The introduction of new vocabulary is not a time for drill or for emphasizing word attack skills. Instead, it is the time to give students oral familiarity with selected words. Typically, a teacher introduces no more than five words at once.

d. Establish purpose. Based on the notion that the establishment of clear, concise purpose for reading a selection determines the quality of the readers' comprehension, the teacher poses questions for the students to answer in their silent reading. The overall question the teacher should consider is, "What are the students reading for?" For example, the teacher must decide whether to set a general purpose for the entire selection, such as "Read to find out the series of events that led to the downfall of the dictator," or if the teacher decides to set more specific purposes for each part of a selection, another example is "Read to find out how the dictator came to power before you go on to other parts of the selection."

The presentation of the readiness stage of the DRA should take approximately five to fifteen minutes but will vary in length and emphasis according to the ability of the students and the complexity of the selections. For less advanced students, it may be necessary to spend a longer time preparing them to read the selection than when preparing more advanced students. Depending upon how the teacher approaches the readiness stage, one component may encompass other aspects of this step. For instance, introducing new vocabulary may create interest and develop concept background simultaneously. With the exception of establishing purpose, which should conclude the readiness stage, the teacher need not present the other components in any established order.

Stage 2: Directed Silent Reading. Following the readiness stage of the DRA, the students should read the selection silently to seek answers to the purpose-questions that the teacher has set. It is emphasized that the teacher have students read the selection silently, and not orally. This way is more rapid, it is more characteristic of everyday reading needs, and it gives the students an opportunity to use their work attack skills without expressed effort.

If readiness activities have been thorough, many students will work efficiently with very little, if any, teacher help. The teacher should encourage students to work out word recognition problems independently; however, he or she might also be available in the event a student requests help with confirmation or analysis. Because silent reading is not a time for word attack drills, it is suggested that teachers guide students who require help to clues that will aid them in unlocking the meaning of unknown words. If students seem unable to decode certain words, the teacher usually will provide these words so that reading may proceed. The teacher can make note of those words that give students particular difficulty and/or those specific skill needs of students as they attempt to decode words. Later, teachers can plan appropriate individual and/or group activities to counteract those difficulties.

Stage 3: Comprehension Check and Discussion. Discussion activities follow each silent reading segment that is assigned. An obvious start of the discussion can be answering the purpose-questions set during the readiness stage, although discussion may begin naturally on the other aspects of the selection. During the discussion it is appropriate to stress and develop comprehension abilities. For example, teachers might formulate discussion questions to extend and challenge the ideas students glean from their reading.

Stage 4: Oral Rereading. This stage of the DRA may occur in conjunction with the previous stage (comprehension check and discussion) or the teacher may use it to set new purposes for reading. The teacher may set these purposes independently, new purposes may develop out of the discussion, or they may serve as a preparation for a follow-up activity. Rereading may also occur if students are confused about one of the discussion questions. If such is the case, the new purpose is for students to read to solve problems that have resulted from the discussion. Students reread rapidly to locate information under question and then orally reread to the group to alleviate the confusion or to verify a point.

Stage 5: Follow-Up Activities. Follow-up activities include experiences that build and extend skill development and activities that add to, or enrich, students' understanding of the concepts in the story. This is also an appropriate time for the teacher to review any skills that were noted to have produced difficulties during the silent reading. Such activities are suitable on an individual basis, in a small group, or in a whole class situation.

The rationale behind this type of follow-up activity is that practice with, and opportunities to use, skills that present difficulty to students will provide them with the reinforcement necessary to learn those skills. As such, the use of basal reader workbooks, teacher-made worksheets, or commercially available material is often suggested to strengthen those specific skills that the DRA showed to be of concern.

Activities that can enrich or extend students' understanding of the story's concepts start with the premise that the application of newly learned concepts to other types of activities will further enhance and broaden new learning. Such extension activities may involve creative work, study activities, or extended reading. Creative work may include writing about personal experiences related to the story, preparing dramatization, and making illustrations for the story. Study activities may include workbook exercises and teacher-made practice material. Students may also do research into the information they gain from the selection in order to organize it into a chart or table format. Examples of extended reading might include selected readings in other texts or library books on related topics, or reading to find answers to questions that arise in the discussion of the story.

Cautions and Comments

The effective use of the DRA requires the teacher to be sensitive to the students' needs, to the differential demands of text, and to the adequacy of the DRA as a lesson framework. In this respect, the DRA seems to have one shortcoming; namely, it seems to be too teacher-dominated, which reduces the opportunities for students to "develop active, inquiring minds" (Nessel, 1989, p. 55). Interactions occurring between teachers and pupils flow mainly from the questions and activities that the teacher prescribes.

Nessel (1989) believes that "the type of instruction that is implemented in today's schools is one identifiable factor contributing to passive reading" (p. 55). As a result, the procedures followed in DRA could develop in students a dependence on teacher direction rather than on their own self-initiated reading-thinking processes. Results gleaned from Blanton and Moorman's (1990) study on reading instruction using the DRA framework convey that

- An inordinate amount of DRA time was consumed by activity unrelated to the lesson
- Teacher behavior reflected more time in questioning, telling, and defining rather than utilizing meaningful higher order thinking skills and processing
- Teachers provided few explanations, rarely modeled, or demonstrated skills for students
- Inconsistencies between teacher focus and instructional outcomes were evident

In addition, studies by Davidson (1970) and Petre (1970) compared the DRA with the Directed Reading-Thinking Activity (DRTA) and found results favoring the DRTA. Nessel (1989) identifies the following as advantages favoring DR-TA:

- Students are actively involved at the higher levels of thinking
- Teachers ask students to speculate rather than telling them what they will read about
- Students anticipate what will happen based on knowledge gleaned from the discussion
- Teachers recognize and praise student thinking and predictions (p. 57)

Another concern about the use of the DRA involves skill development (including oral reading, word recognition, comprehension, and study skills). If implemented properly, and related to the actual reading assignment, skills instruction has the potential to be purposeful and relevant. However, if skills instruction is rote or isolated from a selection, as worksheet exercises often are, then it is often meaningless, as argued by Sachs (1981), Osborn (1984), and Blanton, Moorman, and Wood (1986).

Despite these limitations, the DRA has adaptive potential to teach almost any reading selection. Aspects of other strategies described in this book may serve as supplements to the DRA. For example, teachers can effectively utilize ReQuest (see Unit 7) as a replacement for the readiness stage of the DRA. DRA's potential can serve other subject areas as well.

REFERENCES

Betts, E. A. 1946. *Foundations of reading instruction.* New York: American Book. Presents one of the original descriptions of the general principles and assumptions behind the DRA.

Blanton, W. E., and G. B. Moorman. 1990. The presentation of reading lessons. *Reading Research and Instruction* 29: 35–55. A research study in which the effectiveness of DRA with skill instruction was explored.

Blanton, W. E., G. B. Moorman, and R. G. Wood. 1986. A model of direct instruction applied to the basal skills lesson. *The Reading Teacher* 40: 299–304. Proposes a direct instruction model that extends the DRA framework.

Cunningham, J. W., and L. K. Wall. 1994. Teaching good readers to comprehend better. *Journal of Reading* 37(6): 480–486. Presents a variation of the DRA as used with ninth graders.

Davidson, J. L. 1970. *The relationship between teachers' questions and pupils' responses during a Directed Reading Activity and a Directed Reading-Thinking Activity.* Unpublished doctoral diss., University of Michigan. Presents a research study in which the efficacy of DRA is questioned.

Donlan, D. 1985. Using the DRA to teach literary comprehension at three response levels. *Journal of Reading* 28: 408–415. Explores the use of the DRA as a means of aiding interpretation.

Greabell, L. C., and N. A. Anderson. 1992. Applying strategies from the Directed Reading Activity to a directed mathematics activity. *School Sciences and Mathematics* 92: 142–144. Presents a math lesson on problem-solving utilizing the DRA framework.

Karlin, R. 1975. *Teaching elementary reading: Principles and strategies* (2d ed.). New York: Harcourt, Brace, Jovanovich, 146–151. Describes the steps involved in the DRA when used with a basal reader.

Miller, W. H. 1977. *The first R: Elementary reading today* (2d ed.). New York: Holt, Rinehart and Winston, 59–78. Provides general guidelines for using the DRA in the guise of a basal reader lesson.

Nessel, D. 1989. Do your students think when they read? *Learning* 18: 55–57. Compares the DRA model with the DRTA model of direct instruction.

Neubert, G. A., and E. Wilkins. 2004. *Putting it all together: The Directed Reading Lesson in the secondary content classroom.* Boston: Allyn and Bacon. Includes numerous examples of directed reading lessons for secondary classrooms.

Osborn, J. 1984. The purposes, uses, and contents of workbooks and some guidelines for publishers. In R. C. Anderson, J. Osborn, and R. J. Tierney (Eds.), *Learning to read in American schools: Basal readers and content texts.* Hillsdale, NJ: Erlbaum. Discusses the strengths, weaknesses, and use of workbooks accompanying basal reading lessons.

Petre, R. M. 1970. *Quantity, quality and variety of pupil responses during an open-communication group Directed Reading-Thinking Activity and a closed-communication structured group Directed Reading Activity.* Unpublished doctoral diss., University of Delaware. Presents a research study in which the efficacy of DRA is questioned.

Purves, A. C., L. Papa, and S. Jordan. 1994. *Encyclopedia of English studies and language arts.* New York: National Council of Teachers of English. An excellent resource that contains an extensive collection of more than 800 annotated entries/topics in English Studies and Language Arts.

Sachs, A. W. 1981. *The effects of three prereading activities on learning disabled children's short-term reading comprehension.* Unpublished doctoral diss., George Peabody University. Presents a research study in which the effectiveness of the DRA was examined.

Shepherd, D. L. 1973. *Comprehensive high school reading methods.* Columbus, OH: Charles E. Merrill, 132–138. Outlines steps to adapt the DRA for use in the content fields.

Spache, G. D., and E. B. Spache. 1977. *Reading in the elementary school* (4th ed.). Boston: Allyn and Bacon, 46–53. Provides an outlined procedure for teaching a typical basal reader lesson.

Stauffer, R. G. 1969. *Directing reading maturity as a cognitive process.* New York: Harper & Row, 35–86. Describes an alternative procedure to the DRA—the Directed Reading-Thinking Activity. Using the same fundamental steps as the DRA, this strategy promotes more student involvement.

Wilkinson, I. A. G., and R. C. Anderson. 1995. Sociocognitive processes in guided silent reading: A microanalysis of small-group lessons. *Reading Research Quarterly* 30(4): 710–740. Reports a detailed analysis of small group engaged in Directed Reading Activities and the benefits accrued from reading with others.

Directed Reading-Thinking Activity

Purpose

The Directed Reading-Thinking Activity (DRTA) is intended to develop students' ability to read critically and reflectively. Broadly speaking, it attempts to equip readers with: (1) the ability to determine purposes for reading; (2) the ability to extract, comprehend, and assimilate information; (3) the ability to examine reading material based upon purposes for reading; (4) the ability to suspend judgments; and (5) the ability to make decisions based upon information gleaned from reading.

Rationale

Russell Stauffer (1969) developed the DRTA to provide conditions that would produce readers who could think, learn, and test. Stauffer suggests that these readers

> will learn to have the strength of their convictions and the courage to deal with ideas. They will not be fearful but courageous; not blind, but discerning; not hasty, but deliberate; not deceitful, but honest; not muddled, but articulate; not acquiescent, but militant; not conceited, but modest; not imitative, but original. (p. 84)

Stauffer based his notions upon the belief that reading is a thinking process that involves the reader in using his or her own experiences to reconstruct the author's ideas. The reconstruction begins with the generation of hypotheses based upon the reader's doubts and desires. It continues with the reader's acquisition of information and the generation of further hypotheses during reading. The reconstruction terminates with the resolution of the reader's doubts and desires. Stauffer puts this into practice with the DRTA as follows:

> either the reader declares his own purposes or if he adopts the purposes of others, he makes certain how and why he is doing so. He also speculates about the nature and complexity of the answers he is seeking by using to the fullest his experience and knowledge relevant to the circumstances. Then he reads to test his purposes and his assumptions. As a result, he may: one, find the answer he is seeking literally and completely stated; two, find only partial answers or implied answers and face the need to either restate his purposes in light of the new information gained or to suspend judgment until more reading has been done; three, need to declare completely new purposes. (p. 40)

Intended Audience

As with the Directed Reading Activity, the teacher can easily adapt the DRTA for any selection at any level of difficulty. Toward a balanced reading program, Stauffer suggests the extension and differentiation of the DRTA for both group and individual use. With groups, he suggests using it with from eight to twelve students. Shepherd (1978) has also suggested using the DRTA with content fields.

Description of the Procedures

The DRTA has two parts—a process cycle and a product. The process cycle involves the reader in the following: setting purposes for reading, adjusting the rate and the material for these purposes, reading to verify purposes, pausing to evaluate understanding, then proceeding to read with the same or with different purposes. The product of the DRTA is the extension and refinement of students' ideas and thinking.

Stauffer suggests procedures for a group DRTA, which the teacher can extend and adapt into an individualized version.

1. Group DRTA. There are certain essential phases in the implementation of a group DRTA. The first phase involves directing reading-thinking processes. The second phase involves fundamental skill training.

a. Phase 1: Directing the reading-thinking process. Directing the reading-thinking process involves the reader in three steps: predicting, reading, and proving. As students proceed through a selection, they predict or define purposes for reading; they read and select relevant data; and they evaluate and revise predictions, using the information they acquire.

Maria (1989) argues that since background knowledge is an important factor in reading, it is imperative that the teacher develop an appropriate introduction to the reading selection that incorporates student diversity and experiences. It is possible that some students come to school with "limited experiences with regard to reading comprehension which are more common for middle class children, and are thus taken for granted by authors of children's texts" (Maria, 1989, 296). Because of this fact, the teacher must "bridge the gap by finding an anchor point in what all children know and what they need to know to understand the text" (Maria, 1989, 298). In doing so, "the teacher shifts the focus from the text to the children and estimates what kind of background knowledge they have for these central concepts" (Maria, 1989, 298). Maria (1989) provides the following guidelines to assist teachers in bridging this gap: (a) implement a variety of prereading strategies that will maintain student motivation and interest, (b) utilize the prereading strategy that will be the most effective and suitable for the particular text, (c) teacher scaffolding and visual props may be needed to build background experiences, (d) utilize activities that merge prior knowledge with active participation, such as group discussions and brainstorming, partner or small-group interactions, and visual props to integrate and display knowledge (pp. 297–299).

The teacher, the material, and the group are all essential to the success of this activity. The teacher has to create an environment that will arouse students' curiosities and meet their reading needs. The group serves to audit and extend the thinking of its members. The material provides, Stauffer states, "the substance for cognition" (1969, 46). To this end, he suggests the material should be well written, appealing in content, and of an appropriate difficulty level. For the purpose of directing the reading-thinking processes, the teacher may treat the selection in segments. Here is an example of how teachers might implement this phase with a selection divided into segments.

1. Each student either receives or locates a copy of the selection; the teacher directs the student to study either the title or the pictures on the first page.

- **a.** What do you think a story with this title might be about?
- **b.** What do you think might happen in this story?
- **c.** Which of these predictions do you agree with?

The teacher encourages students to make several different suggestions and to discuss agreement or disagreement with one another's suggestions. The teacher promotes this interaction. Richek (1987) argues that an important element to the success of the DRTA is positive dynamics and interactions. Richek (1987) proclaims that it "builds anticipation and sharpens the thinking process. In addition, students often serve as effective models for each other" (p. 635).

2. When the teacher introduces the DRTA, he or she first familiarizes students with the strategy for dealing with unknown words. That is, if students encounter unknown words, the teacher would expect the students to implement the following steps in the specified order:

- **a.** Read to the end of the sentence
- **b.** Use picture clues, if available

c. Sound out the word
d. Ask the teacher for help

Before asking for teacher assistance, the student should try to figure out the word and, according to Stauffer, the teacher should give the student the opportunity to do so.

3. The teacher directs the students to read a segment of the story silently to check their predictions. The teacher is responsible for ensuring that students read for meaning, observing reading performance, and helping students who request help with words. When the latter occurs, the teacher might have the student suggest a word it might be, explain what the student did to figure out the word, and, if the word is still unknown, the teacher provides it. Note that the teacher introduced no vocabulary prior to reading the story. Stauffer suggests this is unnecessary, given the vocabulary controls and systematic word identification programs found in basal readers.

4. After students have read the first segment, the teacher asks them to close their books and the comprehension check begins.

Questions serve to guide the students' examination of the evidence, their evaluation of their previous predictions, and their generation of new predictions.

"*Were you correct?*" or "*What do you think now?*" force students to examine the proof of their predictions. Oral reading of a particular sentence directs students to share their evidence with other group members.

"*What do you think now?*" or "*What do you think will happen?*" encourage students to screen their ideas and to make predictions about events to come.

5. The students read the next segment of text and with each new segment of reading material, continue the predicting-reading-proving cycle. As students proceed, they come upon more and more information; divergent conjectures begin to converge. At the beginning of the selection, predictions usually tend to be divergent. Toward the end of the reading, predictions should tend to converge.

b. Phase 2: Fundamental skill training. After the students have read the selection, the teacher has completed the first phase of the DRTA—directing the reading-thinking of the selection. Now the second phase begins. Stauffer refers to this phase as the phase when "skill training of a different kind is accomplished" (1969, 64). The second phase entails reexamining the story, reexamining selected words or phrases, and pictures or diagrams, for the purpose of developing systematically and concurrently the students' reading-thinking abilities and other reading-related skills. These might include word attack, the use of semantic analysis, concept clarification and development, power of observation, and reflective abilities. The format of these activities varies but, in many cases, is also similar to the suggested exercises in the teacher's edition, the workbooks, or the skillbooks that accompany most basal reading systems.

2. Individualized DRTA. Individualized DRTAs apply, extend, and refine the skills and abilities that students acquire in group DRTAs. Stauffer claims that individualized DRTAs afford a systematic method by which students can learn about themselves in terms of their own interests, tasks, judgments, and thinking abilities.

Teachers can introduce individualized DRTAs after group DRTAs or in conjunction with them. Familiarity with group DRTA procedures is a prerequisite for introducing an individualized DRTA.

There are several features that distinguish an individualized DRTA:

1. It does not use traditional grouping; instead, each student is free to work with a minimum of interruption, in pursuit of his or her interests. If interests coincide, students may occasionally work together.

2. The teacher expects students to know why they are to select materials, what materials they might select, and how they should select them. To this end, the teacher schedules time for selection of material and for discussion of selection techniques. The teacher may help students either individually or in groups to formulate interests, needs, and methods for selection.

3. Students should generate their own reading purposes and be familiar with the predicting-reading-proving cycle of the DRTA. Either worksheet or student record cards might direct these processes.

4. At scheduled times, students should share their work or what they have read with others. This process might involve the use of posters, bulletin boards, dramatizations, reports, and the like.

5. As the need arises, students receive incidental or systematic skills instruction, individually or in groups.

6. Students should abide by class rules that are established to ensure individual rights and efficient learning.

7. Students should keep meaningful records on a daily or weekly basis. These records might track students' activities, the stories they read, or their skill needs.

8. Students can develop other language-related skills (oral expression, written expression, listening) through presentations, reports, verbal sharing, and other activities.

9. Throughout the individualized DRTAs, the teacher should serve various functions, including the following:

- **a.** Organizing groups for projects and skill training
- **b.** Organizing the schedule to ensure flexibility and efficiency
- **c.** Pacing the various activities to afford maximum success and a minimum of frustration
- **d.** Establishing operating rules to facilitate learning and thinking
- **e.** Maintaining meaningful records to map individual progress and planning future activities
- **f.** Guiding, directing, and assisting students

Richek (1987) provides four variations of DRTA that can assist teachers in meeting the needs of students at various stages of their development (p. 635). These include

- Eliciting Predictions without Justification

  This format can be utilized when students are unable or unwilling to support their predictions. Once students experience success and gain confidence, the teacher can prompt for justifications.

- Directed Listening-Thinking Activity (DLTA)

  This procedure can be implemented with students who speak English as a second language. "Students listen to the text rather than read it." Through active listening, students "learn what to expect from difficult narratives, yet, are freed from reading text that is above their instructional level. This also increases their facility with language which transfers to reading. The key is to provide challenging listening selections" (p. 635).
- Silent Directed Reading-Thinking Activity (Silent DRTA)

  This variation "encourages independence in reading and has the added benefit of requiring a written response. It eliminates potential public embarrassment and intimidation and allows students to pace their own reading" (p. 635).
- Directed Reading-Thinking Activity Source (DRTA Source)

  "This form helps students reflect upon the role that they play as readers in the reading process. When making predictions, students specify which part of the prediction was engendered by the text and by background knowledge" (p. 636).

Cautions and Comments

As lesson frameworks, the Directed Reading Activity and the DRTA are suitable for use with almost any reading selection. But the DRTA has certain features that distinguish it from the Directed Reading Activity. First, the DRTA places a heavy emphasis upon the relationship between reading and thinking. It encourages students to be aware of and to develop their own reading-thinking processes through initiating their own purposes for reading and making predictions. DRTA invites "free participation by all students regardless of reading abilities. The only possible response is one made by the child, utilizing both information gleaned from the text in conjunction with existing knowledge. As the reader is required to prove his/her prediction, s/he must actively interact with the text's message" (Widomski, 1983, 308). Second, the role of the teacher is different. Stauffer (1968) describes the teacher's role "as one of an intellectual agitator facilitating discussion among and between students about a particular text" (Widomski, 1983, 308). Unlike the DRA, the DRTA materials govern teacher-pupil interactions and students' purposes for reading; the teacher's questioning does not prescribe this interaction. The teacher does not assume the role of either questioner or judge. Instead, the teacher becomes a moderator and a facilitator. Third, vocabulary is treated differently; the student does not meet words prior to reading but as they occur in context. In those studies in which comparisons have been made of the two procedures, the DRTA has fared better (Davidson 1970; Petre 1970). To see some of these differences more clearly, consider the use of both the DRA and DRTA with a single selection (see the sample lesson plan in this section).

Widomski (1983) suggests incorporating DRTA with semantic webbing, which "enables students to construct a visual display emphasizing ways for readers to organize and integrate concepts of a story in aiding comprehension of text" (p. 309). She argues that using "information gained in semantic webbing to test predictions for DRTA will produce the following benefits:

- Builds story schema and story grammar
- Establishes insights into varying author styles
- Strengthens inferential and evaluative skills
- Builds generalizations and deductive reasoning" (p. 312).

Davidson (1982) believes the DRTA is a sophisticated procedure when used appropriately. In order for this to occur, teacher in-service and training must be provided. Davidson provides suggestions for teachers to "help them refine and develop the needed skills" (58). Stieglitz and Oehlkers' (1989) findings reveal that teachers respond positively to innovative teaching procedures when provided appropriate in-service training and materials. For teachers familiar with traditional reading materials, the DRTA affords a useful alternative, but one that they should not use repeatedly. For example, teachers might wish to vary both the treatment of the reading-thinking phase and the format of activities within the fundamental skill phase, because with repeated use, children become "programmed" to the strategy rather than becoming involved in reading-thinking interactions. If teachers find their students unable or unwilling to make predictions, they may supplement the approach with games and activities that encourage predictive behaviors. Teachers may find the presentation of either incomplete pictures, jigsaw pieces, or cartoons useful devices for generating predictions. And teachers may sometimes read a story to students for the purpose of either introducing or supplementing the predicting-reading-proving cycle. Other examples of the DRTA and its use can be located via internet-based web searches.

Sample Lesson Plan for a Directed Reading Activity and a Directed Reading-Thinking Activity

To compare the use of a Directed Reading Activity and a Directed Reading-Thinking Activity, here are two lesson plans for the same selection. One lesson plan represents what a teacher might typically do using a Directed Reading Activity approach. The other lesson plan represents what a user might typically do with a Directed Reading-Thinking Activity.

The Selection

The selection we chose for this purpose is a story entitled "The Surprise," suitable for use in a second grade classroom. "The Surprise" tells what happened to a child's box of cookies. The child had made the cookies for his or her teacher. The teacher inadvertently sits on the box, crumbling the child's cookies. The story ends happily, with the children and the teacher having a party.

Directed Reading Activity

I. *Introducing the Selection*
In the Directed Reading Activity, the teacher introduces the selection by attempting to do four things: build an interest in the story, build concept background, introduce new vocabulary, set purposes. Show children a white box. Ask them what they think the box is (create interest). Explain to students that what you have is a surprise. Have them tell about surprises they have received (concept background). Write the words *surprise* and *children* on the chalkboard. Have the students say the words and use them in a sentence

Directed Reading-Thinking Activity

I. *Introducing the Selection*
In the Directed Reading-Thinking Activity, the teacher encourages the students to make their own predictions concerning what they are about to read. The teacher neither introduces vocabulary nor sets purpose. Show children a white box. Ask them what they think the box is. Explain to students that what you have is a surprise. Have them turn to the story entitled "The Surprise" and have them make predictions about the surprise. Ask questions like: *What do you think will happen in this story?* (The teacher might refer them to the

(introduce vocabulary). Direct children to the story entitled "The Surprise" and have them read the first page to learn who is getting the surprise (setting purpose).

II. *Directed Silent Reading*
As the students silently read the designated section, the teacher stands by to help. If the student has difficulty with a word, the authors suggest the teacher provide it immediately. Once the students have located the answer to the question, the teacher directs them either to mark with their finger, or to remember the word, sentence, or section that told them the answer.

III. *Comprehension Check and Skill Building*

IV. *Oral Rereading*
The teacher asks the students to answer this previous question: *Who was the surprise for?* The students share their answers and verify them by orally rereading the sentences or sentence that yielded the answer. The teacher asks other related questions: *Who is Miss Day? Who is Jay?*

Repetition of Phases I, II, III, & IV

As the students progress through the rest of the selection in segments, the teacher sets further purposes for their reading, the teacher checks their comprehension, and the students orally reread to verify answers.

picture clues.) Direct students to read the first page to learn about their predictions.

II. *Directed Silent Reading*
As the students silently read the designated section, the teacher stands by to help. If a student has difficulty with a word, there is a set procedure to follow. This procedure involves

1. Reading to the end of the sentence;
2. Using picture clues, if available;
3. Sounding out the word; and
4. (If the students still do not recognize the word) asking the teacher.

Once the students have finished the designated page, they turn over their books and await the teacher.

III. *Comprehension Check and Skill Building*

IV. *Oral Reading*
The teacher asks the students how accurate their predictions were. The students produce the proof they used to verify their predictions by orally rereading the sentences or sentence that yielded the answer. The teacher asks students to share what else they now know.

Repetition of Phases I, II, III, & IV

As students progress through the rest of the selection in segments, the teacher asks them to make further predictions, to silently read to verify them, to revise, and to evaluate these predictions. Students refine predictions with more information, as in the phase described under *Introducing the Selection.* Students repeat Directed Silent Reading, Comprehension Check, Skill Building, and Oral Rereading.

A teacher may use the patterns exemplified here for teaching a story or article at any level; however, there may be some differences. The teacher may or may not break the selection into segments. What the teacher actually does within each phase will vary, depending on the selection, the students themselves, and their purposes for reading.

Follow-Up Activities

In the Directed Reading Activity, various and sundry follow-up activities usually occur. In the

Follow-Up Activities

In the Directed Reading-Thinking Activities, the follow-up activities are virtually the same as

(continued)

(continued)

main, they center upon developing the following skills:

1. Comprehension
2. Word identification
3. Study skills
4. Literary appreciation and understanding
5. Vocabulary
6. Oral reading

those we propose for a Directed Reading Activity. Indeed, a teacher might use the examples here across both strategies. To follow up the Directed Reading-Thinking Activity, Stauffer suggests Fundamental Skill Activities that would be similar to the follow-up activities suggested in most basal programs.

REFERENCES

Bear, D. R., and M. Invernizzi. 1984. Student directed reading groups. *Journal of Reading* 28: 248–252. Explores the benefits of group DRTAs.

Davidson, J. L. 1970. *The relationship between teachers' questions and pupils' responses during a Directed Reading Activity and a Directed Reading-Thinking Activity.* Unpublished doctoral diss., University of Michigan. Presents a research study in which the efficacy of DRA is questioned.

———. 1982. The DRTA: Avoiding common pitfalls. *Reading Horizons* 23: 54–58. Provides solutions to the common misconceptions of DRTA.

Dixon, C. N., and D. D. Nessel. 1992. *Meaning making: Directed Reading and Thinking Activities for second-language students.* Englewood Cliffs, NJ: Prentice-Hall. A good source for use with ESL students.

Gill, J. T., and D. R. Bear. 1988. No book, whole book, and chapter DR-TAs. *Journal of Reading* 31: 444–451. Explores the use of the DRTA without books, with entire books, or chapters.

Haggard, M. R. 1988. Developing critical thinking with the Directed Reading-Thinking Activity. *The Reading Teacher* 41: 526–535. Provides an extended discussion of the DRTA, its rationale and use.

Maria, K. 1989. Developing disadvantaged children's background knowledge interactively. *The Reading Teacher* 42: 296–300. Describes knowledge to increase children's reading comprehension.

Nessel, D. 1987. The new face of comprehension instruction: A closer look at questions. *The Reading Teacher.* 40: 604–606. Provides sample questions for teachers to ask during a reading lesson.

Petre, R. M. 1970. *Quantity, quality and variety of pupil responses during an open-communication group Directed Reading-Thinking Activity and a closed-communication structured group Directed Reading Activity.* Unpublished doctoral diss., University of Delaware. Presents a research study in which the efficacy of DRA is questioned.

Purves, A. C., L. Papa, and S. Jordan (Eds.). 1994. *Encyclopedia of English studies and language arts.* New York: National Council of Teachers of English. An excellent resource that contains an extensive collection of more than 800 annotated entries/topics in English studies and language arts.

Richek, M. A. 1987. DRTA: 5 variations that facilitate independence in reading narratives. *Journal of Reading* 30: 632–636. Describes the variations of DRTA that a teacher can implement in order to meet individual student needs and development.

Shepherd, D. L. 1978. *Comprehensive high school reading methods* (2d ed.). Columbus, OH: Merrill. Presents a discussion of how the Directed Reading-Thinking Activities might be used in the content areas.

Stauffer, R. G. 1960. Productive reading-thinking at the first grade level. *The Reading Teacher* 13: 183–187. Presents a brief description of the use of reading-thinking strategies with first graders.

———. 1969. *Directing reading maturity as a cognitive process.* New York: Harper & Row. Intended for the graduate or advanced student, this text presents a detailed description of the procedure and its rationale.

———. 1970. *The language-experience approach to the teaching of reading.* New York: Harper & Row, 132–176. A readable description of the strategy and its use.

———. 1976. *Teaching reading as a thinking process.* New York: Harper & Row. Intended for the less advanced student, this text presents the procedure in detail, but with less theory.

Stauffer, R. G., and M. M. Harrel. 1975. Individualized reading-thinking activities. *The Reading Teacher* 28: 765–769. Describes a program for individualizing Directed Reading-Thinking Activities.

Stieglitz, E. L., and W. J. Oehlkers. 1989. Improving teacher discourse in a reading lesson. *The Reading*

Teacher 42: 374–379. A research study depicting the effects of teacher in-service on behaviors and DRTA procedures.

Valeri-Gold, M. 1987. Previewing: A directed reading-thinking activity. *Reading Horizons* 27: 123–126. Provides sample questions for teachers to ask when engaged in a DRTA lesson.

Widomski, C. L. 1983. Building foundations for reading comprehension. *Reading World*. 22: 306–313. Provides an overview of the effectiveness of combining two techniques, DRTA with semantic webbing, to increase reading comprehension.

Scaffolded Reading Experience

Purpose

The Scaffolded Reading Experience (SRE) was developed by Graves and Graves (1994) as a framework to assist students in successfully understanding, learning from, and enjoying a text selection. The SRE is designed as a set of prereading, during reading, and postreading activities that teachers fit to the students and the texts.

Rationale

Graves and Graves state that the Scaffolded Reading Experience was developed out of an educational need and has its foundation in classroom experience, research, and common sense. The two key principles behind SREs are the notion of scaffolding and the importance of student success in learning. Graves and Graves credit Jerome Bruner with coining the term *scaffolding* based upon his research with mothers' verbal interactions with their children when reading to them. They quote Bruner as defining scaffolding as "a process that enables a child or novice to solve a problem, carry out a task, or achieve a goal which would be beyond his [or her] unassisted efforts" (Wood, Bruner, and Ross, 1976, 90). In the case of the SRE, Graves and Graves describe reading a text as taking a journey; the more unfamiliar the territory, the greater is the need for assistance in preparation, guidance, and follow-up for the trip. The SRE was designed with scaffolding in mind as it provides students the essentials for making the journey through the text both meaningful and worthwhile.

Graves and Graves also point out that, to enjoy reading and get the most out of what is read, students need to be actively involved in the text. Assignments that require students to read the text and answer questions at the end of the selection will probably not foster students' engagement with text and may even turn them off to reading and learning. Students need to be provided the kind of learning experiences that allow them to integrate their prior knowledge and interest with a purpose for reading, guide them as they read, and enable them to synthesize and evaluate the information they glean from the text. Experiences that promote these opportunities for students also provide the opportunity for them to succeed.

It is with these principles in mind that Graves and Graves developed the Scaffolded Reading Experience. Although the activities they describe in the SRE are similar to other instructional frameworks (e.g., Directed Reading Activity, Directed Reading-Thinking Activity; see this Unit), Graves and Graves point out that the SRE differs significantly from them because it is not a preset prescription for dealing with whatever text is encountered. Instead, they view the SRE as a flexible framework that provides teachers with options in which they are able to select the most appropriate ones to use with particular students, texts, and purposes for reading. At the same time, it should be mentioned that where the DRA might teach students a particular comprehension strategy as part of the lesson, the SRE is not designed to do that. Teaching strategies, instructing students how to do something they do not know how to do, require more time than the SRE allows, according to Graves and Graves.

Intended Audience

Although seemingly intended for the elementary grades when first conceived, other descriptions of the SRE have indicated its use with students in all grades, 1–12, and with students of all ability levels. Graves and Graves also indicate the SRE can be used with all types of texts—novels, short stories, folk tales, text chapters, magazine articles, and cookbooks.

Description of the Procedures

The SRE has two major phases: (1) planning, and (2) implementation.

1. Phase One: Planning. In planning, teachers take into account their knowledge of the students' abilities, interests, and background knowledge, the topic of the selection and the difficulty it may present, and the purpose(s) for reading it. This allows teachers to decide what options to consider in planning which prereading, reading, and postreading activities to use with students to help them understand and enjoy the selection. For instance, if fifth-grade students of average ability are to read a text selection on the Constitution and the goal is to learn the important information in the text, then in prereading you could consider a motivational activity, an activity that acquaints students with some difficult vocabulary, and a questioning activity that focuses on the who, what, when, where, why, and how questions that should be answered in the text. In reading, you could choose to orally read part of the text to students, followed by them reading the rest of it looking for answers to the questions they have formulated about the text. Finally, in postreading students could break into small groups to answer their questions about the text; the groups then could come together to share their answers in a large group discussion.

Graves and Graves point out two characteristics of SREs that emphasize their flexibility. First, looking at the previous example, for instance, there is not usually only *one* set of options in planning what combination of prereading, reading, and postreading activities teachers could select in designing an effective lesson. In this example a writing activity in postreading might easily be added. Second, instead of following a prescribed set of activities as in other frameworks, teachers make their own decisions about what activities to use based upon their knowledge of their students and the text. For instance, if the same set of students were going to read *Maniac Magee* by Jerry Spinelli and you wanted students merely to enjoy reading the novel, you would not want to put students through a series of prescribed activities that a DRA or DRTA would have you do or through the structure you would use with a text chapter. In this case you simply could do a brief motivational activity, have students read the story silently, and then talk or write about the parts of it they found the most interesting. In this example a lot of instruction would be unnecessary because the story itself and the purpose for reading it, as well as the students' abilities, do not require it. Planning takes into account not only the factors mentioned—the students, the text, and the purpose(s)—but also how they are interrelated. Decisions about one factor constrain the choices to be made about the other factors.

2. Phase Two: Implementation. The implementation phase of the SRE consists of engaging students in the prereading, reading, and postreading activities planned for the lesson. In each of these components of the instructional lesson, Graves and Graves provide a number of options for teachers to consider.

a. Prereading. Prereading activities are designed to arouse students' interest, activate their prior knowledge, or preteach vocabulary or concepts that may be difficult. Prereading activities include

- Motivating
- Activating background knowledge
- Building text-specific knowledge
- Relating the reading to students' lives
- Preteaching vocabulary
- Preteaching concepts
- Prequestioning
- Predicting
- Direction setting
- Suggesting comprehension strategies

Motivating activities refer to any activity designed to interest students in the text to be read and motivate them to read it. Although many of the prereading activities that will be described can be motivating, Graves and Graves feel that an activity which focuses solely on building interest in and of itself is very appropriate.

Activating background knowledge involves bringing to bear any prior knowledge students may have of a topic for the purpose of having them consciously use it to assist in their understanding of the text. For example, before reading a text on the Rockies, students' knowledge about mountains in general can be activated.

Building text-specific knowledge refers to the notion of providing students information from the text beforehand, particularly if the text selection is conceptually difficult or has an abundance of information that is important. For instance, if there are six main topics in a text on the animal kingdom, these can be given to the students. This text-specific information serves as an advance organizer of sorts for students as they read.

Relating the reading to students' lives is a powerful way to engage students in a text and facilitate their comprehension. Before reading a text about people's reactions to someone who is disfigured, teachers might have students talk about times when they were treated wrongly for something they did.

Preteaching vocabulary involves teaching words to students that are new labels for concepts they already know. An example of this would be teaching students the word *barter* when they already know the word *trade.*

Preteaching concepts, on the other hand, consists of teaching students new and possibly difficult ideas. For instance, it would be important to take the time to teach the concept of a *depression* if students were to read a text selection dealing with America's depression of the 1930s. Preteaching new ideas will take significantly more time than preteaching new labels.

Prequestioning, predicting, and *direction setting* all involve focusing students' attention on what is important to look for as they encounter the text. These activities will help students distinguish between key ideas and those that are peripheral.

Suggesting comprehension strategies to students means telling them what strategies they should employ as they read a text. These would be strategies they already know, for instance, suggesting students use their knowledge of a cause-effect text structure to aid them in understanding a text that employs that structure.

b. Reading. Reading activities are those activities students can do as they read or those things teachers can do to assist them as they read. Reading activities that are options in an SRE include

- Silent reading
- Reading to students
- Guided reading
- Oral reading by students
- Modifying the text

Graves and Graves believe that *silent reading* should be the most frequently used activity during reading. Because most of the reading students will do throughout life will be silently reading, they need to be given as many opportunities as possible to achieve proficiency. Therefore, teachers must take care to choose text selections that students are able to read and then adequately prepare them to do so.

Reading to students provides teachers an opportunity to give students the pleasure of listening to a selection while, at the same time, modeling what good oral reading is. Reading the first part of a selection also can serve as a means to entice students into reading the rest of the text silently. In some cases difficult but important material might have to be read aloud to make it accessible to students.

Guided reading refers to any activity that teachers might use to focus students' attention on particular aspects of a text. Thus, it might be used most often with expository text material, but it can be used with narrative texts to guide students' appreciation and enjoyment of the selection. Guided reading usually begins as a prereading activity and is carried out during the reading.

Depending on the type of text, *oral reading by students* might be used by teachers. For instance, when examining alternate interpretations of text, oral reading might be helpful. Additionally, oral reading can be used with poetry or a particularly touching passage of a text.

Sometimes *modifying the text* is necessary to make a difficult or lengthy text more accessible to students. This might be done through the use of audio or video tape, changing the format of the text, and even shortening it.

c. Postreading. Postreading activities provide opportunities for students to synthesize and organize ideas obtained from a text and evaluate their understanding of it. They also allow students to respond to a text in a number of interesting ways. Postreading activities for an SRE include

- Questioning
- Discussion
- Writing

- Drama
- Artistic, graphic, and nonverbal activities
- Application and outreach activities
- Reteaching

Questioning is probably the most frequently used postreading activity. Although students should not always be faced with this type of accountability, questioning does provide teachers the opportunity to encourage higher level thinking on the part of students. Questioning can also be varied by having students ask questions of one another or of the teacher.

Another frequently used postreading activity is *discussion.* This activity, whether in small groups or the whole class, is an opportunity for students to clarify their understanding of the text and to offer their own interpretations of it. Discussion also provides students the opportunity to talk about the strategies they employed to understand a text and learn how they might approach their reading of a similar text.

Writing is another way for students to demonstrate and extend their understanding of a text. However, before writing is used, teachers should have some assurance that students understood what they read.

Drama refers to informal performances by students involving action, movement, and speech and allows them to become actively involved in responding to a text. Drama includes skits, short plays, pantomimes, and Readers Theatre (see Unit 10) and shows students that ideas can not only be read, but also may be seen, heard, and felt.

Artistic, graphic, and nonverbal activities are a broad category which includes visual art; graphics such as diagrams, maps, charts, and schematics; music; dance; and media productions such as slide shows and videos. These activities allow students to express themselves in ways that may be different from the usual school tasks and can be both fun and meaningful (see Sketch to Stretch, Unit 10).

Application and outreach activities include concrete applications, as in cooking a dish after reading a recipe about it, and activities which could take place off of school grounds, such as a field trip to an aquarium after reading about marine life. This category of activities is quite broad and includes many options.

Reteaching may be warranted when it becomes apparent that students have not achieved the level of understanding expected. Reteaching may simply be rereading parts of a text, or it may entail presenting a short lesson on a part of the text that is problematic.

Cautions and Comments

There is no doubt that the Scaffolded Reading Experience provides teachers with a framework that is flexible and allows for maximum teacher decision-making in lesson planning and construction. SREs also help students succeed in their reading, since they assist the students in understanding, enjoying, and learning from the text selections they read. Graves and Graves recommend that the SRE be employed once a week, particularly in the lower grades, but also state they might be used more frequently in the content areas because of the challenges that type of reading demands. They point out, though, that the SRE is not a complete reading framework. SREs do not teach students phonics or vocabulary, for instance; nor, as stated previously, do they teach comprehension strategies. Therefore, teachers who use this framework will need to add the teaching of essential skills to the SRE.

According to Graves and Graves, the general rule in providing scaffolding using this framework is to provide enough for students to be successful but not so much that they do not feel challenged, become bored, or feel as if they are being spoon fed. This requires teachers to be knowledgeable enough about their students and the texts they use to employ the appropriate amount of scaffolding with the SRE. Teachers also need to be flexible in using the many prereading, reading, and postreading options available to them. They need to be able to make instruction decisions about which options are most appropriate and how many of these options they will use. Too many options employed might be overkill, and too few might be inadequate to enhance students' learning. It should also be mentioned that, in addition to the numerous options Graves and Graves suggest with the SRE, many of the strategies discussed in this text can be incorporated into the SRE. For instance, an Anticipation Guide (see Unit 7), Possible Sentences (see Unit 8), and the Graphic Organizer (see Unit 12) could be added to the SRE. In fact, most of the strategies described in Units 7, 8, 10, and 12 might be used with this framework.

Finally, while Graves and Graves ground the SRE in the theoretical notions of learning and student success, no research has been carried out concerning the SRE. It should be pointed out, however, that such research might be difficult to carry out since there is no prescribed set of steps to use when employing the SRE. Without a set procedure, it would be difficult to do a comparison study of the SRE's effectiveness versus that of another instructional framework.

Also, Graves and Graves leave undeveloped issues surrounding the selection of material that will best meet the needs of the developing readers. While they stress the role of reading appropriate material to meet the students' needs, they offer little guidance in choosing appropriate material and deciding upon next steps.

REFERENCES

Avery, P. G., and M. F. Graves. 1997. Scaffolding young learners' reading of social studies. *Social Studies and the Young Learner* 9(4): 10–14. An application of the SRE to 5th-grade social studies.

Fournier, D. N. E., and M. F. Graves. 2002. Scaffolding adolescents' comprehension of short stories. *Journal of Adolescent and Adult Literacy* 46(1): 30–39. Describes the use of a Scaffolded Reading Experience (SRE) to assist seventh-grade students' comprehension of individual texts.

Graves, M. F., and P. G. Avery. 1997. Scaffolding students' reading of history. *The Social Studies* 88(3): 134–138. An application of the SRE to high school history.

Graves, M. F., and B. B. Graves. 1994. *Scaffolding reading experiences: Designs for student success.* Norwood, MA: Christopher-Gordon. Text offering a complete description of SREs, with many examples.

———. 1995. The scaffolded reading experience: A flexible framework for helping students get the most out of text. *Reading* 24: 29–34. A condensed description of SREs.

———. 2003. *Scaffolding reading experiences: Designs for student success* (2nd ed.). Norwood, MA: Christopher-Gordon. Updates the previous edition.

Graves, M. F., B. B. Graves, and S. Braaten. 1996. Scaffolded reading experiences for inclusive classes. *Educational Leadership* 53(6): 14–16. Describes the use of SREs with special education students.

Rothenberg, S. S., and S. M. Watts. 1997. Students with learning difficulties meet Shakespeare: Using a scaffolded reading experience. *Journal of Adolescent and Adult Literacy* 40: 532–539. Use of the SRE within a Shakespearean play for 8th–9th graders with learning difficulties.

Watts, S. M., and M. F. Graves. 1997. Fostering students' understanding of challenging texts. *Middle School Journal* 29: 45–51. Another application of SREs in middle school.

Wood, D. J., J. S. Bruner, and G. Ross. 1976. The role of tutoring in problem-solving. *Journal of Child Psychology and Psychiatry* 17(2):89–100. Article describing the notion of scaffolding, the basis of SREs.

Direct Instruction

Purpose

Direct Instruction procedures represent a teacher-directed approach to reading instruction using curriculum design tenets involving carefully sequenced and detailed teaching objectives emanating from an analysis of the necessary component skills.

Rationale

While Direct Instruction has been defined in various by different persons who use the term, it tends to be governed by a consideration for instructional design that places a heavy emphasis on teacher-directed learning based on an analysis of complex tasks divided into their component skills, teaching these components skills, modeling to students how these components are combined, and scaffolding the learning of these skills with review to ensure that learning has occurred.

Advocates of Direct Instruction tend to draw on a range of findings that support the direct and explicit teaching of component skills based on a needs assessment of students and the development of an instructional design that ensures that teachers model the component skills separately and in combination and attempt to ensure that the students learn the skills that are deemed essential. Whereas early models of Direct Instruction drew on the work of Englemann (1980), which focused on learning what many considered to be isolated language units, more recent models of Direct Instruction focus on a more integrated and text-based approach to literacy. What has not changed is the focus on teacher-directed and in some ways teacher-scripted approach.

DISTAR as instantiated by Englemann (1969) and others (e.g., Englemann and Osborn, 1987) is considered by many the dominant precursor of Direct Instruction, carrying with it scripted directions to teacher for how to present phonic elements and ensure that students repeated and eventually learned these elements separately and in combination. As Kameenui, Chard, and Dickson (1997) suggest, the approach has underlying tenets of the instructional design assumptions of Englemann. As they stated:

> Direct Instruction is made distinctive, pedagogically and philosophically, by its originator, Siegfried Engelmann, and the 40 or so curriculum programs that he and his colleagues have authored over the past 25 years. It is simply not possible to speak of Direct Instruction without giving attention to the assumptions on which Direct Instruction curriculum programs are based.
>
> 1. The teacher is responsible for the learning and performance of the children
> 2. The first and most important step is to discover what the child has failed to learn
> 3. There are individual differences between children, but these differences must be expressed in such a way that the teacher can do something about them
> 4. The more carefully skills are taught, the greater the possibility that the child will learn them
> 5. Teach children in a way that provides maximum feedback
> 6. He doesn't merely learn, he learns specific facts and relations
> 7. Children failing to learn is unacceptable (pp. 61–62)

In more recent instantiations of Direct Instruction, especially by Carnine, Silbert, and Kameenui, Direct Instruction includes a fuller consideration for what has emerged in conjunction with the virtues of integration, including reading–writing connection, as well as application of skills in meaningful contexts.

Advocates for Direct Instruction claim there exists substantial research evidence for Direct Instruction tied to research syntheses of effective teaching by Rosenshine (1983) and others as well as studies of the effectiveness of Direct Instruction versus other approaches in the teaching of specific skills such as in Follow Through Project evaluation, which focused on the success of Direct Instruction.

Intended Audience

Direct Instruction procedures are intended to meet the needs of all students, but especially those who are incurring difficulty learning to read.

Description of the Procedures

Direct Instruction approaches are expected to reflect:

- Objectives that are stated as specified observable behaviors and sequenced to ensure that essential skills are learned first in an appropriate order.
- Strategies that are carefully constructed to be both learnable and teachable with an understanding of what students need to learn and do over time. In particular, the strategy "must be translated into a format that specifies exactly how the teacher is to present the strategy. The strategy must include what to say, what words to emphasize, what to ask, how to signal, how to correct appropriately etc." (Carnine and Silbert, 1979, p. 15). They stress that teachers need to be concrete rather than vague or abstract and must focus on one skill at a time and suggest that the detailed format ensures that teachers can focus on student performance.

To illustrate and introduce the approach, Carnine et al. (1979, 1997, 2004), in *Direct Instruction Reading,* offer a series of vignettes around students incurring problems. The first vignette involves a student, Arthur, who is able to read the assigned texts with only 60 percent word accuracy and is unable to complete the written exercises. According to Carnine et al., a Direct Instruction teacher would likely suggest placing Arthur where he would have better likelihood of success at the same time an analysis is done of the critical component skills that are lacking and need development, "examining the tasks to determine the critical component skills and devising strategies to teach these skills" (p. 8). A second vignette involved Janice, a first grader who has been taught to memorize the words *map, sat, rat,* and *can* but misidentifies *at* for *it* and *hum* for *him.* As they stated, a Direct Instruction teacher would check her knowledge of the phonic element "i" and how she approaches reading words and would look for any deficiency in skills. A directed approach to teaching would likely include modeling and practice with support until mastery is achieved. A third vignette involved Dale, a sixth grader who is identified as having difficulty recalling and applying a strategy for looking up information in a textbook. Here Carnine, Silbert, and Kameenui suggest that Direct Instruction would reteach the skill and provide more practice after teaching until mastery. They explain that across the three situations, a distinguishing feature of Direct Instruction is teaching focused on essential component skills following a task analysis of the essential prerequisite skills prior to reading or the performance of a task. Again, task analysis is seen as essential for identifying what skills are essential and need to be taught directly and practiced adequately until mastery.

The teacher's role is seen as occurring in two phases: at the beginning of the year and then day to day. At the beginning of the year, the teacher is expected to invest a great deal of time setting up the program, which includes assessing students, determining skill needs priorities and sequencing, selecting material, and organizing resources. The guidelines for the analysis of skills and sequencing involve recognition that preskills for a strategy are taught before the strategy itself, instances that are consistent are addressed before inconsistencies, high-utility skills are introduced first, and easier concepts are presented before harder ones. On a day-to-day basis the teacher is expected to organize the skill instruction and practice exercises, which involves intensive teacher–student interaction prior to independent reading and writing experiences, which the students will likely do without direct teacher support.

There are ranges of other elements that are also deemed key to success. They include the examples that are selected; the practice that is provided including the support, presentation techniques, small-group instruction presentation, and unison oral responding; ways to signal response; the pacing of instruction; and how teachers should monitor students, including judging performance, correcting and other forms of feedback, and doing formal checks on learning including delayed tests. In terms of passage selection, at the lower elementary levels, decodable texts, which apply the skills, might be used. As students proceed to the intermediate level, the text becomes more varied, but an attempt is made to include texts that address the skills under consideration.

To illustrate how the skill portion might proceed, here is an example of the format suggested for teaching phonics and a format for passage reading. Both are for the primary grades.

Example: Rhyming Words

Teacher model: "Listen. I am going to rhyme with [pause] *at*. What word?"
Teacher signals response. Students respond with *at*.
Teacher says:

Rhymes with *at* begins with *s*. Sat
Rhymes with *at* begins with *f*. Fat
Rhymes with *at* begin with *m*. Mat.

Teacher leads. "Lets do it together. We are going to rhyme with [pause] *at*. What word [signals]?" "At."
Teacher and students together say:

Rhymes with *at* and begins with *s*. What word? [clap] Sat
Rhymes with *at* and begins with *f*. What word? [clap] Fat
Rhymes with *at* and begins with *m*. What word? [clap] Mat

Teacher responds one or two times until students appear not to need leading. Teacher directs students to try this by themselves and then tests some individuals.

Example: Paragraph Reading. Teacher introduces story by reading the title. The teacher directs the students to read the title. Teacher says, "Let's see what the story says about the cat and the mouse. Read the passage silently, and then lets read it aloud together."

Teacher points to the end of the second paragraph. Students do so. Teacher tells students to read silently the two paragraphs then tells them to place their fingers on the first word of the first paragraph. The teacher observes students eyes as they read silently. When everyone is finished the teacher calls on different students to read different sentences. Individual students read the sentences aloud. The teacher then asks questions to check if they know what the story is about. The process continues until the teacher feels that the students are able to proceed in pairs.

Various strategies within this text are illustrative of Direct Instruction. For example, two strategies, Synthetic Word Families and Syllabaries, in Unit 5, Phonics and Word Identification, reflect many of the instructional design features of Direct Instruction. In Unit 7, Comprehension Development and Thinking Critically, the strategy Explicit Teaching of Reading Comprehension is governed by the tenets of scaffolding and modeling as espoused by Direct Instruction advocates. Likewise, there are a number of other strategies including some of those discussed in these and other units. Certainly, some of the multisensory approaches have adopted scripts similar to those proposed in Direct Instruction. Further, the discussion of whole language includes a lengthy discussion of some of the tenets that distinguish whole language from Direct Instruction. Finally, Carnine, Silbert, and Kameenui's *Direct Instruction Reading* includes more detail about the approach and for the interested reader should be used as a primary source for an understanding of the approach.

Cautions and Comments

Direct Instruction has received renewed attention in conjunction with the increased emphasis that evidence-based practice has received, especially in the context of a narrow definition of what constitutes "scientific research" as well as claims that such research offers support for direct teaching over other approaches.

Critics of direct instruction have expressed a range of concerns. For example, it has been suggested that the scripted nature of the Direct Instruction could have a detrimental effect on teachers. For example, as Allington (2002) and McNeil (2000) discuss, there is a loss of professional engagement of teachers in approaches that perpetuate a scripted approach. Whereas advocates of Direct Instruction would suggest that the format is based on careful consideration of what should be targeted for instruction and how that instruction should be delivered to ensure effectiveness, the approach is perceived as detracting from what teachers need to do in the moment-by-moment nature of learning and classroom life. For Direct Instruction advocates, their lock-step approach ensures that learning will proceed as they prescribe.

It has also been suggested that the emphasis on component skills assumes an approach to learning to read that proceeds from part to whole rather than interactive and that is based more on a stimulus response learning model than on constructivist approaches. Further, the emphasis on learning the components and then applying them may be problematic for some students for whom the transfer or application of skills in context is not straightforward. In longitudinal studies, the importance of integrated approaches to teaching reading is supported, especially if student performance after several years is examined.

Most educators see a role for some of the elements of Direct Instruction. Indeed, notions of scaffolding, modeling, demonstrations, reviews, and needs-based assessment are included in most approaches. What is distinctive is the care with which the instructional planning occurs with Direct Instruction and the extent to which the orientation is on a teacher-centered approach in which the teacher offers the models versus a student-centered or more interactive orientation in which the teacher might take the lead from the student.

REFERENCES

Allington, R. L. 2002. *Big brother and the national reading curriculum: How ideology trumped evidence.* Portsmouth, NH: Heinemann. Discusses concerns with scripted teaching and the need for a dynamic approach to teaching.

Baumann, J. F. 1983. A generic comprehension instructional strategy. *Reading World* 23: 284–294. Presents an instructional strategy based on tenets of Direct Instruction

Carnine, D., and J. Silbert. 1979. *Direct Instruction reading* (2d ed.). Columbus, OH: Merrill. Represents a thorough discussion of the assumptions, arguments, claims, and elements that constitute teaching explicit and synthetic phonics from the perspective of those advocating Direct Instruction.

Carnine, D. W., J. Silbert, and E. J. Kameenui. 1997. *Direct Instruction reading* (3d ed.). Columbus, OH: Merrill. Provides a detailed examination of the tenets of Direct Instruction with illustrations and guidelines for practice.

———. 2004. *Direct Instruction Reading* (4th ed.). Columbus, OH: Merrill. More recent edition of the aforementioned book updated in terms of research and with additional illustrations.

Englemann, S. 1969. *DISTAR reading program.* Chicago: Science Research Associates. Presents the reading program which is the primary example of Direct Instruction.

———. 1980. *Direct Instruction.* Englewood Cliffs, NJ: Prentice-Hall. The original volume discussing direct instruction.

Englemann, S., and J. Osborn, 1987. *DISTAR Language I.* Chicago: Science Research Associates. Presents the language program that followed from DISTAR reading.

Kameenui, E. J., D. C. Simmons, D. Chard, and S. Dickson. 1997. Direct Instruction reading. In S. A. Stahl and D. A. Hayes (Eds.), *Instructional models in reading.* Mahwah, NJ: Erlbaum, 59–84. Discusses the tenets and historical antecedents of Direct Instruction.

McNeil, L. M. 2000. *Contradictions of school reform: Educational costs of standardized testing.* New York: Routledge. Discusses the experiences of Houston teachers with overly scripted instruction.

Rosenshine, B. V. 1983. Teaching functions in instructional programs. *Elementary School Journal* 83: 335–351. Reviews the process/product research on teaching and learning and discusses Direct Instruction.

Queensland's New Basics and Rich Literacy Tasks

Purpose

Allan Luke and Peter Freebody, in conjunction with the Queensland Department of Education (Australia), developed a literacy framework, or new "literacy strategy," intended to move literacy programs for the future. In particular, the framework is intended to provide teachers with guidelines for transitioning classrooms and schools to meet the changes arising from information-based cultures, economies, and technologies. In terms of literacy, this includes the shift beyond print-based literacies to multiple literacies.

Rationale

Our description of Queensland's New Basics focuses on literacy; however, New Basics cuts across curriculum areas. Indeed, New Basics is described as a transdisciplinary approach with four basic categories: (1) Life pathways and social futures (Who am I and where am I going?) (2) Multiliteracies and communication media (How do I make sense of and communicate with the world?) (3) Active citizenship (What are my rights and responsibilities in communities, cultures, and economies?) and (4) Environment and technologies (How do I describe, analyze, and shape the world around me?).

The integration occurs somewhat in conjunction with the pursuit of a curriculum that connects with the real world, culminating in the completion of what is labeled Rich Tasks, which have the following characteristics:

> A capstone function or culminating experience akin to Ted Sizer's notion of demonstration (Sizer, 1994)
>
> Assessment activities aligned with real-world problem solving and teacher professional judgment versus high stakes assessment
>
> Tasks involving problem solving that have relevance and power in everyday life and in today's new worlds of work
>
> A range of cognitive, cultural, and social skills that need to be acquired developmentally

Accordingly, New Basics pedagogy focuses on the quality of student intellectual engagement, connectedness, and integration en route to a less crowded curriculum. It provides ways to provide a supportive classroom environment, recognizing differences and distinctiveness, and is introduced to suggest an alternative to a priori defined approaches to teaching. The term *productive pedagogy* is introduced to bring to the fore teaching practices that stress teacher judgment, including adjustments and customization to meet different situations with different students. As Luke suggested:

> Productive pedagogies are an approach to creating a place, space and vocabulary for us to get talking about classroom instruction again. It isn't a magic formula (e.g., just teach this way and it will solve all the kids' problems), but rather it's a framework and vocabulary for staff room, in-service, preservice training, for us to describe the various things that we can do in classrooms—the various options in our teaching "repertoires" that we have—and how we can adjust these, play with these . . . to get different outcomes. This isn't a "one approach fits all model of pedagogy." It has the possibility of providing a common grounds and dialogue between teachers, school administrators, teacher educators, student-teachers and others about these repertoires and about which aspects of our teaching repertoires work best for improved intellectual and social outcomes for distinctive groups of kids. . . . The tasks for teachers would be inductive rather than deductive, holistic rather than positivist. . . . [T]he teacher would begin from the whole tasks that have visible value in the everyday lifeworlds of work, education, citizenship, etc. and then use their professional knowledge and judgment to distill down knowledges, subskills, practices and competences for teaching—instead of beginning from the skills. (Luke, 1999, 5–7)

In terms of literacy, New Basics pedagogy is closely aligned with the notions of multiliteracies emanating from the work of a team of leading literacy scholars who called themselves the "New London Group" and the Pedagogy of Multiliteracies to which they are committed (New London Group, 1996). These groups argue for a commitment to prepare all students to participate in public, community, and economic life, the achievement of which involves significant broadening of our views and pedagogies of literacy.

As the New London Group (1996) stated:

> Literacy pedagogy . . . has been a carefully restricted project—restricted to formalized, monolingual, monocultural and rule-governed forms of language. . . . [W]e attempt to this

> understanding of literacy and literacy teaching and learning to include negotiating a multiplicity of discourses. First, we want to extend the idea and scope of literacy pedagogy to account for the context of our culturally and linguistically diverse and increasingly globalized societies, for the multifarious cultures that interrelate and the plurality of texts that circulate. Second, we argue that literacy pedagogy now must account for the burgeoning variety of text forms associated with information and multimedia technologies. This includes understanding and competent control of representational forms that are increasingly significant in overall communications environment, such as visual images and their relationships to the written word. . . . [T]he proliferation of communications channels and media supports and extends cultural and subcultural diversity . . . the question of difference becomes critically important.

Along similar lines, the Queensland New Basics proponents define literacy as "the flexible and sustainable mastery of a repertoire of practices with the texts of traditional and new communication technologies via spoken, print and multimedia" (1996, 9).

> Flexible and sustainable mastery requires not only "basic skills," but also the capacity to stretch, blend, expand and exchange these skills for others across the life span. It is productive to think of literacy in terms of a repertoire of practices that, like the skills of a musician or tradesperson, expands and develops as one faces new technologies and techniques, new possibilities, problems and contexts. (Education Queensland, 2000a, 11)

Drawing on the work of Freebody and Luke and others (Freebody and Luke, 1990; Luke and Freebody, 1998; New South Wales Department of Education and Training, 1997), the New Basics include as the repertoire of practices the following roles for students:

- Code Breaker: The practices required to crack the codes and systems of written and spoken languages and visual images;
- Meaning Maker: The practices required to build and construct cultural meanings from texts;
- Text User: The practices required to use texts effectively in everyday, face-to-face situations;
- Text Analyst: The practices required to analyze, critique and second-guess texts. (Education Queensland, 2000a, 11–12).

In turn they suggest examining literacy practices or planning literacy along two axes: media of communication and roles.

Roles/Modes	**Oral**	**Print**	**Media**
Code Breaker			
Meaning Maker			
Text User			
Text Analyst			

Intended Audience

Parents, students, and teachers in K–12 settings are the primary audience for the framework.

Description of the Framework

A key assumption with the New Basics Program is that the approach is intended as a framework for planning and supporting the development of multiliteracies rather than a prepackaged approach that prescribes a uniform set of themes or units and a set of a priori lessons.

Indeed, as the Queensland Department of Education has introduced New Basics it has done so by inviting schools to participate in a manner akin to experimentation around emerging possibilities rather than in a manner that is formulaic or preset in terms of day-to-day activities. The approach expects schools to identify meaningful integrated engagements with projects that enlist multiple literacies over extended periods of time, which could extend to weeks or even months.

These extended literacies experiences, or Rich Tasks, serve as the foundation for teachers and students planning a range of literacy learning experiences involving various modes of communication and different roles. Rich Tasks are seen as extended projects spread over varying spans of time. They would be seen as being generative, facilitating transdisciplinary and integrated projects that connect with the everyday world and new world of work in ways that engage students with new literacies as well as old. Further, Rich Tasks absorb and reduce the extent to which learning is crowded, piecemeal, and removed from situations. In these learning contexts, teachers in partnership with other teachers would be engaged in planning how to support the students in ways including providing the resources and scaffolding necessary for success and mastery of the skills (traditional and new) that students will need. Initially, it was suggested that there would be as few as five Rich Tasks for grades 1–3, seven for grades 4–6, and eight for grades 7–9.

It was intended that teachers would in a sense work backward from the Rich Tasks. In other words, the teacher or teachers (perhaps in partnership with the community) would select Rich Tasks and use their professional judgment to break them down into sequences of instruction around targeted repertoires of practices (strategies and knowledge) befitting the Rich Task and informed by the teachers' knowledge of skills and tool development that might be needed.

Consistent with these notions, the Queensland Department of Education set the guidelines to characterize Rich Tasks and what might follow. In so doing, they appear to be suggesting rather than any prescribing preset Rich Tasks. They have also set about supporting a range of pilots across the state that are quite varied and meet the different needs of students in different settings. The range is diverse and includes such Rich Tasks as the following which would then spur a number of substeps including skill and tool development activities:

> A suggested Rich Task for years four to six involved the design, development and display of a product. In particular, students were expected to design or improve the design of a purposeful product—indeed, make the product or a working model or prototype. In turn, as part of the display they were to generate a marketing plan and explore mass manufacturing.
>
> A suggested Rich Task for years seven to nine involved improving the well being in the community. In particular, students would be engaged in working with a local community to

> develop a plan for improving an aspect of the well being of this community and enact the plan modifying it as necessary. They will evaluate the level of success they experience in enacting the plan and, where necessary, recommend future action. (Education of Queensland, 2000b)

Initially these tasks are seen as accounting for 40 to 60 percent of school time.

In terms of assessment, the Queensland Department of Education argues for a range of measures including the notion of demonstration, exhibitions or portfolios, a variety of tasks, and teacher judgment. They stress the need for parents to be better informed about the weaknesses of tests and the limitations and multiple interpretations of different test results. Rich Tasks serve as a form of overarching concept from which performance assessment would emerge. Accordingly, they would be expected to vary in accordance with the nature of the problems that are being pursued.

Cautions and Comments

The New Basics draws from critical and insightful examination of the research literature and assessment data as well as exploration of key issues. In terms of research findings, New Basics advocates strongly support a range of research findings as informing practice. They stress that there is no silver bullet or single approach, method, or package that should be endorsed. But while they highlight the limitations of past research and the problems with applying research settings to different settings, they do suggest that research tends to support the worth of the following practices:

- Scaffolded and focused pedagogical strategies for specific groups of students
- Investment in initial, ongoing, and continuous professional development of teachers

Perhaps the central undergirding pedagogical concept is the notion of Rich Literacy Tasks, which are viewed as integrated and cross-disciplinary initiatives with which students are intended to engage for extended periods of time. These Rich Literacy Tasks are expected to serve as the basis for planning students' engagement in real-world tasks and problem solving using the aforementioned modes of communication, including multimedia. In many ways these Rich Literacy Tasks are a form of situated learning and serve as the foundation for students engaged in scaffolded support and developing expertise as Code Breakers, Meaning Makers, Text Users, and Text Analysts.

The New Basics and Rich Literacy Tasks are clearly cutting edge in a number of ways. To date, few literacy programs or frameworks have engaged students and teachers in literacy experiences that are directed in a planful fashion toward the new literacies—especially multimedia. Although the pursuit of such possibilities may be constrained by the digital technologies currently available to students, growing numbers of schools are increasing the access to multimedia-based technologies especially as laptops, wireless environments, digital imaging, and other software afford more ubiquitous mobile and flexible use to these tools.

New Basics could be seen by some as an approach to curriculum that is tied to notions of units, projects, and themes. Rather than have the curriculum set up a predefined approach and sequence of skill development, such projects would serve as the context and basis for determining what to teach when and how. For the Australian teacher who has had a history of program development rather than program adoption (as their U.S. counterparts have) doing so would be familiar.

New Basics evolved from a careful consideration of the future needs of students and drew heavily from a thoughtful consideration of research, assessment data, and assumptions about learning, culture, equity, and professional practice. The approach is intended to spur changes in practice, which will in turn influence changes in the guidelines for New Basics. In hopes of promoting such synergies, various pilots are established that are informing future guidelines and engaging in collaborative exchanges around professional issues.

One of the hallmarks of New Basics is a definition of and approach to difference. Their proponents discuss a range of issues around difference and bring to the fore notions of distinctiveness and the disconnection between schools and the experiences of some students. This includes the curriculum itself—especially the content—as well as the lack of congruence between teachers and students who need support. While being critical of past assessments of diverse groups of students, they do suggest that there appears to be convergence in that certain groups show consistently low levels of performance on tests. These groups include boys, aboriginal students, students for whom English is not a first language, and students living in limited economic circumstances. They do stress that one should approach the needs of different groups with the understanding that certain students and settings are underresourced. As they state, "there is systematic under-provision of literacy education to certain categories of students and communities rather than these kinds of students from these kinds of backgrounds are under-achieving" (Education Queensland, 2000a, 31).

In terms of the debates over methods, New Basics appears to accommodate the various concerns of literacy scholars, whether they be advocates of a genre approach, whole language, or a code emphasis. The four roles advocated for students ensure that traditional literacy skills as well as other areas associated with multiliteracies are addressed. The focus on Rich Literacy Tasks ensures that teaching and learning of various strategies are related to real-world problem solving. In some ways the New Basics approach has elements in common with integrated theme-based curriculum together with approaches to skill and strategy development, which are scaffolded.

A range of material detailing New Basics and Rich Literacy Tasks is available at the Queensland Department of Education website: http://education.qld.gov.au/corporate/newbasics.

REFERENCES

Education Queensland. 2000a. *Literate futures: Report of the literacy review for Queensland state schools.* Brisbane, Australia: Education Queensland. A core document that provides the undergirding tenets, research literature, and data sources describing New Basics.

Education Queensland. 2000b. *New Basics: Curriculum organizers.* Brisbane, Australia: Education Queensland.

Freebody, P., and A. Luke 1990. Literacies programs: Debates and demands in cultural contexts. *Prospect* 5: 7–15. Provides a discussion of how New Basics address the debate about cultural context.

Luke, A. 1999. *Education 2010 and new times: Why equity and social justice still matter, but differently.* Education Queensland online conference. October 20, 1999. Discusses the tenets of New Basics, especially the undergirding research and theory.

Luke, A., and P. Freebody. 1998. The social practices of reading. In S. Muspratt, A. Luke, and P. Freebody (Eds.), *Constructing critical literacies.* Creskill, NJ: Hampton Press. Provides some of the early discussion of reading practices in terms of social processes and institutions.

Luke, A., J. Ladwig, B. Lingard, D. Hayes, and M. Mills. 1998. *School reform longitudinal study (SRLS).* St. Lucia, Australia: University of Queensland. A report of the research that directly influenced the development of New Basics.

New London Group. A pedagogy of multiliteracies: Designing social futures. *Harvard Educational Review* 66(1): 60–92. This often cited article is viewed as central to the discussion of multiple literacies, especially in terms of establishing a rationale.

New South Wales Department of Education and Training. 1997. *State Literacy Strategy.* Sydney: Department of Education and Training.

Sizer, T. 1992. *Horace's hope: What works for the American high school.* Boston: Houghton-Mifflin. Provides a discussion of a number of notions that inform New Basics, in particular Sizer's discussion of demonstrations and exhibitions as a means of assessing students' engagement in meaningful integrated learning.

UNIT 2

Holistic, Whole-Language, Learner-Centered, and Literature-Based Approaches

UNIT OVERVIEW

This unit deals with approaches to literacy for which a central focus involves engaging students in meaningful literacy experiences through inquiry and workshops as well as a range of other activities via reading and writing projects and units. These practices are informed by a range of theories and research in conjunction with various forms of exploration of practice, including traditional empiricism.

The holistic label for the strategies in this unit may be a misnomer if the term carries with it the notion that these approaches view the literacy development without regard to how students orchestrate their engagements with a variety of texts by using a variety of strategies in combination. Most of the approaches are multifaceted in terms of their goals and their focus while retaining an overriding goal of meaningful literacy involvements. Most of the approaches in this unit involve a mix of reading and writing together with strategy development or an approach that is not interactive or pedagogical.

Over the past decade, literacy has been the focus of considerable political attention in the United States and elsewhere. Certain views seem to have become the target for considerable criticism while others have been able to garner a great deal of support and even legislated mandates to ensure that reading is taught in a predetermined fashion. The U.S. Congress has now mandated a definition of reading tied to a certain view of reading (versus others) as well as what counts as research (and what doesn't). Politicians also argue that the reading debates on beginning approaches (especially phonics and whole-language) are over as a new integrated approach is touted.

Jerome Harste discussed his encounters with the changing political climate in the October 1998 NCTE *Council Chronicle* in an article entitled "A Model of Difference." As he stated:

> I think we are in a McCarthy era in reading and it concerns me.
>
> All of a sudden we are supposed to be pleased with research reports on reading that take us back to a Bloomfield view of reading. Reports in which reading is not being seen as an instance of language. That is why they need not review this literature. Goodman doesn't exist. Reports in which reading and writing relationship research, other than the early literacy stuff, can be ignored. Now Graves doesn't exist.

> These are decisions that strike at the very heart of our profession. What is particularly insidious is that all of this is being done in the name of science.
>
> Recently, I was asked to respond to *Preventing Reading Failure in Young Children* at AERA where a panel of the researchers presented sections of this final report published by the National Reading Council.
>
> Specifically I criticized the report on its many flawed conceptions of reading. I argued that the report positioned itself as having ended the reading wars and in so doing perpetuated the myth that the problems with reading in this country are a result of whole language and phonics wars and that somehow this mess has weakened reading instruction and resulted in declining literacy scores. I suggested that the panel visit schools so they could see for themselves that there is not enough whole language going on in this country to have affected reading scores either positively or negatively. I concluded this first point by arguing that I thought they had the big picture wrong. My second criticism rested on their conception of the reading process. While their exact definition of reading is rather slippery, for the most part they advocate a linguistic model of reading where "real reading" begins with phonological awareness and graphophonemic processing. Everything else is cast as a factor that affects reading. . . . My third criticism of the document was that it posed itself as a document about pedagogy when it was really about power. I used the fact that the report's conclusions already had become legislative action as data to support this hypothesis.
>
> When I got done with my critique, several respected colleagues expressed their disappointment with my remarks. One said he just couldn't understand what it was I disliked about this report. Another said it was a little bit like having a skunk show up at a rose garden party. Still another thought it was most unfortunate I took the position I did and that I should use my position as vice president of NCTE to get behind the report.
>
> . . . Now I personally know that these colleagues of mine have broader views of reading than are reflected in this report. But why, I ask, is no one speaking out?
>
> . . . From what I can tell the only people who benefit are basal publishers. They are going to have a heyday. Everyone is interpreting these reports as saying they have to put in place a systematic phonics program and a formal spelling program
>
> . . . Another experience happened just last week. I attended the first meeting of the new National Reading Panel formed by NICHD (National Institute of Child and Human Development). While I was a visitor and not given an opportunity to speak, it amazed me how, with two or three options on the floor, chairman Donald Langenberg simply declared that they seemed to have reached consensus and moved on.

While the present unit addresses a range of practices that might not be deemed as "politically correct" by selected sectors that seem to have garnered enormous political advantage, they represent noteworthy strategies which we would deem as making significant and positive contributions to the improvement of literacy programs. The strategies and frameworks in the present unit described include Whole-Language, Theme-Based Units, Author-Reader-Inquirer Cycle, Reading-Writing Workshop, Book Club, Uninterrupted Sustained Silent Reading, and Individualized Reading. This should not be viewed as an exhaustive list of strategies that could be labeled Holistic, Whole-Language, Learner-Centered, or Literature-Based approaches. It should be noted that many of the other units include strategies or approaches that could be so labeled.

Whole-Language. Whole-Language is a view of literacy, literacy-learning, and teaching that is driven by key assumptions about how students learn. Whole-Language has its antecedents in the student-centered notions of Dewey and the psycholinguistic assumptions of Kenneth Goodman, Smith, and others. In recent years, these assumptions have been used as the basis for suggesting classroom practices which befit some of these tenets.

Theme-Based Units. Theme-Based Units incorporates projects as a means of providing opportunities for learners to pursue integrated learning experiences wherein learners as individuals and members of different groups set goals, plan, research, compose/construct, and share ideas gleaned from their exploration of topics and issues demanding the integration of resources and tools from different subject areas.

Author-Reader-Inquirer Cycle. Like Whole-Language, the Author-Reader-Inquirer Cycle represents not so much a collection of strategies for reading and writing as an approach to learning and curriculum development. The Author-Reader-Inquirer Cycle, as explained in Short, Harste, and Burke (1996), uses literacy as a means for inquiry rather than as an end in itself. By engaging students as author in a cycle of experiences around inquiry of their worlds, writing serves as the backdrop for stimuli of, and in synergism with, reading, talk, and other ways of engaging students separately and together in shared explorations.

Reading-Writing Workshop. The Reading-Writing Workshop represents a comprehensive approach to reading and writing that attempts to engage students in meaningful literacy activities and to develop strategic approaches to reading and writing. The workshop approach draws from holistic approaches to teaching and learning, including process writing and Whole-Language tenets and related strategies.

Book Club. Book Club began as an attempt to engage students more fully in conversations about books. In pursuing this goal, Book Club has expanded and become a framework to guide teachers "as researchers" in developing reading and writing instructional activities to ensure that students can be as fully engaged as possible in literacy activities. Book Club's genesis and continued development are tied to the efforts by Susan McMahon and Taffy Raphael to explore the possibilities that emerge from changing views of literacy learning. They have been guided by a commitment to ongoing teacher research as well as certain key theoretical and pedagogical assumptions largely emanating from a combination of a sociocultural perspective and reader response theory that emphasizes the active and social nature of learning as well as the central role of language in the process of literacy learning.

Uninterrupted Sustained Silent Reading. Uninterrupted Sustained Silent Reading is among the few strategies that have as their central focus opportunities for students to engage in sustained reading and to do so alongside others, including the teacher and sometimes others within a school, such as school personnel who provide services other than instruction.

Individualized Reading. Individualized Reading, which centers on the child rather than on the material, seeks to counter the orientation away from individual characteristics. Based upon the notion of seeking, self-selection, and self-monitoring, Individualized Reading redirects reading instruction toward reading real books and toward students assuming responsibility for monitoring their own progress.

REFERENCES

Harste, J. 1998. A model of difference. *NCTE Council Chronicle,* October 8, 220.

National Research Council. 1998. *Preventing reading failure in young children.* Washington, DC: National Academy Press.

Taylor, D. 1998. *Beginning to read and the spin doctors of science: The political campaign to change America's mind about how children learn to read.* Urbana, IL: National Council of Teachers of English.

Whole-Language

Purpose

Whole-Language is a view of literacy, literacy learning, and teaching that is driven by key assumptions about how students learn. In recent years, these assumptions have been used as the basis for suggesting classroom practices for students.

Rationale

Whole-Language has antecedents in the student-centered notion of Dewey, but its modern-day roots and articulation stem from the work of psycholinguists that began in the late sixties and early seventies. Early proponents of Whole-Language were Smith and Goodman. In an article entitled "On the Psycholinguistic Method of Teaching Reading," they explained what remains as a key tenet—Whole-Language is a set of beliefs, not an approach. In this article, Whole-Language was synonymous with a "psycholinguistic approach." As they stated:

> a "psycholinguistic approach" to reading would be the very antithesis of a set of instructional materials. . . . The child learning to read seems to need the opportunity to examine a large sample of language, to generate hypotheses about the regularity underlying it, and to test and modify these hypotheses on the basis of feedback that is appropriate to the unspoken rules that he happens to be testing.
>
> None of this can, to our mind, be formalized in a prescribed sequence of behaviorally stated objectives embalmed in a set of instructional materials, programmed or otherwise. The child is already programmed to learn to read. He needs written language that is both interesting and comprehensible and teachers who understand language-learning and appreciate his competence as a language-learner. (1971, 179–180)

This concern over making a distinction between beliefs and practice was stressed by Altwerger, Edelsky, and Flores. In response to the question "Whole-Language: What is it?" they stated:

> First and foremost: Whole-Language is not practice. It is a set of beliefs, a perspective. It must become practice, but it is not the practice itself. Journals, book publishing, literature study, thematic science units and so forth do not make a classroom "Whole-Language." Rather these practices become Whole-Language-like because the teacher has particular beliefs and intentions. (1987, 145)

Weaver (1990) further defines the beliefs and practices of Whole-Language as:

> a way of thinking about children and their learning, a set of beliefs that increasingly guides instructional decision-making for those committed to this educational philosophy. Thus, if we talk about a whole language approach, we mean instructional practices that stem from this philosophy, not a system that can be embodied in sets of prepackaged materials. (p. 22)

Several key theoretical premises inform Whole-Language. In terms of assumptions about language, these premises seem aptly described by Altwerger, Edelsky, and Flores (1987), who suggest:

> Whole-Language is based on the following ideas: (a) language is for making meanings, for accomplishing purposes; (b) written language is language—thus what is true for language in general is true for written language; (c) the cuing systems of language (phonology in oral, orthography in written language, morphology, syntax, semantics, pragmatics) are always simultaneously present in any instance of language use; (d) language use always occurs in a situation; (e) situations are critical to meaning making. (p. 145)

Gursky (1991) defines Whole-Language as

> an entire philosophy about teaching, learning, and role of language in the classroom. It stresses that language should be kept whole and uncontrived and that children should use language in ways that relate to their own lives and cultures. In the whole language classroom, the final product—the "answer"—isn't as important as the process of learning to define and solve problems. Whole language advocates believe that the ideal classroom is a child centered one in which students enjoy learning because they perceive that the material has meaning and relevance to their lives. (p. 23)

In terms of assumptions about learning and teaching, Goodman and Goodman (1982) have offered several guidelines. In general, Whole-Language holds the view that teaching should be guided by what is known about language learning. The further teaching moves away from how students learn naturally, the more difficult the task is for students. In accordance with this view, a great deal of respect is given to the child's natural language learning processes and the fact that a child learns literacy from a very early age in a similar way to proficient readers. As Goodman and Goodman (1982) state:

> In this method there are no pre-reading skills, no formalized reading readiness. Instead, learning is expected to progress from whole to part, from general to specific, from familiar to unfamiliar, from vague to precise, from gross to fine, from highly contextualized to more abstract. Children are expected to read, first, familiar meaningful wholes—easily predictable materials that draw on concepts and experiences they already have. These may be signs, cereal boxes, or books. From this perspective readiness is intrinsic when language is real. Children are ready when they see need and have confidence in themselves. By carefully building on what children already know, we assure their readiness. (p. 127)

In accordance with this view, Whole-Language does not support reading and writing curriculum that is overly structured or constrained by attempts to sequence a hierarchy of reading and writing experiences. The use of controlled vocabulary aimed at giving students control of a predetermined set of words is seen as being artificial, meaningless, and misdirected. Likewise, the isolation of skills and the tendency to teach skills to mastery are seen as inappropriate. As Goodman and Goodman (1982) state:

> Learning to read is not learning to recognize words, it is learning to make sense of texts. In the whole-language program there is no separate phonics instructions. . . . Readers in a whole-language program do form rules for relating print to speech as they are reading meaningful texts. But these self-developed rules are not overlearned and artificial as they would be if they were imposed by a structured phonics program. (p. 127)

One of the key principles underlying Whole-Language is that language is learned best when the learner's focus is on use and meaning.

Whereas descriptions of Whole-Language principles may vary somewhat, they tend to focus on respect for the learner, for learning in meaningful situations, and for the learner's natural language-learning tendencies. In conjunction with these tendencies, Whole-Language values approximation, immersion, engagement, and exploration rather than mastery of conventions and piecemeal learning. In an attempt to summarize some of these key tenets, Goodman and Goodman offered the following list of selected principles:

1. Learning in school and out of school should not be different. In both situations learning should be functional and literacy should be an extension of natural language learning.
2. Function should be considered a necessary precondition for the development of form or learning about form.
3. Literacy development, including the learning of strategies, should occur during functional, meaningful, and relevant language use.
4. Literacy abilities are acquired by children from a very early age in conjunction with their personal and social development. They have already made strong beginnings in developing literacy and literacy learning principles before they come to school.
5. Teaching and learning do not have a one-to-one correspondence. "The teacher monitors development, provides relevant appropriate materials, and provides timely experiences to facilitate learning" (Goodman and Goodman 1982, 126). The learner extracts from that environment elements that are meaningful to him or her and expands upon those elements.
6. Risk taking is an essential part of language learning. Learners should be encouraged to speculate, predict, and generate their own hypotheses about meaning and meaning-making. Errors/mistakes should not be viewed as problematic but as an essential part of development.
7. Materials to be read and written should be functional rather than constrained by attempts to control texts and contexts artificially.
8. Fragmentation of language and language learning should be avoided.
9. Meaning should always be the focus, and learners should be urged to ask continually, "Does this make sense to me?"
10. Learning should proceed from the literacy base that the learner brings to school.

In an attempt to summarize some of the key tenets, researchers such as Goodman and Goodman (1982), Weaver (1990, 22–27), and Ruddell (1992, 613) offer the following list of selected principles for "language and literacy acquisition which serve to clarify the meaning of a whole language philosophy, define a whole language perspective, and guide the development of our instructional methodology" (Ruddell, 1992, 614).

1. Children, from a very early age, are active theory builders and hypothesis testers. Children grow and learn most readily when they actively pursue their own learning.
2. Materials to be read and written should be functional rather than constrained by attempts to control texts and contexts artificially. The driving force is children's need to obtain meaning; learners are encouraged to continually ask, "Does this make sense to me?"
3. Language performance is directly related to the language environment. Learning in and out of school should not be different. In both situations learning should be functional and literacy should be an extension of natural language learning. Learning should proceed from the literacy base that the learner brings to school.
4. Oral and written language acquisition are parallel and interactive in development. Fragmentation of language and language learning, learning part-to-whole, should be avoided.
5. Oral and written language development, including the learning of strategies, are directly related to and interactive with literacy acquisition and development.
6. Risk taking is an essential part of language learning. Learners, teachers, and students alike should become decision makers in the learning process. They are encouraged to speculate, predict, and generate their own hypotheses about meaning and meaning making. Errors/mistakes should not be viewed as problematic but as an essential part of development.
7. Ongoing and periodic assessment is intertwined with learning and teaching.
8. Interdisciplinary learning fosters the kinds of attitudes and behaviors needed in a technologically advanced, democratic society.

Cambourne (1988) presents a model of literacy learning (see Figure 2.1) that directly relates the Whole-Language philosophy with classroom instruction.

Intended Audience

Whole-Language is a view of literacy learning that is intended to guide literacy programs at any level.

Description of the Procedures

Rather than offering a prescription for practice, Whole-Language educators develop literacy learning environments based upon the needs and experiences of students and, within these environments, provide careful guidance that responds to the child's endeavors. In recent years, certain techniques and practices have become almost synonymous with Whole-Language. In an attempt to make Whole-Language more concrete, we will describe some of these techniques with the recognition that they should not be regarded as a formula for Whole-Language. For purposes of organization, we will discuss these techniques under three headings: Beginning Reading, Developing Reading, and Remediation or Revaluing.

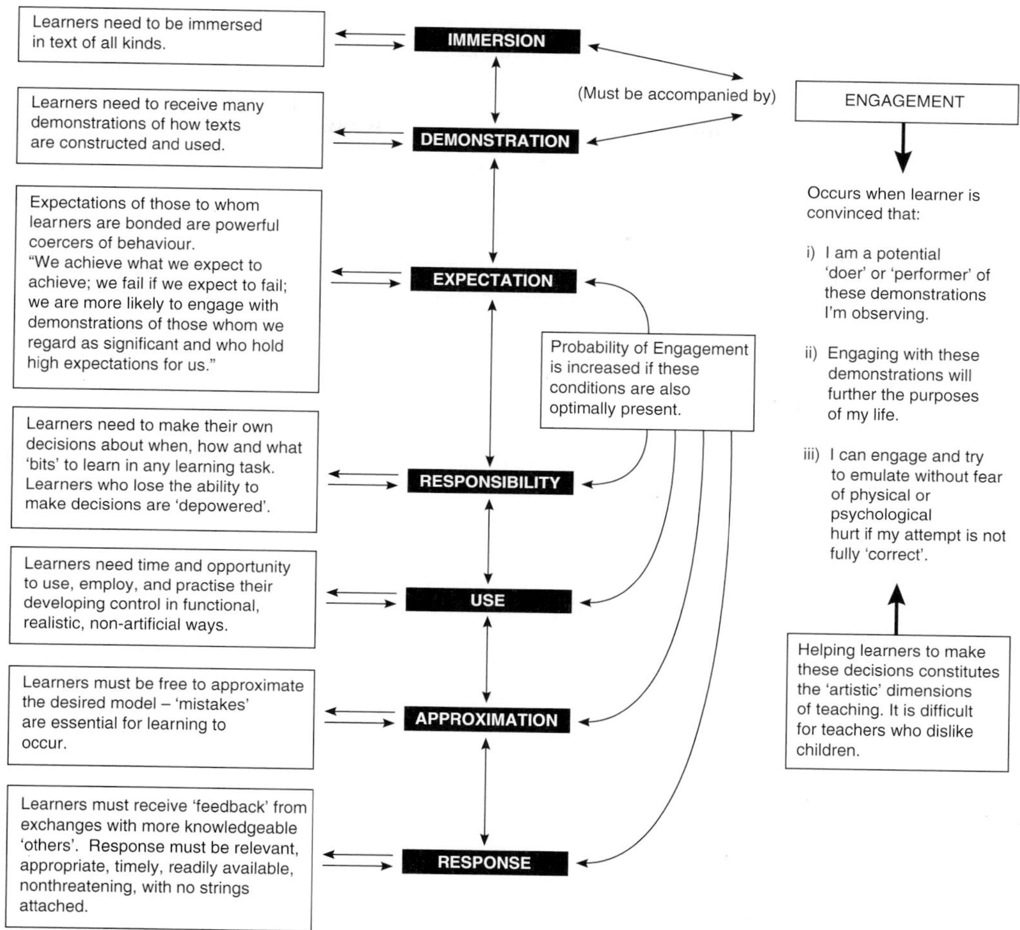

FIGURE 2.1 A Schematic Representation of Brian Cambourne's Model of Learning as It Applies to Literacy Learning

Beginning Reading. Among the goals typically associated with a Whole-Language view of beginning reading are the following:

1. To build on children's developing awareness of functions of print, environmental reading, and informational reading
2. To create a literate environment in the classroom
3. To expand the learner's awareness of books
4. To expand the child's sense of style and form
5. To help the child develop strategies for making sense of print

In accordance with these goals, a Whole-Language classroom is apt to be rich in print resources and lively in terms of meaningful/functional experiences with print. The classroom is likely to be surrounded by artwork, children's writings, class writings, books, and labels and other vehicles (charts, bulletin boards, menus, recipes) by which students can see, contribute to, and be part of a print environment. Excursions, simulations, role-playing, and so on, in which print is an integral part (e.g., a shopping list for a visit to a store, telephone messages) of the experience may be commonplace. Literature circles, writing centers, peer conferences, and reading areas are likely to be integral to providing the students with a sense of immersion, exploration, and opportunity to develop and use print. Likewise, students' writing, dictated stories, shared book experiences, and assisted reading will likely be recurring activities as the teacher encourages student involvement with trade books (especially reading predictable books with familiar content and reading their own and each other's writing). The point is, "The children are growing into literacy under the guidance of their teachers. They are not carefully taken into it skill by skill" (Goodman and Goodman 1982, 129).

Developmental Reading. Goodman and Goodman (1982) suggest that there are three major "focal points" in using Whole-Language as students grow as readers. They are: (1) involving the students in lots of reading; (2) creating an environment that "accepts and encourages risk-taking"; and (3) maintaining a focus on meaning.

Based on these notions, a number of Whole-Language educators have proposed what they consider to be essential elements. For example, Watson and Crowley (1988) suggest that although not every classroom will look the same, the following similarities are likely to exist. As they state:

> In their own unique ways all whole-language teachers facilitate certain activities and procedures.
>
> 1. They find out about students' interests, abilities, and needs. And then they go an important step further—they use that information in planning curriculum.
> 2. They read to students or tell them stories every day.
> 3. They see to it that students have an opportunity to participate in authentic writing every day.
> 4. They see to it that students have an opportunity to read real literature every day.
> 5. They initiate discussions in which students consider the processes of reading and writing.
> 6. They know that kids can help other kids many times and in many ways that no one else can; therefore, they take advantage of the social nature of literacy (reading and writing) in order to promote it. (Watson and Crowley 1988, 235)

In a similar vein, Andrea Butler (not dated) suggests that a balanced Whole-Language program typically includes all of the following elements:

- *Reading to children.* Quality literature, books owned by the children, and sometimes more demanding than those they read alone.
- *Shared book experience.* (A discussion of this practice is provided in this unit.)
- *Sustained silent reading.* (A discussion of this practice is provided in this unit.)
- *Guided reading.* This involves the teacher's working with a small group of children in the reading of picture books, short stories, or novels. In conjunction with the reading, the children are involved in independent reading, discussion, response activities, and sharing activities. (For a discussion of this practice see Unit 1.)

- *Individualized reading.* (A discussion of this practice is provided in this unit.)
- *Language experience.* (For a discussion of this see Unit 3.)
- *Children's writing.* Most of the guidelines emanating from Donald Graves's work in writing relate directly to Whole-Language.
- *Modeled writing.* Modeled writing involves the teacher's modeling good writing behavior. As Butler (not dated) states: "It involves composing in front of children, articulating the processes they are going through, and explaining why they are doing what they are doing. It can also take the form of teachers scribing as they and the students compose text collaboratively" (p. 30).
- *Opportunities for sharing.* Sharing time involves providing students the opportunity to present a finished product (response to reading, own writing, drama, report of play).
- *Content area reading and writing.* In the Whole-Language classroom the aforementioned activities extend to the content areas. As Butler states: "the nine elements . . . do not just apply to the time allocated to the specific teaching of language. They apply all day in every content area."

Goodman and Goodman (1982) also emphasize that "Children are helped to broaden the scope and range of their reading and to build specific strategies which will be helpful with different kinds of texts" (p. 129). They go on to suggest the use of strategy lessons. (For an expanded discussion of strategy lessons, see Unit 5, Goodman's Reading Strategy Lessons and Retrospective Miscue Analysis.) Or, as Watson and Crowley suggest: "Strategy lessons take advantage of the strengths of a reader, and they are often brief and always to the point. Equally important, they lead to a discussion of the reading process" (p. 258). Apart from strategy lessons, a deliberate attempt is made to hold conferences with the children (either individually or in group) in an attempt to bring the reading to a conscious level. As Watson and Crowley (1988) contend:

> Whole-Language teachers do talk about the reading process in both formal and informal ways with their students. They talk with students at the teachable moment—that is, when they need and can make immediate use of the information; furthermore, the teachers build on what readers are doing right, not what they are doing wrong. Additionally, teachers bring reading to the students' awareness by discussing strategies involved in real reading . . . those strategies involve the reader's sampling from print, predicting . . . confirming . . . correcting . . . instead of drilling on skills, children in Whole-Language classrooms are asked to reflect on the strategies they use. (p. 257)

Remediation or Revaluing. Goodman and Goodman (1982) argue that remedial programs enlist practices that tend to be in opposition to a Whole-Language view. For example, they suggest that remedial programs tend to focus on weaknesses rather than strengths, word-level rather than meaning-seeking strategies. In accordance with a Whole-Language view, they argue that instruction for troubled readers should focus on helping readers revalue themselves—that is, "help them to value what they can do and not be defeated by what they can't do, to trust themselves and their linguistic intuition . . . specifics of a revaluing program include a great deal of Whole-Language, meaningful reading and of nonpressuring support" (p. 131).

Goals	Code Emphasis	Other Approaches*	Meaning Emphasis
What are the skills taught?	Subskills, e.g., sound-symbol correspondences, such as identification of initial and final vowels, consonants, syllables, and morphemes; dividing words into components and then sounding them out; understanding syntactic relationships; building a sight word vocabulary.		As they engage in communicative experiences, students acquire basic understandings of how language functions and is used. At the same time as students are involved in "total" reading experiences from the beginning, they become aware of what they are learning in terms of language conventions and discuss strategies they use as they read, write, and experience communication. The teacher's task is to capitalize upon and encourage the students to be their own informants.
Instruction *What is the order in which instruction takes place?*	Letter, sound, and word recognition taught first; comprehension skills become focus after students develop automaticity; preskills of a strategy are taught before the strategy itself is presented; high utility skills are introduced before less useful ones; easy skills are taught before more complex ones. Skilled comprehension strategies are taught beginning in the intermediate grades.		Students are encouraged to be active participants in their reading experiences. Rather than be taught subskills, they are provided experiences for understanding a variety of texts read for student self-initiated purposes. Students learn strategies and skills in conjunction with those communicative experiences. These experiences can emanate from the students' initial writing experience, from reading activities involving reading predictable texts, simple directions, stories, etc., or from print-related activities related to everyday activities (e.g., grocery lists, responding to signs and notices).
How are skills taught and practiced?	Subskills are taught in a specific sequence and are practiced until they are mastered. Complex skills are broken down into components. The teacher demonstrates the steps in a strategy and then provides structured practice in using the strategy. The students practice until they recognize when the strategy is called for in a situation. Practice includes a concentrated presentation of examples, with review across several lessons. Unison reading; individual oral responding, usually in small groups; game activities.		As children are involved in reading experiences for which they have self-propelled purposes, they are encouraged to consider the strategies they might use or do not use to achieve their reading goals. The teacher's task is to encourage the student to explore these learnings and try them or test them. Thus, skills/strategies are developed in conjunction with meaningful reading and learning experiences.
What kinds of learning experiences do students have?	Learning by practicing the same skill over and over again, gradually moving to more and more complex skills. Most children move through the various levels of a basal reader supplemented by high interest reading materials.		Learning is primarily experience based, using children's problems/purposes to direct selection of texts or using children's own written materials. Within these contexts, learning occurs through student discovery and exploration rather than teacher direction. Practice occurs naturally as students test their strategies in a variety of communication contexts. Practice involves testing as well as refining what is learned. Students are recognized as accomplished language learners who are apt to learn when experiences are meaningful and goals for learning are self-propelled.
What is the setting in which learning takes place?	Primarily in school, using a commercially published basal reader series and supplementary materials. Many classrooms have a reading corner where high-interest books are available to the children.		Children's experiences outside of school are used to create a functional, meaningful base for learning. Emphasis on taking the children into a variety of settings to build on their experience base. Classroom materials are many, varied, and predictable—they grow out of the children's and teacher's interests.
How is the learning situation structured?	Highly structured, with skills to be learned in a specific order. Some students will not be interested in learning. The teacher can show them that they can succeed in reading by designing lessons effectively, and that there is a reward in learning to read by using extrinsic rewards such as physical contact and by eventually developing intrinsic motivation in these students. Children are divided into small groups based on their ability. More time is generally spent with low-ability groups. Continuing diagnosis allows for restructuring of groups based on needs of students.		The teacher serves as a group facilitator. The teacher arranges the environment, provides relevant, appropriate materials, and provides timely experiences to facilitate learning. The learner extracts from the environment those elements which are most meaningful. When language is functional, motivation to learn is high. Children know when they are successful because they have met their own needs. No external reward system is necessary. Teachers work with children individually and in small groups. Much time is given to self-selected reading. Lessons tend to focus on developing strategies for getting meaning from print.

(continued)

FIGURE 2.2 A Comparison of Whole-Language/Meaning Emphasis with a Code Emphasis (Reed and Ward, 1982)

Goals	Code Emphasis	Other Approaches*	Meaning Emphasis
How do teachers respond to students' creativity?	Student creativity is not a focus of the beginning reading program.		The entire focus of the reading program is to build and maintain students' interest in reading. Students are encouraged to be as creative as they can be.
How are student "errors" viewed?	Specific skill deficits are diagnosed by the teacher based on identification of recurrent error patterns. The correction procedure involves praise for correct responses, modeling the correct response and leading the child (responding with the child), testing the child until he or she responds correctly every time, and giving the child a delayed test later in the lesson.		Self-exploration of problems on the part of students is a critical part of the learning process. Errors are accepted as a natural part of that process. Students' own motivation to learn results in the correction of errors. The teacher serves as a guide and facilitator in this process.
How is instruction in various skill areas or content areas coordinated or integrated?	This is highly individualized. It is recommended that teachers of intermediate children incorporate reading activities into all content area instruction; however, strategies for reading content materials are seldom taught.		Content areas are integrated within a problem-solving curriculum. Particular concern is given to the reading of content materials in mathematics, science, and social studies. Students work at the development of special strategies for reading and understanding these materials. Much emphasis is placed on written and oral language use together with reading.
Assessment			
How is learning assessed?	Children are tested, usually with informal reading inventories, at the beginning of the school year to determine their skill levels and to place them in the appropriate small groups. For ongoing evaluation, teachers use individual skills tests and have students read aloud individually.		Teachers observe and monitor the progress children are making in developing literacy. They observe students using language and informally apply their knowledge of language development to achieve an understanding of students' strengths and needs. Teachers evaluate the program on the basis of evidence that children have acquired and use comprehension strategies.

*These lines represent other possible approaches to reading instruction.

FIGURE 2.2 Continued

Cautions and Comments

In our aforementioned discussion we attempted to highlight the notion that Whole-Language represents a viewpoint rather than a set approach. In presenting a description of key elements of Whole-Language, it should be reemphasized that Whole-Language is not a set of activities but a belief-driven approach that will and should vary. Certainly Whole-Language can be distinguished from approaches to reading that are highly structured and that presume a sequence of skills and strategies, including teaching suggestions that isolate separate skills and strategies. A useful comparison of Whole-Language with a decoding emphasis was developed by Reed and Ward (1982). It is shown in Figure 2.2. Dahl and Freppon (1995) and Dahl, Sharer, Grogan, and Lawson (1998, in press) provide significant support for Whole-Language teaching versus more skills-based teaching.

One should not assume that a Whole-Language orientation is easy to achieve. As Altwerger, Edelsky, and Flores (1987) have explained, to become a Whole-Language teacher requires more than simply putting in place certain practices or activities. To achieve effective Whole-Language classrooms, teachers need to develop an understanding of some key facets of language learning, adopt an attitude of teaching as a continuous experiment, and open their eyes to what children are doing, can do, and might be sensitively guided to achieve.

Weaver points out that "many teachers prefer the safety of basals to the unpredictable vagaries of whole language." She emphasizes that "if teachers haven't made the shift in models of learning, they're going to take nice trade books and do all the awful things that have been done with basals, namely use the literature to teach isolated skills" (Gursky, 1991, 28). Smith (1992) concurs by saying "teachers could also mistake whole language as just another method rather than an entirely new approach to teaching. Such teachers still do not trust children to learn unless their attention is controlled and their progress monitored and evaluated" (p. 440).

Educators who do not fully understand the tenets of Whole-Language find that their concerns usually are among the many myths and misconceptions of what Whole-Language really is. Newman and Church (1990) and Weaver (1990) identify the following as the most frequently cited myths associated with Whole-Language:

- Phonics, spelling, and/or grammar are not taught in Whole-Language classrooms.
- Whole-Language means a literature-based curriculum.
- Whole-Language is a way of teaching the language arts without integrating the other subject areas.
- Teachers do not teach in Whole-Language classrooms.
- A Whole-Language classroom is not structured.
- Evaluation does not exist in Whole-Language classrooms.
- "Anything goes" in a Whole-Language classroom.
- Whole-Language teachers focus only on the process of learning.
- There is little research supporting Whole-Language.
- Whole-Language is a methodology.
- Commercial Whole-Language materials make a Whole-Language teacher.
- There is one right way to do Whole-Language.
- Whole-Language is for the "super teacher."
- Change occurs only in the classrooms; administrators are not affected.
- Whole-Language is another name for whole word, look-say method, and language experience approach.
- Whole-Language teaching is a matter of teaching skills in context, rather than in isolation.
- All you have to do to implement Whole-Language is to mandate it.

An ongoing challenge for Whole-Language teachers, according to Villaume and Worden (1993), "is the close examination of the student voices that emerge from classrooms" (p. 462). They state, "literate voices seek out and value different viewpoints in order to define their understandings of themselves and their world. Literate voices listen to others but do not expect to be told how to respond to exercises; their responses are personal, yet thoughtful. Literate voices are awake, alive, and stimulated by the complexity of the world around them" (p. 468).

Goodman (1992, 359–360) redefines the role of the teacher within a Whole-language environment. He proclaims that "Whole-language teachers must

- Accept their status as professionals
- Have power (as professionals and faculties)

- Be supportive
- Reject certain traditional roles
- Seek to support learning, not control it
- Seek collaboration, not compete with peers and pupils
- Continually evaluate self, pupils, and the system in which they teach
- Assume professional roles as listed below:
  - The teacher as initiator
    The teacher invites students to participate in relevant and appropriate learning experiences
  - The teacher as mediator
    The teacher mediates learning, but does not dictate or interfere with the learning process
  - The teacher as kid watcher (Goodman, 1978)
    The teacher spends much time observing students in academic and social settings.
  - The teacher as liberator
    The teacher must provide opportunities for students to take on more responsibility for their own learning. "They must seek to free the minds and creative energies of pupils for the greatest gains in their intellectual, physical, and social development" (p. 360).
  - The teacher as curriculum maker
    The teacher must provide authentic experiences and a meaningful curriculum that builds upon "the personal and social experiences of the pupils" (p. 360).

Staab (1990) defines a successful Whole-Language teacher as:

> an individual who creates an exciting print environment and allows children to engage in meaningful literacy experiences. She continually provides mediation which means to lead from behind (Newman, 1990), thus discovering what a child is attempting to do and helping the child accomplish it. (p. 548)

Koepke (1991) further describes Whole-Language teachers as:

> those individuals who declare their independence from the constraints of the centralized, highly regulated education system and share with students the power to make decisions about what is learned and how learning takes place. They need to be less like technicians, implementing programs and strategies without questioning their effectiveness, and more like explorers, observing and responding to students. (p. 36)

Gursky (1991) concurs by stating:

> the teacher is not an authoritarian, but a resource, a coach, and co-learner who shares power with the students and allows them to make choices. Learning in such a classroom is a social act, and children learn from and help each other. The challenge to the teacher is to adapt the curriculum and activities to the interest and talents of the children, to provide a content-rich environment, and to assure that they are constantly engaged in learning. The common techniques of whole language teaching—daily journal and letter writing, a great deal of silent and oral reading of real literature, and student cooperation, to name a few—are the philosophy in action. (p. 23)

Certain support groups have emerged in Canada and the United States that afford teachers interested in Whole-Language the opportunity to share. These groups are known by names such as TAWL (Teachers Applying Whole Language), CAWL (Children and Whole Language), and CEL (Child-centered, Experience-based Learning).

"More whole language groups are started for the same reason—because teachers want to teach the way students learn best. These teachers draw strength from each other, and through that strength, they gain confidence and power—power to change the way they teach" (Hood, 1989, 62).

Judging the validity of Whole-Language has been problematic. Certainly there are ample affidavits supporting the enthusiasm with which the approach has been embraced by teachers and students. In school situations in which students have received an overdose of skills and appear deprived of reading and writing, Whole-Language seems to have the potential to reestablish a set of more appropriate priorities. But several questions remain as to whether the current set of Whole-Language beliefs are valid and as to the relationship that should be in place between beliefs and practices. In past years the beliefs have been subjected to revision, reconsideration, or refinement as new understandings of language learning have emerged. The irony of Whole-Language may be that some of the practices being suggested—well-nigh tentatively—may constrain the ongoing reexamination and continued development of Whole-Language.

The authors of this compendium debated whether Whole-Language should be included in the book. Whole-Language is not an approach but a set of beliefs about readers, about learning to read, and about reading instruction. In the end, our decision to include Whole-Language was prompted by the attention that Whole-Language received in the late eighties and the number of teachers who asked the question "What is Whole-Language?" We hope the previous discussion offers at least a partial explanation.

Since students in a Whole-Language classroom "have an investment and an interest in their learning, they are encouraged to: (a) share in the decision making process, (b) suggest and negotiate projects, and (c) set their own goals as readers and writers. As a result, they become active participants in their literacy learning, they develop a sense of belonging, and learn to work responsibly and independently" (Weaver, 1990, 31).

Research with various populations of students has offered positive demonstrations of the worth of Whole-Language. One of the most notable studies was done by Dahl et al., who demonstrated the positive impact on student's strategic learning as a result of a Whole-Language orientation. Other research has included its use with various student populations whose first language is not English. Whole Language has also been successful used with students who are challenged by visual or hearing impairments (D'Alessandro, 1990; Schulz, 1991; Zucker, 1993).

Unfortunately, Whole-Language has been subjected to a form of scapegoating, as if it has contributed to divisions and debate in the field, which in turn are harmful for education. We would argue with this characterization for a number of reasons. Consensus may or may not be a desirable goal, and we see debate as provoking conversation and consideration of alternatives.

Beyond scapegoating, Whole-Language has been sidelined by some in conjunction with the political developments that are defining so narrowly and artificially what counts as best practice and research that might inform best practice. Cambourne (2002) provides one of the most substantial discussions of some of the guiding principles of Whole-Language.

REFERENCES

Altwerger, B., C. Edelsky, and B. Flores. 1987. Whole-Language: What's new? *The Reading Teacher* 27: 144–154. Presents one of the most substantive discussions of what Whole-Language is and is not.

Au, K. H., and J. A. Scheu. (1996). Journey toward holistic instruction: Supporting teachers' growth. *The Reading Teacher* 49(6): 468–477. Describes the exploration of holistic instruction in Hawaii and the impact upon teachers and students.

Balajthy, E. 1989. The printout: Holistic approaches to reading. *The Reading Teacher* 42(4): 324. Provides eight guidelines supporting the implementation of technology in a literature-rich environment.

Baskwill, J., and P. Whitman. 1986. *Whole-Language source book.* Toronto, Ont.: Scholastic. Presents a variety of ideas purported to be consistent with a Whole-Language viewpoint.

Bruneau, B. J. 1997. The Literacy Pyramid organization of reading/writing activities in a whole language classroom. *The Reading Teacher* 51(2): 158–160. The Literacy Pyramid is a blending together of eight instructional events of guide thinking about Whole-Language teaching.

Butler, A. Not dated. *The elements of the whole-language program.* Crystal Lake, IL: Rigby. Describes in detail, including lesson plans, a Whole-Language approach.

———. Not dated. *Whole-language—a framework for thinking.* Crystal Lake, IL: Rigby. Discusses basic premises underlying Whole-Language.

Cambourne, B. 1988. *The whole story—natural learning and the acquisition of literacy in the classroom.* Auckland, New Zealand: Ashton Scholastic. An excellent reference supporting a model of literacy learning that defines seven conditions which must be present within a literate environment in order for learning to occur.

———. 1994. The rhetoric of "the rhetoric of whole language." *Reading Research Quarterly* 29(4): 330–332. Critiques the rhetoric of those critiquing Whole-Language critique.

———. 1995. Toward an educationally relevant theory of literacy learning: Twenty years of inquiry. *The Reading Teacher* 49(3): 182–190. Cambourne expands upon his conditions for learning.

———. 2002. Holistic, integrated approaches to reading and language arts instruction: The constructivist framework of an instructional theory. In A. E. Farstrup and S. J. Samuels (Eds.), *What research has to say about Reading Instruction.* Newark, DE: International Reading Association, 25–47. Thoughtful discussion of holistic teaching from a constructivist perspective; explores assumptions about curriculum, teaching, and research. Especially useful in comparison with nonholistic approaches.

Crafton, L. 1994. *Challenges of holistic teaching: Answering the tough questions.* Norwood, MA: Christopher-Gordon Publishers. Provides a discussion of selected classroom practices tied to holistic teaching.

Dahl, K. L., and P. A. Freppon. 1995. A comparison of innercity children's interpretations of reading and writing instruction in the early grades in skills-based and whole language classrooms. *Reading Research Quarterly* 30(1): 50–74. A study focusing upon learners' interpretations of beginning reading and writing instruction.

Dahl, K. L., and P. L. Scharer. 2000. Phonics teaching and learning in Whole Language classrooms: New evidence from research. *The Reading Teacher* 53: 584–594. Discusses Dahl et al. 1999, and its findings and their implications for teachers.

Dahl, K. L, L. Scharer, L. Lawson, and P. R. Grogan. 1999. Phonics instruction and student achievement in Whole Language first grade classrooms. *Reading Research Quarterly* 34(3): 312–341. Careful examination of the Whole-Language classroom in terms of phonic strategy development.

D'Alessandro, M. 1990. Accommodating emotionally handicapped children through a literature-based reading program. *The Reading Teacher* 44: 288–293. Describes how a special educator implemented a literature-based program to accommodate the personal, social, and academic needs of her elementary emotionally handicapped children.

Doake, D. 1987. *Changing the assumptions for literacy learning: A revolution in progress.* Monographs on Literacy Learning, Acadia University, Nova Scotia. Discusses the key assumptions underlying Whole-Language as well as practices that might emanate from these assumptions.

Edelsky, C. 1991. *With literacy and justice for all.* Philadelphia: The Farmer Press. "This volume documents the author's decade-long involvement with socially critical, holistic approaches to the everyday problems and possibilities facing teachers and language and literacy." (Editor's Introduction, p. viii).

Edelsky, C., B. Altwerger, and B. Flores. 1991. *Whole-Language—What's the difference?* Portsmouth, NH: Heinemann. Clarifies Whole-Language from a theoretical and historical perspective.

Freeman, Y. S., and D. E. Freeman. 1992. *Whole-Language for second language learners.* Portsmouth, NH: Heinemann. Provides guidelines for teachers where some or all of the students' English is another language.

Freppon, P. A., and K. L. Dahl. 1998. Balanced instruction: Insights and considerations. *Reading Research Quarterly* 33(2): 240–251. Explores the claims for balanced instruction and explores Whole-Language in terms of providing for it.

Goodman, K. S. 1986. *What's Whole-Language?* Richmond Hill, Ont.: Scholastic-TAB. Represents a primary source for understanding the tenets of Whole-Language.

———. 1992. Why Whole-Language is today's agenda in education. *Language Arts* 69: 354–363. Defines Whole-Language in terms of the constructivist's perspective, curriculum design, learning context, and teacher role.

———. 1994. Deconstructing the rhetoric of Moorman, Blanton, and McLaughlin: A response. *Reading Research Quarterly* 29(4): 340–346. Provides a further critique of the critical analysis of the rhetoric of Whole-Language.

———. 1997. Putting theory and research in the context of history. *Language Arts* 74(8): 595–599. Details the notions of Ken Goodman and their implications for literacy.

Goodman, K. S., and Y. Goodman. 1979. Learning to read is natural. In L. B. Resnik and P. A. Weaver (Eds.), *Theory and practice of early reading,* Vol. 1. Hillsdale, NJ: Erlbaum. Discusses beginning reading development and the implications for teaching.

———. 1981. Twenty questions about teaching language. *Educational Leadership* 38: 437–442. Addresses key questions about Whole-Language.

———. 1982. A Whole-Language comprehension centered view of reading development. In L. Reed and S. Ward (Eds.), *Basic skills: Issues and choices,* vol. 2. St. Louis: CEMREL, 125–134. Includes a thorough description of Whole-Language tenets and their implications.

Goodman, K. S., Y. M. Goodman, and W. J. Hood. 1988. *The Whole-Language evaluation book.* Portsmouth, NH: Heinemann. An edited volume of attempts by teachers to evaluate literacy in Whole-Language classrooms.

Goodman, Y. M. 1980. The roots of literacy. In M. P. Douglass (Ed.), *Claremont Reading Conference; Forty-fourth yearbook.* Hillsdale, NJ: Erlbaum. Presents a coherent description of Whole-Language tenets and practices.

Goodman, Y. M., W. J. Hood, and K. S. Goodman. 1991. *Organizing for Whole-Language.* Portsmouth, NH: Heinemann. An edited text that provides practical ways for organizing classrooms to reflect holistic learning and teaching.

Gunderson, L. 1997. Whole Language approaches to reading and writing. In S. Stahl and D. A. Hayes (Eds.), *Instructional models in reading.* Mahwah, NJ: Erlbaum. Discusses the underlying principles of Whole-Language and research that has informed its use and demonstrated its effectiveness.

Gunkel, J. 1991. "Please Teach America": Keisuke's journey into a language community. *Language Arts* 68: 303–310. A personal account of the activities the author implemented to extend the learning of an ESL student.

Gursky, D. 1991. After the reign of Dick and Jane. *Teacher Magazine* (2)9: 22–29. Describes and defines the art of teaching literacy development from the Whole-Language and the more traditional viewpoints.

Harlin, R., S. E. Lipa, and R. Lonberger. 1991. *The Whole-Language Journey.* Markham, Ont.: Pippin. Provides practical ideas, references, resources, and suggestions for teachers shifting to a Whole-Language way of teaching.

Harste, J. C., K. Short, and C. Burke. 1988. *Creating classrooms for authors.* Portsmouth, NH: Heinemann Educational Books. Represents a practical book for teachers planning Whole-Language classrooms.

Harste, J. C., V. Woodward, and C. Burke. 1984. *Language stories and literacy lessons.* Portsmouth, NH: Heinemann Educational Books. Presents a rich discussion of emergent literacy and assumptions emanating from selected findings.

Holdaway, D. 1979. *The foundations of literacy.* Gosford, N. S. W.: Ashton Scholastic. A basic source for details on teaching reading using selected Whole-Language tenets.

Hood, W. 1989. Whole-Language: A grass roots movement catches on. *Learning* 7: 61–62. Depicts the journey two teachers took on their way to becoming Whole-Language teachers. Information is also available for TAWL support groups.

Jeynes, W. H., and S. W. Littell. 2000. A Meta-analysis of studies examining the effect of Whole Language instruction on the literacy. *Elementary School Journal* 101(1): 21–34. Examines whether Whole-Language instruction increases the reading skills of low-SES students in grades K–3.

King, D. F., and D. J. Watson. 1984. Reading as meaning construction. In B. A. Busching and J. I. Schwartz (Eds.), *Integrating the language arts in the elementary school.* Urbana, IL: National Council of Teachers of English, 70–77. Demonstrates how children learn in Whole-Language classrooms.

Koepke, M. 1991. The power to be a professional. *Teacher Magazine* 2(9): 35–41. An in-depth account of one teacher's growth, challenges, and changes when shifting to a Whole-Language way of teaching.

Korkeamaki, R., & M. J. Dreher 1996. Trying something new: Meaning-based instruction in a Finnish first-grade classroom. *Journal of Literacy Research*

28(1): 9–34. Reports a study examining impact of predictable books, literature centers, and mini books.

Krashen, S. 2002. Defending Whole Language: The limits of phonics instruction and the efficacy of Whole Language Instruction. *Reading Improvement* 39(1): 32–42. Discusses the efficacy of Whole-Language in terms of the development of reading skills with special focus on phonics.

Ladestro, D. 1991. Making a change for good. *Teacher Magazine* 2(9): 42–45. A description of the journey two middle schools made when moving toward a more holistic way of teaching.

McCauley, J. K., and D. S. McCauley. 1992. Using choral reading to promote language learning for ESL students. *The Reading Teacher* 45: 526–532. Describes one reading strategy implemented with ESL students to enhance language acquisition.

McWhirter, A. M. 1990. Whole language in the middle school. *The Reading Teacher* 4(8): 562–565. Describes how a middle-school teacher captured students' interest in learning through literature and writing, using dialogue journals and reading workshop.

Mills, H., and J. A. Clyde. 1990. *Portraits of whole language classrooms learning for all ages.* Portsmouth, NH: Heinemann. This resource portrays actual descriptions of how teachers immerse their students in authentic literacy activities. The classrooms are from varying educational settings and with diverse student populations.

Moore, M. A. 1991. Electronic dialoguing: An avenue to literacy. *The Reading Teacher* 45: 280–286. An informative article describing how technology can enhance literacy learning.

Moorman, G. B., W. E. Blanton, and T. McLaughlin. 1994. The rhetoric of Whole-Language. *Reading Research Quarterly* 29(4): 309–329. Critiques the rhetoric of Whole-Language advocates in terms of the metaphors they use.

———. 1994. Rhetoric and community in Whole-Language: A response to Cambourne, Willinsky, and Goodman. *Reading Research Quarterly* 29(4): 348–351. *A response to the responses of their original critique.*

Newman, J. (Ed.) 1985. *Whole-Language—Theory into use.* Portsmouth, NH: Heinemann Educational Books. Represents a primary source for information on Whole-Language tenets and practices.

Newman, J., and S. Church. 1990. Myths of whole language. *The Reading Teacher* 44: 20–26. Identifies and examines the most commonly known myths of Whole-Language.

Pang, V. O., C. Colvin, M. Tran, and R. H. Barba. 1992. Beyond chopsticks and dragons: Selecting Asian-American literature for children. *The Reading Teacher* 46: 216–224. Provides an in-depth discussion on criteria to use when selecting children's books for culturally diverse populations.

Purves, A. C., L. Papa, and S. Jordan (Eds.). 1994. *Encyclopedia of English studies and language arts.* New York: National Council of Teachers of English. This encyclopedia has more than 800 annotated entries/topics that succinctly address this topic and related areas.

Quintero, E., and A. Heueta-Macias. 1992. Bilingualism and biliteracy. *The Reading Teacher* 44: 306–312. Provides a description of the FIEL (Family Initiative for English Literacy) project.

Reed, L., and S. Ward. 1982. *Basic skills issues and choices,* Vols. I and II. St. Louis: CEMREL. Compares various holistic versus atomistic approaches to teaching in different curriculum areas, including reading and writing.

Reimer, K. M. 1992. Multiethnic literature: Holding fast to dreams. *Language Arts* 69: 14–21. Identifies several important issues pertaining to the authenticity of multicultural children's literature books.

Reutzel, D. R., and R. B. Cooter. 1990. Whole-Language: Comparative effects on first-grade reading achievement. *Journal of Educational Research* 83: 252–257. Reveals that students immersed in a Whole-Language approach score as well, or better, than those participating in a basal reader approach when given a traditional reading standardized achievement test at the end of their first-grade year.

Rich, S. 1985. Restoring power to teachers: The impact of Whole-Language. *Language Arts* 62: 717–724. Provides a demonstration of Whole-Language at work.

Richgels, D. J. 1995. Invented spelling ability and printed word learning in kindergarten. *Reading Research Quarterly* 30(1): 96–109. Explores the relationships between alphabet knowledge, word reading ability, and invented spelling ability.

Routman, R. 1997. Back to the basics of Whole Language. *Educational Leadership* 54(5): 70–74. Explains the use of Whole-Language in terms of developing basic skills.

Ruddell, R. B. 1992. A Whole-Language and literature perspective: Creating a meaning making instructional environment. *Language Arts* 69: 612–619. Provides an in-depth discussion on Whole-Language by focusing on how teaching facilitates learning in the classroom.

Scharer, P. L., and D. B. Detweiler. 1992. Changing as teachers: Perils and possibilities of literature-based language arts instruction. *Language Arts* 69: 186, 192. Describes the challenges and successes the teacher experienced when shifting from a traditional model to an integrated model of teaching.

Schulz, E. 1991, August. Nourishing a desire to learn. *Teacher Magazine,* 2(9): 30–34. Describes how three elementary teachers designed their classrooms and literacy activities from the Whole-Language perspective.

Shapiro, J. 1994. Research perspectives on Whole Language. In V. Froese (Ed.), *Whole Language: Practice and theory.* Boston: Allyn and Bacon, 433–470. Discusses research that informs and supports the use of Whole-Language.

Smith, F. 1971. *Psycholinguistics and reading.* New York: Holt, Rinehart and Winston. Includes selected articles that address basic tenets of Whole-Language.

———. 1981. Demonstrations, engagement, and sensitivity: A revised approach to language learning. *Language Arts* 58: 103–112. Discusses key assumptions underlying Whole-Language.

———. 1992. Learning to Read: The never ending debate. *Phi Delta Kappan* 73: 432–441. Describes the reading process from the traditional language perspective.

Smith, F., and K. Goodman. 1971. On the psycholinguistic method of teaching reading. *Elementary School Journal,* 177–181. Represents a seminal article on Whole-Language.

Staab, C. F. 1990. Teacher mediation in one whole literacy classroom. *The Reading Teacher* 43(8): 548–552. Describes how a first grade classroom mediates the learning process in a Whole-Language classroom.

Storeygard, J., R. Cummons, M. Stumpf, and E. Pavloglou. 1993. Making computers work for students with special needs. *Teaching Exceptional Children* 26: 22–24. Describes a computer and writing program utilized in a middle school to assist the needs of special-needs students and reluctant writers.

Sumara, D., and L. Walker. 1991. The teacher's role in Whole-Language. *Language Arts* 68: 276–285. Provides an account of the changing roles of two teachers when shifting toward a Whole-Language way of teaching.

Temple, C., A. M. Hache de Yunen, and L. Montenegro. 1994. The "Global Method" of Celestin Freinet: Whole-Language in a European setting? *The Reading Teacher* 48(1): 86–89. Discusses the notions of a French school teacher, Celestin Freinet, as they relate to Whole-Language.

Turbill, J., and B. Cambourne. 1987. *Coping with chaos.* Portsmouth, NH: Heinemann Educational Books. Provides a rich description of Whole-Language classrooms.

Turner, J. C. 1995. The influence of classroom contexts on young children's motivation for literacy. *Reading Research Quarterly* 30(3): 410–441. Explores differences in motivation for reading for first graders involved in basal versus Whole-Language classrooms.

Vacca, R. T., and T. V. Rasinski. 1992. *Case studies in Whole-Language.* Forth Worth, TX: Harcourt Brace Jovanovich. Describes how preschool and elementary teachers define their role within a Whole-Language framework.

Villaume, S. K., and T. Worden. 1993. Developing literate voices: The challenge of Whole-Language. *Language Arts* 70: 462–468. Provides an in-depth review of the issues pertaining to literature discussion groups.

Walker-Dathouse, D. 1992. Using African-American literature to increase ethnic understanding. *The Reading Teacher* 45: 416–422. Provides a personal account of how the author designed and implemented a literature unit to promote deeper understanding and knowledge of the African-American culture.

Watson, D., and P. Crowley. 1988. How can we implement a Whole-Language approach? In C. Weaver (Ed.), *Reading process and practice.* Portsmouth, NH: Heinemann Educational Books. Represents a detailed description of Whole-Language principles and practices.

Weaver, C. 1990. *Understanding Whole-Language from principles to practice.* Portsmouth, NH: Heinemann. An excellent reference for teachers, parents, and administrators regarding theory and practice of Whole-Language.

———. 1998. Experimental research: On phonemic awareness and on Whole Language. In C. Weaver (Ed.), *Reconsidering a balanced approach to reading.* Urbana, IL: National Council of Teachers of English, 321–371. Discusses the findings from recent syntheses on phonemic awareness and the role of a Whole-Language orientation in developing students' phonemic awareness and reading.

Wepner, S. B. 1990. Holistic computer applications in literature-based classrooms. *The Reading Teacher* 44: 12–19. Provides a description of the software programs that are available to complement any literature-based or Whole-Language program.

Whitt, A. G. 1994. Whole-Language revitalizes one high school classroom. *Journal of Reading* 37(6): 488–493. Describes a high school teacher's shift to Whole-Language.

Willinsky, J. 1994. Theory and meaning in Whole-Language: Engaging Moorman, Blanton, and McLaughlin. *Reading Research Quarterly* 29(4): 334–339. Discusses Whole-Language critique in terms of Whole-Language theory.

Zucker, C. 1993. Using Whole-Language with students who have language and learning disabilities. *The Reading Teacher* 46: 660–670. Provides a description of a language arts program emphasizing the Whole-Language philosophy within an elementary language learning disabilities classroom.

Theme-Based Units

Purpose

The purpose of Thematic Units is to provide opportunities for learners to pursue integrated learning experiences wherein learners as individuals and members of different groups set goals, plan, research, compose/construct, and share ideas gleaned from their exploration of topics and issues demanding the integration of resources and tools from different subject areas.

Rationale

The concept of interdisciplinary learning dates back to the educational philosophy and practice of Locke, Pestalozzi, Froebel, Rousseau, Spencer, and Dewey. These educators viewed learning as a process that reflected real-life experiences. Children learned to explore, experiment, and manipulate objects through sensory orientation. All child-initiated activities and observations were encouraged and reinforced.

Spencer, at the end of the nineteenth century, proposed a shift in curricular development that encompassed a "radical change in the type of curriculum and teaching methods instituted in the school" (Kazamias, 1966, 22). This educational reform, also known as the scientific movement in education (Kazamias, 1966, 28), incorporated "natural experimental methods of science which involved manipulating objects rather than focusing on textbook learning. This procedure enabled students, with the guidance of the teacher, to proceed from simple to complex tasks (Kimball, 1932, 127) thereby promoting individuality and self-development. This process invited children to make their own investigations, to draw their own inferences, and to individually discover as much as possible" (Cavenagh, 1932).

The Progressive Educational Movement, under the guidance of John Dewey in the early 1900s, reinforced the restructuring efforts of previous educators. Dewey's efforts, however, prompted a shift in the theoretical framework that emphasized "learning by doing" in a child-oriented setting in addition to curriculum restructuring. His platform addressed meaningful and realistic activities that valued physical freedom, play, and self-discovery in accordance with an individual's realm of physical, mental, and emotional development (Caswell and Campbell, 1937, 393–394). Classrooms promoted and implemented these learning situations through an Activity Curriculum program. Activities, according to Caswell and Foshay (1957), were defined as

> learning situations brought about by the strong purpose of a child or group of children to achieve a worthy end desirable to themselves which draws upon a large number of different kinds of experiences and many fields of knowledge. (p. 254)

Dewey's definition, on the other hand, inferred a more individualistic and cognitive structure. He believed that a good activity

> drew from many subject areas for developmentally appropriate content. It had to be purposeful so that each step or procedure opened up a new field, raised new questions, aroused a demand for further knowledge, and suggested what to do next on the basis of what had been accomplished and the knowledge thereby gained. (Caswell and Campbell, 1937, 604)

This activity program launched a new development in curriculum revitalization that emphasizes subject matter integration. This restructuring, through an integrated program approach, invites students to become collaborators in curriculum planning and social participants in the learning process. As a result, this "authentic integration takes place in the minds of the learners," thus enabling them to "explore, gather, process, refine, and present information about topics they want to investigate without the constraints imposed by traditional subject barriers" (Pigdon and Woolley, 1993, 6). Figure 2.3 compares the characteristics of an integrated approach to those of the traditional subject approach.

Integration, according to Roehler (1983), is "a strategy for intentionally combining subject matter so that students are aware of this during implementation" (p. 28). Routman (1991) defines integration as "an approach to learning and a way of thinking that respects the interrelationships of language processes—reading, writing, speaking, and listening—as integral to meaningful teaching across any area of the curriculum" (p. 276).

Over the years a number of educators have proclaimed the importance of curriculum integration for student learning and the availability for making connections between personal experiences and school knowledge. For instance, Dewey (1916) argued "that the great waste in school comes from the inability to utilize the experiences one gets outside of school in any complete and free way; while on the other hand, one is able to apply in daily life what one learns in school" (p. 75). In addition, Vacca and Rasinski (1992) claim that when "students are engaged in activities that genuinely meet their needs, purposes, interests, and experiences, then the curriculum is fun, relevant, and meaningful" and participation in authentic literacy events provides opportunities for them to "bring the world outside of school into the classroom" (p. 20). An avenue to incorporate students' personal experiences within the school curriculum is through the techniques of integrated curriculum units, thematic units, and thematic cycles.

FIGURE 2.3 Characteristics of the Integrated Approach and Traditional Approach

Possible Characteristics Typical of Traditional Approach
vs. Inquiry Driven/Integrated Approach

Traditional Approach	Inquiry Driven Approach
Purpose	Purpose
Factual recall and focus upon preselected ideas	Inquiry Emerging understandings Questioning and learning how to learn
Approach	Approach
Teacher directed Preset activities Reading assignment with worksheets Teacher questioning Teacher as expert	Teacher support of student engagement Emerging plans & flexible projects, exploration of issues Discussion and group exploration Students as authorities
Outcomes	Outcomes
Assignments Quiz	Portfolios Sharings Future goals

Integrated curriculum units focus on the inquiry approach, which provides opportunities for learners to participate by taking control of their learning, making predictions, testing hypotheses, gathering and organizing information, synthesizing findings, and building on prior knowledge. As a result, Pigdon and Woolley, among others, claim that learners reflect on their experiences, begin to value differing opinions, viewpoints, and interests, and become risk takers (Pigdon and Woolley, 1993, 16). These units, according to Pigdon and Woolley (1993), provide opportunities for students to: (a) develop understandings through sustained interaction, conversation, or discussion about concepts, ideas, values, and modes of presenting information, (b) develop an understanding of the variety of ways in which we can present, represent, and transfer ideas about the world, (c) build on and extend their personal, out-of-school experiences, and knowledge, (d) understand the difference between real-world, factual experiences, and exploration of knowledge, and fictional imagined worlds, and (e) develop a sense of reflection about their world and their environment that leads to action, control, and conservation (p. 16). An illustration and description of the framework for designing integrated curriculum units are provided in the procedure section (see Figure 2.5).

A related and sometimes synonymous approach is thematic approaches—for example, Thematic Units and Thematic Cycles.

Thematic Units enable students to "study various subject areas through one common theme or topic which is extended into the subject areas" (Vacca and Rasinski, 1992, 259) that is "meaningful and relevant to the curriculum and student lives" (Routman, 1991, 278). Pigdon and Woolley (1993) suggest that activities within these units must be selected so that they "offer the possibility for the learners to further develop their ideas about the fields of knowledge they're studying" (p. 59). Planning for thematic units varies according to the teacher's classroom setup and curriculum orientation. For instance, within a Whole-Language classroom, teachers usually plan integrated units collaboratively with their students. Routman's (1991) guidelines for integrated unit planning are described under the procedures section (see Figure 2.6).

When developing Thematic Units, Weaver, Chaston, and Peterson (1993) suggest five principles of learning that need to be considered when (a) teachers and students negotiate significant aspects of the curriculum, and (b) students participate in authentic language activities in and out of the classroom that relate to whole text reading and writing.

These five principles include:

1. The curriculum should not consist of work sheets and dittos but of opportunities to select and engage in a variety of natural reading, writing, discussion, experimentation, and research activities.
2. The curriculum must be negotiated between the teacher and the students. The topics and themes must be of interest to the students while providing much opportunity for language and literacy development. Decision making must encompass both long- and short-term planning.
3. Thematic units activities must be functional and purposeful. Learning must utilize authentic language and complete texts.
4. Direct and indirect teaching of skills is on an individualized basis. Focus is always on what the student currently needs in order to move forward in learning. Skills are always taught within whole texts and are not used as an isolated lesson.

5. Teaching occurs as a direct response to the student's actions, inquiry, or when the need arises.

Thematic Units, according to Lukasevich (1991), focus around a central theme, selected collaboratively between teacher and students, where subject areas are integrated and explored. He recommends a seven-step process when developing Thematic Units. An illustration and description of these steps are provided in the procedures section (see Figure 2.7).

Edwards (1990) further develops Thematic Units by focusing on mathematical concepts. These units, known as *Thematic Maths,* provide opportunities for students to (1) develop creative and divergent thinking skills, (2) utilize their own knowledge of the real world while fostering new areas of inquiry and learning, and (3) explore, experiment, and expand their knowledge of mathematical and other language arts concepts rather than locating, retrieving, and computing in order to find the "right answers" (Edwards, 1990). Edwards (1990) claims that when children are presented with a challenge in the form of these units, they work for longer periods of time seeking a variety of solutions through questioning, explaining, defending, confirming, and validating their thoughts by conferencing with peers (p. 8).

Advantages for utilizing Thematic Maths include the following: (1) relevant to real-life situations, (2) activities lead to inquiry, investigation, exploration, observations, and self-discovery, (3) challenges current levels of knowledge and thinking, (4) encourages discourse and integration of language learning, (5) encourages risk-taking and problem-solving, (6) puts responsibility of learning onto the child, (7) students gain inner control and confidence in learning.

Thematic Cycles utilize subject areas to investigate a topic. The cycle begins with a question that becomes the focal point of the study. "The content areas are brought to bear on the topic as needed to answer the question or one of the questions that might spin-off from the original" (Vacca and Rasinski, 1992, 259). Vacca and Rasinski (1992) further denote that Thematic Cycles "use art, music, literature, social studies, and sciences for exploring, expanding, and answering the question that defines the central topic." Because of this, "subject areas are more closely connected" (p. 260).

Harste, Short, and Burke (1988) concur that curriculum must be negotiated between teacher and students. He states that "the curriculum that results from the coming together of teachers and students reaches toward new potentials for knowing" (p. 366). An illustration depicting the steps when developing Thematic Cycles is provided in the procedures section (see Figure 2.8).

Pappas, Kiefer, and Levstik (1990, 1995) emphasize the importance of integration through personal characteristics and cultural backgrounds. They state, "children bring their complex customs or styles of integration to their activities or projects. Children from different cultural backgrounds have different rules for communication. Collaboration is crucial and negotiation is the means by which participants can deal with the varying ways of participating and interacting" (1990, p. 40).

As experienced in previous educational reforms, our schools today continue to fall short in helping students "learn tolerance and appreciation of other cultures and persons who are members of those cultures" (Rasinski and Padak, 1990, 576). It appears we have attempted to foster "tolerance, patience, appreciation, and friendship among children of dif-

FIGURE 2.4 Four Models for Integrating Ethnic/Multicultural Content into the Curriculum

Level 1: Contributions Approach	At this level, literature is used in isolated lessons to address holidays, heroes, and customs of a particular culture.
Level 2: Additive Approach	Literature depicting content, concepts, and/or themes of other cultures are added into the curriculum, but not woven through the curriculum.
Level 3: Transformation Approach	Students are encouraged to address different problems, themes, and concerns from another cultural group's perspective. This allows students to see the "interconnectiveness" of the various ethnic cultures with the dominant culture.
Level 4: Decision-Making and Social Action Approach	At this highest level, students are asked to identify social problems and concerns, problem solve, and take actions to help remedy the problem they have identified. This *empowers* them to take ownership in their own learning.

Source: From Rasinski, T., and N. Padak. 1990, October. Multicultural learning through children's literature. *Language Arts* 67: 576–580.

ferent backgrounds and cultures" (Rasinski and Padak, 1990, 576) through curriculum development as denoted in Banks's (1989) four models of multicultural integration. Banks states that "these models are hierarchically arranged in terms of their sophistication in making multicultural issues a central part of the integrated program" (p. 577). Descriptions of these models are listed in Figure 2.4.

Intended Audience

Thematic units may be used with students at any level. Program planning and implementation may differ according to grade level organization and emphasis.

Description of the Procedures

Pigdon and Woolley (1993) identify the framework for designing Integrated Curriculum Units. Descriptions of components are as shown in Figure 2.5.

The framework for Thematic Units as described by Routman (1991) (Figure 2.6) and Lukasevich (1991) (Figure 2.7) includes the following steps:

A. *Planning the Unit*

1. Select the topic that is developmentally appropriate, inviting, and that meets the academic and interest needs of students.
2. Brainstorm and web the possibilities that visually describe the connection between the topic and other subject areas, activities, literature, technology and media, community leaders and agencies.

FIGURE 2.5 Integrated Curriculum Units Framework

A. PROGRAM LEVEL PLANNING

- **1** Selection of a topic for the unit
- **2** Writing specific understandings for the unit

B. ACTIVITY LEVEL PLANNING

- **3** Tuning in
- **4** The shared experience
- **5** Sorting out the shared experience
  - (a) Art activities
  - (b) Drama activities
  - (c) Math activities
  - (d) Language activities
  - (e) Generalizations
- **6** Related experiences
- **7** Sorting out the related experiences
- **8** Values clarification
- **9** Reflection and action

C. RECORD KEEPING AND EVALUATION

- **10** Evaluation of the teaching strategies and materials
- **11** Evaluation of the learner's development
- **12** Future planning

FIGURE 2.6 Guidelines for Planning an Integrated Unit Collaboratively with Students

1. Planning the Unit
- select topic
- brainstorm ideas
- web possibilities
- list questions to be explored
- plan activities for development
- gather resources
- teach for genre of factual writing
- inform, include, and invite parent participation
- long-range planning; fieldtrips, speakers, outside assistance
- organize and set up environment which is conducive to learning

2. Implementation
- justification for studying the unit is shared and discussed
- introduce and teach needed information gathering skills: note taking, research gathering, and report gathering
- provide time for exploration, investigation, and information processing
- group students flexibly
- promote opportunities of collaboration, free choice-self selection
- maintain a climate of inquiry: investigating, collecting data, gathering information, problem solving, revising, and rethinking

3. Evaluation
- allow for student choice such as oral presentation, debate, written reports, published writing, graphs, drama, murals, dance, and song
- provide time for sharing, speaking, and listening
- balance teacher, peer, and self evaluation

Source: From Routman (1991, 279–280).

FIGURE 2.7 The Seven Steps in Developing a Thematic Unit According to Lukasevich, 1991

1. Selection of an interesting theme around which to study other subject areas.
2. Brainstorm/web directions to take the theme. Consider how the theme can impact on the various subject areas through learning activities.
3. Set goals and objectives for the unit.
4. Collect relevant resources and materials.
5. Plan an introduction to the unit. Focus on developing student interests and questions about the topic.
6. Plan learning activities and experiences. Include activities for whole class, small groups, and individual students. Organize activities by subject areas or teaching strategies.
7. Plan a culmination experience. The experience should help you pull together or summarize the unit of study for students.

Source: From Vacca and Rasinski (1992, 260).

3. Through planning, goal setting, and listing objectives the teacher and students have means to document instructional strategies and student progress.
4. An abundance and variety of materials and resources enable the students to experiment, explore, and manipulate the materials through multimodality learning.

B. Implementation

1. The orientation to the unit should pique students' interest. Opportunities for students to share personal experiences and knowledge is critical. Encourage students to develop questions that will lead to further inquiry, problem-solving, study, and investigation.
2. Provide an environment that promotes collaboration, self-selection, discussion, approximation, decision-making, and flexibility.
3. Instructional activities and experiences should be planned to incorporate whole group, small group, and individualized learning. Direct and Indirect teaching is utilized within a language-oriented context using authentic materials.
4. Culminating activities provide an opportunity for students to share their knowledge in collaborative and creative ways.

C. Evaluation

1. Observations, anecdotal entries, conferences, discussion groups, and student self-reflections are ongoing.
2. Opportunities for sharing, reporting, listening, and speaking are encouraged.
3. Students choose how they will report their investigations, findings, and reflections.
4. There must be a balance between teacher, student, and peer evaluation.

Figure 2.8 illustrates the steps for developing Thematic Cycles described by Harste et al. (1988).

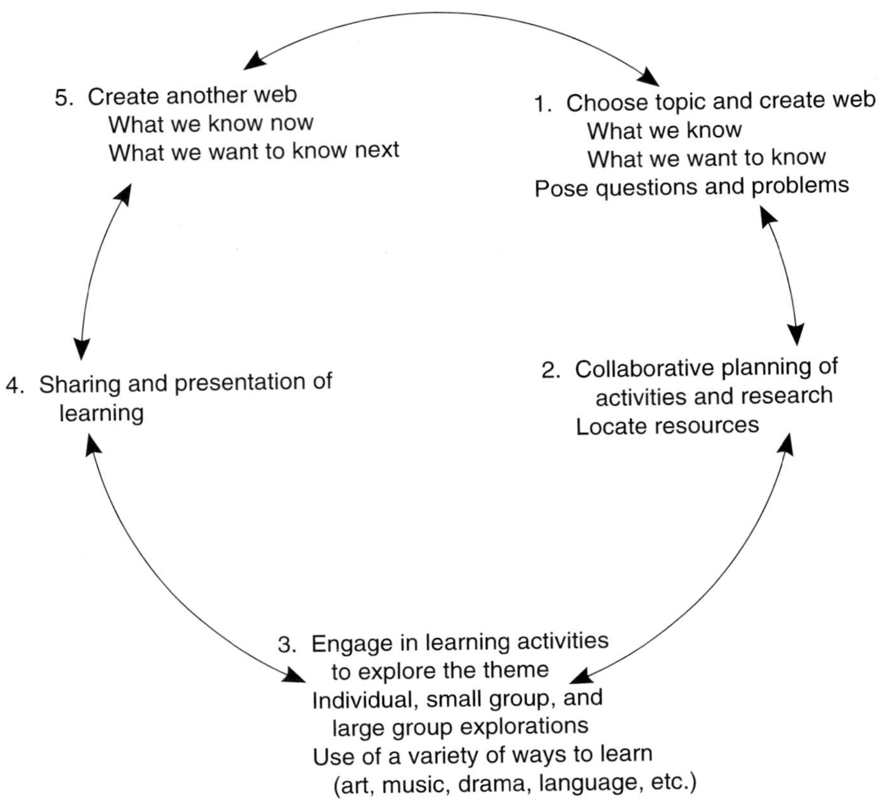

FIGURE 2.8 Generative Theme Cycle

Cautions and Comments

Many limitations have surfaced regarding thematic units. One drawback involves "the superficial integration of the theme and the connection between subject areas" (Vacca and Rasinski, 1992, 260). Another limitation is the "inability to link ways which maximize opportunities for students to make the connections between school and home environments and between subject areas" (Pigdon and Woolley, 1993, 13). Another limitation involves the activities within thematic units. Pigdon and Woolley (1993) claim that "all activities must provide opportunities for students to learn more about the content and not just participate in available extension tasks" (pp. 12–13).

A fourth limitation might be the emphasis given to obtaining information. Rather than addressing one's own questions or delving into the ideas as a way of solving problems, or their application to the real world, units can be for purposes of downloading and sometimes simply copying ideas from one place to another. Sometimes the goal becomes the presentation of the unit, rather than what is gained in conjunction with the exploration, or transactions with other sets. Another limitation may emerge as a result of an emphasis upon the comprehensive treatment of a topic through textbooks, and so on, hands-on experience, and the use of primary sources may be slighted. Likewise, the approach pursues an approach to subject matter learning that is comprehensive and general rather than delving, focused, or caselike. Instead of students delving into issues and subtopics, they are encouraged to develop a surveylike understanding. Many fear that the opportunity to delve may precede a survey understanding, but not vice versa. Finally, the issue of multiculturalism and achieving different perspectives is slighted in this work. (For a detailed discussion of some of these notions as they are applied in the area of social studies, the reader is referred to the Bradley Report.) With the advent of multimedia technologies, the notion of integrated units, project-based learning, and Rich Literacy Tasks (see Unit 1) has resulted in a resurgence of interest in and shift in the purpose, processes, and outcomes of frameworks akin to units. Multiple literacies and Rich Literacy Tasks advocate for a stronger connection between real-world literacies, including digital literacies, and school assignments (New London Group, 2000). These multimedia literacies have the power to create more flexible and multifaceted engagements with ideas, including varying depth of digital images and in multivocal and multilingual ways.

REFERENCES

Alvermann, D. 1991. The discussion web: A graphic aid for learning across the curriculum. *The Reading Teacher,* 45: 92–99. Describes the steps to follow when implementing this instructional tool to promote discussion, comprehension, and reflective responses to any reading material.

Anderson-Inman, L., M. A. Horney, D. Chen, and L. Lewin. 1994. Hypertext literacy: Observations from the ElectroText project. *Language Arts* 71: 279–287. Explores the use of the Internet in conjunction with various literacy activities.

Banks, J. A. 1989. Integrating the curriculum with ethnic content: Approaches and guidelines. In J. A. Banks and C. A. McGee Banks (Eds.), *Multicultural education: Issues and perspectives.* Boston: Allyn and Bacon, 189–207. Describes a hierarchical model for integrating multicultural literature into the curriculum.

Bargiel, S., C. Beck, D. Koblitz, A. O'Connor, K. M. Pierce, and S. Wolf. 1997. Bringing life's issues into classrooms. *Language Arts* 74(6): 482–490. Presents books that deal with life's issues from abuse to war, life to death, etc.

Barton, D., M. Hamilton, and R. Ivanic (Eds.). 2000. *Situated literacies: Reading and writing in context.* London: Routledge. Discusses real-world literacy practices informing notions of situated integrated literacies.

Bergeron, B. S., and E. A. Rudenga. 1996. Seeking authenticity: What is "real" about thematic literacy instruction? *The Reading Teacher* 49(7): 544–551. Provides a framework for analyzing the authenticity of thematic literacy instruction in terms of purpose, choice, audience, resources, and relevance.

Bertelson, C. D. (1992). *A study of an integrated, personalized reading program for special needs students that reinforces the relationship between the home and school environments.* Unpublished master's thesis, Ohio State University, Columbus. This study examines how an integrated reading program impacts early literacy development and parental involvement of two primary developmentally handicapped children.

Bradley Commission on History in Schools. 1988. *Building a history curriculum: Guidelines for teaching history in schools.* Washington, DC: Educational Excellence Network. This report examines the teaching of history across the grades and the curriculum and includes major recommendations for shifting the nature of teaching and learning. References are made to notions such as multiple perspective taking, the use of primary sources, and focused study of topics vs. surveylike examinations.

Brodzik, K., J. Macphee, and S. Shanahan, 1996. Using thematic units in the classroom. *Language Arts* 73: 530–541. Provides a bibliography of professional literature to help teachers develop Theme-Based Units.

Busching, B. A., and S. W. Lundsteen. 1983. Curriculum models for integrating the language arts. In B. A. Busching and J. I. Schwartz (Eds.), *Integrating the language arts in the elementary schools.* Urbana, IL: National Council of Teachers of English, 3–27. Provides a detailed model for integrating the language arts into existing curriculum structures.

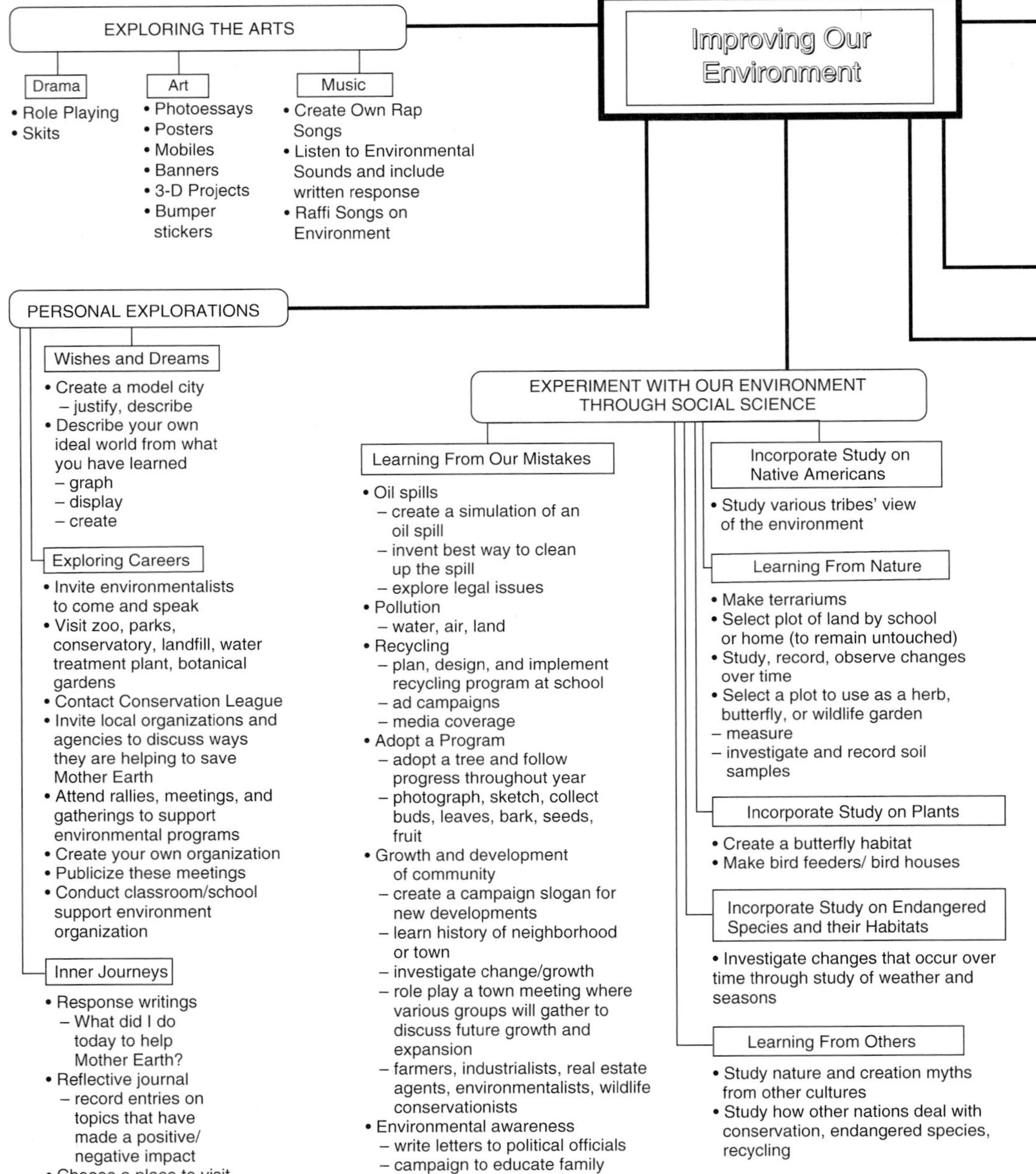

Improving Our Environment
EXPLORING THE ARTS
Drama
• Role Playing
• Skits
Art
• Photoessays
• Posters
• Mobiles
• Banners
• 3-D Projects
• Bumper stickers
Music
• Create Own Rap Songs
• Listen to Environmental Sounds and include written response
• Raffi Songs on Environment
PERSONAL EXPLORATIONS
Wishes and Dreams
• Create a model city
– justify, describe
• Describe your own ideal world from what you have learned
– graph
– display
– create
Exploring Careers
• Invite environmentalists to come and speak
• Visit zoo, parks, conservatory, landfill, water treatment plant, botanical gardens
• Contact Conservation League
• Invite local organizations and agencies to discuss ways they are helping to save Mother Earth
• Attend rallies, meetings, and gatherings to support environmental programs
• Create your own organization
• Publicize these meetings
• Conduct classroom/school support environment organization
Inner Journeys
• Response writings
– What did I do today to help Mother Earth?
• Reflective journal
– record entries on topics that have made a positive/ negative impact
• Choose a place to visit often
– observe how it changes over time
– graph, record, illustrate
– describe ways people and wildlife use this space
EXPERIMENT WITH OUR ENVIRONMENT THROUGH SOCIAL SCIENCE
Learning From Our Mistakes
• Oil spills
– create a simulation of an oil spill
– invent best way to clean up the spill
– explore legal issues
• Pollution
– water, air, land
• Recycling
– plan, design, and implement recycling program at school
– ad campaigns
– media coverage
• Adopt a Program
– adopt a tree and follow progress throughout year
– photograph, sketch, collect buds, leaves, bark, seeds, fruit
• Growth and development of community
– create a campaign slogan for new developments
– learn history of neighborhood or town
– investigate change/growth
– role play a town meeting where various groups will gather to discuss future growth and expansion
– farmers, industrialists, real estate agents, environmentalists, wildlife conservationists
• Environmental awareness
– write letters to political officials
– campaign to educate family and community
– create household products that are environmentally safe
Incorporate Study on Native Americans
• Study various tribes' view of the environment
Learning From Nature
• Make terrariums
• Select plot of land by school or home (to remain untouched)
• Study, record, observe changes over time
• Select a plot to use as a herb, butterfly, or wildlife garden
– measure
– investigate and record soil samples
Incorporate Study on Plants
• Create a butterfly habitat
• Make bird feeders/ bird houses
Incorporate Study on Endangered Species and their Habitats
• Investigate changes that occur over time through study of weather and seasons
Learning From Others
• Study nature and creation myths from other cultures
• Study how other nations deal with conservation, endangered species, recycling

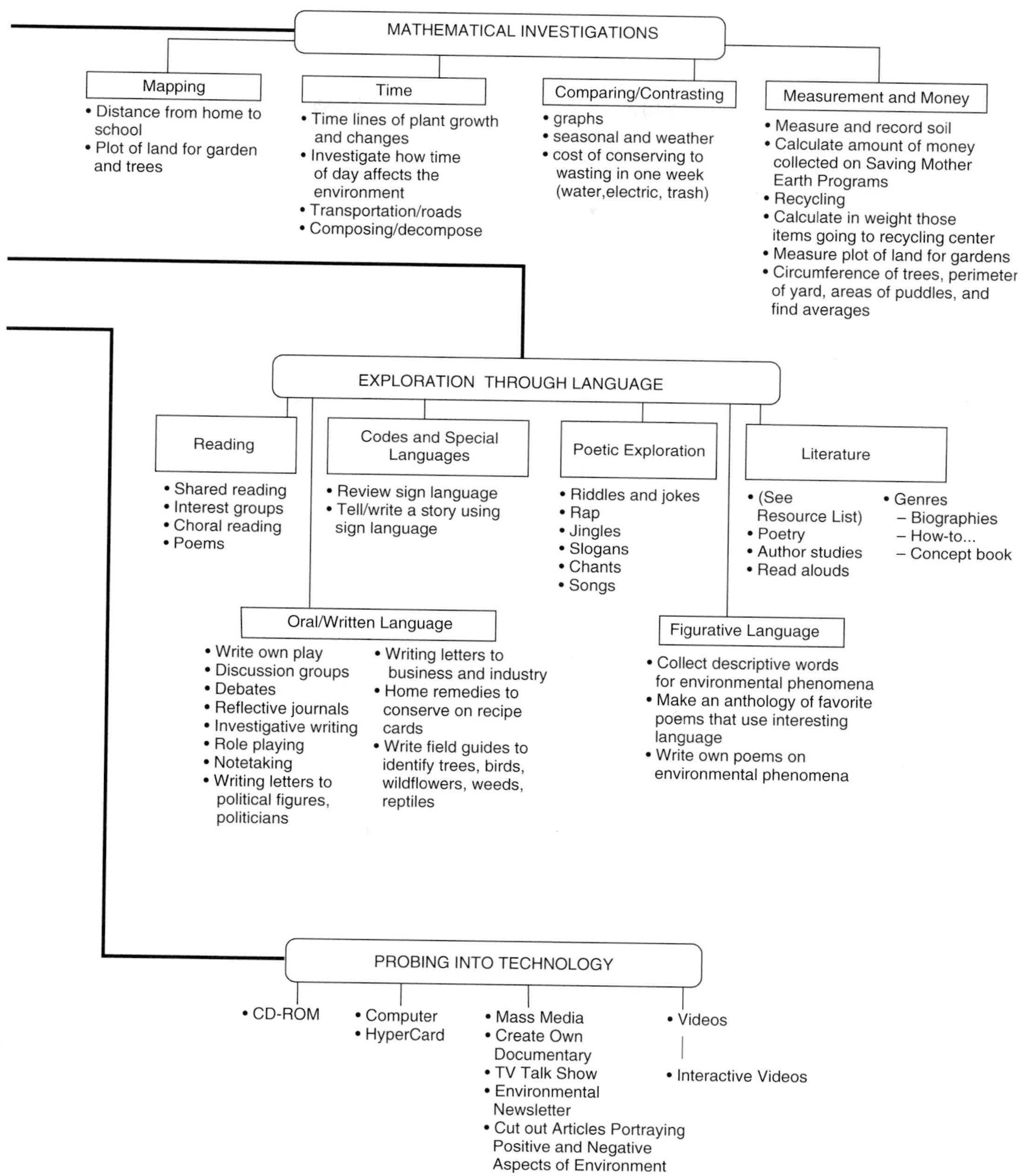
MATHEMATICAL INVESTIGATIONS
Mapping
• Distance from home to school
• Plot of land for garden and trees
Time
• Time lines of plant growth and changes
• Investigate how time of day affects the environment
• Transportation/roads
• Composing/decompose
Comparing/Contrasting
• graphs
• seasonal and weather
• cost of conserving to wasting in one week (water,electric, trash)
Measurement and Money
• Measure and record soil
• Calculate amount of money collected on Saving Mother Earth Programs
• Recycling
• Calculate in weight those items going to recycling center
• Measure plot of land for gardens
• Circumference of trees, perimeter of yard, areas of puddles, and find averages
EXPLORATION THROUGH LANGUAGE
Reading
• Shared reading
• Interest groups
• Choral reading
• Poems
Codes and Special Languages
• Review sign language
• Tell/write a story using sign language
Poetic Exploration
• Riddles and jokes
• Rap
• Jingles
• Slogans
• Chants
• Songs
Literature
• (See Resource List)
• Poetry
• Author studies
• Read alouds
• Genres
– Biographies
– How-to...
– Concept book
Oral/Written Language
• Write own play
• Discussion groups
• Debates
• Reflective journals
• Investigative writing
• Role playing
• Notetaking
• Writing letters to political figures, politicians
• Writing letters to business and industry
• Home remedies to conserve on recipe cards
• Write field guides to identify trees, birds, wildflowers, weeds, reptiles
Figurative Language
• Collect descriptive words for environmental phenomena
• Make an anthology of favorite poems that use interesting language
• Write own poems on environmental phenomena
PROBING INTO TECHNOLOGY
• CD-ROM
• Computer
• HyperCard
• Mass Media
• Create Own Documentary
• TV Talk Show
• Environmental Newsletter
• Cut out Articles Portraying Positive and Negative Aspects of Environment
• Videos
• Interactive Videos

Carraquillo, A., and C. Hedley. 1993. *Whole language and the bilingual learner.* Norwood, NJ: Ablex. Provides a framework for integrating literacy learning with language development.

Cassady, J. K. 1998. Wordless books: No-risk tools for inclusive middle-grade classrooms. *Journal of Adolescent & Adult Literacy* 41(6): 428–433. Discusses the use of wordless books in conjunction with theme-based approaches for students incurring difficulties learning to read.

Caswell, H. L., and D. S. Campbell. 1937. *Readings in curriculum development.* New York: American Book Company. Discusses the challenges of curriculum development and incorporates viewpoints of educational scholars on educational issues, problems, and concerns.

Caswell, H. L., and A. W. Foshay. 1957. *Education in the elementary school.* New York: American Book Company. Describes the major findings relating to elementary education from goals/aims to organization, policies, and practices.

Cavenagh, F. A. 1932. *Herbert Spencer on education.* London: Cambridge University Press. Describes Herbert Spencer's life and his contributions to American Education.

Cena, M. E., and J. P. Mitchell, 1998. Anchored instruction: A model for integrating the language arts through content area study. *Journal of Adolescent & Adult Literacy* 41(7): 559–561. Discusses the integration of content areas including the steps teachers might take to choose the anchor.

Colasent, R., and P. L. Griffith, 1998. Autism and literacy: Looking into the classroom with rabbit stories. *The Reading Teacher* 51(5): 414–420. Describes the utility of a theme-based approach for working with children with autism.

Crafton, L. 1994. *Challenges of holistic teachings: Answering the tough questions.* Norwood, MA: Christopher-Gordon. A resource for teachers that addresses key questions about holistic teaching.

Crawford, K., C. Crowell, G. Kauffman, B. Peterson, L. Phillips, J. Schroeder, C. Giorgis, and K. Short, 1994. Finding ourselves as people and as learners. *The Reading Teacher* 48(1): 64–74. Explores themes tied to the theme of finding yourself as a learner, in a book, in the world, etc.

Cunningham, P. M., and R. L. Allington, 1994. *Classrooms that work: They can all read and write.* New York: Harper Collins. Provides an overview of various activities that might be used to support the development of an integrated classroom.

Dewey, J. 1916. *Democracy and education: An introduction to the philosophy of education.* New York: Macmillan. This book described how theory is translated into practice.

Dillner, M. 1994. Using hypermedia to enhance content area instruction. *Journal of Reading* 37(4): 260–270. Describes the use of hypermedia in conjunction with students' exploration of different topics.

Edwards, D. 1990. *Math in context. A thematic approach.* Portsmouth, NH: Heinemann. Describes how one teacher utilizes math themes with her elementary children. Sample units are included.

Ernst, G., and K. J. Richard, 1994. Reading and writing pathways to conversation in the ESL classroom. *The Reading Teacher* 48(4): 320–326. Discusses uses of reading and writing activities tied to themes in terms of meeting the needs of ESL students.

Exploring Nature with Jean Craighead George Web. *The WEB*, 9,* 1, 1–23. Columbus: Ohio State University. Fall, 1984. (Themed issue)

Gavelek, J. R., T. E. Raphael, S. M. Biondo, and D. Wang. 2000. Integrated literacy instruction. In M. L. Kamil, P. B. Mosenthal, P. D. Pearson, and R. Barr (Eds.), *Handbook of reading research,* Vol. III, Mahwah, NJ: Erlbaum, 587–608. Substantial theoretical discussion exploring the tenets of units and integrated literacies.

Gee, J. M. 1994. *Multiple discourse use by intermediate grade students engaged in a unit approach to learn social studies content.* Unpublished dissertation. Columbus: The Ohio State University.

Glasgow, J. N. 1997. Let's plan it, map it, and show it! A dream vacation. *Journal of Adolescent & Adult Literacy* 40(6): 456–467. Describes high schoolers' use of a theme based upon planning a dream vacation.

Hansen-Krening, N., and D. T. Mizokawa. 1997. Exploring ethnic-specific literature: A unity of parents, families, and educators. *Journal of Adolescent & Adult Literacy* 41(3): 180–189. Explores ethnic-specific literature that might be used in classrooms.

Harste, J., K. G. Short, and C. Burke. 1988. *Creating classrooms for authors.* Portsmouth, NH: Heinemann. Provides a framework for holistic learning, including a section on Thematic Cycles.

Heller, M. F. 1997. Reading and writing about the environment: Visions of the year 2000. *Journal of Adolescent and Adult Literacy* 40(5): 332–341. Describes middle schoolers' engagement in Theme-Based Units tied to concepts of conservatory preservation and estimation.

Hydrick, J. 1990. Diskovery: Kids and technology—revelry or rivalry? *Language Arts* 67: 518–524. Describes how computers can be incorporated into the curriculum as an instructional tool.

Katz, L. G., and S. C. Chard. 2000. *Engaging children's minds: The project approach* (2d ed.). Stamford, CT: Ablex. Provides a description of principles and practices of the project approach with examples of the approach can be applied to students.

Kazamias, A. 1966. *Herbert Spencer on education.* New York: Teachers College Press. Describes Herbert Spencer's four essays on education and the implications for American education.

Keeper of the Earth Web. *The WEB*, 16,* 3, 20–27. Columbus: Ohio State University. Spring/Summer 1992. (Themed issue)

Kettel, R. P., and N. L Douglas. 2003. Comprehending multiple texts: A theme approach incorporating the best of children's literature. *Voices from the Middle* 11(1): 43–49. Discusses the use of single-theme, multiple-text instruction to help students understand the theme from a variety of perspectives.

Kimball, E. P. 1932. *Sociology and education: An analysis of the theories of Spencer and Ward.* New York: Columbia University Press. Provides a framework on how Spencer's theory of education relates to other leading educational theorists.

Labbo, L. D., and S. L. Field. 1998. Visiting South Africa through children's literature: Is it worth the trip? African educators provide the answer. *The Reading Teacher* 51(6): 464–475. In conjunction with discussing children's literature of South Africa, suggestions for a theme-based approach are provided.

Lukasevich, A. 1991. Organizing Whole-Language classrooms. In V. Froese (Ed.), *Whole Language: Practice and Theory.* Boston: Allyn and Bacon, 221–253. Provides a framework for developing Thematic Units.

Martinez, M., and M. F. Nash, 1995. Talking about children's literature. *Language Arts* 72: 368–375. Provides a listing of books dealing with relationships.

———. 1997. Talking about children's books. *Language Arts* 74: 50–56. Provides suggestions for books dealing with heroes and heroines.

Matthews, S., R. Reid, A. Sylvan, L. Woolard, and E. Freeman, 1997. Children's books: Explorations. *The Reading Teacher* 50(8): 680–687. Offers suggestions for books tied to various themes around the general topic of exploration.

McMillen, L., S. Shanahan, K. Dowd, J. Macphee, and J. Hester, 1997. Integrating technology in the classroom. *Language Arts* 74: 137–149. Explores the use of the Internet in conjunction with various literacy activities.

Morrow, L., and L. Gambrell. 2000. Literature-based reading instruction. In M. L. Kamil, P. B. Mosenthal, P. D. Pearson, and R. Barr (Eds.), *Handbook of reading research,* Vol. III. Mahwah, NJ: Erlbaum, 563–587. Explores literature based themes in terms of research and theory.

Morrow, L. M., M. Pressley, J. K. Smith, and M. Smith, 1997. The effect of a literature-based program integrated into literacy and science instruction with children from diverse backgrounds. *Reading Research Quarterly* 32(1): 54–76. Reports a study which explores the impact of a literature-based program upon achievement, use of literature, and attitudes.

New London Group. 2000. A pedagogy of multiliteracies. In B. Cope and M. Kalantzis (Eds.), *Multiliteracies: Literacy learning and the design of social futures.* London: Routledge, 9–37. Provides the rationale for a shift to the new literacies and rich literacy tasks.

O'Brien, D. (1998). Multiple literacies in a high school program for "at risk" adolescents. In D. Alvermann, K. Hinchman, D. Moore, S. Phelps, and D. Waff (Eds.), *Reconceptualizing the literacies in adolescents' lives.* London: Erlbaum, 27–50. Explores the notion of multiple literacies in terms of possible uses with adolescents.

Palmer, R. G., and R. A. Stewart. 1997. Nonfiction trade books in content area instruction: Realities and potential. *Journal of Adolescent and Adult Literacy* 40(8): 630–641. Describes how middle school teachers and students use trade books in a theme-based approach.

Pappas, C. C., B. Z. Kiefer, and L. A. Levstik. 1990. Planning thematic units. In *An integrated language perspective in the elementary school: Theory into action.* New York: Longman. 49–70. Describes how to plan and implement Thematic Units.

———. 1995. *An integrated language perspective in the elementary school.* White Plains, NY: Longman. A key resource for exploring the rational possibilities of theme-based units.

Pigdon, K., and M. Woolley. 1993. *The big picture: Integrating children's learning.* Portsmouth, NH: Heinemann. Provides a model for integrating language learning.

Purves, A. C., L. Papa, and S. Jordan (Eds.). 1994. *Encyclopedia of English studies and language arts.* New York: National Council of Teachers of English. Has more than 800 annotated entries/topics that succinctly address this topic and related areas.

Rasinski, T., and N. Padak. 1990. Multicultural learning through children's literature. *Language Arts,* 67: 576–580. Defines authentic ways to integrate multicultural learning into classrooms.

Roehler, L. R. 1983. Ten ways to integrate language and subject matter. In B. A. Busching and J. I. Schwartz (Eds.), *Integrating the language arts in the elementary school.* Urbana, IL: National Council of Teachers of English, 28–34. Describes ways to effectively integrate language and subject matter.

Rose, D. H., and A. Meyer, 1994. The role of technology in language arts instruction. *Language Arts* 71: 290–294. Explores the use of the Internet in conjunction with various literacy activities.

Routman, R. 1991. *Invitations to changing as teachers and learners K–12.* Portsmouth, NH: Heinemann. An excellent teacher resource to assist teachers when integrating the curriculum.

Ryder, R. J., and M. F. Graves, 1996. Using the Internet to enhance students' reading, writing, and information-gathering skills. *Journal of Adolescent and Adult Literacy* 40(4): 244–254. Describes the uses of the Internet to enhance students' explorations of themes.

Shanahan, T. (1997). Reading-writing relationships, thematic units, inquiry learning: In pursuit of effective integrated literacy instruction. *The Reading Teacher* 51(1): 12–19. Reviews research on reading-writing relationships in conjunction with the use of theme-based units.

Shanahan, T., B. Robinson, and M. Schneider, (eds.) 1995. Avoiding some of the pitfalls of thematic units. *The Reading Teacher* 48(8): 718–719. Discusses the what, why, and problems of thematic units.

Short, K. G., and K. M. Pierce. 1990. *Talking about books.* Portsmouth, NH: Heinemann. Describes how educators and students can create, implement, and sustain literate communities within the school environment.

Spiegel, D. L. 1990. Materials for integrating science and social studies with the language arts. *The Reading Teacher* 44: 162–165. Provides a set of six criteria to use when evaluating instructional resources. Also provides a listing of resources for teachers to utilize when implementing thematic units in the science and social studies areas.

Stokes, S. M. 1997. Curriculum for Native American students: Using Native American values. *The Reading Teacher* 50(7): 576–584. Details theme-based curriculum tied to a consideration of the values of Native Americans.

Tierney, R. J., L. Stowell, L. Desai, and R. Keiffer. 1993. New possibilities for literature teaching and technology. In G. E. Newell and R. K. Durst (Eds.), *Exploring texts: The role of discussion and writing in the teaching and learning of literature.* Norwood, MA: Christopher-Gordon, 175–190. Describes ways technology can aid and complement instructional practices.

Vacca, R. T., and T. V. Rasinski. 1992. *Case studies in whole language.* Fort Worth: Harcourt Brace Jovanovich. Describes how preschool and elementary teachers define their role within a Whole-Language framework.

Vogt, M. E. 1991. An observation guide for supervisors and administrators: Moving toward integrated reading/language arts instruction. *The Reading Teacher* 45: 206–211. Provides the guidelines and a model for supervisors and administrators to use when promoting and supporting districtwide change toward a more integrated approach to teaching.

Walmsley, S. A. 1994. *Children exploring their world: Theme teaching in elementary school.* Portsmouth, NH: Heinemann. Explores a rationale for themes and various ideas for putting them together.

Weaver, C., J. Chaston, and S. Peterson. 1993. *Theme exploration: A voyage of discovery.* Portsmouth, NH: Heinemann. Describes the personal journey and growth three teachers experienced when participating in a thematic research project with first and fourth graders.

Wepner, S. B. 1992. Technology and thematic units: A primary example. *The Reading Teacher* 46: 260–263. Describes how software can be implemented within a thematic unit to enhance learning. A sample "technological web" is included.

Wharton-McDonald, R., M. Pressley, J. Rankin, J. Mistretta, L. Yokoi, and S. Ettenberger, 1997. Effective primary-grades literacy instruction = Balanced literacy instruction. *The Reading Teacher* 50(6): 518–521. Describes the classroom characteristics often reported by effective primary-level teachers.

Woodman, M., P. Hershey, B. Stiles, M. Unanue, N. Storrs, and K. M. Pierce, 1994. Systems. *The Reading Teacher* 48(2): 164–171. Describes books that might be used in themes related to systems (e.g., solar system, ecosystems, etc.).

Yokota, J. 1994. Books that represent more than one culture. *Language Arts* 71: 212–219. Provides books that present comparisons and contrasts across multiple cultures.

Author-Reader-Inquirer Cycle

Purpose

The Author-Reader-Inquirer Cycle is an extension of the curriculum framework for creating rich conditions for learning with literacy via the Author-Reader Cycle proposed in the Harste, Short, and Burke (1988) book. These notions are extended in the Short, Harste, and Burke (1996) book to embrace the notion that inquiry is a key element in literacy curriculum development.

Rationale

The Author-Reader-Inquirer Cycle is a reading and learning curricular framework that is tied to the writing process. Harste, Short, and Burke (1988) use a complex notion of authorship as it relates to learning:

> Webster's Ninth New Collegiate Dictionary provides two definitions of author. The first definition is "the writer of a literary work (as a book)," but the second is more general—"one that originates or gives existence." Although the creation of written texts is certainly important, children have repeatedly shown us that authoring means much more. Authoring and literacy involve "making" meanings through any of the available communication systems (language, art, drama, etc.) to achieve personal and social goals. . . .
>
> Current theories of cognition . . . have shown that learning is not simply a matter of transferring information from the outside world to some sort of in-head storehouse. Instead, learners must actively construct knowledge for themselves—a process that is affected by learners' current beliefs, hypotheses, interests, needs, and purposes.
>
> In the final analysis, our interest in reading and writing is also an interest in learning. (p. 5)

Even the learning of science and mathematics is a part of authorship. The child develops or authors his or her own understandings using systems of communication. The Author-Reader-Inquirer Cycle takes this learning process and makes it into the basis for school curriculum:

> As a curricular frame, the authoring cycle constituted an attempt to orchestrate the how and what of teaching. By organizing curriculum around a learning cycle, participants experience, see demonstrated, and come to value how they might use literacy strategically to learn. From this perspective, authoring was a metaphor for learning, while learning is what literacy is all about. (p. 181)

While the Author-Reader-Inquirer Cycle resembles, in terms of the activities it includes, other literacy approaches (e.g., Whole-Language, Reading/Writing Workshop, theme-based curriculum), this approach can be defined by what Harste, Short, and Burke (1988) would call the "deep structure" of the process:

> Although [a particular teacher] handles science somewhat differently than [another teacher], the open and invitational nature of her curriculum is similar. [The teacher] understands that children do not need to engage in the same activity to have an equivalent experience. Rather than be concerned with the surface structure of lessons—whether the students are studying birds, animals, magnets, and so on—she is worried about the deep structure—whether the students are experiencing and coming to value the process of learning using the perspective of whatever discipline they are studying. (p. 188)

The Author-Reader-Inquirer Cycle uses literacy as an approach to inquiry across the content areas, based on an understanding that all knowledge is available through and represented by literacy:

> A visitor to [the teacher's] room may well have difficulty knowing what phase of the authoring cycle children are in or when the reading and writing period has occurred. What

they see is children reading and writing as they actively explore a topic. The authoring cycle is not perceived as something endemic to language arts, but as a general learning cycle. Children begin with what they know (life experiences), talk, sketch, read, write, listen, rethink, revise, edit, synthesize, and present. Although this is the authoring process, it is also the learning cycle. During the course of a unit of study, this cycle is engaged in over and over again. (p. 190)

While students' products may differ widely from each other, the process they use to learn is similar. Figure 2.9, from Harste, Short, and Burke (1996, 263), shows the process through which the children go even while their particular subject matters differ greatly.

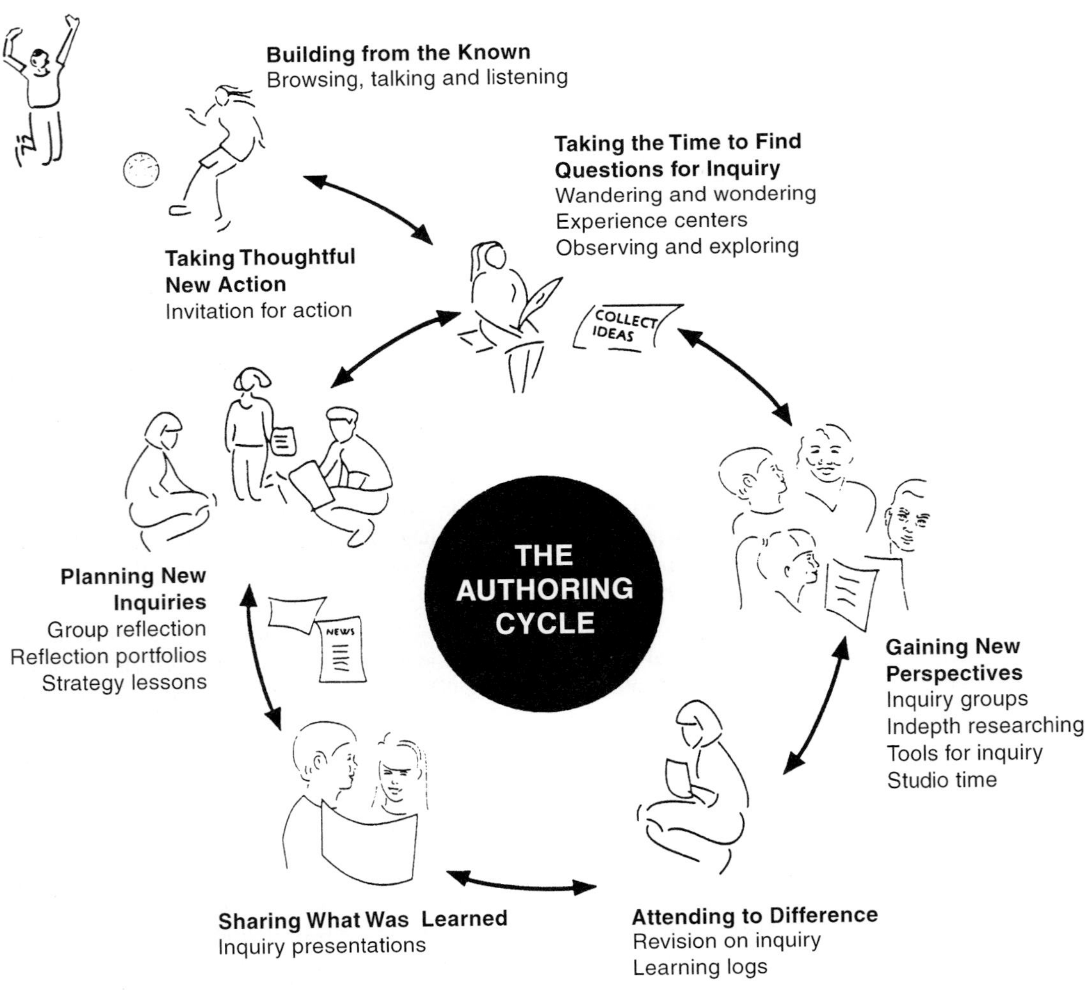

FIGURE 2.9 The Authoring Cycle as a Curricular Framework for Inquiry

Finally, the authors cite several tenets on which the Author-Reader-Inquirer Cycle is based:

- It focuses on process, defining the language arts curriculum in terms of psycholinguistic and sociolinguistic strategies, and suggests that the content of instruction be the strategies of successful language use and learning . . .
- It views reading and writing as a disciplined creative activity that can be analyzed, described, and taught by creating supportive contexts in which the strategies of successful language use and learning can be experienced, demonstrated, and valued . . .
- It emphasizes that reading and writing are ways of learning and developing as well as communicating what has already been learned . . .
- It identifies cognitive universals across all language users regardless of age and posits experience rather than developmental stage as the key variable in the evolution of literacy . . .
- It suggests that in terms of what the mind does, reading and writing share much in common . . .
- It suggests that current approaches to the evaluation of a process curriculum have failed . . .
- It suggests that literacy is relative, an open potential, dependent on context of situation . . .
- It is holistic, viewing reading and writing as multimodal events and one of several systems of knowing . . .
- It highlights the functional nature of literacy both psychologically and sociologically . . .
- It teaches strategies whereby students can solve problems and learn how to learn using reading and writing as tools for learning . . .
- It stresses the inherently social nature of language and language learning . . .
- It stresses the principle that reading and writing teachers should be people who read and write with children to provide demonstrations of the strategies involved in successful written language use and learning . . .
- It sees learning as continuous and the function of curriculum as setting up the learning cycle. It suggests that teaching children the strategies involved in how to learn are the real strategies of literacy . . .
- It sees the past and future of literacy and curriculum as potentials rather than problems . . . (Harste, Short, and Burke, 1996, 208–210)

Rather than being an approach to learning literacy skills (particularly in isolation from everything else children learn), the Author-Reader-Inquirer Cycle is an approach to learning that employs literacy; at the same time that children use their literacies for learning, they expand their literacy strategies.

In the 1996 book, the transition to inquiry represents a major shift in the focus of the cycle. It places inquiry in the center of all of the activities. As they state:

> Curriculum as inquiry is not something that happens from one o'clock till three o'clock in the afternoon in school. It is not a clever device for integrating the curriculum through themes. Nor is it a skill we can teach by doing a unit on the experimental method in science. . . . Teaching reading as inquiry is different from teaching reading as comprehension. All of a sudden we are more interested in the tension different interpretations offer than we are in arriving at consensus as to what the story means. Writing as inquiry is more than teaching writing as a skill that is to be mastered. Inquiry is more than problem solving.

> Problem solving suggests a right answer; inquiry suggests alternative answers as we unpack the complexity of issues. Problems are not something to be avoided, but opportunities to inquire. The very act of teaching itself becomes a process of inquiry. Teachers and students are all inquirers. (p. 51)

Intended Audience

The Author-Reader-Inquirer Cycle can be used at all ages. The authors cite instances of heterogeneous groups of children with a range of interests, backgrounds, and abilities finding challenge and satisfaction with this approach to learning. In fact, the authors tend to avoid grouping children by grade or reading level.

Description of the Procedures

The Author-Reader-Inquirer Cycle is characterized by three goals, around which all the procedures are built:

> From a language arts perspective, our first goal is to create a self-maintaining environment for authors and authorship by providing time, functional reading and writing activities, and opportunities for children to meet, learn from, and come to see themselves and their classmates as authors, readers and inquirers. A second goal is to juxtapose reading and writing so that the sense of authorship students acquire in writing is a basis for taking ownership of reading and vice versa. A third goal is to litter the environment with print so that children are provided with numerous reading and writing invitations. (p. 117)

Certainly, they have now extended their cycle to address inquiry. In terms of inquiry, they draw upon several essential views that lead to reorientation to their previous notions. First is the notion that the learner needs the opportunity or time to be curious or (as they stated, drawing upon Eve Merriam's notions) students need time to wander and wonder. Second, they view that inquiry is tied more to problem-posing than problem-solving, wherein differences and tensions in findings or lack of unity and ongoing unsolved issues are the ongoing fuel and result of inquiry. Third, they stress the need to engage students in achieving multiple perspectives and even perspectives on their perspective-taking, as well as problem-solving. This may also entail having students consider what benefits are achieved by the inquiry and by whom.

With these goals in mind, the authors suggest certain activities that would meet these goals and engage students in ongoing inquiry.

1. Environment. Both the physical classroom and the classroom schedule need to reflect the centrality of the Author-Reader-Inquirer Cycle. Children need to have access to plenty of good reading materials on a variety of levels; therefore it is paramount to have a good classroom library. Likewise, children need to have access to many different kinds of writing supplies—including different kinds of paper, blank books, journals, and the like. Finally, the class schedule should include regular Work Time—large blocks of time (whole mornings) on which children can depend, and during which children can work on their reading and writing.

2. Juxtaposition of Reading and Writing. The Author-Reader-Inquirer Cycle can be supported by numerous activities that build connections between reading and writing. Harste, Short, and Burke (1988) mention several, which appear in this book—Author's Chair, Readers Theatre, Shared Book Experience, literature response activities, and so forth—as happening frequently in Author-Reader-Inquirer Cycle classrooms. Like the Reading-Writing workshop, the Author-Reader-Inquirer Cycle uses strategy lessons, tailor-made for students' current interests and concerns. Yet the Author-Reader-Inquirer Cycle is not limited to a particular set of activities, strategy lessons, or curriculum; to do so would be antithetical to the philosophy that undergirds this approach to literacy.

3. Invitations. Provide opportunities and time to "wander and wonder." "Litter the environment with print"—the bases for many of the invitations to read in the Author-Reader-Inquirer Cycle-based classroom. Every center—cooking, science, math—can include invitations to read. Even very young children can assist with classroom procedures that require reading. The classroom library is part of the invitation to read, as is Author's Chair—including the teacher's daily reading to children. As with reading, the writing invitations are numerous, and interconnected with reading: various kinds of journals, a classroom publishing program, pen pals, a message board for use by everyone in the class, written conversations, and theme studies across the curriculum.

Oftentimes, the work in Author-Reader-Inquirer Cycle classrooms takes place in the form of units of study (see theme-based curriculum), which may be initiated from a collaboration of the teacher or the students. Although different groups of children may explore different areas, they tend to use a similar process. For example, students might go through the following steps during several weeks of a particular exploration:

1. *Selecting area for exploration*

Look for problems or issues to inquire in conjunction with exploring students' interests and curiosities in a particular area

Look for various kinds of information sources including engaging in conversation and exploration using writing, talking, sketches, and the like

2. *Gaining perspectives: collaboration, investigation, and transmediation*

Use different lenses and points of view to explore the topic
Look for other sources of information and different perspectives
Make the questions and differences visible

3. *Attending to differences: tensions, revisions, and unity*

Look for tensions, unanswered questions, what is new, what is different
Think of ways to think about ideas differently and to show patterns
Get feedback on your ideas
Revise central ideas if needed

4. *Sharing what was learned: transformation and presentation*

Share your central ideas with other classmates
Get feedback
Begin planning your presentation using multimodal texts

5. *Planning new inquiries: reflection and reflexivity*
   Retrace the journey taken in the exploration
   Consider what was new, surprising, useful, and so on
   Consider the worth of what you have explored for yourself and others
   Consider what should be explored next and how

As can be seen in Figure 2.10, all the subject matters can be taught through the Author-Reader-Inquirer Cycle.

Coupled with unit-type studies the Author-Reader-Inquirer Cycle also includes a publishing program that emphasizes writing process as well as the use of other media. This publishing process helps children to make the connections between their own experiences and the experiences they have during unit study through developing their own texts.

While the publishing process of course includes written and other forms of texts, the authors cite instances of a writing process-type approach being used for the creation of other materials:

> In this [Author-Reader-Inquirer Cycle] classroom, the teachers and children also valued texts authored in other communication systems, as demonstrated by a group of children who explored space and rockets. After looking at books and talking together, several of the children began using their knowledge of rockets to make paper rockets. All but Aaron used the same process of paper folding and gluing in their rocket constructions. While they all had used a paper cylinder for the rocket body, Aaron had devised a different way to fold and attach fins to the rocket body than the other boys. When they met together to share their "rough draft" rockets, the other boys made fun of Aaron's rocket, which looked different from theirs. Aaron, however, explained why and how he was making his rocket, and as he talked, the other boys realized that he had some good ideas. Following their Authors' Circle on the rocket constructions, the other boys made modifications in their rockets. (Harste, Short, and Burke, 1988, 35)

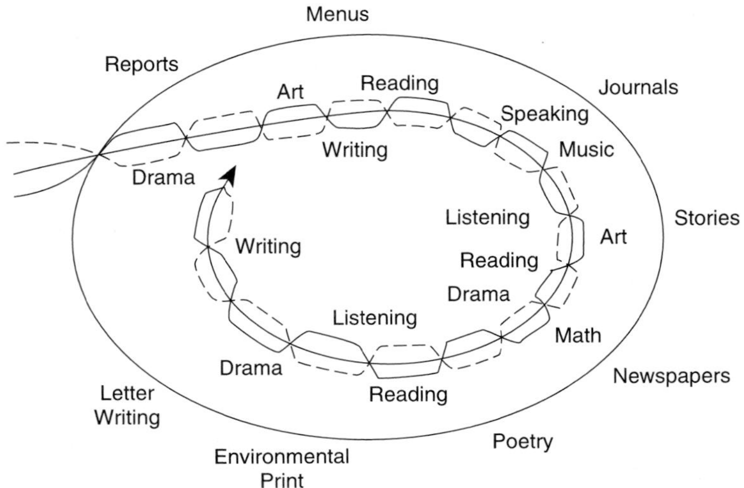

FIGURE 2.10 The Authoring Cycle

As a way of judging the merits of the Author-Reader-Inquirer Cycle practices, Short, Harste, and Burke (1996) suggest asking the following kinds of questions:

- Are we connecting to what students know and are interested in exploring?
- Do all voices get heard?
- Have students been provided ample time to wander and wonder en route to finding their inquiry questions?
- What new perspectives will be gained?
- What new conversations will be started?
- How are the tensions being used to put everyone's explorations on edge and to fuel further inquiry?
- Have opportunities to share what is learned and explored been put into place?
- Are learners supported in reflecting upon and planning their inquiries?
- Have structures for continuing new conversations been planned so that thoughtful new actions can be taken?

Cautions and Comments

The Author-Reader-Inquirer Cycle combines strategies that are well known, e.g., Author's Chair, Shared Book Experience, Reading-Writing Workshop, and so forth, but it does so in a way that places emphasis on the use of literacy for learning, illustrating the point that Gadamer (1976) makes about understanding:

> The understanding of a text has not begun at all as long as the text remains mute. But a text can begin to speak. . . . When it does begin to speak, however, it does not simply speak its word, always the same, in lifeless rigidity, but gives ever new answers to the person who questions it and poses ever new questions to him who answers it. To understand a text is to come to understand oneself in a kind of dialogue. This contention is confirmed by the fact that the concrete dealing with a text yields understanding only when what is said in the text begins to find expression in the interpreter's own language. Interpretation belongs to the essential unity of understanding. One must take up into himself what is said to him in such fashion that it speaks and finds an answer in the words of his own language. (p. 57)

The Author-Reader-Inquirer Cycle ultimately helps children to be able to use and understand the texts to pose and explore problems through the dialogue made possible with the publishing process.

As stated above, the Author-Reader-Inquirer Cycle might incorporate other reading strategies mentioned in this unit (Whole-Language, Theme-Based Units, Reading-Writing Workshop) and in other units (e.g., Sketch to Stretch). In fact, many of the teachers mentioned in Harste, Short, and Burke (1988) and the second edition (Short, Harste, and Burke, 1996) began using these other strategies but then expanded to Author-Reader-Inquirer Cycle work as they began to approach other subject matters using literacy techniques. The major difference, then, between the Author-Reader-Inquirer Cycle and other strategies is that the emphasis in the Author-Reader-Inquirer Cycle is on literacy as a means for finding points of engagement and inquiry between the self and the world.

Of concern to those implementing the Author-Reader-Inquirer Cycle is the role of the teacher. Because this framework is complex, the teacher roles become numerous and challenging, including: (1) developing a curriculum that stems from the interests of the children and areas for inquiry, (2) being an effective diagnostician, (3) responding to the individual needs of the children, (4) being able to respond to children's diverse responses to the material, and (5) helping establish and guide inquiry.

As with other related strategies and frameworks, this framework may appear daunting to the novice. Teachers may wish to implement the Author-Reader-Inquirer Cycle in one part of their classroom (reading and writing are an obvious place to start) using the materials and methods for which there are many excellent resources (see the bibliographies in this unit under Theme-Based Units, Whole-Language, and Reading-Writing Workshop). As teachers become comfortable with these methods, they can expand into other subject matters as well.

Perhaps the area that will need a great deal of support is in helping teachers develop an understanding of the inquiry process. As Short, Harste, and Burke (1996) note, most teaching is driven by content rather than inquiry. Teachers may need to explore how to engage students in inquiry including the steps that are involved and the attributes of an inquiring mind to which students might aspire and be guided.

It may well be difficult, as well with the Author-Reader-Inquirer Cycle, to ensure that students are provided with the range of opportunities for reading and writing across genres, for example, offered by more structured approaches.

One of the main strengths of the approach is that it goes beyond a statement of beliefs to a discussion of an actual practice without being overly prescriptive. Because this approach is so student-centered in philosophy, it is an ideal one to support a culturally diverse classroom. Children can be invited to read multicultural children's literature, to write about their own experiences, and to study cultures that are different from their own.

Computer technology is particularly well suited to the Author-Reader-Inquirer Cycle. Harste, Short, and Burke (1988) mention the advantages of having a computer in the classroom for the publication process. Yet the possibilities for computers extend far beyond simple word processing capabilities. The multimedia and Internet possibilities of the computer are congruent with the interconnected processes of reading and writing around inquiry that comprise the Author-Reader-Inquirer Cycle. As computers become more prevalent in classrooms, teachers may want to invite children to explore applications that afford opportunities for researching and "wandering and wondering," and which combine image, sound, and print in innovative ways to create complex documents that can be read in different ways by different readers.

The Author-Reader-Inquirer Cycle uses many strategies that are familiar to teachers who run student-centered classrooms and who place a great deal of emphasis on literacy. The main difference between the Author-Reader-Inquirer Cycle and other approaches lies in the ideas that govern the implementation of the strategies: The Author-Reader-Inquirer Cycle is based on the use of literacy for inquiry—literacy as a means to pose and explore problems. Teachers who wish to implement the Author-Reader-Inquirer Cycle are encouraged to read Short, Harste, and Burke (1996) for the ideas on which the Author-Reader-Inquirer Cycle are based. The Author-Reader-Inquirer Cycle evolved in conjunction with engagements by the authors in schools in Arizona and Indiana, where it has been used as the cornerstone of curriculum development efforts in selected schools with significant success.

REFERENCES

Atwell, N. 1987. *In the middle: Writing, reading, and learning with adolescents.* Portsmouth, NH: Heinemann. Provides ways of working with adolescents; practical "mini-lessons" that might be adapted to Author-Reader-Inquirer Cycle.

Barksdale-Ladd, M. A., and A. R. Nedeff. 1997. The worlds of a reader's mind: Students as authors. *The Reading Teacher* 50(7): 564–573. Describes a student-as-author project in West Virginia.

Gadamer, H. G. 1976. *Philosophical hermeneutics.* Berkeley: University of California Press. A philosophical approach to ideas about reading.

Harste, J., K. Short, and C. Burke. 1988. *Creating classrooms for authors: The reading-writing connection.* Portsmouth, NH: Heinemann. Outlines the ideas about the Author-Reader-Inquirer Cycle as a learning cycle. Also contains numerous strategies for implementing the Author-Reader-Inquirer Cycle in the classroom.

Newman, J. (Ed.) 1985. *Whole-Language: Theory into use.* Portsmouth, NH: Heinemann. Represents a primary source for information on Whole-Language tenets and practices.

Purves, A. C., L. Papa, and S. Jordan (Eds.). 1994. *Encyclopedia of English Studies and Language Arts.* New York: National Council of Teachers of English. This encyclopedia has more than 800 annotated entries and topics that succinctly address this topic and related areas.

Purves, A. C., T. Rogers, and A. O. Soter. 1990. *How porcupines make love II: Teaching a response-centered literature curriculum.* New York: Longman. Response to literature activities might be adapted to the Author-Reader-Inquirer Cycle approach.

Short, K., J. Harste, and C. Burke. 1996. *Creating classrooms for authors and inquirers.* Portsmouth, NH: Heinemann. In this edition there is a major shift to inquiry as being at the heart of curriculum and the guiding force in the cycle previously defined as Author-Reader Cycle.

Tierney, R. J., L. Stowell, L. Desai, and R. Keiffer. 1993. New possibilities for literature teaching and technology. In G. E. Newell and R. K. Durst (Eds.), *Exploring texts: The role of discussion and writing in the teaching and learning of literature.* Discusses a multimedia approach to a social studies-type unit.

Reading-Writing Workshop

Purpose

The Reading-Writing Workshop represents a comprehensive approach to reading and writing that attempts to engage students in meaningful literacy activities and to develop strategic approaches to reading and writing. The workshop approach draws from numerous sources and is compatible with other literacy approaches (e.g., Whole-Language, Author-Reader-Inquirer Cycle, and so forth). It has been formalized into an approach by Nancie Atwell through her work as a teacher of young adolescents and through her research.

Rationale

As Atwell (1987, 1998) points out, teachers have implicitly communicated to students certain ideas that actually impede reading, including:

- Reading is difficult, serious business.
- Reading is a performance for an audience of one: the teacher.
- "Errors" in comprehension or interpretation will not be tolerated.
- Student readers aren't smart or trustworthy enough to choose their own texts.
- Readers break whole texts into separate pieces to be read and dissected one fragment at a time.

- Re-reading a book is . . . cheating; so are skimming, skipping, and looking ahead.
- There's another kind of reading, a fun, satisfying kind you can do on your free time or outside of school.
- You can fail English yet still succeed at and love this other kind of reading. (Atwell, 152–153)

Yet good adult readers do not always finish every book they start, look up every word they don't understand, read only "great" literature, read without errors, or read according to the many expectations we have of children in reading classes. If we want children to become lifelong readers, we need to approach reading from an authentic perspective.

Likewise, traditional school practices with writing do not reflect the writing process that real writers use. As Atwell points out, for example, most writers write numerous drafts in the course of producing a finished work (she cites Hemingway's 39 drafts of the ending for *A Farewell to Arms*). Writers also write about matters that are fundamentally interesting to themselves. Finally, the traditional response to children's writing—correction after the writing has finished—does not help children become better writers.

Atwell further suggests that good readers use many of the same strategies that writers use:

Writing and Reading as Process

Writers and readers REHEARSE, planning and predicting:

- What will I write?
- What will it be like?
- How will it be shaped by my prior experiences as a writer?
- What will I read?
- What will it be like?
- How will it be shaped by my prior experiences as a reader?

Writers and readers DRAFT, discovering meaning:

- Where will these words I am writing take me?
- What surprises, disappointments, problems, questions,and insights will I encounter along the way?
- Where will these words I am reading take me?

Writers and readers REVISE, reseeing and reseeking meaning:

- Is this what I expected, what I hoped for?
- What do I think of the words on the page?
- What new thoughts do I think because of the words on the page?
- What makes sense? What needs to be changed so sense can be made?

(Atwell, 155)

The Reading-Writing Workshop, then, supports students as they acquire the same kinds of reading and writing habits that good adult readers and writers have: the ability to choose books to read and topics to write about, numerous strategies used in the context of reading and writing, ways of talking about the books they are reading and pieces they are writing, and, most important, a personal identity as a reader and writer.

Intended Audience

The Reading-Writing Workshop was developed originally for adolescents, but can be extended to children in the lower grades (see Cautions and Comments for information about using the Writing Workshop component with children in the primary grades). This approach to reading and writing has been successfully used with at-risk and learning-disabled children, as well as deaf students. An advantage of using the Reading-Writing Workshop component is that children are not limited to mainstream literature or topics. They can have opportunities to explore multicultural literature and their own experiences in writing; these opportunities may be especially helpful for children of diverse ethnic origins.

Description of the Procedures

There are two main ideas behind the Reading-Writing Workshop approach. First is that students own their own reading and writing. Students are in charge of choosing their own books to read, subject to the guidelines mentioned below, and their own subjects on which to write. Secondly, the role of the teacher is as expert reader-writer and guide rather than judge. The teacher actually reads for his or her own purposes along with the students and shares his or her reading experiences with the students. He or she writes with the students, as well, and shares that writing. Along with its guiding principles of student ownership of reading and teacher as mentor, the Reading-Writing Workshop procedure has four elements:

1. Time to read and write
2. Forums for response
3. Conferences with the teacher
4. Mini-lessons

1. Time to Read and Write. Various sources indicate that students in the intermediate grades read independently for only 15 minutes of their day. If students are going to become lifelong readers, they need to have the time to do it. In providing stretches of time during the school day for independent reading, the school gives the message to students that reading is important and worthwhile. Likewise, as Atwell points out, students do not take on the writer's identity based on writing a "complete" piece once a week in class. Young writers need two to three hours a week of writing time.

The bulk of Reading-Writing Workshop time is spent reading and/or writing. Because of the Maine state curriculum, Atwell's students have both reading and writing workshops at different times of the day. Some teachers might plan two days per week of Reading Workshop and three days per week of Writing Workshop. Morris (1991) gave his at-risk students choices: They could read or write, as long as they were doing one or the other of those activities.

Nancie Atwell provides some rules for the Reading Workshop aspect that help students to use this time constructively:

Rules for Using Reading Workshop Time

1. Students must read for the entire period
2. They cannot do homework or read any material for another course. Reading workshop is not a study hall.
3. They must read a book (no magazines or newspapers where text competes with pictures), preferably one that tells a story (e.g., novels, histories, and biographies rather than books of lists or facts where readers can't sustain attention, build up speed and fluency, or grow to love good stories).
4. They must have a book in their possession when the bell rings; this is the main responsibility involved in coming prepared to this class. (Students who need help finding a book or who finish a book during the workshop are obvious exceptions.)
5. They may not talk to or disturb others.
6. They may sit or recline wherever they'd like as long as feet don't go up on furniture and rule #5 is maintained . . .
7. There are no lavatory or water fountain sign-outs to disturb me or other readers. In an emergency, they may simply slip out and slip back in again as quietly as possible.
8. A student who's absent can make up time and receive points by reading at home, during study hall (with a note from a parent or study hall teacher), or after school. (Atwell, 159–160)

Likewise, Atwell has guidelines for the Writing Workshop time:

> This year, we're going to have a writers' workshop every day. Every day all of you will be working in some way on your writing. And in this writers' workshop, we're going to have certain rules.
>
> First, there's no erasing. Save that record of your thinking and how it's changed. I'm interested in how writers think and change their minds; when you change your mind, simply draw a line through.
>
> Next, write on one side of the paper only. Writers often cut and paste—cut their writing apart and reorganize the pieces. That's hard to do when there's writing on the other side of the page.
>
> The next rule is, save everything. You're creating a history of yourself as a writer this year, and what you decide against is as much a part of your writing as what you decide to keep. So hold on to all those false starts and ideas that don't work out and notes and doodles and preliminary drafts.
>
> You should also date and label everything. By label I mean mark it DRAFT #1, DRAFT #2, and so on. Or NOTES, which is how I'd label the ideas for stories you just jotted down.
>
> The next rule is, speak in quiet voices only. Beyond all else, writing is thinking. It's hard to think as a writer thinks when your thoughts are interrupted. During writing time I'll always speak softly and expect you to do the same. If you'd like to read your writing to a friend, there are places to go to quietly confer. All your writing conferences with each other will take place in the four conference corners.
>
> And the final rule of writing workshop is, work really hard. (Atwell, 83–84)

Reading and Writing workshops provide time for students to read and write. They feature guidelines for students' behaviors that help all members of the classroom to respect the reading and writing that are taking place and to keep reading and writing central to the activities in the classroom.

2. Forums for Response. Along with time to read and write, students also need to have several ways to be able to respond to their reading and writing—with the teacher and with each other. Adult readers often talk to each other about books; response is an authentic reading activity. Further, a student's enthusiastic response about a book may encourage other students to read that book next. Writers also need opportunities for response to their work. As Atwell points out, the teacher should be responding to writers during the process of writing and not after the student feels the project is finished—even if students do read "after the fact" responses from the teacher, the suggestions might not transfer to the student's next writing project. Peer responses can be helpful for writers as well; students need to have an audience for their writing that is larger than the teacher.

Responses can take verbal or written form. Verbal forms include literature response groups, peer conferencing, group sharing of writing, conferencing with the teacher (see below), and the kind of discussion that takes place in the mini-lessons (see below). Atwell discusses the importance of listening to students, particularly when responding to students' writing. Part of this listening involves recognizing the student's interest in working further on a piece and the directions in which the student wants to take the piece. Atwell also typically asks questions to find out how the students are thinking (instead of offering suggestions for how to solve problems; for example, she asks the student to list some of the options he or she might use—and then she adds a possibility to that list based on her own experiences). She cautions teachers to avoid responding like teachers (quizzing students, focusing on details of the reading and writing) and to try to respond to students as readers, writers, and mentors.

Atwell recommends using the Dialogue Journal (see Dialogue Journals, Unit 9) between teacher and student. Response journals allow the teacher individual contact on a regular basis. Students can also be encouraged to write notes to each other about their reading. Students might make their responses outside of class, or the last few minutes of class might be reserved for making responses to reading.

3. Conference with the Teacher. The main form of evaluation for the Reading-Writing Workshop focuses on conferences with the teacher, which can occur periodically during the school year. Reading and writing conferences provide students with chances to review their progress toward old goals and to set new ones.

Atwell discusses four kinds of writing workshop conferences. The status of the class conference occurs at the beginning of every writing workshop, in which students indicate to Atwell exactly what they plan to work on during that session. They may set deadlines and goals for themselves during this three-minute whole-class conference. This conference helps Atwell to keep track of what each individual student is working on and it helps her to help students follow through with their goals.

The second type of conference, the topic conference, helps students to come up with ideas for writing. Atwell uses open-ended questioning (e.g., "Tell me about _______" or "What kinds of writing would you like to try?") to help students come up with topics for writing:

> In this [topic conference] . . . my job isn't to tell [the writer] what he should write but to help him find out what he knows, show him I'm interested in what he knows, and then give it back to him from my perspective. (p. 101)

The third type of conference focuses on students' writing drafts. Atwell offers guidelines for these conferences, which occur throughout the writing period:

1. Keep conferences short, just a quick minute or two. . . . It's important to remember that you're not asking to hear every word every student writes; if you do, you're taking control and making each of those pieces of writing your responsibility . . .
2. See as many writers as possible. If you can't get to everyone on a given day, make a note on the status-of-the-class chart of who you didn't get a chance to check in with and see them first in the next workshop.
3. Go to your students so you can control the length of the conference and see many writers . . .
4. Make eye contact with the writer. This means kneeling or sitting alongside their desks as you talk and listen . . .
5. Don't tell writers what should be in their writing, or, worse, write on their pieces. Remember the centrality of ownership to students' growth as writers. The piece of writing belongs to the writer.
6. Build on what writers know and have done, rather than bemoaning what's not on the page or what's wrong with what is there. Remember that in general students do the best they can. As you help them move forward, their best will get better.
7. Resist making judgments about the writing . . . Avoid generalized or contrived praise, too. . . . Instead, praise by becoming involved in the writing, by paying and calling attention to what students know. And praise by describing the effects specific techniques have on you as reader/listener . . .
8. In questioning students, ask about something you're curious about as an inquisitive human being. . . . What would you like to know more about? What didn't you understand? Then focus on just these one or two issues, taking care not to overwhelm the writer. (pp. 94–95)

A fourth type of conference is the evaluative conference, which takes place in both reading and writing workshops. This conference consists of a meeting between teacher and student in which the teacher interviews the student and his or her reading and/or writing, they discuss the student's previous goals, and they come to agreement on new goals for the next grading period (see unit on assessment).

4. Mini-lessons. While mini-lessons are brief in length, they are an important contribution to the success of the Reading Workshop. Mini-lessons can include a variety of activities, from readings of poetry and literature, through short discussions of an author the students may be interested in, to the presentation of reading strategies that will benefit students. The key to mini-lessons is that they be relevant to the students' actual reading or writing. The teacher makes choices about which mini-lessons to present based on students' dialogue journals, informal and formal conferencing, and his or her own revelations about reading and writing.

While reading and writing mini-lessons may differ in terms of their subject matter, their format is essentially the same. It is important to choose a topic that can be addressed in a relatively short period of time. Larger topics can be broken up into mini-lessons that can be used successively.

One important kind of mini-lesson is one that helps students to build strategies. The following is an example of a reading lesson that gives students choices about reading strategies.

Prediction and Self-Questioning Strategies Mini-Lesson

In conjunction with a teacher's recognizing that a subset of her students do not engage as actively as they might in reading selections, especially content area material, the teacher decides to pull together the students and focus upon helping them make predictions and ask their own questions. To this end, the teacher presents a book that is new to the classroom. She shows the children the cover and asks:

> What do you think this is about?
> How can you tell what it might be about?

She then discusses with them the need to be actively involved in using clues as a basis for making predictions and asking themselves questions. Students discuss the types of clues that help them formulate their own questions and afford them predictions. They brainstorm a list of clues they might use:

> Think about what you want to learn
> Check the title, illustrations, headings, etc., as a way of suggesting questions or narrowing possibilities

She then brainstorms other things that help them decide upon their questions and to figure out what the book might offer.

As an extension she gets the children involved with coming up with examples of when they might use that strategy, perhaps by doing what-ifs: What if the cover was missing? What if you didn't know the name of the author? What if the book was not in English?

She then directs them to apply the strategies to their own reading and emphasizes that it's okay if the predictions don't turn out to be true. The point of making predictions is not to outguess the author but to have a starting point for reading the book. This mini-lesson could be done at least twice, once with a book that is fairly predictable and once with a surprising book—so that children can savor the surprise but still practice prediction. After reading she has the students reflect upon what they read and also talk about questions and predictions that they pursued.

Skolnick (1989) has an example of a writing mini-lesson:

> Mini-lessons are a natural time for teachers and children to explore the craft of the writer. . . . To help her second graders understand that authors choose words carefully as they write, during a mini-lesson Jane Fraser told the class: "Earlier this morning, as we shared Lilian Moore's *I'll Meet You at the Cucumbers,* I noticed that Moore used special language. Remember the way she described the truck coming down the road? 'At first he thought two small stars had tumbled out of the sky. Then he realized that what he saw were two headlights. The farmer's truck was coming down the road, home from the city.' I love the way she said that: 'two small stars had tumbled out of the sky.' Those words give me a crystal-clear image. Moore didn't say, 'He could see the lights on the truck' or just, 'He saw the truck coming down the road.' The language she chose has a special sound. As you write today, think about the words you choose. What picture do you want to give the reader? What special language will *you* try in your story today?" (p. 55)

In both of these mini-lessons, the children are invited to participate—in the first via discussion and in the second via writing. The second mini-lesson in particular exemplifies the community of readers and writers that characterizes the Reading-Writing Workshop classroom: The teacher talks about her response to a book—as a reader, and not as a teacher. She is able to articulate what in particular she likes about the writing and she offers alternatives that the writer could have chosen. Finally, she issues a single challenge—what special language will you try in your story today?

Cautions and Comments

Nancie Atwell (1987, 1998) cites numerous instances in which students have begun reading in the Reading Workshop because that was the expectation and ended up reading because they enjoyed it. Additionally, Oberlin and Shugarman (1989) have found that the Reading Workshop approach benefits learning-disabled readers—specifically contributing to a positive change in their attitudes toward reading.

Since Atwell's much-cited book, others have made suggestions about ways to implement the Reading Workshop. Reutzel and Cooter (1991) suggest that mini-lessons not only benefit the students, but they are a way that teachers can satisfy school and district curriculum demands while providing students with choice and support in authentic reading situations. The authors suggest selecting curriculum material for presentation in the form of mini-lessons as the material applies to readers' needs. Spencer (1991) provides an account of an elective Reading Workshop class set up for ninth graders. Students responded favorably to this class as an elective, and she suggests expanding the possibility to the higher grades as well. With some trepidation, Morris (1991) began to implement Reading and Writing Workshop into his class of at-risk high school students and found that the students responded—not dramatically, but there was a discernable positive response. Nower (1991) has implemented the writing workshop approach with deaf students, and Harris-Martine (1991) uses it in her classroom in an inner-city school. This approach supports the wide range of students that might be found in a culturally diverse classroom.

McAuliffe (1993) and others have pointed out children's tendencies to write strongly gendered work. In fact, boys and girls often have a hard time relating to and even understanding each other's stories. In her study of second graders, McAuliffe found that through peer feedback available in writers' workshops, children began to change their writing so that more of their classmates could engage with it. Writing workshop, then, offers children a chance to move beyond some of the narrow confines of socialization.

Other authors have challenged some of Atwell's ideas. While Ash (1990) acknowledges the importance of student ownership of reading, she also makes a case for an occasional class-read text. She found, through having her students read a James Thurber story, that her students were not engaging with the material because they weren't hearing the voices in the text. This class reading became the basis for working on an important reading strategy. Abrahamson and Carter (1991), finally, suggest that Atwell privileges fiction/narrative at the expense of great nonfiction. They suggest that despite Atwell's third rule (see above), students may find nonfiction books that don't fall into her categories to be absorbing.

REFERENCES

Abrahamson, R. F., and B. Carter. 1991. Nonfiction: The missing piece in the middle. *English Journal* 80: 52–57. The authors argue that reading workshop should include nonfiction as well as fiction.

Ash, B. H. 1990. Reading assigned literature in a reading workshop. *English Journal* 79: 77–79.

Atwell, N. 1987. *In the middle: Writing, reading, and learning with adolescents.* Portsmouth, NH: Heinemann. A thorough and comprehensive book on reading and writing workshops.

———. 1998. *In the middle: New understandings about reading, writing, and learning.* Portsmouth, NH: Heinemann. Extends the previous editions with rich examples and further discussion as well as support for teachers.

Barnitz, J. G. (Ed.). 1998. Revising grammar instruction for authentic composing and comprehending. *The Reading Teacher* 51(7): 608–611. Describes grammar workshop for use in conjunction with authentic reading and writing.

Brent, R., and P. Anderson. 1993. Developing children's classroom listening strategies. *The Reading Teacher* 47: 122–126. Uses a mini-lesson format for teaching listening strategies. Offers a good process for teaching mini-lessons.

Dorn, L. J., and C. Soffies. 2001. *Scaffolding young writers: A writers workshop approach.* Portland, ME: Stenhouse. Discusses some of the notions of the workshop approach to working with writers.

Harris-Martine, D. 1991. Reading, writing, and literature in a Harlem second grade. In J. T. Feeley, D. S. Strickland, and S. B. Wepner (Eds.), *Process reading and writing: A literature-based approach.* New York: Teachers College Press. Describes the use of reading and writing workshop-type strategies with children in Harlem.

Lancia, P. J. 1997. Literary borrowing: The effects of literature on children's writing. *The Reading Teacher* 50(6): 470–475. Describes a second-grade teacher's use of literature as a model for writing.

Lunsford, S. H. 1997. "And they wrote happily ever after": Literature-based mini-lessons in writing. *Language Arts* 74: 42–48. Describes a primary teacher's use of mini-lessons to meet the needs of her students.

McAuliffe, S. 1993. Toward understanding one another: Second graders' use of gendered language and story styles. *The Reading Teacher* 47: 302–310. Describes a study of children's changing their use of language during a school year.

Meehan, P. 1997. Beyond a chocolate crunch bar: A teacher examines her philosophy of teaching reading. *The Reading Teacher* 51(4): 314–324. Presents a model with practices akin to the Reading-Writing Workshop.

Morris, C. W. 1991. Giving at-risk juniors intellectual independence: An experiment. *English Journal* 80: 37–41. Morris implemented reading and writing workshop with students who had repeatedly experienced failure.

Nower, B. 1991. So it doesn't disappear in air. *The Volta Review* 93: 123–137. Describes a writing workshop approach with deaf students.

Oberlin, K. J., and S. L. Shugarman. 1989. Implementing the reading workshop with middle school learning-disabled readers. *Journal of Reading* 32: 682–687. This study found that learning-disabled students improved in their attitudes toward and involvement with books following a reading workshop approach.

Opitz, M. F., and D. Cooper. 1993. Adapting the spelling basal for spelling workshop. *The Reading Teacher* 47: 106–113. For teachers who are not ready to or cannot give up the spelling basal, here is an approach that integrates it into a workshop.

Reutzel, D. R., and R. B. Cooter, Jr. 1991. Organizing for effective instruction: The reading workshop. *The Reading Teacher* 44: 548–554. Describes several strategies for organizing reading workshops.

Rucinski, C. A., and G. E. Garcia. 1996. Teachers' concerns about curriculum change: Adapting to the "Reading Workshop." In C. K. Kinzer and D. J. Leu (Eds.), *Multidimensional aspects of literacy research, theory, and practice.* Chicago, IL: National Reading Conference, 537–542. Explores issues of teacher change in the context of exploring Reading Workshop.

Skolnick, D. 1989. When literature and writing meet. In N. Atwell (Ed.), *Workshop I by and for teachers: Writing and literature.* Describes several literary mini-lessons that connect reading and writing.

Spencer, P. S. 1991. Recovering innocence: Growing up reading. *English Journal* 80: 65–69. At the behest of a student, Spencer developed an optional reading workshop that became popular with the students.

Taylor, M. M. 2000. Nancie Atwell's "In the Middle" and the ongoing transformation of the writing workshop. *English Journal* 90(1): 46–52. Explores Atwell's writing workshop approach and its transformative qualities for writing.

Book Club

Purpose

Book Club began as an attempt to engage students more fully in conversations about books. In pursuing this goal, Book Club has expanded and become a framework to guide teachers "as researchers" in developing reading and writing instructional activities to ensure that students can be as fully engaged as possible in literacy activities.

Rationale

Book Club's genesis and continued development are tied to the efforts by Susan McMahon and Taffy Raphael (now largely Taffy Raphael and her colleagues) to explore the possibilities that emerge from changing views of literacy learning. They have been guided by a commitment to ongoing teacher research as well as certain key theoretical and pedagogical assumptions largely emanating from a combination of a sociocultural perspective and reader response theory that emphasize the active and social nature of learning as well as the central role of language in the process of literacy learning. In recent years it has been renamed Book Club Plus to differentiate the approach from any actual book club and to highlight the instructed components extending from it.

The Book Club Plus program involves the ongoing development and refinement of instruction that teachers and others might create to ensure that students have the support and contexts necessary for acquiring and developing literacy abilities and strategies (i.e., reading, writing, and oral language) to be successful. It is designed as an alternative to literacy instruction based upon asking the question: What are the implications of a sociocultural perspective for literature-based reading instruction?

As they state:

> As we considered how a sociocultural perspective contributed to the design of the Book Club program, we identified four key principles. First, language develops thinking and learners construct meanings—which are eventually internalized—in their interactions with others. Second, learning is best facilitated as more knowledgeable others guide the learner with appropriate tasks. Third, individuals construct a sense of self as they participate in social contexts; this identity includes their own and others' roles in the group. Fourth, individuals construct meanings for language within their experiences and develop speech genres particular to given social contexts. The research exploring reader response provided the basis for three additional principles. First, we believed readers interact with texts within a social context and that meaning results from this transaction. Second, readers respond to text in multiple ways, so a reading program should promote variations in the kinds and ways students represent their responses. Third, since response varies depending on readers' stances and points of progression through a text, a student should have opportunity to respond throughout the reading process. (McMahon and Raphael, 1997, p. 18)

Therefore, key assumptions and principles undergirding their development of Book Club Plus include:

- The foundational nature of oral and written language development to any kind of literacy development.
- The key role that authentic reading materials can play and the importance of authentic oral and written activities connected to such reading experiences.
- The active nature of meaning making—tied to the view of the reader and writer as constructing meanings.
- The importance of social interaction in defining the nature of reading and writing. In turn, the importance of others and the classroom community in developing successful learning.
- The important role a teacher has in developing and supporting contexts for learning as well as providing guidance and scaffolding.

Intended Audience

Book Club Plus can be developed to meet the needs of students of all ages, including students with special needs.

Description of the Procedures

The Book Club is at the heart of the Book Club Plus Program, but the program extends beyond Book Club per se to include what they describe as four "contexts" for instruction and participation in language and literacy. They are:

1. Community share
2. Book Club discussion groups
3. Reading
4. Writing

1. Community Share. Community share is the time when whole class activities occur. These activities are seen as the place where classroom community building activities occur and where various groups' activities may stem or merge. Community share time is seen as "a complex and critical component . . . providing a public and social forum within which students hear and use the language of literacy and literary discussion . . . It is the context in which the individual students and their independent book clubs come together to form a discourse community with shared knowledge (Raphael and Goatley, 1996, 46). During this time the teacher may afford students opportunities to share what has evolved in group discussions or in conjunction with other activities.

Prior to Book Club, it may serve as an opportunity for the teacher to introduce and model a host of strategies including conversational strategies, raise issues that the teacher wants students to consider, as well as model reading and writing strategies that the teacher is trying to foster for all the students. Or, it may serve to introduce the students to literacy conventions as well as vocabulary.

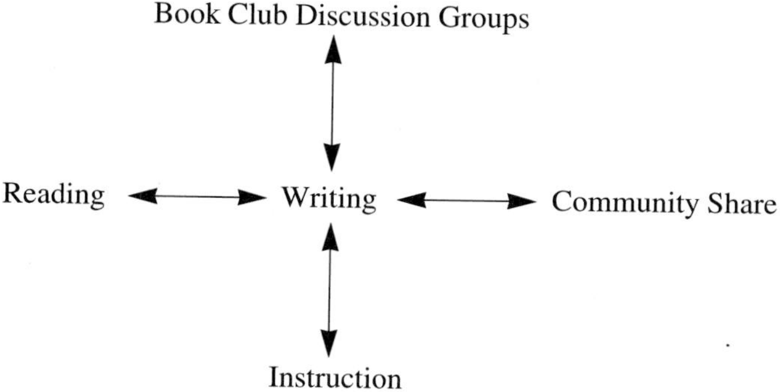

Components of Book Club

After Book Club, it may serve as a time to follow up on issues (such as debate or extend conversation around an issue presented or make connections to other books) or to reexamine the nature and quality of discussion for purposes of improving students' engagements in future Book Club discussions. The teacher plays three roles: participant, facilitator, and scaffolder. Sometimes the teacher will take a back seat to the students' responding; at other times, the teacher will read aloud, direct, or introduce via explanation key concepts. These community share times may occur prior to a unit or day's activities or at various times when the teacher considers that a meeting of the class community would be worthwhile. At other times, the teacher may use these times to discuss connections across several units.

2. Book Club Plus Discussion Groups. The Book Club Plus discussion groups are carefully planned discussions by small groups around a book or books. In planning the Book Club discussions the teacher considers a range of possible grouping versus defaulting to ability grouping. Raphael and McMahon (1994) stress that Book Clubs are not intended to perpetuate the norms of most class discussions, which emphasize turntaking and individuality to the detriment of authentic conversation as among people interested in books. In their view authentic conversations are less competitive and more supportive. To illustrate, they offer numerous examples of conversations which seem procedural rather than authentic. In addition, they show how students will move from appreciating what each other contributes (especially to learning) rather than whose work is best. Here is one example:

> When Eva saw the similarity between Joshua's reading log and her own, she called him a copy cat despite the fact that they were responding to the same prompt. Eva and her peers did not realize that the activity had been designed to help them explore ideas central to the story and apply their own background knowledge, experiences, and strategies as they constructed their understanding of the story. One of our goals was to help students learn the differences between their preconceptions about book discussion and authentic discussion that arises when students are engaged with their texts. (Raphael and McMahon, 1994, 105)

They also stress the importance of students' engagements in the ideas of the text and ways that they might prepare students for book clubs with reading and writing support to ensure their engagement. In support of the Book Club Plus discussions, Raphael and her colleagues stress the development of reading strategies in concert with, and often in preparation for, the discussions. These might include teacher modeling as well as workshops on comprehension or word recognition, including vocabulary. They also stress writing activities as a means of engaging students in pulling together ideas within and across texts. Over time, students develop control over and their own ways of preparing for Book Club discussions.

Book Club Plus stresses that the material students read needs to be carefully selected by teachers as they consider what will spark student interest and what is instructionally viable as well as other factors. Book Club is committed to including trade books and various periodicals, but the final selection and the subsequent procurement of multiple copies follows lengthy deliberations of the range of material, the quality of the material, the curriculum goals and possibilities (both skills and themes), teacher and student interest, and issues of representation of diversity. The authors note that commitment to trade books was facilitated by their willingness to ensure (to school district personnel) that skills and strategies could be taught through these materials.

*3. **Reading.*** Reading opportunities involve a mix of sustained reading opportunities (at least 15 minutes per day or the equivalent across the week) as well as other more focused reading opportunities. In some classrooms the teacher might afford the students a sustained reading opportunity daily; in other classrooms the teacher might do once per week and then use the other four days for skill and strategy development. In addition, students are afforded a variety of opportunities (reading with peers, reading aloud by teachers) to ensure that they are afforded a range of texts written in different styles/genres. Emphasis is also given to reading strategy development as well as a focus upon the students' engagement with characters, events, and themes. Across these various reading experiences a range of supporting activities are enlisted, including webs and logs as well as other forms of writing experiences that might accompany reading.

*4. **Writing.*** Writing activities are seen as essential for ensuring personal responses as well as ways to contextualize strategies while extending thinking including analysis and synthesis of texts. To these ends, proponents of Book Club Plus expect students to be engaged in a host of daily writing activities that might support the reading directly. Such would include reading logs and think sheets that students complete in response to reading. In addition, extended writing (including planning, revision, and publishing) are seen as ways to engage in more extended meaning making. Furthermore, such opportunities are seen as invaluable in helping teachers achieve a window into student thinking, interests, and strategy development.

Cautions and Comments

Since its inception, Book Club or Book Club Plus has been seen as an approach that offers students integrated learning opportunities emanating from their engagements with literature. The elements are viewed by many literacy educators as key for a balanced and integrated literacy program (Duffy and Hoffman, 2002; International Reading Association, 2002). Numerous explorations of its use have been made and discussed by Raphael and her colleagues, and there is a website (www.planetbookclub.com) that offers accounts of its use, discussion of its effectiveness in various settings, and guidance on how it might be used. Its use in schools seems to be burgeoning.

The various educators who have been engaged in the collaborative development of Book Club Plus have also engaged in an examination of Book Club upon students' engagement in reading and writing, as well as more traditional measures of performance. Most of their analyses have focused on the meaningfulness of the discussions themselves, including the impact of the various ways groups have been constituted and supported. As you might expect, the collaborative team has been interested in using this information to refine their thinking and spur further explorations. While they have garnered support for organizing diverse groups, they have also pursued other issues. It is important to remember that an essential goal of Book Club Plus is tied to the rationale that we want students to be literate and this entails being able to be engaged in the kind of literate behaviors espoused by Book Club Plus.

The dynamic nature of Book Club Plus should be stressed. Book Club Plus is a program which does not overly prescribe a certain regimen. If one were to identify a regimen, it would entail the practice of ongoing collaborative research and development among teachers. Certainly Book Club Plus offers a framework, but the framework is defined broadly and flexibly rather than narrowly and rigidly.

Nonetheless, there are some features that distinguish Book Club Plus. We would posit that they include: the notion of engaging students in discussion as a goal of literacy rather than a means to enhancing literacy achievement, the various methods of grouping other than ability grouping, the engagement of students in student-led discussions including ways to upgrade them, and the commitment to ongoing research and development through collaborative research. To date, advocates of Book Club Plus have provided plenty of examples to illustrate a range of possibilities.

REFERENCES

Bisesi, T. L., and T. E. Raphael. 1997. Aligning curriculum, instruction, and assessment in the Book Club program. In S. I. McMahon and T. E. Raphael (Eds.), *The Book Club connection: Literacy learning and classroom talk.* New York: Teachers College Press, 184–204.

The Book Club Plus Network. 1999. What counts as teacher research? An essay. *Language Arts* 77(1): 48–52. Discusses the role of teacher research in exploring and reflecting on the use of Book Club.

Commeyras, M., and G. Summer. 1996. Literature discussions based on student-posed questions. *The Reading Teacher* 50: 262–265. Describes a study dealing with student-led literature-based discussion.

Duffy, G., and J. V. Hoffman. 2002. Beating the odds in literacy education: Not the "betting on" but the "bettering of" schools and teachers. In B. Taylor, M. Pressley, and P. David Pearson (Eds.), *Teaching reading: Effective schools, accomplished teachers.* Mahwah, NJ: Erlbaum, 375–387. Discusses the elements involved in effective literacy instruction in conjunction with offering a critique of the National Reading Panel report.

Harmon, J. M. 1998. Vocabulary teaching and learning in a seventh-grade literature-based classroom. *Journal of Adolescent and Adult Literacy* 41: 518–529. Details practices for literature use and discussion, together with explicit reading of vocabulary.

———. 2000. Vocabulary teaching and learning in a seventh-grade literature-based classroom. In D. W. Moore, D. E. Alvermann, and K. A. Hinchman (Eds.), *Struggling adolescent readers: A collection of teaching strategies.* Newark, DE: International Reading Association, 174–188.

International Reading Association. 2002. *Evidence-based reading instruction: Putting the National Reading panel report into practice.* Newark, DE: Authur, 232–236. Presents a rationale for evidence based practices and key elements constituting an effective literacy program.

Kong, A., and E. Fitch. 2002. Using Book Club to engage culturally and linguistically diverse learners in reading, writing, and talking about books. *The Reading Teacher* 56(4): 352–362. Discusses how Book Club improved students' comprehension.

McGinley, W., K. Conley, and J. W. White. 2000. Pedagogy for a few: Book Club discussion guides and the modern book industry as literacy teacher. *Journal of Adolescent and Adult Literacy* 44(3): 204–214.

McMahon, S. I., and T. E. Raphael. 1997. Theory and research underlying the Book Club program. In S. I. McMahon and T. E. Raphael (Eds.), *The "Book Club" connection: Literacy learning and classroom talk.* New York: Teachers College Press, 3–25. Explores some of the initial research undergirding book club.

McMahon, S., and T. Raphael (Eds.). 1997. *The Book Club connection.* New York and Newark, DE: Teachers College Press and the International Reading Association. An edited volume of articles detailing theory and practice pertaining to Book Club as well as several teacher researcher articles. The volume includes the article by Raphael and Goatley referenced below.

Raphael T. E. 2000. Balancing literature and instruction: Lessons from the Book Club Project. In B. M. Taylor, M. F. Graves, and P. Van Den Broek (Eds.), *Reading for meaning: Fostering comprehension in the middle grades.* New York: Teachers College Press, 70–94. Explores the issue of balance between reading literature and strategy lessons.

———. 2001a. Book Club workshop: Learning about language and literacy through culture. In J. Many (Ed.), *Instructional practices for literacy teacher-educators*. Mahwah, NJ: Erlbaum, 39–49. Explores the use of some of the Book Club elements in conjunction with students addressing issues of identity, including culture.

———. 2001b. Literacy teaching, literacy learning: Lessons from the Book Club Plus project (NRC Presidential Address.) *National Reading Conference Yearbook* (50): 1–20. Discusses the origins of Book Club along with the research findings from studies of its use.

Raphael, T. E., K. Damphousse, K. Highfield, and S. Florio-Ruane. 2001. Understanding culture in our lives and work: Teachers' literature study in the Book Club program. In P. R. Schmidt and P. B. Mosenthal (Eds.), *Literacy in the new age of pluralism and multiculturalism, Vol. 9: Advances in reading/language research*. Greenwich, CT: Information Age, 367–387. Explores culture in conjunction with reflections by teachers of Book Clubs.

Raphael, T. E., S. Florio-Ruane, and M. George. 2001. Book Club Plus: A conceptual framework to organize literacy instruction. *Language Arts* 79(1): 159–168. Presents some of the undergirding concepts of Book Club with discussion of the possibilities that they suggest.

Raphael T. E., and J. R. Gavelek. 2001. Book Clubs for children. In B. E. Cullinan and D. G. Person (Eds.), *Encyclopedia of children's literature*. New York: Continuum International. A concise description of Book Club.

Raphael, T. E., and V. J. Goatley. 1996. The teacher as "more knowledgeable other": Changing roles for teachers in alternative reading instruction programs. In C. K. Kinzer & D. J. Leu (Eds.), *Multidimensional aspects of literacy research, theory, and practice*. Chicago: National Reading Conference, 527–536. Explored the teachers' roles and nature of discussions and their function, as well as the content of such.

———. 1997. Creating literacy communities through "community share." In S. I. McMahon and T. E. Raphael (Eds.), *The Book Club connection: Literacy learning and classroom talk*. New York: Teachers College Press, 26–46. Explores notions of community development in conjunction with Book Club.

Raphael, T. E., M. Johnston, C. Pocius, K. Highfield, K. Pentzien, K. Brimmer, and M. George. In press. Questioning practices in the classroom. In B. Guzzetti (Ed.), *Literacy in America: An encyclopedia*. Santa Barbara, CA. ABC-CLIO. Explores questioning strategies with reference to Book Club.

Raphael, T. E., M. Kehus, and K. Damphousse. 2001. *Book Club for middle school*. Lawrence, MA: Small Planet Communications. Explores the use of Book Club in the middle school context.

Raphael, T., and S. McMahon. 1994. Book Club: An alternative framework for reading instruction. *The Reading Teacher* 48: 102–116. Provides an overview of the Book Club with illustrations of its use.

Raphael, T. E., L. S. Pardo, and K. Highfield. 2002. *Book Club: A literature-based curriculum* (2d ed.). Littleton, MA: Small Planet Communications. The primary source, and the second edition represents an updated discussion of Book Clubs incorporating extensive explorations of its use.

Uninterrupted Sustained Silent Reading

Purpose

Generally recognized objectives of Uninterrupted Sustained Silent Reading (USSR) are (1) to provide students with a quiet time to practice their silent reading, (2) to provide students with models of good silent reading behavior, and (3) to increase students' abilities to sustain silent reading for longer periods of time.

Rationale

Much time is spent teaching students *how* to read; however, USSR is tied to the notion that classroom teachers should provide students with a model for reading or the opportunity to read materials for pleasure.

According to McCracken and McCracken (1978), this program provides students the following messages:

- Reading books is important
- Reading is something anyone can do
- Reading is communicating with an author
- Books are meant to be read in large sections
- Children are capable of sustained thoughts
- The teacher believes that the pupils are comprehending (because he or she doesn't bother to check)
- The teacher trusts the children to decide when something is well written, when something important has been read (because the teacher expects pupils to share after USSR). (p. 408)

In a similar vein, Sadoski (1984) suggests that USSR provides students the opportunity to practice the art of reading; to become actively involved in the reading act with materials of their own choosing, and to become better readers by reading and seeing others read.

Intended Audience

Uninterrupted Sustained Silent Reading is appropriate for students at kindergarten levels through senior high school. College and adult reading programs also could profit from the use of the technique. The technique may be used by an elementary teacher with a self-contained classroom, by a content teacher in a departmentalized program, or by a total school staff during a predetermined period of the school day (Ganz and Theofield, 1974).

Description of the Procedures

USSR contains three vital elements:

1. Preparation
2. The reading period
3. Follow-up

1. Preparation. Perhaps the key to the success of a USSR program is this vital first step. Students should understand what they are going to be doing during the activity, why it is important, and how it will be carried out.

The idea of USSR should be discussed with students several days in advance of the first reading session. The emphasis at this stage should be on the fact that the students will be allowed to select whatever reading material they desire to read during this period. Although students should be encouraged to bring their favorite reading material to class for USSR sessions, several students predictably will forget on occasion; therefore, the teacher should collect a variety of reading materials that will remain in the classroom and can be used during USSR sessions. The collection should be changed occasionally to provide a variety of offerings.

Teachers also should be sure to inform their administrator(s) and colleagues of what they are doing and should ask them not to interrupt unless an emergency arises.

It is essential that all students in the class understand the rules of USSR. Presentation of the rules a day or two before the start of USSR allows students and teachers to discuss why these particular regulations are necessary. It is suggested that the rules be reviewed just prior to the first USSR session. The three cardinal rules of USSR are:

a. Everybody reads. Both students and teacher will read something of their own choosing. Completing homework assignments, grading papers, and similar activities are discouraged. The reading should be for the pleasure of the reader.

b. There are to be no interruptions during USSR. The word *uninterrupted* is an essential part of the technique. Interruptions result in loss of comprehension and loss of interest by many students; therefore, questions and comments should be held until the silent reading period has concluded.

c. No one will be asked to report what they have read. It is essential that students feel that this is a period of free reading, with the emphasis on reading for enjoyment.

2. The Reading Period. The USSR period begins as soon as the students have been given a sufficient amount of time to select their reading materials and the teacher has reviewed the rules briefly. Following the first session, it may be necessary only occasionally to remind the students of the rules.

a. Setting the time. The time length of the very first USSR session should be such that the majority of the students within the class can easily sustain their silent reading. For the lower grades, this may mean three to five minutes; for upper elementary grades, five to ten minutes; and for secondary classrooms, ten to fifteen minutes. It is probably better initially to underestimate students' ability to sustain silent reading, since one of the goals of USSR is to increase gradually the time devoted to the activity. Depending on the ability and interest levels of the students, reasonable goals might be fifteen to twenty minutes for primary level classrooms; twenty to thirty minutes for the middle grades; and thirty minutes for high school classes. These times should be considered only as guidelines.

b. Timing USSR. Most teachers have found that a kitchen timer or an alarm clock works best as the timing device for USSR sessions. The timer should be set for the agreed-upon time and then placed in such a position that students are unable to see the face of the device. This procedure solves the problem of the "clock watchers" within a classroom. For this same reason, a large classroom clock should not be used as the timing device. Another advantage of the alarm clock or kitchen timer is that it provides a definite end to the USSR session. The sound of an alarm clock leaves no doubt that the reading period has come to an end, and that it is time to move on to other activities.

c. The role of the teacher. During the USSR period, the teacher is doing exactly what all the students in the class are doing—reading for pleasure. The teacher has the very important role of showing good, sustained silent reading behavior. For some students in the classroom, this may be the first opportunity to observe an adult who is reading for pure enjoyment.

It is important to keep this one activity in mind. There are a number of things that a teacher should not do during USSR. The class instructor should not correct papers, plan lessons, take attendance, or perform similar school-related activities. By doing this type of activity, teachers are, in effect, saying to students, "Reading is an important activity for you, but not for me." Likewise, the teacher should not move around the classroom to seek out students who are not reading or those who are potential troublemakers. Besides not serving as an adequate model, a teacher in the monitoring role becomes a potential "interrupter" of the reading process.

d. Interruptions during USSR. It is not unusual for interruptions to occur occasionally, especially in the initial phase of using the procedure in the classroom. Interruptions that cause the classroom teacher and a large number of students to look up from their reading should generally result in an end to the reading period for that day. However, persons guilty of interrupting should not be reprimanded; rather, the classroom teacher may simply say, "I'm sorry, but that concludes our USSR session for today. Please put your reading material away and we will proceed with our next lesson." The instructor should be prepared to move quickly to the next scheduled activity without providing the individual who interrupted with the attention that the student might be seeking. The activity immediately following the USSR also should not appear to be arranged as a means of punishment, i.e., tests and other equally unpopular activities are best scheduled at other times.

After the habit of silent reading has been firmly established, minor and unintentional interruptions may be handled smoothly without resulting in an end to the reading session. In these situations, the teacher might respond in this manner: "I hope that the interruption did not cause you to completely lose your train of thought. Do you think you can return to your reading without any problems?" If most students respond affirmatively, then the teacher provides a model by returning immediately to reading. Very minor disturbances that cause the instructors and only one or two students to look up from their reading should be ignored. After quickly evaluating the situation, the teacher should return immediately to the reading. This action has the effect of saying, "No problem. Let's continue our reading."

e. Concluding the reading period. USSR ends with the sound of the timer. The instructor should be prepared to move on to the next scheduled activity. Occasionally, teachers may provide students a few additional minutes of reading time. This "buffer" period allows students an opportunity to read until a more appropriate stopping point is reached.

3. Follow-Up. McCracken (1971) suggested that after the first week of USSR, the teacher may begin to think of ways to encourage sharing what has been read during the silent reading sessions. The teacher can set an example by making a brief comment about interesting ideas the students have read, by keeping a log of the books and the number of pages read, and by similar actions that show a sincere interest in the reading act. These sharing activities can result in greater student interest in reading.

It must be emphasized that such sharing activities should not begin until after the USSR activity has been firmly established. If the teacher begins to prompt students to share too early in the beginning sessions, USSR might deteriorate into something other than reading for enjoyment.

Cautions and Comments

Although USSR is a simple technique and can easily be implemented in classrooms at any level, it is very difficult to evaluate. It should not be surprising that research studies, in which the influence of USSR upon achievement and attitude has been studied, have yielded quite mixed results. For instance, this program provides the following strengths:

- Interest in reading
- Awareness of a variety of books
- Feelings of community within a classroom
- Awareness of the reading program and its purpose
- Information to assist in school or leisure time activities
- Appreciation of reading, which affords pleasurable experiences when engaged with books
- Improvement in writing as a result of exposure to wide reading

Possible negative aspects of this procedure are:

- Lack of teacher and/or administrator modeling, due to attitudes
- Provisions not made for students lacking sufficient materials
- Classroom materials not meeting students' needs
- Disruptions within the classroom or in the hallways
- Lack of longitudinal data
- Inadequate planning and availability of materials
- Older students' attitudes differ greatly from those of younger students

Whereas few literacy educators would disagree with the worth of engaging students in reading independently, the manner with which these engagements occur has been queried. Although the National Reading Panel expressed concern for the lack of research on independent reading, the panel questioned whether unfocussed engagement was likely to contribute to success for all students (National Reading Panel, 2000). Results from studies on special populations indicate that careful planning and implementation are needed in order for this procedure to be successful. Grubaugh (1986) states that, "potential poorer readers must be carefully matched with materials. If these students aren't able to engage in silent reading, adjustments should consist of small groups reading aloud" (p. 170). Allington (1975) expanded this belief by stating that "remedial readers must have unlimited opportunities for reading contextual material rather than skill instruction." It is imperative that "they be given time to engage themselves with stories and books in order to become fluent readers" (p. 263). Gutkin (1990) proclaimed that kindergarten children need time for book perusal and "reading." She has instituted a sustained loud reading (SLR) time, which encourages students to partner-read and share books that fascinate them. She states, "When I saw and heard the excitement from my students, I decided that, at this stage in my students' careers, silence would be more of an obstacle than a relaxing tool to enhance their relationships with books" (p. 490).

Despite the lack of consistency in data results, this program should not be overlooked. The strategy provides teachers a manageable procedure for increasing reading time. Furthermore, the teacher, by the very act of reading, is communicating the *value* of reading to the students. Conversely, any lack of interest or enthusiasm by the teacher can result in a similar reaction by the students.

Indeed, teachers are likely to be instrumental in the success of this program. They can promote positive attitudes toward and achievement in reading by: (a) planning reading activities children like; (b) providing large quantities and a variety of materials that are related to children's interests and needs; (c) promoting regular intervals of recreational and quiet reading within the school schedule; (d) demonstrating and modeling a personal valuing of reading; (e) providing a pleasant, relaxed classroom atmosphere; (f) reducing pressure to report on what was read; and (g) providing opportunities for sharing (Langford and Allen, 1983, 195). A way for teachers to promote student interest and motivation in this activity is by creating a catchy title through acronyms. Those most commonly used include:

- SQUIRT (Silent, quiet, uninterrupted, individualized reading time)
- DEAR (Drop everything and read)
- DEER (Drop everything else—read)
- OTTER (Our time to enjoy reading)

USSR can be extended to the home setting by parents. Home Sustained Silent Reading (HSSR) can be used to "promote a love for reading that extends into the home while providing additional support for children and a common goal for home and school" (Demos, 1986, 263). When participating in HSSR, Demos and Fitzpatrick suggest that parents (a) "foster an interest in reading by creating an environment that places a high priority on the printed word" (Fitzpatrick, 1982, 50), (b) "support the development of attitudes and habits conducive to lifelong learning and reading for enjoyment, (c) extend reading opportunities outside the school environment, and (d) provide additional practice and application of school learning" (Demos, 1986, 263–264).

REFERENCES

Allington, R. 1975. Approaches to reading and writing. *Language Arts* 52: 813–815. Describes approaches to silent reading and the importance of self-selecting materials.

Anderson, C. 2000. Sustained Silent Reading: Try it, you'll like it. *The Reading Teacher* 54(3): 258–259. Discusses rules and regulations for the implementation of SSR.

Benedict, G. 1982. Making reading a habit for students. *Reading Improvement* 19(1): 48–53. Reports how a school district developed student reading habits through USSR and parent program.

Berglund, R. L., and J. L. Johns. 1983. Primer on uninterrupted sustained silent reading. *The Reading Teacher* 36: 534–539. Discusses the "ins" and "outs" of implementing USSR.

Clary, L. M. 1988. Helping parents help their children. *Reading Horizons* 28: 172–177. Describes techniques parents can utilize at home to increase students' reading attitude and achievement.

Demos, E. S. 1986. Parents, schools, and HSSR. *Reading Horizons* 26(4): 262–265. Presents a model for parents when designing a home sustained silent reading program.

Dwyer, E. J., and V. Reed. 1989. Effects of sustained silent reading on attitudes toward reading. *Reading Horizons* 29: 283–293. Describes a study that investigates students' reading achievement and attitudes.

Evans, H. M., and J. C. Towner. 1975. Sustained silent reading: Does it increase skills? *The Reading Teacher* 29: 155–156. Describes a study comparing the use of USSR with the use of basal supplements.

Fitzpatrick, K. 1982. Attention parents! Your pre-school child and reading. *Reading Improvement* 19: 50–53. Outlines techniques parents can utilize when working with their preschooler at home.

Fresch, M. J. 1995. Self-selection of early literacy learners. *The Reading Teacher* 49(3): 220–227. Explores the nature of self-selection of books by six-year-old children in relation to their instructional levels.

Gambrell, L. B. 1978. Getting started with sustained silent reading and keeping it going. *The Reading Teacher* 32: 328–331. Discusses preparation for and management of the USSR.

Ganz, P., and M. B. Theofield. 1974. Suggestions for starting USSR. *Journal of Reading* 17: 614–616. Provides recommendations for initiating a USSR program on a schoolwide basis.

Goostree, R. C. 1981. *A study of reading interests and attitudes of 4th, 5th, and 6th grade gifted children in Missouri.* MA Thesis, Southwest Missouri State University. A study depicting the reading interests and attitudes of upper elementary gifted students.

Grubaugh, S. 1986. Initiating sustained silent reading in your school. *Clearing House* 60: 169–174. Summarizes the principles of a USSR program and how a school can plan and successfully implement this program.

Gutkin, R. J. 1990. Sustained ——— reading. *Language Arts* 67: 490–491. Recounts a kindergarten teacher's experience with USSR and its effectiveness for her learning.

Halpern, H. 1981. An attitude survey of uninterrupted sustained silent reading. *Reading Horizons* 21: 272–279. An instructional tool to be used with students to "determine their attitudes toward silent reading," p. 276. The survey and description of its use are included.

Hunt, L. C. 1971. Six steps to the individualized reading program (IRP). *Elementary English* 48: 27–32. Describes the intent and procedures for implementing USSR.

Kaisen, J. 1987. SSR/Booktime: Kindergarten and first grade sustained silent reading. *The Reading Teacher* 40: 532–537. Modifies SSR for use in kindergarten and the first grade.

Langford, J., and E. G. Allen. 1983. The effects of U.S.S.R. on students' attitudes and achievement. *Reading Horizons* 23: 194–200. A study depicting the attitudes and achievement of fifth and sixth graders participating in a USSR program.

Marshall, J. C. 2002. *Are they really reading? Expanding SSR in the middle grades.* Portland, ME: Stenhouse. Expansion of traditional concepts of SSR to include read-alouds, writing, and accountability to scaffold struggling middle-grade students.

McCracken, R. A. 1971. Initiating sustained silent reading. *Journal of Reading* 14: 521–524, 582–583. Recommends six rules teachers must follow to implement USSR successfully.

McCracken, R. A., and M. J. McCracken. 1972. *Reading is only the tiger's tail.* San Rafael, CA: Leswing Press. Provides recommendations for initiating a USSR program.

———. 1978. Modeling is the key to sustained silent reading. *The Reading Teacher* 31: 406–408. Describes how and what a teacher does during and after silent reading; also defines what students do.

Moore, J. C., C. J. Jones, and D. C. Miller. 1980. What we know after a decade of sustained silent reading. *The Reading Teacher* 33: 455–450. Reviews the research on USSR.

Morrow, L. M., and C. S. Weinstein, 1986. Encouraging voluntary reading: The impact of a literature program on children's use of library centers. *Reading Research Quarterly* 21: 330–345. Reports a study that examined whether children's voluntary use of library centers and attitudes toward reading could be enhanced by involvement in a literature program emphasizing enjoyment in books.

National Reading Panel. 2000. *Teaching children to read: An evidence-based assessment of the scientific research literature on reading and its implications for reading instruction* (Report of the Subgroups). Washington, DC: U.S. Department of Health and Human Services, Public Health Service, National Institutes of Health, and the National Institute of Child Health and Human Development.

Parker, A., and E. Paradis. 1986. Attitude development toward reading in grades one through six. *Journal of Educational Research* 79: 313–315. A study discussing reading attitudes relating to gender and grade level.

Purves, A. C., L. Papa, and S. Jordan, eds. 1994. *Encyclopedia of English studies and language arts.* New York: National Council of Teachers of English. An excellent resource that contains an extensive collection of more than 800 annotated entries/topics in English Studies and Language Arts.

Sadoski, M. C. 1984. SSR, accountability, and effective reading instruction. *Reading Horizons* 24: 119–123. Reviews research on USSR.

Sanacore, J. 1994. Lifetime literacy through independent reading: The principal is a key player. *Journal of Reading* 37(7): 602–606. Discusses the key role played by the principal.

Schaudt, B. A. 1983. Another look at sustained silent reading. *The Reading Teacher* 36: 934–936. Reviews research studies and guidelines suggested for implementation of USSR.

Wiesendanger, K. D., and E. D. Birlem. 1984. The effectiveness of SSR: An overview of the research. *Reading Horizons* 24: 197–201. Provides an overview of USSR research.

Worthy, J., M. Turner, and M. Moorman. 1998. The precarious place of self-selected reading. *Language Arts* 75(4): 296–304.

Individualized Reading

Purpose

Based on the notion of seeking, self-selection, and self-pacing, Individualized Reading is designed to: (1) focus reading instruction on the individual needs of each child, and (2) aid teachers in guiding children toward assuming responsibility and initiative for their own growth in reading.

Rationale

As with any reading method, Individualized Reading is designed to develop a reader's abilities and interests. However, the basic premise in Individualized Reading differs greatly from that in other methods. Olson (1949) suggested three major principles that have become the foundation of Individualized Reading: seeking, self-selection, and self-pacing. Olson explained that students are continually exploring their own environment in search of experiences that fit with their growth and needs. Applied to reading, this means that the most conducive environment for reading growth would be one in which students are surrounded by materials to explore and select from and to read at their own pace. Such exploration is done in accordance with students' own needs and interests. In terms of actual reading instruction, the procedure that has evolved from this point of view was summarized briefly by Smith (1963) as follows:

> Each child selects a book that he wants to read. During the individual conference period, the teacher sits in some particular spot in the room as each child comes and reads to her. As he does so, she notes his individual needs and gives him appropriate help. Finally, she writes what the child is reading, his needs and strengths, on his record card. Then another individual conference is held and so on. If several children need help on the same skills, they may be called together in a group for such help. (p. 142)

One important aspect of individualized reading is that time and opportunity be afforded to students to read. It is important that students "be engaged with the print in the book while reading. If not, they are not benefiting from the reading opportunity provided by the classroom setting" (Fielding and Roller, 1992, 678). If students aren't benefiting from this instruction, then teachers must find ways to "make difficult books accessible and easy books acceptable" for students (Fielding and Roller, 1992 680). Such guidelines (Fielding and Roller, 1992, 680–681) available to teachers include:

- Modeling use and enjoyment of books
- Altering purposes for easy reading
- Utilizing books on tape
- Challenging students with easier books through book discussions, book sharing sessions
- Making nonfiction more available and familiar to student
- Preceding more difficult books with an easy book
- Providing opportunities for partner reading or read alouds

Intended Audience

Although Individualized Reading has been more widely used in the elementary grades, the technique readily lends itself to teaching in the content areas, particularly where a multiple-textbook approach is employed to expose students to various ideas and opinions.

Description of the Procedures

An Individualized Reading program is heavily dependent on: (1) self-selection, (2) ample supply of reading material, (3) student-teacher conference, (4) extended contracts, (5) flexible needs grouping, and (6) sharing books.

1. Self-selection. Possibly the most basic ingredient in the Individualized Reading program is that every student be taught reading with materials that the student chooses. As Veatch (1978) suggested, the student is taught to select reading material based on two criteria: (1) I like it, and (2) I can read it.

Obviously, an important teacher function is to expose students constantly to the variety of material available for reading. Through brief, enticing descriptions of these materials, the teacher can encourage the student to select the most desirable and motivating material. This, in essence, is the first responsibility of the teacher in planning—to make sure each student is given suitable material during the reading program.

2. Ample Supply of Reading Material. Essential to a program of self-selection is an ample supply of reading material for the student. A variety of material is needed if a student is to select a book he or she can handle with comfort. Veatch (1978) recommended that in order to maintain an adequate supply of reading material in the classroom, there should be available at least three to five titles per student.

Books are needed on many grade levels, since the range of ability in a classroom is wide. Typically, the range of difficulty should extend from one or two grade levels below the slowest reader to one or two grades above the best reader in the class. Thus, for example, in a typical first-grade class, the teacher selects books for students ranging from picture books of the earliest prereading level to those books of at least fifth-grade difficulty.

In addition, even though bright readers can effectively deal with materials of greater difficulty than average readers, their interests may be similar. Hence, a variety of books dealing with the same topic on different levels is necessary.

There are many possible sources available for a teacher who is trying to gather three to five titles for each student in the class. The school librarian can be an invaluable aid and a tremendous source of information concerning books. Public libraries and bookmobiles provide other sources of reading material for the classroom. Book fairs also can be a means of securing additional materials for the students.

Paperback books are another source for stocking the classroom library, since they are relatively inexpensive when compared to the price of hardcovers. Book clubs, such as those of Scholastic Book Services, often provide discount rates for paperbacks. Often neglected, but still excellent sources of reading materials, are magazines and newspapers. Again, they are relatively inexpensive, and a teacher can request that the students bring in old magazines or newspapers from home to maintain an adequate supply.

Finally, abandoned or old sets of basal readers can be used to supplement the book supply. Basal readers do have stories that attract children; the individual story selections can be separated into small books for distribution as "mini-books." Teachers of different grade levels can exchange a certain number of basal readers among themselves.

3. Student-Teacher Conference. Central to the Individualized Reading program are the individual sessions a student has with the teacher. These conferences essentially determine the character of the reading program, since during them, the student receives important personal direction in reading activity. The teacher needs to have specific purposes in mind and the ability to analyze and understand the reading performance of each student. This is essential in order to conduct a speedy, but thorough, conference and in order to ensure that each student gets the necessary amount of individual attention and instruction that will provide for optimum growth.

A teacher does not check on everything a child reads, but rather concentrates on what the child has selected and prepared for presentation. Veatch (1978) described four areas that should be explored in the conference session:

1. The mechanical aspects of the student's reading ability
2. The student's ability to read critically
3. The student's personal involvement
4. The ability to hold an audience while reading aloud

In the area of mechanical skills, the teacher might ascertain the student's ability to use word attack skills when encountering words that present difficulty. When reading critically, the student should be able to get the overall sense of the story, as well as be able to delve into the author's purposes. Knowing why a certain book is chosen is considered important for the student, not only for the student's own personal development but also for gaining the ability to recommend the book to others in the class. Personal involvement with characters in the book also should be explored. Finally, the area of oral reading with expression should be explored.

Essential to the individual conference are the records the teacher keeps on each student. It is with these annotations that the teacher can guide the student in reading and also plan for grouping activities. The following is an example of such a record:

Juan	8.5 Age	2.5 Rdg. Ach.
9/5	Horton Hatches the Egg (p. 21, oral) Saw value of commitment Group: checking organization of details Ind. Assign.: Vocabulary exercises	

From such an annotative record, the teacher can plan the next day's reading activities for the student. For example, the student Juan might work in a group to improve his skill in reading for details. In addition, he will work on his own with vocabulary activities, or the teacher can wait until several children have the same skill need and group them together to work on that area.

4. Flexible Needs Grouping. Groups are formed based upon the observations and diagnoses teachers have made during individual conferences and other observations made during the school day. When the teacher sees that at least two students have the same need, a group can be formed.

It is to be emphasized that groups be formed in an individualized program when at least two students need to know something or do something that the others in class do not need to know or do. These groups are flexible in the sense that they are formed only temporarily to fill a need and then are disbanded.

This is contrary to the usual practice of grouping, which is organized on the basis of low, middle, and high reading abilities. This conventional grouping plan is usually indefinite and allows for little flexibility in instruction. In addition, such grouping allows for the negative aspects of peer pressure and labeling—the low group (e.g., "the Buzzards") become "dummies," and everyone knows it!

Groups may be formed easily when the teacher keeps good records of the individual conferences. By looking over these records, the teacher can readily see those students who are having common difficulties. For instance, the teacher can see that Juan, the student mentioned in the sample record, is only one of five students who are having difficulty with organizing their ideas. Thus, the teacher can save valuable time by grouping the five together. Instead of spending time teaching each student individually, time is efficiently used by helping all of them with the same thing at the same time.

Groups may also be formed for other purposes, some of which may be highly specific. Interest groups may be organized around a common concern. On the other hand, a few students can be grouped together for the specific purposes of finding more challenging reading material or for help in selecting a book at their reading level.

5. Sharing Books. Individualized Reading provides students with an opportunity to share their reading experiences. In common practice, the sharing of books is accomplished through written reports that, unless creatively used, become tedious. As an alternative, teachers might give students a variety of ways to share books. These sharing activities might range from simple reflection on the content of the book to a dramatic presentation of an inspiring part of the book. Role playing, pantomiming, moving scripts, advertisements, radio scripts, posters, and puppetry are suggested alternatives from which the children might select.

Cautions and Comments

Individualized Reading presents the teacher with a viable alternative to other approaches, by emphasizing personal involvement and decision making on the part of the student. However, there are some major deterrents to its use.

Since Individualized Reading is predicated upon the idea of self-selection, and self-selection from an ample supply of books, these two factors may affect the success of the program. For example, the lack of a large number of appropriate titles from which to choose may limit the self-selective process, and students may not find a title that matches both their interests and their reading abilities.

A problem that seems to arise is the pressure to complete as many individual conferences as possible in each day. Ideally, the teacher will not neglect anyone, even the brightest of readers. In reality, overly long conferences with some students will result in less available time for the other students. Thus, some students may not get the individual attention necessary to progress adequately in reading.

Similarly, the success of an Individualized Reading program is in part dependent on the vitality of the teacher-student conferences and sharing experiences. To ensure student involvement, both student conferences and sharing experiences will need to be meaningful and varied according to individual reading experiences.

A variation of individualized reading has been useful to educators in Montgomery County, Maryland. The program, Students Achieving Independent Learning (SAIL), assists low-achieving students in becoming active participants and decision makers in the learning process. The impetus of this program is to "raise students' consciousness of the strategic responses that successful readers make" (p. 20) by utilizing a four-step conceptual framework grounded within a theoretical model. Within this program, a four-step process is utilized, which consists of (a) getting ready to read, (b) before reading, (c) while reading, and (d) after reading. The purpose of the first step is to get students to set personal goals and to find a connection between the curriculum and personal aspirations. Since this program is to "convince students that constructing meaning is the core activity of reading (Bergman and Schuder, 1992, 20), the teachers must get students to delve into the reading materials as often as possible. Step 2, before reading, attempts to get students to self-select the reading material, set their own purpose for reading, and individually decide on how to process the task of reading. Step 3, while reading, requires that the students think about, select, and utilize a problem-solving and monitoring strategy that promotes individuality and responsibility for the reading task. Throughout this program, students are taught four monitoring strategies: (a) predict-verify-decide, (b) visualize-verify-decide, (c) summarize-verify-decide, (d) think aloud. In the last step, after reading, students are encouraged to choose and implement an evaluation strategy that relates to the reading task they have just completed.

Finally, Individualized Reading represents a viable alternative for the classroom teacher. Like most approaches, it demands that teachers possess an adequate understanding of the reading process and the reading curriculum. However, as an Individual Reading practice, it demands extensive teacher preparation and record keeping.

REFERENCES

Bergman, J. L., and T. Schuder. 1992. Teaching at-risk students to read strategically. *Educational Leadership* 50: 19–23. Provides an in-depth discussion on how the SAIL program (Students Achieving Independent Learning) impacts on low-achieving readers.

Blakely, W. P., and B. McKay. 1972. Individualized reading as part of an eclectic reading program. In W. H. Miller (Ed.), *Elementary reading today: Selected articles.* New York: Holt, Rinehart and Winston, 111–120. Presents the results of an investigation that lends credibility to Individualized Reading procedures.

Fader, D. N., J. Duggins, T. Finn, and E. B. McNeil. 1976. *The new hooked on books.* New York: Berkeley. Updates a discussion of a saturated book program.

Fielding, L., and C. Roller. 1992. Making difficult books accessible and easy books acceptable. *The Reading Teacher* 45: 687–685. Provides guidelines for helping students become more active when participating in individual reading.

Frymier, J. November, 1992. Children who hurt, children who fail. *Phi Delta Kappa,* 257–259. Provides a brief overview of the study conducted on at-risk students and lists the instructional techniques that were successful with these students.

Greenwood, S. C. 1985. Use contracts to motivate and manage your secondary reading class. *Journal of Reading* 28: 487–491. Explores how contracts, which include SSR, study skills, etc., affect student participation.

Groff, P. 1972. Helping teachers begin individualized reading. In W. H. Miller (Ed.), *Elementary reading today: Selected articles.* New York: Holt, Rinehart and Winston, 101–106. Reviews 12 basic questions and points of concern when planning and initiating a program of Individualized Reading.

Hunt, L. 1970. Effect of self-selection, interest, and motivation upon independent, instructional, and frustration levels. *The Reading Teacher* 24: 146–151. Examines the effect of major tenets of Individualized Reading on the traditional concepts of reading levels.

Lysaker, J. T. 1997. Learning to read from self-selected texts: The book choices of six first graders. In C. K. Kinzer, K. A. Hinchman, and D. J. Leu (Eds.), *Inquiries in literacy theory and practice.* Chicago: National Reading Conference, 273–282. Explores the book choices of six first graders in conjunction with their learning to read.

Olson, W. C. 1949. *Child development.* Boston: D.C. Heath. Presents the basic principles of Individualized Reading.

Purves, A. C., L. Papa, and S. Jordan (Eds.). 1994. *Encyclopedia of English studies and language arts.* New York: National Council of Teachers of English. This encyclopedia has more than 800 annotated entries/topics that succinctly address this topic and related areas.

Sartain, H. W. 1972. Advantages and disadvantages of individualized reading. In L. A. Harris and C. B. Smith (Eds.), *Individualizing reading instruction: A reader.* New York: Holt, Rinehart and Winston, 86–96. Provides the pros and cons of an Individualized Reading program.

Smith, N. B. 1963. *Reading instruction for today's children.* Englewood Cliffs, NJ: Prentice-Hall, 129–162. Traces the historical development of Individualized Reading and presents examples of its use.

Veatch, J. 1978. *Reading in the elementary school* (2d ed.). New York: John Wiley and Sons. Provides the basic plans from which to establish an Individualized Reading program with particular emphasis on classroom management.

Veatch, J. 1996. From the vantage of retirement. *The Reading Teacher* 49(7): 510–516. Discusses individualized reading that she developed.

Worthy, J., and S. S. McKool. 1996. Students who say they hate to read: The importance of opportunity, choice, and access. In D. J. Leu, C. K. Kinzer, and K. A. Hinchman (Eds.), *Literacies for the 21st century: Research and practice.* Chicago: National Reading Conference, 245–256. Investigates students who have negative reading attitudes in terms of issues of choice and opportunity.

UNIT 3

Developing Literacies through Language Experiences, Shared Reading, and Use of Multiple Representations

UNIT OVERVIEW

For many years teachers have recognized the worth of the child's own oral language and experiences as basic ingredients in beginning reading instruction. As far back as 1908, Edmund Huey reported the use of a sentence method that drew on the child's language and experiences to describe pictures. Through the first half of this century, numerous educators cited and recommended an experience-based approach to teaching reading (e.g., Storm and Smith, 1930; Gans, 1941; Lamoreaux and Lee, 1943; Sullivan, 1986). In the middle of the 1960s researchers and educators in their search for the *one* best method for teaching reading turned their attention to language acquisition and the psycholinguistic nature of the reading process. The resulting approach became widely recognized and identified by its now familiar label, "the language experience approach." In the 1970s and early 1980s, the approach became widely used throughout the world. For example, Breakthrough to Literacy developed for use in Great Britain became widely used throughout the British Commonwealth (McKay, Thompson, and Schaub, 1970). Various offshoots of the approach that appeared as developments in other areas have dovetailed with the approach. For example, the procedure has been accepted for use with adolescents (e.g., McWilliams and Smith, 1981; Stratton, Grindler, and Postell, 1992), adult immigrants (Wales, 1994), and ESL students (Dixon and Nessel, 1983), strategies have been developed for extending comprehension abilities with the procedure (Sulzby, 1980; Heller, 1988), and it has been adapted for use with students with invented spellings (Coate and Castle, 1989) and adapted to the teaching of science (Tragash, 1987).

As these developments occurred with the language experience approach, researchers began exploring more intensely young children's encounters with print in the environment and during shared reading experiences with parents. What emerged in conjunction with these developments were approaches that further capitalized on the language experiences of young children.

The rationale of these approaches was based on the notion that children are born with a prowess for language acquisition and that this prowess can and should be directed toward the acquisition of reading abilities. To this end, proponents of the language experience approach and the role of environmental print advocated taking advantage of the experiences that children bring to reading. By conveying these experiences through language, children can move back and forth from oral to written expression. From this foundation, children develop quite naturally the ability and interest to read widely, deeply, and fluently.

One of the key understandings that has occurred since the development of the language experience approach has been the growing awareness of the nature of reading and writing development from the earliest years. Tierney (1992) discusses several longitudinal studies:

> To date, a number of researchers have offered a longitudinal perspective on the understandings children acquire as they write. Read (1971) and Chomsky (1979) have described in some detail the assumptions which tend to undergird a child's invented spellings. Harste, Burke and Woodward (1984 a & b) have offered several examples of how young children's writing develops across time. Bissex's (1980) and Baghban's (1984) case studies of their children are devoted primarily to tracing their early writing development. Graves (1982) and Calkins (1982) have offered rich descriptions of writing development across time as students begin writing and conferencing with others. . . . Taken together, the longitudinal research on early reading and writing to date has confirmed some beliefs at the same time as it has added definition and stimulated a number of issues. The view of the child as an active meaning maker constructing his or her own hypotheses in the context of daily negotiations with print and others is substantiated repeatedly. (p. 180) [Studies mentioned in this excerpt are cited in bibliography.]

In conjunction with these developments, some key and interrelated understandings about the development of children's literacy have emerged:

> *Emergent Literacy.* Children learn to read and write in a fashion that is not unlike how they learn to talk—with opportunities to experiment, to take risks, to be engaged in meaningful interactions, and to be able to invent ways of reading and writing using their own rule systems.
>
> *Invented Spelling.* Carol Chomsky (1979) points out the role of children's use of invented spelling as they learn to read:
>
> > Children who have been writing for months are in a very favorable position when they undertake learning to read. They have at their command considerable phonetic information about English, practice in phonemic segmentation, and experience with alphabetic representation. These are some of the technical skills that they need to get started. They have, in addition, an expectation of going ahead on their own. They are prepared to make sense, and their purpose is to derive a message from print, not just to pronounce the words. (pp. 51–52)
>
> *Interplay of Reading, Writing, Talking, Drawing, and Peer Relationships.* Reading and writing are not isolated activities; they occur with and in relation to a number of meaning-making experiences that children have. Tierney and Shanahan (1991) demonstrate this through citing two important studies:
>
> . . . in conjunction with exploring the nature of literacy learning in a day-care environment for 3- and 4-year-olds, Rowe (1987) concluded that there are two general types of "intertextual"

> connections that are important. The first type is the *formation of shared meanings* through conversations and demonstrations so that these young literacy learners are members of a community that affords communication with others. The second type involves linking current literacy experiences to past experiences. . . . Based upon her observations of first graders, Short (1986) argues that the potential for learning and thinking are changed when the classroom environment facilitates intertextuality. A collaborative and meaning-centered learning environment engages learners more fully and actively in learning and encourages higher levels of thinking. (p. 272) [italics original]

Additionally, Dyson (1989) concludes an extensive study of children's writing by stating:

> Thus, in studying the efforts of Regina, Jake, Manuel, Mitzi, and the other young writers who shared this classroom, the focus was not on their writing alone, because writing does not evolve only from writing. Rather, the focus was on the meanings each child intended to communicate, that is, on the symbolic worlds being deliberately formed. And those worlds were revealed in the children's drawing, talking, and playing, as well as in their writing. . . . In brief, from the perspective of this book, writing development is viewed as evolving within and shaped by children's interactions with other symbolic media and other people, including their peers. Both the developmental challenges children face as writers and the resources they lean upon are found in the varied symbolic and social worlds within which they, and all authors, work. (p. 255)

Later, Dyson discusses the ramifications of her work for our understanding of literacy acquisition:

> Parents and children alike expect students to learn to read and write in school, presumably to the eventual betterment of children's social and economic futures. And, for children whose background is considered out of the "mainstream," for whatever reason (most often because the children are not middle class and/or not Anglo), becoming literate is considered a process of moving, through individual achievement, beyond present ground, beyond their families and neighborhoods.
>
> This way of thinking about school literacy needs some rethinking. Within the context of this project, children's growth as literate people was linked to the social practices that surrounded them, that is, to their discovery of literacy's rich relevance to their present interactions with friends and to their reflections on their experiences. Literacy that helps children to articulate their todays and to make ongoing connections with others may be more likely to grow with them into their tomorrows. (p. 276)

The work that has led to these three conclusions has extended and sometimes challenged past language experience approaches, especially those that may not have been developed with some of these same appreciations and understandings. As a result, some language experience approaches carry too great a focus on "correct conventions," they delay writing until after reading, and they do not work with or take advantage of the interplay of reading and writing with drawing, talking, and peer relationships.

A further major development that has affected approaches for early literacy development has been the development of digital technologies for the classroom, especially with the advent of multimedia applications. Reinking and Bridwell-Bowes (1991) mention five advantages to using computers with reading and writing. They can:

1. Enhance the ability of readers and writers to interact with text.

2. Permit the external control of written language processes.

3. Lessen the drudgery associated with some aspects of reading and writing.

4. Provide individualized help and guidance during independent reading and writing activities.

5. Contribute to the development of purposeful communication in school, and thus they can bring together reading and writing activities.

The New London Group and various researchers invested in multimedia have discussed the emergence of new multiple literacies (see New London Group, 1996; Hagood, 2003; Kress, 2003). Further, numerous different types of programs exist that enhance learning through word processing combined with speech synthesis, story development software, and desktop publishing (see Sampson, Allen, and Sampson, 1991; Stratton, Grindler, and Postell, 1992; El-Hindi, 1998; and McMillen, Shanahan, Dowd, Macphee, and Hester, 1997, for specific applications of computer technology with such approaches).

The present unit describes six strategies for developing early literacies.

The Reggio Emilia Approach. The Reggio Emilia Approach is an internationally renowned program that represents a culturally relevant and community-supported initiative, which enlists multiple symbolic representations as a key means by which students engage inquiry, discovery, and reflection.

Allen's Language Experience Approach in Communication. The Language Experiences in Communication represent an attempt by Roach Van Allen to develop a comprehensive language-based approach to reading. Most people credit Allen with nurturing the evolution of the language experience approach. Allen's intent has been to develop an approach that provides the language competencies essential to promote reading. In comparison with others, this approach provides the most comprehensive and detailed suggestions for teaching reading as a language experience.

Ashton-Warner's Organic Reading. Organic Reading is an experience-centered approach to reading instruction based upon Sylvia Ashton-Warner's teaching experiences with Maori children in New Zealand. It is designed to bridge the gap between the language world of the child and the language world of books through the use of each child's key vocabulary.

Stauffer's Language-Experience Approach. The Language-Experience Approach represents Russell Stauffer's conceptualization of the language experience approach for teaching beginning reading. His approach focuses on the use of individual- and group-dictated stories, the use of word banks, and the use of creative writing activities. As a beginning reading approach, it can serve either to supplement or to substitute for traditional basal reading programs.

Shared Book Experience. Shared Book Experience adopts some of the features of early reading experiences between young children and their parents to the classroom. As described by Doake (1985) and Holdaway (1979), Shared Book Experience is intended as a means of establishing early reading experiences that capitalize on the children's natural prowess with stories and that dovetail story experiences with other language activities.

Patterned Language Approach. Patterned Language Approach by Bridge adopts the use of predictable story material and a structured language experience approach to provide teachers with a whole-part procedure for introducing students to reading. The procedure is intended for use with beginning readers to develop an initial vocabulary, as well as readers' use of meaning cues, syntactical cues, and graphophonic features of words.

REFERENCES

Baghban, M. F. M. 1984. *Our daughter learns to read and write: A case study from birth to three.* Newark, DE: International Reading Association.

Barksdale-Ladd, M. A., and A. R. Nedeff. 1997. The worlds of a reader's mind: Students as authors. *The Reading Teacher* 50(7): 564–573. Describes a student-as-author project in West Virginia.

Barnitz, J. G. (Ed.). 1998. Revising grammar instruction for authentic composing and comprehending. *The Reading Teacher* 51(7): 608–611. Describes grammar workshop for use in conjunction with authentic reading and writing.

Bissex, G. 1980. *Gyns at wrk: A child learns to read and write.* Cambridge: Harvard University Press. Diary account of the emergent literacy of a child.

Calkins, L. 1983. *Lessons from a child.* Portsmouth, NH: Heinemann.

Calkins, L. M., with S. Harwayne. 1990. *Living between the lines.* Portsmouth, NH: Heinemann. Discusses various writing experiences and accompanying lessons that engage reading and writing in a reciprocal relationship.

Chomsky, C. 1979. Approaching reading through invented spelling. In L. B. Resnick and P. A. Weaver (Eds.), *Theory and practice of early reading,* Vol. 2. Hillsdale, NJ: Erlbaum.

Coate, S., and M. Castle. 1989. Integrating LEA and invented spelling in kindergarten. *The Reading Teacher* 42: 516–519. Explores the use of invented spelling and reading-writing connections in conjunction with the LEA.

Dixon, C. N., and D. Nessel. 1983. *Language experience approach to reading (and writing).* Hayward, CA: The Alemany Press.

Doake, D. 1985. Reading-like behavior: Its role in learning to read. In A. M. Jaggar and M. T. Smith-Burke (Eds.), *Observing the language learner.* Newark, DE: International Reading Association/NCTE.

Dyson, A. H. 1989. *Multiple worlds of child writers: Friends learning to write.* New York: Teachers College Press.

El-Hindi, A. E. 1998. Beyond classroom boundaries: Constructivist teaching with the Internet. *The Reading Teacher* 51(8): 694–700. Explores the use of the Internet in conjunction with various reading-writing activities.

Gans, R. 1941. *Guiding children's reading through experiences.* New York: Teachers College Press.

Graves, D. 1982. Patterns of child control of the writing process. In R. D. Walshe (Ed.), *Donald Graves in Australia.* Portsmouth, NH: Heinemann.

Hagood, M. C. 2003. New media and online literacies: No age left behind. *Reading Research Quarterly* 38(3): 387–391.

Harste, J. C., V. A. Woodward, & C. L. Burke. (1984a). Examining our assumptions: A transactional view of literacy and learning. *Research in the Teaching of English* 18: 84–108.

———. (1984b). *Language stories and literacy lessons.* Portsmouth, NH: Heinemann.

Heller, M. F. 1988. Comprehending composing through language experience. *The Reading Teacher* 42: 130–135. Discusses an adaptation of LEA intended to enhance comprehension.

Holdaway, D. 1979. *Foundations of literacy.* Gossford: Ashton, Scholastic.

Huey, E. G. 1908. *The psychology and pedagogy of reading.* New York: Macmillan.

Kress, G. 2003. *Literacy in the new media age.* London: Routledge.

Lamoreaux, L., and D. M. Lee. 1943. *Learning to read through experiences.* New York: Appleton-Century-Crofts.

Lancia, P. J. 1997. Literary borrowing: The effects of literature on children's writing. *The Reading Teacher* 50(6): 470–475. Describes a second-grade teacher's use of literature as a model for writing.

Lunsford, S. H. 1997. "And they wrote happily ever after": Literature-based mini-lessons in writing. *Language Arts* 74: 42–48. Describes a primary teacher's use of mini-lessons to meet the needs of her students.

McKay, D., B. Thompson, and P. Schaub. 1970. *Breakthrough to literacy: Programme in linguistics and English teaching.* London: Schools Council (Longman).

McMillen, L., S. Shanahan, K. Dowd, J. Macphee, and J. Hester. 1997. Integrating technology in the classroom. *Language Arts* 74: 137–149. Explores the use of the Internet in conjunction with various literacy activities.

McWilliams, L., and D. Smith. 1981. Decision stories. *Journal of Reading* 25: 142–145.

New London Group. 1996. A pedagogy of multiliteracies: Designing social futures. *Harvard Educational Review* 66: 60–92.

Read, C. 1971. Pre-school children's knowledge of English phonology. *Harvard Educational Review* 41: 1–34.

Reinking, D., and L. Bridwell-Bowles. 1991. Computers in reading and writing. In R. Barr, M. Kamil, P. Mosenthal, and P. D. Pearson (Eds.), *Handbook of reading research,* Vol. II. New York: Longman, 310–340.

Rose, D. H., and A. Meyer. 1994. The role of technology in language arts instruction. *Language Arts* 71: 290–294. Explores the use of the Internet in conjunction with various literacy activities.

Rowe, D. W. 1987. Literacy learning as an intertextual process. In J. E. Readence and R. Scott Baldwin (Eds.), *Research in literacy: Merging perspectives.* Rochester, NY: National Reading Conference.

Sampson, M., R. V. Allen, and M. Sampson. 1991. *Pathways to literacy: A meaning-centered approach.* Fort Worth: Holt, Rinehart and Winston.

Short, K. G. 1986. *Literacy as a collaborative experience.* Unpublished doctoral dissertation. Bloomington: Indiana University.

Storm, G. E., and N. B. Smith. 1930. *Reading activities in primary grades.* Boston: Ginn.

Stratton, Beverly D., M. C. Grindler, and C. M. Postell. 1992. Discovering oneself. *Middle School Journal* 24: 42–43.

Sullivan, J. 1986. The global method: Language experience in the content areas. *The Reading Teacher* 39: 664–669.

Sulzby, E. 1980. Using children's dictated stories to aid comprehension. *The Reading Teacher* 33: 772–778.

Tierney, R. J. 1992. Studies of reading and writing growth: Longitudinal research on literacy development. In J. Flood, J. M. Jensen, D. Lapp, and J. R. Squire (Eds.), *Handbook of research on teaching the English language arts.* New York: Macmillan Publishing Co.

Tierney, R. J., and T. Shanahan. 1991. Research on the reading-writing relationship: Interactions, transactions, and outcomes. In R. Barr, M. Kamil, P. Mosenthal, and P. D. Pearson (Eds.), *Handbook of reading research,* Vol. II. New York: Longman.

Tierney, R. J., and M. Sheehy. 2002. What longitudinal studies say about literacy development/what literacy development says about longitudinal studies. In J. Flood, J. Jensen, D. Lapp, and J. R. Squire (Eds.), *Handbook of research on teaching the language arts,* Vol. II. New York: Macmillan.

Tragash, J. R. 1987. *Teaching difficult learners science: Hands-on experiments.* Monograph #17, University of Florida Multidisciplinary Diagnostic and Training Program. ERIC Document 353-743.

Wales, M. L. 1994. A language experience approach (LEA) in adult immigrant literacy programs in Australia. *Journal of Reading* 38(3): 200–208. Describes the use of the LEA with adult immigrants enrolled in literacy programs in Australia.

The Reggio Emilia Approach

Purpose

The Reggio Emilia Approach offers a learner-centered framework whereby educators can provide children opportunities for explorations and inquiries through extended culturally relevant and community-situated learning opportunities, which enlist multiple symbolic representations as a key means by which students engage inquiry, discovery, and reflection.

Rationale

The Reggio Emilia Approach has an extraordinary history emanating from the dedicated efforts of a northern Italian community and teachers, especially Loris Malaguzzi, who were attracted to the possibility of creating a school with a remarkable set of values and philosophy that drew on the leading developmental psychologists (Vygotsky, Piaget, Bruner, Bettleheim) and educators of the past century, including Italy's Montessori.

As Howard Gardner noted, what sustains the approach is the community of dedicated educators and the community members and children who support the approach, activities, and philosophy. As he stated: "Nowhere else in the world is there such a seamless and symbiotic relationship between a school's progressive philosophy and its practices" (Gardner, 1995, x). Indeed the building of relationships between community and school and parents is at the core of the Reggio Emilia Approach. North American educators such as Lillian Katz and others who have visited the Reggio schools have noted that the classes have a "homelike closeness and intimacy" (Katz, 1995, 32), which seems to occur as a result of community engagement, an extended commitment to the same teacher across years and in some classrooms the use of mixed age groupings. Loris Malaguzzi (1995) indicates that "the goal is to create an amiable school, where children, teachers, and families feel at home" (p. 58).

A commitment to child-centeredness is pervasive. As Malaguzzi stated:

> What children learn does not follow as an automatic result from what is taught. Rather it is in large part due to the children's own doing as a consequence of their activities and our resources. . . . Always and everywhere children take an active role in the construction and acquisition of learning. (p. 59)

In many ways the approach resembles a project approach, but its richness and emphasis on representation make for an approach to learning that builds on the use and study of multiple literacies to engage students in the exploration of their world. As Forman (1995) suggests "there is a belief that all children learn best when they can use multiple symbol systems to understand complex relations, particularly when these complex relations are part of a real-world project that gives these relationships a holistic gestalt" (p. 188).

Intended Audience

The Reggio Emilia Approach is intended for early childhood settings, but the tenets lend themselves to most educational endeavors.

Description of the Procedures

The commitment to community and child-centeredness would be difficult to prescribe or even to describe adequately in a summary fashion. We would encourage those truly interested in the Reggio Emilia Approach to explore the possibility of a visit to the schools or to access some of the writings, which will provide a fuller discussion, and description of the elements of the approach. Indeed, we have restricted our discussion of the Reggio Emilia

Approach to its use of projects—especially in the orientation to multiple literacies. We stress that our discussion is limited and that the Reggio Emilia Approach involves considerably more than these projects. For discussions of the community nature of the approach, professional development model, various resources and a range of other key elements, other sources need to be examined.

George Forman (1998) and a number of others have used the Long Jump Project as a way of illustrating some of the elements of the Reggio Emilia approach. The Long Jump Project involved the development of an athletic event by a subgroup of Reggio Emilia students who volunteered to plan the event with some input from the class. Some of the activities emerged; others were planned with teacher and classmate input. The teachers identified the long jump event as viable given what they discerned as its potential for measurement, research, representation, and student involvement. The project was initiated with the goal of the class holding a long jump event and then setting the students the task of investigating the possibility—researching the long jump in conjunction with exploring the event at the Olympics, discussing videos of athletes jumping, and then doing so for themselves. The exploration involved the students' discussing what they might do, especially in the context of an event with which all of the students would be involved. This entailed thinking about issues such as space for running and jumping, as well as spots for spectators and judges. To this end, the students developed plans and then a model with replicas and problem-solved how they would compare the length of jumps with strings. Sometimes in conversations peers advised one another, compared observations, discussed simulations, pursued replays, and so on en route to making decisions as to how they would carry out the event and its planning for participants, judges, and spectators with different needs and interests. The list of issues that were discussed and planned ranged from rules for runners (starting, run up, foot placement, clothing) to rules for judging, measurement, disqualification, and etiquette as well as advertising, announcements, applications to participate, awards, and so on.

During the exploration, teachers supported the students and prompted comparisons, speculations, and planning and especially ways to represent using various symbol systems as a means of exploring a range of issues, maintaining records, engaging in simulations, and communicating. As Forman stated, sometimes the discussion focused on the worth of different symbolizations and created "the type of constructive conflict we deem to be the power of this multi-symbolic approach to education" (1995, 187). Further, as he stated:

> As these children sought to gain a more coherent understanding of time, distance, and rules of equity, they externalized their nascent theories as icons, gestures, speech, text, pictograms, diagrams and notations. These symbols were embedded in the coherence of the real-world event which in turn helped convert a random list of symbols into a symbol system. This holism assures that the symbol system will ultimately converge to deepen knowledge rather than increase facts. (p. 188)

There has been a range of other projects described in various Reggio Emilia sites, especially as preschools in the United States and elsewhere have emulated the practices. Tierney and Damarin (1998) described the Creature City Project at the Sophie Rogers preschool at the Ohio State University, where their teachers adopted a project orientation based on the Reggio Emilia tenets.

The Creature City Project emerged from discussion between the teacher and the children who decided to build the city, including buildings, schools, parks, sports stadiums, and a zoo. The project took months as the children went on excursions around their community to study their own city and photograph buildings and streets en route to sketching, gathering all sorts of material as they contemplated their own city. The project involved working together on the different city constructions, using each other's emerging expertise about the city, including construction issues such as how to represent grass on the baseball field, relative heights and distances, plans for showing people or developing games, and other activities to go along with their city as well as refining the city by the addition of signage, photographs, and so on. Throughout the project the children used parents and friends as advisors as well as participants. Finally, the city was laid out on boards of plywood and everyone was invited for a final celebration of their city.

In discussing the underlying principles for these projects, Edwards and Forman (1998) suggest the following guidelines.

Staging the Project. The projects emerge from reconnaissance, although themes removed from everyday experience are not excluded nor are large and challenging projects or emotionally laden issues. Brainstorming and a consideration of the display and communication possibilities of the project are enlisted to think through possibilities, including curriculum connections. An effort is made to group children into collaborations involving 2 to 6 children.

Representational Strategies. A range of sketches, photographs, pictures, maps, and so on are used. To help students explore topics and issues, various forms of representation (photos, sketches, etc.) are used and discussed in terms of their worth. The students explore the worth of the representations as a means of learning, planning, and unpacking the children's thinking—especially important is the use of art as a thinking tool rather than merely as an aesthetic consideration.

Cross-modal explorations are encouraged as well as the invention of symbols, icons, and notations as a means of exploring issues of representation across settings and time.

Group Dynamics. The learning that can occur socially through collaboration is supported; teachers should consider ethnicity and gender, differences and dynamics. They encourage comparisons and criticisms as a way of learning rather than judging.

Teaching Strategies. Teachers support the discussion of the worth of different representations and follow the children's lead while also doing things that might expand or challenge their thinking. Some technical skills might be taught directly. Further, teachers encourage thinking about goals and encourage more in-depth probes. Teachers support the exchange of expertise by students and explore ways to use relationships with others to support individual or group learning.

Included are discussions of incomplete work. A stress is placed on documenting what is occurring and sharing this documentation with others as a basis for reflection. Further, the teachers are encouraged to review what has occurred, including their own and the students' documentation, for purposes of thinking about what is happening and about the available possibilities.

Comments and Cautions

The Reggio Emilia Approach deserves the attention that it has received worldwide and recognition as a model of early childhood education, which is historically significant. The approach has achieved what many educators have only aspired to—namely, a child-centered, culturally relevant situated learning enlisting multiple literacies in ways that engage students in creative discovery, inquiry, and critique.

Of considerable significance to literacy educators is the means used to engage students in multiple literacies or multiple symbol representations. The approach involves students inventing, taking risks with media separately and together and then reflecting on their use of these literacies for purposes of thinking, communication, documentation, engagement, learning, and display.

Unlike many approaches to literacy, the Reggio Emilia Approach adopts an orientation to literacy as socially constructed over time in a manner that is powerfully intertextual in ways that support synergies and dynamics that are often omitted or underprescribed in other approaches. In many ways the approach to literacy is quite extraordinary especially in terms of the extent to which literacies through multiple representations occur.

The Reggio Emilia Approach seems to have parallels to the work by the New London Group on multiple literacies and others, especially notions of the Rich Literacy Task advocated by the Queensland Department of Education as well as advocates of learner-centered curriculum and culturally relevant approaches that draw on parental and community engagement and build a curriculum around extended exploration of everyday events (see Unit 1).

The Reggio Emilia preschool model has a history dating back to postwar Italy, but it did not receive much attention until 15 years ago. Nowadays it is world renowned and has been the subject of educators' attention and analysis. Various preschool sites around the world are trying to emulate Reggio Emilia practice, and a body of work describing the approach has emerged. Among Internet links with a focus on Reggio Emilia are http://ecap.crc.uiuc.edu/info/reggio.html, and www.emtech.net/reggio.html.

REFERENCES

Cadwell, L. B. 1997. *Bringing Reggio Emilia home: An innovative approach to early childhood education.* New York: Teachers College Press. Explores various dimensions of Reggio Emilia Approach.

Edwards, C., and G. Forman. 1998. Conclusion: where do we go from here? In C. Edwards, L. Gandini, and G. Forman (Eds.), *The hundred languages of children: The Reggio Emilia Approach—Advanced reflections* (2d ed.). Greenwich, CT: Ablex, 305–312. An excellent source that reviews the overall principles of the Reggio Emilia Approach.

Edwards, C., L. Gandini, and G. Forman (Eds.). 1993. *The hundred languages of children: The Reggio Emilia Approach to early childhood education.* Norwood, NJ: Ablex.

———. 1998. *The hundred languages of children: The Reggio Emilia Approach—Advanced reflections* (2d ed.). Greenwich, CT: Ablex. The original and revised volumes trace the history and explore the evolution and core practices of Reggio Emilia through interviews with teachers and analyses by various U.S. scholars including Carolyn Edwards, George Forman, Howard Gardner, Lillian Katz, and others.

Forman, G. 1995. Multiple symbolization in the Long Jump Project. In C. Edwards, L. Gandini, and G. Forman (Eds.), *The hundred languages of children: The Reggio Emilia Approach—Advanced reflections* (2d ed.). Greenwich, CT: Ablex, 171–188. Discusses the nature and role of representation in a Reggio Emilia project, which has received a lot of attention among educators.

Gandini, L. 1984. Not just anywhere: Making child-care centers into "Particular" Places. *Beginnings*

(Spring): 17–20. Gandini explores the values that undergird the Reggio Emilia preschool.

Gardner, H. 1995. Foreword: Complementary perspectives on Reggio Emilia. In C. Edwards, L. Gandini, and G. Forman (Eds.), *The hundred languages of children: The Reggio Emilia Approach to early childhood education.* Norwood, NJ: Ablex, ix–xiv. Discusses the tenets of Reggio Emilia Approach and what he believes to be its significance.

Katz, L. 1990. Impressions of Reggio Emilia preschools. *Young Children* 45(6): 11–12. Offers overall impressions of Reggio Emilia with comparisons to other early childhood educational theorists.

Katz, L. G. 1995. What can we learn from Reggio Emilia? In C. Edwards, L. Gandini, and G. Forman (Eds.), *The hundred languages of children: The Reggio Emilia Approach to early childhood education.* Norwood, NJ: Ablex, 19–37. Discusses overriding lessons to be learned about curriculum and effective programs.

Katz, L. G., and B. Cesarone (Eds.). 1994. *Reflections on the Reggio Emilia Approach.* Champaign, IL: ERIC Clearinghouse on Elementary and Early Childhood Education. Discusses the Reggio Emilia Approach, especially as it compares with project-based approaches.

Malaguzzi, L. 1995. History, ideas, and basic philosophy. In C. Edwards, L. Gandini, and G. Forman (Eds.), *The hundred languages of children: The Reggio Emilia Approach to early childhood education.* Norwood, NJ: Ablex, 41–89. An interview with Malaguzzi (by Gandini) detailing the origins and keys to the approach.

New, R. 1990. Excellent early education: A city in Italy has it. *Young Children* 45(6), 4–10. Explores various dimensions of the Reggio Emilia Approach—the role of community, teachers, representational matters, and the projects.

———. 1991. Projects and provocations: Preschool curriculum ideas from Reggio Emilia. *Montessori Life* (Winter): 26–28. Explores curriculum ideas derived from the tenets of Reggio Emilia Approach.

———. 1991. Early childhood teacher education in Italy: Reggio Emilia's master plan for "master" teachers. *The Journal of Early Childhood Teacher Education* 12: 3. Describes the role of teachers in Reggio Emilia.

———. 2000. The Reggio Emilia Approach: It's not an approach—it's an attitude. In J. Roopnarine and J. Johnson (Eds.), *Approaches to early childhood education.* Columbus, OH: Merrill. Explores the underlying tenets of the Reggio Emilia Approach and the values that undergird how it has evolved.

Tierney, R. J. 1997. Learning with multiple symbol systems: Possibilities, realities, paradigm shifts, and developmental considerations. In J. Flood, S. B. Heath, and D. Lapp (Eds.), *A handbook for literacy educators: research in teaching the communicative and visual arts.* New York: Macmillan. Explores Reggio Emilia's Long Jump project in terms of literacies development.

Tierney, R. J., and S. Damarin. 1998. Technology as enfranchisement, cultural transformation and learning practices. In D. Reinking (Ed.), *Handbook of literacy and technology: Transformations in a post-typographic world.* Hillsdale, NJ: Erlbaum. Discusses the Creature City Project in terms of issues of multiple literacy and cultural transformation and equity.

Allen's Language Experience Approach in Communication

Purpose

The language experience in communication represents the Language Experience Approach as advocated by Roach Van Allen (1976). It is designed to develop the language competencies essential for the promotion of reading. To this end, it provides each child with opportunities to: (1) experience communication in various situations, (2) study aspects of communication, and (3) relate the ideas of others to self.

Rationale

Historically, the writings and material of Roach Van Allen have been largely responsible for this approach's recognition and evolution. Allen's rationale for the Language Experience Approach stems largely from a project sponsored by the Department of Education, San Diego County, California, where researchers pursued the question, "Of all the language experiences available for study in the elementary school years, which ones have the greatest contribution to make to reading?" This work served to identify twenty essential language experiences and give the approach its now familiar label, *language experience.*

With the approach's evolution, these twenty experiences have been organized into a design for a total language arts/communication curriculum. Figure 3.1 shows its design (Allen, 1976, 13). Within the design, the twenty language experiences fall within a framework of three strands and occur through the development of four types of activities. The three strands are: experiencing communication, studying communication, and relating communication of others to self. The four types of activities integral to the development of these experiences are language acquisition, language prediction, language recognition, and language production.*

The implementation of Allen's curriculum design is guided by certain principles and assumptions about language and the learner, and the interactive nature of the two. The assumption is that students acquire reading and writing skills in the same way that they acquire oral language skills. It is suggested that teachers recognize that students vary in language and language acquisition in accordance with their habits, age, socioeconomic group, and geographic region; teachers should further recognize that language changes slowly, continuously, creatively, and personally. To this end, it is Allen's premise that the "one big responsibility of a teacher at any level of instruction is to help each child to habituate, and to internalize certain truths about self and language" (Allen, 1976, 52). The conceptualization of these truths became the approach's trademark. This conceptualization was:

> What I can think about, I can talk about.
> What I can say, I can write (or someone can write about).
> What I can write, I can read.
> I can read what others write for me to read.
>
> (Allen and Allen, 1966, Level 1, 6)

In more recent years this conceptualization has evolved into the following:

> I can think about what I have experienced and imagined.
> I can talk about what I think about.
> What I can talk about I can express in some other form.
> Anything I can record I can tell through speaking or reading.
> I can read what I can write by myself and what other people write for me to read.
> As I talk and write, I use some words over and over and some not so often.
> As I talk and write, I use some words and clusters of words to express my meanings.
> As I write to represent the sounds I make through speech, I use the same symbols over and over.
> Each letter of the alphabet stands for one or more sounds that I make when I talk.
> As I read, I must add to what an author has written if I am to get full meaning and inherent pleasure from print.
>
> (Allen 1976; reprinted by permission)

*Language acquisition is directed toward increasing students' inventory of words, knowledge of ways to express themselves, and ability to explain the unfamiliar. Language prediction entails developing students' abilities to anticipate aspects of language and language patterns in their reading and listening. Language recognition is directed toward having students see the relationship between their language and the printed language of others. It includes developing their awareness of the characteristics of print and certain word identification skills. Language production involves having the student communicate through a variety of different media, associating most communications with speaking and writing, and realizing that ideas can be expressed, written, and read.

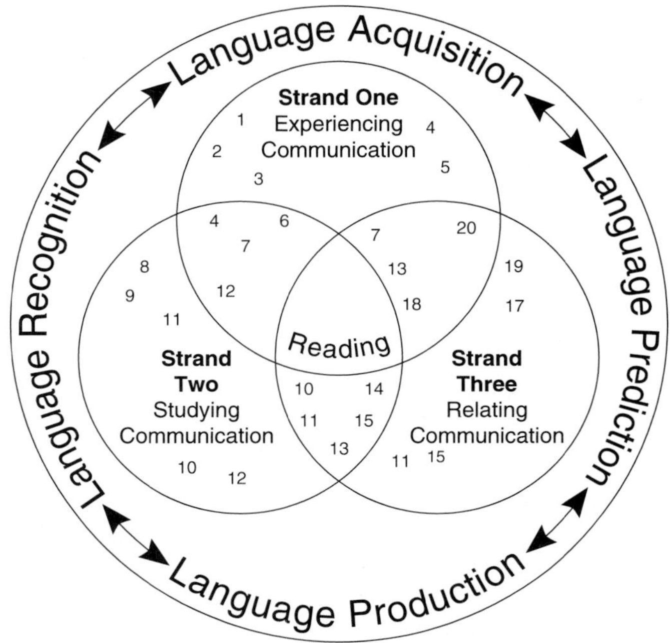

Reading in a Language Experience Approach

I. Experiencing Communication

1. Oral sharing of ideas
2. Visual portrayal of experiences
3. Dramatization of experiences
4. Responding rhythmically
5. Discussing and conversing
6. Exploring writing
7. Authoring individual books

II. Studying Communication

8. Recognizing high-frequency words
9. Exploring spelling
10. Studying style and words
11. Studying language structure
12. Extending vocabularies
13. Reading non-alphabetic symbols

III. Relating Communication of Others to Self

14. Listening to and reading language of others
15. Comprehending what is heard and read
16. Organizing ideas
17. Assimilating and integrating ideas
18. Searching out and reseaching multiple sources
19. Responding in personal ways
20. Evaluating communication of others

FIGURE 3.1 Design for Total Language Arts/Communication Curriculum

Intended Audience

Allen's Language Experience Approach can be used with students of all ages and abilities. It provides for a total language arts curriculum that can be implemented within a single group, a whole classroom, or across a whole school. The approach works with whole-class, group, or individual instruction.

Description of the Procedures

According to Allen, it is not his intention to suggest exactly how to develop a Language Experience Approach, but to suggest ways in which it might be implemented. In so doing, he assumes that teachers understand the philosophy of this approach, its curriculum rationale, learning center organization, and the use of multiple materials.

The language classroom proposed by Allen can be characterized by direct and indirect teaching activities within the framework of an instructional schedule. The direct and indirect teaching procedures entail the use of: (1) patterns of teacher-pupil interaction, (2) learning centers, and (3) planned programming. These provide the skeleton or organizational framework to which the instructional schedule clings. For purposes of discussion, the organizational framework is presented, and a presentation of specific teaching suggestions follows.

Organizational Framework

1. Patterns of Teacher-Pupil Interactions. Depending upon the nature of the activity, Allen suggests whole-class, group, or individual organizational patterns. Whole-class activities are suggested for the following:

- **a.** Reading aloud to or by children
- **b.** Oral discussion of topics of interest
- **c.** Oral composition of stories
- **d.** Films, filmstrips, and other audiovisual presentations
- **e.** Introduction and demonstrations of games or learning centers
- **f.** Seminars on various skills
- **g.** Singing, rhymes, choral reading, or unison reading

Group activities are suggested for the following:

- **a.** Teacher taking dictation for one child
- **b.** Children working, reading, or playing games with each other
- **c.** Teacher reading with individuals or groups
- **d.** Meeting a group's skill needs
- **e.** Completing work initiated with class
- **f.** Editing manuscripts for publication
- **g.** Planning and rehearsing dramatizations

Individual activities are suggested for the following:

- **a.** Conferring with students about writing individual books
- **b.** Conferring with students concerning their progress

c. Helping with spelling or word recognition
d. Taking dictation from individuals for whom sharing would be inappropriate

2. Learning Centers. To meet the specific needs of the approach, Allen suggests and describes a variety of permanent and temporary learning centers for the language classroom. Several of his suggestions are described below.

a. Strand learning centers. Once children have internalized the curriculum rationale, large centers made up of subcenters are suggested for each strand. For example, within a larger center for self-expression (Strand 1), there might be various subcenters for directing art expression, creative writing, and creative dramatics. Within a center for language study (Strand 2), there might be subcenters for editing manuscripts, review of language skills, and dictation experiences. Within a third, larger center for reflection (Strand 3), there might be subcenters for leisure reading, puppets, listening, and reading instruction.

b. The discussion center. Allen sees the discussion center as the hub of the language classroom. It is where the teacher introduces activities, stimulates interest, shares stories, establishes classroom procedures, and evaluates the program. It is where the students share and present ideas to other classmates.

c. The arts and crafts center. An arts and crafts center is suggested to provide the students a "treasure house" of creative materials and to serve as a "launching pad" for expression. This center is where children express themselves through various media within a recreational setting. Allen sees this expression as furnishing the raw materials essential for speaking, listening, reading, and writing.

d. The discovery center. A discovery center serves to highlight the language of science and encourages children to discover new things or look at familiar things with new perspectives. Toward these ends, it is equipped with microscopes, magnifying glasses, and collections of plants, insects, and minerals.

e. The dramatization center. A dramatization center serves to encourage children to discover themselves and relate to others through dramatization. The center is equipped with masks, puppets, and clothing.

f. The language study center. A language study center provides students a variety of different activities by which to acquire aspects of language, such as word study, language anticipation, grammar, and sight words.

g. Reading research center. A reading research center provides the students a place to browse, research, and read a variety of material. Intended for relaxation reading and research, it contains reference material, recreational reading materials, books written by the children, and magazines.

h. Writing/publishing center. A writing/publishing center is a place where children find both resources and motivation. Here children are stimulated to write, edit, review, and publish manuscripts. Here, newspapers, magazines, and previously published books of other children might be located.

Allen provides a number of other suggestions for learning centers that might be activated with program planning. Among his major suggestions are a music center, a cooking center, a viewing/listening center, and, for relaxation and contemplation, a quiet place.

3. Program Planning. Program planning is another essential aspect of Allen's organizational framework for teaching reading as a language experience. Program planning serves to structure learning experiences; for this purpose, Allen provides guidelines for recording, charting, and implementing the language experience program. His specific guidelines include the following suggestions:

a. Major language goals should be selected and implemented regularly and systematically. For example, language goals should be selected from each of the three strands and emphasized for no less than one week. Over a month or six weeks, each of the twenty language experience substrands should be emphasized by the teacher.

b. To serve the language concepts being emphasized, the teacher should develop learning centers to meet the students' needs and adjust the class grouping plans to afford maximum benefits.

c. Teacher-pupil interactions should be suited to the activities and needs of the students.

d. Evaluation procedures should be selected that can assess the program in terms of its objectives.

The chart in Figure 3.2 is suggested by Allen to guide program planning (Allen, 1976, 88).

Specific Teaching Suggestions. In addition to the organizational framework, Allen makes several specific teaching suggestions for establishing certain learning experiences. In an effort to provide a representative and detailed examination of some essential aspects of Allen's approach, his suggestions for dictated stories are presented.

Suggestions for Dictated Stories. Dictated stories are an integral part of Allen's language experience approach. They afford students the opportunity to learn about language through experiencing, studying, and reflecting on oral communications.

Allen breaks his suggestions for dictated stories into thirteen basic steps. They are:

1. Visit with the student for the purpose of discussing a topic of interest. Have students tell the names for things and describe their color, size, shape, function, parts, feelings, taste, smell, quantity, and related actions or events.

2. Decide whether the goal is for the student to provide description or to tell a story of some kind. If telling a story is the goal, have the student tell the whole story; then decide whether to write all of the student's ideas or some of them. Allen points out that often the goals for the dictation can be served by writing only one or two of the student's ideas. As the stories or labels are written, the teacher and student should talk about the letters, their

Name ____________ Class ____________ Dates ________ to ________

Theme or language emphasis: ____________

Activities from the Three Strands	Classroom Organization*			Learning Centers Activated† (with materials and equipment needed)	Evaluation‡			
	TC	SG	I		In	CR	St	PC
Experiencing communication								
Studying communication								
Relating communication of others to self								
Other activities								

*TC – total class
SG – small group
I – individuals

†Learning centers available: Discussion, Arts and Crafts, Cooking, Dramatization, Game, Reading/Research, Viewing/Listening, Writing/Publishing, A Quiet Place

‡In – informal inventory
CR – criterion reference
St – standardized test
PC – personal conference

FIGURE 3.2 Chart to Guide Program Planning

Source: Allen (1976); reprinted by permission.

names, their formation, the sounds they represent, and their structure. As Allen (1973) suggests:

> Talk about alphabet symbols you are using to represent the sounds the child made. (Let other children listen.) Let it be known that the letters have names, that some words begin with capital letters, that the same letters are used over and over as the first letters of words, that the same words appear over and over, that some ending sounds appear over and over, and they may tell us "how many" or "when." (p. 1)

3. After writing the story or the student's ideas, read the text back to the student and ask if the text is what the students said. The student might be asked to read along or to read some words or sentences alone.

4. Display the students' ideas or stories in the room and invite the students either to tell about their ideas or stories or to read them to the group. Some sentences might be read in unison to show the proper phrasing during reading. Have students compare their stories for word study. For example, students might study two or three characteristics of words, such as words that are the same, words that rhyme, words that begin or end the same, words with similar meanings, and words that are names. Allen suggests that teachers and students might identify these characteristics by underlining with different-colored pens.

5. Students might be invited either to read words, phrases, or sentences, or to read along in unison. Allen points out that involvement is more important at this point than correctness or the identification of poor readers.

6. The teacher or students might identify words that appear five or more times in students' stories and place them on a chart entitled "Words We All Use." Allen suggests this chart can be used as an aid for developing a reading vocabulary, as a source for word games, as a resource for the correct spelling of words, and as a way to determine if the student is ready for book reading. In terms of the latter purpose, Allen suggests a student is ready for book reading only when the vocabulary on this chart matches the vocabulary of books.

7. The students' dictated stories are copied onto ditto masters, duplicated, bound, and distributed to each student. Eight or ten stories are suggested for each book.

8. When students become interested in writing, Allen suggests that they trace their recorded story.

9. After tracing, students might be encouraged to copy stories on spaces left between each line.

10. The students move from copying below each line to copying on a separate sheet of paper.

11. The students write their own stories on the chalkboard.

12. A group or the whole class listens to the stories and makes suggestions for editing. The edited story is written on a story strip and displayed.

13. Students involve themselves in writing and refining their own stories at the writing center. For students who cannot write, the writing center can include independent tracing, copying, and other activities.

Cautions and Comments

Allen (1976) suggests that certain features about the Language Experience Approach to teaching communication distinguish it from traditional approaches to reading and from other aspects of language experience approaches. These features include:

1. Students' oral language grows and is used to develop language acquisition, production, recognition, and prediction abilities.

2. Vocabulary control occurs naturally rather than artificially through the students' natural use and acquisition of the vocabulary they use.

3. Students' vocabulary acquisition is accelerated through developing an understanding of words and language, rather than through drills.

4. Individualization, grouping, and teaching patterns vary with students' individual and group needs and not solely with their abilities.

5. In comparison to other Language Experience Approaches, the language experience approach to teaching communication affords a comprehensive curriculum design for creating learning environments and for screening activities.

6. Word identification skills are taught directly and in relationship to writing and spelling.

7. Students initially read familiar rather than unfamiliar story material. This provides them with a basis and the confidence for reading other material.

8. Students read initially within the context of their own linguistic environment, rather than within a language environment that is unfamiliar to them.

9. Students learn about language through expression and through exposure to the various language media. These experiences afford them an understanding of language patterns and the writing system.

10. Students gain exposure to a wide variety of reading material, including newspapers, magazines, recreational reading material, reference material, and stories written by their peers.

11. The use of a variety of multimedia materials stimulates the students' interests and expression.

12. Students are afforded opportunities to become fully involved in personalized learning experiences. Their ideas are valued and used as the basis for these experiences.

13. Students internalize a pattern of thinking about reading. This pattern suggests that ideas can be spoken, written, or read.

14. Students learn to read as a result of their increased sensitivity to their environment, their language, and their discovery of how reading meets their personal needs.

The approach does distinguish itself from other traditional approaches to teaching reading and from other Language Experience Approaches. It does, as Allen suggests, provide teachers a wealth of suggestions for implementing a comprehensive language-arts-based approach to teaching reading. But certain of these suggestions might be questioned. For example, Allen states that reading, writing, speaking, and listening are closely interrelated. However, he assumes that in practice these activities can be taught concurrently and interchangeably. During the dictation of a story, the teacher would refer students to a study of how letters are formed and how they sound. As Smith (1973) suggests, reading, writing, speaking, and listening should not be taught concurrently when the interchange detracts from meaningful and purposeful communication. The emphasis on the mechanics of writing would tend to do just that. Perhaps subsequent revisions of this approach could place more stress on using "invented spellings" which, in turn, would diminish the need for dictation and require a reconsideration of the emphasis on mechanics.

Other examples of questionable practices include Allen's suggestions for direct rather than indirect word identification skills instruction, his emphasis upon words and the acquisition of a sight vocabulary, and his suggested use of choral and unison reading. Again, advocates of a psycholinguistic notion of reading (Smith, 1973) would claim this approach overemphasizes the mechanics of word-perfect reading.

Research evidence to support Allen's approach is rather limited, and what is available tends to be negative (Kendrick and Bennett, 1966). In defense of Allen, the research that has been implemented has seemed rather insensitive to the subtleties of the goals he outlined. Measurement procedures and analysis techniques have seemed inadequate to truly evaluate the effectiveness of this approach.

Allen did not invent the Language Experience Approach, but he should be given a great deal of credit for its emergence, popularity, and evolution. His Language Experience Approach to teaching communication represents his most recent efforts and his response to demands for a more comprehensive and structured language experience approach. The enigma of the approach may be that while it is not sufficiently prescriptive for some teachers, it may be too prescriptive for others.

Sampson, Allen, and Sampson (1991) bring some new issues to using Allen's Language Experience Approach. They suggest that this approach is particularly good for supporting students from diverse cultural and linguistic backgrounds:

> Meaning-centered curricula value the differences that children bring to the classroom. Many children have failed in school because . . . their language and culture were rejected as new language and new ways were imposed on them. They were considered deficient, and many failed because their self-esteem was destroyed and because the techniques used to teach a second language of "standard English" were so different from the way they had learned their first language. (p. 358)

Difference is not only inevitable in the classroom, it is valuable. The different lives children lead allow them to bring many different experiences into the classroom to share; when the class values children's experiences, it is enriched by them as well. Further, as Dyson (1989) points out, children acquire literacy in connection with their experiences; a classroom that values children's experiences is one that gives children, as Dyson says, a literacy that "may be more likely to grow with them into their tomorrows" (p. 276).

Sampson, Allen, and Sampson (1991) also discuss the use of computer technology in relation to the Language Experience Approach. They describe several software packages that are available, software that is several steps beyond the early "skill and drill" packages that used to characterize "educational" software. Because the software arena is changing so quickly, the software packages will be discussed as types of software rather than in terms of specific packages. Other types of software that may be useful and interesting to students are being developed very rapidly; this list, then, is provisional.

- Word processing programs. These allow teachers to record children's dictated texts and to print out typed copies. Word processing programs designed for children are easy to use and allow children to edit their texts very easily. Some word processors include speech synthesizers, which allow the computer to read the text out loud. Although speech synthesis can be problematic, some speech synthesis programs allow the teacher to correct the computer's pronunciation.

- Text development software. These are more than word processors. They often have a graphics package, which allows the children to combine words and pictures in their work. For example, some packages help children to create comic books; the graphics include characters drawn in comic book style and speech balloons for the texts that children write. Story development software allows children to create their own stories and to select from graphics libraries to illustrate their stories.

- Fiction software. Story exploration software connects with children's books and allows children to extend their reading experiences through further exploration of the world of the particular story. Some of the stories currently available are not very engaging for children. Adventure games may use a story world or a new world. Children interact with that world through text and pictures. Children control the plot and often write in conjunction with using choose-your-own-adventure-type stories or open-ended adventure stories.

In his review of the use of computers in teaching language arts, Bruce (1991) mentions five possible roles for the computer:

> 1. *A tutor.* It can individualize instruction, provide learning material at a controlled pace, and record student progress.
> 2. *A tool.* It aids in reading; it allows students to produce and format texts easily; it facilitates revision of texts; it checks for spelling errors. It stores in a compact and easily accessible form all sorts of information that learners need, from style sheets to encyclopedic data.
> 3. *A way to explore language.* It makes the regularities, the beauties, and the difficulties of language something that students can examine and interact with in new ways.
> 4. *A medium.* It makes possible new modes of communication, and "hypertexts," or "hypermedia," which allow the intermixing of tables, charts, graphs, pictures, sounds, video, and text.
> 5. *An environment for communication.* It is a new social realm that permits new forms of meaningful communication and reconfigures the relationship among students and teachers. (p. 536) [italics original]

Computer technology can be a valued asset in classrooms in which Allen's Language Experience Approach is being used.

Finally, Allen's Language Experience Approach is congruent with and might be used in conjunction with other reading strategies, e.g., Whole-Language, Theme-Based Units, and the Author-Reader-Inquirer Cycle.

REFERENCES

Allen, R. V. 1968. How a language experience program works. In E. C. Vilscek (Ed.), *A Decade of innovations: Approaches to beginning reading.* Newark, DE: International Reading Association. Provides a brief overview of the approach's rationale and guiding principles.

———. 1973. *Suggestions for taking dictation.* Unpublished paper, University of Arizona. Describes his suggestions for taking students' dictation.

———. 1976. *Language experiences in communication.* Boston: Houghton Mifflin. Provides a detailed discussion of the approach's rationale and methods of implementation.

Allen, R. V., and C. Allen. 1966–68. *Language experiences in reading, Levels I, II, and III.* Chicago: Encyclopedia Brittanica. Provides extensive resource material, including suggestions for lessons, teaching methods, materials, and activities, for use with elementary school students.

———. 1969. *Language experiences in early childhood.* Chicago: Encyclopedia Brittanica. Provides extensive resource material, including suggestions for lessons, teaching methods, materials, and activities for use in first-grade or early childhood programs.

———. 1976. *Language experience activities.* Boston: Houghton Mifflin. Contains more than 250 activities for use with the approach and in learning centers.

Aukerman, R. C. 1984. *Approaches to beginning reading.* (2d ed.). New York: John Wiley and Sons, 331–338. Provides a detailed discussion of the approach's development, rationale, methods, and materials.

Bruce, B. 1991. Roles for computers in teaching the English language arts. In J. Flood, J. M. Jensen, D. Lapp, and J. R. Squire (Eds.), *Handbook of research on teaching the English language arts.* New York: Macmillan. Discusses five roles for computers and research related to their use in language arts programs.

Dyson, A. H. 1989. *Multiple worlds of child writers: Friends learning to write.* New York: Teachers College Press. Longitudinal study of children using reading, writing, drawing, and talking in their development of literacy.

Hoover, I. W. 1971. *Historical and theoretical development of a language experience approach to teaching reading in selected teacher education institutions.* Ed.D. thesis, College of Education, University of Arizona, Tucson. Presents a survey of the Language Experience Approach's historical development and its introduction in teacher education institutions.

Kendrick, W. M., and C. L. Bennett. 1966. A comparative study of two first-grade language arts programs. *Reading Research Quarterly* 2: 83–118. Reports a research study comparing the Language Experience Approach with a traditional basal method.

Lee, D. M., and R. V. Allen. 1963. *Learning to read through experience.* New York: Appleton-Century-Crofts. Presents a 146-page overview of the Language Experience Approach.

Purves, A. C., L. Papa, and S. Jordan (Eds.). 1994. *Encyclopedia of English studies and language arts.* New York: National Council of Teachers of English. This encyclopedia has more than 800 annotated entries/topics that succinctly address this topic and related areas.

Sampson, M., R. V. Allen, and M. Sampson. 1991. *Pathways to literacy: A meaning-centered approach.* Fort Worth: Holt, Rinehart and Winston. This is a reading textbook that is based on Allen's Language Experience Approach.

Smith, F. 1973. Twelve easy ways to make reading difficult. In F. Smith (Ed.), *Psycholinguistics and reading.* New York: Holt, Rinehart and Winston, 183–196. Discusses the problems associated with selected instructional principles and practices.

Ashton-Warner's Organic Reading

Purpose

Organic Reading (Ashton-Warner, 1958) is an experience-centered approach to reading instruction based upon Sylvia Ashton-Warner's twenty-four years of teaching experiences with New Zealand Maori children. It is designed to provide a bridge from the known to the unknown, a bridge that can help students move from their own experiences to sharing the written experiences of others.

Rationale

In her various books, *Spinster* (1958), *Teacher* (1963), and *Spearpoint* (1972), Ashton-Warner presents the rationale and details of her procedure. She states that Organic Reading is derived from the notion that learning experiences should begin with the "intrinsic" rather than with the "extrinsic"; she suggests that students should relate to their own innermost thoughts before relating to the thoughts of others. Her goal as a teacher is to "release" the native imagery and use it for working material (Ashton-Warner, 1972, 17).

Along this line of reasoning, the student's initial exposure to reading should afford an organic, instinctive reaction to reading. As Ashton-Warner suggests:

> First words must mean something to a child. First words must have intense meaning for a child. They must be a part of his being.
>
> How much hangs on the love of reading, the instinctive inclination to hold a book! Instinctive. That's what it must be. The reaching out for a book needs to become an organic action, which can happen at this yet formative age. Pleasant words won't do. Respectable words won't do. They must be words organically tied up, organically born from the dynamic life itself. They must be words that are already part of the child's being. (Ashton-Warner, 1963, 30)

Ashton-Warner claims that the longer the student's reading is organic, the stronger it will become. She suggests that teachers should reach into the minds of students to touch this key vocabulary; when a number of words are acquired, students should be given opportunities to write and read stories based upon this vocabulary. Ashton-Warner suggests that in so doing, the foundation to a lifetime of reading can be laid.

Intended Audience

Organic Reading is suited for use on either an individual, a group, or a classroom basis with any student. It was proposed as a beginning reading method with children from divergent cultures, specifically New Zealand Maori children, but has also been used in the United States.

Description of the Procedures

Sylvia Ashton-Warner describes the Organic Reading Approach as integral to the total curriculum. Organic reading would be one aspect of the organic teaching program. During a school day, students would be scheduled to do "organic work" and "standard work." Both these aspects of the school program would involve what Ashton-Warner refers to as "input" and "output" periods. As suggested by Ashton-Warner, the typical school day would entail the following activities (1963, 101):

Typical Day's Activities

Morning

Organic Work

Output period (approximately 1 hour, 45 minutes)

- conversation, art activities, craft activities, singing, creative dance, key vocabulary, organic vocabulary, etc.

Input period (approximately 1 hour)

- key vocabulary (for little ones), organic vocabulary, organic discussion, stories, pictures, etc.

Afternoon

Standard work

Output period (approximately 1 hour)

- nature study and numbers

Input period (approximately 50 minutes)

- standard vocabulary, standard reading, Maori book vocabulary and reading, supplementary reading, stories, songs, poems, letters (for little ones)

Organic Reading involves four movements or periods in the student's development. The first movement begins with the students' generating words they wish to learn. The latter movements involve the students in writing and reading stories.

First Movement. The first movement entails, as Ashton-Warner puts it, reaching into the child's "inner mind" to discover the child's key vocabulary. Ashton-Warner suggests that each student has a key vocabulary, which, if it is to be reached, requires a great deal of teacher sensitivity and patience. It is probed during the morning output period when the teacher holds personal conferences with each student. The teacher elicits these key words from the student and writes each on a 12 × 5-inch card as it is spoken. The student then takes the work, traces it, studies it, and, when ready to move on to other activities, places it in the teacher's word box.

Later that same morning, each student is given further experiences with these same words. Namely, a check is made to see if the words are remembered. An opportunity is given for the student to use them in organic writing and spelling activities. In the latter activities, the student will: (1) write either a sentence or a story using the key vocabulary words and (2) be presented with the words for either naming or spelling. The chalkboard rather than paper is used extensively for these activities.

Several other techniques are used to learn and check each student's key vocabulary. At the beginning of each school day, students receive their cards mixed together and emptied on the classroom floor. When the students enter, they have to scramble to find their own word cards. Ashton-Warner suggests that the recalled cards represent the student's "living" key vocabulary. Following this line of reasoning, words that are not recalled are removed and destroyed. To facilitate further learning, each student then sits with a partner, and they hear and help each other say their words.

According to Ashton-Warner, each student's key vocabulary reflects the student's inner self. The words in this key vocabulary center upon the student's primitive instincts. Specifically, they reflect ideas related to fear and sex. Among the fear words often suggested were ghost, frightened, cry, and wild. Among the sex words often suggested were kiss, love, dance, and together.

Second Movement. As the students' vocabulary develops, they progress through the other movements. By the time the second movement has been reached, the student has acquired a sizable key vocabulary and has begun suggesting words from "outside" rather than "inside," such as *happy days* and *snowy mountains.* In this movement, the use of two words replaces the use of single words; longer, yellow cards replace the white word cards. The student again traces the words written on the card, puts them in a story, and, during the morning input period, writes them on the chalkboard and spells them. Early every morning, the students will once again arrive to find their new cards piled on the floor and will begin a search for them. During this movement, the students begin to read either homemade or teacher-made books that use key vocabulary words. These are the students' stories, made from their own words by their teacher or their parents. The students read these books to themselves and each other.

Third and Fourth Movements. As the students continue to progress, they move through Ashton-Warner's third and fourth movements. During these movements, the student progresses from writing his or her own small stories with teacher assistance to writing small stories without teacher assistance to writing rather sophisticated stories.

During these movements the student's vocabulary is ever changing; Ashton-Warner suggests that words appear and disappear with their changing appeal. Whenever the student adds a new word, the teacher writes it in the back of the student's own story book. These back pages assume the role of a personal dictionary for the student.

During these movements, time is also allotted to vocabulary building, reading, sharing, and discussing stories. During vocabulary periods, students write their words on the chalkboard and spell them aloud. During organic reading and sharing, students not only read and master their own stories but also share them with others. Following organic reading and sharing, the students discuss each other's stories, then proceed to use the Maori readers. These readers contain stories collected from the work of previous children. They are intended as an introduction to reading published books.

During the afternoon input and output periods, the students are presented with standard school experiences in accordance with their level of development. These experiences purport to introduce the students to the culture at large. Experiences would include nature study, numbers, standard vocabulary, standard reading, listening experiences, songs, and poems. For students at the key vocabulary level, they would also include letter-writing activities.

Cautions and Comments

There have been a number of evaluations of Ashton-Warner's ideas (Packer, 1970; Duquette, 1972). These evaluations have yielded mixed results in terms of the carry-over of the approach to published reading programs, but they do support Ashton-Warner's claim that her approach affords a more enjoyable and meaningful approach to developing beginning readers' attitudes and abilities. As she suggests in her own evaluation of the use of the approach with American children (1972), Organic Reading may have differential success in accordance with the general attitude and desire of children for learning.

Teachers should recognize that the approach necessitates a great deal of daily preparation. Teachers would have to be aware of and record each student's developmental level and scheduled activities, and, in particular, to teach the student's key vocabulary. Teachers would need to be able to provide the mechanisms for generating stories based upon the students' vocabularies and for having students write their own stories.

It should be noted that certain aspects of Ashton-Warner's approach lack adequate development. For example, while her suggestions for using and generating key vocabulary seem reasonable, some of her proposed methods are ill-defined and poorly reasoned. In places her approach lacks sufficient definition to be understood or implemented, and some of her suggestions lack a base either in theory or in research, e.g., her procedures for spelling and writing words.

As with other language experience approaches (see introduction to this unit), computer technology can be helpful in the implementation of this strategy. Desktop publishing programs and versatile word processing programs (those that allow the user a lot of flexibility in formatting) can expedite the making of books. Word processing can be used to keep track of students' vocabulary, as well.

Given that Ashton-Warner developed her reading method as she was teaching a group of minority children in New Zealand, she has a new historical presence in the current efforts to respond to the needs of children in culturally diverse classrooms. One finds congruencies between Ashton-Warner's method and the three principles that Farr (1991) suggests are important in the effective teaching of language arts to nonmainstream students:

> The most important principle of effective instruction for nonmainstream students is that of ethnosensitivity. . . . It is crucial that teachers understand that their own views of the world, or ways of using language in that world, are not necessarily shared by others. . . . A second principle involves structuring activities that comprise functional and interactive communication and allow students to feel "ownership" of their own writing. That is, writing intended as actual communication is much more effective in engaging students in literacy learning. A third principle is . . . the need for abundant experience with written texts. Such texts are replete with the linguistic responses of Western literacy. . . . The more experience students have with such texts, the more easily they will acquire the particular linguistic devices and cultural orientation that they contain. (pp. 368–369)

Like other language experience approaches, Ashton-Warner's approach does not simply create a "tolerance" in the classroom for cultural diversity, it actually uses children's own experiences as a basis from which to build learning. Cultural diversity in the classroom becomes a strength.

Finally, as Veatch (1991) points out, Ashton-Warner's work is compatible with the Whole-Language approach. It is also compatible with other reading strategies, notably, Reading-Writing Workshop, Author-Reader-Inquirer Cycle, and Theme-Based Units.

REFERENCES

Ashton-Warner, S. 1958. *Spinster.* New York: Simon and Schuster. Describes aspects of her life as a teacher of New Zealand Maori children and refers to her organic teaching methods.

———. 1963. *Teacher.* New York: Simon and Schuster. Provides a detailed description of her organic teaching methods, their rationale, and their use with New Zealand children.

———. 1972. *Spearpoint.* New York: Alfred A. Knopf. Describes Ashton-Warner's experiences with her method while teaching in Colorado.

Aukerman, R. C. 1984. *Approaches to beginning reading* (2d ed.). New York: John Wiley and Sons, 368–371. Provides a summary description and discussion of the organic teaching methods.

Duquette, R. J. 1972. Research summary of Barnette-Duquette study. *Childhood Education* 48: 438–440. Presents a summary of a research study in which Ashton-Warner's key vocabulary concept was used with students of varying reading ability in different United States cities.

Farr, M. 1991. Dialects, culture, and teaching the English language arts. In J. Flood, J. M. Jensen, D. Lapp, and J. R. Squire (Eds.), *Handbook of research on teaching the English language arts.* New York: Macmillan. Summarizes research on cultural differences and teaching language arts.

Packer, A. B. 1970. Ashton-Warner's key vocabulary for the disadvantaged. *The Reading Teacher* 23: 559–564. Presents the findings of a United States study in which words in students' key vocabulary were compared with basal word lists.

Purves, A. C., L. Papa, and S. Jordan (Eds.). 1994. *Encyclopedia of English studies and language arts.* New York: National Council of Teachers of English. This encyclopedia has more than 800 annotated entries/topics that succinctly address this topic and related areas.

Veatch, J. 1978. *Reading in the elementary school* (2d ed.). New York: John Wiley and Sons, 343–357. Discusses key words and their relation to beginning reading.

———. 1991. *Whole language and its predecessors: Commentary.* Paper presented at the Annual Meeting of the College Reading Association. ERIC Document 341–035. Points out similarities in philosophy between several older reading strategies and Whole-Language.

———. 1996. From the vantage of retirement. *The Reading Teacher* 49(7): 510–516. Reflects upon Sylvia Ashton-Warner's key word approach.

Veatch, J., F. Sawicki, G. Elliot, E. Barnette, and J. Blakey. 1979. *Key words to reading: The language experience approach begins* (2d ed.). Columbus: Charles E. Merrill. Provides a description of how key vocabulary can be integrated into an individualized reading program.

Wasserman, S. 1972. Aspen mornings with Sylvia Ashton-Warner, *Childhood Education* 48: 348–353. Describes a teacher's exposure to organic teaching through a workshop run by Ashton-Warner.

Stauffer's Language-Experience Approach

Purpose

The purpose of the Language-Experience Approach advocated by Russell Stauffer (1970) is to take advantage of the linguistic, intellectual, social, and cultural wealth a student brings to school so that the transfer from oral language to written language can be made.

Rationale

In the preface to his book *The Language-Experience Approach to the Teaching of Reading* (1970), Stauffer makes the following statement:

> The best label that can be applied to the Language-Experience Approach is "The Eclectic Approach to Reading Instruction." It embraces the best practices regardless of their sources and does so in a functional communication-oriented way.

He suggests that essential to the Language-Experience Approach are the relationships that exist among language, thought, and experience, and among the communicative skills of reading, writing, speaking, and listening. More specifically, he suggests:

1. Reading, writing, speaking, and listening occur within the context of purposeful communication.
2. The interests, curiosities, creativity, culture, capacity, percepts, and concepts of each individual are used.
3. The use of word recognition and word identification is developed in a meaningful context ensuring the use of meaning clues.
4. Reading skills which are taught are assimilated and used.
5. Individual interests and understandings are extended and refined.
6. An appreciation of the value and uses of reading is afforded.

To these ends, the Language-Experience Approach is a total language arts approach that relies heavily upon dictated stories, word banks, and creative writing.

Intended Audience

The Language-Experience Approach is designed for use as a beginning reading approach with students of various ages and abilities. It is appropriate for use either on a one-to-one, a group, or a whole-class basis. The Language-Experience Approach has been used with a wide variety of students, from kindergarten through middle school, and with students of varying abilities. Several variations of the Language-Experience Approach have been found to be successful with students who have language deficiencies (e.g., Franklin, 1992, and Leverett and Diefendorf, 1992). In a case study of a child with severe expressive language delay and a phonological disorder, Franklin records the importance of the Language-Experience Approach to the child's progress:

> Ryan's teacher also took dictation from the individual children in her group each week, which proved to be an important tool for Ryan's development in written language. In October of the second year, when Ryan reread his dictations during sharing time, he began to sweep his finger under the words as he had seen his teacher do when she reread language experience stories. By February, he began to add his own writing to his dictations and drawings. . . . A year later, Ryan began to prefer to do his own writing rather than dictate. (p. 47)

Additionally, Leverett and Diefendorf (1992) suggest that the Language-Experience Approach provides children who have language deficiencies with both common language to use about shared experiences and an individualized approach to reading. Finally, Dixon and Nessel (1983) have used a variation of Stauffer's approach for English as second-language learners.

Description of the Procedures

The following description of Stauffer's Language-Experience Approach is not intended to be exhaustive but instead to represent its major characteristics. The interested reader is directed to Stauffer's book *The Language-Experience Approach to the Teaching of Reading* (1970) for further details. Those aspects we will discuss include: (1) dictated experience stories, (2) word banks, and (3) creative writing.

1. Dictated Experience Stories. Dictated experience stories are the core of Stauffer's Language-Experience Approach. They provide students with the opportunity to learn to read much as they learn to talk. They also provide a means of getting started with reading and for developing, refining, and extending reading skills.

As a way of getting started, Stauffer suggests the use of whole-class dictated stories. During the first few weeks, the whole-class dictated stories provide the students an opportunity to become familiar with the procedure and to get acquainted with each other linguistically, culturally, and socially. Once familiar with the procedure, the students engage in group-dictated stories and, ideally, individual-dictated stories.

Across whole-class-, group-, and individual-dictated experience stories, the procedures used by the teacher are quite similar. For this reason, they will be discussed together.

a. Generating the dictated experience story. To generate the dictated experience story requires that the teacher locate a stimulus with which the student can associate and through which, Stauffer suggests, students can "examine more carefully the world about them, to see new horizons, to view the past and the future, and to act upon it intellectually" (Stauffer, 1970, 55). The stimulus might be an event, an idea, or a concrete object. It might involve something the students can see, touch, or feel, and, with the help of teacher questioning, discuss.

When the teacher feels the students are able and willing to generate some dictation, the stimulus is put aside and the students gather around a chart set up for dictation. For class-dictated stories, a lined chart approximately 2 × 3 feet is suggested; for group-dictated stories a chart approximately 12 × 15 inches. For individual-dictated stories, letter-size paper is suggested.

The teacher now asks the students to tell about the stimulus; as the students offer ideas, these are recorded by the teacher. In a whole-class or a group situation, only selected students would be given an opportunity to dictate sentences. Once the several sentences are recorded, the teacher might terminate the generation activity and reread the sentences to check if the recorded ideas are stated appropriately.

b. Reading the story and follow-up activities. Once the students' dictated story is completed, it is read. First the teacher reads the story; then the teacher and students read the story in unison. As the story is read and read again, the teacher points to each word. The teacher may then direct the students to draw a picture depicting their story, to identify known words in the story, or to begin other activities.

On the second day, the students are again referred to their dictated experience story. If the story is a class effort, the class is first divided into groups, with at least one child who contributes to the story in each group. Typically, the activities of the second day are sequenced in this way:

1. Each student follows along, either individually or in groups, as the teacher reads their individual, group, or class stories.

2. As the teacher points to each word, the story is read by the teacher and student in unison.

3. The whole story or portions of the story are read by selected individuals or by the author of the story.

4. The students match, name, or locate selected words.

5. The students locate and underline words they know or the whole group knows.

6. To check on known words, the teacher has the student(s) reread the dictated story orally. If the student fails to recognize a word previously underlined, the underlining is crossed, e.g., *donkey.* This marking indicates that *donkey* is no longer a known word.

On the third day, students in the class are given the opportunity to do more intense study of their stories. When stories are dictated with the whole class, the teacher reproduces the story and distributes it to each student. Individually, students read over the story and underline known words. Stories are then placed in class and personal folders. The students whose stories are generated individually or in a group are given an opportunity to reread their stories and check (after a reasonable "forgetting period") whether they still remember their words from the previous day. For the purpose of providing a schedule for group dictation, Stauffer (1970) suggests the following activities across a week:

Group Dictating Study

	Group I (least mature)	**Group II**	**Group III**	**Group IV (most mature)**
Monday	dictating	other activities	other activities	dictating
Tuesday	re-reading and word study	dictating	dictating	re-reading and word study
Wednesday	re-reading and word study	re-reading and word study	re-reading and word study	other activities
Thursday	dictating	re-reading and word study	other activities	dictating
Friday	re-reading and word study	dictating	dictating	re-reading and word study

2. Word Banks. As Stauffer describes the word-bank file, it is "a personalized record of words a pupil has learned to read or recognize at sight" (Stauffer, 1970, 74). The file of words emanates from the dictated stories generated by the student. It includes only words that the student has identified as being known across successive days. These are words that have been underlined at least twice. As a check on the students' recognition of these words, the teacher has them identify their words. For this purpose, a small window card is suggested (see Figure 3.3). The window frame is placed over each underlined word in random order. The random ordering of presentation prevents the student's use of context.

The students' known words form the deposits and reserves of their individual word banks. Each known word is written or typed on a card (approximately 3/8 × 1 1/2 inches) and filed. As the word bank expands beyond thirty cards, an alphabetic filing system is introduced. Thus, each student gains a personalized file of known words, which acts both as a resource and as a dictionary. To use the word bank cards as a resource, Stauffer suggests a variety of activities: composing stories, word attack activities, discrimination activities, categorization activities, and finding other occurrences of the words in print.

3. Creative Writing. Another facet of Stauffer's Language-Experience Approach grows out of the students' word banks—creative writing. Stauffer defines creative writing as "a composition that reflects a child's own choice of words, ideas, order, spelling, and punctuation" (Stauffer, 1970, 78).

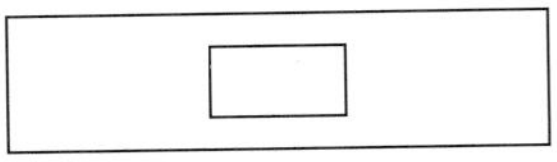

Window Card

Henry

Henry is my very best friend.
He is an ant that I keep in an
ant house beside my bed. He has
six legs and is brown and red.

FIGURE 3.3 Window Card for the Word-Bank File

The students' first encounter with writing is expected to occur with the writing of names and recognition of words. But creative word usage begins with the construction of sentences from words in the word banks. Using their word cards, students' first creative writing experiences occur when they lay out simple sentences and stories with their cards. When a word not in their card bank is required, they begin to learn to write and spell, using their new word recognition skills.

To begin creative writing experiences, Stauffer suggests the use of 12 × 18-inch paper. To provide a space for illustration, he suggests leaving the top half unlined. To guide lettering and to afford ample spacing between lines, he suggests ruling five lines with 3/4-inch spacing, and lines 3/8-inch wide between each two of these lines across the bottom of the page.

As described by Stauffer (1970, 82–83), the following guidelines may help the teacher in developing creative writing abilities from these beginnings:

a. Students should want to write rather than be coerced into writing.

b. Instructions to students should be simple and direct.

c. Creative writing topics may be suggested, but students should be encouraged to write about anything they wish.

d. Students should be encouraged to write legibly and spell accurately, but not at the expense of interfering with the flow of their ideas.

e. Students' ideas should be encouraged to flow freely through teacher assistance and questioning when needed.

f. Students' writing should be evaluated in terms of quality of expression and not purely by "adult standards."

Cautions and Comments

Stauffer's Language-Experience Approach provides the teacher with a comprehensive, well-articulated, and experience-based language-arts program for initial reading. The approach seems suitable for use with students of varying ages and capabilities. It provides for a variety of language-experience activities in all four facets of the language arts. Eventually it may be used either to supplement or to substitute for a total reading program. Stauffer's approach affords incidental instruction for the development, extension, and refinement of word identification skills, spelling skills, writing skills, concept development skills, and general comprehension.

As evidence of the approach's use and value, Stauffer provides a wealth of actual examples taken from teachers in different settings and also cites theory and research. Several related research studies are abstracted in the appendices to his book (Stauffer, 1970).

However, the approach does seem to have at least one major shortcoming. Namely, it appears that the approach places an undue emphasis on the recognition of isolated words. This emphasis occurs in the pointing to words during reading, in the identification and mastery of single words, and in the word banks composed of single, known words. Students with whom the approach is used are in danger of becoming nonfluent readers and word callers, if they give each word the power these activities suggest. If reading for meaning is our goal, the approach should place less emphasis upon word-perfect reading and the acquisition of single, known words and should give more emphasis to reading with understanding.

There are some concerns to consider in the practice of this strategy. Since the Language-Experience Approach relies on using children's own words and sentence patterns, teachers are cautioned to be sure they are using the child's own syntax and vocabulary, even if those language patterns are not shared by the teacher. This process requires careful listening to the child, since it is so easy to automatically "correct" regionalisms or ethnic dialects to "standard" English. The power of the Language-Experience Approach is that the child can read what she wrote because it is her language; if "I be six" is "corrected" to "I am six," the child will not be reading and will have to be corrected when she produces "her" sentence.

Obviously, using children's own language may be problematic in the classroom if the child uses offensive language or if the child chooses a subject matter that is not appropriate to the classroom. In these situations, the teacher may negotiate with the child about different ways to say something or the subject matter of a text. Again, this must be done in a nonjudgmental fashion (e.g., "Can you think of another word to use?"). If a story is not appropriate for general classroom consumption, you may want to encourage the child to tell that story in a different context and to choose another story for reading work (e.g., "Have you told your mom how you feel about that?").

Computer technology, as was pointed out in the introduction to this unit, can be used with language-experience approaches. Casey (1984) used a computer not only in the process of working with print but also as the subject of the language experience. Certainly classroom resources such as informational texts on CD-ROM can be exciting experiences about which children may want to write. Fiction software (as described in Sampson, Allen, and Sampson, 1991) in which children interact with stories on the computer (e.g., "adventure" games) might also be good subjects for language experience stories. Stratton, Grindler, and Postell (1992) combined word processing and photography in a Language-Experience Approach with middle school students.

Word processing and desktop publishing are helpful resources for making children's language experience stories into books and for keeping track of children's vocabularies. Additionally, word processing features, such as spelling checkers and the ability to cut and paste text, help children to create quality texts with much less frustration than the texts they create in hand-writing.

Word processing may be particularly helpful in the Language-Experience Approach. Although the process of keyboarding is a concern for many teachers (should children use a computer before they know how to type correctly?) the word processor is less frustrating than hand-writing for many children, and the computer itself is intrinsically motivating. The multimedia capabilities of computers (e.g., combinations of hypertext, animation, video, written text, still images, and sound bytes) lend themselves to the Language-Experience Approach.

Finally, the Language-Experience Approach is congruent with and supportive of other reading approaches, especially Whole-Language, Theme-Based Units, and the Author-Reader-Inquirer Cycle.

REFERENCES

Casey, J. M. 1984. *Beginning reading instruction: Using the LEA approach with and without micro-computer intervention.* ERIC Document 245–192. An account of a research project in which Language-Experience Approach was used both with and without word processing/voice synthesis. Computer technology contributed significantly to the effectiveness of the method. Includes case study of a reluctant reader.

Dixon, C., and D. Nessel. 1983. *Language-Experience Approach to reading (and writing): Language-experience reading for second language learners.* Hayward, CA: The Alemany Press. Activities and methods for using LEA with English as a second language students.

Franklin, E. 1992. Learning to read and write the natural way. *Teaching Exceptional Children* 24: 45–48. Shows how Whole-Language and Language-Experience Approaches can be used with children who have special needs.

Leverett, R. G., and A. O. Diefendorf. 1992. Students with language deficiencies. *Teaching Exceptional Children* 24: 30–35. Reviews several strategies that can be used, including the Language-Experience Approach.

Purves, A. C., L. Papa, and S. Jordan (Eds.). 1994. *Encyclopedia of English studies and language arts.* New York: National Council of Teachers of English. This encyclopedia has more than 800 annotated entries/topics that succinctly address this topic and related areas.

Sampson, M., R. V. Allen, and M. Sampson. 1991. *Pathways to literacy: A meaning-centered approach.* Fort Worth: Holt, Rinehart and Winston. This is a reading textbook that is based on Allen's Language Experience Approach.

Stauffer, R. G. 1965. The Language-Experience Approach. In J. Kerfoot (Ed.), *First grade reading programs.* Newark, DE: International Reading Association. Provides additional information concerning Stauffer's Language-Experience Approach.

———. 1969. *Directing reading maturity as a cognitive process.* New York: Harper & Row, 186–238. Presents a detailed discussion of aspects of Stauffer's Language-Experience Approach.

———. 1970. *The Language-Experience Approach to the teaching of reading.* New York: Harper & Row. Presents a detailed account, with examples, of the rationale and procedures of this approach.

Stauffer, R. G., and W. D. Hammond. 1967. The effectiveness of language arts and basic reader approaches to first-grade reading instruction—extended into second grade. *The Reading Teacher* 20: 740–746. Presents research findings in which Stauffer's approach is compared favorably with basic reading program instruction.

Stauffer, R. G., and W. D. Hammond. 1969. The effectiveness of language arts and basic reader approach to first-grade reading instruction—extended into third grade. *Reading Research Quarterly* 4: 468–499. Presents an extension of previous research findings concerning the Stauffer approach.

Stratton, B. D., M. C. Grindler, and C. M. Postell. 1992. Discovering oneself. *Middle School Journal* 24: 42–43. Discusses a language experience project with middle school children.

Shared Book Experience

Purpose

Shared Book Experience is an attempt to adapt the principles of early book experiences between parent and child to the classroom and to refine the procedures to be a very powerful system of learning. As described by David Doake and Donald Holdaway, Shared Book Experience is intended as a means of affording groups of students early reading experiences that are intimate and that dovetail with other language activities.

Rationale

Shared Book Experience began in New Zealand in an attempt to unite the language learning experiences of students by shifting to the center of early reading experiences "the enjoyment of a rich, open literature of favorite stories, poems and songs" (Park, 1982). Holdaway (1979), who has been one of the major advocates of this approach, has suggested that the model underlying the Shared Book Experience has its roots in the same developmental tenets of learning spoken language and acquiring other learnings. He suggests, for example, that Shared Book Experience has its basis in learning experiences similar to the bedtime story situation. Just as it is important for a bedtime story to be enjoyable, interesting, and presented in relaxed circumstances, so Holdaway argues that stories should be introduced to classes in a relaxed, nonthreatening, and motivating setting. Similarly, the read-it-again phenomenon, which is a characteristic of bedtime stories, is integral to maximizing the utility of stories. In particular, stories that students look forward to rereading can be used: (1) as independent reading material, even if children role-play as readers, and (2) to focus the reader's attention on certain aspects of the text; for example, words and predictable features of language.

The major tools of the Shared Book Experience are what might be considered oversized books. These books are intended to be at the center of the reading and writing program. They serve two basic functions: They take advantage of good literature, and they capitalize upon the social dynamics of a classroom. Indeed, the initial name for Shared Book Experience was "cooperative reading." The rationale behind the enlarged text is, as the New Zealand Department of Education has suggested:

> When a teacher is working with an enlarged text . . . the right climate and the right auditory and visual conditions exist for effective skills teaching. The enlargement of print enables precise, accurate attention to be focussed on word and every letter detail. (p. 3)

As the above comments suggest, Shared Book Experience is not seen as separate from other aspects of the reading and writing program. Doake (1985) and Holdaway (1979) have viewed the use of Shared Book Experience as working hand in hand with a language experience approach and as a precursor to individualized reading. In Figure 3.4 Holdaway has depicted how the Shared Book Experience might work in conjunction with other activities. Apart from this general depiction of the interrelationships, Holdaway has discussed at length a number of reading and writing activities that might use the raw material of the books as their base.

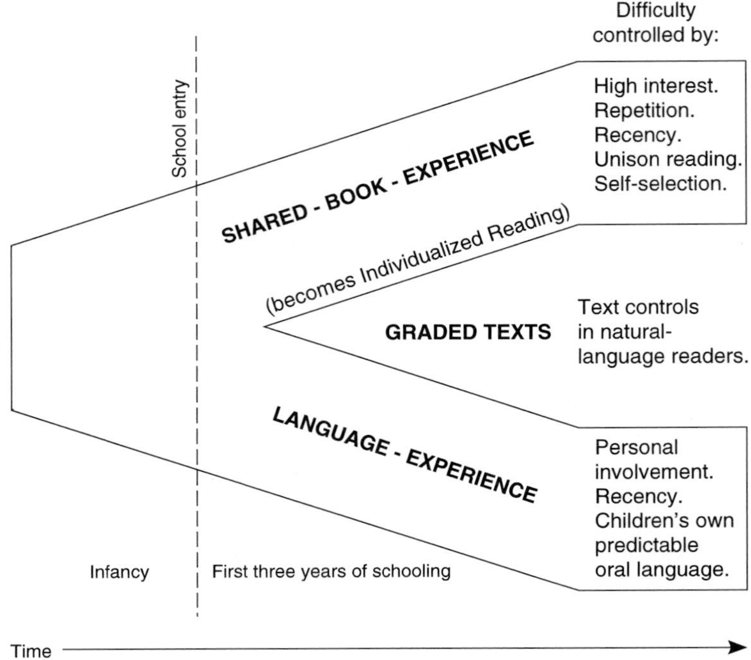

FIGURE 3.4 Balancing Approaches and Materials

Holdaway has claimed that there are innumerable benefits that might be accrued from the use of the Shared Book Experience. His suggestion of the benefits and their cyclic nature are presented in Figure 3.5. At the heart of his advocacy of the Shared Book Experience is his belief, as he has stated, that:

> Gathered around a book as a natural, sharing community children learn more from participation than from direct instruction: they learn from the teacher's model, from their own sensible involvement, and from each other, without any sense of competition or pressure. They also learn from judicious instruction which is more intelligible because of its real and obvious purposes. (Park, 1982, 819)

Slaughter (1993) suggests that the importance of this technique "is its sequencing of instruction. Children first become familiar with an entire story; teachers then use this familiarity to help students attend gradually to smaller segments of text—sentences first, then phrases and words within sentences, and finally letters within words" (p. 7).

Shared Book Experiences enable children to "become readers competent in themselves and their developing abilities, enjoy predictable stories, participate in meaningful, goal-directed activities, develop a sense of belonging within the classroom community, never experience a feeling of failure since reading is encouraged—never demanded—therefore, creating an atmosphere conducive to learning" (Slaughter, 1993, 12).

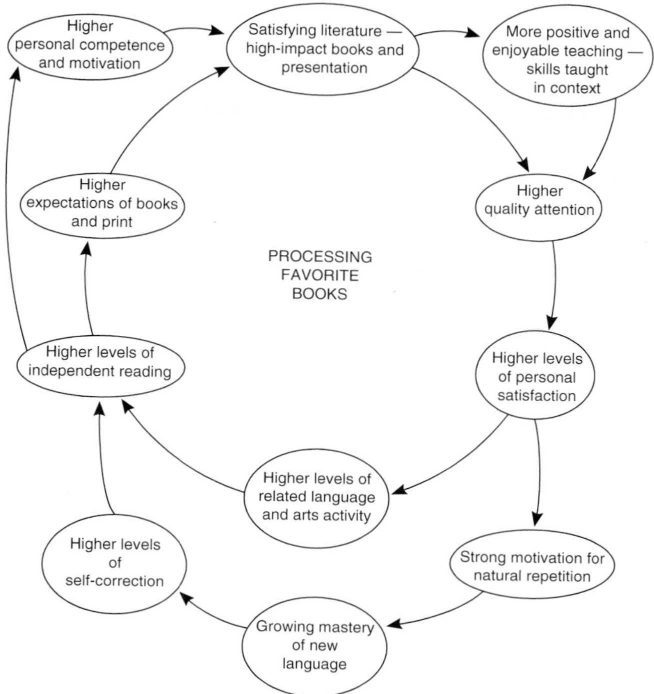

FIGURE 3.5 The Cycle of Success in Shared Book Experience

Strickland and Morrow (1989) maintain that reading to young children "increases their interest in books and in learning to read. It enhances their background information and sense of story structure, and familiarizes them with differences between written and oral language." They contend that "reading to children helps them understand how print functions and how it is used. Through this social interaction, they learn early book strategies such as book handling, directionality, recognizing story structure, and the concept of authorship" (p. 322). Carger (1993) suggests that "the use of engaging and motivating children's literature can offer second language readers an exciting entrance into second language literacy by:

- Reading books portraying familiar faces and events to which children can link their own schemata makes comprehension easier and school less threatening
- Providing them with a basis for meaningful communication as they share reactions to stories
- Offering natural opportunities for generating language in reacting to and retelling stories with puppets or other props (p. 543)
- These storybook readings, retellings, and pretend readings of favorite storybooks afford second language children the opportunity to construct language creatively within a comfortable, meaning-centered activity.
- By participating in storybook activities, second language learners can "communicate their reactions and interpretation connected with the world they encountered without barriers" (p. 547)

Intended Audience

A Shared Book Experience approach can be used in almost any situation when the teacher wants to focus a group's attention on a single text. As described by Holdaway (1979), it is most suited to use in preschools or the first grade, but can be extended to language-delayed children and children with learning disabilities and effectively implemented in middle and high school classrooms.

Description of the Procedures

The Shared Book Experience centers around the use of enlarged books or overheads of good quality that are predictable stories and that can be presented to a class or group of students. These enlarged copies of different books are intended to be sufficiently interesting and predictable to engage young readers in anticipating what will happen in the story and in participating whenever selected words or phrases are repeated. As the story is read aloud to the children, the teacher will enlist the use of a pointer to ensure the children follow along. After reading, students are given language extension experiences and time to read independently either the new story or one of their previous favorites (Figure 3.6). "Little books" or small versions might be made available along with listening stations so that children who cannot handle the story or who just wanted to listen will be able to follow along.

For instance, a class that has been involved in reading a big book copy of "The Three Billy Goats Gruff" might be involved in dramatizing the story and in choral reading. Also they might choose to learn about goats or write their own story based upon this tale. The stories that the class generate might be published and used as further reading material for the class. In essence, the story serves as the stimulus for other literacy learnings. A typical Shared Book Experience involves the following activities:

1. Tuning In. The enjoyment of poetry and song. Here the students are given opportunities to participate in and enjoy singing or reading along with the class.

2. Rereading of a Favorite Story. If possible, students are encouraged to make predictions and read along with the story. Sometimes children can direct the reading.

3. Learning about Print and about Language. This entails what is termed functional skills teaching and innovation. Functional skills teaching includes developing comprehension skills, listening skills, learning conventions such as left to right and reference labels, prediction, confirmation and self-correction, sight vocabulary, auditory discrimination, letter-sound associations, letter names, punctuation, and intonation patterns. For this purpose, masks might be used to cover parts of words, phrases, sentences, or lines from a story as a way of focusing students' attention on elements of the print. At other times, it might entail using windows to highlight words or other activities (Figure 3.7).

Innovation is the creation of a new statement based on a familiar pattern or theme. At the simplest level, it might involve changing the name of a character in a story. At other times, it might involve changing a number of different words in the context of sentences.

FIGURE 3.6 Children Enjoying Shared Book Experience during Independent Time

Additional activities that can be part of a shared book experience are:

1. Introduction of a new story
2. Independent reading of favorite stories
3. Expressive activities arising from the literature such as writing, dramatization, art, creative movement, etc.

As Holdaway (Park, 1982) says, the choice of material, especially the material that is enlarged, must be very carefully selected. It must be able to grip students, have a good plot, be predictable, include interesting pictures, and, if possible, have repetitive elements, patterns, and maybe rhyme.

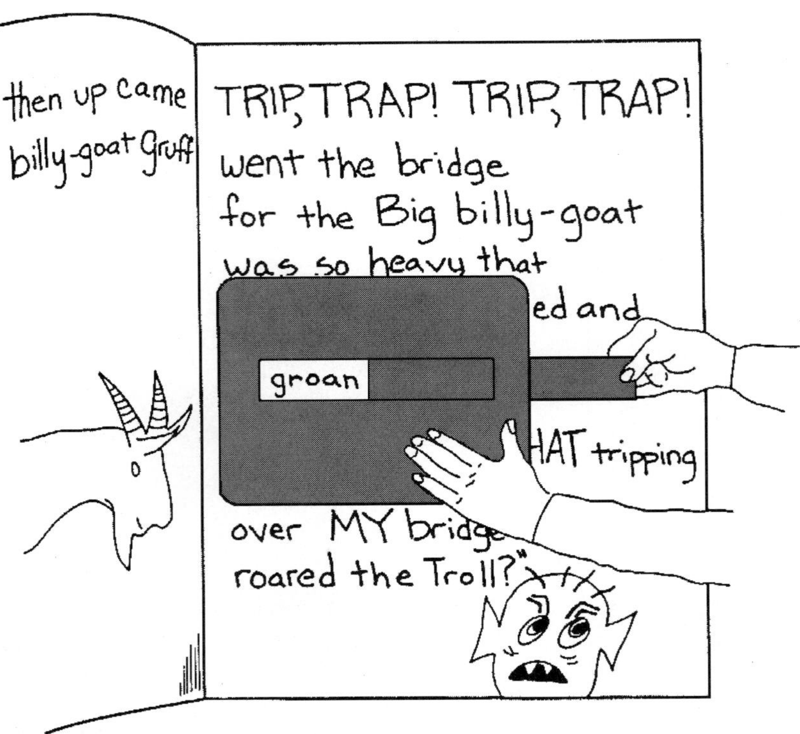

FIGURE 3.7 Follow-Up Activity Involving Word Masking

After students develop some security with these materials, Holdaway suggests that teachers might include among the independent reading materials some of the graded readers, assuming that they are not overly stilted.

McTeague (1992), in advocating the use of shared reading activities with older learners, suggests three strategies: reading response journals, listening logs, and guiding book talks. The *reading response journal* is "a notebook or writing folder in which students record a measure of their enjoyment of a book they have chosen for silent reading under the guidance of the teacher. They record their personal responses to the reading experience" (p. 15). *Listening logs* are used "as a response to the teacher's daily reading aloud from a literary work not otherwise available to the students." This activity enables the teacher to "deepen the authentic and personal response of every student by guiding each one to wider reading and more reflective writing" (p. 17). McTeague (1992) poses the following as potential questions while listening:

- What's going on in your mind?
- What pictures occur in your head?

- What feelings do you experience?
- What do you expect to happen?
- What questions occur to you?
- What are you thinking about? (p. 17)

Guiding student book talks, according to Chambers (1985), is a technique that enables students to explore a text as a whole class activity by listing their likes, dislikes, confusions, and emerging patterns found in the text. Chambers (1985) recommends teachers to adhere to the following points when implementing this approach:

- Process can be used with whole class or small group
- The teacher's role is to guide students and to facilitate the discussion
- Students need and should feel ownership in the discussion
- Process should be a shared discovery that leads the group or class to deeper levels of understanding, interpretation, and appraisal. (p. 20)

Cautions and Comments

In the 1990s, the Shared Book Experience had become an element included in most reading programs. In recent years, it has received less attention as the direct instruction of skills has become more prominent. This is unfortunate because the worth of Shared Book Experience remains. Holdaway emphasizes, however, that Shared Book Experience is not a panacea and can be easily misused. He warns that the Shared Book Experience should not be viewed as a license to enlarge just any story. He emphasizes, as do others, that careful selection of interesting and predictable story material is essential.

Other problems that may emerge with the use of the Shared Book Experience may be inherent in the approach itself. The procedure requires a teacher who is willing to explore story readings with his or her students and a view of learning to read that is more Whole-Language than piecemeal. It is important to realize that students learn reading not by word mastery or skill mastery.

In recent years the use of Shared Reading has become widespread. It has come to be viewed as the appropriate way to introduce reading to children and analogous in some ways to invented spelling. Just as invented spellings offer the young writer with rudimentary mechanical skills a way to write, so shared reading affords a reader involvement in reading. What seems key is the license big books offer with respect to moving away from vocabulary control and the view that children must master a set use of words prior to being able to read.

This approach is flexible in that it can be implemented as a comprehensive approach unto itself, or it can supplement the contemporary reading program. According to Slaughter (1993), the Shared Book Experience is "comprehensive, flexible, imaginative, stimulating, and provides teachers with an ideal basis for guiding children in their acquisition and development of literacy" (p. 14). Most reviews of research of early literacy development include discussions of shared reading and its role.

REFERENCES

Au, K. 2002. Balanced literacy instruction: Implications for students of diverse backgrounds. In J. Flood, J. Jensen, D. Lapp, and J. R. Squire (Eds.), *Handbook of research on teaching the language arts,* Vol. II. New York: Macmillan, 955–966. Discusses the effectiveness of Shared Reading in conjunction with programs in Hawaii.

Butler, A. Not dated. *Shared book experiences.* Crystal Lake, IL: Rigby. Represents a straightforward guide to the use of big books.

Carger, C. L. 1993. Louie comes to life: Pretend reading with second language emergent readers. *Language Arts* 70: 542–547. A research study describing the experiences of second language learners participating in a literature-rich environment.

Chambers, A. 1985. *Introducing books to children.* London: Heinemann. Provides a description of how to plan and implement guided book talks with students.

Coombs, M. 1987. Modeling the reading process with enlarged texts. *The Reading Teacher* 40: 422–426. Describes how teachers can utilize enlarged texts to enhance children's reading development. She presents findings supporting its use with readers of varying ability.

Dickinson, D. K., and M. W. Smith. 1994. Long-term effects of preschool teachers' book readings on low-income children's vocabulary and story comprehension. *Reading Research Quarterly* 29(2): 105–122. Examines talk about books in 25 classrooms serving 4-year-old low income children.

Doake, D. B. 1979, May. *Book experience and emergent reading behavior.* Paper presented at the International Reading Association, Atlanta. Describes study of Shared Book Experience.

———. 1985. Reading-like behavior: Its role in learning to read. In *Observing the language learner,* edited by A. M. Jaggar and M. T. Smith-Burke. Newark, DE: International Reading Association/NCTE. Describes how Shared Book Experiences contribute to learning to read.

Dulbow, M. 2003. On the same page: Shared reading beyond the primary grades. *Journal of Adult & Adolescent Literacy* 47(1): 100. Explores the use of Shared Reading with adolescents.

Eldredge, J. L., D. R. Reutzel, and P. M. Hollingsworth. 1996. Comparing the effectiveness of two oral reading practices: Round-robin reading and the shared book experience. *Journal of Literacy Research* 28(2): 201–225. A study comparing Shared Book Experiences with round-robin reading on second graders' reading growth.

Hammett, L. A., A. Van Kleeck, and C. J. Huberty. 2003. Patterns of parents' extratextual interactions during book sharing with preschool children: A cluster analysis study. *Reading Research Quarterly* 38(4): 442–467. Provides insights into the nature of the interactions that support reading development in conjunction with Shared Reading.

Handel, R. D. 1992. The partnership for family reading: Benefits for families and schools. *The Reading Teacher* 46: 116–126. Describes how the family literacy projects were started in Newark, NJ, and the importance of family-school collaboration.

Harste, J., K. Short, and C. Burke. 1988. *Creating classrooms for authors.* Portsmouth, NH: Heinemann. Explores the use of shared reading in the classroom.

Heald-Taylor, B. G. 1987. Big books. In D. Watson (Ed.), *Ideas with insights: Language arts K–6.* Urbana, IL: National Council of Teachers of English. Offers practical suggestions for using big books.

Holdaway, D. 1979. *Foundations of literacy.* Sydney: Ashton-Scholastic. Presents a thorough discussion of the Shared Book Experience, including theoretical rationale, examples from classrooms, and information pertaining to how the approach relates to the total school literacy program.

Johns, J. L., and S. D. Lenski. 2001. *Improving reading: Strategies and resources* (3d ed.). Dubuque, IA: Kendall/Hunt. A practical resource with examples that can be used in a range of classrooms.

Klesius, J. P., and P. L. Griffith. 1996. Interactive storybook reading for at-risk learners. *The Reading Teacher* 49(7): 552–560. Describes the implementation of a lap reading between parent and child for kindergartners deemed "at risk."

Lynch, P. 1986. *Using big books and predictable books.* Richmond Hill, Ontario: Scholastic-TAB. Provides practical suggestions for using big books and predictable books in the classroom.

Martinez, M. G., and W. H. Teale. Classroom storybook reading: The creation of texts and learning opportunities. *Theory into Practice* 28: 126–135. An analysis of current research on storybook reading and the implications for classroom use.

McGee, L. M., L. Courtney, and R. G. Lomax. 1996. Teachers' roles in first graders' grand conversations. In C. K. Kinzer and D. J. Leu (Eds.), *Multidimensional aspects of literacy research, theory, and practice.* Chicago: National Reading Conference, 517–526. Explores the roles played by teachers in grand conversations.

McTeague, F. 1992. *Shared reading in the middle and high school years.* Portsmouth, NH: Heinemann. Provides an overview of how shared reading and collaboration between teachers and students can be implemented with older readers.

New Zealand Department of Education. 1978a. *Shared book experience procedures, Unit 6, Early reading inservice course.* Wellington: E. C. Keating, Government Printer. Provides an overview of the approach, including suggestions for activities, material, and slides demonstrating the approach.

———. 1978b. *Suggestions for making enlarged books, Early reading inservice course.* Wellington: Department of Education. Presents graphically procedures for enlarging books, including illustrations, print, choice of paper, assembling and storage.

Nister, R. J., and A. Maiers. 2000. Stopping the silence: Hearing parents' voices in an urban first-grade family literacy program. *The Reading Teacher* 53(8): 670–680. Discusses a parental involvement program that improves children's literacy development.

Park, B. 1982. The big book trend—A discussion with Don Holdaway. *Language Arts* 59: 815–821. Presents an interview with Donald Holdaway in which the Shared Book Experience is thoroughly discussed.

Peetoom, A. 1986. *Shared reading: Safe risks with whole books.* Richmond Hill, Ont.: Scholastic-TAB. Offers suggestions for using big books with less confident readers.

Purcell-Gates, V. 2000. Family literacy. In M. L. Kamil, P. B. Mosenthal, P. D. Pearson, & R. Barr (Eds.), *Handbook of reading research,* Vol. III. Mahwah, NJ: Erlbaum, 853–870. Discusses the role of a range of family literacy practices in developing readers and writers.

Purves, A. C., L. Papa, and S. Jordan (Eds.). 1994. *Encyclopedia of English studies and language arts.* New York: National Council of Teachers of English. An excellent resource that contains an extensive collection of more than 800 annotated entries/topics in English Studies and Language Arts.

Reutzel, D. R., P. M. Hollingsworth, and J. L. Eldredge. 1995. Oral reading instruction: The impact on student reading development. *Reading Research Quarterly* 29(1): 41–59. Shared Book Experience is compared with Oral Reading Recitation in terms of second graders' reading development.

Rosenhouse, J., D. Feitelson, B. Kita, and Z. Goldstein. 1997. Interactive reading aloud to Israeli first graders: Its contribution to literacy development. *Reading Research Quarterly* 32(2): 168–183. Explores the impact of reading aloud to first graders assigned to different treatment groups.

Slaughter, J. P. 1993. *Beyond storybooks: Young children and the shared book experience.* Newark, DE: International Reading Association. Describes the possibilities of using Shared Book Experiences with students—teaching tips, integrated shared books with other learning, etc.

Strickland, D. S., and L. M. Morrow. 1989. Interactive experiences with storybook reading. *The Reading Teacher* 42, 322–333. Provides an overview of the importance of reading to young children and on early reading development.

———. 1990. Storybook reading: A bridge to literary language. *The Reading Teacher* 44: 264–268. A research study focusing on the value of storybook reading with Arab kindergartners.

Tierney, R. J., and M. Sheehy. 2002. What longitudinal studies say about literacy development/what literacy development says about longitudinal studies. In J. Flood, J. Jensen, D. Lapp, and J. R. Squire (Eds.), *Handbook of research on teaching the language arts,* Vol. II. New York: Macmillan, 171–191. Explores the role of Shared Reading or the equivalent in conjunction with longitudinal studies by various researchers.

Trachtenburg, P., and A. Ferruggia. 1989. Big books from little voices: Reaching high risk beginning readers. *The Reading Teacher* 42: 284–289. Discusses the positive aspects of utilizing big books in a primary classroom for beginning readers.

Watson, D., and P. Crowley. 1987. How can we implement a whole-language approach? In C. Weaver (Ed.), *Reading process and practice.* Portsmouth, NH: Heinemann. Offers an extended discussion of big books in conjunction with describing Whole-Language.

Yaden, D. B., D. W. Rowe, and L. Macgillivray. 2000. Emergent Literacy: A matter (polyphony) of perspectives. In M. L. Kamil, P. B. Mosenthal, P. D. Pearson, and R. Barr (Eds.), *Handbook of reading research,* Vol. III. Mahwah, NJ: Erlbaum, 425–454. Includes a discussion of Shared Reading and other practices in promoting literacy development.

Yamada, Y. 1983. How much can children learn from a single book? *The Reading Teacher* 36: 880–883. A research study describing a sixth-grade Japanese class participating in a directed group reading project.

Yopp, H. K. 1995. Read-aloud books for developing phonemic awareness: An annotated bibliography. *The Reading Teacher* 48(6): 538–543. Presents various read-aloud books that lend themselves to developing phonemic awareness.

Patterned Language Approach

Purpose

The Patterned Language Approach (Bridge, 1979; Bridge and Burton, 1982; Bridge, Winograd, and Haley, 1983) is intended to provide students success in their initial encounters with books through the use of a combination of a structured language experience approach with patterned or predictable stories. The strategy has been shown to be useful for purposes of developing an initial vocabulary, a positive attitude to reading, and the use of context.

Rationale

The Patterned Language Approach represents an adaptation of three proposals: (1) the notions of Bridge and Burton (1982) on the use of predictable stories, (2) the suggestions by Cunningham (1979) for using structured language experience stories, and (3) some of Martin and Brogan's (1971) guidelines for using patterned books. The authors of the approach claim that the approach represents a response to Frank Smith's (1978) belief that students learn to read by reading and a suggestion by K. Goodman (1976) that predictability is an essential ingredient for early reading material. The question the Patterned Language Approach addresses is: How are beginning readers to practice reading when they cannot yet read?

They respond to this question with the claim (and data supporting this claim) that patterned books, if used appropriately, are a most effective way for beginning reading. As Bridge, Winograd, and Haley stated:

> Patterned books contain repetitive structures that enable readers to predict the next word or line or episode. After hearing such material read aloud, children can join in and "read" along even though at that point they are probably not able to recognize the individual words. However, repeated opportunities to recognize high frequency words in dependable contexts help them develop a sight vocabulary that can soon be recognized in other contexts. (1983, 884)

Sentence-matching activities and dictated stories are used to avoid the possibility that children just memorize the story "and are not really reading."

Intended Audience

The Patterned Language Approach is intended for use in the first grade or kindergarten. With suitable material, the approach seems suited to use with students at any age level.

Description of the Procedures

The procedure is based on the careful selection of appropriate "patterned stories," which are used in a whole-to-part fashion. Students begin with what Martin and Brogan (1971) refer to as "whole book success" in which they role-play successful readers, as well as develop a trust of print. Their attention is then focused on sentences and words for purposes of developing flexible reading strategies and an initial vocabulary.

To aid in the selection of appropriate material, Bridge (1979) and Bridge, Winograd, and Haley (1983) offer sources and guidelines for using and selecting predictable stories, as well as generating dictated stories.

The sequence of lessons to be followed with any single book or the children's own dictated story is as follows:

1. The teacher reads the book to the group and then reads it again, inviting the students to join in when they are able to predict what is coming. The group may then be divided into subgroups for various choral readings in which they change parts. When dictated stories are used, the lesson is the same, except the first lesson is preceded with a discussion and the generation of a story is dictated by the students.

2. The teacher and students read the story from the book together. Then the story is read from a chart without the picture clues or, if a big book (see Shared Book Experience in Unit 2) is being used, with the pictures covered.

3. The teacher and students read the story from the chart. The students are given sentence strips containing lines of the story. They match the steps with the corresponding line in the story by placing the strip under the line.

4. The students as a group read the story from the chart. They are then given word cards to match with words on the chart.

5. The students as a group read the story from the chart. In random order, the teacher places word cards from the story at the bottom of the chart. The students locate each of these words on the story and place them in the order in which they occurred in the story. The procedure is requested for each section of the story.

Cautions and Comments

In two studies, a Patterned Language Approach has been shown to be equal or superior to a "typical" basal approach with first graders. Bridge, Winograd, and Haley (1983) have reported that the use of a Patterned Language Approach—in contrast to a typical basal approach—spurred the acquisition of sight vocabulary, induced students to use context clues, and created more positive feelings about reading. In a second study, Bridge and Burton (1982) were not able to show significant differences, but suggested similar trends were evident in their data.

As a method for beginning formal reading instruction, the Patterned Language Approach shares a great deal in common with Holdaway's procedure for using a Shared Book Approach and R. V. Allen's Language Experience Approach for reading. What the patterned approach offers that these other approaches do not are straightforward procedures for having students simultaneously attend to meaning, the flow of a text, the syntax, and graphophonic features. What also distinguishes the approach from others is the examination of its efficacy by Bridge and others. Too few strategies are subjected to the scrutiny that systematic research examinations can provide.

What may be a limitation of the procedure is the routine itself. If followed repetitively, the specific steps suggested may become more tedious than educative. Otherwise, a great deal of care needs to go into the presentation of the material or varying the word- and sentence-matching procedures. What is also a limitation of the procedure is the failure of Bridge and her colleagues to spell out how predictable story material should be selected or produced by the teacher. When suggesting that teachers direct students' attention to words, Bridge and her colleagues never indicate which words or how many should be identified and matched.

Despite these limitations, the approach does serve the purposes for which it was intended. It represents an approach that allows students to learn to read by reading.

REFERENCES

Bridge, C. 1979. Predictable materials for beginning readers. *Language Arts* 50: 503–507. Describes the use of predictable or patterned stories and how they might be used by teachers.

Bridge, C., and B. Burton. 1982. Teaching sight vocabulary through patterned language materials. In J. A. Niles and L. A. Harris (Eds.), *New inquiries in reading research and instruction.* Washington, DC: National Reading Conference, 119–123. Presents a research study in which "patterned" stories were used.

Bridge, C., P. Winograd, and D. Haley. 1983. Using predictable materials vs. preprimers to teach beginning sight words. *The Reading Teacher* 36: 884–891. Represents the primary source for a Patterned Language Approach.

Cunningham, P. 1979. Beginning reading without readiness: Structured language experience. *Reading Horizons* 19: 222–227. Describes a structured approach for using students' dictated stories.

Goodman, K. S. 1976. *Reading: A conversation with Kenneth Goodman.* Glenview, IL: Scott, Foresman. Discusses how psycholinguistic thinking applies to beginning reading.

Heald-Taylor, G. 1987. Predictable literature selections and activities for language arts instruction. *The Reading Teacher* 41: 6–12. Explores the use of predictable books with suggestions for sources and a checklist to assess aspects of reading behavior (e.g., book handling).

Martin, B., and P. Brogan. 1971. *Teachers guide to the instant readers.* New York: Holt, Rinehart and Winston. Provides guidelines and suggestions for using predictable stories.

Purves, A. C., L. Papa, and S. Jordan, (Eds.). 1994. *Encyclopedia of English studies and language arts.* New York: National Council of Teachers of English. This encyclopedia has more than 800 annotated entries/topics that succinctly address this topic and related areas.

Rhodes, L. K. 1979. Comprehension and predictability: An analysis of beginning reading materials. In J. C. Hartse and R. Carey (Eds.), *New perspectives on comprehension.* Bloomington: Indiana University, School of Education. Presents a research study in which the worth of patterned stories was examined.

Rhodes, L. K. 1981. I can read! Predictable books as resources for reading and writing instruction. *The Reading Teacher* 34: 511–518. Discusses the use of patterned or predictable stories in a classroom.

Smith, F. 1978. *Understanding reading* (2d ed.). New York: Holt, Rinehart and Winston. Presents a theoretical discussion of reading and learning to read based upon psycholinguistic thinking.

UNIT 4

Intervention Programs for At-Risk Readers

UNIT OVERVIEW

The term *at risk* became widely used as schools, legislatures, and industry became increasingly concerned that: (1) students were failing to achieve the basic literacy skills to participate fully and productively in society; (2) most attempts to address the needs of this population have not been successful; (3) the costs of students failing were immense, especially when measured over time; and (4) special "pullout" or clinic programs seemed to offer little in the way of long-term benefits. No longer is it satisfactory to have the child show growth in the clinical or "pullout" setting; it is now essential that the transition back to a regular classroom be achieved—that is, the student should have the skills and strategies to maintain the ability to read and to grow as a reader. Unfortunately, developments have occurred that may have had a positive impact on programs to meet the needs of students at risk. In situations in which school funding has been cut, often support for one-to-one tutoring by qualified professionals has been replaced with approaches that are less costly. These cutbacks have occurred sometimes without regard to the long-term impact and costs of short-changing students in the early years.

A further development that may have been positive has been the attempt to identify best practice based on a narrow definition of research—in particular, the findings offered by the National Reading Panel. The end result has been an attempt by program developers to adjust their programs to fit these findings despite the limitations of the syntheses and the narrowness of the research and issues that they consulted.

This unit describes several of the more notable attempts to meet the needs of at-risk readers. They include strategies dating back over 50 years as well as some more current ones.

Reading Recovery and Success for All represent two of the most widely enlisted programs for students deemed "at risk." Early Steps represents one of the many tutoring programs that have emerged in recent years. However, unlike most other programs, it is now used in school settings. (See our reference list for some others.) The remaining three strategies are included for their historical significance.

Reading Recovery. The Reading Recovery program is a one-to-one intervention program for the poorest readers in the first grade and an intensive training program for teachers. These students receive Reading Recovery interventions for 30 minutes every day with a trained teacher until they develop the self-improvement system needed to return to the regular classroom.

Success for All. The Success for All program is a schoolwide tutoring program for readers in grades one to three who are experiencing difficulties. The program emphasizes early, intensive intervention and prevention and focuses much of its thrust on disadvantaged schools.

Early Steps. Early Steps (or the Howard Street Tutoring Program) was developed as an after school tutoring program for second and third graders who were falling behind in reading. The program has expanded to use in schools with students in grades one through three.

Gillingham-Stillman Method. The Gillingham-Stillman method represents an approach that emphasizes students' auditory abilities in learning to read. Based on the theories of Samuel Orton, the Gillingham-Stillman procedure provides an alphabetic method by which words are built through associations involving students' visual, auditory, and kinesthetic processes. It purports to provide teachers of disabled readers a systematic approach to teach reading in a progression from letters to words, from words to sentences, and from sentences to stories.

Fernald Technique. The Fernald technique has been perhaps the most historic practice for teaching remedial reading. It represents a comprehensive approach to developing reading abilities from low to normal ability based initially on multisensory learning.

Internet searches will yield current website discussions and materials pertaining to the various approaches.

REFERENCES

Allington, Richard L. 2002. *Big brother and the national reading curriculum: How ideology trumped evidence.* Portsmouth, NH: Heinemann. Includes several papers critiquing the National Reading Panel report.

Caserta-Henry, C. 1996. Reading Buddies: A first-grade intervention program. *The Reading Teacher* 49(6): 500–503. Describes a year of "Reading Buddies"—a first-grade intervention program.

Coles, G. 2002. *Great unmentionables: What national reading reports and reading legislation don't tell you.* Portsmouth, NH: Heinemann. Critique of the National Reading Panel report and the reading legislation that led to these and other initiatives.

Cunningham, J. W. 2001. The national reading panel report. *Reading Research Quarterly,* 30(3): 326–335. Reviews issues concerning the definition of scientific research.

Erickson, K. A., and D. A. Koppenhaver. 1995. Developing a literacy program for children with severe disabilities. *The Reading Teacher* 48(8): 676–684. Discusses technology resources and how they might be used in classrooms to help readers incurring difficulties and with severe disabilities.

Fox, B. J. 1997. Connecting school and home literacy experiences through cross-age reading. *The Reading Teacher* 50(5): 396–403. Describes cross-age tutoring program called "Storymates," which connects school and home literacy programs for nine-, ten-, and eleven-year-olds.

Gaskins, I. W. 1998. There's more to teaching at-risk and delayed readers than good reading instruction. *The Reading Teacher* 51(7): 534–547. Provides a description of the lessons learned at the Benchmark School for children with reading difficulties.

Hiebert, E. H., and B. M. Taylor. 2000. Beginning reading instruction: Research on early interventions. In M. L. Kamil, P. B. Mosenthal, P. D. Pearson, and R. Barr (Eds.), *Handbook of reading research,* Vol. III. Mahwah, NJ: Erlbaum. Review of various approaches to beginning reading, including some of the programs intended to meet the needs of students at risk. Delineates various generalizations of effective programs.

Juel, C. 1996. What makes tutoring effective? *Reading Research Quarterly* 31(3): 268–289. Describes a study of tutoring in an attempt to discuss what makes tutoring effective.

Klenk, L., and M. W. Kibby. 2000. Re-mediating reading difficulties: Appraising the past, reconciling the present, constructing the future. In M. L. Kamil, P. B. Mosenthal, P. D. Pearson, & R. Barr (Eds.), *Handbook of Reading Research,* Vol. III. Mahwah, NJ: Erlbaum. Critiques notions of remediation and the constructs underlying them.

National Reading Panel. 2000. *Teaching children to read: An evidence-based assessment of the scientific research literature on reading and its implications for reading instruction* (Report of the Subgroups). Washington, DC: U.S. Department of Health and Human Services, Public Health Service, National Institutes of Health, and the National Institute of Child Health and Human Development. Reports the purposes, methods, and findings of the synthesis in several areas including discussions of what may meet the need of students incurring difficulty.

No Child Left Behind Act of 2001, Pub. L. No. 107-110, 115 Stat. 1425. (2002).

Pikulski, J. J. 1994. Preventing reading failure: A review of five effective programs. *The Reading Teacher* 48(1): 30–39. Reviews critical features of five successful reading programs for at-risk first-graders.

Snow, C. E., M. S. Burns, and P. Griffin. 1998. *Preventing reading difficulties in young children: A report of the National Research Council.* Washington, DC: National Academy Press. Reports the views of a panel of researchers and educators on what may contribute to effective reading instruction

Taylor, B. M., B. E. Hanson, K. Justice-Swanson, and S. M. Watts. 1997. Helping struggling readers: Linking small-group intervention with cross-age tutoring. *The Reading Teacher* 51(3): 196–209. Describes a study of a reading intervention program for older students in need of support.

Taylor, D. 1998. *Beginning to read and the spin doctors of science. The political campaign to change America's mind about how children learn to read.* Urbana, IL: National Council of Teachers of English. Critiques the discussion of federal pronouncements regarding reading research findings.

Wasik, B. A. 1998. Using volunteers as reading tutors: Guidelines for successful practices. *The Reading Teacher* 51(7): 562–570. Discusses components that seem essential for the success of volunteer tutoring programs.

Reading Recovery

Purpose

The major goals of Reading Recovery are to reduce reading failure through early intervention and to help students develop a "self-improving system" for continued growth in reading.

Rationale

The Reading Recovery program is a one-to-one intervention program for the poorest readers in first-grade classrooms (i.e., the lowest 20 percent). These students, deemed at risk, are placed in a program that provides 30 minutes daily (in addition to their regular classroom teaching) with a trained Reading Recovery teacher who uses a specific lesson framework. The students continue receiving this instruction until they are brought up to the average of their class and have developed the necessary self-improvement strategies to maintain that level. The power of Reading Recovery is purported to be "in the framework of the lesson itself and in the development of teacher knowledge and problem-solving ability" (Pinnell, DeFord, and Lyons, 1988, 2).

A number of principles guide the Reading Recovery teachers. They are:

1. Reading is a strategic process that takes place in the reader's mind. A goal of Reading Recovery is to help readers develop a meaning orientation to print that includes the ability to enlist effective strategies in a flexible and integrated way.

2. Reading and writing work together to enhance basic understandings of both processes. Throughout the Reading Recovery program, reading and writing are used flexibly to help children make connections between the two.

3. Children learn to read by reading. A basic tenet of Reading Recovery is the notion that for children to make accelerated growth they must actively engage in reading. As Pinnell, DeFord, and Lyons (1988) state:

> Almost every minute during the lesson, children actively engage in reading or writing messages and stories. Familiar material helps children build fluency and experience success; new materials challenge children to do independent problem solving. (1988, 13)

4. Children need to develop fruitful concepts of what reading is. Reading Recovery assumes that children need to develop both a reader-based view and a text-based view of meaning making. They need experiences that focus on integrating reader-based and text-based processes.

5. It is expedient and productive to help children early. Reading Recovery claims that difficulties in learning to read emerge early and should be dealt with as soon as possible.

6. Children who have difficulty can and do make accelerated progress. A goal of Reading Recovery is to engage in fast pacing as the student and teacher work together en route to accelerating growth and student development of independent learning strategies.

The Reading Recovery approach is an early intervention program designed for at-risk first graders having difficulty learning to read. Daily individual lessons, explicit teaching for strategies, and following the child rather than a prescribed curriculum are three features that distinguish this program.

Clay's observational findings on low and high progress readers are the cornerstone of the program. She differentiates these types of readers by saying,

> . . . low progress readers tend to operate on a narrow range of strategies. They rely on what can be invented from memory for the text by paying little or no attention at all to visual details. . . .Whereas high progress readers operate on print in an integrated way in search for meaning, which results in high accuracy and high self-correction rates. . . .The ability to shift to higher and lower strategies, also known as "toing and froing," enables the high progress readers to monitor their reading, integrate knowledge about directional rules of printed language, space formats, and punctuation cues. This increases the likelihood for reading to become automatic. (Clay, 1988, 7)

Reading Recovery was originated by M. Clay in New Zealand. According to Clay, the program emerged in response to a request by readers to initiate a research and development effort aimed at helping young children with reading difficulties. As a result, Clay "spent two years observing children and teachers in tutoring situations and then a year in field trials of the procedures that we considered had worked well" (Clay, 1982a, 173). In particular, Clay's research team constructed a framework for teachers working one-to-one with at-risk students. In 1979, Reading Recovery became a nationwide program in New Zealand; in 1984 it was introduced in the United States and Australia.

Intended Audience

Reading Recovery is a program for at-risk students who are in the first grade.

Description of the Procedures

For a fuller description of Reading Recovery, books and articles on the reference list should be consulted. What follows is only a partial description of the program. The description includes an overview of the following: (1) diagnostic procedures and roaming around the known, (2) lesson framework, (3) exiting principles, (4) teacher training procedure.

Diagnostic Procedures and Roaming around the Known. Several principles undergird Reading Recovery diagnostic practices. First, Reading Recovery relies on a battery of diagnostic procedures for input on a student's reading behavior. As Clay emphasized, "Teachers are advised to apply as many as possible to the children. . . . Reducing the scope of our observations increases the risk that we will make erroneous interpretations" (Clay, 1979b, 10). Second, the use of an initial screening procedure should not diminish the fact that Reading Recovery is involved in ongoing diagnosis of students throughout their involvement in the program as well as in conjunction with their transition back to the classroom. Third, the diagnostic procedures are not intended to displace teacher observation. Reading Recovery teachers are expected to notice significant behaviors apart from what is tested.

The initial screening done of students in American schools involves using a combination of the classroom teacher's ranking, kindergarten teacher's opinion (if available), scores and observed responses on the six tasks of the Observation Survey, and a qualitative synthesis of these responses written on the Observation Summary. The six tasks include:

1. Letter identification (upper and lowercase letters)
2. Word test (high frequency words)
3. Concepts about print (Clays's assessment of child's knowledge of print and book handling)
4. Writing vocabulary (exhaustive list of child's known words, beginning with own name, ability to write high frequency words, writing samples from class)
5. Hearing and recording sounds in words (Dictation test) (assessing knowledge of 37 phonemes presented in a sentence)
6. Text reading (running record for purposes of determining the nature of the reader's errors and highest level at which 90 percent accuracy is attained)

The summary of the Observation Survey "brings together what the teacher has observed. She describes what the child can do, what is partially known at the boundaries of his knowledge as it were" (Clay, 1993a, 71). The goal of this initial assessment is threefold: to justify special help or involvement in the Reading Recovery program; to acquire some baseline data for use in documenting growth; and to acquire a sense of where and how to start.

"Roaming around the known" represents the student's introduction to the program. "The most important reason for roaming is that it requires the teacher to stop teaching from her preconceived ideas. She has to work from the child's responses. This will be her focus throughout the programme" (Clay, 1993b, 13). These ten days of exploration are intended to serve a variety of purposes:

- Provides the teacher and child the opportunity to develop a relationship of trust
- Enables the teacher to see what the child initiates as well as what the child can and cannot do outside the constraints of the testing situation and away from the classroom
- Provides opportunities for systematic observation
- Gives the child a feeling he is "really reading and writing"
- Provides a foundation for further learning on which the teacher can build the individualized program (Clay, 1993b, 13)

Lesson Framework. A Reading Recovery lesson has seven components that emphasize reading, writing, problem-solving strategies, and much student-teacher interaction. Within this model, students are taught to be strategic learners, which leads to the development of a "self-extending system." Within this framework, the teacher becomes the focal point rather than the curriculum. The teacher is perceived as the instructional decision maker and the researcher. She constantly observes the child's behavior, quickly reflecting on why the child reacted as she or he did, and responds with appropriate praise or prompts to extend this child's learning.

The components of the daily 30-minute lesson follow:

1. Familiar rereading of two or more books

Students self-select at least 2 books that are known stories to read aloud. "A familiar book is not a memorized book," says Clay. This rereading encourages "confidence and fluency, and provides practice in orchestrating reading behaviors while also allowing the reader to discover new things about print" (Clay, 1993b, 38). During the reading of these books the focus is on the meaning of the text and the student's use of strategies as he or she reads fluently. With this in mind, the teacher talks to the child about the story rather than correcting him/her.

The teacher's goal is to find the hardest book (natural language rather than controlled vocabulary) that the child can handle with 90 percent accuracy. The intent is to find books that are easy enough for the child to use effective strategies, and difficult enough for independent problem solving.

2. Running Record on the previous day's new story

This book reading enables the teacher to become an observer of the child reading the story and engaging with the text using problem-solving strategies, and is also one way to attain an ongoing record of the child's progress—especially strategy development. The teacher records student's reading behaviors and will select one or two to use as teaching points. (For a discussion of the Running Record, see Unit 14.)

3. Letter identification and/or word making and breaking

This component provides opportunities for students who know few letters and words to learn how to look at print as a cuing source when reading and writing. "For consistency, always do a little letter work after taking the Running Record in the lesson. When most of the letters are known, shift to some speedy work on making and breaking words (using magnetic letters) and giving attention to generating new words from known words" (Clay, 1993b, 25).

4. Writing a story and hearing sounds in words

The child-generated written story helps the child "think about the order of sounds in spoken words and to help analyze a new word he wants to write into its sequence of sounds" (Clay, 1979a, 1988, 64). This child is asked to repeat the story so that this model can be used as a framework on which to monitor his own writing (Clay, 1993b).

When the child comes to a problem word, the sounds (at least the initial sound) are predicted/isolated. Sometimes phonic segmentation is used, based upon Elkonin (1975). These procedures break the sounds represented by the letters into boxes, e.g.,

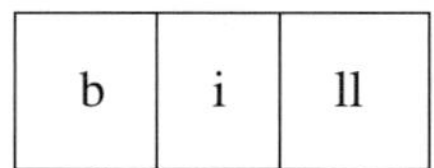

Clay has stressed that it is important that children become aware of sound sequences in words.

As she stated:

> We have worked with some children who find it extraordinarily difficult to hear the sounds that go to make up words. For example, some children consistently focus on the final sounds of a word, and for them, this completely masks the initial sounds.
>
> The teacher has to work with such children individually and act as an analyzer of words into sounds. This is analogous to acting as his scribe at first when he cannot write. The teacher articulates the words very slowly and gradually develops the same skill in her pupil (Clay, 1979b, 5).

As Clay suggests, an essential feature of Reading Recovery is helping students to segment words. Initially, this is pursued with counters, not letters. This approach ensures that children learn that there may be more than one letter for every sound. When the child has a good grasp of segments, he or she is then moved into associating the letters with the segments. As with the early segmentation activities (for counting syllables and so on), Elkonin boxes are used. As the students develop competence, the emphasis on sound segmentation is more incidental and may not entail using the boxes.

5. Cut up story

Just as children are encouraged to segment words into sounds, so, too, are they involved in cutting up stories into a descending order of language units (phrases, words, structural segments, clusters of letters, single letters). . . . The cut-up sentence provides practice with "assembling sentences, one-to-one correspondence of words spoken and written, directional, checking, and monitoring behaviors, breaking oral language into segments, and word study (from occasionally cut up words)" (Clay, 1993b, 35).

A cutting up activity, for example, might begin by having the child choose a portion of the story that was liked. The teacher and/or child would write that portion of the story twice and the child, with or without the teacher's help, would read the text pointing to each word. The teacher would then cut up the text, starting with the first word, emphasizing its word components. The child would then be expected to reassemble the text, initially with the story model present and later without it. Depending upon the child's familiarity with the names of letters, plastic letters on a magnetic board might also be used to assemble known words.

It should be noted that the procedures for helping students link sounds to letters, acquiring word analysis procedures, developing fluency, and so on, extend beyond these activities. Clay's *Reading Recovery: A Guidebook for Teachers in Training* (1993b) should be consulted for details.

6. New book introduction

Book selections are seen as vital to the success of the lesson. The book selected must be "within the child's control, uses words and letters he knows or can get to using his present strategies, and should be a minimum of new things to learn if the teaching goal is the integration of skills" (Clay, 1979a, 1988, 68).

During the new-book orientation, Clay (1993b) contends that "the child must know what the story is about before he reads it" (p. 37). In order to do this, the teacher makes the child familiar with the story, by discussing pictures, new words, and story language. The goal is to ensure that the child has the ideas and language he/she needs to read the story in his or her head.

7. New book attempted

This component enables the student to read the book with help. The overall aim is to provide opportunities for students to orchestrate and monitor their use of strategies and for teachers to confirm and reinforce these behaviors. To this end, Clay has developed quite elaborate procedures to ensure that teachers know how to help students develop ways of effectively initiating appropriate reading behaviors and monitor their use. The second reading of this book is to get fluency. On subsequent days, the book is reread and placed in a box with other books the child has read. As Clay (1979b) has suggested, "A child on the way to independence needs as many books as possible at his level" (p. 54).

The basic framework of the Reading Recovery lesson should be viewed as a partial guide. Within this framework, every child's program will differ as he or she reads and writes different materials and as various skills and strategies are developed. The teachers who work in Reading Recovery undergo intensive training in the use of various procedures to help them plan each child's program and develop each one's reading abilities. For example, each teacher receives extensive training in an elaborate array of teaching strategies intended to help students acquire and be able to orchestrate a repertoire of strategies, including directional movement, self-monitoring, cross-checking, use of multiple cue sources, and self-correction. In other words, teachers are trained to have enormous skills at helping students based on a repertoire of teaching strategies they themselves are expected to acquire and be able to enlist thoughtfully with different students. For example, the teacher is encouraged to enlist a variety of probes and encouragements to have the child think aloud as he or she enlists meaning cues, visual cues, structure cues, sound cues (both together and separately), cross-checking to ensure accuracy. Comments such as: Does it make sense? Does that look right? What would you expect to see? You made a mistake; can you find it? How did you know? Will you check to see if what you read looks right? and so on, pervade the teacher's responses to the child as the teacher aims to help students develop the self-improving strategies necessary to be independent.

Clay has pointed out that the goal is to develop readers who improve whenever they read. They have strategies by which to monitor, search for cues, discover new things for themselves, cross-check cues, confirm by repeating or reviewing, self-correct, and solve new problems as they develop fluency with longer and less predictable texts that have less familiar language.

Exiting Principles. There is no set time for exiting the program. The program continues for the child until he or she is reading at about the average level for his/her school or class and when the child has acquired the strategies needed to continue without extra help. Typically, the program lasts 12 to 16 weeks. As Clay states:

> There is no fixed set of strategies nor any required levels of text nor any test score that must be attained to warrant discontinuing. It is essential that the child has a system of strategies which work in such a way that a child learns from his own attempts to read. (1979a, 1988, 87).

Some of the things a child ready for discontinuing will be able to do will include (Clay, 1993b, 58–59):

- Directional movement
- One-to-one matching
- Self-monitor reading
- Cross-checking
- Use of multiple cue sources
- Self-correction

It should be noted that although Reading Recovery lessons may cease, extensive follow-up is carried out to ensure that students receive continued support in the classroom context.

Teacher Training Procedure. It is claimed that the key to successfully implementing Reading Recovery does not lie with a set of procedures but in the staff development that enables teachers to work with students insightfully and adeptly. Reading Recovery teachers are certified teachers who volunteer for the program, have had at least three years' experience in teaching young children, possess proven ability to establish rapport with children, and undergo one year of intensive Reading Recovery training, as well as annual follow-ups. The demanding one-year program involves a full-time commitment to learning Reading Recovery procedures through working with four students (individually), demonstrations, seminars, analyses of lessons, close monitoring of their own teaching, observing and interpreting reading behaviors, and so on. After the initial training year, they are expected to continue to pursue active contact with Reading Recovery procedures as they meet with fellow Reading Recovery teachers, view demonstration lessons, and refine organization skills.

When implementing Reading Recovery instruction in a school, several organizational models are suggested. (Teachers work with at least four children each day for half a day.) Sometimes a Reading Recovery teacher will work with a regular class for half the day and then work with four children for the other half. Other models involve having a separate Reading Recovery teacher who works with the teacher.

Apart from training teachers, an integral feature of Reading Recovery is the preparation of Reading Recovery teacher leaders. These teacher leaders undergo a very rigorous training that goes beyond the regular teacher training to learning how to assume a leadership role. In many ways the experience is akin to an internship program. The teacher leaders work with other teacher leaders as they work with children and with Reading Recovery teachers also working with children. At the same time, they learn how to initiate, operate, and direct the preparation of Reading Recovery teachers.

To be a Reading Recovery teacher requires training by authorized teacher leaders who themselves have been trained to serve in those roles. It should be emphasized that the aforementioned description provides some information about Reading Recovery, but should not be viewed as comprehensive or as a substitute for the necessary training.

Cautions and Comments

Reading Recovery has been acclaimed as one of the most successful early innovative programs for at-risk students. Whereas attempts to pull out at-risk students have a long history of failure—especially when the students return to the regular classroom—Reading Recovery boasts a very high success rate.

If you examine the references below, you will discover that Reading Recovery has been subjected to considerable scrutiny. Some educators would argue that Reading Recovery may be identifying students too early. For example, they would suggest that the first month of the first grade may be a time of massive adjustment for the child and might not indicate how well the child might perform thereafter. Educators, sensitive to the differences in the social situation of Reading Recovery and the regular classroom, may question the extent to which discontinued students have acquired the self-improving social skills necessary to succeed in the regular classroom. The development of a classroom-based Reading Recovery model such as the Ohio Early Literacy Learning Initiative addresses some of these concerns. (For some background on this model see Guided Reading in Unit 1.) Advocates of a more Whole-Language orientation might argue that the approach has a tendency to place more stress on mediating skills such as letter-sound correspondence, sound blending, accurate word recognition, and so on, than might be justified. Educators interested in reading comprehension might consider the approach more text-based than reader-based. For example, strategies such as brainstorming, visualizing, self-questioning, engagement, and so on, appear to receive only indirect emphasis. Teacher educators might argue that the teacher training procedures appear somewhat formulaic as teachers are expected to commit themselves to the principles and practices advocated by Clay (1979a, 1988). Still others argue about the costs associated with such a program. However, the differences entailed in costs over time are less problematic when the costs associated with alternatives are fully considered.

Apart from these concerns, few educators can argue that Reading Recovery has not amassed a distinguished record of success and a rather unique commitment to accountability in terms of expectations for students, training teachers, training teacher leaders, and, above all, research that scrutinizes these enterprises and their impact. Although Reading Recovery has been closely scrutinized and critiqued, it is still considered to be highly effective and seems to be the standard by which other programs are judged and to which they strive. Reading Recovery remains a program committed to the development of highly qualified professionals and ongoing reflection and research of their initiatives. Although the National Reading Panel report does occasionally focus on some of the research on Reading Recovery and adaptations, the report does not offer a comprehensive review of research on Reading Recovery or a critique of the various elements that inform its program. Conversely, Reading Recovery has delineated how Reading Recovery incorporates elements suggested as key by the National Reading Panel—for example, phonemic awareness, systematic phonics, fluency, and balanced reading (Pinell, 2000). Furthermore, Reading Recovery has delved into various research findings en route to arguing that the program is more effective than other programs. Reading Recovery offers support materials, including research discussion and exploration of related issues on its websites. Guided Reading (see Unit 1) explores some of the elements of Reading Recovery applied at a classroom level.

REFERENCES

Allington, R. 1992. How to get information on several proven programs for accelerating the progress of low-achieving children. *The Reading Teacher* 46: 246–248. An overview of three programming efforts, extended to at-risk students, to help accelerate learning.

Barnes, B. L. 1997. But teacher you went right on: A perspective on Reading Recovery. *The Reading Teacher* 50(4): 284–292. Barnes critiques her training as a Reading Recovery teacher and discusses her concerns with the approach used.

Begoray, D. L. 2001. The Literacy Groups Project: Investigating the use of Reading Recovery techniques with small groups of grade 2 students. *The Alberta Journal of Educational Research* 47(2): 141–155. Explores classroom uses of some of the techniques advocated by Reading Recovery advocates.

Browne, A., M. Fitts, B. McLaughlin, M. J. McNamara, and J. Williams. 1997. Teaching and learning in Reading Recovery: Response to "But teacher you went right on." *The Reading Teacher* 50(4): 294–300. Five Reading Recovery teachers respond to Barnes' article in conjunction with discussing issues of time, writing, discipline, training, record keeping, etc.

Center, Y., K. Wheldall, L. Freeman, L. Outhred, and M. McNaught, 1995. An evaluation of Reading Recovery. *Reading Research Quarterly* 30(2): 240–263. Explores the effectiveness of Reading Recovery in ten primary schools in New South Wales, Australia.

Clay, M. M. 1975. *What did I write?* Portsmouth, NH: Heinemann. Illustrates authentic writing samples of emergent writers as they develop written language.

———. 1979a, 1988. *The early detection of reading difficulties.* Auckland, New Zealand: Heinemann. Represents the primary source for information on Reading Recovery, including diagnostic and instructional procedures.

———. 1979b. *Reading: The patterning of complex behavior.* Auckland, New Zealand: Heinemann. Presents a detailed account of Clay's views on reading and reading instruction.

———. 1982a. *Observing young readers: Selected papers.* Portsmouth, NH: Heinemann. A compilation of research reports that depict early learners' growth and progress over time.

———. 1982b. Reading Recovery: A follow-up study. In M. M. Clay (Ed.), *Observing young readers: Selected papers.* Exeter, NH: Heinemann. Reports the findings of a follow-up study along with implications.

———. 1989. Concepts about Print in English and other languages. *The Reading Teacher* 42: 268–276. Describes the purpose for this observational instrument and the modifications made to be statistically effective with emergent learners of other languages.

———. 1991. *Becoming literate: The construction of inner control.* Portmouth, NH: Heinemann. Describes the patterns of change that emergent learners experience when engaged in authentic literacy activities.

———. 1991. Developmental learning puzzles me. *Australian Journal of Reading* 14: 263–275. Provides a discussion on the definition of developmental learning.

———. 1991. Why is an in-service programme for Reading Recovery teachers necessary? *Reading Horizons* 31: 355–372. This article provides a rationale for utilizing an intensive in-service model for training teachers, teacher leaders, and teacher leader trainers.

———. 1993a. *An observation survey of early literacy achievement.* Portsmouth, NH: Heinemann. This text was written for teachers and researchers who work with young readers and writers and describes the procedures to follow when administering and scoring the six assessment tasks in the Observation Survey and when utilizing a Running Record.

———. 1993b. *Reading Recovery: A guidebook for teachers in training.* Portsmouth, NH: Heinemann. This text is used by teachers in training. It describes the components and procedures of a Recovery lesson.

———. 1998. *Different paths to different outcomes.* York, Maine: Stenhouse Publishers. A collection of several key articles by Marie Clay that focus on what children know and how they develop.

DeFord, D. E., C. A. Lyons, and G. S. Pinnell. 1991. *Bridges to literacy learning from Reading Recovery.* Discusses how teachers and students can work within a collaborative setting while focusing on literacy learning.

DeFord, D. E., G. S. Pinnell, C. A. Lyons, and P. Young. 1987. *Report of the follow-up studies—Columbus, Ohio—Reading Recovery project 1985–1986, 1986–1987.* (Technical Report). Columbus: Ohio State University. One of several reports on the impact of Reading Recovery on at-risk students.

———. 1987. *Report of the follow-up study, Reading Recovery project, Vol. IX.* Columbus: Ohio State University. One of several reports on the impact of Reading Recovery on at-risk students.

Dudley-Marling, C., and S. Murphy, 1997. A political critique of remedial reading programs: The example of Reading Recovery. *The Reading Teacher* 50(6): 460–468. Pursues a critique of Reading Recovery with suggestions for change.

Elbaum, B., M. T. Vaughan, M. T. Hughes, and Moody 2000. How effective are one-to-one tutoring programs for elementary students at risk for reading failure? A meta-analysis of the intervention research. *Journal of Educational Psychology* 92(4): 605–619. Reviews findings of one-to-one tutoring including Reading Recovery.

Elkonin, D. B. 1975. USSR. In J. Downing (Ed.), *Comparative reading: Cross-national studies of behavior and processes in reading and writing.* New York: Macmillan. Provides a description of the phonic segmentation that served as a basis for Clay's phonic practices.

Fountas, I. C., and G. S. Pinnell. 1999. *Matching books to readers: Using leveled book n guided readings, K–3.* Portsmouth, NH: Heinemann. Discusses a variety of reading systems and provides graded book lists as a support for instruction.

Geeke, P. 1988. *Evaluation report on the Reading Recovery field trial in Central Victoria, 1984.* Australia: Centre for Studies in Literacy, University of Wollongong. Represents a critical evaluation of Reading Recovery in Australia.

Hicks, C. P., and S. K. Villaume. 2000–2001. Finding our own way: Critical reflections on the literacy development of two Reading Recovery children. *The Reading Teacher* 54: 398–412. Explores firsthand the use of Reading Recovery with students via the reflections of teachers.

Hiebert, E. H., and B. M. Taylor. 2000. Beginning reading instruction: Research on early interventions. In M. L. Kamil, P. B. Mosenthal, P. D. Pearson, and R. Barr (Eds.), *Handbook of reading research,* Vol. III. Mahwah, NJ: Erlbaum. Review of various approaches to beginning reading including some of the programs intended to meet the needs of students at risk. Delineates various generalizations of effective programs.

Holland, K. 1987. *The impact of Reading Recovery program on parents and home literacy contexts.* Unpublished doctoral diss., Ohio State University, Columbus. Examines the effects of Reading Recovery on home literacy and parents.

Huck, D., and G. Pinnell. 1985. *The Reading Recovery project in Columbus, Ohio: Pilot year 1984–1985* (Technical Report). Columbus: Ohio State University. Describes the Reading Recovery project during its initiation in Columbus, Ohio.

Jones, N. K. 1991. Helping to learn: Components and principles of Reading Recovery training. *Reading Horizons* 31: 422–438. Provides an in-depth overview of the components within the Reading Recovery teacher training program.

Klein, A. F., P. R. Kelly, and G. Pinnell. 1997. Teaching from theory: Decision making in Reading Recovery. In S. A. Stahl and D. A. Hayes (Eds.), *Instructional models in reading.* Mahwah, NJ: Erlbaum, 161–179. Explores some of the tenets and research informing Reading Recovery and illustrates with transcripts the nature of teacher decision making.

Klenk, L., and M. W. Kibby. 2000. Re-mediating reading difficulties: Appraising the past, reconciling the present, constructing the future. In M. L. Kamil, P. B. Mosenthal, P. D. Pearson, and R. Barr (Eds.), *Handbook of reading research,* Vol. III. Mahwah, NJ: Erlbaum. Critiques notions of remediation and the constructs underlying them.

Krueger, E., and N. Townshend, 1997. Reading clubs boost second language first graders' reading achievement. *The Reading Teacher* 51(2): 122–127. Reading clubs are an adaptation of the Reading Recovery program developed to meet the needs of "at risk" second graders.

Letters to the Editor. 1998. *The Reading Teacher* 51(8): 632–636. Various letters to the editor regarding Reading Recovery.

Lyons, C. A., G. S. Pinnell, A. McCarrier, P. Young, and D. DeFord. 1988. *The Ohio Reading Recovery project: Volume X and State of Ohio Year 1987–1988.* Columbus: Ohio State University. One of several reports on the impact of Reading Recovery.

Lyons, C. A., G. Pinnell, K. Short, and P. Young. 1986. *The Ohio Reading Recovery project: Volume IV pilot year. 1985–1986.* (Technical Report). Columbus: Ohio State University. One of several reports of the impact of Reading Recovery.

Lyons, C., G. Pinnell, P. Young, and D. E. DeFord. 1987. *Report of the Ohio Reading Recovery project, State of Ohio, Year One 1986–1987,* Vol. VIII (Technical Report). Columbus: Ohio State University. One of several reports on the impact of Reading Recovery.

Mackenzie, K. K. 2001. Using literacy booster groups to maintain and extend Reading Recovery success in the primary grades. *The Reading Teacher* 55(3): 222–234. Explores Reading Recovery and ways to engage in a more systemic fashion within the primary grades.

Peterson, B. 1987. *The characteristics of text which support beginning readers.* Unpublished doctoral diss., Ohio State University, Columbus. Explores the features of text that work best with young students.

Pinnell, G. S. 1986. Helping teachers help children at risk: Insights from the Reading Recovery program. *Peabody Journal* 62: 70–85. Explores issues pertaining to helping teachers help children who are at risk.

———. 1987. Helping teachers see how readers read: Staff development through observation. *Theory Into Practice* 26: 51–58. Discusses staff development issues as they pertain to Reading Recovery.

———. 2000. Reading Recovery: An analysis of research-based reading intervention. Columbus, OH: Reading Recovery Council of North America. Suggests ten principles for what accounts for effective reading instruction.

Pinnell, G. S., D. E. DeFord, and C. A. Lyons. 1988. *Reading Recovery: Early intervention for at risk first graders.* Arlington, VA: Educational Research Service. Presents an overview of Reading Recovery, including results of studies of its effects.

Pinnell, G. S., D. E. DeFord, C. A. Lyons, and A. S. Bryk. 1995. Response to Rasinski. *Reading Research Quarterly* 30(2): 272–275. Response to Rasinski's critique of Reading Recovery.

Pinnell, G. S., M. D. Fried, and R. M. Estice. 1990. Reading Recovery: Learning how to make a difference. *The Reading Teacher* 43: 282–295. Provides an in-depth discussion on Reading Recovery lessons and procedures, the teacher training model, and research findings within the USA.

Pinnell, G. S., C. A. Lyons, D. E. DeFord, A. S. Bryk, and M. Seltzer. 1994. Comparing instructional models for literacy education of high-risk first graders. *Reading Research Quarterly* 29(1): 9–39. Compares Reading Recovery to three other instructional models across ten school districts.

Pinnell, G. S., K. Short, C. A. Lyons, and P. Young. 1986a. *The Reading Recovery project in Columbus, Ohio: Volume II. Year One 1985–1986.* (Technical Report). Columbus: Ohio State University. One of several reports on the impact of Reading Recovery.

———. 1986b. *The Reading Recovery project in Columbus, Ohio: Volume III. Year One 1985–1986* (Technical Report). Columbus: Ohio State University. One of several reports on the impact of Reading Recovery.

Purves, A. C., L. Papa, and S. Jordan (Eds.). 1994. *Encyclopedia of English studies and language arts.* New York: National Council of Teachers of English. An excellent resource that contains an extensive collection of more than 800 annotated entries/topics in English studies and language arts.

Rasinski, T. V. 1995. Commentary on the effects of Reading Recovery: A response to Pinnell, Lyons, DeFord, Bryk, and Seltzer. *Reading Research Quarterly* 30(2): 264–270. A commentary on the article by Pinnell et al.

Rasinski, T. V. 1995. Reply to Pinnell, DeFord, Lyons, and Bryk. *Reading Research Quarterly* 30(2): 276–277. As the title implies, Rasinski responds to the earlier response to his initial critique.

Roehrig, A. D., M. Pressley, and M. Sloup. 2001. Reading strategy instruction in regular primary-level classrooms by teachers trained in Reading Recovery. *Reading & Writing Quarterly* 17: 323–348. Explores strategy development with Reading Recovery.

Schwartz, R. M. 1997. Self-monitoring in beginning reading. *The Reading Teacher* 51(1): 40–48. Discusses self-monitoring and searching behaviors in conjunction with Reading Recovery.

———. 2001. The relationship of research findings and recommendations: A response to Elbaum et al. 2000 meta-analysis of one-to-one tutoring interventions. Available at www.readingrecovery.org/sectiopns/home/elbaum.asp. Discusses the findings of Elbaum's meta-analysis and corrects the conclusions by highlighting the advantage that Reading Recovery delivered by professionals versus tutoring delivered by nonprofessionals.

Shanahan, T., and R. Barr. 1995. Reading Recovery: An independent evaluation of the effects of an early instructional intervention for at-risk learners. *Reading Research Quarterly* 30(4): 958–996. Critically explores the learning gains of Reading Recovery against the costs.

Smith-Burke, M. T. 2001. Reading Recovery: A systemic approach to early intervention. In L. M. Morrow and D. G. Woo (Eds.), *Tutoring programs for struggling readers: The America Reads Challenge.* NY: Guilford Press, 216–236. Discussion of Reading Recovery in one volume is based on original papers presented by the authors at the symposium on Tutoring Programs for Struggling Readers at the Rutgers Graduate School of Education.

Spiegel, D. L. 1995. A comparison of traditional remedial programs and Reading Recovery: Guidelines for success for all programs. *The Reading Teacher* 49(2): 86–96. Compares traditional programs associated with Chapter 1 against Reading Recovery principles.

Success for All

Purpose

Success for All (Slavin, Madden, Karweit, Livermon, and Dolan, 1990) is a schoolwide tutoring program that emphasizes prevention and early, intensive intervention. It is designed for schools that have large disadvantaged populations, and its intention is to make sure that all children are successful in basic skills, especially reading, the first time they are taught. Success for All uses certified teachers acting as one-on-one tutors for students who are experiencing difficulty in reading in grades one to three.

Rationale

Wasik and Slavin (1993) suggest that four theoretical tenets provide the background for Success for All. First, children do not learn to read through isolated exercises about print; reading and learning to read should be done through interaction with meaningful text. Second, as a strategy for cracking the code, phonics should be taught systematically. Although children engage in reading meaningful and interesting text, the stories should use a vocabulary that is phonetically controlled. Third, emphasis should be placed on meaning as children are taught to see the relationship between the words they read and the understanding that they gain from them. Merely recognizing the words is not enough. Finally, children should be directly taught strategies that will make them successful readers. Those children with problems in reading do not possess the effective metacognitive strategies that will help them read. Children should be taught the when, how, and why of using reading strategies.

Therefore, the following instructional components of reading are emphasized in practice: decoding, prior knowledge, reading strategies, inference making, metacognition and error detection, and error correction. Success for All emphasizes that reading occurs in the reader's mind, it is a strategic process, and direct teaching of strategies is crucial.

Intended Audience

Success for All is a preventive tutoring program in reading intended for low-achieving children in the early grades.

Description of the Procedures

Success for All will be described using its seven programmatic components:

1. Reading tutors
2. The program
3. Assessments at eight weeks
4. Preschool and kindergarten
5. Family support team
6. Program facilitator
7. Teachers and teacher training

1. Reading Tutors. A major component of Success for All is the reading tutors, certified teachers with experience in teaching primary reading, Chapter I, and/or special education. They tutor in one-on-one situations with children who are not successful in their reading groups. Twenty-minute sessions drawn from an hour-long social studies period are used to support what is being taught in the regular reading groups. However, the tutors also identify learning problems and seek to use different strategies to make reading progress.

During daily reading/language arts periods, tutors reduce class size to 15 to 20 by serving as additional reading teachers. To coordinate the instructional approaches with individual children, teachers and tutors record children's specific problems and needs on communication forms and meet at regular intervals.

Tutors also give informal reading inventories to each child. From the information gained, decisions are made about reading-group placements and the need for tutoring. Additional assessments, which include teacher judgment and more formal assessments, are given at eight-week intervals and are used to make revised decisions about group placement and tutoring. Priority for tutoring is given to first graders because of the major function of Success for All, to help all readers become successful from the beginning and avoid becoming remedial readers.

2. The Program. During most of the day, students are assigned to age-grouped, heterogeneous classes of 25, but during the 90-minute reading period the students are regrouped by reading ability into homogeneous classes of 15 to 20 students. For example, the one to two reading class might contain students from grades one to three, as they are all reading at that level. Regrouping allows the teacher/tutor to teach the whole class simultaneously, without the need to put them into smaller groups; this organization becomes more efficient as it reduces the time spent in seat work and increases time for direct instruction. In turn, this eliminates the need for workbooks and other follow-up activities that would be found in normal, multigrouped classrooms.

At all levels teachers begin the reading class by reading children's literature to the students and discussing it to improve their comprehension, oral vocabulary, and story structure knowledge. In grades kindergarten to one, Success for All emphasizes the development of basic language skills through the use of storytelling, retelling, and dramatizing with literature. Big books, language development kits, and oral/written composing activities serve to develop children's print concepts, knowledge of story structure, and receptive/expressive language.

In the second semester of kindergarten beginning reading is introduced. Letters and sounds are introduced through oral language activities and moved to written symbols. Learned letter sounds are reinforced by reading stories using those same sounds. The reading program uses phonetically regular but meaningful minibooks and emphasizes the following: repeated oral reading to partners and the teacher, instruction in story structure and comprehension skills, and integrated reading and writing lessons.

When kindergartners reach the primer reading level, they are introduced to reading and composition activities based on cooperative learning using the school's basal series. These activities emphasize prediction, story structure, story-related writing and summarization, vocabulary, and decoding practice. Working in teams the students share their writing, engage in structured discussions and partner reading, and work on their vocabulary from an understanding of the story. In addition to basal instruction, teachers provide teams direct instruction in comprehension skills. Teachers are also provided classroom libraries of trade books at students' reading levels, and students are asked to read at home for 20 minutes each night. These independent readings are shared in class through presentations, summaries, and puppet shows twice weekly.

In the second year of Success for All, programs for writing/language arts based on cooperative learning are introduced. These programs use a structured writing process approach and focus on teaching students to respond to and facilitate each other's writing.

3. Assessments at Eight Weeks. Each eight weeks teachers assess the progress of each student. These results determine the need to receive tutoring, change group assignment, modify instruction, and identify other forms of assistance such as vision screening or family intervention.

4. Preschool and Kindergarten. Success for All schools attempt to provide a half-day preschool and/or a full-day kindergarten for eligible children. These programs focus on giving students developmentally appropriate learning experiences and emphasize language development and use. Additionally, nonacademic art, music, and movement activities are provided in a series of thematic units.

5. Family Support Team. Parents are considered to be essential to the success of the program. At each school site a support team works to make families comfortable with the school and provides specific services. Depending on the resources of the school, this team might consist of social workers, attendance monitors, assistant principals, counselors, and any other appropriate person already in the school. The team works to get parents to support what the children are doing in school, and it contacts parents to see what help can be provided to get children who are frequently absent to school. Parenting education is also provided for interested families. Finally, family support assistance is provided when students are having academic difficulties due to problems at home.

6. Program Facilitator. At each school an experienced teacher works as a program facilitator to oversee the operation of Success for All. This individual helps plan the overall program, works on scheduling, and visits classes and tutoring sessions to provide help as individual problems arise. The facilitator works directly with teachers on matters of curriculum and classroom management and coordinates any activities that concern the instructional staff and the family support team.

7. Teachers and Teacher Training. The staff development model used in Success for All provides brief initial training for teachers mixed with extensive classroom follow-up and group discussion. Teachers and tutors receive two days in-service at the year's beginning and a detailed teacher's manual. The in-service sessions focus on implementing the reading program; the teacher's manual provides general teaching strategies and specific lessons. Tutors receive an additional day of in-service training for tutoring strategies and assessment. Throughout the year the facilitator organizes other in-service sessions on topics such as classroom management or cooperative learning, as needed. Facilitators also organize informal sessions with groups of teachers for sharing, problem solving, and discussion of changes for individual children.

Cautions and Comments

Success for All seems to present a highly structured, intensive, and well-thought-out program of reading-problem prevention. Students are challenged and kept moving forward. The tutor acts as a model of strategies that the student should be using for effective reading. While one might argue with various components of the program, the research has indicated that Success for All is effective at least in terms of improving overall achievement measures.

Further, the developers of Success for All (especially Slavin) represent their program as having a solid and sound "scientific" research base to merit consideration as an evidence-based program. In terms of the National Reading Panel, they have represented the program as being informed by the research results for a balanced reading program as well as practices such as phonemic awareness, the systematic teaching of phonics, fluency, and reading comprehension (see www.successforall.net/resource). Slavin has been a strong advocate of the narrow definition of scientific-based research as well as what merits a designation as evidence-based practice. While the program developers are engaged in ongoing research of the impact of Success for All on reading development, comparisons with other programs have yielded mix results in terms of its effectiveness. In addition, it seems to suffer from shortcomings in terms of the engagement by teachers and ongoing professional development—especially compared with initiatives such as Reading Recovery.

Nonetheless a summary of the results for various studies on Success for All indicates that students made substantial increases in achievement when compared to their matched counterparts not participating in the program. Additionally, assignments to special education because of learning problems were greatly reduced, and retentions were virtually eliminated. These findings are particularly impressive when one considers the fact that these programs took place in high-at-risk, disadvantaged schools. Still, further research needs to look qualitatively at the program for consistency across school sites as well as across tutoring sessions. Claims regarding the efficacy of Success for All compared with other programs such as Reading Recovery need to be critically examined—especially comparisons based upon economic arguments alone. In terms of sustained achievement, Reading Recovery's record seems stronger.

REFERENCES

Borman, G., and G. Hewes. 2002. The long-term effects and cost-effectiveness of Success for All. *Educational Evaluation and Policy Analysis,* 24(4): 243–266. Reports research exploring the costs versus the long-term returns of the program.

Hurley, E. A., A. Chamberlain, R. E. Slavin, and N. A. Madden. 2001. Effects of Success for All on TAAS Reading: A Texas statewide evaluation. *Phi Delta Kappan,* 82(10): 750–756. Results for Texas are reported.

Madden, N. A., R. E. Slavin, N. L. Karweit, L. J. Dolan, and B. A. Wasik. 1993. Success for All: Longitudinal effects of a restructuring program for inner-city elementary schools. *American Educational Research Journal* 30: 123–148. Presents a longitudinal study documenting the positive effects of the program.

Sanders, W. L., S. P. Wright, S. M. Ross, and L. W. Wang. 2000. *Value-added achievement results for three cohorts of Roots & Wings schools in Memphis: 1995–1999 outcomes.* Memphis: University of Memphis, Center for Research in Education Policy. Explores an evaluation of Success for All in Memphis schools.

Slavin, R. E. 1995, Winter. A model of effective instruction. *The Educational Forum* 59: 166–176. Discusses the research that they have pursued on the effectiveness of Success for All.

———. 1996. Research for the future: Research on cooperative learning and achievement: What we know, what we need to know. *Contemporary Educational Psychology* 21(0004): 43–69.

———. 1999. *How Title I can become the engine of reform in America's schools.* Baltimore: Johns Hopkins University, Center for Research on the Education of Students Placed at Risk. Discusses notions of evidence based practice and scientific research in the context of Title I funding.

Slavin, R. E., and A. Cheung. 2003. *Effective reading programs for English language learners: A best-evidence synthesis.* Baltimore: Johns Hopkins University, Center for Research on the Education of Students Placed at Risk. Slavin et al.'s own exploration of Success for All alongside other programs in terms of their effectiveness.

Slavin, R. E., N. L. Karweit, and B. A. Wasik. 1993, January. Preventing early school failure: What works? *Educational Leadership:* 10–18. Reviews an examination of various intervention programs.

Slavin, R. E., and N. A. Madden. 1999a. *Effects of bilingual and English as a second language adaptations of Success for All on the reading achievement of students acquiring English.* Baltimore: Johns Hopkins University and Success for All Foundation. Explores the effectiveness of adaptations of Success for All for second-language learners.

———. 1999. *Roots & Wings: A comprehensive approach to elementary school reform.* In J. Block, S. Everson, and T. Guskey (Eds.), *Comprehensive school reform: A program perspective.* Dubuque, IA: Kendall/Hunt. Provides the rationale and bases for Success for All.

———. 2000. Research on achievement outcomes of Success for All: A summary and response to critics. *Phi Delta Kappan,* 82(1): 38–40, 59–66. Responds to critics of Success for All.

———. 2003. *Success for All/Roots & Wings: 2003 summary of research on achievement outcomes.* Baltimore: Johns Hopkins University, Center for Research on the Education of Students Placed at Risk. Summary of Success for All research pursuits involving achievement results.

Slavin, R. E., N. A. Madden, L. J. Dolan, and B. A Wasik, 1996. *Every child, every school: Success for All.* Newbury Park, CA: Corwin. Presents an overview and a description of the elements of Success for All.

Slavin, R. E., N. A. Madden, L. J. Dolan, B. A. Wasik, S. M. Ross, and L. J. Smith, 1994. Whenever and wherever we choose: The replication of Success for All. *Phi Delta Kappan* 75(8): 639–647. Presents the first replication of Success for All beyond its Baltimore origins.

Slavin, R. E., N. A. Madden, N. L. Karweit, L. J. Dolan, and B. A. Wasik. 1991. Research directions: Success for All: Ending reading failure from the beginning. *Language Arts* 68: 404–409. A description of the program.

Slavin, R. E., N. A. Madden, N. L. Karweit, B. J. Livermon, and L. J. Dolan. 1990. Success for All: First-year outcomes of a comprehensive plan for reforming urban education. *American Educational Research Journal* 27: 255–278. Report of the first-year results of the program.

Smith, L. J., S. M. Ross, and J. Casey, 1996. Multi-site comparison of the effects of Success for All on reading achievement. *Journal of Literacy Research* 28(3): 329–353. Presents a multi-site (four cities) comparison of the effects of Success for All and the difficulties implementing the program from afar.

Wasik, B. A., and R. E. Slavin. 1993. Preventing early reading failure with one-to-one tutoring: A review of five programs. *Reading Research Quarterly* 28: 179–200. A review of the positive effects of Success for All.

Early Steps

Purpose

Early Steps, or the Howard Street Tutoring Program, was originally developed by Darrell Morris (Morris, Shaw, and Perney, 1990) as a one-to-one tutorial program which was intended as an early intervention program to help students in grades one through three that had fallen behind or were deemed at risk.

Rationale

Developed in conjunction with a partnership between National Louis College faculty and a community group (Good News Educational Workshop), Early Steps, sometimes referred to as the Howard Street Tutoring Program, was intended as an after school program where second and third graders received tutoring help from volunteers. The goal of the program was "to provide quality, after school reading instruction to second- and third-grade public school children who had fallen significantly behind their peers in reading" (Morris et al., 1990, p. 135). Since its inception, the program has grown and now extends to its use as an intervention program during school hours.

As originally conceived, the use of volunteers after school was perceived as a way of addressing the lack of resources to meet the needs of students lagging behind in reading opportunities—especially in those school situations where resources are inadequate. Partially because volunteers may be neophytes relative to helping students with reading, the program was initially reserved for second and third graders who had fallen behind, rather than first graders.

The reading instructional program assumes the following:

a. Children learn to read by reading, not unlike "they learn to ride a bicycle by jumping on and trying to ride it" (Morris et al., 1990, 137);

b. Children need the support of good stories—including the syntactic and semantic characteristics of natural versus artificial or contrived language;

c. Word study should play an important role—minimally knowledge of the spelling patterns of English (CVC, CVCe, CVVC)—"so that they can draw efficiently on this word knowledge in their contextual reading and writing efforts" (Morris et al., 1990, 137).

Intended Audience

Early Steps is intended for students who may fall behind others in the development of reading abilities—especially in grades one through three. Students are selected based upon an informal reading inventory and spelling tests.

Description of the Procedures

Variations in the implementation of the program exist. In school settings with younger students, the frequency and amount of time may vary. For instance, Santa and Hoein (1999) describe daily sessions of 30 minutes. After school programs that may involve tutoring sessions are one hour, four times per week. Also, as we will discuss, there is some variation in how the activities are implemented across its various components.

Early Steps lessons involve the following components: (1) contextual reading at the child's instructional level, (2) word study, (3) writing, (4) easy contextual reading, and (5) reading to the child and introducing new books.

1. Contextual Reading at the Child's Instructional Level. The first part of the lesson involves the child reading or rereading leveled, well-written books or stories. The tutor may support the student's reading by initially choosing patterned stories or doing echo reading in which the teacher reads and then the child, or by taking turns reading. At the lower levels they recommend avoiding basals—especially those basal selections that include the stilted and artificial language which often characterizes the earliest basal materials. The length of time devoted to this contextual reading may vary. In some locations, they keep to 8 to 10 minutes; in other locations, they recommend 15 to 20 minutes in situations where the time for the program is more extended.

2. Word Study. Depending upon the child's word knowledge, various letter and/or word sorts or categorization activities are pursued (sorts of beginning consonant elements, word families or rhyming words, and vowel patterns). This portion of the lesson takes the child through letter knowledge to consonant sounds to the most common word families. As described by Santa and Hoein (1999) in conjunction with the use of Early Steps with first graders:

> For many children the first weeks of the lessons involved learning how to name and write the letters. Once children demonstrated knowledge of the alphabet, they next practiced discriminating initial consonant sounds by sorting picture cards representing different initial letters. After students could discriminate the sounds with pictures, they learned the names on the initial letters corresponding to the sounds of picture names. Next they progressed to word sorting, where they simultaneously examined visual and auditory patterns. The children started with word families (rhyming patterns) and then progressed through short- and then long-vowel patterns. (p. 34)

The students are expected to demonstrate skill with a given sort prior to progressing to a subsequent sort (in the case of word patterns this entails the ability to read and spell the words with confidence). A typical word sort entails placing three words across a table reflecting a word pattern and then a stack of cards with words to be sorted according to the patterns of the three words. For example, the teacher might place the following words on cards on a table: *bit, tin,* and *lip.* The teacher might check to see if the student knows the words; if not, the words might be introduced to be sure they are known prior to proceeding. Students are then presented with a stack of words representing these patterns. The students are expected to sort the word at the same time as the teacher is reinforcing the spelling and recognition of the word. Morris (1992) and Santa and Hoein (1999) include more details on word sorts and the lists of words for these sorts. These word sorts may take 5 to 6 minutes or 10 to 12 minutes depending upon the time available.

3. Writing. Children are enco: raged to write sentences or short stories based upon their interests and experiences. After a short discussion of their experiences, children will be encouraged to write, saying aloud each word as they write. The teacher encourages the child to write down the letters and sounds the child hears. Invented spelling is encouraged in first-draft writing. Periodically (e.g., every two weeks) the tutor is encouraged to have the student choose his favorite piece for editing. With younger students sentence strips are also used. This entails the tutor also writing the students' sentence(s) on a strip and then cutting the sentence apart and then putting the sentence together. The time allocated for writing may vary from 5 to 15 minutes.

4. Easy Contextual Reading. To develop sight vocabulary, confidence, and interest, as well as fluency, children are given the opportunity to read aloud easier material—either rereading a favorite book or perhaps partner reading a new, but easy, book. Typically, the reading is done in trade books including books such as little book libraries. The time allocated for the easy contextual reading may be 10 to 15 minutes. In some sites, easy contextual reading is not a separate part of the tutoring program.

5. Reading to the Child and Introducing New Books. In conjunction with the after school tutoring program, tutors will close the lesson with the reading of a chapter or short book including fables, pictures books, or a chapter from a book. In some sites (Early Steps as developed by Santa and Hoein, 1999), the session may close with the introduction of a new book that the child will be expected to read without much help the next day at the beginning of the lesson. The book is intended to be a slightly more advanced letter than the books the child had previously read (e.g., look at pictures, discuss relevant interests, and talk about vocabulary). The teacher will introduce the book and support the child as she or he reads, that is to say, with coaching or encouragement to figure out the words. They place a high emphasis upon the child becoming strategic. As Santa and Hoein stress, tutors are expected to encourage children to reflect upon their strategies during book reading opportunities with prompts similar to the following:

> What can I do to figure out the word by myself?
> What strategies might I use—read the line again, how does the word start?
> What other words is the word like? What is the pattern?

Tutors are encouraged to carefully monitor the level of the material that the child reads. As Morris et al. (1990) state, "there is an optimal level of task difficulty that will produce the biggest gains in learning—a level where the reader is sufficiently challenged but not overwhelmed . . . we continually try to identify each child's current 'instructional level,' moving the student forward quickly when performance warrants such a move" (p. 137). For the out of school tutoring program, the trained supervisor is responsible for monitoring the tutor and ensuring that the student's needs are being met and progress is paced appropriately. After each lesson the tutor is expected to make notes which inform the supervisor as the next lesson is prepared. Upon arrival for the next lesson, the tutor will find a new lesson prepared and be expected to locate the necessary materials.

Cautions and Comments

Early Steps represents an intervention program that pulls together spelling development and reading development as well as other elements to ensure the adequacy of the program design as well as the delivery. It has been carefully developed based upon certain key assumptions and ongoing research and development based upon feedback from various implementations. Indeed, the developers have been quite intrepid in their pursuit of various case studies as they have pursued both an assessment of their program and refinement of their practices. The program appears to emphasize many of the elements stressed by other successful intervention programs: the need to engage students with meaningful texts and to engage students in developing and using various strategies, especially in context and transferred to carefully selected text selections.

Research of the effects of the program does suggest that, with appropriate pacing, sustained involvement with these tutoring programs will lead to students achieving significant gains that appear to be sustainable. Some students will make enough progress to be able to maintain their progress with the mainstream; others will make as much gain within the year, although they may not have caught up with their peers; still others will show progress but slower than what is expected for most of the other students.

It should be stressed that such growth is achieved after a considerable investment in time by both the tutor and child as well as a trained supervisor. As Morris et al. stated, "it took 50 hours of well-planned closely supervised one-to-one tutoring" (pp. 146–147) to achieve just a one-half year difference in reading achievement between groups receiving tutoring and the peers with whom they were comparing themselves.

The volunteer tutors have included undergraduate students, retirees, and suburban homemakers. Tutors begin working with someone who is an actual teacher. For the first three to four sessions, the supervisor models the teaching and prepares the lessons for the tutor as well as oversees the tutor's implementation. After the initial period the supervisor still prepares the lessons for the tutor.

In recent years, there has been an attempt to measure the effectiveness of intervention programs against the costs entailed. Such assessments seem problematic for a number of reasons. Any tutoring program has enormous costs, which are rarely factored into such a determination (e.g., donated time and materials), and what is missing is the commitment as well as negotiations that must be pursued for resources, including space and time to run the program. In addition, issues such as communication and cooperation (especially across communities, agencies, schools, families, tutors, supervisors, etc.) are also not factored into the determination.

REFERENCES

Morris, D. 1992. *Case studies in teaching beginning reading: The Howard Street tutoring manual.* Boone, NC: Fieldstream Publications. Provides a very comprehensive description of the program including its development and assessment, with sample lessons.

———. 1995. *The First Steps: An early reading intervention program.* (ERIC Documentation Reproduction Service No. ED 388956.) Provides a description of the tutoring program.

———. 1999. *The Howard Street tutoring manual: Teaching at-risk readers in the primary grades.* New York: Guilford Press. Manual is a tool for volunteer tutors and student teachers, classroom teachers, and reading specialists.

———. 2001. The Howard Street tutoring model: Using volunteer tutors to prevent reading failure in the primary grades. In L. M. Morrow and D. G. Woo (Eds.), *Tutoring programs for struggling reader. The America Reads Challenge.* New York: Guilford Press, 177–192. Summarizes Early Steps/Howard Street Tutoring models as part of a conference volume exploring a range of tutoring programs.

Morris, D., C. Ervin, and K. Conrad. 1996. A case study of middle school reading disability. *The Reading Teacher* 49: 368–377. Explores a case study of a sixth grader who is having difficulty learning to read. The instructional approach is aligned with Morris' other tutoring endeavors.

Morris, D., B. Shaw, and J. Perney. 1990. Helping low readers in grades 2 and 3: An after school volunteer tutoring program. *Elementary School Journal* 91: 133–150. Describes the tutoring program and research comparing its effects upon second and third graders. Offers suggestions and guidelines for establishing the program including community involvement.

Morris, D., and R. E. Slavin. 2003. *Every child reading.* Boston: Allyn and Bacon. Defines the problem of early reading and provides a developmental perspective on teaching reading in K–1. Discusses one-on-one intervention and provides an overview of Success for All.

Santa, C. M., and T. Hoein. 1999. An assessment of Early Steps: A program of early intervention of reading problems. *Reading Research Quarterly* 34: 2–29. Describes and reports the results of the implementation of the tutoring program in a school setting in Montana with first graders.

Wasik, B. 1998. Volunteer programs in reading: A review. *Reading Research Quarterly* 33: 266–292. Article reviewing the research findings from 17 volunteer programs involved in the America Reads Challenge Act of 1997.

Gillingham-Stillman Method

Purpose

The purpose of the Gillingham-Stillman method (Gillingham and Stillman, 1997) is to provide the reader, "disabled" or "potentially disabled," who has a specific language difficulty, with a method for learning to read that is consistent with the evolution of language functions.

Rationale

Gillingham and Stillman (1997) argue that students with specific language disabilities will learn to read successfully only with methods that are consistent with the evolution of language functions. The system they have suggested is based upon the theoretical position and work of Samuel Orton. As suggested in the foreword to Gillingham and Stillman's 1965 text, *Remedial Training for Children with Specific Disabilities in Reading, Spelling, and Penmanship,* their goal was to organize remedial techniques to make them consistent with Orton's (1937) working hypothesis.

According to Gillingham and Stillman, Orton hypothesized that specific language disabilities he observed may have been due to hemispherical dominance in specific areas of the brain. He related certain instances of reading disability to the difficulty students might potentially have when dealing with inconsistencies that result from mixed dominance. Mirror writing and reversals seemed to be evidence of these difficulties.

The method, as it was developed by Gillingham and Stillman, purports to be new, different, and exclusive. It purports to be new and different in that it provides a "phonetic method" consistent with the evolution of language functions. It purports to be exclusive in that students using it engage in this and only this method. Gillingham and Stillman have claimed that the best teachers for this method are those familiar with traditional reading and spelling instruction. These teachers, it is argued, are cognizant of the need for and utility of Gillingham and Stillman's method.

Intended Audience

The Gillingham-Stillman method is intended for use with students who, due to specific language disabilities, have had or may have difficulty learning to read or spell. These disabled readers or potentially disabled readers should not include students who show either low mental abilities or sensory deficiencies. The method is intended for use with third graders through sixth graders, but has been adapted for use with older and younger students.

Description of the Procedures

To introduce students to the system, Gillingham and Stillman suggest a narrative entitled "The Growth of Written Language." The narrative is intended to provide a positive mind-set; it traces, with examples, the evolution of communications from spoken language to picture writing to alphabetic writing. The narrative ends with a description of the Gillingham-Stillman method and an explanation to the students that the difficulty they have incurred with reading it is not unique. As Gillingham and Stillman (1973) suggest, the latter message might be handled as follows:

> Now I am going to begin with you in an entirely different way. We are going to use the Alphabetic Method. You are going to learn the sounds of the letters, then build them into words. You will find it real fun and it will be nice for you to be attempting something which you can do.
>
> There are a great many children, more than you have any idea of, who have had the same kind of trouble that you have. Some of them have grown to be famous men and women. Boys and girls now doing well in college and business were taught to read and write as I am going to teach you. (p. 37)

Thereafter, a sequence of exercises beginning with the learning of letters and letter sounds, then blending sound to words, and finally to sentence and story reading is suggested. Within this framework, the technique will be described in this sequence:

1. Letters
2. Words
3. Sentences and stories
4. Other

1. Letters. The first principle of the technique is to teach the sounds represented by letters and then build these into words. To this end, each word family is taught by associations involving visual, auditory, and kinesthetic processes.

There are three associative processes involved. The first associative process involves two parts:

a. The teacher shows the student a letter and says it. It is then repeated by the student.

b. The same procedure is followed for the sound represented by the letter. The teacher says it. The student repeats it.

The second associative process involves responding with the name of a letter to the sound represented by the letter. That is, the teacher makes the sound represented by the letter and the student names the letter represented.

The third associative process involves learning the letter form. Learning of letter forms takes place in the following manner:

a. The teacher writes and explains the letter form.

b. The student traces the teacher's lines, copies them, writes the word from memory, and then writes the word without looking at what is being written.

There are several guidelines for the teacher to follow across these associative processes:

a. Letters are always introduced by a key word, such as *b,* and would be presented in the context of *boy;* when the *b* card is shown, the pupil would be expected to respond with *boy.*

b. Drill cards are used to introduce each letter, provide repetition, and improve the accuracy of sound production.

c. Students learn to differentiate vowels and consonants by the manner of their production and through the use of different-colored cards, e.g., white for consonants, salmon for vowels.

d. The first letters presented to the student should represent clear sounds and nonreversible letter forms.

e. An "echo" speech procedure in which the teacher drills the student in reproducing sounds is suggested for students incurring pronunciation difficulties.

f. For reinforcement purposes, students who know the name and sound represented by a letter are asked to respond to the names of letters with the sounds they represent.

g. In instances where writing takes place, cursive writing is preferred and suggested over manuscript writing.

2. Words. After ten letters are well known, blending them into words begins. Drill cards forming a word are placed in front of the student, and the student is required to blend the sounds represented by these letters, such as *h-i-m, t-a-p, a-t, i-f, h-i-p.* It is the teacher's responsibility to devise ways of drilling words effectively. These words, printed on colored cards, are placed in what has been termed the student's "Jewel Case." Time drills are imposed; in some instances, students' growth in accuracy is graphed.

After a few days of sound blending, the student is required to reverse the procedure and analyze words into the component sounds. For example, the teacher might say the word *m-a-p* slowly and have students name and find the cards for each sound. As further reinforcement, the student might write the word. As the student writes the word, each letter is named and then the word is spoken.

Typically, not more than one or two additional sounds are introduced each day. When a letter might represent more than one sound, only one of the sounds would be introduced. As word families are introduced, the drill card and Jewel Case card files are expanded. On a single day, the various activities might be organized as follows:

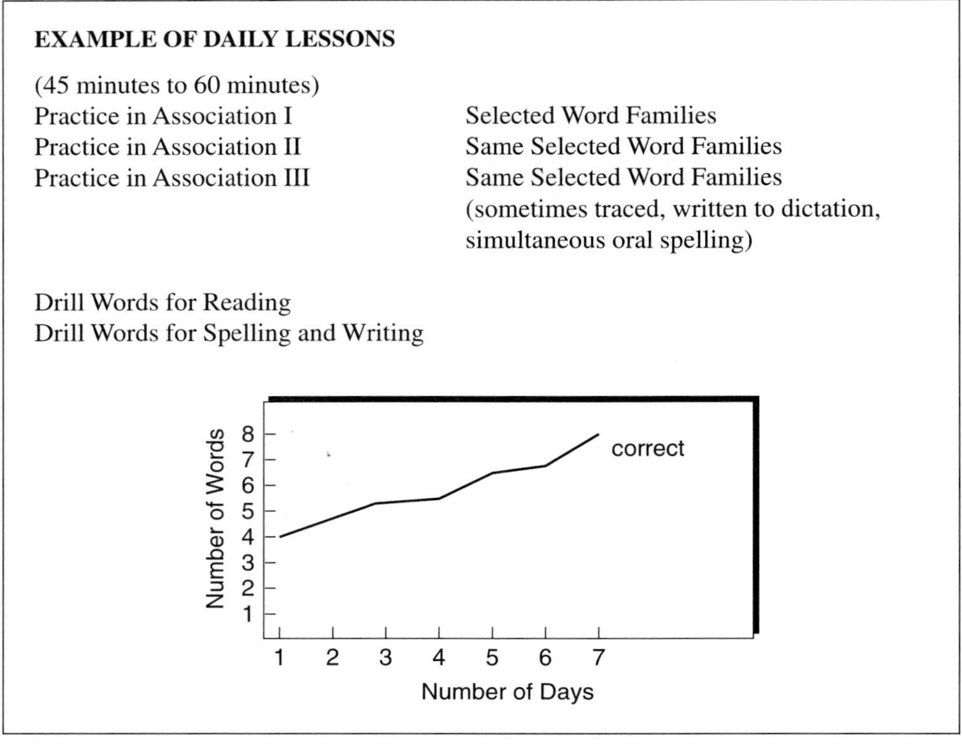

EXAMPLE OF DAILY LESSONS

(45 minutes to 60 minutes)

Practice in Association I	Selected Word Families
Practice in Association II	Same Selected Word Families
Practice in Association III	Same Selected Word Families (sometimes traced, written to dictation, simultaneous oral spelling)

Drill Words for Reading
Drill Words for Spelling and Writing

3. Sentences and Stories. After students can read and write any three-letter "perfectly phonetic" word, sentence and story reading is begun. It begins with simple, highly structured stories, referred to as "Little Stories," which are presented to the student to read and write.

Several of these Little Stories are available from Gillingham and Stillman. The following is an example:

> Pat sat on the mat.
> She had a hat.
> The hat was on Pat.
> A rat sat on the mat.
> Pat ran.
> The rat ran.

For both sentence and story reading, students are required to prepare silently. Their task is to read the story or sentence silently until they can read it perfectly. Any words with which the students may have difficulty are either sounded out, or, in cases where words may be unfamiliar, such as "phonetically irregular words," pronunciation is provided. The students are encouraged to be accurate and to avoid guessing. For sentence and story writing, Little Stories are dictated by the teacher. As the teacher dictates the story, avoiding unnecessary repetitions, the students write the words.

4. Other. As the students' reading skills develop, the teacher may want to use further guidance provided by Gillingham and Stillman:

a. Students learn that polysyllabic words are formed by syllables in the same way monosyllabic words are formed by letters. To this end, students are presented with and asked to combine detached syllables, and are taught to identify the appropriate accent by trying the accent on each syllable.

b. Dictionary use is taught for the purpose of identifying the pronunciation of words.

c. To deal with a few selected words which are phonetically irregular, whole-word drill is suggested.

d. Finally, until the student completes a major portion of the phonics program, he or she is discouraged from reading independently.

Gillingham and Stillman suggested that the technique would yield substantial benefits, assuming that sufficient time is provided. At a minimum, they suggest the technique requires a commitment of five lessons per week for no less than two years. Eventually, they suggest, the student will be able to return to a regular class; but unless returning students can read their texts and assignments fluently, they should be assisted in reading them.

Cautions and Comments

There appear to be several important similarities and differences between the Gillingham-Stillman technique and other multisensory approaches—for example, the Fernald technique. Both the Gillingham-Stillman and Fernald techniques emphasize constant reinforcement and repetition through the use of visual, auditory, and kinesthetic modalities; both prefer cursive writing to manuscript; and both attempt to develop a positive mind-set in the reader prior to the commencement of remediation. In terms of differences, Gillingham and Stillman insist upon a letter-by-letter, structured, synthetic phonics approach, in contrast to Fernald's concern that students not proceed letter by letter but select their own words to learn, and initially learn through all modalities.

Although the Gillingham-Stillman technique purports to yield positive results, there are reasons to caution potential users. First, very few contemporary authorities still accept the theoretical position of Orton as tenable. Second, students who learn by these methods may have a tendency to emphasize pronunciation over meaning. This synthetic letter-by-letter approach, with its emphasis upon word-perfect reading, places an undue emphasis on the mechanics rather than reading for meaning. In recent years, the Gillingham-Stillman approach has received a great deal of attention especially among educators who support a strong emphasis on phonics instruction. While the findings of the National Reading Panel report tend to support eclecticism and suggest the limitations of phonics for comprehension development beyond the second grade, supporters of the Gillingham-Stillman draw on the findings of the National Reading Panel report to argue for their program. Certainly, the Gillingham-Stillman technique was one of the programs that has been studied in a number of meta-analyses, but support for the approach needs to be tempered with the fuller set of findings as well as the criticisms that have been made (see the bibliography list accompanying the overview to this unit; see also Unit 5).

REFERENCES

Chall, J. 1967. *Learning to read: The great debate.* New York: McGraw-Hill, 169–170. Presents an evaluation and discussion of Orton's notions of reading disability and Orton's suggestions for remedial reading methods.

Gearhart, B. R. 1973. *Learning disabilities: Educational strategies.* St. Louis: C. V. Mosby, 103–107. Presents a detailed discussion of the major aspects of the technique.

Gillingham, A., and B. W. Stillman. 1997. *Remedial training for children with specific disability in reading, spelling and penmanship* (8th ed.). Cambridge, MA: Educators Publishing Service. Provides the rationale and history, and serves as the manual, for the Gillingham-Stillman technique.

Harris, A. J., and E. R. Sipay. 1975. *How to increase reading ability* (6th ed.). New York: David McKay, 396–397. Discusses briefly the theory and procedure of the technique.

Kaluger, G., and C. J. Kolson. 1969. *Reading and learning disabilities.* Columbus, OH: Charles E. Merrill, 267–268. Presents a brief summary and discussion of this and other techniques.

Orton, S. 1937. *Reading, writing, and speech problems in children.* New York: W. W. Norton. Discusses Orton's theory for specific disabilities in reading.

———. 1966. The Orton-Gillingham approach. In J. Money (Ed.), *The disabled reader.* Baltimore: Johns Hopkins University Press, 119–146. Summarizes Orton's theory and discusses the technique.

Fernald Technique

Purpose

The Fernald technique (Fernald, 1943, 1988) has two basic purposes: (1) to teach the student to write and read words correctly; and (2) to extend the student's reading to various materials other than personal compositions.

Rationale

Fernald claims that many cases of reading disability, both "partial" and "extreme," are due to teachers' failure to use methods that allow students to learn in the manner most appropriate to their individual abilities. Fernald claims that the use of limited methods blocks the learning process. As an alternative, Fernald's own procedure, which incorporates a multisensory strategy, purportedly caters to the varied needs of individuals.

Intended Audience

The Fernald technique is intended for use with cases of extreme and partial reading disability. Extreme disability refers to the totally disabled student with zero reading ability. Partial disability refers to the student with some reading skills, who is unable to acquire adequate reading skills within the instructional framework of the class. It is intended that the teacher use the procedure on a one-to-one basis with each student; however, the technique can be adapted for use with groups.

Description of the Procedures

Fernald divides her technique into four stages in accord with varying levels of individual reading ability and development. In the first stage, the student traces the word with a finger, saying each part of the word aloud as it is traced, until it can be written without looking at the copy. By the final stage, the student is eager to read. The student can begin to generalize about words and to identify new ones.

Stage 1. The first stage is highly structured and for this reason will be described in some detail. In this stage, the student selects any word or words that he or she wants to learn, regardless of length. Each word is written with crayon on a strip of paper in large, chalkboard-size cursive writing, or manuscript print. The student then traces the word with finger contact, pronouncing each part of the word as it is traced. This tracing procedure is repeated as many times as necessary until the student can write the word on a separate piece of paper without looking at the copy. As new words are learned in this manner, they are placed in an alphabetized word file by the student.

After several words are taught in this way, the student begins to realize that he or she can read and write words. At this time, "story-writing" activities are introduced. Subsequent learning of words occurs whenever the student cannot write a word for the story. Sometimes the student may have to learn every word by this tracing technique before the story can be written. After the words are learned and the story is written, the story is typed by the teacher within 24 hours. The story is then read by the student, who proceeds to file the words under the proper letter in the word file.

The following points are stressed by Fernald for using this initial stage:

1. For maximum efficiency, unknown words should always be traced with the finger in contact with the paper.

2. In order to avoid breaking the word into meaningless units, the student should write the word from memory rather than from copy.

3. Similarly, if any error or interruption occurs during the student's writing of the word, the word should be rewritten entirely.

4. To ensure that the student understands the meaning of the word, words should always be used in context.

The following dialogue between a student and teacher is presented to illustrate the use of the first stage of the Fernald technique with a totally disabled reader.

TEACHER: Good morning, my name is Mr. Stewart and I'm your teacher. Please sit here at my side.

STUDENT: Oh, all right.

TEACHER: I have a new way of learning to read which I'd like you to try. Many bright people have had the same difficulty you have had in learning to read and have learned easily by this new method. Now, give me any word that you want to learn to read.

STUDENT: Dinosaur.

TEACHER: Dinosaur?

STUDENT: Dinosaur.

TEACHER: Now, watch what I do and listen to what I say. Are you ready?

STUDENT: Yeah.

[The teacher should use a crayon and a piece of paper which is approximately 4 inches by 12 inches.

1. The teacher says the word before writing it.
2. As the word is written, each syllable is said.
3. If the word is written in cursive style (as the word is said again), the *t*'s are crossed and the *i*'s are dotted, etc.
4. As the word is said again, each syllable is underlined.
5. The word is said again.]

TEACHER: Now again, watch what I do and listen to what I say. Are you ready?

STUDENT: Yeah.

TEACHER: [The teacher follows exactly the steps as above, only the teacher uses a finger instead of a crayon.] I want you to do exactly as I did until you think you can write the word without looking at it. Now watch again what I do and listen to what I say. Ready? [Teacher repeats tracing procedure.]

STUDENT: Let me try.

TEACHER: Do what I did and say what I said until you can write the word without looking at it.

STUDENT: [The student traces the word following the procedure demonstrated.]

TEACHER: [Teacher checks student's tracing technique. Whenever the student hesitates or makes an error, the teacher stops the student and, if necessary, demonstrates the technique again. The number of times the student traces the word is recorded.]

STUDENT: (After several tracings): I think I know the word now.

TEACHER: [Teacher removes copy of word and places a blank sheet of paper and a crayon in front of the student.] Write the word on this piece of paper using the same procedure. [If the student makes a mistake, the student is stopped immediately. Do not erase the word. Instead, fold or turn paper over and allow the student to try again.]

STUDENT: [Student writes the word using the same procedure followed when tracing the word.] Finished.

TEACHER: Are you correct?

STUDENT: I sure am.

TEACHER: Check and see if you are correct.

STUDENT: [Student turns over the copy and compares attempt.]

TEACHER: Were you correct?

STUDENT: Yeah.

TEACHER: Do you think you can write it correctly twice? Try writing the word again. [The teacher turns copies of the word down and gives student another blank sheet of paper.]

[Student proceeds to write the word correctly a second time.]

TEACHER: Check to see if you are correct again.

[Student checks word.]

TEACHER: Congratulations! That's great! Now place the word in your word file under the proper letter.

[Student proceeds to place word under the letter *d* in the word file.]

TEACHER: Now tell me another word you wish to learn.

Two, three, or maybe four words might be learned using this same procedure during a single session over each of the first few days. As soon as the student realizes that words can be learned by this procedure, story-writing is started. Words are learned as they are needed for the story the student is writing.

Stage 2. The length of the tracing period (Stage 1) will vary from student to student and is phased out when the student is able to learn without it. This becomes evident when there is a decrease in the number of tracings required to learn a word, and when some words are learned with single or no tracings. At the point when the need for any tracing disappears, the student is ready to embark upon Stage 2. On the average, the tracing period lasts about two months, with a range from one to eight months.

During Stage 2, the student learns words simply by looking at the word while saying it over and over. As with Stage 1, words to be learned are derived from unknown words in stories the student has written. These words are presented to the student in print or in cursive form for study. The word is learned by saying the word several times, over and over again, until it can be written from memory.

Stage 3. Stage 3 is basically the same as Stage 2, except that the student has now reached the stage where learning occurs merely by looking at a word and saying it. The student is permitted to read anything and as much as he or she desires. Whenever an unknown word is met, the student is told the word. At this stage, the student learns directly from the printed page. It has become unnecessary to write or print each new word on a card. The student looks at the word in print, pronounces it a number of times, and then is able to write it from memory. As with the previous stage, new words are reviewed after reading, filed, and, at a later stage, reviewed again.

Stage 4. In Stage 4, the student is able to recognize new words from their resemblance to words or parts of words already learned. As with Stage 3, the student is expected to read a variety of materials. However, unlike Stage 3, the student is able to work out many words. For example, such words might be learned from the context, or from generalizations about words or word parts. The student is told only words for which it is not possible to determine the meaning. For purposes of retention, such words are usually written down by the student.

Fernald emphasizes the need for student involvement in the content of what is being read. For this reason, she suggests that the student be encouraged to survey a paragraph to clear up the meaning of unknown words prior to reading. She argues that this will prevent distraction and enable the student to concentrate on the content of the reading material. Toward the goal of reading for meaning, she discourages the sounding out of words during reading, either by the teacher or by a student, and suggests that any word that the student does not know be provided.

Cautions and Comments

Empirical evidence of the success of the Fernald technique comes from various studies. Kress and Johnson (1970), Berres and Eyer (1970), Enstrom (1970), and Coterell (1972) have all reported positive results with this approach. Fernald herself provides a great deal of documented support for the strategy's success in *Remedial Techniques in Basic School Subjects* (1943).

While there seems to be a consensus that the Fernald technique yields positive results and has several desirable features, there also seems to be agreement that it suffers from some major drawbacks.

On the positive side, the desirable features of the Fernald method include:

1. It reinforces the acquisition of word form cues and the ability to use context.

2. Methods seem consistent with aims and take into account variations in the child's rate of learning and specific needs and interests.

3. Motivation and reading of interesting materials are emphasized.

On the negative side, objections to the use of the technique include:

1. The procedure tends to be very time-consuming and demanding of the teacher, especially in the early stages. Often more expedient methods for teaching disabled readers can be developed.

2. Reading books is deemed important, but delayed.

3. Syllabic division within words may distort the pronunciation of certain words, e.g., *fat/her.*

4. Readers may develop who are too busy sounding out words to either concentrate on meaning or understand the purposes of reading. In this respect, it can be argued that Fernald suggests the need, but not the methods by which students will read for meaning.

REFERENCES

Berres, F., and J. T. Eyer. 1970. John. In A. J. Harris (Ed.), *Casebook on reading disability.* New York: David McKay, 25–47. Describes a case history example of the use of the procedure.

Birsch, J. R. (Ed.). (1999). *Multisensory teaching of basic language skills.* Baltimore: Paul H. Brookes. Explores multisensory techniques for developing various language skills.

Bond, G. L., and M. A. Tinker. 1973. *Reading difficulties: Their diagnosis and correction.* 3d ed. Englewood Cliffs, NJ: Prentice-Hall, 498–501. Presents a brief discussion on the procedure and its uses.

Chall, J. 1967. *Learning to read: The great debate.* New York: McGraw-Hill, 170–172. Presents a brief discussion of aspects of Fernald's work with disabled readers.

Coterell, G. 1972. A case of severe learning disability. *Remedial Education* 7: 5–9. Describes an example of the procedure's successful use.

Enstrom, E. A. 1970. A key to learning. *Academic Therapy* 5: 295–297. Describes a successful example using the procedure.

Fernald, G. 1943. *Remedial techniques in basic school subjects.* New York: McGraw-Hill. (The book was reprinted by Pro-Ed [Austin, Texas] in 1988). Presents a detailed description of the procedure and results of its use.

Gearhart, B. R. 1973. *Learning disabilities: Educational strategies.* St. Louis: C. V. Mosby, 76–90. Presents a detailed discussion of the procedure and provides examples of its use through case histories.

Harris, A. J., and E. R. Sipay. 1975. *How to increase reading ability* (6th ed.). New York: David McKay, 393–396. Presents a brief discussion of the procedure and its use with students experiencing reading difficulty.

Kaluger, G., and C. J. Kolson. 1969. *Reading and learning disabilities.* Columbus, OH: Merrill, 263–267. Presents a theoretical discussion of the procedure and its use.

Kress, R. A., and M. S. Johnson. 1970. Martin. In A. J. Harris (Ed.), *Casebook on reading disability.* New York: David McKay, 1–24. Describes an example of the use of the procedure through a case history.

Meyer, C. A. 1978. Reviewing the literature on Fernald's technique of remedial reading. *The Reading Teacher* 31: 614–619. Reviews studies examining the effectiveness of Fernald's technique.

UNIT 5

Phonics and Word Identification

UNIT OVERVIEW

No aspect of reading instruction has been the subject of more debate than that dealing with phonics and word identification instruction (Stahl, Duffy-Hester, and Stahl, 1998). Unfortunately, these debates may lead one to think that instruction in word identification, particularly in phonics, is the single most important ingredient in the entire reading program. Such arguments seem to disregard the notion that word identification includes skills other than phonics skills. These arguments ignore the notion that word identification and phonics are only a means to an end: reading for understanding. The issue addressed in this unit is not *whether* to teach, but *how* to teach, word identification skills. Of particular concern is the problem of preparing readers to deal with unknown words they encounter as they read.

The unit presents the theoretical bases and procedures for some of the alternative ways to teach word identification. In so doing, it provides a backdrop for examining alternatives. Beyond these descriptions, selected books and articles should be reviewed. In 1990, a report by M. Adams was released; in 1989, the magazine *Phi Delta Kappan* devoted several issues to this topic. Stahl et al. (1998), Stanovich (1991), and Cunningham (1992) provided a review of the literature on word identification and phonics. Goodman (1993) developed his book *Phonics Phacts* as a response to the increased demand for teaching phonics first. In 1998, the U.S. Congress passed its controversial Reading Excellence Act, which defines reading as more dependent upon phonics than most experts would suggest, and narrowly defined what would count as scientific studies. In turn, the formation of the National Reading Panel and their review of scientific studies of reading in the area that they termed *alphabetics* resulted in a focus on phonics instruction including phonemic awareness and fluency. Further, the review tended to perpetuate an emphasis on the role of phonics instruction despite findings that supported a balanced approach. In particular, while the National Reading Panel report offers support for some phonemic awareness, it emphasizes that such an approach should be short in duration and may be unnecessary for some students. Further, while the panel supports the teaching of phonics, it does not suggest that any one approach (synthetic or analytic) has an advantage over another. While the panel supports the impact of phonics on achievement through grade one, the members of the panel suggest that positive effects are unlikely to carry over beyond grade two unless the approach is balanced with an emphasis on meaning. If the scope of research is extended to include other reviews and other research, one can find strong support for a more whole-language orientation (see Dahl, Scharer, Lawson, and Grogan, 1999).

The majority of practices included in this unit involve what the National Reading Panel and others refer to as systematic and explicit phonics. As they describe the various systematic phonics approaches:

> These include synthetic phonics, analytic phonics, embedded phonics, analogy phonics, on-set rhyme phonics, and phonics through spelling . . . and some phonics programs combine two or more of these types of instruction. . . . Although differences exist the hallmark of systematic phonics is that they delineate a planned sequential set of phonic elements and they teach these elements explicitly and systematically. (National Reading Panel, 2000, 2–89)

In addition, this unit also includes two sets of strategies that are more holistic and meaning-centered in their orientation—namely, Retrospective Miscue Analysis and Goodman's Reading Strategy Lessons. These two sets of strategies represent practices consistent with the Whole-Language approach described in Unit 2. It should be noted that the preceding units include details of approaches that include a focus on phonics instruction. In Units 1 through 4 most of the approaches include phonics as one of the areas of instructional emphasis. Many of the approaches are primarily analytic but often include a mix—especially Guided Reading, Shared Reading, Directed Reading Activity, New Basics/Rich Literacy Tasks, and the various Language Experience–oriented approaches. Four Squares represents an approach tied to the notion of analogy phonics or syllabaries. Direct Instruction, Monroe Methods, and Gillingham-Stillman represent synthetically oriented approaches.

Six strategies designed to improve the reader's word identification skills are presented here. The strategies represent both traditional and contemporary suggestions for developing word identification abilities. Three of the strategies (Analytic, Synthetic, and Syllabaries) might be viewed as core, since elements of these approaches are usually combined in most phonics and word identification practices. Word Study is representative of a strategy that combines many of these elements as well as the elements drawn from an understanding of the relationship between spelling development and word identification. Retrospective Miscue Analysis and Goodman's Reading Strategy Lessons represent an approach to phonics and word identification that is both contextualized and meaning-centered. A brief summary of the strategies provides a preview of the unit.

> *Word Study.* Word Study (Bear, Invernizzi, Templeton, and Johnston, 1996) is a comprehensive approach to teaching not only phonics but also vocabulary, spelling, writing, and concept development. It involves students categorizing words and pictures according to the likenesses and differences they see in them. It allows students to make logical decisions about the way in which they think about the elements in words, including their sound, patterns, meaning, and use.
>
> *Analytic Method.* The Analytic Method is among the most widely used of the traditional methods for teaching phonics. This method is designed to have readers use known words to discover strategies for decoding unknown words. In recent years it has been referred to as the implicit method of teaching phonics.

Synthetic Word Families. The Synthetic Word Families approach is another widely used traditional method for developing phonic and word identification abilities. It is designed to serve three purposes: (1) to help readers learn the sounds represented by letters and some methods of blending these sounds into words; (2) to increase the student's sight vocabulary through the use of consonant substitution; and (3) to aid students in word identification skills through the use of blending and minimally contrasting word elements. In recent years it has been referred to as the explicit method of teaching phonics. In addition, Direct Instruction offers a very scripted version of this approach.

Syllabaries. The Syllabaries strategy evolved in the 1970s, but has received increased attention in recent years. This approach is designed to improve word identification skills through the use of the syllable as the unit of pronunciation.

Retrospective Miscue Analysis. Retrospective Miscue Analysis was developed by Goodman and Marek (1996) as a strategy that engages readers of all ability levels in revaluing their reading by reflecting upon and evaluating the reading process through analyzing their oral reading miscues.

Goodman's Reading Strategy Lessons. Reading Strategy Lessons represent an earlier attempt to translate the theories of Kenneth Goodman (1967, 1975) into practice. Advocates of Goodman's psycholinguistic perspective on reading designed these lessons to help readers focus on, and strengthen their use of, the syntactic or grammatic, the semantic or meaning, and the graphophonic or sound-symbol cueing systems involved in reading.

REFERENCES

Adams, M. J. 1990. *Beginning to read: Thinking and learning about print.* Cambridge: MIT Press.

Cunningham, P. M. 1992. What kind of phonics instruction will we have? In C. K. Kinzer and D. J. Leu (Eds.), *Literacy research, theory, and practice: View from many perspectives.* Forty-first Yearbook of the National Reading Conference. Chicago: National Reading Conference, 17–31.

Dahl, K. L, L. Scharer, L. Lawson, and P. R. Grogan. 1999. Phonics instruction and student achievement in whole language first grade classrooms. *Reading Research* 34(3): 312–341.

Ehri, L., and S. Numes. 2002. *The role of phonemic awareness in learning to read.* In A. Farstrup and S. J. Samuels (Eds.), *What research has to say about reading instruction* (3d ed.). Newark, DE: International Reading Association, 101–139.

Goodman, K. S. 1993. *Phonics phacts.* Portsmouth, NH: Heinemann.

Hiebert, E. H., and B. M. Taylor. 2000. Beginning reading instruction: Research on early interventions. In M. L. Kamil, P. B. Mosenthal, P. D. Pearson, and R. Barr (Eds.), *Handbook of Reading Research,* Vol. III. Mahwah, NJ: Erlbaum.

International Reading Association (IRA). 1997. *The role of phonics in reading instruction: A position statement of the International Reading association.* Newark, DE: Author.

Morrow, L. M., and D. H. Tracey. 1997. Strategies used for phonics instruction in early childhood classrooms. *The Reading Teacher* 50: 644–651. Details the type of phonics instructional strategies used by teachers between preschool and kindergarten, and first and second grades.

National Reading Panel. 2000. *Teaching children to read: An evidence-based assessment of the scientific research literature on reading and its implications for reading instruction* (Report of the Subgroups). Washington, DC: U.S. Department of Health and Human Services, Public Health Service, National Institutes of Health and the National Institute of Child Health and Human Development.

Snow, C. E., M. S. Burns, and P. Griffin. 1998. *Preventing reading difficulties in young children: A report of the National Research Council.* Washington, DC: National Academy Press.

Stahl, S. A., A. M. Duffy-Hester, and K. A. D. Stahl. 1998. Everything you wanted to know about phonics (but were afraid to ask). *Reading Research Quarterly* 35: 338–355.

Stanovich, K. E. 1991. Word recognition: Changing perspectives. In R. Barr, M. L. Kamil, P. Mosenthal, and P. D. Pearson (Eds.), *Handbook of reading research,* Vol. II. New York: Longman, 418–452.

Strickland, D. S. 1998. *Teaching phonics today: A primer for educators.* Newark, DE: International Reading Association. Explores issues associated with the teaching of phonics and argues for a balance between systematic, intensive code-driven and holistic, embedded, and meaning-driven approaches.

United States Congress H. R. 2614 Reading Excellence Act.

Word Study

Purpose

Word Study (Bear, Invernizzi, Templeton, and Johnston, 1996) is an active process whereby students categorize words and pictures according to the likenesses and differences they see in them. It allows students to make logical decisions about the way in which they think about the elements in words, including their sound, patterns, meaning, and use.

Rationale

Students develop rich speaking vocabularies before they enter school. The first written words students come to know are those that they already understand in their oral language, for example, their own names and those of people significant in their lives, followed by the names of animals, objects, and ideas that are meaningful to them. In other words, they represent concepts. In school a shift occurs in which emphasis is no longer on learning the written forms of the concepts they already understand but rather on building and expanding those concepts through exposure to our writing system, or orthography. By this exposure to print, their orthographic knowledge grows as students see the relationships among words through the varying types of information represented: alphabetic, pattern, and meaning. Alphabetic information is the knowledge that letters match up to sounds in a left-to-right sequence. Pattern information is the knowledge that groups of letters can function as a single unit to represent sounds, for example, knowing that *beat* follows a CVVC spelling pattern and that the vowel combination usually has a long vowel sound with the second vowel silent. Finally, meaning information is the knowledge that groups of letters can represent the meaning units that make up words, for example, suffixes or prefixes. Through activities that enable students to explore and study words, their commonalities and differences, their orthographic knowledge grows and, thus, their vocabularies.

Intended Audience

Bear et al. state that Word Study can be used through the grades and on into fluency, but the strategy is most closely associated with students in the elementary grades who are emerging readers and who are not yet fluent in their reading.

Description of the Procedures

The discussion of the Word Study strategy is organized in two parts: (1) assessing orthographic knowledge, and (2) organizing for Word Study instruction.

1. Assessing Orthographic Knowledge. At the beginning of the school year or when a new student enters the class, Bear et al. recommend that teachers assess students so they can plan an effective program of Word Study which will help them learn to read and write. In particular, students' orthographic knowledge needs to be assessed, and they recommend the use of a spelling inventory to determine the stage of orthographic development of the students. In this way teachers can find out what students already know about orthography, what they use but confuse about spelling, and what is missing in their ability to spell.

a. Stages of orthographic development. Before discussion of the spelling inventory, it would be helpful to describe the stages of orthographic/spelling development into which students may fall so effective instruction can be planned. The stages of spelling development were first described by Henderson in 1981. In the research he conducted over the years Henderson found that students' spelling errors were not random, and they evolved over time. From this he developed various stages of spelling development and what occurred at each level. Bear et al. (1996) use the following stage names because they believe they are descriptive of students' spelling behavior and the basic strategies they use to spell. The stages of spelling are:

Preliterate
Early Letter Name
Middle and Late Letter Name
Within Word Pattern
Syllable Juncture
Derivational Constancy

The *preliterate* stage of spelling is the emergent period of literacy and is characterized by random scribbling, the drawing of pictures, and some letters and numbers. Drawing and scribbling are sometimes confused with writing, and also letters are confused for one another. What is absent may be directionality and a complete command of sound-symbol correspondences.

Students in the *early letter name* stage of spelling may be characterized as beginning readers. Students are able to use most beginning and ending consonants and have solid command of sound-symbol correspondences. However, consistent use of all vowels and consonant blends and digraphs is still not present.

The *middle and late letter name* stage of spelling is characterized by students who are less hesitant in their reading, know a vowel occurs in most syllables, and have increasing command of most regular short vowel patterns and consonant blends and digraphs. They will also begin to spell some common long vowel words (e.g., *hope*). However, these students will substitute a regular word pattern for low frequency vowels (e.g., *tot* for *taught*).

Students in the *within word pattern* stage of spelling are approaching fluency and show increasing command of regular and r-controlled short vowels and consonant blends and digraphs. They are becoming more comfortable with single-syllable long vowel sounds and are beginning to use common Latin suffixes (e.g., *-tion* in *invention*). However, they still confuse some letters within words such as long vowel markers (e.g., *maik* for *make*) and some consonant patterns (e.g., *brock* for *broke*). What is still absent is consonant doubling (e.g., *poped* for *popped*).

Bear et al. discuss the *syllable juncture* and *derivational constancy* stages of orthographic development together because many of the features that describe each stage are shared. In these stages students read fluently as their word recognition is automatic. Meaning takes on greater influence at these stages. In the syllable juncture stage students are negotiating the rules that apply to pattern-to-sound relationships at places where syllables meet and when adding affixes to words. The level of meaning is focused on affixation. In the derivational constancy stage students are exploring how the derivations and spellings of parts of words remain the same across different words. The level of meaning in this stage is on root words and the Latin and Greek origins of polysyllabic words.

b. Word Study spelling inventory. To determine the stage of orthographic development, teachers need to document the way students spell. The spelling inventory Bear et al. recommend is quick and easy for teachers to administer. Instead of singling students out to complete the inventory, it should be administered in small groups; this provides a more relaxed atmosphere for students. Let students know you are administering the inventory to learn about how they spell; students should also be told that the inventory is not a test; rather it is to help you become a better teacher. Bear et al. suggest the following script to introduce the inventory:

> I am going to ask you to spell some words. Try to spell them the best you can. Some of the words will be easy to spell; some will be more difficult. When you do not know how to spell a word, spell it the best you can; write down all the sounds you feel and hear. (p. 38)

The inventory is administered in sets of five words. Say each word once; then say it in a sentence and repeat the word once more. Generally, the younger the students are, the fewer sets of words need to be given. Terminate the administration after students miss 3 out of 5 words in a set. Following are the words Bear et al. suggest for the spelling inventory:

Set 1: bed, ship, drive, bump, when
Set 2: train, closet, chase, float, beaches
Set 3: preparing, popping, cattle, caught, inspection
Set 4: puncture, cellar, pleasure, squirrel, fortunate
Set 5: confident, civilize, flexible, opposition, emphasize

The inventories are next scored for the number of correct spellings and analyzed for the type of errors made. In this way the stage of orthographic development and what each student knows and what is used but confused can be determined. Bear et al. suggest the following guidelines for determining the range of development based on the number of correct spellings. Zero correct indicates the preliterate or letter name stage; 1–5 correct indicates the letter name or the within word pattern stage; 5–10 correct indicates the within word pattern stage or the syllable juncture stage; and 10–25 correct indicates the syllable juncture or derivational constancy stage. Counting the number of words spelled correctly is a starting point for determining the stage of development and planning instruction, but a more detailed analysis of the errors is needed. Although Bear et al. provide a spelling checklist and an error guide to help teachers in doing this detailed analysis, they suggest that an hour or two of practice will be enough to eliminate the need to use these aids. By examining what each student knows and determining what is used but confused allows teachers to categorize students into stages. Once this is done, teachers can plan for instruction.

2. Organizing for Word Study Instruction. Word Study is an active process of comparing and contrasting whereby students categorize pictures and words. Therefore, integral to a program of Word Study are picture sorts and word sorts.

a. Word Study sorts. These sorts are phonics, spelling, and vocabulary activities that use categorization to determine similarities and differences among pictures and words. Students are asked to match pictures or words to designated key pictures or words. These key pictures or words indicate the basic categorizations that students are to examine during their sorting. The repetition of these categorization activities allows students to discover the patterns that pictures and words make and learn the sounds associated with those patterns. An average of 15 minutes daily should be allotted for directed Word Study. Bear et al. describe a number of different sorts in which students can participate.

Picture sorts. Picture sorting is a basic categorization task which asks students to group pictures with similar sounds in their name (e.g., initial consonant sounds, consonant blends and digraphs, rhyming families, vowel sounds). For instance, students might be given the letters *b, m,* and *s* and pictures that depict the following: *ball, mouse, sock, bat, man, smile, box, moon,* and *sun.* Students in pairs or groups are asked to say the names of the words the pictures depict and categorize the pictures under the correct sounds the letters say. As with all sorts, this task should first be modeled by the teacher and guidance provided to students as appropriate. This type of activity is appropriate for students in the preliterate, letter name, and early within word pattern of spelling development. Bear et al. state that picture sorting, as with all other sorts, differs from traditional phonics activities in three ways: (a) it proceeds from the known to the unknown; (b) it is analytic, versus synthetic, in approach; and, (c) it relies on critical thinking to make categorical decisions rather than drill or memorization.

Word sorts. Word sorting is like picture sorting except that printed words are used. Word sorts are useful for students who possess a functional sight word vocabulary, that is to say, students who are in the letter name stage of development or above. Depending on the stage of development, word sorts might have students categorize words into groups that share the same: beginning sounds, vowel patterns, the way vowel sounds are spelled, or syllable structure.

Word hunts. In this activity students hunt through their reading and writing for words that are additional examples of the patterns they are studying. For instance, students look for examples of long and short vowels in a text they've just finished reading. These examples would be listed under the appropriate category of sounds.

Closed sorts. These are sorts chosen by the teacher. Most of the sorts Bear et al. recommend are closed sorts.

Open sorts. These are sorts chosen by the students. They are more diagnostic in scope as teachers have the opportunity to see what categories students choose.

Blind sorts. Blind sorts are a form of a closed sort, with the category chosen by the teacher. The teacher or a buddy in a pair call out words; students point to the key word with which it belongs. This activity is useful for students who need to attend to sounds rather than the visual patterns of words.

Writing sorts. Writing sorts are a variation of both blind sorts and closed sorts. A word is called out by the teacher or a buddy; students write the word in the correct category using the key word.

Speed sorts. Speed sorts are the same as regular open or closed picture or word sorts except students try to complete the task as quickly as possible. This activity is only appropriate when accuracy is assured.

Bear et al. recommend that directed Word Study be done in small groups, suggesting that teachers look for groupings by thirds. Of course, this will depend on the spread of students into stages and the number of students with which teachers like to work in small groups. The spread of students will likely be greater in the lower grades and decrease in the upper grades as students develop their orthographic knowledge. Time should also be set aside for students to sort independently or in pairs to study further the orthographic features they are learning.

b. Principles of Word Study instruction. Although Bear et al. point out that teachers do not need to be experts on spelling before they begin Word Study instruction, they do provide ten guiding principles for implementing this program.

1. *Look for what students use but confuse.* Working with features with which students are experimenting comprises the teachable moment. Students will learn best when they are using something but using it inconsistently. The orthographic features with which students are currently negotiating should be targeted. On the other hand, it is highly unlikely that students will learn something that is absent from their experimentation with spelling. Students who spell *coat* as *cote* are ready to examine long vowel patterns; students who spell it as *cot* are not experimenting with these patterns and probably would not benefit from lessons on long vowels.

2. *A step backward is a step forward.* Simply put, provide success experiences for students in Word Study instruction. Start with something that students know before providing an activity that is new. For instance, start with initial consonants for success, and then move quickly to short vowels if that is the target.

3. *Use words students can read.* Learning to spell requires students to achieve a match between spoken language and the orthography. Therefore, the words students are examining must be words they can pronounce.

4. *Compare words that do with words that don't.* Conceptually speaking, in order to learn what something is, you must also learn what it is not. In other words, to learn orthographic features they must be contrasted with nonfeatures. For example, to learn words that double consonants (e.g., hit-hitting), they must be contrasted with words that don't (e.g., make-making).

5. *Sort by sight and sound.* Students need to be able to examine words both by how they are spelled and by how they sound. Sorts should be provided which focus on sounds as well as visual patterns (e.g., while *rain* and *cane* sound alike, they have different spelling patterns).

6. *Begin with obvious contrasts first.* To avoid potential confusion for students, start with distinctive differences for effective learning. If you are working on initial consonants, do not start with *B* and *P* as they share too many visual and sound features; *B* and *F* would be better as their differences are greater.

7. *Don't hide exceptions.* Exceptions will occur, but there is no reason to hide them. Exceptions can form the basis for new generalizations. For instance, *dove* and *live* do not conform to a long vowel pattern but may form the basis for a new pattern (e.g., words that have a *v* in them).

8. *Avoid rules.* Do not tell students rules for spelling and pronunciation; let students discover their own patterns and form generalizations from them. It is the teacher's job to make sure these generalizations are obvious in the sorts they develop.

9. *Work for automaticity.* It is not enough for students to be accurate in their sorting; they must also become fluent. Students need enough exposure in their sorting to move from being hesitant to being automatic.

10. *Return to meaningful texts.* After students have practiced with their sorts, they should be given the opportunity to look for other examples to add to their sorts. These hunts should take place in real texts.

c. Matching Word Study activities to development. In order to set up a Word Study program for your students, you will need to target activities appropriate for the developmental level you found from the spelling inventory you administered. For each level Bear et al. have recommended some general reading and writing activities as well as the focus the Word Study activities should take.

Preliterate stage. Reading and writing activities include reading to students, directed listening activities, dramatics, oral language activities, short dictations of one to two sentences, group language experience charts, drawing, and storytelling.

Word Study activities should include learning to recognize the alphabet and using concept sorts, which are sorting tasks designed to help students differentiate and expand upon their existing concepts and labels for those concepts (e.g., animals, seasons, school activities).

Early Letter Name Stage. Appropriate reading and writing activities for this stage are reading to students, concept of word activities using rhymes and pattern books, writing in journals, and rereading dictations.

The Word Study focus should be sorts of pictures and words by initial consonants, collecting known words for students' word banks, and introducing consonant blends and digraphs.

Middle and late letter name stage. In this stage reading and writing activities include reading to students, reading longer dictations, process writing, and encouraging invented spellings.

Word Study includes sorts of pictures and words by families (e.g., *-at),* short vowels, and the CVC pattern, continuing with consonant blends and digraphs, expanding students' word banks, and open and closed sorts and games with short vowels.

Within word pattern stage. In the within word pattern stage, reading and writing activities include beginning to read simple chapter books, reading to students, and writers' workshops, conferencing, and publication.

Word Study should focus on beginning a Word Study notebook which records sorts, emphasizing closed sorts of known words, sorts of long versus short vowels, examining long vowel patterns through open and closed sorts, and initiating an examination of homographs and homophones (e.g., *main* and *mane*), low frequency short vowels with consonant digraphs (e.g., *taught*), and r-controlled short vowels (e.g., first).

Syllable juncture stage. Syllable juncture reading and writing activities include reading chapter books of up to 200 pages, reading to students, beginning to work on outlining skills and adjusting reading rate to purpose, and continuing to explore reading and writing styles and genres.

In this stage Word Study should include continuing with students' notebooks, examining consonant doubling and plurals, using words to study from students' reading and writing, sorts on prefixes and suffixes, studying polysyllabic words for stress and accent, and linking meaning with spelling.

Derivational constancy stage. Activities for reading and writing include focusing on recreational reading, plenty of reading and writing experiences, and developing study skills such as notetaking, textbook reading, reference work, and report writing.

Word Study includes continuing the activities of the syllable juncture stage plus examining vowel alternations, Latin and Greek roots, and content-related words from foreign languages, and developing an interest in etymology in the content areas.

Cautions and Comments

It is obvious from this description of Word Study that it is more than just a strategy to teach phonics and word identification. It is a comprehensive approach to teaching not only phonics but also vocabulary, spelling, writing, and concept development. All aspects of Word Study seem to have been thoroughly researched over a sustained period of time. It is systematic in how it prescribes instruction based on assessment. It should be commended for how it proceeds from what students bring to the learning situation and trying to capitalize upon what they know. Through the use of discovery and critical thinking, Word Study seems to overcome the drawbacks of drill and memorization on which traditional phonics approaches seem to rely. Additionally, assessment through the use of the spelling inventory seems easy and straightforward. Indeed, a side benefit of Word Study assessment may be that it helps teachers in their ability to examine students' writing.

As with any new approach, teachers may encounter some difficulty in getting started. Orchestrating Word Study activities for a whole class or a number of classes simultaneously could be time-consuming. Indeed, informal feedback on the implementation of Word Study would indicate management issues are the major problem, particularly if teachers decide to use four to five small groups and try to implement the games at the same time they are trying to do the sorts. It might be recommended that teachers implement the approach at a slower pace rather than try to do all the activities of Word Study at once. Indeed, this may help students who are used to traditional spelling instruction and are having problems adjusting to the type of instruction appropriate for Word Study.

In recent years, the Word Study approach has been refined and expanded as feedback from various sites has informed practice and as needs have arisen. Although the approach may not have been subjected to study using traditional randomized groups design, the various elements offer a well-tested approach to word analysis with many of the elements cited as important by the National Reading Panel as well as others (e.g., Cunningham and Cunningham, 2002).

REFERENCES

Bear, D. R., M. Invernizzi, S. Templeton, and F. Johnston. 1996. *Words their way: Word study for phonics, vocabulary, and spelling instruction.* Upper Saddle River, NJ: Prentice-Hall. A book about studying words, based upon the various stages of orthographic development and designed to complement the use of any existing phonics, spelling, and vocabulary programs.

———. 2003. *Words their way: Word study for phonics, vocabulary and spelling instruction.* Upper Saddle River, NJ: Prentice-Hall.

———. 2004a. *Words their way* [Video]. Upper Saddle River, NJ: Prentice-Hall. The 67-minute, *Words their way* video presents actual classroom footage.

———. 2004b. *Words their way: Letter name.* Upper Saddle River, NJ: Prentice-Hall. Supplements *Words their way,* expanding and enriching that word study, specifically Letter Name–Alphabetic Spellers.

———. 2004c. *Words their way: Within word.* Upper Saddle River, NJ: Prentice-Hall. Supplements *Words their way,* specifically Within Word–Word Pattern Spellers.

Cunningham, P. M. 1995. *Phonics they use: Words for reading and writing* (2d ed.). New York: HarperCollins. A book of activities used by teachers designed to help students learn phonics.

Cunningham, P., and J. Cunningham. 2002. What we know about how to teach phonics. In A. Farstrup and S. J. Samuels (Eds.), *What research has to say about reading instruction* (3d ed.). Newark, DE: International Reading Association, 87–109.

Henderson, E. 1981. *Learning to read and spell: The child's knowledge of words.* DeKalb: Northern Illinois Press. The original source for the description of the stages of spelling development.

Pinnell, G. S., and I. C. Fountas. 1998. *Word matters: Teaching phonics and spelling in the reading/writing classroom.* Portsmouth, NH: Heinemann. Discusses analytic procedures for teaching phonics and spelling.

Richgels, D. J., K. J. Poremba, & L. M., McGee. 1996. Kindergartners talk about print: Phonemic awareness in meaningful contexts. *The Reading Teacher* 49(8): 632–642. Explores a contextualized approach to developing phonemic awareness. It is perceived as an approach that maintains student initiative.

Topping, K. J. 1995. Cued spelling: A powerful technique for parent and peer tutoring. *The Reading Teacher*

48(5): 374–383. Explores a structured approach to spelling to complement regular spelling instruction. It is a technique for use with trained tutors.

Zutell, J. 1996. The Directed Spelling Thinking Activity (DSTA): Providing an effective balance in word study instruction. *The Reading Teacher* 50(2): 98–108. The Directed Spelling Thinking Activity (DSTA) is a technique that engages students in actively looking for categories and relationships for words.

Analytic Method

Purpose

The Analytic Method, or implicit method, of phonics instruction is designed to provide students with strategies for decoding unfamiliar words; in this method, students are encouraged to employ their knowledge of the phonic elements within familiar words.

Rationale

As was indicated in the overview to this unit, most of the practices described in Units 1 through 4 incorporate phonics instruction as one of the areas for instructional emphasis. In Units 1 through 4 many of the approaches are primarily analytic but often include a mix, especially Guided Reading, Shared Reading, Directed Reading Activity, New Basics/Rich Literacy Tasks and the various Language Experience–oriented approaches.

The authors of the National Reading Panel report characterizes analytic phonics as follows: "Analytic phonics avoids having children pronounce sounds in isolation to figure out words. Rather children are taught to analyze letter-sound relations once the word is identified" (National Reading Panel, 2000, 2–89). The analytic method of phonic instruction is based on the premise that words can be analyzed into their common phonic elements. The student is introduced to a number of common words, from which an analysis of component parts can follow. That is, when the student has a bank of words with the same phonic features, phonics instruction begins. For example, students might be asked to discover this generalization: the common sound of the letter *b* as in *bat, ball,* and *boy.*

In essence, this method places stress on meaning and on the importance of building a bank of known words as the basis for acquiring certain phonic understandings. Letter sounds are never learned in isolation, thus avoiding the distorted notion that isolated letters have sounds. Phonic elements are learned through discovery, rather than through rote memorization.

Intended Audience

The Analytic Method of phonics instruction is suggested for use with beginning readers, where the emphasis is placed on learning sound/symbol relationships. The method may be used in conjunction with existing classroom materials or as a substitute for them, either in a group or in an individual situation.

Description of the Procedures

The discussion of the actual teaching of an Analytic phonics lesson focuses on the following steps: (1) auditory and visual discrimination, (2) auditory discrimination, (3) word blending, and (4) contextual application.

1. Auditory and Visual Discrimination. Hearing and seeing the likeness and differences in sound and letters are essential parts of phonics instruction. It is from this base that an analytic phonics lesson begins. If a teacher were to present a phonics lesson concerning the single consonant *d,* the first thing to do would be to put a sentence on the board, underlining the word containing the target element in this way:

The <u>dog</u> bit the boy.

Rather than call attention to the sentence at this time, the teacher writes other words on the board that have the same phonic element. The words should all be known words. Children are asked to look at the words and read them. It is suggested that the students, rather than the teacher, pronounce the words. Since language differences may exist between the teacher and the children, the sounds produced by the teacher may differ from those produced by the children; some confusion may arise.

Words that might be listed could include:

Dick
dot
dig
duck

Emphasis is placed upon the beginning sound as each is pronounced, but the phonic element is never separated from the word. Through questioning and discussion, the teacher would elicit the following from the students: (a) the words all start alike, and (b) the words all sound alike in the beginning.

2. Auditory Discrimination. Now that students have seen and heard that the words start alike, the next step is to reinforce further the targeted phonic element through the student's listening vocabulary. A new group of words is read by one of the students, rather than by the teacher, again to avoid possible language confusion caused by differences in sound production between the teacher and students. The students are now asked to decide whether these words begin in the same way as the group of words on the board. The new words are not written on the board. Words that might be used here could include:

dock	bank	deep
went	dark	rich

Finally, students are asked to generate words that begin the same way as the targeted phonic element:

dumb do Doug dear

3. Word Blending. If students are successful with the first two steps of the teaching procedure, they will be ready to learn to generalize from known words how the targeted phonic element sounds in new words. A sight word is written on the board, and below this word, another one with the targeted element:

mad
dad

Students are asked to focus on the similarities and differences between the word that they know and the new word with the phonic element they are learning. They should observe that: (a) the words end alike; (b) they sound alike at the end; and (c) they differ in the beginning. Once students have observed the above, the teacher draws their attention to the fact that the new word starts like the group of words on the board.

Students are now asked to interchange the beginning consonant elements; thus, the *m* is replaced with a *d*. Students must remember how words with *d* sound in order to pronounce the new word, *dad.* This process is continued with a few more pairs of words, to ensure that students can use their newly learned phonic element. Other pairs that might be used are:

bay	rip	fairy
day	dip	dairy

4. Contextual Application. The last step in this teaching strategy requires that students apply their new learning in an actual reading situation, where phonic learning is more natural than in isolation. Students are now asked to read their newly acquired words in short sentences:

My dad is at work.
What day is today?
Dip your brush in the paint.
Milk comes from a dairy.

After reading these sentences successfully, the students are asked to go back to the original sentence that started the lesson and read it:

The dog bit the boy.

Students may respond to the original sentence in different ways. Some may rhyme *log* with *dog,* substituting the initial consonant; others may have mastered the sound of *d* and use it in conjunction with context clues to decode *dog.* The important thing to remember is that nowhere in the lesson was the *d* separated from real words, thus avoiding any distortion that may result when the students sound letters in isolation.

Cautions and Comments

Substantial claims have been made by proponents of both synthetic and analytic phonics approaches as to which is the better method. Certainly, the more holistic approach taken by analytic phonics seems to be the more appropriate learning strategy. Research that bears on the influence of the variations in these approaches upon oral reading performance has yielded predictable results. As Allington (1984) indicated:

> The errors of children in meaning-emphasis programs continue to reflect greater sensitivity to contextual constraints, while those of readers in code-emphasis programs reflect greater sensitivity to graphemic cues and less awareness of context. (p. 848)

Two comments are in order concerning the use of either analytic or synthetic phonics. First, some professionals argue that the exclusive use of one approach over the other limits students' chances to master phonic principles. Moving back and forth between the two approaches may be a productive procedure if it enhances the students' abilities to deal with the abstract principles of phonics. It also may prove to be nonproductive, causing confusion rather than developing understanding.

Second, no matter which approach is chosen, it must be remembered that the ultimate test of a student's ability to use phonics is whether the student is able to read successfully for meaning and to apply such skills in contextual situations. Regardless of the method used, it is possible that a student would acquire adequate phonic skills and still remain a poor reader. With respect to either the analytic or the synthetic phonic method, it would seem imperative that students' newly acquired phonic understandings be applied to actual reading situations. In longitudinal studies of reading development, Tierney and Sheehy (2002) has reported a clear and consistent advantage for meaning-centered approaches versus decontextualized phonics instruction. A study by Dahl, Scharer, Lawson, and Grogan (1999) provides complementary evidence of the advantages of systematic phonics within meaning-centered approaches and consistent with calls for a balanced approach (Cunningham and Cunningham, 2002; Duffy and Hoffman, 2002; International Reading Association, 2002; National Reading Panel, 2000; Taylor, Pressley, and Pearson, 2002).

REFERENCES

Allington, R. L. 1984. Oral reading. In P. D. Pearson, R. Barr, M. L. Kamil, and P. Mosenthal (Eds.), *Handbook of reading research.* New York: Longman. Presents a review of research findings dealing with oral reading including the effects of different phonics approaches.

Cunningham, P., and J. Cunningham. 2002. What we know about how to teach phonics. In A. Farstrup and S. J. Samuels (Eds.), *What research has to say about reading instruction* (3d ed.). Newark, DE: International Reading Association, 87–109. Describes guidelines for teaching phonics in schools including a call for a balanced approach.

Dahl, K. L., P. L. Scharer, L. L. Lawson, and P. R. Grogan. 1999. Phonics instruction and student achievement in whole language first grade classrooms. *Reading Research Quarterly* 34(3): 312–341. Presents an extensive set of case studies of the teaching of phonics in whole language classrooms and the impact on student learning.

Duffy, G., and J. V. Hoffman. 2002. Beating the odds in literacy education: Not the "betting on" but the "bettering of" schools and teachers. In B. Taylor, M. Pressley, and P. D. Pearson (Eds.), *Teaching reading: Effective schools, accomplished teachers.* Mahwah, NJ: Erlbaum, 375–387. Discusses the limitations of the notion of best practice and offers suggestions for practice.

Durkin, D. 1983. *Teaching them to read* (4th ed.). Boston: Allyn and Bacon, 177–205. Describes both the content of and the various teaching procedures used in phonics.

Foorman, B. 1995. Research on "the great debate": Code-oriented versus whole language approaches to reading instruction. *School Psychology Review,* 24(3): 376–392. Argues for a synthetic approach to phonics in the context of discussing code-oriented versus whole language issues.

International Reading Association. 2002. *Evidence-based reading instruction: Putting the National Reading panel report into practice.* Newark, DE: Author, 232–236. Discusses the endorsed recommendations from the International Reading Association, includes reference to the limitations of the notion of best method for and advocates for a balanced approach to teaching reading.

Johnson, D. D., and P. D. Pearson. 1978. *Teaching reading vocabulary.* New York: Holt, Rinehart and Winston. Examines word identification in both the analytic and the synthetic approaches.

———. 1984. *Teaching reading vocabulary* (2nd ed.). New York: Holt, Rinehart and Winston. A revised edition of their earlier book.

National Reading Panel. 2000. *Teaching children to read: An evidence-based assessment of the scientific research literature on reading and its implications for reading instruction* (Report of the Subgroups). Washington, DC: U.S. Department of Health and Human Services, Public Health Service, National Institutes of Health, and the National Institute of Child Health and Human Development. Reports the purposes, methods and findings of the synthesis in several areas including discussions of what may meet the need of students incurring difficulty.

Stahl, S. A. 1992. Saying the "p" word: Nine guidelines for exemplary phonics instruction. *The Reading Teacher* 45: 618–625. Discusses guidelines for effective phonics instruction.

Strickland, D. S. 1998. *Teaching phonics today: A primer for educators.* Newark, DE: International Reading Association. Discusses the teaching of systematic phonics in a meaning centered fashion.

Taylor, B., M. Pressley, and P. D. Pearson. 2002. Research-supported characteristics of teachers and schools that promote teaching achievement. In B. Taylor, M. Pressley, and P. D. Pearson (Eds.), *Teaching reading: Effective schools, accomplished teachers.* Mahwah, NJ: Erlbaum, 361–373. Discusses the essential elements in defining effective schools and the need for a balanced approach to teaching reading.

Tierney, R. J. 1992. Studies of reading and writing growth: Longitudinal research on literacy acquisition. In J. Flood, J. Jensen, D. Lapp, and J. R. Squire (Eds.), *Handbook of research on teaching the language arts.* New York: Macmillan.

Tierney, R. J., and M. Sheehy. 2002. What longitudinal studies say about literacy development/what literacy development says about longitudinal studies. In J. Flood, J. Jensen, D. Lapp, and J. R. Squire (Eds.), *Handbook of research on teaching the language arts,* Vol. II. New York: Macmillan, 171–191. An updated review of longitudinal studies of reading development.

United States Congress H.R. 2614 Reading Excellence Act. Presents a definition of reading in support of a selected view of reading and reading research.

Synthetic Word Families

Purpose

The purpose of Synthetic Word Families, or explicit phonics, is to: (1) increase vocabulary through the use of consonant substitution and (2) aid students in word identification skills by employing the strategy of blending letter sounds with contrasting word elements.

Rationale

The authors of the National Reading Panel report characterizes synthetic phonics as programs that teach children to convert letters into sounds or phonemes and then blend the sounds to form recognizable words (National Reading Panel, 2000, 2–89). In Units 1 through 4 a number of approaches and practices incorporate phonics instruction as one of the areas for instructional emphasis. In terms of synthetic phonics, Direct Instruction, Monroe Methods, Gillingham-Stillman, and Success for All represent synthetically oriented approaches, although many approaches adopt practices that are somewhat synthetic in orientation. Taken together, the discussion of synthetic approaches and these aforementioned strategies provide for a solid representation of synthetic approaches to teaching phonics. However, it should be noted that the National Reading Panel mentions those included in the compendium as well as a few that are not, but most of these are published reading programs that are purposely not included in the book.

To a large extent, Synthetic Word Families often become the cornerstone of the synthetic approach. Word families are word elements that contain both vowel and consonant elements, to which can be synthetically blended an initial consonant element. For instance, the word family *at* can be blended with the sounds of *b, c, f,* and *h* to form *bat, cat, fat,* and *hat.* Word families have also been variously referred to as phonograms, graphemic bases, and spelling patterns; they form the basis for reading systems claiming a linguistic approach.

The use of word families is based upon the principle that English is an alphabetic writing system employing a methodical code that is easily broken. This code consists of many contrasting patterns (word families), which the student can take advantage of when learning to read. Therefore, reading instruction centered around the patterns of language and the contrasting elements that may be generated from those patterns might be highly conducive to success in identifying unknown words and in learning to read. Less importance is placed on learning words in context, since instruction with Synthetic Word Families begins with parts and proceeds to form wholes.

When using word families in conjunction with consonant substitution, the instructor can capitalize on the principle of minimal contrast and the student's knowledge of letter sounds. After a model word (a known word) has been explored for its elements, the word family (vowel and consonant elements) can be used to generate new words through consonant substitution. Learning is accomplished by building on what is already known, varying that known element only minimally. Thus, the identification of new words is centered around maximum similarity and minimum difference—the maximum similarity being the word family, and the minimum difference being the synthetically blended consonant.

Intended Audience

The use of Synthetic Word Families is commonly associated with beginning reading instruction in the primary grades. Although Synthetic Word Families are intended to be used as the total reading program, they may also be used as a supplement for other materials designed to teach word identification skills.

Description of the Procedures

Some background information is in order before dealing with the teaching procedure. The following would be representative of the use of Synthetic Word Families in books known as linguistic readers:

Nat is a cat
Is Nat fat?
Nat is fat.
Nat is a fat cat.*

*C. C. Fries, A. C. Fries, R. Wilson, and M. K. Randolph, *Merrill linguistic readers: First reader.* (Columbus, OH: Charles E. Merrill, 1965) 4.

The above is a prime example of the use of initial consonant substitution and minimal contrasts within the word family *at.*

Aukerman (1984) has described the variety of ways word families are used in linguistic readers. Synthetic Word Families are built upon a base sound that may be a sound in any position—beginning, medial, or ending. For instance, using the short vowel sound of *a* (aah) with both initial and final consonant substitution, a number of combinations may be generated:

fa (fat)	pa (pal)	na (nab)
da (dad)	sa (sad)	va (van)
ma (mad)	ba (bat)	la (lap)
	or	
at	ax (axe)	ap (apt)
am	ad (add)	ak (ack)
an (ant)	ag	as

Nonsense combinations are encouraged in linguistic material, since they may be parts of meaningful words that the student may meet later.

A second method would be to use a medial position and word family, such as *-an,* and build words or nonwords that are larger in length:

ban	bans	band
bant	banx	banp
bang	banz	bank

Using different initial consonant sounds, numerous other combinations may be built, both with and without meaning.

Word pairs may also be used as follows:

lamp	belt	tilt	band
ramp	felt	pilt	cand

On the other hand, if more regularity is desired, an identical base with the five short vowel sounds could be used, to which initial consonant sounds might be added:

b-all	g-all	p-all
c-all	h-all	s-all
f-all	m-all	t-all
	or	
b-ell	j-ell	p-ell
d-ell	m-ell	s-ell
f-ell	n-ell	t-ell

Used in the previously mentioned ways, the Synthetic Word Family concept can produce innumerable word combinations.

To present a more manageable application of Synthetic Word Families, and to show how they may be fit into a teaching procedure to augment other types of instruction in word identification, we will focus our discussion of Synthetic Word Families on: (1) prior concepts, (2) teacher guidance, and (3) student independence.

1. Prior Concepts. There are certain prior concepts or learnings that students may need to have before the teacher can initiate a Synthetic Word Families approach. These include: (a) a small bank of known words, (b) rhyming words, and (c) consonant sounds.

A first pedagogical principle is that learning proceeds from the known to the unknown. In accordance with this principle, the Synthetic Word Families approach begins with a small bank of known words to serve as a referent from which to generate new words. It is recommended that whole words, rather than elements of words, be used to initiate this procedure. For example, *b-ell* might be easier to learn than *-ell.*

Students must be sensitive to rhyme. They must be able to recognize that words that look alike at their end (possess the same word family) probably rhyme in most cases. In addition, students must know which parts of rhyming words sound alike, and which parts do not. To this end, students should be given auditory discrimination activities to ensure that they can differentiate between the rhyming and nonrhyming words.

Finally, knowledge of individual consonant sounds is necessary, so that students may effectively synthesize these sounds with word families. Needless to say, it will be difficult to rhyme words without a knowledge of consonant sounds.

2. Teacher Guidance. Again, as with most teaching procedures, it must not be assumed that even if students have mastered all necessary prerequisites, they will be able to use word families effectively to improve word identification abilities. The teacher must guide the students toward independence.

Initially, teachers should select a model word that is part of the student's known vocabulary. New words are generated by using: (a) the same word family as the model word and (b) differing beginning consonant sounds, which may be placed next to the model. An example might be:

dog
bog
fog
hog
log

Through observation and teacher encouragement, students will see that the new words look like the model except for the initial consonant. Students who have mastered consonant sounds will be able to read the minimally contrasting words. By doing this, students will recognize that all words sound alike. The teacher may point out that detecting word family elements can aid in pronouncing unfamiliar words.

Exercises as described above should be continued by using other words the students know as a basis and blending known consonant sounds to them. Gradually, the teacher should allow the students to generate new words. Later on, the use of diagraphs and blends as possible initial substitutes should be explored and demonstrated.

By going through these exercises diligently, the teacher can be confident that the students are able to use the concept of Synthetic Word Families in substitution exercises. However, there may not be any transfer to "real" reading and to student independence from these exercises alone.

3. Student Independence. Exercises like these do not necessarily ensure that students will be able to match mentally the word families they know with the unfamiliar words they encounter in reading. To help students gain independence in using word families, Cunningham, Moore, Cunningham, and Moore (1983) have recommended a teaching procedure to aid students in mentally processing word matches to identify unfamiliar words in their reading.

The first step in this strategy is to create five cards with known words for each student. For instance, the five word cards may be: *tell, can, dog, it,* and *bump.* The teacher writes a word on the board, such as *bell,* and students are expected to find a match among their cards. This is followed by the teacher, or more preferably, by a student volunteer, demonstrating how the words look alike (word family) and how they differ (initial consonant), and then pronouncing both words. Searching through their small bank of word cards to secure a match will aid students in eventually gaining the facility to match words on their own when reading print. Word cards are continually added, and this procedure is continued, until students have mastered 15 word cards as well as possible matches.

The second step of this strategy is for students to match a word printed on the board without the aid of the word cards. This is the point where students start to use their total mental processes to provide a match. All 15 words are used in this step.

The third step involves the extension of the 15 words to include all the words the students know. A new model word is given, and students are asked to figure out the unknown word by attempting to match it with a known word in their heads. In this way, they gain further independence in using Synthetic Word Families to decode unknown words.

The fourth and final step is for students to apply this concept to their reading. When a student encounters difficult words, the teacher should encourage the student to think of a word family that ends like the unknown word, to aid in identifying it. It is here that students face the true test of using Synthetic Word Families, i.e., word families to aid in decoding unknown words.

Cautions and Comments

When using Synthetic Word Families as an aid to improving word recognition, teachers need to be aware of some possible problems. For example, using word families in isolation without helping students use them in actual reading situations may be problematic. Students need to be shown the relevance of word families to reading text selections. Indeed, the use of word families may deteriorate into a game of word calling if students are merely asked to play with words, no matter how exciting this activity may become. Furthermore, students taught using synthetic methods may be prone to become overdependent on graphic clues.

Some problems may arise in generating new words using word families. Nonsense words, though advocated by linguistic approaches to reading, should be avoided. By definition, these words are meaningless, despite the linguistic consistency they provide. They are likely to contribute to readers' substituting nonsense words for unknown words in text where real words should apply.

The second area of concern is that of irregular words. For instance, does *bow* rhyme with *cow* or *row?* Furthermore, consonant sounds may become distorted when sounded separately, as with the sound of *b-buh.* Should *bat* be pronounced as *buh-at?*

An alternate use of Synthetic Word Families has been developed by LaPray (1972) for use with poor readers. Those students who have mastered little else in reading except their names are asked to list spontaneously their names and other words they may know. Utilizing the few words generated, new words can be built from their known parts. For example, if a student lists only *Bill, dog, and mom,* new words may be built and learned, first by sound and then by context, by putting them into a short phrase or sentence.

Perhaps the best known example of a synthetic phonics approach is Direct Instruction, which is an integral part of an approach called Reading Mastery. Despite claims of the success of the approach through the second grade, most students do not appear to retain an advantage and may lag behind students who have received systematic phonics in more meaning-centered approach (Dahl, Scharer, Lawson, and Grogan, 1999; Foorman, 1995; Grisson, 1988; Tierney, 1992; Tierney and Sheehy, 2002).

Finally, to leave the reader some food for thought, Kenneth Goodman's (1976) comments on the efficacy of phonic instruction are worthy of note.

> You have to put skills in the context of meaning. That's where they have the most value. That's where they maintain their proper proportion. And there they won't lead to the development of problems which eventually interfere with learning to read. In fact, children learn best this way because skills taught in context don't result in incorrect generalizations which then have to be overcome.
>
> Take the common emphasis on phonic skills. When you isolate a letter or a sound, you make it more abstract, and you also change its relative value. If I give kids the sentence, "The girl is in the garden," I can talk about the initial letter of girl and the sound that it relates to. But if I give the lesson backwards, if I start with the sound of g, then I'm saying that each letter has a value—a meaning. That's not true. The value is dependent on the sequence that it's in. And the importance of noticing and using a particular graphic cue is exaggerated because in context it works together with everything else. (p. 7)

In a similar vein, the findings of the National Reading Panel emphasize the importance of balancing a synthetic approach with an emphasis on meaning and stress the importance of teachers focusing on the purpose of phonics instruction in terms of developing readers' ability to apply their skills in context. Likewise, various other discussions of the role of phonics express similar concerns (e.g., Cunningham and Cunningham, 2002).

REFERENCES

Aukerman, R. C. 1984. *Approaches to beginning reading* (2d ed.). New York: John Wiley and Sons, 177–220. Discusses the use of Synthetic Word Families as one basic approach to phonics instruction. Also describes, in detail, linguistically oriented materials used in beginning reading instruction.

Carnine, D., and J. Silbert. 1979. *Direct instruction reading* (2d ed.). Columbus, OH: Merrill. Represents a thorough discussion of the assumptions, arguments, claims, and elements that constitute teaching explicit and synthetic phonics from the perspective of those advocating direct instruction.

Carnine, D. W., J. Silbert, and E. J. Kameenui. 1997. *Direct instruction reading* (3d ed.). Columbus, OH: Merrill. Provides a detailed examination of the tenets of direct instruction with illustrations and guidelines for practice.

———. 2004. *Direct instruction reading* (4th ed.). Columbus, OH: Merrill. More recent edition of the aforementioned book with updated research and additional illustrations.

Cunningham, P., and J. Cunningham. 2002. What we know about how to teach phonics. In A. Farstrup & S. J. Samuels (Eds.), *What research has to say about reading instruction* (3d ed.). Newark, DE: International Reading Association, 87–109. Describes guidelines for teaching phonics in schools, including a call for a balanced approach.

Cunningham, P. M., S. A. Moore, J. W. Cunningham, and D. W. Moore. 1983. *Reading in elementary classrooms: Strategies and observations.* New York: Longman. Advocates the use of consonant substitution with word families to build sight vocabulary.

Dahl, K. L., P. L. Scharer, L. L. Lawson, and P. R. Grogan. 1999. Phonics instruction and student achievement in whole language first grade classrooms. *Reading Research Quarterly* 34(3): 321–341. Presents an extensive set of case studies of the teaching of phonics in whole language classrooms and the impact on student learning.

Duffy, G., and Hoffman, J. V. 2002. Beating the odds in literacy education: Not the "betting on" but the "bettering of" schools and teachers. In B. Taylor, M. Pressley, and P. D. Pearson (Eds.), *Teaching reading: Effective schools, accomplished teachers.* Mahwah, NJ: Erlbaum, 361–373. Discusses the limitations of the notion of best practice and offers suggestions for practice.

Durkin, D. 1983. *Teaching them to read* (4th ed.). Boston: Allyn and Bacon. Describes different phonic approaches, but especially the synthetic.

Englemann, S. 1969. *DISTAR reading program.* Chicago: Science Research Associates. Presents the reading program that is the primary example of Direct Instruction.

———. 1980. *Direct instruction.* Englewood Cliffs, NJ: Prentice-Hall. The original volume discussing direct instruction, including a form of synthetic phonics.

Foorman, B. 1995. Research on "the great debate": Code-oriented versus whole language approaches to reading instruction. *School Psychology Review,* 24(3): 376–392. Argues for a synthetic approach to phonics in the context of discussing code-oriented versus whole language issues.

Goodman, K. 1976. *Reading: A conversation with Kenneth Goodman.* Glenview, IL: Scott, Foresman. Goodman comments on reading.

Grossen, B. (in press). The research base for Reading Mastery, SRA http:\\darkwing.uoregon.edu/~adiep/rdgtxt.htm. Presents a detailed rationale for direct instruction and research that arguably supports the approach.

Hoffman, J. V., M. Sailors, and E. U. Patterson. 2001. Decodable texts for beginning reading instruction: The Year 2000 Basals. *Journal of Literacy Research* 34(3): 269–298.

Jenkins, J. R., and P. F. Vadasy. 2000. Tutoring first-grade struggling readers in phonological reading skills. *Learning Disabilities Research and Practice* 15(2): 75–85. Retrieved from the Academic Search Premier database. Provides details about *Sound Partner,* a tutoring program designed to supplement classroom reading instruction.

Juel, C., and C. Minden-Cupp. 2000. Learning to read words: Linguistic units and instructional strategies. *Reading Research Quarterly* 35(4): 458–492. Presents research on a synthetic approach to teaching word recognition

Kameenui, E. J., D. C. Simmons, D. Chard, and S. Dickson. 1997. Direct instruction reading. In S. A. Stahl and D. A. Hayes (Eds.), *Instructional models in reading.* Mahwah, NJ: Erlbaum, 59–84. Discusses the tenets and historical antecedents of Direct Instruction, which incorporates a synthetic approach to teaching phonics.

LaPray, M. 1972. *Teaching children to become independent readers.* New York: Center for Applied Research in Education. Advocates the use of Synthetic Word Families as a means to establish success-oriented instruction with students experiencing reading difficulties.

National Reading Panel. 2000. *Teaching children to read: An evidence-based assessment of the scientific research literature on reading and its implications for reading instruction* (Report of the Subgroups). Washington, DC: U.S. Department of Health and Human Services, Public Health Service, National Institutes of Health, and the National Institute of Child Health and Human Development. Reports the purposes, methods, and findings of the synthesis in several areas including discussions of what may meet the needs of students incurring difficulty.

Strickland, D. S. 1998. Teaching phonics today: A primer for educators. Newark, DE: International Reading Association. Discusses the teaching of systematic phonics in a meaning centered fashion.

Taylor, B., M. Pressley, and P. D. Pearson. 2002. Research-supported characteristics of teachers and schools that promote teaching achievement. In B. Taylor, M. Pressley, and P. D. Pearson (Eds.), *Teaching reading: Effective schools, accomplished teachers.* Mahwah, NJ: Erlbaum, 361–373. Discusses the essential elements in defining effective schools and the need for a balanced approach to teaching reading.

Tierney, R. J. 1992. Studies of reading and writing growth: Longitudinal research on literacy acquisition. In J. Flood, J. Jensen, D. Lapp, and J. R. Squire (Eds.),

Handbook of research on teaching the language arts. New York: Macmillan.

Tierney, R. J., and M. Sheehy. 2002. What longitudinal studies say about literacy development/what literacy development says about longitudinal studies. In J. Flood, J. Jensen, D. Lapp, and J. R. Squire (Eds.), *Handbook of research on teaching the language arts,* Vol. II. New York: Macmillan, 171–191. An updated review of longitudinal reading development studies.

U.S. Congress H.R. 2614 Reading Excellence Act. Presents a definition of reading in support of a selected view of reading and reading research.

Syllabary/Analogy Method

Purpose

The purpose of the Syllabary/Analogy Method is to: (1) teach word identification skills through the use of the syllable as the unit of instruction; and (2) use a comparison-contrast strategy to decode words by proceeding from known word parts to unknown word parts.

Rationale

The Analogy Method of teaching phonics or the Syllabary approach teaches children to use parts of written words they already know to identify new words. The Syllabary/Analogy Method of improving word recognition skills is based upon the use of the syllable as the unit of pronunciation. It is an alternative to traditional phonics, which is based upon the use of phoneme/grapheme correspondence.

Phonemes, the basic sounds of language, become distorted when pronounced in isolation; i.e., the sound of the letter *b* pronounced in isolation is *buh.* Some students seem to have difficulty learning to pronounce these units and even more trouble blending them together; i.e., *buh-ah-tuh* = *bat.* Although the use of phonics to decode unknown words presents difficulty to some, most students do have the facility to segment words into syllables (Gibson and Levin, 1975).

The Syllabary, seemingly a more natural unit of pronunciation for some students, may provide a sound means to overcome those phonological problems by beginning with those units (syllables) that are more easily recognized and pronounced in isolation (Gleitman and Rozin, 1973). To illustrate this point with the word *paper,* note the difference in ease of pronunciation between *puh-aper* (only first letter sound in isolation) versus *pa-per* (two syllables in isolation). This premise and the use of a comparison-contrast strategy to decode unknown words form the basis of the Syllabary, which was developed as a means to teach word recognition skills.

There are some differences among the teacher strategies advocated by the various materials for teaching beginning readers decoding skills; however, it can be inferred that: (1) certain rules must be applied by readers to identify unfamiliar words, and (2) they must be applied in some certain order. To identify an unknown word, readers are taught to apply an ordered set of syllabication rules and then to apply phonic rules with each of the individual syllables.

Cunningham provides this example with the word *recertify* to illustrate the word identification processes a reader might typically use:

1. Reader decides on the number of syllables by counting the vowels (remembering that the *y* at the end of a word is a vowel): four vowels = four syllables.

2. Reader divides the word in syllables by applying the following ordered rules:
   a. Divide between a root word and a prefix: *re certify.*
   b. Divide between two intervocalic consonants (except final consonant, of course): *re cer tify.*
   c. Divide before a single intervocalic consonant: *re cer ti fy.*

3. Reader applies rules to the letters in each syllable.
   a. *re:* ends in a vowel—long *e* sound; think long *e* sound—blend with *r*—pronounce *rē.*
   b. *cer:* *c* before *e, i,* or *y* usually has the *s* sound; *e* is controlled by *r.* Blend *c* with *er*—pronounce *ser.*
   c. *ti:* just like first syllable, if it ends in a vowel; try the long sound—pronounce *tī.*
   d. *fy:* when it is a vowel rather than a consonant, *y* can be pronounced as in *cry* or as in *daddy.* Try *fi.*

4. Reader blends all four syllables together: *re ser ti fi.* Reader does not recognize word as one he or she has heard before or knows a meaning for, so reader tries different sound correspondences.

5. Reader tries a different sound for the syllables. Perhaps it is a *y* as in *daddy: rē ser tī fē.* Still not a word reader knows; perhaps this is a word the reader has never heard of before?

6. Finally, reader remembers about unaccented syllables and tries a schwa in different places until he happens upon the correct pronunciation: *rē ser t'fī.* "Oh, like what happens if you forget to renew your license and have to be recertified to get another license."

7. Reader continues reading (Cunningham, 1975–76, 129–130).

Although it may seem difficult, if not impossible, for this process to take place in a reader's mind as he or she attempts to identify an unknown word, this current mode of word identification processes is advocated and taught to elementary school students.

To provide an alternative to the theory that students apply an ordered set of rules in word identification, Cunningham (1975–76) proposes a synthesized theory of mediated word identification, based on these premises:

1. Words and word parts are stored in the human memory.

2. Word identification does not involve the application of teacher-taught rules; rather, it involves a search through this memory-store, comparing the unknown with the known.

3. Unfamiliar words not recognized on sight are segmented into units.

4. These units are compared/contrasted with known words, with word parts, or with fragments, for identification.

5. Recombining the units results in a word for which the reader knows a meaning or a sound referent.

6. Readers form their own rules (they are not taught rules) for decoding unfamiliar words by comparing/contrasting the unknown with the known.

Applying the synthesized theory of word identification to the previous example with *recertify,* it can be assumed that the reader has numerous words and word parts in his memory-store and has also developed the ability to compare the unknown to the known. Segmenting an unfamiliar word occurs not by successively applying adult-taught syllabication rules, but by recognizing known parts in the unknown whole.

The reader can identify the unfamiliar whole *recertify* through a variety of comparisons such as:

1. If *certify* is in the reader's memory-store, along with either the word part *re* or other words beginning with *re* (*reexamine; relay*), the resulting combination of the two parts is tested against words for which the reader has sound and/or meaning referents.

2. If *certify* is not in the reader's store, it might be segmented into more manageable units. For instance, the reader might have *identify* or *sanctify* for the segment *tify.* The reader could identify *re* as described. *Cer* might be secured from parts of *certainly* or *ceramics.* Again, the reader would combine parts for comparison against the reader's sound and/or meaning referents.

3. If a wrong match is chosen from the reader's word-store (*recreation* instead of *relay,* or *ceremony* instead of *certainly*), the reader will be unable to identify it as there will be neither sound nor meaning referent. The reader will reenter his or her memory-store for a more appropriate match.

Intended Audience

Gleitman and Rozin (1973) suggested three possible ways to incorporate the use of the Syllabary in reading instruction in the elementary grades. First, it may be used as an introductory system to make phonics utility more accessible to students. Second, the Syllabary may be used as a substitute for teaching many phonics principles, thus minimizing the quantity of instruction in that area. Finally, Gleitman and Rozin recommend that the Syllabary could be used as a remedial approach to word recognition in cases where students cannot master phonics principles. It is the latter use that Cunningham (1975–76) demonstrated successfully in a study investigating the use of the syllable as a means to improve word recognition skills. Therefore, the Syllabary seems most appropriate for augmenting other forms of word recognition instruction for beginning readers or for readers experiencing difficulty with sound/symbol relationships.

Description of the Procedures

To employ the Syllabary strategy to improve readers' word identification skills, the teacher would follow these steps:

1. Teacher-dominated training
2. Student-oriented practice
3. Meaningful reading

1. Teacher-Dominated Training. The teacher must not assume that students will readily grasp the thrust of the Syllabary. Teachers should start with familiar one-syllable words before moving on to less familiar polysyllabic words. Beginning the training with familiar monosyllabic words ensures that students will be able to call upon their own word-store.

The teacher might begin with words like *pen, sill, for,* and *wind* to illustrate how words like *penny, pencil, silly, before, windy, window,* and *windowsill* may be identified. In this way, words or word parts that are known become established in the word-store, enabling the students to use these known words in comparing unknown polysyllabic words. For example, knowledge of the words *wind* and *silly* will enable a student to make the appropriate comparisons to identify the word *windowsill.* Teacher questioning should accompany this step of acquainting students with the use of the Syllabary to ensure the match between syllables and the known word parts. Gleitman and Rozin (1973) have recommended the use of pictures as an aid to identifying unknown words by their syllabic parts. Some examples are shown in Figure 5.1.

2. Student-Oriented Practice. At this point in the strategy, the students are ready to begin more independent work with the concept of the Syllabary. Polysyllabic words are introduced for students to decode using the comparison/contrast strategy. Work may be done individually, but is probably best accomplished in pairs or in small groups until students have a firm grasp of the concept. An illustration of this type of practice follows.

Words like *sleepless, blanket,* and *pillow* might be introduced. The teacher is cautioned that it may be necessary to guide the students through a few practice words before they can work independently. For instance, using the syllabary to decode *sleepless,* the teacher can show children *less,* which might be a word in their memory-store or a word part, as in *unless.*

Again, the teacher is illustrating how to compare unknown words to known words or word parts in the students' word-stores. As students gain skill and confidence in using the comparison/contrast strategy, more complex words may be introduced. It is suggested that as students are exposed to new words, these words be written on word cards for review and reinforcement. The comparisons students have made from their word-stores may be written on the back of the card and may be referred to by the student if any difficulty arises during the review. Review with flash cards may be accomplished by pairing the students.

3. Meaningful Reading. It is to be remembered that the implementation and usage of the Syllabary has occurred only when unknown words were seen in isolation. The ultimate test of any form of word identification occurs when the student becomes able to decode unknown words from a meaningful context. Hence, the follow-up step in the use of the Syllabary is to develop students' ability to deal with unknown words in story reading.

FIGURE 5.1 Use of Pictures to Identify Unknown Words

It is recommended that a short story consisting of a few paragraphs be constructed, using many of the words students have studied in isolation. Variations of those words or similar words should also be incorporated. For example, the polysyllabic words used in Section 2, student-oriented practice, should be used, but the teacher should attempt to use the variations (*sleeping; pill*) as well. In this way, the teacher can be assured that the comparison/contrast word identification strategy is being successfully implemented and has been transferred to real reading. An illustration of a short story using these words is included.

Nim looked very sleepy.
He threw his pillow on the floor.
He removed his blanket.
He had not gotten to sleep.
It had been a sleepless night.

Cautions and Comments

There are apparent merits to a word identification strategy employing the Syllabary; however, there are also a number of cautions of which teachers should be aware. First, although the syllable may be more easily pronounced in isolation than a phoneme, there are thousands of separate syllables in the English language. The task of dealing with each of these units might be overwhelming. For this reason, it should be used in conjunction with sound/symbol relationships.

Second, dialect differences in readers make for differences in syllable pronunciations. What may seem to be an obvious comparison with an individual's word-store may be obvious only to the teacher who also has a particular dialectical pattern. The students may not necessarily be contemplating the obvious comparison because of differences in their speech.

Third, the syllable is very much influenced by the stress it receives, i.e., the sound shifts with the stress (Goodman, 1973). For example, *site* becomes *situate* by adding more meaning units to the original word. This could very easily produce confusion for the younger reader.

Despite these problems, the Syllabary/Analogy approach has been supported by research. Cunningham (1975–76, 1978) found differences between a group trained to use the Syllabary concept and a control group, when both groups attempted to decode unknown words.

Elements of the Syllabary/Analogy Method—namely, the use of known words as cues to unknown words—have been incorporated successfully in strategies developed and used by Benchmark school in Pennsylvania (Gaskins et al., 1997), Gunning (1995), and by Lovett, Warren-Chaplin, and Ransby (1990).

REFERENCES

Cunningham, P. M. 1975–76. Investigating a synthesized theory of mediated word identification. *Reading Research Quarterly* 11: 127–143. Reports the results of an experiment designed to improve the word identification abilities of second graders using a Syllabary approach.

———. 1978. A compare/contrast theory of mediated word identification. *The Reading Teacher* 32: 774–778. Reports a follow-up to the earlier study with fourth and fifth grade students.

———. 1995. *Phonics they use* (2d ed.). New York: HarperCollins. In exploring phonics instruction, Cunningham details the use of the Analogy approach.

Gaskins, I. W., L. C. Ehri, C. Cress, C. O'Hara, and K. Donnelly. 1997. Procedures for word learning: Making discoveries about words. *The Reading Teacher* 50(4): 312–327. Details the development of the word-learning procedures for learning key words used in the Benchmark Word Identification Program.

Gaskins, R. W., and I. W. Gaskins. 1997. Creating readers who read for meaning and love to read: The Benchmark School Reading Program. In S. A. Stahl and D. A. Hayes (Eds.), *Instructional models in reading*. Mahwah, NJ: Erlbaum, 131–159. Explores the antecedents and nature of the Analogy approach used at Benchmark School.

Gibson, E. J., and H. Levin. 1975. *The psychology of reading*. Cambridge: MIT Press. Describes the use of the syllabic method as a means to learn to read in various languages.

Gleitman, L., and P. Rozin. 1973. Teaching reading by use of a syllabary. *Reading Research Quarterly* 8: 447–483. Reports the successful use of the Syllabary with pictures as an introductory method to teach reading to both inner-city and suburban children.

Goodman, K. S. 1973. The 13th easy way to make learning to read difficult. *Reading Research Quarterly* 8: 484–493. Challenges the use of the Syllabary as a means of teaching word identification skills.

Gunning, T. G. 1995. Word building: A strategic approach to the teaching of phonics. *The Reading Teacher* 48(6): 484–488. Word building is a system for teaching phonics that capitalizes on the tendency of students to seek out word parts. It incorporates analogy, phonics, and word parts.

Lovett, M., P. Warren-Chaplin, and M. Ransby. 1990. Training the word recognition skills of reading disabled children: Treatment and transfer. *Journal of Educational Psychology* 82: 769–780. Presents findings from an exploration of the effectiveness of the Analogy approach.

Rozin, P., and L. R. Gleitman. 1977. The structure and acquisition of reading II: The reading process and the acquisition of the alphabetic principle. In A. Reber and O. Scarborough (Eds.), *Toward a psychology of reading*. Hillsdale, NJ: Erlbaum, 55–142. Describes research, theory, and practice built around the Syllabary approach.

Retrospective Miscue Analysis

Purpose

Retrospective Miscue Analysis was developed by Goodman and Marek (1996) as a strategy that engages readers of all ability levels in revaluing their reading by reflecting upon and evaluating the reading process by analyzing their oral reading miscues.

Rationale

One of the key concepts of Retrospective Miscue Analysis is the notion of revaluing the reader versus remediating the reader in trouble. Central to the strategy is the view that students, regardless of ability (especially when they are incurring reading difficulty) can improve their reading by self-reflection on their own processes. In particular, such reflection can simultaneously shift a reader's views, values, and approach to reading—especially if the reader applies a sociopsycholinguistic lens to examining their own reading processes. As support for these notions and undergirding the approach espoused, several case studies have been pursued.

Retrospective Miscue Analysis is both an extension of miscue analysis and a shift in orientation in its use. Retrospective Miscue Analysis builds upon the notion that miscue analysis affords a window into the reading process of students and extends its use as an assessment tool to serve teachers' needs toward meeting the needs of the readers themselves as a way of self-examining, understanding, and improving their own processes. In some ways, the strategy is not unlike video replay, which has been used as a teaching tool for providing feedback and monitoring improvements in various activities. As Goodman and Marek (1996) suggest:

> . . . it can help them come to revalue themselves as readers. . . . readers discover for themselves that reading is a process of predicting, inferring, sampling, confirming, and correcting . . . they dismantle the notion that good reading is represented by error-free reproductions of text . . . in short, . . . a strategy that has been effectively used to demonstrate to readers what we know about the reading process. . . . Much in the same way that researchers learned about the reading processes using reading miscue analysis, readers analyze their own miscues to discover the reading process for themselves. In a typical retrospective miscue session, readers listen to a previous tape recording of themselves reading a text. Then one by one they analyze several miscues, asking questions like: Did the miscue make sense? Was it corrected? Should it have been? Why was the miscue made? Did it affect my understanding of the text? (pp. ix–x)

Goodman and Marek (1996) claim that the strategy can result in readers shifting from what they term as a "skill-based text-reproduction model of the reading process" (p. x) to one that is more confidently transactional and meaning-centered.

Undergirding the strategy is a solid foundation of collaborative efforts with teachers focused upon case studies with readers as well as a history of involvement in miscue analysis research that has led to a theory of the reading process which began with Ken Goodman. The discussion of various strategies in the current volume present these notions (see Whole-Language, Unit 2, as well as Goodman's Reading Strategy Lessons, this unit). The work in Retrospective Miscue Analysis extends these notions in a number of ways in conjunction with their explorations of the nature and value of the self-reflection that they have been examining across case studies with teachers.

Case studies of readers of varying ability have been essential to the development of their notion and refinement of the strategy. From these case studies, as Goodman and Marek (1996) note, they refined their understanding of how to better approach revaluing or guide the retrospective analysis. For example, certain initial observations were made:

- All the readers brought to the reading process a wealth of linguistic and world knowledge
- Each reader had misconceptions of the reading process and most undersubscribed to a constructing meanings approach while oversubscribing to a dependence upon skills, and many had contradictions in what they viewed as characteristics of effective strategies
- All the readers had misconceptions about their proficiency as readers
- All the readers seem to have been influenced by the instructional emphases that they received in school and oftentimes these emphases had a negative impact
- Regardless of their view of reading, all readers had the potential for understanding the complexity of the reading process, the qualitative nature of the reading process, and the importance of reading for meaning
- Each reader had the ability to become more proficient.

Retrospective Miscue Analysis differs from programs intended to meet the needs of students having problems in two distinct ways. Whereas many programs approach the students with a view to remediation with predetermined interventions, Retrospective Miscue Analysis focuses upon having students revalue their own reading by reflecting upon their own processes. Whereas approaches to explicit training of strategies (based upon developing a metacognitive language for strategizing) often assume that students (especially poorer students) do not have a metalinguistic awareness of their own processes, Retrospective Miscue Analysis research has found otherwise. As Goodman and Marek (1996) argue:

> Rather than assuming that good readers have metalinguistic abilities and poor readers do not, it is more useful to discover what any reader, regardless of proficiency label, believes about the reading process, how they use their knowledge, and what they do when their beliefs conflict with what they do as they read.
>
> . . . we do not find terms metacognitive and metalinguistic awareness very useful for school settings or as a label for reading proficiencies. We prefer more direct and clear terminology. We simply state that engaging students in talking and thinking about language is one important part of reading instruction. (Marek in Goodman and Marek, 1996, p. 103)

Intended Audience

Retrospective Miscue Analysis could be enlisted as a strategy for enhancing all readers' understanding or valuing of their reading and strategies for reading.

Description of the Procedures

The procedures for implementing Retrospective Miscue Analysis are described in some detail in Goodman and Marek (1996) from which most of the following description has been drawn. Four elements are included in their description of the procedure:

Initial sessions and screening with the reader
Developing a plan for guidance
Conducting a session with the reader
Follow-up and discontinuance of the sessions

Initial Sessions and Screening with the Reader. The initial one or two sessions are intended to introduce the reader to the purposes of the reading miscue analysis, obtain some background information on the reader's history and practices as a reader, and, time permitting, to engage the reader in some oral reading.

Goodman and Marek (1996) stress the importance of apprising the reader of the purpose and nature of the initial session and subsequent series of sessions and, in so doing, address concerns and establish some rapport. Once established, the initial screening focuses upon the reader's history (including instructional history) as well as the nature of the reading (and writing) with which they are currently engaged both occupationally as well as recreationally or avocationally. There are a host of ways that such information might be pursued, and Goodman and Marek (1996) include an example interview form that may be used. It should be stressed that the interview should attempt to develop an understanding of the literate events with which the reader is engaged, including the kinds of readings they do. They might encourage the reader to share their portfolio (if they have such) or the readings they are expected to pursue or with which they are engaged. Notes are taken on the initial interview.

This initial interview serves as the basis for deciding upon a reading selection to be used for initial observations of their reading process. To this end, the observer will have the reader orally read one or more selections of sufficient length to begin to glean or understand the reader's processes for dealing with one or more texts. Following the oral reading of each selection, each reader is asked to retell what they read and sometimes develop webs or sketches depending upon the selection and the reader. Tape recordings are made of the oral reading and retelling for subsequent explorations.

Developing a Plan for Guidance. The teacher/coach will examine the tapes and notes en route to developing a plan for the subsequent sessions. The oral reading will be examined in detail in conjunction with using a miscue analysis in an attempt to understand the reader's use of various cueing systems (syntactic, semantic, phonological) as well as overall meaning-making tendencies. The teacher needs to have knowledge of miscue analysis and have had experience in understanding/interpreting oral reading patterns en route to developing a profile of the reader. Goodman and Marek (1996) stress the teacher-researcher nature of these explorations and the need to be engaged in ongoing reflection, refinement, and rethinking of what they do and might do.

In conjunction with planning for the sessions, they suggest the teacher choose to focus on certain kinds of miscues rather than all the miscues of the reader and, oftentimes, on miscues that help build the reader's confidence. For example, the teacher might focus on omissions that are syntactically or semantically acceptable. To this end, they encourage the teacher to identify certain specific miscues (from the oral reading collected) prior to the first session. As an aid to considering possible foci, Goodman and Marek (1996) offer some reader profile characteristics, or tendencies, they have encountered and possible ways these manifest themselves as miscues.

Reader Tendencies

- Reads slowly or hesitantly; miscues seem graphophonically consistent with text but may disrupt meaning
  Select miscues that are acceptable and have no graphophonic similarities.
  Select omission and insertion miscues that are acceptable.
- Seldom self-corrects
  Select miscues that represent effective prediction, disconfirmation, and self-correction strategies. Contrast with those that do not.
- Produces non-word substitutions for words in reader's oral vocabulary
  Compare miscues that are acceptable with nonword substitutions.
- Overcorrects despite semantic and syntactic acceptability of miscues
  Select fully acceptable miscues where correction is unnecessary.
- Is satisfied with focus on surface features rather than on making meaning
  Compare miscues that do and do not make sense.
  Select miscues that highlight manipulation of syntax in insertions and omissions.
- Does not consistently read efficiently
  Select miscue examples that highlight efficiency of reading.
- Unaware of the strength shown in making higher quality miscues
  Select miscue examples that highlight quality of miscues.

In subsequent sessions, they encourage teachers to examine what they have done—especially whether they engaged the reader in reflections and the quality of these discussions.

Conducting a Session with the Reader. The actual session with the reader involves the reader in a guided discussion with the teacher and coach over the tape-recorded and transcribed oral reading that was pursued. To this end, the teacher would have a tape-recorder to replay the oral reading, as well as a copy of the text read, and a copy of the same text with the miscues of the reader marked. The teacher would focus the student on preselected portions of the text that contain certain miscues and then discuss with the reader the nature and quality of their miscues. Goodman and Marek (1996) suggest the following set of questions as a start:

1. Does the miscue make sense? If not, does the miscue look like what was on the page? . . . sound like what was on the page?
2. Does the miscue sound like language?
3. Was the miscue corrected? Should it have been?
4. Why do you think that you made this miscue?
5. Did the miscue affect your understanding of the text?

Each miscue is expanded into a discussion by asking "Why do you think so?" or "How do you know?" In some cases, the teacher might not preselect the miscues. Instead, the reader is told to stop the tape-recorder when they hear something unexpected.

Goodman and Marek (1996) stress the importance of engaging the student in a meaningful discussion of his or her own miscues and stress that the conversation and questions should be pursued in a formulaic fashion. They stress that readers might need to be reoriented to the selection that they read and understand what they'll be doing, including apprising them of the focus of the session and the overriding goal of considering what they do that makes sense. They encourage teachers to experiment with ways of engaging students in these discussions—especially questions that work with different readers. Again, they stress the importance on focusing on what the reader does that is successful rather than just what they could rethink or revalue.

No single session can be exhaustive, and consideration needs to be given to the length of the session. In some cases, more than a single session is planned to discuss the miscues from a single reading or the extent the same selection can be used for subsequent discussions. Usually, the session involves the reader reading and retelling another selection to be used in the next session. It should be noted that the session requires two tape-recorders—to replay the tapes from the prior session and one to tape the current session.

The authors note that managing the Retrospective Miscue Analysis is very labor intensive. However, they indicate they have had some success in having students, in groups or in pairs, do forms of reflections with one another over their miscues. This affords students the possibility of reflecting upon their own processes as a result of being able to contrast/compare them with others. In addition, the teacher can have students bring their own materials, and rather than preselect the miscues, the teacher can select them (with the readers) in the actual sessions.

Overview of RMA Session

I. Initial Session with Reader

Preparations: Tape-recorder, background information sheet, note paper, interest inventory, and typescript for miscue markings

Steps:

1. Establish rapport, introduce session, and provide overview
2. Collect background information and conduct interview about their reading experiences and instructional history as well as views of what a good reader does
3. Tape-record reading and retelling (may occur at second session)

II. Prepare for RMA Session

Preparations: Tape-recorder, tape of previous session, typescript of text(s), RMA coding form, RMA session organizer or equivalent

Steps:

1. Check and mark typescript from previous reading
2. Code miscues
3. Preselect miscues for RMA session
4. Find and mark numbers on tape-recorder
5. Prepare organizer, listing tape numbers and identifying information

III. Conduct RMA Session

Preparation: Two tape-recorders, tape of previous reading, marked and unmarked typescripts of previous reading, two blank tapes, new reading material, and typescripts

Steps:

1. Tape-record RMA session
2. Use organizer to locate and identify preselected miscues
3. Mark the miscue with student on blank typescript
4. Discuss miscues using RMA questions as guides
5. Optional: Tape-record new reading and retelling

IV. Analyze RMA Session

Preparation: Tape-recorder, tape of RMA session, RMA response forms

Steps:

1. Listen to RMA session tape-recording and take notes
2. Transcribe significant portion of tape recording
3. Begin preparation for next RMA session

Follow-Up and Discontinuance of the Sessions. Subsequent to each session and prior to the next session, each teacher is encouraged to reflect upon the session, including doing further miscue analysis of the selection read. They are encouraged to consider what has transpired in the session, including what has been learned about predispositions as well as what the reader may reorient. Over time, the reader might bring his or her own texts to the session.

Ownership and independence are two primary goals for readers, and the Retrospective Miscue Analysis sessions pursue these and view their achievement as an ongoing endeavor for all readers. At the point in time when readers display the kind of self-engagement of appropriate reading strategies as evidenced by their miscues, and a kind of self-improving system or reflection, then the sessions are ended with a debriefing for the reader. This is intended to afford the teacher feedback on what subsequent support might be in place.

Cautions and Comments

Retrospective Miscue Analysis differs from most instructional programs that follow a cycle of pretesting students based upon a predetermined set of objectives en route to implementing an instructional program based upon a predetermined set of options. Very few programs approach readers with the goal of developing truly customized support. Retrospective Miscue Analysis is the exception. Retrospective Miscue Analysis attempts to observe readers in the act of their everyday reading and to style a program emanating from their own reflections. Most of us would appreciate having a coach watch and support our reading in this learner-centered fashion. However, I suspect that we would be keen that the coach had an in-depth understanding of the nature of reading and was able to cater to a wide array of readers.

Retrospective Miscue Analysis has the benefit of being informed by a solid foundation of research. Suggestions for implementing the strategy draw upon numerous observations of readers as well as a well-developed model of the reading process as guideposts to probing readers' reflections of their reading processes. Furthermore, the strategy has been explored over a number of sessions involving different readers (of various abilities and backgrounds) and different coaches. But, because of the interpretative and emergent nature of the guidance, the knowledge and artfulness of the coach must be considered as paramount. Indeed, a key feature of the Retrospective Miscue Analysis are practices that ensure that the teacher/coach is reflecting upon his or her own analyses and interpretations while proceeding with students. Repeatedly guidelines are provided whereby the teacher or coach observes and contemplate their guidance and directions. Further, a number of articles have begun to appear that afford a discussion of the technique in the context of its use in classrooms and on a one-to-one basis (e.g., Moore and Brantingham, 2002).

The engagement of readers in self-reflection seems underutilized in reading except as an assessment device with few links to helping readers revalue and reorient themselves. Certainly, Retrospective Miscue Analysis moves us in an important new way toward learner-centered strategies that are developmental and less intrusive.

The lens one uses to look at oneself as a reader, as well as the process used to scrutinize such snapshots, is crucial. One's image of oneself is defined in part by the lens used and the interpretative processes or orientation that guides discussion of the images. Retrospective Miscue Analysis uses oral reading (especially miscues) as the lens and the framework of a sociopsycholinguistic orientation to interpretation. Perhaps other lenses (e.g., video of students interacting with others) could be used as well as other frameworks (interactions within groups). Perhaps an additional lens might engage the students in discussing their retellings.

REFERENCES

Goodman, Y. 1996. Revaluing readers while readers revalue themselves: Retrospective Miscue Analysis. *The Reading Teacher* 49: 600–609. Details the variations of Retrospective Miscue Analysis.

Goodman, Y. M., and A. M. Marek. 1996. *Retrospective Miscue Analysis: Revaluing readers and reading.* Katonah, NY: Richard C. Owens. Provides a detailed description of the rationale and procedures for Retrospective Miscue Analysis with contributions from Kenneth Goodman as well as other educators who have explored the use of the practice in their classrooms.

———. 1998. *Retrospective Miscue Analysis: Two papers.* Occasional paper no. 19, University of Arizona, College of Education, Program in Language and Literacy. Describes some of the initial thinking of the possibilities of using Retrospective Miscue Analysis, with examples of its use.

Marek, A. M. 1987. *Retrospective Miscue Analysis as an instructional strategy with adult readers.* Unpublished doctoral dissertation, University of Arizona, Tucson. Details foundational research using Retrospective Miscue Analysis with adult learners.

Martens, P. 1998. Using Retrospective Miscue Analysis to inquire: Learning from Michael. *The Reading Teacher* 52(2): 176–180. Describes the use of Retrospective Miscue Analysis with a fourth grader, Michael.

Moore, R. A., and C. M. Aspegren. 2001. Reflective conversations between two learners: Retrospective Miscue Analysis. *Journal of Adolescent and Adult Literacy* 44(6): 492–503. Explores the use of Retrospective Miscue Analysis with adolescent readers.

Moore, R. A., and K. L. Brantingham. 2002. Nathan: A case study in reader response and retrospective miscue analysis. *The Reading Teacher* 56(5): 466–474. Explores the use of Retrospective Miscue Analysis in the context of a case study.

Goodman's Reading Strategy Lessons

Purpose

The purpose of the Reading Strategy Lessons (Y. Goodman and Burke, 1972) is to increase students' awareness of the language and thought clues available during reading. The lessons are intended to: (1) help readers focus on aspects of written language not being processed effectively, and (2) support and strengthen readers' use of clues already being used.

Rationale

In Unit 2, Whole-Language was partially described and Reading Strategy Lessons were alluded to. Reading Strategy Lessons are based on Kenneth Goodman's (1967, 1975) notions of reading that suggest that there are certain universal reading processes. These processes are applied by all readers with varying levels of proficiency across different reading material. Toward the end of acquiring meaning, these processes include:

1. The reader's selecting the appropriate and necessary language cues to make predictions
2. The reader's verifying these predictions, and
3. The reader's reprocessing language cues if predictions prove untenable

A diagram developed by Y. Goodman, Burke, and Sherman (1974), given in Figure 5.2, depicts these notions.

The general goal of the Reading Strategy Lessons is to involve students in a meaningful reading situation that does not distract them from reading with understanding. To this end, some general guidelines are suggested:

1. The language of the material used should be similar to the language of the reader and of worthy literary quality.
2. The language of the material should not be ambiguous.
3. The language of the material should use redundant information naturally.
4. The content of the material used should be both interesting and significant to readers.
5. Lessons should afford students the opportunity to apply learnings from strategy lessons to actual reading situations.

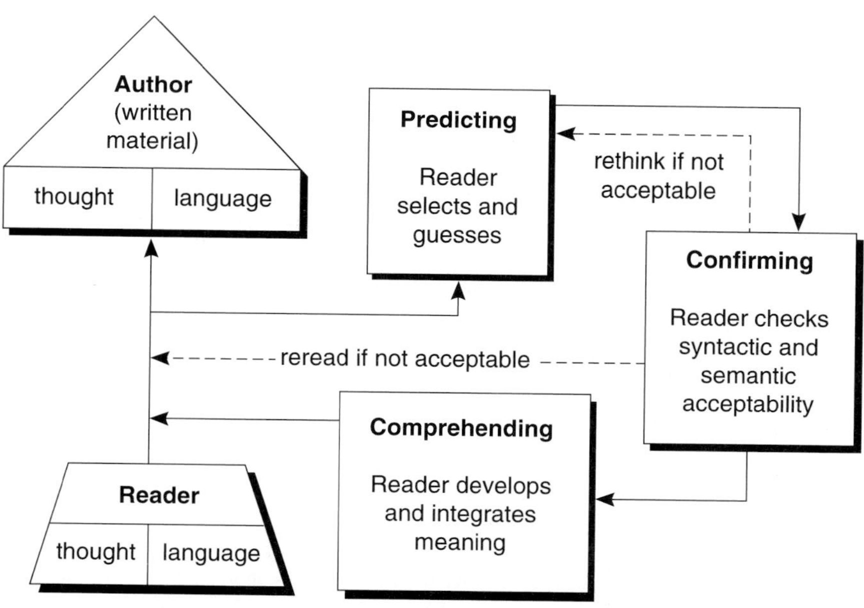

FIGURE 5.2 Proficient Silent Reading Model*

*The reader selects the appropriate language cues in order to *predict* as best he can, based upon his knowledge of language and his background experience. He *confirms* his predictions by testing these hypotheses or predictions. He does this by checking the syntactic and semantic acceptability of what he thinks he is reading against his knowledge of language and the world. Finally, he *comprehends* those items he believes to be significant. He integrates this new meaning or knowledge into an established meaning system. He then interacts with the print again. The process is continuous, and as we read, we constantly add, alter, or reorganize the meanings.

Source: Y. M. Goodman, Burke, and Sherman, 1974, 18; used by permission of the author.

6. Lessons should be related to students' ongoing learning experiences.

7. Lessons should be initiated when students' needs arise and terminate with students' boredom, disinterest, or accomplishment.

Intended Audience

It is suggested that almost all readers can benefit from Reading Strategy Lessons. The lessons may expand proficient readers' actual reading experiences and help them to build confidence. They can improve and support the strategies used by readers who exhibit evidence of effective, but inconsistent, use of strategies, or for whom the development of effective strategies has been disrupted.

Description of the Procedures

Reading Strategy Lessons are planned situations in which the use and availability of selected reading strategies are highlighted and reinforced. The situations are not intended to be panaceas for reading difficulties. Instead, teacher insight and teacher adaptation of the various strategies are suggested as essential if the needs of students at specific times are to be met.

The following description presents selected and representative strategy lessons. These descriptions have been organized under these headings:

1. Meeting the needs of inefficient readers
2. Meeting the needs of inconsistent readers
3. Meeting the needs of proficient readers

1. Meeting the Needs of Inefficient Readers. Y. Goodman (1975) describes inefficient readers this way:

> They use effective reading strategies occasionally in short phrases or sections of written material, but in most reading situations, these readers tend to omit words they think they do not know; they do not predict acceptable grammatical or semantic structures as they read; they read word for word using sounding out techniques without concern for meaning. They do everything they were taught to do in an isolated and unrelated fashion. They look for little words in big words and find fat/her an acceptable solution for father. They separate words between two middle consonants and often read lit/tul for little and prit/tee for pretty. When they do make occasional effective use of reading strategies, they lack confidence in deciding which strategy is most effective. They regress and correct in situations when it is inefficient to do so. For example, if such a reader reads can't for cannot because of the use of an appropriate predicting strategy, this is corrected when the reader picks up additional graphic cues. Such readers often think that graphic input is the most significant aspect of reading. Reading is not to discover something new or for enjoyment, it is to satisfy another person. (Y. M. Goodman, 1975, 39)*

According to Y. Goodman (1975), inefficient readers need first to realize that they are effective language users and that these abilities can help in reading. To this end, strategy lessons by which students become aware of the utility of their language cueing systems are suggested. For example, cloze procedures similar to the following are suggested to enable students to become more aware of their use of grammatical and meaning cues:

> "Stop!" said John. "Stop! Stop!" He could see that the little red _________ was heading straight for the bridge that had been washed away in the last storm. The driver of the _________ must have heard John. He hit the brakes and the _________ stopped. Its motor stopped and the driver jumped out.

To deal with some of the specific inefficiencies of readers, other strategies are suggested.

a. For readers whose omissions or substitutions result in meaning loss, teachers are urged to encourage them to make meaningful substitutions for omissions. Students might produce words that have some related meaning or words with a close meaning. This might be done incidentally, by encouraging the reader to ask, "What word could go in this spot?" "Why do you think so?" The teacher might take a more systematic approach, too, using exercises like these:

1. Present the students with a passage with systematic deletions of words or phrases and encourage readers to use the context to suggest alternative possibilities.

> They _________ around the pool.
>
> _________ enjoyed swimming.
>
> The children ran for the bus. They had slept late. Just as they arrived at the bus stop, _________.

2. Present the students with a passage containing nonsense words for significant verbs or nouns and have students replace them with real words.

> The buemt hopped through the grass and disappeared into its burrow. The buemt had a little tail of white fur and long ears. The buemt loved to nibble on leaves.

3. Either present the students with a passage containing intentional significant miscues, or have the students prepare a passage containing certain intentional miscues. The reader's task would be to locate these miscues.

b. For readers who have developed habitual associations between words or phrases that have close graphic or phonic similarities, such as *for-from, saw-was, though-thought,* lessons using carefully controlled linguistic material are suggested. For example, the students might be asked to read or write stories that use or elicit one of the confused words or use both words nonambiguously.

The following is an example of a suggested method for dealing with students' confusions between *was* and *saw.* First, present the student with sentences containing one of the habitually associated words: for example, "It was father." In this setting, it is not likely that students will produce "It saw father." When the students show evidence of being able to handle one of the habitually associated words, introduce the students to material in which both words are used nonambiguously.

2. Meeting the Needs of Inconsistent Readers. Y. Goodman (1975) describes inconsistent readers in the following statement:

> These readers use effective reading strategies when the material is highly interesting to them or when it is easy because it has a low concept load. However, when these readers find themselves reading material which is complex, they use less efficient reading strategies. They stop searching for meaning and end up sounding out or word calling. When asked how they handle any particular reading problem, such readers often say they sound words out; they may be unaware that they use context to read or they may believe the teacher disapproves of it. Strategy lessons help these readers become aware of the various effective reading strategies they already use when reading easy material, permitting them to transfer effective reading strategies to more difficult reading materials. (Y. M. Goodman, 1975, 138)*

As described by Y. Goodman and Burke in the manual *Reading Miscue Inventory* (1972), inconsistent readers include the reader who makes some effective use of reading strategies and the reader who makes moderately effective use of reading strategies. In natural reading situations, it is suggested that these readers be encouraged to make judgments while reading. They should be encouraged to ask self-monitoring questions such as "Does what I am reading make sense?" "If it doesn't, what should I do about it?" If the material is not making sense, it is suggested that the readers be encouraged either to continue to see if the selection will begin to make sense, or to judge whether to move to an alternative selection.

Strategy lessons for these readers are designed to develop their awareness of the transfer value of effective reading strategies from easy to difficult material. For example, in the context of easy material, readers might become aware of the strategies used to deal with unfamiliar words and to differentiate the significance of words.

Here is an example of a strategy lesson serving these purposes. It is taken from Goodman's article "Reading Strategy Lessons: Expanding Reading Effectiveness" (1975). This story uses a concept or word that is probably not well known.

> The boy was looking for Petoskies. He was walking slowly to make sure he wouldn't miss them. He usually found a number of them each time he went looking for them. They were not easy to find because they were the same color as the sand. He enjoyed looking for Petoskies on the beach. He was helping his mother, too, since she used them in her work. She was an artist and made jewelry with them. Petoskies are usually bluish gray in their natural state with the fossils in them somewhat darker. When Petoskies are polished, the gray color becomes lighter and the fossils take on a brown character. Petoskies are found only on the shores of the Great Lakes. (p. 138)

To help students gain meaning for the unknown word, the teacher would:

> Put this story on an overhead projector and use it with a small group of readers. Tell them not to worry about pronouncing every word as they read. Cover the entire story and move the

> cover down, exposing one more sentence with each move. As each sentence is exposed, ask the children to tell what the word (point to Petoskies) means. After each sentence, ask the children to revise their guesses about the word. Do not pronounce the word for the children, nor should you ask them to pronounce it. If any reader does say the word, the pronunciation should be accepted without comment. Only after the story is completely exposed and the meaning of Petoskies fully discussed should you ask for variations in pronunciation and finally tell the group how you think it may be pronounced. This is an interesting lesson because many teachers may not pronounce Petoskies the same way the people who polish and sell these stones do. (Y. M. Goodman, 1975, 138)*

Other strategy lessons for these readers might be to have students judge the significance or insignificance of words, phrases, or sentences contained in a selection. For example, students might be asked to read a selection and either delete or underline redundant words.

3. Meeting the Needs of Proficient Readers. Proficient readers are considered to be using reading strategies effectively. Therefore, Reading Strategy Lessons afford these readers an opportunity to develop confidence in the use of these strategies. Specifically, strategy lessons might broaden and deepen their reading experiences. To deepen the readers' experiences, they might be encouraged to anticipate plot, theme, and events, to perceive subtleties and inferential meaning, to realize the influence of background and experience on interpretation, and to appreciate that other readers have different interpretations about the same reading experience. To broaden their reading experiences, such students might be given the opportunity to read a variety of different types of reading materials in varying literary styles. Obviously, attention should be centered on improving their reading-to-learn abilities.

Cautions and Comments

Unfortunately, debate in the field and the increased revenue for traditional research has led to an unwarranted discrediting of the worth of word recognition and other strategy development in the context of a Whole-Language approach. Such dismissals are unwarranted; indeed, strategy development in the context of Whole-Language is quite powerful in terms of ongoing reading development and students' meaning making prowesses (e.g., Dahl, Scharer, Lawson, and Grogan, 1999).

Reading Strategy Lessons represent an attempt to extend K. Goodman's notions of the reading process to classroom practices. According to this view, learning to read "ought not to be very much more difficult than the process by which one learns the oral mode of language. That is, provided that the same principles of relevance, meaningfulness, and motivation for communication which characterized the learning of oral language have been adhered to" (Cambourne 1976–77, 610). The ramification of this notion for instruction, specifically phonics instruction, lies in the following assumptions: decoding to speech or sound is not a necessary step between grapheme and reading for meaning; a hierarchy of subskills is not a necessary aspect of learning reading; maximizing the internalized knowledge of a reader should be encouraged; beginning readers use the same process as fluent readers and should learn to read as naturally; and phonics analysis is neither useful nor necessary.

In terms of the latter assumption, Goodman has been critical of both the emphasis upon phonics and the methodologies proposed. He has claimed that phonic approaches to reading are preoccupied with the erroneous notion that reading requires precise letter identification. That is, he disagrees with the notion that reading involves exact, detailed, sequential perception and identification of letters, words, and spelling patterns. His main argument is that we do not and cannot read letter by letter. A good reader is so efficient in sampling and predicting that he uses the least available information necessary. A less proficient reader needs the confidence to engage in sampling and predicting; encouraging less proficient readers to use too many cues, to be cautious, may detract from the readers' addressing meaning.

Harste, Short, and Burke (1988) offer several suggestions for strategy lessons as do Watson and Crowley (1987), Kucer and Rhodes (1986), and Atwell and Rhodes (1984). Likewise, Restrospective Miscue Analysis represents an extension of a strategy lesson by Yetta Goodman and her colleagues (see previous strategy in this unit). Strategy lessons are not intended to be exhaustive, but to illustrate to teachers ways they might develop their own strategies, based upon a reasonable understanding of the reader and the strategy lessons' rationale. In this regard, the suggestions are sufficiently explicit for appropriate instructional adaptations at most levels. They do need further amplification, though, especially to meet the needs of primary level and advanced high school students. Finally, those teachers needing more background before they construct their own strategy lesson with K. Goodman's ideas are directed to the reference section that follows and the description and references for Whole-Language in Unit 2.

REFERENCES

Allen, P. D., and D. J. Watson (Eds.). 1976. *Findings of research in miscue analysis: Classroom implications.* Urbana, IL: National Council of Teachers of English and Educational Resources Information Center. Includes a collection of articles addressing an extended discussion of the research base of Goodman's ideas and its relevance to instruction.

Atwell, N., and L. K. Rhodes. 1984. Strategy lessons as alternatives to skill lessons in reading. *Journal of Reading* 27: 700–705. Offer suggestions for planning and implementing strategy lessons.

Cambourne, B. 1976–77. Getting to Goodman: An analysis of the Goodman model of reading with some suggestions for evaluation. *Reading Research Quarterly* 12: 605–636. Describes the major features of Goodman's model, its implications, and ways in which it might be reevaluated.

———. 2002. Holistic, integrated approaches to reading and language arts instruction: The constructivist framework of an instructional theory. In A. E. Farstrup and S. J. Samuels (Eds.), *What research has to say about reading instruction.* Newark, DE: International Reading Association, 25–47. Thoughtful discussion of holistic teaching from a constructivist perspective. Explores assumptions for curriculum, teaching, and research. Especially useful in comparison with nonholistic approaches.

Dahl, K. L., L. Scharer, L. Lawson, and P. R. Grogan. 1999. Phonics instruction and student achievement in Whole Language first grade classrooms. *Reading Research Quarterly* 34(3): 312–341. Careful examination of the Whole-Language classrooms in terms of phonic strategy development.

Goodman, K. S. 1965. A linguistic study of cues and miscues in reading. *Elementary English* 42: 639–643. Presents aspects of Goodman's research and the bases for Reading Strategy Lessons.

———. 1967. Reading: A psycholinguistic guessing game. *Journal of the Reading Specialist* 6: 126–135. Presents Goodman's original definition of reading and describes its ramifications.

———. 1975. The reading process. In S. S. Smiley and J. C. Towner (Eds.), *Language and reading.* Bellingham: Western Washington State College. Presents an updated model of Goodman's reading process that revises and expands upon the earlier model.

Goodman, K. S., and Y. M. Goodman. 1979. Learning to read is natural. In L. B. Resnick and P. A. Weaver

(Eds.), *Theory and practice of early reading.* Hillsdale, NJ: Erlbaum. Presents a discussion of the rationale behind a wholistic view of reading and teaching reading.

———. 1982. A whole-language comprehension-centered view of reading development. In L. Reed and S. Ward (Eds.), *Basic skills issues and choices: Approach to basic skills instruction,* Vol. 2. St. Louis: CEMREL. Describes a Whole-Language, comprehension-centered reading program and suggests ways to implement such a program in the classroom, including modifying a basal reader program.

Goodman, Y. M. 1975. Reading strategy lessons: Expanding reading effectiveness. In W. Page (Ed.), *Help for the reading teacher: New directions in research* Urbana, IL: National Council of Teachers of English and Educational Resources Information Center, 34–41. Presents the rationale for and several examples of Reading Strategy Lessons.

Goodman, Y. M., and C. L. Burke. 1972. *Reading miscue inventory.* New York: Macmillan. A manual with suggestions for using strategy lessons, based upon students' identified needs.

———. 1980. *Reading strategies: Focus on comprehension.* New York: Holt, Rinehart and Winston. Presents a resource book of reading strategies for teachers.

———. 1987. Miscue analysis and curriculum development. In *Reading miscue inventory: Alternative procedures.* New York: Richard C. Owens. Offers guidelines for developing an individualized program based on miscue analysis.

Goodman, Y. M., C. L. Burke, and B. Sherman. 1974. *Strategies in reading.* New York: Richard C. Owen. A handbook of reading strategies that provides the theory and practice of strategy lessons.

Gunderson, L. 1997. Whole Language approaches to reading and writing. In S. Stahl and D. A. Hayes (Eds.), *Instructional models in reading.* Mahwah, NJ: Erlbaum. Discusses the underlying principles of Whole-Language and research that has informed its use and demonstrated its effectiveness.

Harste, J., K. G. Short, and C. Burke. 1988. *Creating classrooms for authors.* Portsmouth, NH: Heinemann. Offers several classroom activities and strategy lessons.

Jeynes, W. H., and S. W. Littell. 2000. A meta-analysis of studies examining the effect of Whole Language instruction on the literacy. *Elementary School Journal* 101(1): 21–34. Study examines whether Whole-Language instruction increases the reading skills of low-SES students in grades K through 3.

Krashen, S. 2002. Defending Whole-Language: The limits of phonics instruction and the efficacy of Whole Language Instruction. *Reading Improvement* 39(1): 32–42. Discusses the efficacy of Whole-Language in terms of the development of reading skills with special focus on phonics

Kucer, S. B., and L. K. Rhodes. 1986. Counterpart strategies. *The Reading Teacher* 40: 186–193. Includes various strategies that help students use composing as a means of comprehending.

Routman, R. 1997. Back to the basics of Whole Language. *Educational Leadership* 54(5): 70–74. Explains the use of Whole Language in terms of developing basic skills.

Shapiro, J. 1994. Research perspectives on Whole-Language. In V. Froese (Ed.), *Whole-language practice and theory.* Boston: Allyn and Bacon, 433–470A. Discusses research that informs and supports the use of Whole-Language.

Watson, D., and P. Crowley. 1987. How can we implement a whole-language approach? In C. Weaver (Ed.), *Reading process and practice.* Portsmouth, NH: Heinemann. Offers an extended discussion of strategy lessons including several that are oriented to comprehension.

Weaver, C. 1998. Experimental research: On phonemic awareness and on Whole Language. In C. Weaver (Ed.), *Reconsidering a balanced approach to reading.* Urbana IL: National Council of Teachers of English, 321–371. Discusses the findings from recent syntheses on phonemic awareness and the role of a Whole-Language orientation in developing students' phonemic awareness and reading.

UNIT 6

Oral Reading

UNIT OVERVIEW

Current practices seem to indicate that much instructional time in our elementary classrooms is devoted to oral reading. Although there is value in oral reading for beginning reading instruction, there is some question as to the effectiveness of the way the activity may be conducted in the classroom.

The most frequent oral reading activity is that of "round-robin" or "circle" reading. In this activity, each student in turn reads a small portion aloud to his or her reading group or to the class as a whole, while the other students follow along silently. This practice is used primarily in conjunction with the basal reading program.

Despite its widespread use, research does not support this practice. Research by Anderson, Mason, and Shirey (1984), and Wilkinson and Anderson (1995), and research reviews by Allington (1984) and Brulnsma (1981) suggest that the practice of round-robin reading is suspect. They conclude that its use in classrooms is not defensible if comprehension is the goal.

Oral reading is a communication skill. It is a way of delivering information or providing entertainment to listeners. If used in this way, oral reading would seem best done for a specific purpose, and a student's performance would seem best evaluated in terms of its communicative value. Further, research reviewed by the National Reading Panel (2000) indicated that guided repeated oral reading procedures have a positive impact on achievement in word recognition, fluency, and comprehension at a range of grade levels.

For this reason, the four strategies discussed in this unit are designed to aid the teacher in planning oral reading activities that have specific purposes. Two of the strategies are mainly developmental in nature and focus on the communicative aspects of oral reading. The other two strategies tend to be used with students who may be having difficulty in reading. Taken together, these strategies encourage repeated oral reading with feedback and guidance for students, and their implementation can lead to improved reading performance for both good readers as well as those who are struggling. As a preview of this unit, a brief summary of the strategies follows.

Repeated and Choral Reading. Repeated and Choral Reading is a strategy designed to give students practice in reading with the proper expression. Useful as a whole-class reading activity, this strategy provides students with active involvement in print and puts prime emphasis on interpreting meaning.

Radio Reading. Providing practice for students in both reading and listening, Radio Reading focuses instruction on the ultimate goal of oral reading—communicating a message. It is useful throughout the grades wherever oral reading is one of the teaching methods, particularly as a substitute for round-robin reading.

Echo Reading. Echo Reading is designed to foster the acquisition of vocabulary and oral fluency. It is most effective in a one-to-one instructional situation and primarily with students in the elementary grades.

Topping's Paired Reading. In Topping's Paired Reading tutors read along with children and adjust their oral participation to the difficulty the children experience. In this way children not only are given practice in reading but also have a model of fluent reading.

REFERENCES

Allington, R. L. 1984. Oral reading. In P. D. Pearson, R. Barr, M. L. Kamil, and P. Mosenthal (Eds.), *Handbook of reading research.* New York: Longman.

Anderson, R. C., J. Mason, and L. Shirey. 1984. The reading group: An experimental investigation of a labyrinth. *Reading Research Quarterly* 20: 6–39.

Brulnsma, R. 1981. A critique of "round-robin" oral reading in the elementary classroom. *Reading-Canada-Lecture* 1: 78–81.

National Reading Panel. 2000. *Teaching children to read: An evidence-based assessment of the scientific research literature on reading and its implications for reading instruction: Report of the subgroups.* (NIH Publication No. 00-4754). Washington, DC: National Institute of Child Health and Human Development.

Wilkinson, I. A. G., and R. C. Anderson. 1995. Sociocognitive processes in guided silent reading: A microanalysis of small-group lessons. *Reading Research Quarterly* 30: 710–740.

Repeated and Choral Reading

Purpose

The purpose of Repeated and Choral Reading is to: (1) provide practice for students in reading with the expression necessary to add to meaning; (2) develop self-assurance by giving every student a chance to function as part of a group; and (3) aid students in developing an appreciation for oral expression.

Rationale

Artificial barriers are sometimes created by students and between students when oral reading occurs. For example, poorer readers may not like to read orally, and the shy student who rarely volunteers in any class activity will often be hesitant about oral reading. On the other hand, the overly confident student, if given the opportunity, might dominate an oral reading exercise.

Repeated and Choral Reading provides the teacher with a socialization tool. Poor readers as well as shy ones can use the whole-group format to avoid humiliating corrections while they gain confidence in themselves. The obtrusive student may be tempered through the same whole-group format, which discourages that student from showing off. In addition, Repeated and Choral Reading can develop students' interest in the creative forms of language such as poetry, whereas previously students might have had negative feelings toward such a medium.

Finally, Repeated and Choral Reading provides students with the opportunity to become actively involved with print, placing the prime emphasis on interpreting and expressing meaning. Many times, words and not meaning are emphasized in reading activities. Repeated and Choral Reading develops students' abilities to read for meaning—the eventual goal of the act of reading.

Intended Audience

Repeated and Choral Reading is suitable for any school population. Grade level and achievement level are inconsequential because of the group approach of this strategy. Class size also matters little, as the teacher can divide any large group into smaller, more manageable choral groups.

Description of the Procedures

Repeated Reading is a label that has been applied to a range of oral reading activities, from repeated practicing of a text, to oral reading with support (e.g., audiotaped reading of a text), to a set number of repetitions of various forms of support, to preparation for choral reading performances. As a substitute for oral reading as commonly practiced, Repeated Reading with choral procedures presents the teacher with a unique instructional activity that can unite all readers, regardless of ability, in a common reading experience. At the same time, this strategy can provide students with entertainment, group involvement, and practice in reading with self-expression.

In order for Repeated Reading and Choral Reading to be carried out effectively, the teacher must be prepared to deal with:

1. Developing rhythmic sensitivity
2. Casting

1. Developing Rhythmic Sensitivity. Before Repeated and Choral Reading can be accomplished successfully, the students should be guided by the teacher through progressive steps to develop their sensitivity for rhythm. The teacher should not make any assumptions concerning students' ability in Repeated and Choral Reading. By guiding them through the activity first, the teacher is assured that students have the framework to establish eventual independence in that activity.

The concept of modeling is very appropriate with this activity. One way to impress young children is for the teacher to be an example. By showing students that poetry and other creative forms are enjoyable, by sharing these things with the class, and by demonstrating the desired self-expression, the teacher should find that students experience little difficulty in beginning Repeated and Choral Reading.

A variety of selections should be used to aid students in acquiring a sensitivity for rhythm, mood, and voice modulation. The teacher should demonstrate proper phrasing, tempo, and enunciation with the selections for Repeated and Choral Reading and, through discussion, emphasize the importance of proper expression in conveying a poem's mood and meaning.

Repeated and Choral Reading might begin with short selections, preferably memorized. Eventually, longer selections, possibly with the rhythm marked, may be introduced.

To provide additional reinforcement for students, a tape recorder may be used for evaluative purposes. Students may also participate as critical listeners by separating themselves from the choral groups and providing feedback. After a few successful experiences, students may begin, and be encouraged, to suggest other ways selections might be interpreted and read. Sound effects and pantomiming may also be used.

Finally, when selecting material for Repeated and Choral Reading, care should be taken to ensure that selections have an easily understandable theme and a distinct rhythm.

2. Casting. Casting is a term used in Repeated and Choral Reading to refer to the way a selection is divided into parts and assigned to members of the class for reading. Once the rhythm and tempo of a particular selection are understood, the teacher and students should choose from the following methods of organization for Repeated and Choral Reading:

(a) refrain;
(b) dialogue;
(c) line-a-child or line-a-choir;
(d) cumulative; and
(e) unison.

a. *Refrain.* With certain poems that have a chorus, either the teacher or a designated group can recite the narrative, with the rest of the class responding in the chorus. The refrain provides a good beginning for Repeated and Choral Reading.

b. *Dialogue.* Poems with considerable dialogue (often a question-and-answer format) readily lend themselves to a two-part casting. Alternate responses can be made between boys and girls or between high and low voices.

c. *Line-a-child or line-a-choir.* This arrangement engages three or more individuals or choirs in rhythmic response. Some lines also may be spoken in unison by all participants. This type of Repeated and Choral Reading has variety and provides a challenge for students to respond in the exact tempo.

d. *Cumulative.* In this form of Repeated and Choral Reading, the intent is to create a crescendo effect. Unlike the line-a-choir method, the introduction of a new group to the presentation is permanent, not temporary. This is a more difficult form of Repeated and Choral Reading because voice quality, rather than volume, is necessary to attain a significant climax.

e. *Unison.* This is the most difficult type of Repeated and Choral Reading, even though it has the simplest structure. An entire group or class reads every line together. The potential for problems in blending and timing is very great in unison reading. Monotonous reading often results if the children are inexperienced and insufficient direction has been given by the teacher. This method is best suited for intermediate level students.

The following verse from a poem provides an example of how one type of casting may be used in a Repeated and Choral Reading exercise.

The Triantiwontigongolope*

1ST CHILD: There's a funny insect that you do not often spy,

2ND CHILD: And it isn't quite a spider, and it isn't quite a fly;

1ST CHILD: It is something like a beetle, and a little like a bee,

2ND CHILD: But nothing like a woolly grub that climbs upon a tree.

1ST CHILD: Its name is quite a hard one, but you'll learn it soon, I hope.

1ST CHILD: So, try:

CHORUS: Tri-

ALL: Tri———anti———wonti———

CHILDREN: Triantiwontigongolope

The refrain in this selection can be used with one group of students reciting the narrative while the other recites the chorus. Individual lines or stanzas of the poem may also be assigned to groups of students and the line-a-choir, cumulative, or unison casting may be implemented, depending on the sophistication of the students.

Cautions and Comments

The National Reading Panel report suggested that "repeated oral reading with feedback and guidance leads to meaningful improvements in reading expertise" (2000, p. 3-3). Repeated and Choral Reading provides students with a unique and valuable language experience, since it integrates reading with two other linguistic skills: listening and speaking. In addition, Repeated and Choral Reading builds positive attitudes toward participation in groups and develops students' imaginative abilities.

However, Repeated and Choral Reading can contribute little to the reading and language development of students if it is not used properly. A common practice has been for the teacher to select a passage for Choral Reading, teach it to students who either read it well or memorize it, assign parts of it to groups, and then drill the students until the passage sounds good according to the teacher's conception of what good Repeated and Choral Reading is.

This practice negates the instructional objectives of: (1) making the selection meaningful to the students, (2) developing creativity, and (3) developing self-expression. Strict, tense drill directed by the teacher does not set the proper learning conditions, but active involvement on the part of the students does.

Another area of concern in Repeated and Choral Reading is maintaining the students' focus on the meaning being conveyed. Students have a tendency to focus attention on their delivery of the selection and sometimes lapse into overdramatics. It must be emphasized that the Repeated and Choral Reading is on display, not the students themselves.

*"The Triantiwontigongolope" from *A Book for Kids* by C. J. Dennis is reprinted by permission of Angus & Robertson Publishers.

A further meaning-related concern in Repeated and Choral Reading is that all students should have a similar understanding of the selection. This is essential in order to convey effectively, as a group, a depth of feeling and sensitivity to words.

A last area of concern is voice quality. Each word must be enunciated at the same time by the whole group—a difficult task to accomplish for some students. Finally, students must also learn that it is not necessary to read loudly when expressing themselves; rather, they should read with warm but firm voices, and the Repeated and Choral Reading itself will take care of the volume.

REFERENCES

Dowhower, S. L. 1989. Repeated Reading: Research into practice. *The Reading Teacher* 42: 502–507. A description of the benefits of Repeated Reading, with suggestions for classroom practice.

Dowhower, S. L. 1994. Repeated Reading revisited: Research into practice. *Reading & Writing Quarterly* 10: 343–358. An updated review of the literature on Repeated Reading.

Herman, P. A. 1985. The effect of Repeated Readings on reading rate, speech pauses, and word recognition memory. *Reading Research Quarterly* 20: 553–574. Research study demonstrating that repeated practice can increase poor readers' comprehension of text.

Koskinen, P. S., and I. H. Blum. 1985. Paired Repeated Reading: A classroom strategy for developing fluent reading. *The Reading Teacher* 40: 70–75. Describes the use of Repeated and Choral Reading with only a pair of readers.

Lopardo, G., and M. Sadow. 1982. Criteria and procedures for the method of Repeated Readings. *Journal of Reading* 26: 156–160. Describes how to use Repeated Reading in the classroom.

McCauley, J. K., and D. S. McCauley. 1992. Using Choral Reading to promote language learning for ESL students. *The Reading Teacher* 45: 526–533. A discussion of using Choral Reading with second language learners.

National Reading Panel. 2000. *Teaching children to read: An evidence-based of the scientific research literature on reading and its implications for reading instruction.* Washington, DC: National Institute of Child Health and Human Development. Discusses oral reading practices in the context of improving reading fluency.

Samuels, S. J. 1997. The method of Repeated Readings. *The Reading Teacher* 50: 376–381. A classic article, originally published in 1979, on Repeated Reading.

Temple, C. A., and J. W. Gillett. 1984. *Language arts: Learning processes and teaching practices.* Boston: Little, Brown. Provides examples of using Choral Reading in the language arts program.

Radio Reading

Purpose

The purpose of Radio Reading (Greene, 1979) is to provide help for students in: (1) accurately communicating a message through oral reading; (2) comprehending at the listening level; and (3) summarizing and restating an orally read message.

Rationale

Radio Reading provides the teacher with a viable alternative to the common practice of round-robin reading. Too often, oral reading situations deteriorate into word-attack sessions. Unlike round-robin reading, Radio Reading does not allow for prompting or correction. Rather, it focuses instruction on the ultimate goal of oral reading—to comprehend and communicate a message.

Radio Reading derives its name from the analogy between a radio announcer's talking to a listening audience and the oral reading situation. The reader functions as the radio announcer with a script, and the listeners serve as the audience listening to a radio program. It is the purpose of the reader to communicate accurately a message in oral reading. The listeners respond by discussing and restating the message and evaluating whether the passage was clearly rendered.

Intended Audience

Radio Reading is appropriate throughout the grades, whenever oral reading is used in instruction. It is particularly suitable in the elementary grades as a substitute for round-robin reading; however, it is also useful in the content areas, especially where interpretive reading is done. Radio Reading may be used in either a one-to-one or a group setting.

Description of the Procedures

Radio Reading creates a safe, nonthreatening atmosphere for the reader, in which comprehension, not word-perfect reading, is the primary instructional goal. In order to implement a Radio Reading lesson properly, Searfoss (1975) recommended that four steps be followed: (1) getting started, (2) communicating the message, (3) checking for understanding, and (4) clarifying an unclear message.

1. Getting Started. In this step of the lesson, the teacher sets the tone for the proper atmosphere by explaining the procedure to the students. The simple ground rules of radio reading are these: the reader reads and the listeners listen.

The teacher leads the activity by explaining the remaining three steps of the strategy to the students. Emphasis is placed on the responsibility of the reader to communicate a message to the listeners, just as a radio announcer communicates to his audience. Since the audience (listeners) will not have a copy of the material, the teacher instructs them to listen closely.

It is also the job of the teacher to select materials for Radio Reading that are appropriate in difficulty and length. The materials should be challenging, though not frustrating, and can be narrative or expository in nature. For example, short stories or selections from basal-type readers would be appropriate. The material should be of reasonable length so as not to overwhelm the listener. As a guideline, Searfoss (1975) recommended that each reader should orally read only a paragraph or two in the lower grades, progressing up to as much as a page in the intermediate grades.

2. Communicating the Message. Since the job of the reader is to convey a clear message, the reader is permitted to change words, insert new words, or omit words where warranted. The role of the reader in this activity is similar to that of the fluent, silent reader; both are attending to meaning rather than to individual words. The reader is responsible, however, for deciding when he or she needs help with an unknown word. Greene (1979) stated that when giving directions for Radio Reading, the teacher should say, "If you come to a word you need and you cannot figure it out, put your finger beside it and ask, 'What is that word?' "

Again, since Radio Reading is comprehension-oriented, and further delay on a word would increase the probability of short-term memory interference, the teacher or other listeners should refrain from prompting or beginning a word-attack lesson. The reader should be given the word immediately so that he or she can continue, with as little interruption as possible, to process meaning.

3. Checking for Understanding. The listening audience has control over the student's oral reading and, if necessary, over rereading. If an accurate message has been communicated by the reader, the check for understanding will be brief. The discussion of what was heard, whether teacher-led or student-initiated, will move quickly. After a quick summary has been volunteered, other listeners can confirm the message. Allowances are made for inferences and rewording, as long as accuracy is maintained.

Thus, the reader earns the right to continue reading by communicating a clear message. In a group situation, the role of the radio reader may rotate to give every reader an opportunity to read.

4. Clarifying an Unclear Message. If the listeners give conflicting information or are able to detect errors during the discussion, the reader has not communicated a clear message. It is the radio readers' responsibility to clear up the confusion by returning to the story and rereading the portions of concern. It is still the reader's job to achieve clarity in the passage. The listener may decide that the reader needs assistance to achieve that goal. However, as before, prompting must be avoided to maintain the necessary atmosphere for radio reading.

Cautions and Comments

Since Radio Reading differs greatly from current oral reading practices, the teacher should be certain the four steps outlined are followed. Two areas of caution warrant discussion to enable the teacher to maintain the proper instructional climate for Radio Reading.

One area of caution concerns the students' response to the procedural steps of Radio Reading. Ideally, the students will quickly understand the rules and follow them. Radio Reading will then be performed smoothly, i.e., the students will read as well as they can, requesting help when necessary. In reality, students may manifest other types of responses to this instructional format, causing possible difficulties for the teacher in its implementation.

One difficulty is for the reader to request help at an inappropriate time. Such an occasion arises when it is apparent that the reader already knows the word or has adequate word-attack skills to decode the word. The only recourse the listener has in this situation is to tell the reader the requested word.

It is most likely correct to assume that the reader is testing the rules concerning the reader's and the listener's responsibilities for unknown words rather than simply displaying deficiencies in reading. Thus, not responding to a request for help, or prompting the reader, violates the contract between the reader and the listener and makes the rules of Radio Reading worthless. If the reader requests help, it must be immediately supplied.

An additional response that a student may manifest is not to request help when he or she does need it. The reader then will be redirected to render a clear message after the oral reading. On the other hand, failure to respond at all presents the listener with an entirely different situation. In either an individual or a group situation, the appropriate response for the listener, after waiting a reasonable length of time, is simply to say, "What's the rule?"

In an individual situation, it may be necessary for the listener to restate the rule concerning unknown words. If a response is still not elicited, then Radio Reading should be ended for the day. A clarification of the procedural steps is then in order. In a group setting, a no-response situation is much easier to deal with. Anytime the radio announcer (reader) ceases to broadcast, the listeners will tune to a new "station," i.e., the first reader's right to continue reading ceases, and a new radio reader takes over.

A second caution concerning the instructional climate for Radio Reading is the tendency of teachers to prompt, to correct, or to initiate a word-attack lesson when a reader encounters difficulty or requests help. Such tactics are inappropriate with this strategy. It disrupts the process of reading and converts the activity into a word-attack lesson.

If the reader makes an error and the teacher corrects it, the responsibility for correctness shifts to the teacher and deprives the reader of the responsibility for meaningful reading. Prompting also removes from the reader the responsibility for relaying the message.

There is clearly no place for prompting or for correcting in Radio Reading. If an error is made in an oral rendering, the burden of dealing with it rests with the listener, who must be skillful enough to pick it out and remember it until the passage has been read. It is the reader's responsibility alone to render a clear, comprehensible message from the assigned passage.

REFERENCES

Greene, F. P. 1979. Radio reading. In C. Pennock (Ed.), *Reading comprehension at four linguistic levels.* Newark, DE: International Reading Association, 104–107. Discusses the concept of Radio Reading and describes the procedure.

Searfoss, L. W. 1975. Radio reading. *The Reading Teacher* 29:295–296. Outlines four basic steps in implementing Radio Reading.

Echo Reading

Purpose

The purpose of Echo Reading is to increase the reading fluency of students who have had difficulty in reading.

Rationale

Echo Reading was originally conceived by Heckelman (1969) and is also known as the "neurological impress method" or the "impress method." Heckelman hypothesized that current reading methods allow a student to commit many mistakes, which become very deeply imprinted and are not easily corrected. Because of the time and difficulty involved in correcting these mistakes, students do not make any progress in reading.

Heckelman believed that implementing a new learning procedure could suppress the older methods of learning and thus enable children to read. As a result of this thinking, the impress—or echo—method was used. Its intent was to expose readers only to accurate, fluid reading patterns. After a certain length of time for instruction, the correct reading patterns would become deeply impressed and would replace previously learned patterns.

Intended Audience

Echo Reading has been used almost exclusively with readers who have had difficulty progressing in reading. The procedure should be employed in a one-to-one instructional situation.

Description of the Procedures

The Echo method is a technique that involves the student's visual, aural, oral, and tactile abilities in the process of learning to read. It is recommended that the procedure be used for 15 minutes a day in consecutive daily sessions. After a total instructional time of 7 to 12 hours, there is often a significant rise in achievement by the reader.

At the start of Echo Reading, the reading material used should be at a level slightly lower than the reader can handle adequately. By using material on which the reader has already experienced success, the teacher increases the probability that the echo method will get off to a successful beginning. Material to be used with the procedure should be varied to maintain the student's interest. Newspapers, magazines, and fiction and nonfiction books might be used.

Before Echo Reading starts, some preliminary instructions are given to the student. The student is told to disregard accompanying pictures in the story. The teacher also indicates to the student not to be concerned with reading at all; rather, the student is asked to do as well as possible in terms of just saying the words. The student is told only to slide his or her eyes smoothly across the line of print without stopping or going back. At no time does the teacher attempt to correct any mistakes the student may make.

As Echo Reading begins, the reader is seated slightly in front of the teacher with both participants jointly holding the reading material. Both read in unison; the voice of the teacher is directed into the reader's ear at this close range. In beginning sessions, the teacher is supposed to read slightly louder and faster than the student. This aspect allows the reader to make maximum use of the aural and visual senses involved in this strategy.

As the student begins to master the material and gains confidence in saying the words, the teacher may choose to read with a softer voice or even lag slightly behind the student. If the student falters, the teacher should resort to immediate reinforcement by increasing loudness and speed.

In the beginning sessions, the goal is to establish a fluent reading pattern. Therefore, it is often necessary for the teacher and student to repeat sentences and paragraphs several times until that goal is reached. Once this is accomplished, the teacher and student may move on to more difficult materials. Usually no more than two or three minutes of repetitive reading is required before a fluent reading pattern is established. It is recommended that the teacher regularly reinforce any success the student meets.

To accompany their voices, the teacher's finger simultaneously moves along the line of print. The finger is placed directly under the word as it is spoken, in a smooth, continual fashion. It is emphasized that the flow of the teacher's finger must coincide with the speed and flow of the oral reading.

Once accustomed to the Echo method, the student can begin to take over this function from the teacher. At first, the teacher may need to help the student by guiding the student's finger until a smooth, continuous movement is established.

The coordination of the movement of the finger with the flow of the oral rendition is essential. It is argued that if the teacher's finger is not placed under the word as it is spoken, the aural and oral sensory modes will not be operating in conjunction with the visual and tactile modes (Heckelman, 1969).

The major concern of the Echo method is the style, not the accuracy, of the oral rendition. At no time during the reading is the student questioned on the material, either for word recognition or comprehension. However, if the student volunteers any information, the teacher permits it.

If success with the method has not been achieved by the fourth hour of its use, the procedure should be terminated. A changeover to another method is then suggested.

Cautions and Comments

Particularly in the beginning stages of Echo Reading, a student may experience some difficulty, due to the novelty of the situation or to the conflict that can arise between aural and visual input. A teacher might counter student complaints of not being able to keep up by urging the student to disregard mistakes and to continue reading. Slowing down slightly to a more comfortable speed or rereading some initial lines may eliminate student discomfort with the technique. However, forcing students to process visual and auditory information concurrently may require them to change their natural processing procedures for these types of input. This change may cause undue difficulty and warrant termination of this time-consuming procedure.

Echo Reading seems to place an undue emphasis on the psychomotor skills involved in reading, rather than upon the reading-thinking processes that direct those skills. If reading-thinking processes direct the use of aural and visual skills, then, logically, reading improvement should begin with these reading-thinking processes. In other words, the emphasis given psychomotor skills within Echo Reading seems misplaced and in danger of detracting from meaningful reading experiences by which the student might acquire visual and aural skills both naturally and incidentally.

REFERENCES

Heckelman, R. G. 1969. A neurological-impress method of remedial-reading instruction. *Academic Therapy* 4: 277–282. Introduces and describes the concept of the impress method.

———. 1986. N. I. M. re-visited. *Academic Therapy* 21: 411–420. An update on the impress method.

Hollingsworth, P. M. 1978. An experimental approach to the impress method of teaching reading. *The Reading Teacher* 31: 624–626. Describes results from the use of the impress method.

Memory, D. M. 1981. The impress method: A status report of a new remedial reading technique. *Journal of Research and Development in Education* 14: 102–114. A review of the literature of the impress method.

Topping's Paired Reading

Purpose

The purpose of Topping's Paired Reading (Topping, 1987a) is to provide a simple system where tutors with little training could improve the reading performance of tutees of lesser reading ability.

Rationale

Originally conceived as a means to use the untapped talents of parents to help improve their children's reading ability, Paired Reading now has expanded to include pairings of adults (Scoble, Topping, and Wigglesworth, 1988) and children (Topping, 1989) in peer tutoring situations. In all cases a tutor of greater reading ability is paired with a reader of lesser ability in a reading-together situation. The tutor provides immediate support to the tutee when an error may occur, which frees the reader from word-by-word decoding and allows him or her to develop fluency. The tutor acts as a participant model in which a continuous prompt for correct reading is given to the reader.

Topping's Paired Reading is thought of as a very inexpensive way to deal with the multitude of people whose reading ability is not adequate. The technique employed is simple to learn and use, therefore enabling it to be used widely in a variety of learning situations.

Intended Audience

Topping's Paired Reading can be used in virtually unlimited reading situations in which two readers, one of greater and one of lesser ability, work together.

Description of the Procedures

Topping's Paired Reading will be discussed in the following manner. The standard strategy will first be described; then adaptations for peer tutoring with children will be discussed.

1. The Standard Strategy. The Paired Reading session begins with the tutee selecting a book or other reading material at any level of readability that is within the comfort and competence level of the tutor. Thus, the reading interests of both are taken into account to some extent. The tutor also has the responsibility of discussing the book before reading to promote understanding. Additional discussion and questioning may occur throughout the reading.

The pair read out loud together with the tutor adjusting to the tutee's natural reading speed. If the tutee should make an error or gives no response to a word in five seconds, the standard correction procedure is applied. The tutor says the word correctly, and the tutee is required to repeat it before the reading continues. Because the correction procedure is so simple, the possibility of the tutoring situation turning into a word-attack lesson is minimized. At regular intervals the tutor should also praise the tutee for correct reading behavior.

At any point in the reading, or when an easier text is used, a prearranged nonverbal signal to let the tutor know that the tutee wishes to read alone can be used. The tutor can continue to give praise and initiate discussion of the material but does not rejoin the reading until an error is made. As before, the correction procedure is employed and reading together recommences. Figure 6.1 illustrates the procedure for Topping's Paired Reading.

2. Adaptations for Peer Tutoring. Topping's Paired Reading can easily be employed in the classroom when coupled with the notion of peer tutoring. Tutorial pairs can be trained easily, use the high interest materials available in the classroom, and probably be incorporated into the normal routine without much concern. However, care will need to be given to the organization of this peer tutorial endeavor.

Topping suggests starting with a few pairs and letting others ask to become involved. The ability difference between the tutor and tutee should be neither too large nor too small. Another consideration is to avoid mixing strong and weak personalities. The teacher will also need to have standby tutors available should absences occur; these will need to be particularly competent readers as they will deal with a variety of less able tutees. Information will probably need to be sent at least to the parents of the tutors communicating the benefits to all participants; permission of the parents may also be needed.

Since the procedure has the advantage of being able to use any reading material the pair is comfortable with, this will probably not be much of a problem. However, some pairs will need extra guidance in book selection as the tutorial sessions begin. Books that are continually too difficult or too easy will be problematic, as would books on the same topic. Time will have to be made to get to the school library as well as gain access to it. Finally, if the teacher decides to let the pair bring in books from outside the school, some form of quick readability check will need to be taught to the students.

Topping suggests that the pairing be continued for a six-week period, with at least three sessions a week for no more than 15 to 30 minutes per session. Training should begin with a demonstration, and students should be provided with written information as a reminder. The teacher will need to circulate around the room to monitor the quality of each pair's session, giving further information or demonstration where necessary. It is also to be remembered that all students doing this procedure simultaneously will result in substantial noise in the classroom.

As the tutorial sessions continue, teachers will need to be sure that problems do not arise with the technique, book choice, the interpersonal relationship of the pairs, or particularly difficult words or concepts. Students should keep a record of their progress in terms of the books read, and this should be monitored by the teacher. Positive behavior by the tutees should also be noted by the tutors. Teachers may also employ group or individual discussions of the tutoring sessions with the tutees and tutors, separately or together.

After the initial six-week period of Paired Reading has concluded, an evaluation should take place. Topping suggests that a feedback and review meeting be held with all participants. Verbal and written feedback should be sought, with suggestions for improvement. Teachers will find that some pairs will wish to continue; others will want a new partner. Some will seek fewer sessions.

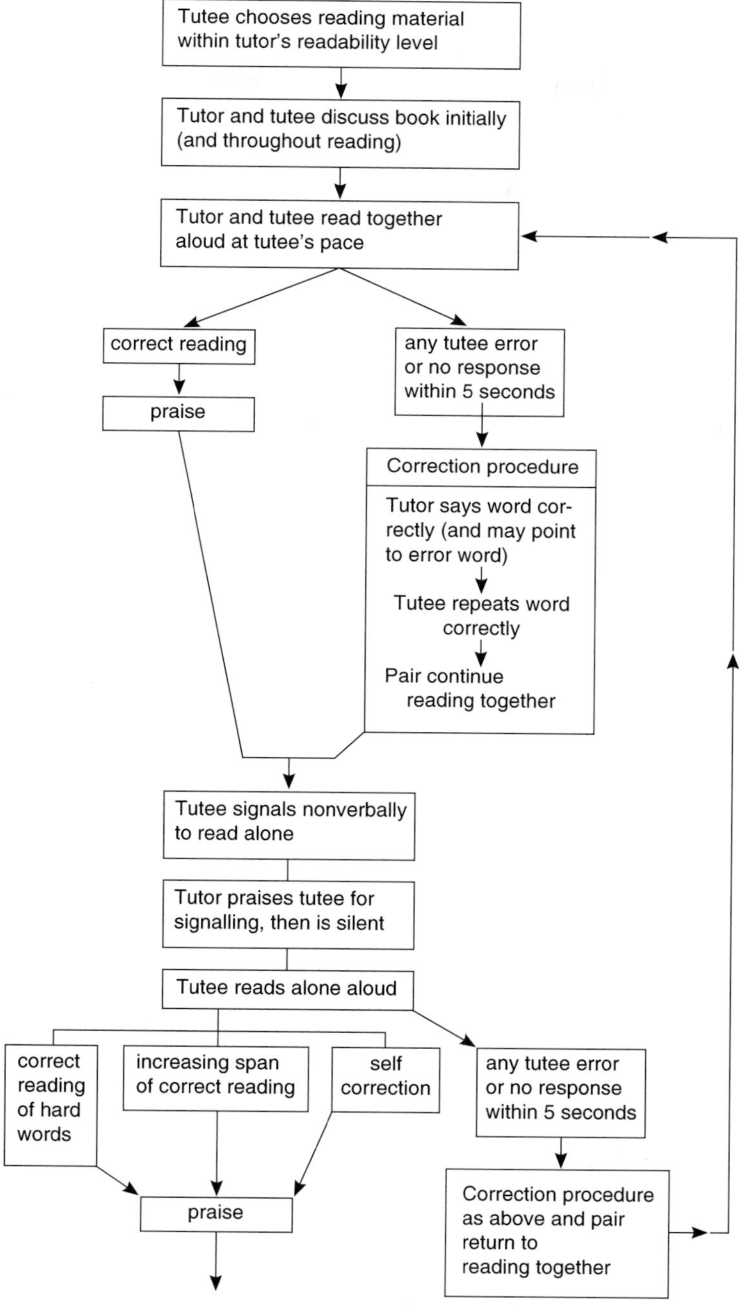

FIGURE 6.1 Paired Reading Procedure

Cautions and Comments

Implementing Topping's Paired Reading in a classroom with peer tutoring will not be without difficulty. Topping himself points out that the noise level may be distracting, and students may not feel comfortable with whole-class tutoring going on. The quality of the tutoring sessions may not be good with less able or young children, or they may suffer because some tutors take on an authoritarian role. Other pairs may become bored without constant fine-tuning of the procedure or the materials. Finally, parents may misunderstand the purpose or the methods and complain.

On the other hand, Topping points out that some children may pick up the procedure more rapidly than some teachers anticipate. In fact, Topping suggests that successful training in Paired Reading is easiest with children, next easiest with parents, and most difficult with teachers. Teachers will also find that the experience of most pairs is positive, and good relationships prosper beyond the tutoring sessions. Paired Reading in the classroom is inexpensive and easy to set up and monitor because the students and the materials are always on hand. This could make the strategy most appropriate to implement in at-risk schools where students have the most to gain. Finally, since both tutors and tutees improve their skills, it is attractive to implement.

Indeed, extensive research has also been reported by Topping (1987b) that demonstrate gains for all participants in Paired Reading. Additionally, the effects of the strategy seem to continue after termination of the tutoring.

REFERENCES

Rekrut, M. D. 1994. Peer and cross-age tutoring: The lessons of research. *Journal of Reading* 37: 356–362. Examines the research on peer and cross-age tutoring, with an emphasis on practice.

Scoble, J., K. Topping, and C. Wigglesworth. 1988. Training family and friends as adult literacy tutors. *Journal of Reading* 31: 410–417. Discussion of Paired Reading for use with adult illiterates.

Topping, K. 1987a. Paired reading: A powerful technique for parent use. *The Reading Teacher* 40: 608–614. A description of the Paired Reading strategy, with the focus on parents working with children.

———. 1987b. Peer tutored paired reading: Outcome data from ten projects. *Educational Psychology* 7: 133–145. Report of various research studies showing the effectiveness of the technique.

———. 1989. Peer tutoring and paired reading: Combining two powerful techniques. *The Reading Teacher* 42: 488–494. A discussion of tutoring programs that combine peer tutoring with Paired Reading techniques.

———. 1995. Cued spelling: A powerful technique for parent and peer tutoring. *The Reading Teacher* 48: 374–383. A paired learning technique to teach spelling.

Topping, K., and G. A. Lindsay. 1992. The structure and development of the paired reading technique. *Journal of Research in Reading* 15: 120–136. A review of the literature on Paired Reading.

UNIT 7

Comprehension Development and Thinking Critically

UNIT OVERVIEW

The basic goals of reading are to enable children to gain an understanding of the world and of themselves, to develop appreciations and interests, to find solutions to their personal and group problems, and to develop strategies by which they can become independent comprehenders. Logically, comprehension should be considered the heart of reading instruction, and the major goal of that instruction should be the provision of learning activities that will enable students to think about and react to what they read—in short, to read for meaning.

The present unit describes 11 strategies for the improvement of reading comprehension and critical thinking. Whereas Unit 11, Discussion and Cooperative Learning, will focus on social aspects of meaning-making, the strategies in this unit focus on "inside the head" processes. Reviews of the research by Tierney and Cunningham (1984), Pearson and Fielding (1991), and a text by Pressley (1998) indicate that there is ample evidence that the use of comprehension strategies will help students learn. However, teachers must demonstrate, model, and explain to students *how* to comprehend as they are implementing these strategies (National Reading Panel, 2000). The strategies in this unit are designed to help teachers in one or more of the following ways:

1. Activate students' prior knowledge
2. Guide students' reading of a text
3. Foster active and engaged reading
4. Reinforce concepts gleaned from the text reading
5. Encourage careful/critical thinking when reading a text
6. Pursue inquiry on different topics

Many of these strategies may substitute or augment parts of the lesson frameworks described in Unit 1. A brief summary of each strategy follows:

Questioning the Author. Questioning the Author is designed to promote student engagement with text through a discussion procedure that differs from a traditional discussion.

K-W-L. K-W-L (What I *K*now, What I *W*ant to Learn, What I *L*earned) is a teaching model designed to help students learn from nonfiction text in any content area. It consists of brainstorming, purpose-setting through questioning, and then examining answers to those questions.

Anticipation Guide. An Anticipation Guide is designed to activate students' prior knowledge about a topic by having them react to a series of statements related to the major concepts to be encountered in their text reading. Thus, it also provides students a guide for their reading.

Text Preview. A Text Preview is a teacher-devised introductory passage used before reading a selection. It is designed to build background knowledge by providing a detailed framework for comprehending a complex narrative or expository text.

ReQuest Procedure. The ReQuest procedure uses a reciprocal questioning technique in an attempt to encourage students to formulate their own questions about material and thereby learn purposeful, thoughtful reading. The ReQuest procedure can be applied to either a reading passage or a picture, and it is suggested for use with students at all levels.

Question-Answer Relationships. Question-Answer Relationships are designed to help students answer comprehension questions by providing them a format for analyzing the task demands of questions.

Explicit Teaching of Reading Comprehension. The Explicit Teaching of Reading Comprehension is a framework for the direct instruction of reading comprehension. Its intent is to get students to independently apply comprehension skills learned through explicit teaching to other reading situations. The strategy is useful for students at all grade levels.

Think-Alouds. Think-Alouds is a modeling procedure based on explicit teaching intended to make students aware of the comprehension processes enlisted as reading is pursued.

Induced Imagery. Induced Imagery is a procedure that teachers model explicitly in hopes of helping students visualize as they read.

Dialogical-Thinking Reading Lesson. The Dialogical-Thinking Reading Lesson is designed to promote critical thinking when elementary students are engaged in reading basal stories and must decide what they believe about a story-specific issue.

Inquiry Chart. The Inquiry Chart is an instructional procedure that uses a data chart of information from multiple sources so that students may critically evaluate a topic under study.

REFERENCES

Duke, N. K., and P. D. Pearson. 2002. Effective practices for developing reading comprehension. In A. E. Farstrup and S. J. Samuels (Eds.), *What research has to say about reading instructions* (3rd ed.). Newark, DE: International Reading Association, pp. 205–241. Provides a review of research on teaching reading comprehension with a focus on strategies.

National Reading Panel. 2000. *Teaching children to read: An evidence-based assessment of the scientific research literature on reading and its implications for reading instruction: Report of the subgroups.*

(NIH Publication No. 00-4754). Washington, DC: National Institute of Child Health and Human Development. Chapter 4 reviews the research on reading comprehension.

Pearson, P. D., and L. Fielding. 1991. Comprehension instruction. In R. Barr, M. L. Kamil, P. B. Mosenthal, and P. D. Pearson (Eds.), *Handbook of reading research,* Vol. II. New York: Longman. Updated review of research on comprehension instruction.

Pressley, M. 1998. *Reading instruction that works: The case for balanced teaching.* New York: Guilford. Text that advocates the use of comprehension strategies.

Tierney, R. J., and J. Cunningham. 1984. Research on teaching reading comprehension. In P. D. Pearson (Ed.), *Handbook of reading research.* New York: Longman. Review of research on reading comprehension.

Questioning the Author

Purpose

Questioning the Author (QtA) was developed by Beck and McKeown (Beck, McKeown, Hamilton, and Kucan, 1997; Beck, McKeown, Sandora, and Kucan, 1996; McKeown, Beck, and Worthy, 1993) as a means to enhance student engagement with both narrative and expository text, particularly text that is difficult and not friendly to the reader.

Rationale

Questioning the Author is based on a constructivist view of learning. That is, learners are not seen as passive extractors of information from text; rather, they are viewed as actively interacting with text information and juxtaposing it with the knowledge and experiences they bring to the text. As learners progress through the text, they combine text information with what they know about language and word meanings, the structure of text, and general information they may have about the content. As reading proceeds, they construct a representation of the author's meaning and continually update it as reading progresses. From a constructivist view, understanding the text involves connecting it to previous knowledge, being able to explain the representation, and using it subsequently.

Additionally, research on social studies textbooks undertaken by Beck and McKeown revealed that the texts had unclear content goals, presumed more extensive prior knowledge on the part of readers than they had, and provided poor explanations (Beck, McKeown, and Gromoll, 1989). Students typically are unable to read such texts with any degree of understanding. When these texts were revised to be more coherent, students were able to read with more understanding and recall more information (Beck, McKeown, Sinatra, and Loxterman, 1991). In trying to revise the texts, Beck and McKeown found that their efforts to make connections and understand the text were exactly like the efforts they presumed students would make to construct meaning from the text. As a result, it occurred to them that they could encourage a constructivist approach by giving students a "reviser's eye" (Beck et al., 1997, 15). It was their thought that a reviser's job was to make a text more understandable, and they wanted students to do this for themselves. As a consequence, they believed this might promote the kind of active engagement with text that needed to take place if learning was to occur. Thus, they developed QtA as a framework for getting students to respond to text through: (1) collaborative discussion, (2) assuming the strategies more mature readers use when they engage text, and (3) promoting a more active search for meaning.

Intended Audience

QtA has been used with elementary and middle grades students with positive results. The procedure probably can be used with any upper grade-level student who is having problems successfully negotiating text material.

Description of the Procedures

QtA will be described in three parts: (1) planning, (2) discussion, and (3) implementation.

1. Planning. In planning their lessons, some teachers rely on their teacher's manual to identify the major ideas of the text and the questions and activities prescribed to get at those ideas. As a result, these teachers may neglect to actually read the material they will be asking students to read. Still other teachers look over the text material and make their own decisions about what ideas to hold students accountable for. This tactic presumes the text is understandable and the authors are infallible.

Beck and McKeown suggest that lesson planning be done differently with QtA. They believe that teachers should attempt to anticipate problems students might encounter as they read a text and think about the support they might offer to help them. Beck and McKeown suggest that teachers should liken themselves to the roles that a director and an actor take in a stage play. That is, as a director in a play teachers should try to anticipate audience reaction, in this case how students will react to the material and how the lesson might develop. As an actor in a play, teachers should try to be ready to improvise, in this case to change the lesson in ways that may not have been anticipated. This calls for a special way in planning; teachers must read the material while thinking about how the text will be encountered by the students who are less skilled readers. Teachers must take the role of students to better facilitate student efforts to construct their own meaning of the text. Thus, Beck and McKeown suggest three goals in planning: (a) identifying major understandings and potential problems, (b) segmenting text, and (c) developing queries.

a. Identifying major understandings and potential problems. Planning in QtA should always begin with a close reading of the text material. In addition to becoming familiar with the text, teachers are reading to identify the major ideas students are to construct and the potential problems they may encounter in doing so, such as the density of the material or its lack of clarity. Unlike traditional planning, teachers' focus should be on the author's meaning or intent with the text. Beck and McKeown reason that this brings the author to the foreground of the material; the author becomes a participant in the discussion and reading becomes more interactive, more like a conversation. The analogy is that in QtA the author is there to be questioned by the reader. The purpose of the conversation is to determine and understand the major ideas the author is presenting.

Additionally, as skilled readers, teachers make sense of text by connecting what they know to the material, even if ideas are not explicitly stated. Students do not do this; therefore, teachers need to predict where students may have trouble with the text. One way for teachers to do this is to consciously monitor their own comprehension and notice where it is they have to work a little harder to understand the material (e.g., where the text has to be reread or where they stop to think about how ideas connect); these spots are likely the ones with which students will have problems.

b. Segmenting text. After reading the text, identifying the major ideas for students to construct, and predicting where trouble spots may occur, teachers must now think about how they want to segment the text. Segmenting entails deciding where to stop students' reading and initiate a discussion toward the construction of meaning. This means segmenting where the major ideas occur or where trouble spots may be. Thus, a single sentence or a series of paragraphs may be where the text is segmented; it should not be where a paragraph ends or on a page break. The number of segments will be dependent on the decisions made during planning.

c. Developing queries. Queries are important in implementing QtA as they link text with discussion and are a driving force in getting students to construct meaning. The major difference between questions and queries is that questions are typically used to assess students' comprehension of text after reading, and queries are used to help students deal with the text as they are attempting to construct meaning *during* reading. Thus, unlike questions, queries are supposed to assist students in their comprehension of text as they focus on the quality and depth of meaning. Additionally, queries facilitate discussion about the author's ideas and enhance student-to-student interactions. This changes the role of teachers from evaluators of comprehension to facilitators of understanding for students as they deal with the text and respond to each others' comments about the author's intent. Queries act to supplement the text and are used at points where the text has been segmented.

Beck and McKeown describe three different types of queries: initiating, follow-up, and narrative. Initiating and follow-up queries may be used with any text; narrative queries were developed to take into account the special nature of narrative text with regard to its authorship, purpose, and structure. Initiating queries are designed to draw attention to the major ideas and make public the notion that these ideas were written by the author. They provide guidance through discussion for students to gain an understanding of the text. Beck et al. (1997, 34) suggest these questions as possible initiating queries:

- What is the author trying to say here?
- What is the author's message?
- What is the author talking about?

Follow-up queries are used for a variety of functions in helping students build a representation of the text. First, they can help students consider the ideas and thoughts behind the actual words of an author, that is, to examine what is meant by the text rather than what the text says. Beck et al. (p. 37) suggest these two queries to accomplish this function:

- What does the author mean here?
- Does the author explain this clearly?

Second, follow-up queries can help students connect ideas previously learned with the text as well as ideas previously read in the text. They may also help students see that a connection is actually missing in the text. Beck et al. (p. 38) suggest these queries:

- Does this make sense with what the author told us before?
- How does this connect to what the author told us here?

Finally, follow-up queries can be used to help students figure out an author's reasons for the inclusion of certain information in the text. To accomplish this, Beck et al. (p. 38) suggest the following queries:

- Does the author tell us why?
- Why do you think the author tells us this now?

Narrative queries are designed to deal exclusively with the unique nature of narrative text, namely to deal with the characters and plot. Beck et al. (p. 42) recommend the following queries to assist students in thinking about characters in the text and their motivations:

- How do things look for this character now?
- Given what the author has already told us about this character, what do you think he's up to?

To focus students' thinking on the plot and how the author has crafted it, Beck et al. (p. 42) suggest two other queries:

- How does the author let you know that something has changed?
- How does the author settled this for us?

2. Discussion. The primary purpose of a QtA discussion is to help students construct an understanding of the ideas they encounter in the text. Beck and McKeown describe a QtA discussion by using the analogy of a maze. The maze comprises the ideas in the text, and the goal of the students is to work their way through the maze to reach understanding. The maze will present interesting twists and turns, there will be dead ends, and strategic maneuvers will be needed to get through. The teacher's job is not to show the way through the maze; rather, it is to help students discover their own way through. Thus, QtA helps students maneuver through a text, but it does not take away their responsibility for discovering how to do it. The key components of a QtA discussion are the students' contributions and the teacher's role.

a. Student contributions. In a traditional discussion students present ideas they have already gleaned from the text, that is, they report information and engage in a shared retrieval of facts and opinions about the text. Participation may be flat. In a QtA discussion, on the other hand, students collaborate on constructing ideas as they are encountered in the text during reading. They become engaged in a shared inquiry of meaning; therefore, participation tends to be active.

b. Teacher's role. In a traditional discussion teachers tend to dominate the thinking that is going on. They seem to do the work of constructing meaning and only signal students to react to the ideas constructed. Students' contributions are usually treated equally, with the goal being to collect and validate all contributions with little focus. In the QtA discussion teachers collaborate with students by differentiating among their contributions, helping them toward the goal of developing an understanding of the text's ideas. Teachers respond to students' contributions strategically; consequently, they are promoting students' thinking by taking their ideas farther whenever possible. Queries are the major tool teachers use to accomplish this. Queries begin the discussion, and then teachers navigate students through the investigation of the text. Besides queries, Beck and McKeown describe other tools that teachers might use to negotiate this process. They point out that *discussion moves* are actions teachers can take to facilitate student discussions; these moves keep students focused on the process of constructing meaning. Beck and McKeown describe six types of discussion moves: marking, turning back, revoicing, modeling, annotating, and recapping.

Marking is a way of drawing attention to a particularly significant comment made by a student. This can be done through paraphrasing or by explicitly acknowledging the idea's importance. Marking becomes the basis for further student discussion. *Turning back* refers to the notion of turning students' attention back to the text for clarification of ideas. It also refers to turning responsibility back to the students for figuring out ideas. Turning students back eliminates the need for teacher explanation, keeps the discussion on track, and allows students to elaborate on ideas or connect ideas with the text or other students. *Revoicing* is a way of taking the unwieldy ideas with which students are struggling and rephrasing them so the students can become part of a productive discussion. This makes it easier for other students to react to the idea, particularly if it is an important comment.

The previous three moves entail different ways to make ideas students have already offered in a discussion more productive; the next three moves bring teachers into the interaction of students more directly. *Modeling* reinforces the notion that the teacher is a collaborator in constructing meaning. For example, modeling can be used when a particularly important but confusing segment of text is encountered or when an idea or word is particularly well presented and teachers want to model their appreciation of the text. It shows students the strategic processes that fluent readers use to grapple with text. *Annotating* is the means by which teachers can provide information to fill in the gaps or add information to the discussion. This becomes necessary because authors sometimes do not provide all the information necessary for students to construct meaning. Annotating allows teachers to give students that information. Finally, *recapping* allows teachers to pull information together and summarize the major ideas students have constructed up to that point. This serves to allow students to move on in the text and in the discussion. Over time students should assume more of a role in recapping.

3. Implementation. This part of QtA deals with how this strategy will be introduced to students, particularly since QtA is different from the traditional way in which students discuss materials. First, Beck and McKeown recommend the classroom be arranged in a U-shape to facilitate discussion; this arrangement allows students to interact with one another more readily, and it allows the teacher to move around more easily. To get a QtA discussion started, students need to be prepared for a procedure they have not experienced before. In essence, this means telling the students that they will be discussing a text in a way they have not done previously.

Next, students need to be introduced to the notion of *author fallibility.* Textbooks are often perceived by students and teachers as authority, above criticism (Baldwin and Readence, 1979). The concept of author fallibility deals with the idea that what students will be reading is just someone else's ideas written down. They need to be told that authors are just people who have written down their ideas, and sometimes their ideas are not as clear as they think they are. The idea here is that authors are just people, and people aren't perfect.

Therefore, sometimes the texts that authors write are not as good or as clear as they think they are. The students' job as readers is to figure out what the authors are trying to say, even if they don't do as good a job in explaining their ideas as they would like. This communicates to students that it is not necessarily their fault if they are unable to understand what it is the author is trying to say. When students understand this notion, they are more likely to want to deal with a text that doesn't make sense to them. This eliminates the fear of being wrong and encourages students to work collaboratively to construct meaning. Additionally, teachers should take this opportunity to explain why authors might be difficult to understand and why a text might seem confusing. Problems of text coherence and clarity on the part of the author can reduce students' tendency to be defensive about not understanding what the author is trying to say.

Beck and McKeown next recommend that teachers demonstrate a think-aloud (see this unit) of a brief text to show them the kind of thinking that goes with constructing a meaning of the text and that characterizes a QtA discussion. In this way students experience what an expert reader mulling over a text does in an attempt to understand it. After the think-aloud has been demonstrated, students should be given the opportunity to discuss the various features of reading and thinking about text that you have shown them. This gives students an opportunity to ask questions about what you were demonstrating and what the author was trying to say in the text. Doing a think-aloud also helps students understand what is involved in learning with text and what a QtA reading is about. Beck and McKeown suggest that the initial experience with QtA be concluded by reminding students that authors are just people putting their thoughts in a text. The job of the students, as readers, is to figure out the author's ideas, and when they do this, they will be doing something called "Questioning the Author."

Cautions and Comments

Questioning the Author is a well-researched and well-planned-out strategy. Beck and McKeown have systematically engaged in a series of research studies designed to provide the foundation for developing QtA and have followed that with studies to investigate the efficacy of the strategy. For this they are to be commended.

While QtA presents students with a novel means to discuss a text, teachers are cautioned that it also presents a novel approach for them, too. Teachers need to be deliberate in their actions in implementing QtA; otherwise, this strategy can deteriorate into a traditional discussion with teachers taking the dominant role. In particular, this might happen when teachers employ the discussion moves, that is, modeling, annotating, and recapping, in which they take a more prominent role in the discussion.

REFERENCES

Almasi, J. F., M. G. McKeown, and I. L. Beck. 1996. The nature of engaged reading in classroom discussions of literature. *Journal of Literacy Research* 28: 107–146. A description of the nature of engagement as students and teachers implemented a QtA approach to reading literature.

Baldwin, R. S., and J. E. Readence. 1979. Critical reading and perceived authority. *Journal of Reading* 22: 617–622. Study showing that texts are perceived as authorities and students suspend their critical reading abilities in lieu of them.

Beck, I. L., M. G. McKeown, and E. W. Gromoll. 1989. Learning from social studies texts. *Cognition and Instruction* 6: 99–158. Research revealing the unfriendliness of social studies textbooks.

Beck, I. L., M. G. McKeown, R. L. Hamilton, and L. Kucan. 1997. *Questioning the Author: An approach for enhancing student engagement with text.* Newark, DE: International Reading Association. A practical guide to help teachers implement QtA.

Beck, I. L., M. G. McKeown, C. Sandora, and L. Kucan. 1996. Questioning the author: A year long classroom implementation to engage students with text. *The Elementary School Journal* 96: 385–414. Study describing the successful implementation of QtA in an at-risk elementary school with a social studies and a reading/language arts teacher.

Beck, I. L., M. G. McKeown, G. M. Sinatra, and J. A. Loxterman. 1991. Revising social studies text from a text-processing perspective: Evidence of improved comprehensibility. *Reading Research Quarterly* 26: 251–276. Study which found that when social studies texts were revised to be more friendly, students were able to understand them better.

Duke, N. K., and P. D. Pearson. 2002. Effective practices for developing reading comprehension. In A. E. Farstrup and S. J. Samuels (Eds.), *What research has to say about reading instruction* (3rd Ed.). Newark, DE: International Reading Association, 205–241. Discusses QtA in the context of a discussion of a range of teaching practices.

McKeown, M. G., I. L. Beck, and J. Worthy. 1993. Grappling with text: Questioning the author. *The Reading Teacher* 46: 560–566. An early description and rationale for using QtA.

K-W-L

Purpose

K-W-L represents a three-step procedure intended to help teachers become more responsive to helping students access appropriate knowledge when reading expository text.

Rationale

Growing out of the research findings that have highlighted the importance of a reader's background knowledge, and concern that teachers have tended to neglect the active engagement of a reader's background knowledge and interest, Ogle (1986a) developed K-W-L to ensure that teachers had a framework to elicit children's background knowledge and engage student interest.

The framework involves well-developed procedures for brainstorming, generating categories for organizing ideas, specifying questions, checking what they have learned, and guiding further reading. The rationale behind these procedures is tied to Ogle's belief in the need for a mix of group and individual activities and procedures that help scaffold students' own ideas and interests. As Ogle stated, the teacher

> helps students keep the control of their own inquiry, extending the pursuit of knowledge beyond just the one article. The teacher is making clear that learning shouldn't be framed around just what an author chooses to include, but that it involves the identification of the learner's questions and the search for authors or articles dealing with those questions. (Ogle, 1986a, 569)

Intended Audience

The framework is intended for use with expository text. Although it is apt to be more widely used with older students, it could be enlisted with students at any age level.

Description of the Procedures

K-W-L involves three basic steps: accessing what I know, determining what I want to learn, and recalling what I did learn as a result of reading. In hopes of making the steps concrete, Ogle suggests the use of a worksheet (see Figure 7.1). For the first two steps of the process the teacher and student engage in oral discussion followed by personal responses; in the third step the sequence reverses.

Step K—What I Know. Step K involves two steps: brainstorming and generating categories for ideas. Prior to reading the selection, students are intended to brainstorm in response to a concept that the teacher puts forth. Guidelines for selecting the concept to be presented for brainstorming are quite detailed and well thought out. Rather than present students with overly general concepts, Ogle suggests beginning with something specific. To illustrate, as Ogle states:

> when the class will read about sea turtles, use the words sea turtles as the stimulus, not "What do you know about animals in the sea?" or "Have you ever been to the ocean?" A general discussion of enjoyable experiences on the beach may never elicit the pertinent schemata. . . . If there appears to be little knowledge of sea turtles in your students' experiences, then ask the next more general question, "What do you know about turtles?" (Ogle, 1986a, 565)

As students offer ideas, Ogle suggests that the teacher might jot down ideas on the board, a chart, or an overhead, and then use them as a basis for encouraging discussion. In terms of the sea turtle example, the students might consider whether facts pertain to all sea turtles. Furthermore, in hopes of deepening thinking and provoking uncertainties to be confirmed by reading, Ogle suggests asking volunteers to indicate: "Where did you learn that?" and "How might you prove it?"

The second part of Step K involves generating categories of information likely to be encountered when students read. For example, prior to reading an article on sea turtles, the teacher might follow the brainstorming with a discussion of possible categories of information. The teacher might say: "Before we read this article on sea turtles, let's think awhile about what kinds of information are most likely to be included. Look at this list of things we already know: Do some of them fit together to form a general category or information (i.e. habitat, enemies)?"

FIGURE 7.1 K-W-L Strategy Sheet

1. K—What we know	W—What we want to find out	L—What we learned and still need to learn

2. Categories of information we expect to use

A.	E.
B.	F.
C.	G.
D.	

Ogle recognizes that students may initially find this approach difficult and proposes that some teacher modeling might be needed. Sometimes it might only be necessary for the teacher to suggest one or two categories before the students will suggest others. At other times, the teacher might find it worthwhile to relate what they will read to other topics that they have learned and the types of categories of information they acquired.

Step W—What Do I Want to Learn? In conjunction with brainstorming and developing categories, students begin to develop interests and curiosities. Sometimes these interests and curiosities are associated with uncertainties; at other times they reflect a drive to learn more about some aspect of the topic. The teacher's goal with Step W is to turn these uncertainties, interests, and so on, into reasons to read. By highlighting gaps in ideas, disagreements, and intriguing ideas, the teacher attempts to provoke questions. After discussing various possible questions for the group, the teacher encourages each student to specify his or her own questions—that is, the questions that he/she is interested in having answered.

Once each student has developed his/her questions, students read the selections. With some selections there may be some teacher preview so that students have some expectations and feel for the article. Again, depending on length, this selection may be read in sections or in its entirety.

Step L—What I Learned. As students complete the article, the students write down what they have learned and check what questions they still need answered. Ogle stresses the importance of going beyond the single selection so that the "clear priority of their personal desire to learn" ensures precedence over "what the author has chosen to include" (Ogle, 1986a, 567). Here is an example transcript taken from Ogle (1986a, 567–569).

TEACHER: Today we're going to read another article about animals. This one is about a special kind of spider—the Black Widow. Before we begin the article, let's think about what we already know about Black Widows. Or if you aren't familiar with this kind of spider, think about some things you know about spiders in general, and we can then see if those are also true for the Black Widow. [Teacher writes Black Widow spider on the board and waits while students think about their knowledge of spiders. Next she elicits ideas from children and writes their contributions on the board.]

TONY: Spiders have six legs.

SUSAN: They eat other insects.

EDDIE: I think they're big and dangerous spiders.

TEACHER: Can you add more about what you mean when you say they're big and dangerous?

EDDIE: They, they, I think they eat other spiders. I think people are afraid of them, too.

STEPH: They spin nests or webs to catch other insects in.

TOM: My cousin got stung by one once and almost died.

TEACHER: You mean they can be dangerous to people?

TOM: Yah, my cousin had to go to the hospital.

TEACHER: Does anyone else know more about the Black Widow? Tammy?

TAMMY: I don't think they live around here. I've never heard of anyone being stung by one.

TEACHER: Where do Black Widows live? Does anyone know? [She waits.] What else do we know about spiders?

JOHN: I think I saw a TV show about them once. They have a special mark on their back. I think it's a blue triangle or circle, or something like that. If people look, they can tell if the spider's a Black Widow or not.

TEACHER: Does anyone else recall anything more about the way they look? [She waits.] Look at what we've already said about these spiders. Can you think of other information we should add?

JOHN: I think they kill their babies or men spiders. I'm not sure which.

TEACHER: Do you remember where you learned that?

JOHN: I think I read an article once.

TEACHER: OK, let's add that to our list. Remember, everything on the list we aren't sure of we can double check when we read.

TEACHER: Anything more you think we should know about these spiders? [She waits.] OK, before we read this article let's think awhile about the kinds or categories of information that are likely to be included. Look at the list of things we already know or have questions about. Which of the categories of information have we already mentioned?

PETER: We mentioned how they look.

TEACHER: Yes, we said they're big and have six legs. And someone said they think Black Widows have a colored mark on them. Good, description is one of the main categories of information we want to learn about when we read about animals or insects. What other categories of information have we mentioned that should be included?

ANNA: Where they live; but we aren't sure.

TEACHER: Good, we should find out where they live. What other kinds of information should we expect to learn from the article? Think about what kinds of information we've learned from other articles about animals.

DIANE: We want to know what kind of homes they make.

RAUL: What do they eat?

ANDY: How they protect themselves.

CARA: How do they have babies? How many do they have?

TEACHER: Good thinking. Are there other categories of information we expect to learn about. [She waits.] We've thought about what we already know and what kinds of information we're likely to learn from an article on Black Widow spiders. Now what are some of the questions we want to have answered? I know we had some things we weren't sure about, like where these spiders live. What are some of the things you'd like to find out when we read?

CARA: I want to know how many baby spiders get born.

RICO: Do Black Widows really hurt people? I never heard of that, and my dad knows a lot about spiders.

ANDY: Why are they called Black Widows? What's a widow?

TEACHER: Good question! Does anyone know what a widow is? Why would this spider be called a "Black Widow"? [After eliciting questions from several students, the teacher asks each child to write their own questions on their worksheet.] What are the questions you are most interested in having answered? Write them down now. As you read, look for the answers and jot them down on your worksheet as you go, or other information you don't want to forget. [The students read the article.]

TEACHER: How did you like this article? What did you learn?

RAUL: The Black Widow eats her husband and sometimes her babies. Yuck! I don't think I like that kind of spider!

STEPH: They can live here—it says they live in all parts of the United States.

ANDY: They can be recognized by an hourglass that is red or yellow on the abdomen.

TEACHER: What is another word for abdomen? [She waits.] Sara, please look up the word abdomen. Let's find out where the hourglass shape is located. While Sara is looking the word up, let's check what we learned against the questions we wanted answered. Are there some questions that didn't get answered? What more do we want to know?

Cautions and Comments

K-W-L represents a thoughtfully developed framework that appears to support student-initiated learning which is text-based but not by a single text or rigid teacher guidance. Ogle claims that the strategy has helped students become better readers of expository text at the same time as it has helped teachers develop a more interactive teaching style—a style that supports student involvement and initiation before, during, and after reading. In her various articles detailing the use of the procedures (including comparison with selections with which the procedure was not used), Ogle indicates that students taught using K-W-L remember what they have pursued and over time become more actively involved in reading. The extent to which they elicit their own background knowledge increases as does their ability to generate categories. Ogle also suggests that teachers have reported to her that students ask if they can use K-W-L, and when they do they read "noisily" with "ahs" and "ohs." At the same time as students seem responsive to the strategy, Ogle claims that teachers seem amenable to its use and aware of the extent to which it facilitates a more interactive approach. Despite these affidavits, the approach should be more rigorously evaluated for purposes of refining its use as well as examining some of the claims.

Since its inception, variations of K-W-L have emerged. For example, Carr and Ogle (1987) suggested K-W-L Plus, which incorporated the use of mapping (Hanf, 1971) and summarization procedures (Brown and Day, 1983). Additionally, Weissman (1996) has suggested using K-W-L with paragraph frames to provide students opportunities for writing, Huffman (1998) has combined K-W-L with focus questions (e.g., who? what? when?

where? why? how?) to make sure essential facts are not overlooked in learning new material, and Bryan (1998) has extended K-W-L to K-W-*W*-L so students can answer the question, *Where* can I learn this?, and get specific information about where to locate the material they need. Finally, Laverick (2002) offered a final variation by suggesting that K-W-L be adapted to B-D-A (before, during, after) for use with high school students.

REFERENCES

Brown, A., and J. Day. 1983. Macrorules for summarizing texts: The development of expertise. *Journal of Verbal Learning and Verbal Behavior* 22: 1–14. Presents guidelines for helping students summarize.

Bryan, J. 1998. K-W-W-L: Questioning the known. *The Reading Teacher* 51: 618–620. Presents a variation of K-W-L that gets at where to locate essential resource information.

Carr, E., and D. Ogle. 1987. K-W-L plus: A strategy for comprehension and summarization. *Journal of Reading* 30: 626–631. Presents a variation on K-W-L and describes its use with ninth graders.

Hanf, M. 1971. Mapping: A technique for translating reading into thinking. *Journal of Reading* 14: 225–230, 270. Presents guidelines for mapping, which has been used as an aid to categorization.

Huffman, L. E. 1998. Spotlighting specifics by combining focus questions with K-W-L. *Journal of Adolescent and Adult Literacy* 41: 470–472. Discusses the addition of focus questions to K-W-L to help students get the essential specifics of a lesson.

Jennings, J. H. 1991. A comparison of summary and journal writing as components of an interactive comprehension model. In J. Zutell and S. McCormick (Eds.), *Learner factors/teacher factors: Issues in literacy research and instruction.* Fortieth Yearbook of the National Reading Conference, 67–82. Chicago: National Reading Conference.

Laverick, C. 2002. B-D-A strategy: Reinventing the wheel can be a good thing. *Journal of Adolescent and Adult Literacy* 46: 144–147. Adaptation of K-W-L for high school students.

Ogle, D. 1986a. K-W-L: A teaching model that develops active reading of expository text. *The Reading Teacher* 39: 564–570. Represents the primary source detailing the use of K-W-L.

———. 1986b. K-W-L group instruction strategy. In A. S. Palincsar, D. S. Ogle, B. F. Jones, and E. G. Carr (Eds.), *Teaching reading as thinking.* Alexandria, VA: Association for Supervision and Curriculum Development. Describes the use of K-W-L in conjunction with developing thinking skills.

———. 1992. KWL in action: Secondary teachers find applications that work. In E. K. Dishner, T. W. Bean, J. E. Readence, and D. W. Moore (Eds.), *Reading in the content areas: Improving classroom instruction* (3d ed.). Dubuque, IA: Kendall/Hunt, 270–282. Describes the use of K-W-L in the content areas.

Sampson, M. B. 2002. Confirming a K-W-L: Considering the source. *The Reading Teacher* 55: 528–532. Adds a confirmation/verification aspect to K-W-L.

Weissman, K. E. 1996. Using paragraph frames to complete a K-W-L. *The Reading Teacher* 50: 271–272. Suggests using paragraph frames with K-W-L to encourage students to write.

Anticipation Guide

Purpose

The Anticipation Guide (Readence, Bean, and Baldwin, 2004) is designed to: (1) activate students' knowledge about a topic before reading and (2) provide purpose by serving as a guide for subsequent reading.

Rationale

The Anticipation Guide attempts to enhance students' comprehension by having them react to a series of statements about a topic before they begin to read or to engage in any other form of information acquisition. It utilizes prediction by activating students' prior knowledge, and it capitalizes on controversy as a motivational device to get students involved in the material to be read.

Numerous studies (e.g., Pearson, Hansen, and Gordon, 1979) have pointed out the efficacy of activating students' knowledge about a topic before they read in order to enhance comprehension. Other ways to promote better comprehension have also been suggested. Herber and Nelson (1986) have recommended that statements be used in lieu of questions as an initial means to get students more involved in their learning because statements require students only to *recognize* and respond, whereas questions require students to *produce* a response. Production of their own questions and statements, which is a more sophisticated learning behavior than recognition alone, becomes the end goal of such instruction. In addition, Lunstrum (1981) suggested that controversy could be used as a motivational technique for reading by arousing students' curiosity about a topic and getting them to use the text to corroborate their stance on an issue.

The Anticipation Guide incorporates all of these comprehension-enhancing strategies by asking students to react to statements that focus their attention on the topic to be learned. Students' previous thoughts and opinions about that topic are activated by using statements that are carefully worded so as to challenge students' knowledge bases and to arouse their curiosity. Students then become motivated to read to resolve the conceptual conflict. In this way, misconceptions about a topic can be brought out and inaccuracies dealt with. Furthermore, the Anticipation Guide can also be used as the basis for postreading discussion wherein students react a second time to the statements, this time dealing with the text information as well.

Intended Audience

The Anticipation Guide can be adapted for use at any grade level and can be used with a variety of print and nonprint media. Statements used in the guide can be modified and read to younger or slower students, who may be unable to read them on their own. In addition, the Anticipation Guide can be used to introduce a film, filmstrip, lecture, audiotape, or field trip, as well as to introduce a text reading assignment. Thus, the guide can be realistically applied in most learning situations.

Description of the Procedures

Readence, Bean, and Baldwin (2004) recommend the following steps to implement an Anticipation Guide:

1. Identify major concepts
2. Determine students' knowledge of these concepts
3. Create statements
4. Decide statement order and presentation mode
5. Present guide
6. Discuss each statement briefly
7. Direct students to read the text
8. Conduct follow-up discussion

1. Identify Major Concepts. The ideas to be learned by reading the text should be determined by a careful perusal of the material and of the teacher's manual, if one is available.

The step is analogous to what normally happens in good lesson planning. The following example of constructing and using an Anticipation Guide is adapted from one provided by Head and Readence (1992). Using a text entitled "Food and Health," the following concepts were identified:

a. Food contains nutrients that your body needs for energy, growth, and repair.
b. Carbohydrates and fats supply energy.
c. A balanced diet includes the correct amount of all the nutrients needed by your body.
d. Every food contains some calories of food energy.

2. Determine Students' Knowledge of These Concepts. In order to determine how the main concepts support or challenge what the students already know, the teacher must consider the students' experiential background. The whole class, as well as individual students, will have to be considered in this step. In our nutrition example, socioeconomic level is one, but only one, factor that may have a bearing on the kinds of statements that eventually result.

3. Create Statements. The number of statements to be created varies with the amount of text to be read and, particularly, the number of concepts that have been identified. In addition, the ability and maturity levels of the students influence statement making. Three to five statements are usually a good number to aim for. The most effective statements are generally those in which the students have sufficient knowledge to understand what the statements say, but not enough to make any of them a totally known entity.

4. Decide Statement Order and Presentation Mode. An appropriate order must be determined to present the guide. Usually, the order follows the sequence in which the concepts are encountered in the text, but that is subject to each teacher's judgment.

The guide may be presented using the chalkboard, an overhead transparency, or a ditto sheet that is handed out individually. A set of directions and blanks for students' responses should be included. The directions must be worded appropriately for the age and maturity levels of the students.

5. Present Guide. Continuing with our Anticipation Guide example on nutrition, the following guide is given to the students:

Anticipation Guide: Food and Health

Directions: Below are some statements about food and nutrition. Read each statement carefully and place a checkmark next to each statement with which you agree. Be prepared to defend your thinking as we discuss the statements.

__________ **1.** An apple a day keeps the doctor away.
__________ **2.** If you wish to live a long life, be a vegetarian.
__________ **3.** Three square meals a day will satisfy all your body's nutritional needs.
__________ **4.** Calories make you fat.

When presenting the guide to students, it is advisable to read the directions and statements orally. You should emphasize that students will share their thoughts and opinions about each statement, defending their agreement or disagreement with the statement. Students can work individually or in small groups to formulate a response.

6. Discuss Each Statement Briefly. A discussion ensues, with the teacher first asking for a show of hands from students to indicate their agreement or disagreement. The teacher tallies the responses. The discussion should include at least one opinion on each side of the issue per statement. As other students listen to the opinions offered, they can evaluate their own view in terms of the others.

7. Direct Students to Read the Text. Students are now told to read the text assignment with the purpose of deciding what the author would say about each statement. As they read, students should keep two things in mind: their own thoughts and opinions as well as those voiced by others, and the way in which what they are reading relates to what was discussed.

8. Conduct Follow-Up Discussion. After reading, the students may respond once again to the statements. This time they should react in the light of the actual text. Thus, the guide now serves as the basis for a postreading discussion in which students can share the new information gained from reading and how their previous thoughts may have been modified by what they understand the reading to say. It should be made clear to the students that agreement with the author is not mandatory.

Cautions and Comments

The Anticipation Guide presents a versatile format for use by teachers to activate students' prior knowledge about a topic to be learned and to motivate them to pursue that information. In essence, the guide provides for the following: (1) active involvement by students in their own learning; (2) the use of prediction as a means to stimulate comprehension; and (3) guidance in the form of purpose-setting behaviors as students interact with the text in their effort to verify their predictions.

In addition, the Anticipation Guide has some diagnostic value for teachers in formulating and executing their instructional plan. As students discuss the statements before reading, teachers can assess the depth and breadth of students' knowledge about a topic. This allows teachers to make tentative instructional decisions about the time required for learning, the kind of materials that may be most appropriate, and what alternative strategies would be beneficial to the students. Lipson (1984) has expressed some concern about the negative effects of inaccurate prior knowledge on learning. Because of this diagnostic character of the Anticipation Guide, teachers can readily take appropriate steps to rectify students' misconceptions when inaccurate or incomplete knowledge is discovered.

Perhaps the most difficult aspect of constructing an Anticipation Guide is selecting appropriate statements to be used. Guide statements must be within students' previous knowledge and, therefore, must be on the experience-based level of comprehension. But the statements must also be on a higher level of generality in order to be an effective teaching and learning strategy. Using statements that are merely fact-based is ineffective. Students should discuss reasons for holding or forming opinions, not simply recite easily found facts.

For instance, if we used a statement in our example guide on nutrition such as "the recommended minimum daily allowance of vitamin A is 1.5 mg," the statement would be virtually useless as a tool to enhance learning. That type of statement is based on fact, not experience. Either students would know it or they wouldn't; in essence, it becomes a true-false statement. If the student does know it, then it has no value as an instructional tool. Conversely, if the student doesn't know it, then it will not serve as a knowledge-activation device. Students must be allowed to use their prior experiences in order to benefit from the use of prereading statements. Teachers are cautioned that, though such statements are more difficult to construct, experience-based statements are crucial to the success of Anticipation Guides or any other guide based on prediction.

REFERENCES

Alvermann, D. E., and J. Swafford. 1989. Do content area strategies have a research base? *Journal of Reading* 32: 388–390. Discusses the research base associated with various strategies and practices.

Duffelmeyer, F. A. 1994. Effective anticipation guide statements for learning from expository prose. *Journal of Reading* 37: 452–457. Presents guidelines for writing effective guide statements.

Ericson, B., M. Hubler, T. W. Bean, C. C. Smith, and J. V. McKenzie. 1987. Increasing critical reading in junior high classrooms. *Journal of Reading* 30: 430–439. Discusses the use of Anticipation Guides as a means to promote critical thinking.

Head, M. H., and J. E. Readence. 1992. Anticipation guides: Enhancing meaning through prediction. In E. K. Dishner, T. W. Bean, J. E. Readence, and D. W. Moore (Eds.), *Reading in the content areas: Improving classroom instruction.* (3rd ed.). Dubuque, IA: Kendall/Hunt, 227–233. Provides a detailed description of the construction and use of Anticipation Guides.

Herber, H. L., and J. B. Nelson. 1986. Questioning is not the answer. In E. K. Dishner, T. W. Bean, J. E. Readence, and D. W. Moore (Eds.), *Reading in the content areas: Improving classroom instruction* (2nd ed.). Dubuque, IA: Kendall/Hunt, 210–215. Discusses the role of statements in learning from text.

Lipson, M. Y. 1984. Some unexpected issues in prior knowledge and comprehension. *The Reading Teacher* 37: 760–764. Describes the problematic effects of inaccurate prior knowledge on comprehension.

Lunstrum, J. P. 1981. Building motivation through the use of controversy. *Journal of Reading* 24: 687–691. Offers controversy as a means to arouse curiosity and enhance comprehension.

Pearson, P. D., J. Hansen, and C. Gordon. 1979. The effect of background knowledge on young children's comprehension of explicit and implicit information. *Journal of Reading Behavior* 11: 201–219. Presents a research study exploring the facilitative effects of prior knowledge on learning from text.

Readence, J. E., T. W. Bean, and R. S. Baldwin. 2004. *Content area reading: An integrated approach* (8th ed.). Dubuque, IA: Kendall/Hunt. Delineates the steps involved in using an Anticipation Guide and provides numerous examples.

Text Preview

Purpose

The Text Preview (Graves, Cooke, and LaBerge, 1983) is designed to: (1) build students' background knowledge about a topic before reading; (2) motivate students to read; and (3) provide an organizational framework for comprehending a text.

Rationale

The major premises behind the use of the Text Preview are similar to that of the Anticipation Guide, namely, that comprehension is enhanced when readers draw on their prior knowledge and are interested in the topic. However, this prereading strategy goes beyond simply drawing on students' prior knowledge; it actually attempts to build their knowledge about a text selection before students read.

When faced with a novel selection, students may have a difficult time with unfamiliar vocabulary, syntax, and/or text structure. This could be further complicated by a narrative where characters, setting, or events are not made explicit and must be inferred. A Text Preview can give readers this information so that when they begin reading the selection they have a framework to understand the characters and events at the text-explicit level and beyond. Text Previews also serve to motivate student interest because explicit connections are made between topics to be read and students' experiences. In addition, students can be further stimulated because the text preview is designed to speak directly to them.

Research support for Text Previews (e.g., Graves, Cooke, and LaBerge, 1983; Graves and Prenn, 1984) have demonstrated the efficacy of using them with students of middle school through high school age who have varying ability levels. Text Previews also have been shown to be effective with both narrative and expository texts. Finally, they have been shown to not only help students understand text selections but also to improve their attitude about reading the texts.

Intended Audience

Text Previews seem most useful for upper elementary through high school students who encounter a variety of text situations, some of which may be novel and/or difficult. They may be especially useful for low ability students who lack sufficient prior knowledge or the necessary motivation to read and understand a potentially difficult text selection.

Description of the Procedures

Graves, Prenn, and Cooke (1985) described the use of previews for narrative selections in two parts: (1) preparation and construction, and (2) presentation.

1. Preparation and Construction of Text Previews. A text preview is a detailed script written in such a way as to provide an organizational framework to enhance students' comprehension of a text selection. Specifically, it consists of three parts: (a) an interest-building section, (b) a synopsis of the selection, which includes a description of characters and setting, and (c) a section that includes a purpose-setting question or directions for reading.

The interest-building section is designed to pique students' interest by asking a few rhetorical questions and making a connection between a familiar topic and the topic of the selection. The synopsis consists of a brief discussion of the story's theme, along with an introduction to the characters and, if appropriate, the setting and point of view. Finally, students are given questions or directions to guide their reading. Included here is a sample text preview written for "The Sniper" (O'Flaherty, 1926).

Text Preview: "The Sniper"*

Trying to get along with other people is very important to most of us. Just imagine what the world would be like if that were the case! Yet, try as we may, we know that is not how people are. Do you remember the last time you got into an argument or fight with someone? What were its consequences? What is even worse is getting into a fight or argument only to find out that it resulted in hurting some other person you really cared for! Has that happened to you? What were your thoughts and feelings when you found out?

In the story you are about to read entitled "The Sniper," the main character is found on a rooftop at night with the sounds of guns in the background. It is wartime. Suddenly, a shot rings out, barely missing the sniper. It is the enemy trying to kill him.

Just then, an enemy car approaches. The sniper performs his duty and kills two of the enemy. Just as he does, another shot rings out, this time wounding the sniper so he can't hold his rifle any longer. Yet, he must do something as daybreak is approaching. The sniper can't be caught on the rooftop in daylight, and his escape is covered by the enemy who wounded him. Then the sniper thinks of an escape plan. After all, this is war and he must survive the enemy, no matter who it may be.

What is the sniper's plan? Will it be successful? And, who is the enemy? You will have to read to find out.

The first step in the construction of a Text Preview is to become thoroughly familiar with the selection. This may mean reading it more than one time. When this is done, it must be decided how to build an analogical bridge between what the students know and the theme or topic of the story. Thus, it is important to think of real-life, day-to-day events that touch the lives of the students. It is this bridge that will become the first part of the Text Preview.

Next, write the synopsis of the story. This should be a brief description of the characters, setting, point of view, and plot up to the point of the climax. This should give students the gist of the story and how it is organized. The last section of the Text Preview suggests the outcome for which the students should be looking as they read the story. It might suggest a general approach or directions for reading. It might also alert them to a special twist they might encounter as they read.

2. Presentation of Text Previews. The use of Text Previews is fairly straightforward. Graves and associates (1985) recommend the following steps:

- Tell students that you're going to introduce a new story.
- Read the interest-building section of the preview to the students. It is best to read the preview rather than paraphrase it since a casual presentation of it belies the care and time involved in its construction.
- Give students a few minutes to relate the information to their prior knowledge and discuss it.
- Read the remainder of the Text Preview.
- Direct students to read the selection.

Previewing a story should take five to ten minutes, including the discussion. The discussion should be focused and is not designed to promote a lengthy dialogue.

*From L. O'Flaherty. 1926. *Spring sowing.* New York: Alfred A. Knopf.

Cautions and Comments

Perhaps the greatest concern in using Text Previews is the amount of time it takes to develop one. Thus, it is recommended that they only be used for particularly challenging and important stories. Teachers must weigh the benefits gained by students with their use versus the amount of time and energy they expend in their creation. However, research on Text Previews seems to show that the effort is well worth it; students report that previews help them to understand the text selections better. Graves and associates (1985) also suggest that (1) Text Previews may only be used with students who are likely to have trouble with a particular text; or (2) briefer previews, using lists of characters or only the interest-building section, might be used. Along that vein of brevity, Baldwin, Readence, and Bean (2004) recommend the use of a shortened version of a text preview, the text appetizer. A text appetizer consists solely of an interest-building paragraph with some accompanying guide questions for reading.

Readence, Bean, and Baldwin (2004) provide additional guidelines for developing Text Previews when using them with expository material. The preview might contain a review of important points along with a definition of key vocabulary terms and focusing questions that move students from text-explicit thinking to more implicit and experience-based thinking. Such changes are necessary to consider because of the nature of expository text.

Finally, as an alternative to the regular use of Text Previews, teachers are encouraged to consider them as potential writing assignments. Once students become familiar with previews, they can be asked to read a story and write a Text Preview for students in other classes. The process of writing a preview will cause students to consider thoroughly the ideas offered in the selection and to think critically about them.

REFERENCES

Baldwin, R. S., J. E. Readence, and T. W. Bean. (2004). *Targeted reading: Improving achievement in middle and secondary grades.* Dubuque, IA: Kendall/Hunt. Discusses the use of the text appetizer, a shortened version of a text preview.

Chen, H. S., and M. F. Graves. 1998. Previewing challenging reading selections for ESL students. *Journal of Adolescent and Adult Reading* 41: 570–571. Discusses why Text Previews would be useful to help ESL students learn with text.

Ericson, B., M. Hubler, T. W. Bean, C. C. Smith, and J. V. MacKenzie. 1987. Increasing critical reading in junior high classrooms. *Journal of Reading* 30: 430–439. Discusses the use of Text Previews as a means to promote critical thinking in English classrooms.

Graves, M. F., C. L. Cooke, and M. J. LaBerge. 1983. Effects of previewing difficult short stories on low ability junior high school students' comprehension, recall, and attitudes. *Reading Research Quarterly* 18: 262–276. Original study that validated the use of Text Previews.

Graves, M. F., and M. C. Prenn. 1984. Effects of previewing expository passages on junior high school students' comprehension and attitudes. In J. A. Niles and L. A. Harris (Eds.), *Changing perspectives on research in reading/language processing and instruction,* Thirty-third yearbook of the National Reading Conference. Rochester, NY: National Reading Conference, 173–177. Research study using eighth-grade social studies students showing that Text Previews can improve comprehension and attitudes, even with expository text.

Graves, M. F., M. C. Prenn, and C. L. Cooke. 1985. The coming attraction: Previewing short stories. *Journal of Reading* 28: 594–598. Review of theoretical and research support on Text Previews and a discussion of their practical applications.

Readence, J. E., T. W. Bean, and R. S. Baldwin. 2004. *Content area reading: An integrated approach* (8th ed.). Dubuque, IA: Kendall/Hunt. Discusses the use of Text Previews as a prereading strategy with examples from both narrative and expository texts.

ReQuest Procedure

Purpose

The ReQuest procedure (Manzo, 1968) is designed to encourage students to: (1) formulate their own questions about the material they are reading and develop questioning behavior; (2) adopt an active, inquiring attitude to reading; (3) acquire reasonable purposes for reading; and (4) improve their independent reading comprehension skills.

Rationale

Manzo, the originator of the ReQuest procedure, suggests that while teacher questioning and purpose setting are important to reading comprehension, of greater importance is the development of the students' abilities to ask their own questions and to set their own purposes for reading. He suggests that these skills facilitate the students' acquisition of an active, inquiring attitude and their ability to examine alternatives and to originate information. These things he considers essential if students are to transfer problem-solving involvement to different contexts.

Intended Audience

ReQuest is suitable for use with students at levels ranging from kindergarten to college. Although it was originally devised for use on a one-to-one basis, it can also work with groups of up to approximately eight persons.

Description of the Procedures

In the ReQuest procedure, an individual student and teacher silently read sections of a selection and then take turns asking and answering each other's questions about that selection. The teacher's function is to model good questioning behavior, to provide feedback to the student about his or her questions, and to assess whether the student has established reasonable purposes for independently completing the passage.

There are six steps teachers should follow in using the ReQuest procedure:

1. Preparation of material
2. Development of readiness for the strategy
3. Development of student questioning behaviors
4. Development of student predictive behaviors
5. Silent reading activity
6. Follow-up activities

1. Preparation of Material. Preparation of the material entails previewing the selection for the purpose of:

- **a.** Selecting material at an appropriate level for the student
- **b.** Selecting material appropriate for making predictions
- **c.** Identifying appropriate points within the selection where the student could plausibly make predictions

2. Development of Readiness for the Strategy. Manzo (1969) suggests the following protocol and guidelines as those appropriate for beginning a ReQuest session.

> The purpose of this lesson is to improve your understanding of what you read. We will each read silently the first sentence. Then we will take turns asking questions about the sentence and what it means. You will ask questions first, then I will ask questions. Try to ask the kinds of questions a teacher might ask in the way a teacher might ask them.
>
> You may ask me as many questions as you wish. When you are asking me questions, I will close my book (or pass the book to you if there is only one between us). When I ask questions, you close your book. (p. 124)

The teacher might also explain these points during or prior to the session: Each question deserves to be answered fully—"I don't know" as an answer is unacceptable; unclear questions are to be rephrased; and uncertain answers should be justified by reference to the text. In addition, it may be necessary at times to introduce some of the vocabulary contained in the selection and/or develop some background for understanding the passage. For example, the teacher may need to give the student oral familiarity with some of the more difficult words in the selection. Also, in order to develop some background for understanding the passage, the teacher might alert the student to the basic concepts involved by a brief and general discussion of the title.

Therefore, in introducing the ReQuest procedure, the teacher should be aware of the need to:

- **a.** Build student interest in the procedure
- **b.** Introduce selected vocabulary
- **c.** Develop some background for understanding the passage
- **d.** Provide the student with an understanding of the rules of ReQuest

3. Development of Student Questioning Behaviors. At this point, both the teacher and the student participate in the reciprocal questioning procedure. As Manzo's protocol suggests, this procedure entails:

a. Joint silent reading. Both the student and teacher read the first sentence of the selection.

b. Student questioning. The teacher closes his or her book, and the student questions the teacher. The teacher responds with an answer, reinforces appropriate questioning behavior, and, if necessary, requests rephrasing of unclear questions.

c. Exchange of roles. The student finishes questioning and removes his or her copy of the material. Then the teacher questions the student.

Throughout this phase, the teacher exhibits good questioning behavior and provides feedback to the student about the student's questions. When taking the role of questioner, the teacher should endeavor to extend the student's thinking. To this end, the teacher might use various types of questions, including questions that build on prior questions and require the student to integrate information. When responding to the student's questions, the teacher could use both verbal and nonverbal reinforcement. For example, a student's question might be reinforced with a statement such as "That's a great question. I really have to . . ." or "I hope I can ask questions that tough that will make you. . . ."

4. Development of Student Predictive Behaviors. At an appropriate point in the procedure (i.e., when the student has read enough to make a prediction about the rest of the material), the exchange of questions is terminated. Assuming the role of agitator, the teacher attempts to elicit predictions and validations from the student. At this point, the teacher might ask, "What do you think will happen? . . . Why do you think so? . . . Read the line that proves it." It may prove helpful to develop a list of suggested predictions and a ranking from most likely to least likely.

If the prediction and verifications are reasonable, the teacher and student can move to the next step—silent reading activity. If the predictions are unreasonable, the teacher and student may continue reading and exchanging questions until another opportunity to elicit predictions arises. However, if the student is unable to make a reasonable prediction after having read three paragraphs, the teacher should terminate this activity. As Manzo suggests, "It may be self-defeating to continue beyond this point" (1969, 125).

5. Silent Reading Activity. The teacher now directs the student to read the remainder of the selection. At this point, the teacher might say, "Read to the end of the selection to see what actually did happen." During this period, the teacher can either read along with the student or stand by to assist. Manzo suggests that it is important to give aid in a manner that does not disrupt the student's comprehension, that is, does not destroy the student's train of thought.

6. Follow-Up Activities. Numerous worthwhile tasks are suitable for follow-up activities. Manzo suggests that readers might engage in activities that verify or apply the information gained from reading. Other useful activities may emanate from a reconsideration and discussion of student predictions. For example, the teacher could encourage the student to consider variations or adaptations of the story.

Cautions and Comments

For those teachers using ReQuest for the first time, Manzo offers a number of suggestions. He advises working with individuals rather than with groups, and for the first encounter, he suggests the use of specific question types: immediate reference, common knowledge, related information, open-ended discussion, personalized discussion, further reference, and translation. With children for whom ReQuest is a new experience, a questioning game or activity may be useful as a starter. Students may wish to underline those ideas about which they want to ask questions; students' confidence in their ability to formulate questions can be vital to their successful involvement in the ReQuest procedure.

At certain times, modifications of the ReQuest procedures may be desirable. For example, in order to provide more varied interactions between questioner and respondent, it may be desirable to alternate the role of questioner after each question. Also, greater flexibility seems desirable in the selection of sections of the passage to be read at one time. Rather than proceed sentence by sentence, one might look for natural breaks within the passage. In a group situation, there are numerous possibilities. One example is where the roles of questioner and respondent either alternate around a circle or proceed at random within the circle. Often a group, as a whole, enjoys challenging the teacher. With kindergarten children, Legenza (1974) has successfully applied a modification of ReQuest using pictures. The suggested protocol in this situation runs as follows:

> Let's ask each other questions about this picture to see if we can learn all the things we can about it. In order to help us to learn all we can, let's both look at the picture first and ask me any questions you can think of about this picture and I'll see if I can answer them—then I'll ask you some questions and you see if you can answer them. (Manzo and Legenza, 1975, 482)

Another possible modification is an incomplete questioning technique. This technique requires the student or teacher to initiate an incomplete question: for example, "Why did John . . . ?" The other party completes the question and directs it at the initiator.

With or without these modifications, the ReQuest procedure appears to be a very effective strategy. The various permutations of the ReQuest procedure provide a viable tool for exploring, extending, and encouraging student hypothesizing. ReQuest facilitates student involvement in problem-solving and necessitates teacher awareness of the student's level of involvement. Studies by Manzo and Legenza (1975) provide empirical support for using ReQuest, and the National Reading Panel (2000) found question generation and question answering, the bases of ReQuest, to be effective strategies for improving comprehension.

Using a modification of the ReQuest procedure and then adding other cognitive strategies, Palincsar and Brown (1984) developed a technique called Reciprocal Teaching to help students comprehend texts better. In addition to question generation akin to ReQuest, students are also taught to summarize, clarify word meanings or confusing text, and predict what the upcoming text will be about. Reciprocal Teaching is done through teacher modeling of these processes followed by guided practice. Teachers gradually release responsibility to the students as the technique ensues. A review of the research by Rosenshine and Meister (1994) found positive effects for using Reciprocal Teaching to improve students' comprehension.

REFERENCES

Alvermann, D. E., and J. Swafford. 1989. Do content area strategies have a research base? *Journal of Reading* 32: 388–390. Discusses the research base associated with various strategies and practices.

Barrentine, S. J. 1996. Engaging with reading through interactive read-alouds. *The Reading Teacher* 50(1): 36–43. Describes conversations around interactive read-alouds and how they contribute to the form of Reciprocal Teaching.

Dermody, M. M., and R. B. Speaker, Jr. 1995. Effects of reciprocal strategy training in prediction, clarification, question generating, and summarization in fourth graders' reading comprehension. In K. A. Hinchman, D. J. Leu, and C. K. Kinzer (Eds.), *Perspectives on literacy research and practice*. Chicago: National Reading Conference, 190–196. Details the results of a study examining the efficacy of Reciprocal Teaching with fourth graders.

Dishner, E. K., and L. W. Searfoss. 1977. Improving comprehension through the ReQuest procedure. *Reading Education: A Journal for Australian Teachers* 2: 22–25. Presents an expanded and more specific set of directions for the ReQuest procedure.

Helfeldt, J. P., and W. A. Henk. 1990. Reciprocal question-answer relationships: An instructional technique for at-risk readers. *Journal of Reading* 33: 509–514. Describes an instructional strategy that integrates ReQuest with Question-Answer Relationships.

Helfeldt, J. P., and R. Lalik. 1979. Reciprocal student-teacher questioning. In C. Pennock (Ed.), *Reading comprehension at four linguistic levels*. Newark,

DE: International Reading Association, 74–99. Reports a study in which ReQuest was shown to be more effective than teacher questioning alone.

Kay, L., J. L. Young, and R. R. Mottley. 1986. Using Manzo's ReQuest model with delinquent adolescents. *Journal of Reading* 29: 506–510. ReQuest is shown to work with incarcerated youths, improving their self-esteem.

King, C. M., and L. M. P. Johnson. (1999). Constructing meaning via reciprocal teaching. *Reading Research and Instruction* 38: 169–186. Research examining the validity of reciprocal teaching with fifth graders.

Legenza, A. 1974. *Questioning behavior of kindergarten children.* Paper presented at Nineteenth Annual Convention, International Reading Association. Describes the use and effectiveness of the ReQuest Picture Treatment with kindergarten children.

Manzo, A. V. 1968. *Improving reading comprehension through reciprocal questioning.* Unpublished doctoral diss., Syracuse University. Primary reference. Describes the original development of the ReQuest procedure, rationale, piloting, and empirical support of its effectiveness.

———. 1969. The ReQuest procedure. *Journal of Reading* 12: 123–126. Manzo's first article based on the ReQuest procedure. Describes the rationale, procedures, and suggestions for use.

———. 1985. Expansion modules for the ReQuest, CAT, GRP and REAP reading/study procedures. *Journal of Reading* 28: 498–503. Updates the use of these study techniques in hopes of increasing student independence.

Manzo, A. V., and A. Legenza. 1975. Inquiry training for kindergarten children. *Educational Leadership* 32: 479–483. Presents the procedures and empirical support for use of ReQuest with kindergarten children.

National Reading Panel. 2000. *Teaching children to read: An evidence-based assessment of the scientific research literature on reading and its implications for reading instruction: Report of the subgroups.* (NIH Publication No. 00-4754). Washington, DC: National Institute of Child Health and Human Development. Chapter 4 reviews the research on reading comprehension.

Palincsar, A. S., and A. L. Brown. 1984. Reciprocal teaching of comprehension-fostering and comprehension-monitoring activities. *Cognition and Instruction* 2: 117–175. Research that found positive results for using reciprocal questioning and other metacognitive strategies for promoting comprehension.

Pearson, P. D., and L. Fielding. 1991. Comprehension instruction. In R. Barr, M. L. Kamil, P. B. Mosenthal, and P. D. Pearson (Eds.), *Handbook of reading research,* Vol. II. New York: Longman. Reviews the research on reading comprehension including Explicit Teaching, Think-Alouds, Induced Imagery, and Text-Based Strategies.

Rosenshine, B., and C. Meister. 1994. Reciprocal teaching: A review of the research. *Review of Educational Research* 64: 479–530. Review of quantitative studies on Reciprocal Teaching.

Rosenshine, B., C. Meister, and S. Chapman. 1996. Teaching students to generate questions: A review of the intervention studies. *Review of Educational Research* 66: 181–221. Review of intervention studies on question asking.

Question-Answer Relationships

Purpose

Question-Answer Relationships (QARs) was developed by Raphael (1982b) as a procedure for enhancing students' ability to answer comprehension questions by giving them a systematic means for analyzing task demands of different question probes.

Rationale

Stemming from her concern that students are frequently asked questions in school but receive little or no guidance in knowing how to answer them, Raphael generated a strategy whereby readers are encouraged to analyze the task demands of questions prior to answering them. The system she devised for students to use involves having students identify three types of questions: text explicit or "right there," text implicit or "think and search," and scriptal or "on my own." This system was based on a taxonomy suggested by Pearson and

Johnson (1978) in which comprehension responses were described as follows: text explicit if the information to be used for the most appropriate response is stated explicitly in the text; text implicit if the response information is located in the text but requires the integration of textual material; and script implicit if the response information is located in the reader's knowledge base.

The system itself is presented to teachers and students in a carefully crafted fashion. Using the research on developing independent comprehenders as a basis (see Tierney and Cunningham, 1984), Raphael applies four principles of instruction to help readers analyze the task demands of questions: (1) give immediate feedback; (2) progress from shorter to longer texts; (3) begin with questions for which the task demand is more straightforward and go on to questions that require the use of multiple sources; and (4) develop independence by beginning with group learning experiences and progressing to individual and independent activities.

Raphael's claims about the efficacy of the strategy has been substantiated by research. Raphael and Pearson (1982) found that students in the fourth, sixth, and eighth grades who had been taught the strategy by a university researcher were more successful in answering questions than students who had not received the instruction. In a follow-up to this study, Raphael, Wonnacott, and Pearson (1983) taught fourth-grade teachers how to use the strategy and obtained similar results. They found that the trained teachers were pleased with the strategy and that students outperformed comparable groups of students who received no such directed learning experiences. In a third study Raphael and McKinney (1983) examined developmental differences in children's performance and training requirements. With older students (eighth graders compared with fifth graders), orientation was as effective as training, and the performance of students improved by training, but not by simply being reminded to apply QARs at the time of testing.

Intended Audience

Raphael has used the procedure successfully with students of varying ability levels from grades four through eight. With some modification the procedure could be used with students at earlier grade levels, especially with those that are less able.

Description of the Procedures

At the heart of QARs is having the student identify the response demands of various questions (either Right There, Think and Search, or On My Own), then using a knowledge of the response demands to generate an answer. For this purpose, Raphael (1982b) offers the following guidelines and student response format as a way of accustoming readers to the strategy. Once the reader has learned the strategy, Raphael suggests that the focus should be on the best possible response to the question.

Initial use of the format entails having students circle the QAR strategy they will use. During this initial period, a student's response to a question is less important than the student's assessment of the task demands. In other words, it would be okay if the reader generated a wrong answer but correctly identified the task demands. Later, when students move to determining and writing in the answer, the actual answer the reader generates becomes important.

To introduce most students to the strategy, Raphael suggests a week of intensive training followed by maintenance activities. Adaptations are recommended if a teacher deems them necessary. Four lessons make up the first week's intensive training.

Lesson 1. The first lesson is intended to introduce students to the task demands of different questions and to provide some initial practice at identifying task demands in conjunction with answering questions. For this purpose, Raphael recommends that instruction similar to the following be given in groups.

Using the previously suggested guidelines and response format (see Figures 7.2 and 7.3), the teacher would explain:

> We are going to talk about different types of questions and the best way to answer them. Sometimes your workbook or I give questions that ask for information you can find quite easily in the book. Other times you won't find the answer there. I will describe three kinds of questions: "Right There," "Think and Search," and "On My Own." Each type can be figured out by deciding where you get the information for the answer. We call this a Question-Answer Relationship, or QAR for short." (Raphael 1984, 189)

Raphael (1984) recommends that initially the teacher discuss the difference between text-based and knowledge-based responses, prior to discriminating between the two text-based strategies. Following the introduction, she suggests that three practice stages can be used with short passages of two or three sentences. In the first stage, she suggests giving students passages to read with questions for which the answer as well as the QARs is identified. During this stage, she suggests discussing the type of QAR each question represents. In the second stage, she suggests giving students passages, questions, and responses to these questions, and having students generate as a group the QAR for each. Finally, in the third stage, she suggests having students determine the QARs and respond with answers.

Lesson 2. The purpose of the second lesson is to provide the students with review and further guided practice as they read slightly longer passages (75 to 150 words). Specifically, Raphael recommends that the teacher begin the lesson with a review of each QAR category and then some guided practice with five questions that require different responses with a passage of approximately 75 to 150 words. She suggests the students do the first passage as a group and then, as a group, that they be given feedback after they finish the second passage independently. As the students proceed with subsequent passages, Raphael emphasizes the importance of giving the students feedback, as well as having them justify their answer to the question and their choice of a QAR. Also she suggests that the teacher explain why an answer is acceptable on the grounds of both accuracy and strategy.

Lesson 3. In the third lesson, Raphael suggests extending the QAR task to a passage approximately the length of a short story selection. She suggests dividing the selection into four sections and generating two questions of each of the three types (a total of six questions) for each section. The first section would be completed in conjunction with reviewing the strategy; students would complete the remaining three sections independently, prior to acquiring feedback.

In the Book QARs

Right There
The answer is in the text, usually easy to find. The words used to make up the question and words used to answer the question are **Right There** in the same sentence.

Think and Search (Putting It Together)
The answer is in the story, but you need to put together different story parts to find it. Words for the question and words for the answer are not found in the same sentence. They come from different parts of the text.

In My Head QARs

Author and You
The answer is *not* in the story. You need to think about what you already know, what the author tells you in the text, and how it fits together.

On My Own
The answer is not in the story. You can even answer the question without reading the story. You need to use your own experience.

FIGURE 7.2 Illustrations to Explain QARs to Students

Lesson 4. For the fourth lesson, Raphael suggests using material typically found in the classroom—a basal story or a social studies or science chapter. She suggests giving the students the passage as a single unit with six questions from each QAR category. The student would be expected to read the passage, determine the QAR for each question, and answer it.

Maintaining QARs. To maintain the use of QARs, Raphael recommends a weekly review lesson and suggests some fun activities (e.g., a courtroom game that requires readers to respond to questions from students who role-play lawyers with the source of answers) that might be reinforcing. To supplement the use of QAR, she suggests that the training program might be extended to more systematic use with content material.

FIGURE 7.3 Passage—"Lighting a Match"

When lighting a match, it is important to follow these steps carefully. First, tear one match out of the matchbook. Second, close the matchbook cover. Third, strike the match against the rough strip on the outside of the matchbook. Finally, after the match has been used, blow it out carefully, and be sure it is cool before you throw it away.

1. What are the first two steps to correctly light and use a match?
   Right There ____________
   Think and Search ____________
   On My Own ____________
2. Why should you be sure the match is cool before you throw it away?
   Right There ____________
   Think and Search ____________
   On My Own ____________
3. What should you do after the match has been used and is still burning?
   Right There ____________
   Think and Search ____________
   On My Own ____________
4. Why should you close the cover before striking the match?
   Right There ____________
   Think and Search ____________
   On My Own ____________
5. What do you strike the match against to light it?
   Right There ____________
   Think and Search ____________
   On My Own ____________

Cautions and Comments

QARs represent one of the more thoroughly researched instructional strategies that have been developed in recent years. Raphael has gone to great lengths to explore its utility thoroughly at different grade levels with students of varying ability. She reports having most success with students of average and below average ability in grades four through eight. She also claims that the strategy can be easily learned by teachers, and she has explored the worth of different in-service training experiences with the technique (see Raphael, 1984). What is lacking from her research data are the long-term benefits or detriments that might arise from using the strategy. We do not know whether students who have been trained to do QARs are better at answering questions after some time has elapsed after training. Nor do we know if the students are better monitors of their own ability to read or answer questions. Furthermore, we have no descriptive data of how QARs influence the reasoning processes that readers use to answer questions and continue reading. Raphael (1984) suggests that with older students there may be interference that arises as a result of considering the task demands.

Two concerns that seem worth mentioning about QAR relate to problems with using the taxonomy. First, the taxonomy was intended to describe question-answer types rather than to facilitate a determination of correct responses. As readers consider answering a question, they might be better advised to consider the goal of the question and the point of the passage rather than whether the answer is forthcoming from such discrete categories as a text or reader. Second, QAR may not enhance comprehension in as straightforward a fashion. To determine the nature of the relationship between a question and answer would seem to follow from rather than precede answering the question. If this be the case, QAR might be best viewed as helping readers achieve feedback on their responses rather than answers to questions. Still, the National Reading Panel (2000) has endorsed the strategy of answering questions as an effective means of improving comprehension.

REFERENCES

Cortese, E. E. 2003–2004. The application of Question-Answer Relationship strategies to pictures. *The Reading Teacher* 57: 374–380. Adaptation of QARs to pictures.

Ezell, H. K., S. A. Hunsicker, M. M. Quinque, and E. Randolph. 1996. Maintenance and generalization of QAR reading comprehension strategies. *Reading Research and Instruction* 36: 64–81. Study demonstrating that QAR training can improve comprehension on text explicit and text implicit questions.

McIntosh, M. E., and R. J. Draper. 1995. Applying the Question-Answer Relationship strategy in mathematics. *Journal of Adolescent and Adult Literacy* 39: 120–131. Description of how to use QARs in mathematics.

National Reading Panel. 2000. *Teaching children to read: An evidence-based assessment of the scientific research literature on reading and its implications for reading instruction: Report of the subgroups.* (NIH Publication No. 00-4754). Washington, DC: National Institute of Child Health and Human Development. Chapter 4 cites the effectiveness of question answering on improving reading comprehension.

Pearson, P. D., and D. D. Johnson. 1978. *Teaching reading comprehension.* New York: Holt, Rinehart and Winston. Presents an overview of the nature of reading comprehension and instructional issues. The taxonomy used by Raphael is described in this book.

Raphael, T. E. 1982a. *Improving question-answering performance through instruction* (Reading Education Report No. 32). Urbana: University of Illinois, Center for the Study of Reading, March. Provides an extensive discussion of the procedure, including pages teachers could use as transparencies or duplicating masters.

———. 1982b. Question-answering strategies for children. *The Reading Teacher* 36: 186–190. Presents a clear description of how students might be taught to use QARs, including lesson plans and guidelines for teachers.

———. 1984. Teaching learners about sources of information for answering comprehension questions. *Journal of Reading* 27: 303–311. Presents an overview of the results of several studies that have explored the utility of QAR.

———. 1986. Teaching question-answer relationships, revisited. *The Reading Teacher* 39: 516–523. Modifies and updates QAR.

Raphael, T. E., and J. McKinney. 1983. An examination of fifth and eighth grade students' question answering behavior: An instructional study in metacognition. *Journal of Reading Behavior* 15: 67–86. Reports an exploration of developmental trends in the use of QARs by students.

Raphael, T. E., and P. D. Pearson. 1982. *The effect of metacognitive awareness training on children's question-answering behavior* (Tech. Rep. No. 238). Urbana: University of Illinois, Center for the Study of Reading, March. Reports the first of three research studies in which QARs were taught to students in grades four, six, and eight.

Raphael, T. E., C. A. Wonnacott, and P. D. Pearson. 1983. *Increasing students' sensitivity to sources of information: An instructional study in question-answer relationships* (Tech. Rep. No. 284). Urbana: University of Illinois, Center for the Study of Reading, July. Reports an attempt to have selected fourth grade teachers trained to teach their students to use QARs.

Simmonds, E. P. M. 1992. The effects of teacher training and implementation of two methods for improving the comprehension skills of students with learning disabilities. *Learning Disabilities Research and Practice* 7: 194–198. Study that demonstrated the superiority of using QARs versus traditional comprehension instruction with learning-disabled students in grades one to nine.

Tierney, R. J., and J. W. Cunningham. 1984. Research on teaching reading comprehension. In P. D. Pearson, R. Barr, M. L. Kamil, and P. Mosenthal (Eds.), *Handbook of reading research.* New York: Longman. Reviews the research on teaching reading comprehension, including QAR and related approaches.

Explicit Teaching of Reading Comprehension

Purpose

The Explicit Teaching of Reading Comprehension is intended as a framework for developing reading comprehension skills and strategies that can be applied to other reading situations without teacher support.

Rationale

In the late 1960s and early 1970s, developmental psychologists began to explore the possibility that reading comprehension and other problem-solving abilities were amenable to change with appropriate intervention. Subsequently, throughout the 1970s and early 1980s, several research studies were pursued in which deliberate and carefully planned attempts were made to explore the instructional characteristics of effective reading comprehension instruction. The question governing these pursuits was: Can students be made aware of reading comprehension strategies or be taught skills that will transfer to independent reading situations? What emerged as a response to this question and from these research pursuits was Explicit Teaching of Reading Comprehension. In other words, as researchers explored different procedures for teaching selected reading comprehension strategies and skills (e.g., summarizing, inferencing, self-questioning, relating background knowledge, finding the main idea and relevant details), several recommendations for instruction seemed forthcoming (Brown, Campione, and Day, 1981; Day, 1980; Hansen and Pearson, 1983; Palincsar and Brown, 1983). These have been pulled together and now are labeled by some educators "Explicit Teaching" (Pearson and Leys, 1984). The features that constitute Explicit Teaching have been discussed in several papers (Brown, Campione, and Day, 1981; Pearson, 1984; Pearson and Gallagher, 1983; Roehler and Duffy, 1984; Tierney, 1982; and Tierney and Cunningham, 1984). The features include:

1. *Relevance:* students are made aware of the purpose of the skill or strategy—the why, when, how, and where of the strategy.

2. *Definition:* students are informed as to how to apply the skills by making public the skill or strategy, modeling its use, discussing its range of utility, and illustrating what it is not.

3. *Guided practice:* students are given feedback on their own use of the strategy or skill.

4. *Self-regulation:* students are given opportunities to try out the strategy for themselves and develop ways to monitor their own use of the strategy or skill.

5. *Gradual release of responsibility:* the teacher initially models and directs the students' learning; as the lesson progresses, the teacher gradually gives more responsibility to the student.

6. *Application:* students are given the opportunity to try their skills and strategies in independent learning situations, including nonschool tasks.

Intended Audience

Explicit Teaching is a generic plan for developing a wide range of strategies. It seems to be an appropriate framework for teaching students at all ages.

Description of the Procedures

During any Explicit Teaching lesson certain key elements will be present; others may be optional. For example, the following is based on those suggested by Pearson and Leys (1984) as an integral part of Explicit Teaching:

Step 1: Introduction to the skill or strategy through examples and review. Refer or expose the students to examples of the skill in the "real world," including the purpose for using the strategy. Discuss how, when, where, and why the strategy or skills are used. If possible, contrast them with other skills; for example, contrast main idea with details, fact with opinion, and good summaries with poor summaries. If the skill has been treated previously, review what they know about the skill.

Step 2 (optional): Have the children volunteer additional examples and discuss them.

Step 3: Label, define, model, and explain the skill or strategy. In this step, the skill or strategy is given a specific label and its application demonstrated with teacher modeling. As the teacher models, students are given guidelines by which they might use the skill or strategy and also examples of faulty strategy usage or skill application.

Step 4: Guided practice. In this step, examples are done together in order to prepare the students for independent practice and to determine who is incurring difficulty with the skill or strategy.

Step 5: Independent practice. The students work through the same type of exercise, but do so independently.

Step 6: Application. Students are given a variety of situations in which they are encouraged to apply the skill and discuss its application. This might entail applying the skill or strategy to other text or to situations outside of school.

What follows is an example of applying this lesson framework to comprehension skills. Specifically, it illustrates the Explicit Teaching of a main idea.

An Example of Explicit Teaching Applied to Main Idea

1. Introduction to the skill or strategy

In the first part of the lesson, examples are provided and the relevance of the strategy established. This can be done by relating what you are going to do to something with which the child has had experience. At the same time, the purpose for teaching the strategy is established.

Ask: "Have you ever had to give a brief description of something? Have you ever wondered what it would be like to give the news on the radio or television? Imagine it was your turn to give the news. Usually you have a few minutes to present in a nutshell the main idea and a few key facts. Now suppose you have been given lots of stories by your classmates. Your task is to present them, but before you do so, you need to isolate the main idea and most relevant details. What would you do?"

2. Labeling, modeling, defining, and explaining

In the next phase the teacher labels, models, defines, and explains the skill. Through teacher modeling and student discussion, the how, when, and where of the strategy is presented. Negative instances (i.e., demonstrations of faulty applications) are given, as well as clear examples of appropriate strategy or skill usage.

The teacher explains that they are going to learn more about how to find the main idea. Students read one of the stories for which the main idea needs to be established.

My name is Sally. I have four gerbils. One is pure white and two have brown spots. The fourth one is all black with a pink nose.

The teacher explains: "The story tells how many different and colorful gerbils Sally has. The reason I know this is the second sentence tells how many gerbils Sally has. The other sentences talk about not the size nor what they eat, but about the color of the gerbils. What is key in finding the main idea is finding out the most important ideas or facts stated about the topic. The main idea is: Sally has four colorful gerbils. Let's look at another story."

3. Guided practice

In this step the teacher and students walk through an example together.

"Let's do the next story together. This is Juan's story. . . ."

4. Independent practice

Students should be given the equivalent of a checklist by which they can not only guide

The teacher directs the children to a third story. The teacher says: "Try one by yourself their own use of the strategy but can also check whether they have succeeded.

this time. Remember the main idea is what is important about the topic. Decide whether the main idea of Pam's story is about:

Adela's home run
Adela's best friend
Adela's favorite sport

Before you make a final decision, ask yourself:

Did you find the important ideas or facts?

Did you decide what they were all about?

Does your main idea cover all the ideas or facts? If not . . . choose another."

The teacher has children share their choice and explain. Other examples follow.

5. Application

The next essential step is application. Your goal should be for the self-initiated and successful use of the strategy or skill without the teacher.

The teacher suggests: "Now try to do some on your own. Remember to use the self-help questions."

After checking these exercises, the teacher says: "Today we have learned about main idea. Can anybody think of where else one might use this skill? Let's see if it could help us with our social studies."

Children are encouraged to discuss how it might help in social studies and take out their social studies books to try it out. Other applications are discussed.

Cautions and Comments

As an approach to developing independent reading comprehension abilities, Explicit Teaching has a large number of advocates, most recently, the National Reading Panel (2000). In support of this approach are a number of research studies in which considerable success was achieved in teaching students selected skills and strategies. At a time when we were well aware of the shortcomings in our methods of teaching reading comprehension, Explicit Teaching seemed a timely solution for upgrading our practices. Furthermore, it was a commonsense approach. It represents what some educators who had looked at effective instruction had specified as key elements (e.g., Rosenshine, 1983).

Despite these qualities, Explicit Teaching should not be accepted without question. The results of experiments in which Explicit Teaching was used were not very well sustained beyond the course of the experiment; and evidence of the application of skills or strategies, either spontaneously or planned, was lacking. Unfortunately, no comparisons exist of Explicit Teaching with learning that is less teacher-centered and more collaborative or discovery-oriented. No data exist by which a determination can be made as to whether an Explicit Teaching procedure might take away from the tendency of some students to self-initiate their own learning strategies. For example, if the approach were more collaborative and less teacher-dependent, perhaps students would be more open to define and use a great many more strategies for themselves at times other than those tied to a teacher's plans.

To compensate for some of the concerns with Explicit Teaching, the National Reading Panel (2000) has suggested a Transactional Strategy Instruction (TSI) approach to reading comprehension. As contrasted with Explicit Teaching, in which the emphasis seems to be on the teachers' ability to provide direct explanations, in TSI teachers not only do that but also focus on their ability to engage students in discussions in which students form collaborative interpretations of text and discuss the explicit mental processes involved in comprehending the text (see the next strategy in this unit, Think Alouds). Thus, in TSI emphasis is placed on the transactions among learners as they collaboratively engage the text.

Apart from these limitations, there are some other issues that stand in the way of the use of the Explicit Teaching model of teaching reading comprehension. Such a model assumes that there are well-defined strategies to teach. Unfortunately, a detailed description of comprehension strategies and skills that are worth teaching—that is, are likely to lead to improvements in comprehension performance—does not exist. The problems facing explicit teaching are compounded by problems in describing how readers actually do use some of the skills that might be taught.

REFERENCES

Anderson, V. 1992. A teacher development project in transactional strategy instruction for teachers of severely reading-disabled adolescents. *Teaching and Teacher Education* 8: 391–403. A research study using TSI.

Baumann, J. F. 1983. A generic comprehensive instructional strategy. *Reading World* 23: 284–294. Presents a reading comprehension instruction based on Explicit Teaching notions.

———. 1988. Direct instruction reconsidered. *Journal of Reading* 31: 712–729. Discusses when direct/explicit teaching is and is not appropriate.

Baumann, J. F., and G. Ivey, 1997. Delicate balances: Striving for curricular and instructional equilibrium in a second-grade, literature/strategy-based classroom. *Reading Research Quarterly* 32(3): 244–275. A qualitative case study exploring what diverse second graders learned through a year-long program of strategy instruction.

Baumann, J. F., and M. C. Schmitt. 1986. The what, why, how and when of comprehension instruction. *The Reading Teacher* 39: 640–647. Discusses features integral to the use of Explicit Teaching.

Brown, A. L., J. D. Campione, and J. D. Day. 1981. Learning to learn: On training students to learn from texts. *Educational Researcher* 10: 14–21. Discusses the research related to developing independent comprehension including ramifications for instruction.

Brown, R., P. B. El-Dinary, M. Pressley, and L. Coy-Ogan. 1995. A transactional strategies approach to reading instruction. *The Reading Teacher* 49(3): 256–258. Describes a transactional strategies approach that draws heavily on teacher Think-Alouds and teacher modeling.

Brown, R., M. Pressley, P. Van Meter, and T. Schuder. 1996. A quasi-experimental validation of transactional strategies instruction with low-achieving second-grade readers. *Journal of Educational Psychology* 88: 18–37. A yearlong study demonstrating the effectiveness of TSI.

Butyniec-Thomas, J., and V. E. Woloshyn. 1997. The effects of explicit-strategy and whole-language instruction on students' spelling ability. *The Journal of Experimental Education* 65: 293–302. Study showing that the combination of Explicit Teaching and Whole-Language instruction helped students' spelling more than either strategy alone.

Day, J. D. 1980. *Teaching summarization skills: A comparison of training methods.* Unpublished doctoral diss., University of Illinois at Urbana-Champaign. Represents a research study in which Explicit Teaching practices were explored.

Dole, J. A., K. J. Brown, and W. Trathen. 1996. The effects of strategy instruction on the comprehension performance of at-risk students. *Reading Research Quarterly* 31(1): 62–88. Describes a study of at-risk fifth and sixth graders' performance in response to strategy instruction.

Duke, N. K., and P. D. Pearson. 2002. Effective practices for developing reading comprehension. In A. E. Farstrup and S. J. Samuels (Eds.), *What research has to say about reading instructions* (3rd ed.). Newark, DE: International Reading Association, 205–241. Provides a review of explicit teaching and reading comprehension in conjunction with a discussion of teaching practices and reading strategies.

Durkin, D. 1978–79. What classroom observations reveal about reading comprehension instruction. *Reading Research Quarterly* 14: 481–533. Presents a dismal picture of the teaching of reading comprehension in schools.

———. 1984. Do basal manuals teach reading comprehension? In R. C. Anderson, J. Osborn, and R. J. Tierney (Eds.), *Learning to read in American schools.* Hillsdale, NJ: Erlbaum. Discusses how basals have approached the teaching of reading comprehension.

El-Hindi, A. E., and K. D. Childers. 1997. Metacognitive awareness, attributional beliefs, and learning strategies of at-risk college readers. In C. K. Kinzer, K. A. Hinchman, and D. J. Leu (Eds.), *Inquiries in literacy theory and practice.* Chicago, IL: National Reading Conference, 127–135. Explores the effectiveness of Explicit Teaching in an academic support college course.

Hansen, J., and P. D. Pearson. 1983. An instructional study: Improving the inferential comprehension of fourth grade good and poor readers. *Journal of Educational Psychology* 75: 821–829. Describes the use of Explicit Teaching in conjunction with research on the influence of attempting to teach students to develop inferential comprehension strategies.

Kameenui, E. J., and P. Shannon. 1988. Point counterpoint: Direct instruction reconsidered. In J. E. Readence and R. S. Baldwin (Eds.), *Dialogues in literacy research.* Thirty-seventh Yearbook of the National Reading Conference. Chicago, IL: National Reading Conference. Debates the pros and cons of direct instruction.

Miholic, V. 1994. An inventory to pique students' metacognitive awareness of reading strategies. *Journal of Reading* 38(2): 84–86. Describes the use of a metacognitive awareness inventory to pique students' strategy development.

National Reading Panel. 2000. *Teaching children to read: An evidence-based assessment of the scientific research literature on reading and its implications for reading instruction: Report of the subgroups.* (NIH Publication No. 00-4754). Washington, DC: National Institute of Child Health and Human Development. Chapter 4 discusses the effectiveness of Explicit Teaching and Transactional Strategy Instruction on improving reading comprehension.

Palincsar, A., and A. Brown. 1983. *Reciprocal teaching of comprehension monitoring activities* (Tech. Rep. No. 269). Urbana: University of Illinois, Center for the Study of Reading. Describes the use of Explicit Teaching in conjunction with having students take the teacher's role in their own learning.

Palincsar, A. S., Y. M. David, J. A. Winn, and D. D. Stevens. 1991. Examining the context of strategy instruction. *Remedial and Special Education* 12: 43–53. A discussion of six models of strategy instruction, including Explicit Teaching.

Pearson, P. D. 1984. Direct explicit teaching of reading comprehension. In G. G. Duffy, L. R. Roehler, and J. Mason (Eds.), *Comprehension instruction.* New York: Longman. Discusses research and theory related to Explicit Teaching.

Pearson, P. D., and L. Fielding. 1991. Comprehension instruction. In R. Barr, M. L. Kamil, P. B. Mosenthal, and P. D. Pearson (Eds.), *Handbook of reading research,* Vol. II. New York: Longman. Reviews the research on reading comprehension including Explicit Teaching, Think-Alouds, Induced Imagery, and text-based strategies.

Pearson, P. D., and M. C. Gallagher. 1983. The instruction of reading comprehension. *Contemporary Educational Psychology* 8: 317–344. Reviews the research on reading comprehension instruction and presents a model for teaching based on the gradual release of responsibility.

Pearson, P. D., and M. Leys. 1984. Teaching comprehension. In T. L. Harris and E. J. Cooper (Eds.), *Reading, thinking and concept development: Strategies for the classroom.* New York: College Board. Describes Explicit Teaching with examples.

Roehler, L. R., and G. G. Duffy. 1984. Direct explanation of comprehension processes. In G. Duffy, L. Roehler, and J. Mason (Eds.), *Comprehension instruction.* New York: Longman. Describes research attempting to make processes explicit.

Rosenshine, B. 1983. Functions of teaching. *Elementary School Journal* 83: 355–351. Presents a framework for teaching based on the research on effective schools.

Tierney, R. J. 1982. Learning from text. In A. Berger and H. Alan Robinson (Eds.), *Secondary school reading.* Newark, DE: International Reading Association. Presents an extended discussion (both pro and con) of Explicit Teaching.

Tierney, R. J., and J. Cunningham. 1984. Research on teaching reading comprehension. In P. D. Pearson (Ed.), *Handbook of reading research.* New York: Longman. Presents a comprehensive review of the research on teaching reading comprehension, including studies using Explicit Teaching.

Think-Alouds

Purpose

Think-Alouds are intended to help readers examine and develop reading behaviors and strategies.

Rationale

Think-Alouds have been used as a means of studying the cognitive processes that readers and writers use as they develop meanings (e.g., Flower and Hayes, 1980; Olshavsky, 1976–77). As an instructional procedure, however, Think-Alouds have rarely been used. Davey (1983) proposes that they might be used as a means of helping poor readers adopt a meaning orientation to print, monitor their comprehension, and apply self-correction strategies. With this in mind, Davey identifies five aspects of a skilled reader's thinking that studies have shown are frequently lacking among poor comprehenders (making predictions, visualizing, linking with prior knowledge, monitoring, and self-correction). Furthermore, she contends that recent work on self-monitoring and problem solving suggests that teachers can help students acquire these skills through modeling by the teacher, followed up by ample practice by the students. As she stated:

> The modeling process is founded on the belief that if teachers describe their own thoughts about a text (so that students can see a mind responding to a specific passage) the students will realize how and when to do the same. (1983, 45)

Such modeling is followed by practice, which includes the use of checklists "to stimulate student involvement and verify that readers were using this procedure" (p. 46).

Intended Audience

Think-Alouds can be used with school-age students at any level.

Description of the Procedures

Davey offers only broad guidelines for the use of Think-Alouds. She suggests four basic steps:

1. Teacher modeling
2. Student partnerships for practice
3. Independent student practice using checklists
4. Integrated use with other materials

1. Teacher Modeling. Initially, Davey suggests that teachers should select passages that "contain points of difficulty, contradictions, ambiguities, or unknown words" (p. 45). These materials are read aloud together with the use of Think-Alouds by the teacher (with students following along silently). As a guide for teachers she offers a number of examples of Think-Alouds:

a. *Making predictions or showing students how to develop hypotheses.*

"From the title I predict that this section will tell how airplane pilots adjust for winds."

"In this next part I think we'll find out what caused these plane crashes."

"I think this is a description of flight simulators."

b. *Describing your visual images.*

"I have a picture of this man in my mind. He looks like a mild mannered, well-dressed business man."

"I can see the horse kicking down the stable door as the flames come closer . . . I can feel the heat of the fire and pressure of the moment."

c. *Sharing an analogy or showing how prior knowledge applies.* Davey refers to this as the "like-a" step.

"This is like a time when I was late for school and it began to thunderstorm."

d. *Verbalizing a confusing point or showing how you monitor developing understandings.*

"This seems to be confusing."

"I am not sure how this fits in."

"This is not what I expected."

e. *Demonstrating fix-up strategies.*

"I need to check this out. I'll read ahead for a moment."

"I need to think about this. Let me rethink what was happening."

"Maybe I'll reread this."

"Perhaps I better change my picture of what is happening."

In conjunction with teacher modeling, Davey suggests that teachers might encourage their students to add their own thoughts.

2. Student Partnerships for Practice. After several modeling experiences, Davey suggests that students might work together with partners to practice Think-Alouds. Each student takes a turn reading and thinking aloud with short passages. The partner listens and offers his or her thoughts. Davey stresses that carefully developed materials should be used initially prior to moving to school materials of various types of lengths.

3. Independent Student Practice Using Checklists. After working with partners, Davey suggests that students should practice independently with the use of checklists to ensure student involvement and verify the use of procedures. (See the example in Figure 7.4.)

4. Integrated Use with Other Materials. After initial experiences with modeling and Think-Alouds, Davey suggests that teachers need to give ample practice with school materials and integrate the use of Think-Alouds with other lessons and content reading. To this end, she suggests occasional demonstrations of how to read, and why and when to use certain strategies. For example, she suggests that the teacher might illustrate his or her thinking prior to reading a content book: "Before I read this, let me think about what this is like and try to get a feel for what this will be about. I'll look over the headings."

Cautions and Comments

The use of think-alouds in conjunction with attempting to help students approach their reading strategically with a meaning orientation is long overdue, and Davey's proposal is worthwhile for offering a feasible framework. Her suggestions for guiding students to read more strategically are thoughtful and systematic. In particular, her list of five possible strategies may not be exhaustive, but it offers a starting point for both teachers and students. Furthermore, her suggestions for teaching modeling, student partnerships, the use of checklists, and help for students in integrating the use of Think-Alouds offer some structure to the approach.

FIGURE 7.4 Example of a Checklist

While I was reading, how did I do?

(Put an X in the appropriate column.)

	Not very much	*A little bit*	*Much of the time*	*All of the time*
Predicting				
Picturing				
"Like-a"				
Identifying problems				
Using fix-up				

Some limitations to the approach should be mentioned. First, apart from Davey's affidavits regarding the effectiveness of their use, little data exist on the long-term benefits of Think-Alouds. Davey, for example, stated that learners with whom she used the strategy, became quite strategic and more positive about reading after three weeks of practicing Think-Alouds. Left unanswered is the extent to which any student gains are sustained and whether the Think-Alouds work with different students and texts. Second, Davey has assumed that students become more strategically oriented if teachers model and guide the use of Think-Alouds. Perhaps a different approach would work as well, if not better. For example, students might become more strategic if they discussed what they did and did not do before, during, and after reading. Perhaps they would gain from being viewed as a co-investigator rather than being expected to aspire to achieve a teacher's Think-Aloud behaviors. In addition, some students may need more concrete or supplemental guidelines to implement strategies effectively. Saying you will do or are doing something may or may not reflect the efficacy with which said strategy is used or the thinking underlying the use of a strategy.

A number of other educators have proposed similar procedures for making thinking explicit. Gordon (1985) has developed a Think-Aloud procedure that encourages students to integrate what they know with ideas they glean from the text. Duffy and Roehler (1987) have suggested a procedure (responsive elaboration) that reflects a more student-based approach. Smith and Dauer (1984) have developed procedures for using Think-Alouds in content reading situations. Paris, Cross, and Lipson (1984) have emphasized group discussions about cognitive strategies that can improve reading using metaphors such as "Be a reading detective."

Finally, the National Reading Report (2000) has stated that comprehension monitoring is an effective strategy for improving comprehension. Since Think Alouds model the process of comprehension monitoring for students, it would stand to reason that this procedure, particularly in combination with other comprehension strategies (e.g., question asking and answering), would help them understand text more efficiently.

REFERENCES

Baumann, J. F., L. A. Jones, and N. Seifert-Kessell. 1993. Using think alouds to enhance children's comprehension monitoring abilities. *The Reading Teacher* 47: 184–193. Describes an instructional program using Think-Alouds to help fourth-graders monitor their comprehension.

Davey, B. 1983. Think-aloud—Modelling the cognitive processes of reading comprehension. *Journal of Reading* 27: 44–47. Presents a thorough description of the use of Think-Alouds.

Davey, B., and S. M. Porter. 1982. Comprehension rating: A procedure to assist poor comprehenders. *Journal of Reading* 26: 197–202. Describes attempts to have students rate their comprehension.

Duffy, G. G., and L. R. Roehler. 1987. Improving reading instruction through responsive elaboration. *The Reading Teacher* 40: 514–515. Offers a detailed description of how teachers can guide students to make their thinking more explicit.

Flower, L., and J. Hayes. 1980. The dynamics of composing: Making plans and juggling constraints. In L. W. Gregg and E. R. Steinberg (Eds.), *Cognitive processes in writing.* Hillsdale, NJ: Erlbaum, 1–50. One of several articles describing the use of Think-Alouds as a research technique for studying writing processes.

Gordon, C. J. 1985. Modeling inference awareness across the curriculum. *Journal of Reading* 28: 444–447. Discusses strategy that encourages students to integrate what they already know with text information in order to make inferences.

Kucan, L., and I. L. Beck. 1996. Four fourth graders thinking aloud: An investigation of genre effects. *Journal of Literacy Research* 28(2): 259–287. A study examining four developing readers' processing of text by asking them to think aloud during reading of narrative and expository text.

Kucan, L., and I. L. Beck. 1997. Thinking aloud and reading comprehension research: Inquiry, instruction, and social interaction. *Review of Educational Research* 67: 271–299. Review of literature that discusses Think-Alouds as a method of inquiry, a mode of instruction, and a means for encouraging social interaction.

Loxterman, J. A., I. L. Beck, and M. G. McKeown. 1994. The effects of thinking aloud during reading on students' comprehension of more or less coherent text. *Reading Research Quarterly* 29: 352–367. Study revealing that both coherent text and Think-Alouds enhance students' performance with text.

National Reading Panel. 2000. *Teaching children to read: An evidence-based assessment of the scientific research literature on reading and its implications for reading instruction: Report of the subgroups.* (NIH Publication No. 00-4754). Washington, DC: National Institute of Child Health and Human Development. Chapter 4 discusses the effectiveness of comprehension monitoring on improving reading comprehension.

Olshavsky, J. 1976–77. Reading as problem-solving: An investigation of strategies. *Reading Research Quarterly* 12: 654–674. Describes various Think-Aloud and introspective techniques to study reading processes.

Paris, S., D. R. Cross, and M. Y. Lipson. 1984. Informed strategies for learning: A program to improve children's reading awareness and comprehension. *Journal of Educational Psychology* 76: 1239–1252. Reports a study directed at one use of metaphors to facilitate thinking about reading.

Pearson, P. D., and L. Fielding. 1991. Comprehension instruction. In R. Barr, M. L. Kamil, P. B. Mosenthal, and P. D. Pearson (Eds.), *Handbook of reading research,* Vol. II. New York: Longman. Reviews the research on reading comprehension including Explicit Teaching, Think-Alouds, Induced Imagery, and text-based strategies.

Smith, R. J., and V. L. Dauer. 1984. A comprehension-monitoring strategy for reading content area materials. *Journal of Reading* 28: 144–147. Explores the use of Think-Alouds with content reading materials.

Induced Imagery

Purpose

Induced Imagery is a procedure for guiding students to generate mental images (about what is read) as a means of enhancing comprehension.

Rationale

In 1984, Tierney and Cunningham concluded from their review of research on reading comprehension that there were "sufficient data for educators to be optimistic that imaging activity is effective" (p. 622). Since their review of the research, additional studies have provided still further support for the positive effects that either training in imaging or spontaneous imaging has on comprehension (Gambrell and Bales, 1984; Sadoski, 1983, 1985). Most recently, the National Reading Report (2000) has advocated the use of mental imagery to improve recall of text.

Based on Gambrell's own research and that of colleagues, Gambrell, Kapinus, and Wilson (1987) developed guidelines for how teachers might enhance the comprehension of readers through training in inducing images. Gambrell et al. cite two values for students' imaging or developing mental pictures. As they state:

> Mental images have two great values: they provide a framework for organizing and remembering information from text, and when students induce images, they expend more energy for integrating information across text. Benefits occur in both comprehension and recall. (1987, 639)

Gambrell's approach to teaching students to develop mental images is based on teacher modeling followed by student practice. Her argument is that the progression from teacher-directed to student-directed learning is "essential for independence in comprehension" (Gambrell et al., 1987, 638).

Intended Audience

The strategy is appropriate for use with students of school age. It was especially developed for poorer students who may not spontaneously develop mental pictures.

Description of the Procedures

Gambrell et al. (1987) offer broad guidelines for helping students develop mental pictures. They suggest three basic steps:

1. Teacher modeling
2. Guided practice
3. Independent practice

1. Teacher Modeling. Teacher modeling is directed at what, why, and how. Gambrell et al. (1987) suggest this statement for introducing students to what mental imagery is: "Today we will concentrate on making mental images. Mental imagery is a reading strategy that helps you comprehend what you're reading." This is followed by an explanation of *why* mental imagery is useful. "Sometimes when we read we can make pictures in our minds about what we're reading. Making mental images—picturing the characters, picturing what is happening—can help us understand what we read, and it can also help us remember what we read" (pp. 639–640).

To introduce students to how readers might evoke mental imagery, Gambrell et al. suggest that teachers offer demonstrations in response to passages that include descriptive detail, and be brief. For example, they suggest that teachers might distribute or place on an overhead a passage such as "The Collision."

> ***The Collision***
> High Street was relatively busy on this dark and cool winter's night. There were a few pedestrians out and a steady stream of cars. Suddenly, every pedestrian's attention turned to the road. A Ford slammed on his brakes—its bright lights shining suddenly as the driver of the next car (a Chevy) hit its brakes. At first, nobody noticed that the brake lights of the Chevy did not shine. Instead they watched as an old BMW went slamming into the back of the Chevy which then slid into the Ford.

The teacher might say, "I have a short passage called 'The Collision' that I'm going to read aloud to you. I'll try to make images in my head as I read. I'll describe how I use mental imagery to understand and remember what I read." The teacher would then read the selection and model his or her thinking.

> "The selection is entitled 'The Collision.' I can imagine a number of collisions; cars, people. As I read on about 'High Street,' 'pedestrians,' and 'a steady stream of cars' on this dark

> night,' I can picture a busy street with car lights and traffic. As I read on I can picture the Ford slamming its brakes followed by the Chevy. I can picture the 'brake lights' of the Ford, followed by the 'dimness' of the Chevy. Then I can picture 'the old BMW' crashing into the rear of the Chevy. My picture now includes the drivers being jerked in their seat belts as glass shatters over the pavement."

The process of teaching the thinking-aloud, Gambrell et al. suggest, should conclude with a comment such as "The images I make in my mind will help me understand what I've read about the collision."

2. Guided Practice. Gambrell et al. (1987) suggest that the teacher initiate guided practice with short passages, perhaps some teacher modeling of the first part of the passage(s), and discussion among the students of the nature of their images. The discussion of the nature of their images and the similarities and differences is intended to help students clarify and refine their use of imagery. With additional brief passages, the students are given "more responsibility for using mental imagery independently" (Gambrell et al., 1987, 640).

3. Independent Practice. In conjunction with helping students develop independence, Gambrell et al. (1987) offer three suggestions: (1) practice with additional texts that lend themselves to mental imagery; (2) encourage imagery use in other reading situations (for example, they suggest reminding students to use imagery while reading content area texts and during leisure reading); and (3) direct/guide students to use additional strategies (e.g., predicting, summarizing, self-questioning) to complement imaging or in those situations that do not lend themselves as readily to imaging.

Cautions and Comments

Inducing students to create mental images as they read represents an important goal. The images students create as they read help them tie together the ideas, contribute to the joy of reading, and mobilize predictions and understandings.

The proposal by Gambrell et al. includes several key features that are worthy of note. First, they emphasize that students should share and compare their images. It should be stressed that there may not be a single correct image, but students should expect to have some details that overlap. Second, Gambrell et al. stress helping students develop independence, including the ability to use images flexibly in various situations. They do not assume that students will transfer the ability to conjure up images without encouragement.

On the negative side, this proposal suffers from a few limitations. The authors' approach to having students develop images is very teacher-centered. Perhaps students could discuss images that they conjure spontaneously rather than be overwhelmed by the teacher's mental pictures. Second, Gambrell et al. seem to assume that students can conjure up images if they hear about others doing so. Perhaps they need to be encouraged to do some other things en route to conjuring up images. It may be that predictions, identification with characters, and so on could help those students who do not generate images so spontaneously.

REFERENCES

Alvermann, D. E., and J. Swafford. 1989. Do content area strategies have a research base? *Journal of Reading* 32: 388–390. Discusses the research base associated with various strategies and practices.

Gambrell, L., and R. J. Bales. 1984. Mental imagery and the comprehension monitoring performance of fourth and fifth grade poor readers. *Reading Research Quarterly* 21: 454–464. Reports a study in which fourth and fifth graders were trained to induce images.

Gambrell, L. B., and P. B. Jawitz. 1993. Mental imagery, text illustrations, and children's story comprehension and recall. *Reading Research Quarterly* 28: 264–273. Study demonstrating that induced imagery, attention to illustrations, and the combination of the two improved children's comprehension and recall of stories.

Gambrell, L., B. A. Kapinus, and R. M. Wilson. 1987. Using mental imagery and summarization to achieve independence in comprehension. *Journal of Reading* 30: 638–642. Describes guidelines for helping students become independent at using mental imagery.

Ignoffo, M. 1993. Theater of the mind: Nonconventional strategies for helping remedial readers gain control over their reading experience. *Journal of Reading* 37(4): 310–321. Explores the use of mental theater exercises to help readers (especially those incurring difficulty) engage.

National Reading Panel. 2000. *Teaching children to read: An evidence-based assessment of the scientific research literature on reading and its implications for reading instruction: Report of the subgroups.* (NIH Publication No. 00-4754). Washington, DC: National Institute of Child Health and Human Development. Chapter 4 discusses the effectiveness of mental imagery on improving recall of text.

Olshansky, B. 1997. Picturing story: An irresistible pathway into literacy. *The Reading Teacher* 50(7): 612–613. Uses picture making and collages as a way of enhancing reading and writing stories.

Pearson, P. D., and L. Fielding. 1991. Comprehension instruction. In R. Barr, M. L. Kamil, P. B. Mosenthal, and P. D. Pearson (Eds.), *Handbook of reading research,* Vol. II. New York: Longman. Reviews the research on reading comprehension including Explicit Teaching, Think-Alouds, Induced Imagery, and text-based strategies.

Sadoski, M. 1983. An exploratory study of the relationships between reported imagery and the comprehension and recall of a story. *Reading Research Quarterly* 19: 110–123. Reports a study in which students self-report images that are related to their comprehension.

———. 1985. The natural use of imagery in story comprehension and recall: Replication and extension. *Reading Research Quarterly* 20: 858–867. Reports a study that replicates his earlier study looking at the relationship between student self-reports of images and comprehension.

Tierney, R. J., and J. Cunningham. 1984. Research on teaching reading comprehension. In P. D. Pearson (Ed.), *Handbook of reading research.* New York: Longman. Includes a discussion of research on inducing imagery.

Dialogical-Thinking Reading Lesson

Purpose

The Dialogical-Thinking Reading Lesson (DTRL) was designed by Commeyras (1990, 1991, 1993) to promote critical thinking for elementary students during their reading instruction. The goal of the DTRL is to engage students in reflection and critical thinking in order to get them to decide what they believe about a story-specific issue during basal reading instruction.

Rationale

Critical thinking plays a key role in developing a responsible citizenry. Commeyras (1993) believes that in order to cope with the information age and its complexity, including a deluge of conflicting, misleading, or erroneous information, students need to be prepared from an early age to think critically. The more emphasis that can be placed on thinking and reflection in reading instruction, the better prepared will be the next generation of citizens to think critically about moral, social, and political issues that may arise. Therefore, Commeyras developed the DTRL as one means to promote careful thinking and "encourage students to (a) return to the text to verify or clarify information; (b) consider multiple interpretations; (c) identify reasons to support interpretations; and (d) evaluate the acceptability and relevance of competing or alternative interpretations" (p. 487).

In developing the DTRL, Commeyras drew insight from work in dialogical thinking, the use of discussion in teaching, and social cognition. Citing Paul (1987), Commeyras defines dialogical thinking as the serious consideration of competing or alternative points of view for issues of significance. The DTRL asks students to engage in dialogical thinking in trying to identify reasons to support alternative conclusions regarding a central story issue. In order to engage in dialogical thinking, Commeyras continues, discussion is required. In the DTRL, discussion becomes the means for students to offer more than one point of view, react to other points of view, develop their understanding of the alternatives provided, and make judgments that are well informed. Finally, since dialogical thinking and discussion involve collaboration with others, aspects of social cognition come into play with the DTRL as students' efforts to think critically are developed and guided by their interactions with their peers and the teacher.

Intended Audience

Commeyras (1990) developed the DTRL for use in teaching sixth graders to critically think about basal stories. Further modification of the procedure occurred in 1991 in a research study with fifth-grade students who were labeled learning disabled. Thus, the DTRL seems appropriate for most elementary students regardless of their learning capabilities.

Description of the Procedures

There are two basic phases for each DTRL: (1) the reading phase, and (2) the discussion phase.

1. Reading Phase. Commeyras states that it is particularly important to select basal stories that lend themselves to a discussion of an issue that can be approached from more than one viewpoint and that students will find interesting or significant. Commeyras (1993) provides a listing of story titles and discussion questions appropriate for use with the DTRL. To illustrate the use of the DTRL the story entitled "Making Room for Uncle Joe," by A. B. Litchfield, was drawn from this listing.

"Making Room for Uncle Joe" is about a family with three children who must open their home to Joe, a Down syndrome adult. Joe's special school has to close so the family, with some misgivings, has to take Joe in until new accommodations can be found. The story describes how the family tries to adjust to Joe and vice versa and the trials and tribulations involved. When a new apartment finally has been located for Joe to live in, everyone is sad that he has to leave. The family decides to invite Joe to stay permanently, and he happily accepts.

Commeyras recommends that the entire selection be read by the students on their own. With less able students who need help reading the story, she suggests a more guided approach wherein each page of the story is read and then shared. Follow-up discussions during this phase are informal, with the goal being simply to reconstruct the story line. Commeyras mentions that regardless of students' ability levels the reading phase should be conducted in such a way as to ensure that all students comprehend the story well enough to participate in the discussion phase that follows.

2. Discussion Phase. This phase of the lesson consumes the most time, as Commeyras considers it conceptually the most important part of the DTRL. The components involved in the discussion phase are: (a) central question, (b) identifying reasons, (c) evaluating reasons, and (d) drawing conclusions. It is suggested that the chalkboard be organized according to these basic components before the discussion phase of the DTRL begins. Thus, the board might look like the following:

Central Question

Support	**Truth**	**Side A**	**Side B**	**Truth**	**Support**

a. Central question. The discussion phase begins with the teacher introducing the central question and the two hypothesized conclusions. In the case of our example story, Commeyras recommends that the central question be: "What should Uncle Joe do?" The conclusions to be discussed would be: (A) "Uncle Joe should stay with the family," and (B) "Uncle Joe should move to the apartment." These are written on the board for students to see.

Based on their understanding of the story, students are asked if they have a preference for either conclusion. Commeyras contends that multiple purposes are served by asking students to take a position before identifying reasons of support for either conclusion. First, it creates initial involvement for students, as they must consider whether or not they actually have a position on the issue. Additionally, it allows the teacher to assess the initial positions of the students for later comparison to their conclusions at the end of the lesson. It also allows the teacher to judge the extent to which individual students might be willing to alter their position in the face of new evidence or to hold back their consideration when there is insufficient evidence. Commeyras views these as two important critical thinking dispositions.

b. Identifying reasons. In this step of the procedure students are asked to explore in depth each hypothesized conclusion by identifying reasons of support for each. Thus, in our example students would be asked to identify reasons to support why Uncle Joe should stay with the family as well as reasons to support why Uncle Joe should move to the apartment. The following are some reasons students might identify:

Side A: Uncle Joe should stay with the family.

1. The family loves Uncle Joe.
2. Uncle Joe cannot take care of himself.
3. It would be best to be around normal people.

Side B: Uncle Joe should move to the apartment.

1. Uncle Joe can take care of himself.
2. It is best that Uncle Joe be with people like himself.
3. He will always be considered to be different from anyone else because he is special.

The students' reasons are written on the board regardless of whether they seem wrong, do not make sense, or may be contradictory. Since students will be asked at a later time to evaluate the truth and relevance of each reason, it is important to accept all reasons at this time. Having the teacher make judgments at this point will deny students the opportunity to examine their own thinking as well as stifle discussion. Commeyras also cautions that the teacher may need to engage in rephrasings and questions with students who need help in identifying and/or articulating their reasons. Additionally, as the discussion leader, the teacher must be judicious and ready to relinquish control over the discussion when it becomes lively and students demonstrate the ability to keep interacting with one another. In the case of our example this could easily happen as students discuss the pros and cons of having Down syndrome and one's ability to function in the real world or the stereotypes people hold about mental retardation.

c. Evaluating reasons. After reasons are identified for each position and listed on the board, the students need to evaluate them in terms of their truth and their relevance. Commeyras advises that a code be used to indicate on the board the students' decision about whether a reason could be true (T), false (F), or depends (D). Since a reason must also be relevant as well as true, students should indicate this, using a (Y) to indicate the reason is relevant or (N) if it is not.

Applying the criteria of truth and relevance to each reason will not always lead to clear-cut answers and consensus, but teachers are advised that what matters in doing this is that only verifiable information be used as the basis for a decision. Some reasons can be verified with the text information while others may be done with prior knowledge or logic. Once a reason has been verified as true, then the students need to judge how strong the support is for a particular conclusion. In this way students are engaged in critically thinking about what is important in making informed decisions about what they believe.

With our example, each reason might not be considered to be true. For instance, in the case of whether or not Uncle Joe can take care of himself, it depends—with some things he might be able to; with others he might not. Further, that Uncle Joe is different due to his retardation might be true, but it may not necessarily be relevant to concluding that he should move to an apartment.

d. Drawing conclusions. Commeyras recommends that to culminate this lesson every student be given an opportunity to state what she or he believes about the central question, given all the thinking and discussion that preceded it. At the same point, some students may still withhold judgment because they have not made up their minds. This is an appropriate option for those students not ready to draw a final conclusion. She suggests that a viable alternative to discussing final conclusions would be to write about them and share them at a later time.

Cautions and Comments

There is no doubt that the Dialogical-Thinking Reading Lesson is teacher-dominated and teacher-controlled. Commeyras acknowledges this but offers alternatives once students understand the structure and intent of the lesson. To shift more responsibility to the students for their own learning, students could become involved in selecting stories, questions, and/or conclusions. As an interim step, teachers might have students work in small groups to evaluate the reasons for one side of a central question and present these to the whole class. Once they are able to do this, then they might be given a story and asked to generate the conclusions that could be drawn from it. On the other hand, it can also be argued that even if the agenda has been previously set, the astute teacher will probably accept alternative conclusions introduced by students as long as they are viable.

Other suggestions for using the DTRL include using it with younger students by simplifying the task. For instance, Commeyras suggests that with first or second graders the teacher might concentrate on just identifying reasons rather than evaluating them, until such time that the students are able to generate alternative reasons on their own. The DTRL might also be coupled with other instructional strategies. It would seem that other strategies in this unit like ReQuest and the Anticipation Guide would be appropriate lead-ins to the discussion phase of this lesson. Likewise, the discussion strategies of Unit 11 are useful with the DTRL. From a topical standpoint, it can also be pointed out that stories dealing with a multicultural emphasis would be most appropriate for use with this technique, as the DTRL allows for an in-depth discussion of varying viewpoints.

REFERENCES

Commeyras, M. 1990. Analyzing a critical-thinking reading lesson. *Teaching and Teacher Education* 6: 201–214. Description of a critical-thinking reading lesson that provided the foundation for the DTRL.

———. 1991. *Dialogical-thinking reading lessons: Promoting critical thinking among "learning-disabled" students.* Unpublished doctoral diss., University of Illinois, Urbana-Champaign. Research that formed the basis for the DTRL.

———. 1993. Promoting critical thinking through dialogical-thinking reading lessons. *The Reading Teacher* 46: 486–494. The description of the steps involved in the DTRL.

Paul, R. W. 1987. Dialogical thinking: Critical thought essential to the acquisition of rational knowledge and passions. In J. B. Baron and R. J. Sternberg (Eds.), *Teaching thinking skills: Theory and practice.* New York: W. H. Freeman. Discussion of the role of dialogical thinking in teaching.

Reutzel, D. R., C. M. Larson, and B. L. Sabey, 1995. Dialogical books: Connecting content, conversation, and composition. *The Reading Teacher* 49(2): 98–109. Describes an approach which engages students in responding to their reading and writing dialogically.

Inquiry Chart

Purpose

The purpose of the Inquiry Chart, also known as the I-Chart (Hoffman, 1992), is to provide a systematic procedure for nurturing critical thinking in the classroom. By using a chart of guiding questions and information gained from multiple sources of information, the I-Chart gives students the opportunity to study a topic in depth and from potentially differing points of view.

Rationale

Critical thinking has received considerable attention in recent years, probably due in large share to a backlash on teaching the basics. Hoffman states that "the results of tests [are] showing that students can do the basics but they are woefully inadequate when asked to think" (p. 122). Hoffman believes that critical thinking skills are learned and that, with good instruction, these skills can be acquired successfully by all students.

Feeling that a reading of any single text to students, regardless of its point of view, only encourages those students to accept arguments in print without question, Hoffman developed the I-Chart as a means for students to examine multiple sources of information for points of consistency/inconsistency and, therefore, provide a rich context for nurturing the skills of critical thinking. Hoffman credits the development of the I-Chart to previous work by Ogle (1986) on K-W-L (see this unit) and McKenzie (1979) on helping students organize reports.

The I-Chart uses a data chart that has students record what they already know about a topic, what they want to learn about it, and a summary of what they did learn from their readings. The I-Chart allows students to gather this information from multiple text sources and organize it on the chart for summarization, comparison, and evaluation.

Intended Audience

Although Hoffman specified no grade level for which the I-Chart was to be used, it seems that this strategy would be appropriate for older students in the upper elementary grades and higher. I-Charts seem to be best used with expository-type material (e.g., history, science) where alternative points of view could be explored.

Description of the Procedures

Hoffman describes the I-Chart strategy as being organized around three phases: (1) planning, (2) interacting, and (3) integrating and evaluating.

1. Planning Phase. The planning phase consists of those activities that teachers engage in before working with the students. Typically these activities involve topic identification, question formation, I-Chart construction, and materials collection.

a. Topic identification. The topic to be used with the I-Chart procedure is identified by the teacher and may be based on the curriculum, the textbook, and/or student interests. For purposes of illustration, our I-Chart topic will be mammals. As Hoffman has indicated, the topic might be almost anything, such as Christopher Columbus, dinosaurs, the Civil War, rocks and fossils, American Presidents, or Adolf Hitler.

b. Question formation. In this step of the procedure the teacher identifies two to four questions of significance that will drive the inquiry process using the I-Chart. Hoffman suggests that for the initial uses of the I-Chart, teachers might use the class textbook and identify the most important ideas that are presented and cast them in the form of questions. To continue with our example topic, the following questions might be identified: (1) What defines a mammal as distinct from other animals? (2) In what ways are mammals alike? (3) In what ways are mammals different? (4) How are mammals grouped?

c. I-Chart construction. The I-Chart is constructed and displayed with the name of the topic and the guiding questions recorded in the top row. It should be large enough (e.g., newsprint, butcher paper) for everyone to see. The structure of the I-Chart is given in Figure 7.5. As the study of the topic progresses, the remaining parts of the I-Chart are filled in.

d. Materials collection. The final part of the planning phase is the collection of the materials dealing with the topic. The sources should include the class textbook as well as other

		GUIDING QUESTIONS					
	TOPIC	1.	2.	3.	4.	Interesting Facts and Figures	New Questions
	WHAT WE KNOW						
SOURCES	1.						
	2.						
	3.						
	SUMMARY						

FIGURE 7.5 Structure of the I-Chart

texts, trade books, encyclopedias, and CD—ROM, among others. When the particular source is used in instruction, Hoffman suggests that the bibliographic information be recorded in the left column of the I-Chart, under Sources.

2. Interacting Phase. The interacting phase of the I-Chart procedure involves those activities in which the teacher and the students work directly, using the students' prior knowledge and the source materials to begin filling out the I-Chart. This phase consists of the exploration of prior knowledge and beliefs, the sharing of interesting facts and new questions, and reading and recording.

a. Exploration of prior knowledge and beliefs. In the initial part of this phase the teacher interacts with the students to probe what prior knowledge they may have related to how the students might respond to each of the guiding questions. The information is recorded on the I-Chart in the row labeled "What We Know" under the appropriate question. This information is recorded regardless of whether it is accurate or is contradictory. In our example of mammals, students might list defining characteristics as "having hair" and "can't fly." Mammals might be alike because "they all have skeletons." They might be different because "only man has hands and legs." Finally, mammals might be grouped by "size."

b. Sharing of interesting facts and new questions. In the last two columns of the "What We Know" row, the teacher should record other information, unrelated to the guiding questions, volunteered by the students. Under the "Interesting Facts" column other information from students' prior knowledge should be written. For instance, students might offer that "both men and kangaroos are mammals." Under the "New Questions" column the teacher should record any question the students may have that is different from the listed questions.

c. Reading and recording. The final step of the interacting phase involves the reading of the various sources collected previously by the teacher and the recording of students' responses from these sources to the questions listed. The amount of time taken in this step will vary from days to weeks depending on many factors including the number of sources and guiding questions. With multiple copies of a source, the teacher could have the students do either independent or guided reading; with single copies of a source, the teacher might choose to read it aloud. Following the reading and discussion of each source, the teacher records any information from each that will answer the questions posed on the I-Chart. Hoffman points out that the recording should be as accurate as possible, even to the point of quoting the material. Any interesting facts and new questions derived from the reading should also be added at this time; with subsequent readings the teacher asks the students to look back at the new questions listed to see if any answers or important insights are forthcoming. It is to be remembered that the eventual size of the I-Chart will be based on the number of sources as well as the number of questions; therefore, the structure given in Figure 7.5 will vary with the I-Chart topic.

3. Integrating and Evaluating Phase. This final phase entails the completion of the I-Chart and sharing of the findings. The steps consist of summarizing, comparing, researching, and reporting.

a. Summarizing. The students are asked to generate summary statements for each of the guiding questions as well as the interesting facts column. They are asked to use all of the information recorded on the I-Chart and synthesize it into a cohesive answer to each question. This will require students to move beyond the facts stated and to account for converging as well as conflicting information in making their summaries. The summaries are recorded in the bottom row of the I-Chart.

b. Comparing. In this step students are asked to compare the information gained from individual sources and their summaries with their prior knowledge and beliefs. Students should examine new information gained as well as reconcile any misconceptions. In examining the prior knowledge recorded from our example of mammals, students would need to correct their beliefs regarding the characteristics of mammals, how they are different, and how they are grouped.

c. Researching. As students continue their research process, new questions accumulate on the I-Chart. It is here that questions that are still unanswered are identified and become the basis for individual or small group research. Students are directed to continue the research process to find answers to these questions.

d. Reporting. In this final step of the procedure students report back to the whole class their findings concerning the unanswered questions identified in the previous step.

Cautions and Comments

Hoffman concedes that his description of the I-Chart procedure is one in which the teacher assumes "a fairly directive/controlling role" (p. 125). However, he states that this must be the case in introducing the procedure to students. Once students are familiar with how to be flexible in using text to support their learning, the goal is to gradually yield responsibility for controlling the inquiry process to the students. In fact, he mentions a number of procedural variations to encourage independent learning by students that teachers might consider once the basic steps of the strategy are known. These include letting the students: (1) identify the topic; (2) generate the questions to be researched; (3) identify the sources to be investigated; and (4) decide the information to be recorded on the I-Chart.

Other suggestions include the use of cooperative learning strategies (see Unit 11: Discussion and Cooperative Learning) in lieu of whole-group procedures. Eventually, the I-Chart could become the basis for independent inquiry. Once students have been successful using the strategy on a whole-group and small-group basis, they might be given a blank I-Chart and asked to work through the inquiry process themselves from beginning to end. Finally, Hoffman feels that the summary statements at the bottom of the I-Chart can become the basic structure for students to expand them into paragraphs and, in turn, for the paragraphs to become the basis for complete written reports. Thus, he sees value in the strategy as a tool for helping students learn to prepare formal reports.

One caution to keep in mind when using the I-Chart procedure is that some students may experience difficulty in synthesizing information into summaries. This is a complex process akin to developing main ideas from supporting details, a process many students will find arduous. Teachers may need to move slowly with this part of the procedure, as it is central to its overall success.

Finally, teachers may find that the I-Chart can be useful in dealing with multicultural issues in the classroom. The in-depth study and its use of multiple sources seem to make this strategy ideal for exploring such topics.

REFERENCES

Hoffman, J. V. 1992. Critical reading/thinking across the curriculum: Using I-Charts to support learning. *Language Arts* 69: 121–127. Describes the rationale and steps for developing and using the I-Chart.

McKenzie, G. 1979. Data charts: A crutch for helping pupils organize reports. *Language Arts* 56: 784–788. Article on helping students organize reports, the basis of part of the I-Chart procedure.

Ogle, D. M. 1986. K-W-L: A teaching model that develops active reading of expository text. *The Reading Teacher* 39: 564–570. Another article that formed part of the basis for I-Charts.

Randall, S. N. 1996. Information charts: A strategy for organizing student research. *Journal of Adolescent and Adult Literacy* 39: 536–542. Example of using I-Charts for students' independent research.

UNIT 8

Meaning Vocabulary

UNIT OVERVIEW

Without a doubt there exists a strong relationship between vocabulary knowledge and reading comprehension (National Reading Panel, 2000). Anderson and Freebody (1985) hypothesized in conjunction with an extensive review of research that "Word knowledge is a requisite for reading comprehension: people who do not know the meanings of words are most probably poor readers" (p. 367). Conversely, it is often presumed that if students are introduced to relevant vocabulary as they encounter it in text, their ability to construct meaning from text will be enhanced (Brett, Rothlein, and Hurley, 1996).

Though there is no doubt that much experience with natural language will enhance vocabulary development (Anderson and Nagy, 1991; Cho and Krashen, 1994; Laflamma, 1997), our rationale is that teachers who have access to a repertoire of strategies that will introduce and reinforce relevant vocabulary words are in a better position to help students learn and retain words. Thus, seven strategies are described in this unit that teachers can use in various aspects of the instructional lesson to promote students' vocabulary development.

Possible Sentences. Possible Sentences is designed to help students determine the meanings of unknown words by pairing them with known words in sentences they think might "possibly" be found in a text. Thus, the strategy enables students to predict word meanings and verify their accuracy as they read.

List-Group-Label. Based upon a strategy originally developed by Taba, List-Group-Label asks students to free-associate terms related to a stimulus topic, and then to group and label these terms. Thus, the strategy serves as a means to activate students' prior knowledge about related concepts or to review concepts gleaned from reading.

Contextual Redefinition. Contextual Redefinition is designed to enable students to use context to make an informed guess about a word's meaning. In addition, it attempts to provide students with a strategy for using context in independent reading situations.

Feature Analysis. Feature Analysis is an attempt to expand and refine students' vocabulary and related concepts after they read. In essence, it uses categorization as a systematic means to reinforce word meaning.

Word Map. The Word Map provides a framework for developing students' understanding of concepts, including the hierarchical structure of these concepts and their attributes.

Vocabulary Self-Collection Strategy. The Vocabulary Self-Collection Strategy is designed to promote growth in either students' general or content area word knowledge. It is based on their prior experiences and encourages independent vocabulary development.

Levin's Keyword Method. The Keyword Method is a mnemonic strategy in which the student devises a keyword, which looks or sounds like the original word to be learned, to associate new information with a mental image to aid in later recall of the target word.

REFERENCES

Anderson, R. C., and P. Freebody. 1985. Vocabulary knowledge. In H. Singer and R. B. Ruddell (Eds.), *Theoretical models and processes of reading* (3rd ed.). Newark, DE: International Reading Association, 343–371. Review of literature on vocabulary and its relationship to comprehension.

Barr, R., M. L. Kamil, P. Mosenthal, and P. D. Pearson, (Eds.). 1991. *Handbook of reading research,* Vol. II. New York: Longman. Chapters by Anderson and Nagy (690–724) and Beck and McKeown (789–814) explore the research literature on word meanings and vocabulary acquisition.

Blachowicz, C. L. Z., and P. Fisher. 2000. Vocabulary instruction. In M. L. Kamil, P. B. Mosenthal, P. D. Pearson, and R. Barr (Eds.), *Handbook of reading research,* Vol. III. Mahwah, NJ: Erlbaum, 503–523. Discusses the research on vocabulary instruction.

Brett, A., L. Rothlein, and M. Hurley. 1996. Vocabulary acquisition from listening to stories and explanations of target words. *The Elementary School Journal* 96: 415–422. Study showing that simple explanations of words before listening to stories increased vocabulary aquisition.

Cho, K., and S. D. Krashen. 1994. Acquisition of vocabulary from the Sweet Valley kids series: Adult ESL acquisition. *Journal of Reading* 37: 662–667. Details vocabulary acquisition through free reading by adolescent readers.

Flood, J., J. M. Jensen, D. Lapp, and J. R. Squire (Eds.). 1991. *Handbook of research on teaching the English language arts.* New York: Macmillan. The chapter by Mason, Herman, and Au (721–731) explores children's developing knowledge of words.

Laflamma, J. G. 1997. The effect of the Multiple Exposure Vocabulary Method and the Target Reading/Writing Strategy on test scores. *Journal of Adolescent & Adult Literacy* 40: 372–381. Describes vocabulary acquisition in the context of reading-writing strategy lessons.

National Reading Panel. 2000. *Teaching children to read: An evidence-based assessment of the scientific research literature on reading and its implications for reading instruction: Report of the subgroups.* (NIH Publication No. 00-4754). Washington, DC: National Institute of Child Health and Human Development. Chapter 4 reviews the research on vocabulary development.

Possible Sentences

Purpose

Possible Sentences (Moore and Moore, 1986) is designed to help students (1) learn new vocabulary to be encountered in a reading assignment; (2) make predictions about sentences to be found in their reading; (3) provide purpose for reading; and (4) arouse their curiosity concerning the text to be read.

Rationale

Possible Sentences was designed as a means to enable students to determine independently the meanings and relationships of unfamiliar words in text reading assignments. Students make predictions about the relationships between the unknown words, read to verify the accuracy of the predicted relationships, and use the text to evaluate and refine their predictions. Thus, prediction is used to create interest and to focus students' attention on the meanings and concepts to be acquired.

Intended Audience

Moore and Moore (1986) specified that Possible Sentences could be used whenever students encounter unfamiliar vocabulary during reading assignments in subject matter classrooms. Therefore, it is implied that Possible Sentences can be used with middle and secondary students in content areas. However, the strategy is probably appropriate for all levels of students reading and learning from expository text.

Description of the Procedures

Possible Sentences is a five-part lesson and consists of the following steps:

1. List key vocabulary
2. Elicit sentences
3. Read and verify sentences
4. Evaluate sentences
5. Generate new sentences

1. List Key Vocabulary. To begin a Possible Sentences lesson, the teacher lists the essential vocabulary of a text selection on the board and pronounces the words for the students. The teacher has determined beforehand that the words are central to the major concepts to be encountered in the text and that they can be adequately defined by their content. For instance, from a text on skin disorders, the following terms might be listed:

Skin Disorders

moles	warts
acne	freckles
boils	athlete's foot
virus	infection
fungus	congenital

2. Elicit Sentences. Students are then asked to use at least two words from the list and make a sentence, one they think might possibly be in the text. The sentences are recorded, one at a time, on the board, and the words used from the list should be underlined. It is important that the sentences be recorded exactly as given, even if students provide incorrect information. This is necessary for the evaluation phase that follows. Students may use words already in previous sentences as long as a new context is created. Continue eliciting sentences until students can produce no more or until a specified length of time has elapsed. However, encourage students to use every word from the list at least once.

Below are some possible sentences students might offer with the list of words related to skin disorders:

1. Warts are caused by an infection.
2. Moles can be a congenital infection.
3. You shouldn't squeeze boils or acne.
4. Moles and freckles are harmless.
5. Either fungus or a virus causes athlete's foot.

3. Read and Verify Sentences. Students are asked to read the text to check the accuracy of the sentences generated.

4. Evaluate Sentences. With the text available for reference, a discussion ensues as each sentence is evaluated. Sentences that are not accurate are either omitted or refined, according to what the text states. The discussion of the sentences calls for careful reading, because judgments as to the accuracy of sentences must be defined by students.

Examining the possible sentences related to skin disorders, sentence 3 is accurate as it stands. Sentence 1 will have to be redefined. Warts are not caused by infections; they are viral in nature. Sentence 2 also needs refinement. Moles can be congenital, but they are not infections. Sentence 4 is technically correct; however, it is more accurate to state that "Moles and freckles are harmless unless irritated." Finally, sentence 5 needs to be modified to state that athlete's foot is caused by a fungal infection.

5. Generate New Sentences. After the original sentences have been evaluated, the teacher asks for additional sentences. This step is taken to further extend students' understanding of the meanings and relationships of the vocabulary terms. As new sentences are generated, they are checked against the text for accuracy. All final sentences should be recorded in their notebooks by the students.

Cautions and Comments

Possible Sentences is a structured language activity that requires students both to recognize the contextual setting of words and to produce their own contextual settings. However, there are some concerns that teachers need to be aware of before implementing a Possible Sentences lesson. Care needs to be taken to ensure that vocabulary can be defined by the context. Authors do not always provide explicit contexts in their writing, and this strategy requires that the context be one in which the meaning of a word is at least directly implied. In addition, the choice of vocabulary terms needs to be considered to conduct a successful lesson. If only unfamiliar words are chosen from a text, students will have difficulty generating sentences. Particularly with passages of a highly technical nature, it is essential also to list some words that will be familiar to students. Otherwise, students will not be able to use their prior knowledge to make connections between what they know and the unfamiliar words they are to learn. Finally, if too many technical words are found in a text or if an absence of defining contexts is noted, then it may behoove the teacher to choose a different strategy or, even more appropriately, a different text.

Possible Sentences provides students an opportunity to use all language processes as they learn new word meanings. Using their prior knowledge, students are asked to make connections between new and known vocabulary words and evaluate them. Students use speaking to express these connections; they use listening to hear other students' ideas and connections. They read to verify the possible sentences generated, and the refined versions are written in their notebooks. Thus, students become actively involved in their new learning, experience multiple exposures to the new words, and use words drawn directly from their reading materials, all principles of effective vocabulary instruction (National Reading Panel, 2000).

There is an additional benefit in using Possible Sentences. Teachers are able to assess what knowledge students bring to the learning task, how they rectify their misconceptions about a topic, and whether or not students have actually learned the word meanings and their related concepts.

REFERENCES

Jansen, S. J., and F. A. Duffelmeyer. 1996. Enhancing possible sentences through cooperative learning. *Journal of Adolescent & Adult Literacy* 39: 658–659. Discusses the use of Possible Sentences with cooperative learning.

Moore, D. W., and S. A. Moore. 1986. Possible sentences. In E. K. Dishner, T. W. Bean, J. E. Readence, and D. W. Moore (Eds.), *Reading in the content areas: Improving classroom instruction* (2d ed.). Dubuque, IA: Kendall/Hunt, 174–179. Describes the rationale, procedures, and suggestions for using Possible Sentences.

Moore, D. W., and S. A. Moore. 1992. Possible sentences: An update. In E. K. Dishner, T. W. Bean, J. E. Readence, and D. W. Moore (Eds.), *Reading in the content areas: Improving classroom instruction* (3d ed.). Dubuque, IA: Kendall/Hunt, 196–202. A refinement and update of the Possible Sentences strategy.

National Reading Panel. (2000). *Teaching children to read: An evidence-based assessment of the scientific research literature on reading and its implications for reading instruction: Report of the subgroups.* (NIH Publication No. 00-4754). Washington, DC: National Institute of Child Health and Human Development. Chapter 4 describes the effective principles of vocabulary development.

Stahl, S. A., and B. A. Kapinus. 1991. Possible sentences: Predicting word meanings to teach content area vocabulary. *The Reading Teacher* 45: 36–43. Research study validating Possible Sentences as an effective means to teach vocabulary and foster recall.

List-Group-Label

Purpose

List-Group-Label (Taba, 1967), also called semantic mapping (Johnson and Pearson, 1978, 1984), is designed to encourage students to (1) improve their vocabulary and categorization skills; (2) organize their verbal concepts; and (3) aid them in remembering and reinforcing new vocabulary.

Rationale

The List-Group-Label (LGL) lesson was originally conceived by Taba as a means to help students deal with the technical vocabulary in science and social studies classes. It is based on the notion that categorizing words can help students organize new concepts and experiences in relation to previously learned concepts. In essence, LGL attempts to improve upon the way in which students learn and remember new concepts.

Intended Audience

List-Group-Label was originally used by Taba with elementary school students. However, the strategy seems appropriate for students at all grade levels.

Description of the Procedures

List-Group-Label is an easy-to-implement three-part strategy that uses (1) listing, (2) grouping/labeling, and (3) follow-up.

1. Listing. The teacher begins the LGL lesson by selecting a one- or two-word topic to serve as a stimulus for listing words. Using a chalkboard, an overhead transparency, or any other means appropriate for recording students' responses, the stimulus topic is written at the top of the board or paper. Topics should be drawn from the materials that students are reading and from which they are learning. For example, if students are about to start a unit on volcanoes, volcanoes might be used as the topic to begin an LGL lesson. On the other hand, almost any topic of which the students have some prior knowledge might be suitable.

Students are asked to brainstorm related to the topic, i.e., to think of any word or expression related to the topic. Using our volcano example, the teacher might say, "Think of any word or words that remind you of the topic 'volcano.' " Responses are recorded, and the teacher should accept all word associations given by the students, unless the response cannot be justified by the student.

The list of words should be kept manageable. Depending on the topic itself and the grade level of the students, approximately 25 responses should be adequate. When most children have had an opportunity to offer a response, the listing portion of the lesson can be terminated by stating, "I'll take only two more words." Below is a list of responses students might generate using volcano as a stimulus topic:

Volcano

lava	Mt. St. Helens	eruption
explosion	ash	rocks
destruction	magma	Pompeii
fire	death	earthquake
dust	smoke	heat
Krakatoa	cinders	molten

2. Grouping/Labeling. To begin this portion of the lesson, the teacher should read the list orally, pointing to each word as it is pronounced. For older students this step may not be necessary, but it is cautioned that even older readers, particularly those of lesser ability, may benefit from it. The students are then instructed to make smaller lists of words related to (in this case) the topic of volcanoes, using only words from the large list that the class generated. These smaller groupings should consist of words that have something in common with one another; and each grouping should have at least three words in it. Words from the large list may be used in more than one smaller group, as long as the groupings are different. Students are also told they must give their group of words a label or title that indicates the shared relationship they possess.

3. Follow-Up. Using another part of the chalkboard or piece of paper, the teacher solicits and records categories of words and their labels from the students, one grouping at a time. After a category is recorded, the student offering the group must state verbally why the words have been categorized in the particular way stated. In this way, all students can see category possibilities that may not have occurred to them.

The following are possible groupings that may be generated from the large list of volcano words:

1. lava, ash, rocks, dust, smoke = things emitted from a volcano
2. Mt. St. Helens, Krakatoa, Pompeii = famous volcanoes
3. explosion, destruction, death, earthquake = results of a volcanic eruption
4. lava, fire, cinders, molten, magma = hot volcanic parts

Cautions and Comments

Perhaps the most beneficial aspects of List-Group-Label are the modeling and sharing that are built into the strategy. It is through this sharing that students are exposed to ideas and concepts that may be beyond their experiential background and, thus, enable learning to occur. Therefore, it is most important that modeling and sharing be emphasized as part of the lesson.

Modeling may also occur as part of the instruction that the teacher provides. For younger or poorer students for whom categorization might prove to be a problem, the teacher should "walk" students through the "how" and "why" of LGL. This might include: (1) constructing the first category and providing a title for it to show students the process of categorization; (2) providing an initial list of words for students to group and label; (3) making the categories yourself and having students label them; and (4) providing the labels and having students find words to fit the category.

Other suggestions for using List-Group-Label include the use of small groups of students to categorize and label rather than just having individual students accomplish this task on their own. This increases the interaction and sharing among individuals, as well as streamlining the whole group discussion that follows groupings and labeling; i.e., instead of individuals reporting their groupings, only a spokesperson for each small group does the talking. For younger students or groups of students, LGL may also be personalized by recording the individual's or group's name by the category that has been offered.

It must also be mentioned that LGL is based on the notion that some prior knowledge is essential for the lesson to be successful. If a teacher assumes prior knowledge on the part of students where little or none exists, LGL stands little chance for success. For instance, using volcano as a stimulus topic for students who are too young will probably result in very few word associations being given. Similarly, using an unfamiliar topic such as "parts of the brain," even with older students, will usually result in failure, too.

Obviously, prior knowledge plays much less of a role in LGL if the strategy is used as a means of reinforcement in the postreading portion of an instructional lesson. In such a case, knowledge gained from the text is going to take precedence over prior knowledge. Therefore, LGL can be an excellent strategy for review purposes, even if the topic was originally unfamiliar. Indeed, Bean, Inabinette, and Ryan (1983) found that secondary students produced significantly higher vocabulary retention scores when LGL was used as a postreading review strategy.

Other problems that may occur with LGL involve aspects of categorization. It is cautioned that semantic, meaning-oriented groupings be emphasized rather than those that focus on surface commonalities of words chosen for a grouping. For example, the following category is perfectly legitimate, though not what is called for in LGL.

explosion, destruction, eruption = three syllable words

If such a category should occur, teachers are cautioned that they must accept the category but point out that meaningful, rather than surface, associations are desired. Another categorization problem that might occur is the propensity of some students to try to make the largest grouping they possibly can. This can be dealt with by simply limiting the number of words that may be used in one group to five or, at the most, to seven words. Finally, some words defy classification. To deal with this, Readence and Searfoss (1986) suggested creating a "misfit" list of all those words that do not fit a category. Exploring why certain words do not fit a category can also prove instructionally beneficial for students.

The diagnostic value of LGL should be mentioned. In a prereading situation, teachers can find out what it is that students know and what it is that will require teacher instruction. In a postreading situation, teachers can find out what students have learned and what will require reteaching. Finally, as a straight vocabulary development lesson, teachers can find a source of words from students' experiences that might require clarification. Finally, though there is little direct research support for LGL, the report of the National Reading Panel (2000) indicates that similar vocabulary strategies that provide for active engagement and multiple exposures to new words are effective.

REFERENCES

Bean, T. W., N. B. Inabinette, and R. Ryan. 1983. The effect of a categorization strategy on secondary students' retention of literacy vocabulary. *Reading Psychology* 4: 247–252. Research study that reports positive effects for the use of List-Group-Label as a postreading strategy.

Heimlich, J. E., and S. D. Pittelman. 1986. *Semantic mapping: Classroom applications.* Newark, DE: International Reading Association. A monograph devoted exclusively to the use of List-Group-Label in the classroom.

Johnson, D. D., and P. D. Pearson. 1978, 1984. *Teaching reading vocabulary.* New York: Holt, Rinehart and Winston. A text that explores vocabulary development in general and List-Group-Label in particular.

Lipson, M. 1995. The effect of semantic mapping instruction on prose comprehension of below-level college readers. *Reading Research and Instruction* 34: 367–378. Research study demonstrating the effectiveness of List-Group-Label with below-level college readers.

National Reading Panel. 2000. *Teaching children to read: An evidence-based assessment of the scientific research literature on reading and its implications for reading instruction: Report of the subgroups.* (NIH Publication No. 00-4754). Washington, DC:

National Institute of Child Health and Human Development. Chapter 4 describes the effective principles of vocabulary development.

Readence, J. E., and L. W. Searfoss. 1986. Teaching strategies for vocabulary development. In E. K. Dishner, T. W. Bean, J. E. Readence, and D. W. Moore (Eds.), *Reading in the content areas: Improving classroom instruction* (2d ed.). Dubuque, IA: Kendall/Hunt, 183–188. Discusses the use of categorization in general and List-Group-Label in particular as a means to develop vocabulary.

Sinatra, R., J. Beaudry, J. Pizzo, and G. Geishart. 1994. Using a computer-based semantic mapping, reading and writing approach with at-risk fourth graders. *Journal of Computing in Childhood Education* 5: 93–112. Study showing the effectiveness of a computer-based approach to List-Group-Label with at-risk fourth graders.

Taba, H. 1967. *Teacher's handbook for elementary social studies.* Reading, MA: Addison-Wesley. Describes the original uses of the List-Group-Label strategy.

Contextual Redefinition

Purpose

Contextual Redefinition (Readence, Bean, and Baldwin, 2004) is designed to help students: (1) use context to unlock the meaning of unknown words, and (2) make informed, rather than haphazard, guesses about word meanings using context.

Rationale

Contextual Redefinition is a strategy that stresses the importance of context in predicting and verifying word meanings. Context enables students to make more informed guesses about the meaning of words in print and to monitor those predictions by checking them for syntactic/semantic appropriateness as reading progresses. Since authors frequently provide clues to the meanings of words in sentences, it is essential that students be able to use those clues as an aid in deriving meaning from print. Contextual Redefinition provides a format for deriving the meaning of unknown words that capitalizes on the use of context and endeavors to give students a strategy that can be used in their own independent reading.

Intended Audience

Contextual Redefinition is appropriate for students of all grade levels who may encounter in their reading a few difficult words that may be defined in the context in which they occur.

Description of the Procedures

Contextual Redefinition may be implemented using a five-step procedure: (1) select unfamiliar words, (2) write a sentence, (3) present the words in isolation, (4) present the words in context, and (5) use a dictionary for verification.

1. Select Unfamiliar Words. Words to be used with this strategy are not randomly chosen; rather, they are identified in conjunction with the reading assignment at hand. Teachers should examine the text to be read to select those words (a) whose meaning may be necessary to understand the important ideas of the text and (b) whose meaning or use may present trouble to students as they read. For the sake of demonstrating this strategy, the following words will be used: hippophagy, carapace, and arachibutyrophobia.

2. Write a Sentence. At least a sentence context needs to be provided so that students have appropriate clues to each word's meaning. If the text already has such a context, use it; otherwise, one will have to be created. If a context is created, it is recommended that various types of clues (e.g., synonyms, comparison/contrast, definition) should be used. In this way students are able to experience the variety of ways authors may provide help in conveying meaning.

With our example the following sentences might be used:

a. The drought had been so long and severe that the cattle had died. Only the horses had survived. Yet, the natives were so hungry that they had to resort to *hippophagy* to avoid starvation.

b. Without its *carapace,* a turtle is subject to certain death from its enemies or the elements.

c. Because Waldo was born with a cleft palate, he would never eat peanut butter. Though he was told by the doctors that he was totally healed, Waldo had developed *arachibutyrophobia.* Because of that, peanut butter was out of the question.

3. Present the Words in Isolation. Using an overhead transparency or a chalkboard, ask students to provide definitions for each word. It is suggested that the teacher pronounce each word as it is introduced so students at least know how the word sounds. When offering their individual guesses, students must provide a rationale for them. As a group, students should try to come to some consensus as to what they believe the best meaning is. Obviously, some predictions may be "off-the-wall" or even humorous. However, this is part of the process of learning; focusing on associations with recognizable parts of the word when it is in isolation robs the reader of the clues provided by a surrounding context. In other words, guesses offered when a word is presented in isolation are usually haphazard and uninformed.

With our example words, it is easy to see that some students could say that *hippophagy* has something to do with hippos, that *carapace* has something to do with a pace car at a race, and that *arachibutyrophobia* has something to do with a fear of spiders.

4. Present the Words in Context. At this point in the lesson, students are presented each word in its appropriate context, using the sentence or sentences from the text or those developed by the teacher. Again, students are asked to offer guesses about the meaning of each word and provide a rationale for each definition. In doing this, less able students are able to experience the thinking processes involved in using context to derive a meaning. In other words, students are able to act as models of appropriate reading behavior for one another. As before, students should try to come to some consensus as to the best meaning of the word offered.

In this part of the strategy, students should learn that context provides much information about the meaning of words and allows for quite informed predictions. In addition, students should learn that simply guessing at a word in isolation to get its meaning is not very accurate and can be frustrating.

5. Use a Dictionary for Verification. In this step, a student or students are asked to consult a dictionary to verify the guesses offered. The dictionary definition is shared with the rest of the class, and a discussion ensues concerning the quality of the predictions given when the words are presented (a) in isolation and (b) in context. It is now that teachers should point out or, even better, have students discover the differences involved in guessing during these two steps of contextual redefinition.

Cautions and Comments

Contextual Redefinition provides teachers with a format to help students learn the use of context in ascertaining the meanings of unfamiliar words. It is easy to implement, requires little extra teacher preparation to use, and does have the potential for transfer to students' other reading situations. Furthermore, the strategy allows students to become actively involved in the discovery of new word meanings rather than just passive receivers of teacher-provided meanings.

It must be remembered, however, that Contextual Redefinition is a strategy to introduce new vocabulary words, not a strategy to teach and reinforce vocabulary words. Therefore, teachers must provide the necessary extension activities for students in order to ensure that the words are retained. In addition, another concern about this strategy is one that Gipe (1978–79) stated in her research on teaching word meanings. Teachers should try to ensure that the words used in explaining a new word are familiar; one cannot expect a student to learn a new word when it is first introduced in a sentence that has other unknown entities in it.

A final mention must be made of the importance of modeling behavior. Built into the strategy is the reading behavior of fluent readers; fluent readers use all available clues (graphophonic, syntactic, semantic) to derive the meaning of an unknown word. Contextual Redefinition tries to demonstrate to students that this is the proper way to cope with unknown words in text reading assignments. Modeling behavior is also used when students explain their thought processes to others in the class. It must not be assumed that all students will deal equally well with the various contexts that can be encountered. As students share their thoughts and ideas with one another, this presents an opportunity for others to pick up on and understand what happens in deriving meaning from print. Finally, it should be stressed that very little research on the use of Contextual Redefinition exists to date, however, the National Reading Panel (2000) has endorsed vocabulary strategies that capitalize on contextual and definitional methodology.

REFERENCES

Gipe, J. P. 1978–79. Investigating techniques for teaching word meanings. *Reading Research Quarterly* 14: 624–644. Research study that found that a vocabulary teaching method emphasizing context proved effective.

National Reading Panel. 2000. *Teaching children to read: An evidence-based assessment of the scientific research literature on reading and its implications for reading instruction: Report of the subgroups.* (NIH Publication No. 00-4754). Washington, DC: National Institute of Child Health and Human Development. Chapter 4 describes the effective principles of vocabulary development.

Readence, J. E., T. W. Bean, and R. S. Baldwin. 2004. *Content area literacy: An integrated approach* (8th ed.). Dubuque, IA: Kendall/Hunt. Presents the steps involved in conducting a Contextual Redefinition lesson in the content areas.

Tierney, R. J., J. E. Readence, and E. K. Dishner. 1990. *Reading strategies and practices: A compendium* (3rd ed.). Boston: Allyn and Bacon. Chapter 6 presents Preview in Context, a vocabulary strategy useful when an existing context provides clues to the meaning of an unknown word and students can be talked through the discovery of its meaning.

Feature Analysis

Purpose

Feature Analysis (also called semantic feature analysis by Johnson and Pearson, 1984) is designed to help students to:

1. Improve their vocabulary and categorization skills;
2. Understand the similarities and differences in related words; and
3. Expand and retain content area vocabulary and concepts.

Rationale

Feature Analysis is a categorization strategy derived from the theoretical construct of cognitive structure as the way in which individuals organize knowledge. Briefly, as human beings process information, categories are established in the cognitive structure based largely on cultural and experiential patterns. Rules (Feature Analysis) are formulated to allocate objects (words or concepts) into these categories. In this way, category interrelationships are established in the cognitive structure so that individuals can search their category systems (knowledge) efficiently to make sense of their experiences. Of practical relevance, Feature Analysis is intended to provide a systematic procedure for exploring and reinforcing vocabulary concepts through the use of categorization.

Intended Audience

Johnson and Pearson (1984) described Feature Analysis as a strategy that could be used with elementary students to develop their vocabulary. However, it can also be used to refine and reinforce vocabulary and related concepts in a postreading situation in content area classrooms.

Description of the Procedures

Feature Analysis may be implemented using the following six steps:

1. Select category
2. List words in category
3. List features
4. Indicate feature possession
5. Add words/features
6. Complete and explore matrix

1. Select Category. The key to Feature Analysis is to start slowly and to begin with something familiar to students. A category topic (e.g., pets) is selected by the teacher. Once students are familiar with the strategy, the kinds and the abstractness of the category topics (e.g., freedom, climate) may increase. For illustration purposes, we use a rather simplistic example with the category of pets.

2. List Words in Category. Once the category topic has been introduced, the teacher provides words that name concepts or objects related to the category. As students become accustomed to the strategy, they should provide these words. In the case of our example of pets, the following words might be introduced initially: (a) dog, (b) fish, (c) hamster, (d) frog, and (e) duck.

3. List Features. The teacher must now decide what features (traits, characteristics) are to be explored in the category *pets.* As before, students should provide these features once they become familiar with the strategy. Since some category topics would have many features that could be explored, as is the case with our example, start with only a few features and build on them later in the lesson. For our example, features to be examined are whether the pet (a) lives on land, (b) lives in the water, (c) has wings, (d) has fins, (e) has legs, and (f) has fur.

After the first three steps of the strategy have been completed, we should have a feature matrix that looks like the following:

Category: Pets

	land	water	wings	fins	legs	fur
dog						
fish						
hamster						
frog						
duck						

4. Indicate Feature Possession. Students are guided through the feature matrix for the purpose of deciding whether a particular pet possesses each of the features. When beginning Feature Analysis, it is recommended that a simple plus/minus (+/–) system be used to indicate feature possession. A more sophisticated system, such as a form of the Likert scale (1 = never; 2 = some; 3 = always), may be substituted once students are familiar with the strategy, and a system that explores the relative degree of feature possession is desired. Feature possession should be based on typical patterns, i.e., though some dogs may not have fur, this is not typical of them. The feature matrix for pets should look as follows using a +/– system:

Category: Pets

	land	water	wings	fins	legs	fur
dog	+	–	–	–	+	+
fish	–	+	–	+	–	–
hamster	+	–	–	–	+	+
frog	+	+	–	–	+	–
duck	+	–	+	–	+	–

5. Add Words/Features. At this point in the strategy, it is time to expand the matrix. The teacher, or preferably the students, should generate new words to be added, followed by new features to be analyzed. Depending on the familiarity of the category or time limitations, the teacher may wish to set a limit on the number of words or features that can be added. This will typically be done automatically as categories become more abstract and begin to rely less on the prior knowledge that students may possess.

In our example, words such as (a) turtle, (b) rabbit, and (c) snake might be added. Features to be added might include (a) has feathers, (b) swims, and (c) flies. Adding words and features to the matrix is an attempt to further expand students' vocabulary and to develop concepts through categorization. The next and final step completes the strategy.

6. Complete and Explore Matrix. Students proceed now to complete the feature matrix by using the identical feature possession system as before with the added words and features. Our final example matrix might look like this:

Category: Pets

	land	water	wings	fins	legs	fur	feathers	swims	flies
dog	+	–	–	–	+	+	–	–	–
fish	–	+	–	+	–	–	–	+	–
hamster	+	–	–	–	+	+	–	–	–
frog	+	+	–	–	+	–	–	+	–
duck	+	–	+	–	+	–	+	+	+
turtle	+	+	–	–	+	–	–	+	–
rabbit	+	–	–	–	+	+	–	–	–
snake	+	–	–	–	–	–	–	+	–

The final part of this step is the exploration of the feature matrix. Students are asked to examine how words in the matrix relate, yet how they are still unique. For instance, it can be noted that even though the dog, the hamster, and the rabbit are different pets, they still have many similar traits. At the same time, they are also different from all the other pets listed and compared. In addition, it can be seen that only certain pets have wings or typically swim.

Exploring the feature matrix is best accomplished when the students, rather than the teacher, note these similarities and differences. Further expansion of the matrix may continue at this point, if the students so desire or the teacher assigns it.

Cautions and Comments

On the positive side, Feature Analysis has been shown to be effective with selected students (Bos and Anders, 1990; Johnson, Toms-Bronowski, and Pittelman, 1983), is relatively easy to implement, and can be fun. On the negative side, it does present some concerns of which teachers need to be aware. Categorization, as espoused in this strategy, is more sophisticated than shown. Some students may find Feature Analysis to be difficult at first. If such is the case, Readence and Searfoss (1980) suggest that simple categorization exercises and strategies such as List-Group-Label (this unit) be used as a means to introduce the concept of categorization and to act as a way into Feature Analysis. A second concern revolves around the plus/minus feature possession system. The strategy looks at typical patterns related to feature possessions, yet there are many exceptions to what is typical. Looking at our example, it can be argued that there are flying fish and that ducks live, at least part of the time, in the water. It is recommended that if Feature Analysis is to be used frequently in the classroom, then teaching students to use a more sophisticated analysis system is warranted. This may lessen the amount of haggling that students do in the analysis process. Finally, as with any strategy, the more actively involved the students become in category selection and in the selection of words and features to be explored, the better the strategy will work.

Categorizing Feature Analysis as strictly a vocabulary development technique for elementary students presents a very narrow view of this strategy. It has great potential in other aspects of vocabulary development, as well as in becoming an integral part of both elementary and secondary reading and content area lessons. Baldwin, Ford, and Readence (1981) have shown how Feature Analysis can be used as an alternative approach to teaching students word connotations. Perhaps the best use, however, of this strategy is when it is used as a means to reinforce the vocabulary and related concepts of text in a content area reading lesson (Readence and Searfoss, 1980; Stieglitz and Stieglitz, 1981). For example, if students were involved in a health unit on drugs, Feature Analysis would be an excellent means to reinforce and review the likenesses and differences of the various drugs. After all, not all drugs are habit forming, create physical dependence, or are hallucinogens! Feature Analysis provides an effective means for examining these characteristics.

REFERENCES

Anders, P. L., and C. S. Bos. 1986. Semantic feature analysis: An interactive strategy for vocabulary development and text comprehension. *Journal of Reading* 29: 610–616. Discusses the theoretical and research bases for Feature Analysis as well as providing a practical example.

Baldwin, R. S., J. C. Ford, and J. E. Readence. 1981. Teaching word connotations: An alternative strategy.

Reading World 21: 103–108. Describes and provides examples of Feature Analysis as a means to help students learn word connotations.

Bos, C. S., and P. L. Anders. 1990. Effects of interactive vocabulary instruction on the vocabulary learning and reading comprehension of junior-high learning disabled students. *Learning Disability Quarterly* 13: 31–42. Research study that found that feature analysis was an effective means of learning new vocabulary for learning disabled students.

Johnson, D. D., and P. D. Pearson. 1978. *Teaching reading vocabulary.* New York: Holt, Rinehart and Winston. A text that explores vocabulary development in general and Feature Analysis in particular.

———. 1984. *Teaching reading vocabulary* (2d ed.). New York: Holt, Rinehart and Winston. An updated version of the aforementioned text.

Johnson, D. D., S. Toms-Bronowski, and S. D. Pittelman. 1983. *An investigation of the effectiveness of semantic mapping and semantic feature analysis with intermediate grade level children.* Program Report 83–3. Madison: Wisconsin Center for Education Research, University of Wisconsin. Presents the findings of a carefully conducted study of the use of the technique.

Pittelman, S. D., J. E. Heimlich, R. L. Berglund, and M. P. French. 1991. *Semantic feature analysis: Classroom applications.* Newark, DE: International Reading Association. Text exploring a variety of classroom uses for Feature Analysis.

Readence, J. E., and L. W. Searfoss. 1980. Teaching strategies for vocabulary development. *English Journal* 69: 43–46. Discusses the use of Feature Analysis as a means to extend vocabulary concepts in the postreading portion of an instruction lesson.

Stieglitz, E. L., and V. S. Stieglitz. 1981. SAVOR the word to reinforce vocabulary in the content areas. *Journal of Reading* 25: 46–51. Discusses Feature Analysis as a means to reinforce vocabulary in the content areas.

Word Map

Purpose

The Word Map (Schwartz and Raphael, 1985), also known as the Frayer model (Frayer, Frederick, and Klausmeier, 1969), is designed to (1) develop students' conceptual knowledge about a topic, and (2) show hierarchical relationships of associated concepts.

Rationale

The Word Map is a systematic teaching technique that attempts to develop students' to-be-learned concepts based upon existing conceptual background. As a result, word concepts are taught by the notion of associating the new to the known.

Thelen (1982) has stated that showing students how concepts are hierarchically related is an important step in helping them learn new concepts, but it might not go far enough. It may be that certain concepts to be learned might need more in-depth processing and that they are better understood when students can generalize the concepts to new situations. Thus, it may be that with certain concepts, just providing a graphic organizer (see Unit 12) may be insufficient for students to fully grasp a concept. Thelen suggested that the Word Map would clarify the task of word learning and was a useful alternative for attaining concepts.

The Word Map also attempts to clarify concepts by showing how they are hierarchically related. However, it suggests that if examples and nonexamples of new concepts, as well as their relevant and irrelevant attributes, are also provided, the students' learning will be even better. Therefore, the strategy examines supraordinate, coordinate, and subordinate aspects of concepts and also stresses those characteristics common to examples of that concept. This clarifying task has been found to be effective in word learning (National Reading Panel, 2000).

Intended Audience

Because of the sophistication involved in the hierarchical arrangement of the Word Map, the strategy is appropriate only for middle and secondary students. Even then, less able middle school students might have difficulty coping with the strategy.

Description of the Procedures

Thelen (1982) recommended that the Word Map be implemented using the following seven steps:

1. Develop the target concept
2. Define the concept
3. Present the concept
4. Finish constructing the hierarchy
5. Guide students to relevant attributes
6. Guide students to irrelevant attributes
7. Complete teaching the concept

1. Develop the Target Concept. A hierarchy should be constructed that incorporates the supraordinate, coordinate, and subordinate aspects of the target concept. A supraordinate aspect of a concept is a term that refers to a common, more general concept of which the target concept is a member. Therefore, if our target concept is *reptiles,* the supraordinate concept might be *vertebrate.* An even more general term would be *animal.*

A coordinate aspect of the target concept is a term that denotes other members of the same general, or supraordinate, concept. For instance, a coordinate concept for reptiles is *amphibians.* Finally, a subordinate aspect of the target concept is a term that possesses specific features of the target concept and is of a lower classification. In the case of reptiles, subordinate terms might be *alligators, snakes,* and *lizards.* Thus, the following hierarchy (Searfoss and Readence, 1994) might be constructed for the target concept *reptiles.*

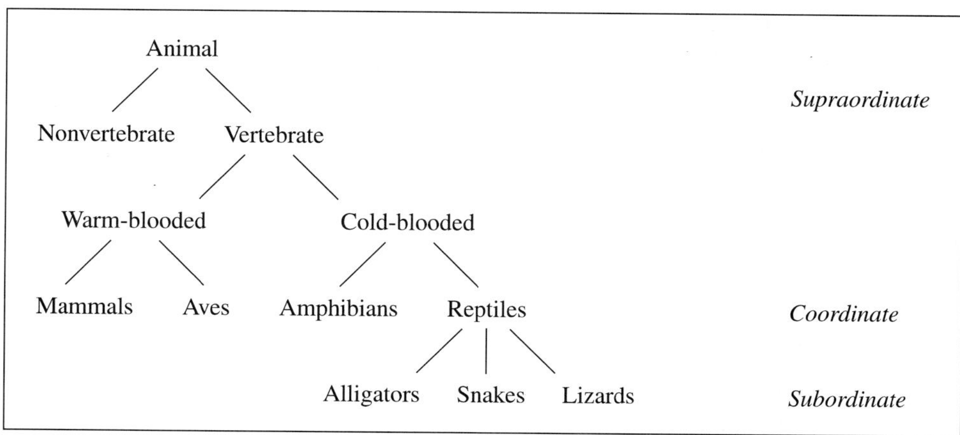

2. Define the Concept. Before presenting the concept, be sure to delineate the relevant attributes for later discussion. Relevant attributes may be defined as characteristics that describe the target concept. Relevant attributes of reptiles, then, might be (a) a vertebrate, (b) breathes air, (c) has scales or bony plates, (d) lays eggs, (e) lacks hair, and (f) is cold-blooded. The examination of relevant attributes of a concept leads students to see not only what an example of it is but also what is not an example of the concept. For instance, a human would not be an example of a reptile, since human beings do not have scales or bony plates, do not lay eggs, are hairy, and are warm-blooded. This provides students the opportunity to see the likenesses and differences involved in attempting to define a concept.

3. Present the Concept. At this time students are provided the target concept to be learned and are asked to contribute examples of it. This can be done either individually or in small groups. The examples can be listed on the board as they are offered. Students may challenge one another's examples as to whether it is an appropriate example. Thus, *gila monsters, chameleons, snakes, alligators, lizards,* and *iguanas* can be categorized as appropriate examples of reptiles. On the other hand, if *toads* or *eagles* were offered, they could be challenged as nonexamples and should be properly classified as amphibians and aves, respectively.

4. Finish Constructing the Hierarchy. Provide students the concept hierarchy that was originally constructed in Step 1. It is essential that the teacher explain why the terms are arranged as they are. The teacher should use questioning techniques to involve the students as much as possible in offering terms that might fit in the resulting diagram to promote fuller understanding.

5. Guide Students to Relevant Attributes. Once all possible examples are given, have students decide what characteristics they have in common (from Step 2). Any misconceptions may be cleared up with regard to what the target concept—in this case, reptiles—is.

6. Guide Students to Irrelevant Attributes. Now have students find differences among the examples offered that do not change the example into a nonexample. In other words, what differences may exist among reptiles that are inconsequential and do not change the example's inclusion as a reptile? Again, this will lead to fuller understanding of the concept. With regard to reptiles, irrelevant attributes might include *whether they walk or slither, what they eat,* or *the size of their eggs.*

7. Complete Teaching the Concept. To complete the Word Map, provide students with other examples and nonexamples they may not have thought of. These could be concepts they may encounter in their reading; doing so will provide additional reinforcement. When this is completed, students will have offered or been supplied the hierarchy from Step 1 and a list of examples, nonexamples, relevant attributes, and irrelevant attributes. With our reptile example, this list might look like this:

1. *Examples*	2. *Nonexamples*
gila monsters	toads
chameleons	eagles
snakes	human beings
alligators	birds
lizards	frogs
iguanas	aardvarks
2. *Relevant Attributes*	4. *Irrelevant Attributes*
vertebrate	walk or slither
cold-blooded	what they eat
lays eggs	size of eggs
lacks hair	color
breathes air	number of eggs
scales or bony plates	where they live

Cautions and Comments

The Word Map provides students with a number of different ways to think about the meaning of word concepts. It allows students to discover how new concepts are related to known concepts and to see what a concept represents as well as what it does not represent. As a consequence, it should help students generalize the newly learned concept to other learning situations. In past research, the Word Map has been used as a basis for developing texts. In studies by Peters (1979) and by Moes, Foertsch, Stewart, Dunning, Rogers, Seda-Santana, Benjamin, and Pearson (1983), such texts were found to be more understandable than texts lacking such a framework.

Key to the success of the Word Map is student involvement and discovery learning. It is essential that students be involved as much as possible in the creation of the concept hierarchy and in the provision of examples, nonexamples, relevant attributes, and irrelevant attributes. It is a fact that a teacher-created hierarchy and teacher-provided examples and attributes will not be as effective a learning environment as one in which students actively participate.

A final problem with the Word Map may be the terminology used in conducting the lesson. The terms *supraordinate, coordinate,* and *subordinate* may be too complex for some students, particularly those who are less able. Teachers may do well to use another set of terminology, such as *more general, equal,* and *more specific* to ensure that the strategy will be effective.

REFERENCES

Frayer, D. A., W. C. Frederick, and H. J. Klausmeier. 1969. *A science for testing the level of concept mastery* (Working paper No. 16). Madison, WI: University of Wisconsin Research and Development Center for Cognitive Learning. Presents some of the original thinking about the Word Map.

Moes, M. A., D. J. Foertsch, J. Stewart, D. Dunning, T. Rogers, I. Seda-Santana, L. Benjamin, and P. D. Pearson. 1983. *Effects of text structure on children's comprehension of expository text.* Paper presented at the National Reading Conference, Austin, TX. Using the Frayer model as a guide to developing text, these researchers compared the effects upon comprehension of the same information presented using different structures.

National Reading Panel. 2000. *Teaching children to read: An evidence-based assessment of the scientific research literature on reading and its implications for reading instruction: Report of the subgroups.* (NIH Publication No. 00-4754). Washington, DC: National Institute of Child Health and Human Development. Chapter 4 describes the effective principles of vocabulary development.

Peters, C. 1979. The effect of systematic restructuring of material upon the comprehension process. *Reading Research Quarterly* 11: 87–110. Studied the effects of using the Frayer model to structure texts.

Rosenbaum, C. 2001. A word map for middle school: A tool for effective vocabulary instruction. *Journal of Adolescent and Adult Literacy* 45: 44–49. Application of the word map strategy to middle school.

Schwartz, R. M. 1988. Learning to learn vocabulary in content area textbooks. *Journal of Reading* 32: 108–118. Use of the Word Map strategy in the content areas.

Schwartz, R. M., and T. E. Raphael. 1985. Concept of definition: A key to improving students' vocabulary. *The Reading Teacher* 39: 198–205. Describes the use of the Word Map strategy.

Searfoss, L. W., and J. E. Readence. 1994. *Helping children learn to read.* 3rd ed. Boston: Allyn and Bacon. Provides a discussion and examples of the Word Map.

Thelen, J. 1982. Preparing students for content reading assignments. *Journal of Reading* 25: 544–549. Delineates the steps involved in implementing the Word Map.

Vocabulary Self-Collection Strategy

Purpose

The Vocabulary Self-Collection Strategy (Haggard, 1986a, 1986b) is designed to help students: (1) generate vocabulary words to be explored and learned, and (2) use their own interest and prior knowledge to enhance vocabulary growth.

Rationale

The Vocabulary Self-Collection Strategy (VSS) is a versatile vocabulary development procedure that can be used to stimulate growth in word knowledge. Haggard based her claims for the utility of VSS on the following premises: "(1) Internal motivation exerts a strong influence on vocabulary acquisition and development, (2) Written text is a major source for new words and terms, (3) Adults develop systematic, personalized strategies for word learning, (4) Words which label or define experience are learned more quickly and easily than those which do not, and (5) The art of collecting words increases sensitivity to new words and enjoyment in word learning" (1986b, 640). In other words, students are asked to use their own interests and prior experiences as the basis for learning words that they will encounter in their reading assignments.

Intended Audience

The Vocabulary Self-Collection Strategy may be used with students at all grade levels, either as an adjunct to class reading assignments or in lieu of regular vocabulary instruction.

Description of the Procedures

The Vocabulary Self-Collection Strategy consists of the following four steps:

1. Selecting the words
2. Defining the words
3. Finalizing the word lists
4. Extending word knowledge

1. Selecting the Words. Students are asked to go through their assigned reading to identify one word they think should be studied further. For instance, in a content lesson students should select words that seem important to understanding the content. Sometimes the class may break up into two- or three-member teams and discuss the words and their meanings before the class as a whole considers them.

If VSS is being used as a spelling lesson, students are asked to "collect" a word that has meaning to their daily lives. These words that students believe the whole class should learn are brought in and presented to the class. No matter what the design of the VSS lesson, the teacher should also select a word. This can become the means by which the teacher ensures that a particularly important word becomes part of the lesson.

2. Defining the Words. Students or teams of students are asked to nominate one word or term they believe should be learned. The teacher does likewise. As the words are recorded on the chalkboard or an overhead, each of them is defined from its original context and reasons for nominating the words are offered. The teacher leads a discussion for clarification and expansion of each word's meaning, adding whatever information the students and teacher have from prior knowledge or gained from the reading selection necessary to come up with the appropriate definition. If necessary or desirable, the dictionary may be checked to verify definitions.

3. Finalizing the Word Lists. Once the discussion is completed, the list of words must be narrowed down by eliminating duplications, words already known, and words that the students do not wish to learn. The words that comprise the final list are redefined so students can record the words and their definitions in their vocabulary journals. Students may decide to record words that were discarded in their personal vocabulary lists.

4. Extending Word Knowledge. Follow-up activities are used to enable students to refine and expand the meanings of the words on the final list. As part of a lesson for general vocabulary development, words can be tested as is normally done if they pertain to the lesson selected. Other activities may need to be redesigned if existing activities do not deal with all the words. With a content selection, the words should be incorporated into the materials for the unit being studied and can be tested as to how they apply to the text.

Cautions and Comments

The Vocabulary Self-Collection Strategy seems easy to implement because the burden of work falls on students. It does seem to provide students with an anchor for new learning as it capitalizes on their experience and word knowledge. In addition, they become actively involved in the lesson through the selection and discussion of words to be learned.

Just as VSS seems versatile in dealing with vocabulary development of various kinds, it can be adapted to be used as a prereading strategy with content material. Though described here as a postreading strategy, VSS can be used with text materials before students actually read them. Students are asked to preview the text before they read it for the purpose of identifying one or two words they feel are important to understanding the text. The words would be defined and recorded as before, except that students would have the opportunity to learn something about the word before they actually read the assignment.

While VSS sounds intuitively appealing as a vocabulary development technique, some concerns about the strategy must be mentioned. First, the strength of the strategy—student self-selection of words—may also be perceived as limiting. The words students may choose as important in a reading assignment may exclude important words. Some teachers would view this as creating a problem if the goal is to have students understand certain text concepts. Second, though not limited to this particular strategy, the necessity of follow-up activities is crucial. Relying on students to develop useful understandings of key concepts should not be left to only a discussion of the words and their recording in a journal. Finally, though little research exists to date on this strategy, it does incorporate many of the principles of effective vocabulary instruction (National Reading Panel, 2000).

REFERENCES

Haggard, M. R. 1986a. The vocabulary self-collection strategy: An active approach to word learning. In E. K. Dishner, T. W. Bean, J. E. Readence, and D. W. Moore (Eds.), *Reading in the content areas: Improving classroom instruction* (2d ed.). Dubuque, IA: Kendall/Hunt, 179–183. The original discussion of the strategy.

———. 1986b. The vocabulary self-collection strategy: Using student interest and world knowledge to enhance vocabulary growth. *Journal of Reading* 29: 634–642. Discusses the use of VSS with a variety of materials and expands upon the theoretical rationale for the strategy.

National Reading Panel. 2000. *Teaching children to read: An evidence-based assessment of the scientific research literature on reading and its implications for reading instruction: Report of the subgroups.* (NIH Publication No. 00-4754). Washington, DC: National Institute of Child Health and Human Development. Chapter 4 describes the effective principles of vocabulary development.

Ruddell, M. R. 1992. Integrated content and long term vocabulary learning with the vocabulary self-collection strategy. In E. K. Dishner, T. W. Bean, J. E. Readence, and D. W. Moore (Eds.), *Reading in the content areas: Improving classroom instruction* (3d ed.). 190–196. Dubuque, IA: Kendall/Hunt. An update of the strategy with particular application to content areas.

Ruddell, M. R., and Shearer, B. A. 2000. "Extraordinary," "tremendous," "exhilarating," "magnificent": Middle at-risk students become avid word learners with the Vocabulary Self-Collection Strategy (VSS). *Journal of Adolescent and Adult Literacy* 45: 352–363. Research study demonstrating the effectiveness of VSS.

Levin's Keyword Method

Purpose

The Keyword Method (Levin, 1983) is a mnemonic strategy that helps students to learn new information by associating it with interactive visual images for later recall.

Rationale

Levin (1983) states that learning new information using the Keyword Method is based on a process of recoding, relating, and retrieving. First, students must recode, or transform, the unknown word to be learned into a more meaningful keyword that looks or sounds like the original. An example might be the word *potable,* which means suitable for drinking. *Potable* is recoded to the familiar word, *pot,* which is then related to the original word by the use of an actual picture or a mental image of a pot of cool spring water sitting in front of you after you have crossed a hot desert. With recoding and relating established, students are now able to use the keyword to retrieve the correct meaning when they encounter the new word. In other words, on seeing the word *potable,* students are reminded of the keyword *pot.* This, in turn, leads them to think of the picture or an appropriate visual image that then leads them to the correct response of "suitable for drinking."

The effectiveness of Levin's Keyword Method is also based upon adherence to three assumptions about picture strategies for learning. First, pictures or images can facilitate learning because they provide a means by which to learn difficult material. Second, the more directly related the pictures or images are to the content to be learned, the more effective the learning will be.

Finally, even given the previous two assumptions, research suggests that the pictures will not be helpful if they are not familiar enough to provide an organizational framework for understanding and retrieving the new information. Levin's Keyword Method meets this assumption and the two aforementioned assumptions by enabling students to recode the new material to be learned into a concrete keyword and relate it within a visual image so that it can be easily retrieved.

Intended Audience

Levin's Keyword Method was originally used to improve college students' ability to learn a foreign language (Atkinson, 1975). Since then, the use of this strategy has expanded to help students, elementary through college, to learn vocabulary and content facts.

Description of the Procedures

Konopak and Williams (1988) described how to use Levin's Keyword Method in the classroom employing the following steps: (1) teacher preparation, (2) modeling, (3) guided practice, (4) independent practice, and (5) transfer.

The strategy will be considered using an example adapted from Konopak and Williams (1988, 685–687). It involves a fifth grade science unit on minerals in which students are asked to recall the names and primary use of various minerals.

1. Teacher Preparation. Using the text passage, the teacher must decide what particular minerals are to be learned and where each of them is used. Next, a keyword must be assigned to each mineral. Then, the visual image of the keyword interacting with its primary use is developed. It is recommended that an actual illustration be used to demonstrate this image; however, an elaborate statement may be used if it can easily create a mental image for the students. The following are example items:

Mineral	*Keyword*	*Primary Use*	*Image*
rhodonite	road	home	a road going through a living room
fluorite	flower	industry	a vase of flowers sitting on a workbench in a factory
corundum	car	home	a car driving through a living room

2. Modeling. Tell students that they will be using a study strategy to help them remember the names of minerals they need to learn and their use. To demonstrate Levin's Keyword Method, use the example of amber. Provide a short description of it and tell them it is used primarily in the home. Explain to them that a keyword, which either looks or sounds like *amber,* will help them learn the information they need to know. Since *hamburger* sounds like the target word, it becomes the keyword for that mineral. Next, students are shown a picture of a hamburger sitting on a chair in a living room. They are informed that by thinking of the picture they will remember that amber (hamburger) is a mineral used primarily in the home (living room). Other demonstrative examples should follow until students understand the concepts of the strategy.

3. Guided Practice. Distribute to the students a short passage about the first target mineral, rhodonite, which is used in the home, and an illustration showing a road going through a living room. The target word, *rhodonite,* and the keyword, *road,* should be used as captions for the illustration. The students are directed to read the passage and examine the accompanying picture for the purpose of recalling the mineral and its use. The picture should be discussed as to how it helps them recall the information.

4. Independent Practice. Break students into small groups of three or four members and have them read the rest of the text information about minerals. Provide them with keywords and have them develop their own mnemonic images, given the examples you previously prepared. These should be shared with the whole class.

5. Transfer. To initiate the successful transfer of this strategy from teacher-provided keywords and illustrations to student-oriented mnemonics, provide additional text information about minerals without supplying a keyword. Students will then need to read the material and develop their own mnemonics to aid in the recall of the material. They will need to be reminded of the study technique and how effective they may have found it. Students will also need encouragement and feedback as they develop their own visual images. Again, these should be shared with the whole class for purposes of feedback.

To further promote transfer, watch for other opportunities for students to use the strategy in their other subject matter areas. They may need to be prompted by the teacher or other students until it is fully learned.

Cautions and Comments

Levin's Keyword Method provides students with the means to recall new content material by employing a workable study strategy that includes familiar, concrete images to facilitate their learning. Unlike most of the strategies described in this unit, Levin's Keyword Method is well documented as a means to help students remember new vocabulary (for reviews, see National Reading Panel, 2000; Pressley, Levin, and Delaney, 1982; Pressley, Levin, and McDaniel, 1987). The strategy has proved to be an effective learning technique for both good and poor readers at all levels on a variety of learning tasks.

Nonetheless, there are a number of disadvantages to the strategy. First, it can be very time-consuming for the teacher to generate keywords and their accompanying images. Second, the visual images initially used are teacher-provided, not student-provided, resulting in potentially less personal involvement by students in their own learning. Third, the extent to which students can transfer the keyword technique to other areas of study is relatively unknown at this time.

REFERENCES

Atkinson, R. C. 1975. Mnemotechnics in second-language learning. *American Psychologist* 30: 82–828. Examines the use of the Keyword Method with second-language learners.

Konopak, B. C., and N. L. Williams. 1988. Using the keyword method to help young readers learn content material. *The Reading Teacher* 41: 682–687. A practical discussion on the background and use of the Keyword Method.

Konopak, B. C., N. L. Williams, and E. S. Jampole. 1991. Use of mnemonic imagery for content learning. *Reading, Writing, and Learning Disabilities* 7: 309–319. Study showing that Levin's Keyword Method was useful with middle level students with learning disabilities in science.

Levin, J. R. 1983. Pictorial strategies for school learning. In M. Pressley and J. R. Levin (Eds.), *Cognitive strategy research: Educational applications.* New York: Springer-Verlag. An examination of the role of pictures in learning.

Levin, J. R., M. E. Levin, L. D. Glasman, and M. B. Nordwall. 1992. Mnemonic vocabulary instruction: Additional effectiveness evidence. *Contemporary Educational Psychology* 17: 156–174. Studies citing the effectiveness of the Keyword Method with elementary and middle school students in individual, paired, and small-group instructional formats.

Levin, J., C. McCormick, G. Miller, and J. Berry. 1982. Mnemonic versus nonmnemonic vocabulary-learning strategies for children. *American Educational Research Journal* 19: 121–136. Research study demonstrating the effectiveness of the Keyword Method with fourth graders.

National Reading Panel. 2000. *Teaching children to read: An evidence-based assessment of the scientific research literature on reading and its implications for reading instruction: Report of the subgroups.* (NIH Publication No. 00-4754). Washington, DC: National Institute of Child Health and Human Development. Chapter 4 reviews the research on Levin's Keyword Method.

Pressley, M., J. R. Levin, and H. D. Delaney. 1982. The mnemonic keyword method. *Review of Educational Research* 52: 61–91. A review of research on the strategy.

Pressley, M., J. R. Levin, and M. A. McDaniel. 1987. Remembering versus inferring what a word means: Mnemonic and contextual approaches. In M. G. McKeown and M. E. Curtis (Eds.), *The nature of vocabulary acquisition.* Hillsdale, NJ: Erlbaum, 107–127. An updated review of research on the Keyword Method.

UNIT 9

Responding to Reading as Writers and Genre Study

UNIT OVERVIEW

Over the past two decades, an upsurge of interest has occurred in teaching writing, which has included a swing toward providing students with many more opportunities to write, including writing in response to what they read and even interacting with each other about their own writing. As a result of these and other changes in practices, students are not only being encouraged to generate ideas but they are also being given feedback on the quality of their thinking. Reading and writing working together has been found to enhance students' ability to think critically, and their engagement as members of a community with voices. In addition, writing is seen as a way of engaging students in a consideration of conventions of print, elements of style, and genre features.

The present unit extends the coverage of strategies and practices that use writing as a means of response, meaning-making, and skill development (see Units 2 and 10). It includes five strategies to help students respond to reading as writers. Each of the strategies has emerged in recent years as a way of having students use writing in conjunction with reading and of responding to the writing.

Author's Chair/Peer Conferencing. The Author's Chair involves having students present to peers their own writing and the writing of other classroom authors or professional authors. In conjunction with peer questioning of what writers did or were trying to do, Author's Chair establishes rich linkages between reading and writing and between authors and readers.

Dialogue Journals. Dialogue Journals provide a more private forum for students to write to their teacher about what they are reading and writing and about experiences they are having. They provide the teacher the opportunity not only to learn what students are thinking and doing but also to share thoughts and suggestions with them.

Style Study. Style Study involves using texts written by professional writers as a basis for comparison with or as stimuli for student writing. It is viewed as a way of enhancing critical reading and alerting students to stylistic options.

Story Impressions. Story Impressions is a prereading writing activity that involves students' using key concepts from a story to develop their own story or impression of how these concepts might fit together.

Expository Reading-Writing Think-Sheets. As students explore topics with their texts, Expository Reading-Writing Think-Sheets offer a framework for developing, refining, and revising reports.

Author's Chair/Peer Conferencing

Purpose

The goal of Author's Chair/Peer Conferencing is to develop readers and writers who have a sense of authorship and readership that helps them in either composing process. This includes developing in students an appreciation of the following: what they read has been written by someone who has certain purposes in mind and control over what they have written; when they write they have a variety of options; and what they write can be interpreted in different ways by different readers.

Rationale

The present description of Author's Chair is taken from the work of several educators (Blackburn, 1982; Boutwell, 1983; Calkins, 1983; Graves, 1983; Graves and Hansen, 1983; Hansen, 2001; Harwayne, 2001) and represents a composite of their ideas. To a large extent, the notion of Author's Chair was shaped in selected classrooms in which teachers had begun exploring the relationships between reading and writing. Most notable among these teachers were Ellen Blackburn and Marilyn Boutwell, whose classrooms are described in several of the articles cited in this section. The term *Author's Chair* was first applied by Graves and Hansen (1983) to activities that took place in these classrooms.

Essentially, the concept of Author's Chair grew from attempts to give writers the opportunity to hear feedback from their peers about their writing. Sometimes this feedback would be used to provide suggestions to a writer who was in the process of writing a story or report and who wanted help; or it would be a sounding board for ideas before proceeding further. Sometimes the feedback would be used to respond to a finished piece of writing or to several works written by a classmate. In time, these Peer Conferences also were used to enable students to discuss professional authors, ranging from C. S. Lewis to Judy Blume.

Researchers interested in reading-writing relationships support such experiences after examining the outcomes (Graves and Hansen, 1983; Tierney, Leys, and Rogers, 1985). They note that children who are involved in Peer Conferences acquire several abilities and sensitivities that seem desirable and are relatively unique. These include: (1) an appreciation that reading and writing involve ongoing constructive activities in which both readers and writers have many options, (2) a richer sense of what the relationship between readers and writers might be, (3) an appreciation of peer input and of the extent to which collaborations might contribute to enhancing both reading and writing skills, and (4) a better sense both of the quality of their own interpretations or written selections and of the strategies that can be used when problems are encountered during reading and writing.

Intended Audience

Although most of the descriptions of Author's Chair/Peer Conferencing emanate from the elementary school, the approaches can be used at any age level and in almost any learning situation—from a second grade reading class to writing an official business memo for a corporation.

Description of the Procedures

The use of peer conferences requires a change in the typical approach used by most teachers. In most reading lessons, teachers guide students through a reading selection with a variety of questions to ensure that they are engaged and come to understand the selection. Upon completing the selection, the teacher is likely to assign more questions or some activities, or develop some comprehension, word recognition, or study skill. Likewise in many classrooms, the teacher assigns students to write on a topic, and as the writing progresses, the teacher may help the students. Upon completing the writing assignment, the student submits the assignment to the teacher for evaluation. These scenarios represent an approach to reading and writing that is in sharp contrast to the use of Peer Conferences or Author's Chair.

The major difference is in the role of the teacher. In Peer Conferencing, the students act as advisers and evaluators along with the teacher. The teacher might orchestrate or facilitate Peer Conferences, but students are given control of many of the questions and other ideas that get introduced. At the heart of Author's Chair or Peer Conferencing is collaboration.

As classes begin to use Peer Conferences and collaboration, various permutations can emerge. For example, in a single class the range of possibilities might include coauthoring, coreading, class discussions of a peer's problem or work in progress, and small group or a paired sharing of work, ideas, or interests. To illustrate the use of Author's Chair or Peer Conferences, three variations of the group conference will be described. They include:

1. Reading and writing in progress conference
2. End of book conference
3. Peer author conferences

Reading and Writing in Progress Conference. At any stage during the reading or writing of a story or a report, it may be appropriate to confer. For example, as readers and writers begin to read or write a story or report, they may want to seek some input on what they are about to read or write. A writer might be unsure as to how he might begin a story, so he might meet with peers to acquire their feedback. Another child might be about to begin reading a book and he would like advice from peers who have read this same or similar books. Sometimes if groups of students are to read the same book or write on the same topic, they might share their plans or simply brainstorm together.

As readers and writers progress through a story or report, they may encounter a problem or want to share what they have done so far and what they plan to do next. Again, Peer Conferences might be organized in which students define the help they need (their reason for asking for a conference), present what they have accomplished so far, and explore reasons for being stuck, or consider what they plan to do next. The student who desired the conference is responsible for entertaining the questions and ideas of his/her peers. This might involve calling for questions from classmates as well as from the teacher. Below is a segment from a conference in which a student is wrestling with a problem in a report he is writing.

FRED: I wanted to call a conference because I'm having trouble finding information on robotics for my report. I have all these books and I started reading them. It seems that there is just too much information. I don't know what to do.

HELEN: Why did you decide upon robotics?

FRED: I'm real interested in robots and how people might use them in everyday life. Also I thought it would be interesting.

SAM: Maybe you could just do one idea of using robots. Sometimes when I do reports I get too much information, so I try to decide what I really want to say. Then I usually just take part of a big idea and use only a few books.

HELEN: You could write about just a few kinds of robots or just a few kinds of things they can do.

FRED: Umhmm. Yeah, that would help. Mr. Flores?

MR. FLORES: So what do you plan to do?

As you can imagine, similar conferences—with or without the teacher—might be held with a variety of different goals in mind. The key is providing peers an opportunity to get an issue on the floor, acquire input, and then discuss how they might use the advice.

End of Book Conference. These conferences provide students the opportunity to share their reading and writing experiences and products. When students finish the stories they have been reading or the reports they have been writing, they can set up a conference for purposes of sharing their accomplishment with their peers. This might involve providing their peers a synopsis of what they have written or read. It might involve reading the entire story or report or interesting sections of a book aloud. Also, it might include discussing what it was like to read or write this story. After sharing, the writer or reader opens the floor to peer reactions, comments, and questions. As Graves and Hansen (1983) suggest, sometimes a reader or writer might need to develop confidence, in which case peers are encouraged to give supportive comments more than interrogative questions. Hansen (1983) has illustrated two such conferences in some examples of writing conferences that took place in Ellen Blackburn's first grade classroom. As Hansen (1983) described them:

> When Scott sits on a little chair . . . and reads his published book to the whole class clustered on the floor in front of him, with their eyes glued upon him, he's scared. Scott is a fragile author. But he knows that when he has finished reading, they will clap. Then lots of hands will go up. However, Scott need not fear because no one plans to ask a question. His friends want to make comments. Regardless of whom Scott calls upon, the child will accept his writing. "My favorite part was when you rode in the ambulance." Or, "The part I liked best was when you looked in the doctor's glasses and under your skin it looked liked fish eggs." His friend didn't ask him to read that part again, but it is also Scott's favorite part and he intends to share it again. . . .
>
> When Jamie shared her book about her nana, a classmate asked, "Why does your Nana have a lump on her back?" Some questions are more pointed. Daniel read his book about his babysitter's cat who got stuck in the dryer, and a friend asked, "Why didn't you tell how the cat got in the dryer?" (pp. 972–973)

Again, such conferences can be used in conjunction with stories and reports that are read by students, as well as written by them. Sometimes such conferences might involve presenting reactions to published authors similar to the following:

> **LISA:** I loved this Judy Blume book. She tells a story about a girl who was overweight. I particularly like the way she let you know the girl's feelings. Let me read you a section. Blume is an excellent author; the only section which I thought she could have improved was her description of the eating by the girl. Also sometimes she left out some important facts. Anyhow I would recommend the book, in fact, I am planning to write a book similar to it.
>
> **FLOR:** Who do you think would like this book?
>
> **LISA:** Anybody who enjoys Blume or stories about people who are real and have everyday problems. I think you would like it.
>
> **PETER:** How come you didn't like so much of the book and still recommend it?
>
> **LISA:** No book is perfect.
>
> **ELIZABETH:** In what ways will your book be similar? etc.

In contrast to reporting on professional authors, conferences about peer work might also be conducted. These are described next.

Peer Author Conferences. Unlike the conferences in which students report on professional authors or their own efforts, Peer Author Conferences refer to conferences that are given by classmates on peer writing. In this situation, the author is present and might be questioned occasionally, but somebody else—a peer reader—reports on the book and fields most of the questions and comments. The author has an opportunity to hear somebody else represent the book, including what they enjoyed, found confusing, and might use. In addition, the author along with peers has an opportunity to ask questions of the readers about their recommendations and evaluation of the book. The person who reads the book has a unique opportunity to share a book of an author whom they know and with whom they may have conferred about the book.

Cautions and Comments

As was mentioned earlier, researchers have suggested that the collaborative experiences afforded by the Author's Chair or Peer Conferencing result in improvements in a student's sense of readership and authorship, as well as an ability to evaluate and problem-solve. In fact, Leal (1993) mentions three positive outcomes of literary peer discussion groups. They are: (1) "a catalyst for learning," (2) "a platform for peer collaboration and peer tutoring," and (3) "an opportunity for exploratory talk with a real audience." She also found that the use of the genre "informational storybook" (books that combine factual information in a fictional narrative framework) was associated with longer discussions by the children, more predictions about the text, and more connections outside the text, such as prior knowledge.

In conjunction with using Author's Chair and other group activities, Brent and Anderson (1993) suggest that teachers help children to develop good listening skills. Specifically, they suggest not only that teachers themselves model good listening skills, but also that they provide instruction in the form of mini-lessons:

> Children can be taught to predict what they might hear, follow directions, appreciate language, identify main ideas and supporting details, draw justifiable inferences, differentiate fact from fiction, and analyze critically. Strategies such as watching the speaker, focusing to block distractions, visualizing, formulating questions, making mental associations, predicting while listening, summarizing, and taking notes are all useful to children as they work to improve their listening abilities. In addition, children should be taught how to select strategies to match the listening situation. (p. 124)

Apart from the benefits of Author's Chair-type discussions, the opportunity to confer provides students with a rich resource that often goes untapped in classrooms—namely, one's own peers. Furthermore, if conferencing opportunities extend to works in progress, teachers can move away from just assigning and assessing reading and writing to developing strategies for use as reading and writing actually occurs. By providing a forum for making public any difficulties and strategies, as Hansen (2001), Graves and Hansen (1983), and Tierney, Leys, and Rogers (1985) have argued, readers and writers are likely to become both better self-monitors and more flexible strategy users.

Finally, providing children with an opportunity to respond to each other's work challenges narrow gender roles, which children may take on in their writing, as McAuliffe's work indicates. Sheila McAuliffe (1993) found that children were very likely to use strongly gendered language and story subjects, such that boys and girls had a hard time understanding each other's stories when sharing them in an Author's Chair-type forum. She found that stories written later in the school year were more likely to feature both male and female story characteristics, stories to which both boys and girls made positive responses. She concludes:

> This yearlong study of a whole language classroom pointed out the importance of *intent* in the process of communication. When understanding broke down, it seemed the students' intent or desire to share meanings caused them to continue to try to understand and be understood. . . . By creating this kind of writers' workshop, a teacher can set up social structures that encourage learners to try to understand one another. When writers ask their audience for response, they want the responders' views of their written messages. These views, including those of the other gender, are then available to use for clarifying original drafts.

Author's Chair may also help children to respond in less ethnocentric ways, provided that children who are outside the dominant culture of the class feel supported in and respected for their readings of and responses to their peers' work.

Three obstacles appear likely to stand in the way of successful conferencing in many classrooms. First, most teachers place themselves on center stage; a conferencing approach requires them to establish quite a different social setting for reading and writing. Second, a teacher may find that children do not automatically take to the approach. Their comments may seem off-base, too general, or too tentative. Some students need encouragement, support, and repeated opportunities before the conferences seem worthwhile. In a recent study, Hittleman had a great deal of success establishing more effective Peer Conferences, using a combination of peer and teacher modeling (Hittleman, 1983). Third, many of the conferences that were described are based on two tenets: (1) students should have the opportunity to write for longer than 30 minutes twice a week (they should be given enough time to write extended stories and reports of their own choosing); and (2) writing experiences contribute to reading. Unless these two tenets are observed in a classroom, some of the conferences described could not take place.

REFERENCES

Atwell, N. 1987. *In the middle: Writing, reading and learning with adolescents.* Portsmouth, NH: Boynton/Cook-Heinemann. Describes her use of Peer Conferencing and Author's Chair in the middle grades.

Blackburn, E. 1982. The rhythm of writing development. In T. Newkirk and N. Atwell (Eds.), *Understanding writing.* Chelmsford, MA: Northeast Regional Exchange. Describes several of her experiences in the first grade as she observed her students writing and interacted with them.

Boutwell, M. 1983. Reading and writing: A reciprocal agreement. *Language Arts* 60: 6, 723–730. Describes the features of her classroom that supported a reciprocal agreement between reading and writing, including the conferences that were initiated.

Brent, R., and P. Anderson. 1993. Developing children's classroom listening strategies. *The Reading Teacher* 47: 122–126. This article identifies important listening strategies and components of lessons for helping children to acquire these strategies.

Calkins, L. M. 1983. *Lessons from a child.* Portsmouth, NH: Heinemann. In this story of one child's growth in writing, Calkins illustrates what influences and classroom procedures are woven into the child's development.

———. 1986. *The art of teaching writing.* Portsmouth, NH: Heinemann. Describes the rationale and procedures for Peer Conferencing.

Flint, A. S., K. van Sluys, Y. G. Lo, and D. East. 2001. I never thought a first grader could teach me how to write: Examining beliefs and positions in author's circles. In *51st yearbook of the National Reading Conference* 51: 164–175. Chicago: National Reading Conference. Explores the use of Author's Chair in a first-grade setting.

Graves, D. 1983. *Writing: Teachers and children at work.* Exeter, NH: Heinemann. Provides a full description of how teachers might teach writing in conjunction with the use of a conference approach. Graves provides extensive guidelines for how teachers might confer with students, which can be applied to Peer Conferencing.

Graves, D., and J. Hansen. 1983. The author's chair. *Language Arts* 60:176–183. Describes the nature and benefits derived in a first-grade classroom that initiated the use of Author's Chair.

Hansen, J. 1983. Authors respond to authors. *Language Arts* 60: 970–976. Describes several different types of conferences with examples from her observations in classrooms.

———. 1987. *When writers read.* Portsmouth, NH: Heinemann. Describes Author's Chair in the context of many other strategies that support children's reading and writing.

———. 2001. *When writers read* (2d ed.). Portsmouth, NH: Heinemann. Updated discussion of classrooms engaged in reading–writing experiences using many of the elements of Author's Chair.

Harste, J. C., K. G. Short, and C. B. Burke. 1989. *Creating classrooms for authors.* Portsmouth, NH: Heinemann. Presents several activities and suggestions for implementing sharing by authors and readers.

Harwayne, S. 2001. *Writing through childhood: Rethinking process and product.* Portsmouth, NH: Heinemann. Explores Author's Chair and many of the elements that support its use.

Hawkins, T. 1977. *Group inquiry techniques for teaching writing.* Urbana, IL: ERIC Clearinghouse on Reading and Communication Skills/NCTE. Describes several procedures for organizing and developing discussion of writing by peers.

Healy, M. K. 1980. *Using student writing response groups in the classroom.* Berkeley: University of California, Bay Area Writing Project. Describes the use of peer response groups in classrooms.

Hittleman, C. G. 1983. *Peer conference groups and teacher written comments as influences on revisions during the composing processes of fourth grade students.* Unpublished doctoral diss., Hofstra University. Presents a thorough study of the use of Peer Conferencing in the fourth grade.

Karelitz, E. B. 1993. *The Author's Chair and beyond: Language and literacy in a primary classroom.* Portsmouth, NH: Heinemann. Describes several reading and writing strategies, including Author's Chair.

Leal, D. J. 1993. The power of literary peer-group discussions: How children collaboratively negotiate meaning. *The Reading Teacher* 47: 114–120. Analyzes examples of children's discussions and shows the kinds of meanings children engage with and derive from them.

McAuliffe, S. 1993. Toward understanding one another: Second graders' use of gendered language and story styles. *The Reading Teacher* 47: 302–310. Describes a study of children's gender use in their stories and how this changed through peer response in a Whole-Language classroom.

Newell, G. E., and R. K. Durst (Eds.). 1993. *Exploring texts: The role of discussion and writing in the teaching and learning of literature.* Norwood, MA: Christopher-Gordon Publishers. Collection of articles, many of which discuss Author's Chair-type techniques.

Purves, A. C., L. Papa, and S. Jordan (Eds.). 1994. *Encyclopedia of English studies and language arts.* New York: National Council of Teachers of English. This encyclopedia has more than 800 annotated entries/topics that succinctly address this topic and related areas.

Purves, A. C., T. Rogers, and A. Soter. 1990. *How porcupines make love II: Teaching a response-centered literature curriculum.* New York: Longman. Discusses many ways of helping students respond to literature, including Author's Chair-type techniques. Focuses on older students.

Tierney, R. J., M. Leys, and T. Rogers. 1985. Composition, comprehension, and collaboration: An analysis of two classrooms. In T. Raphael and R. Reynolds (Eds.), *Contexts of literacy.* New York: Random House. Describes the classroom parameters for a conferencing approach for both reading and writing and the comments and responses of some fourth-grade students.

Villaume, S. K., and E. G. Brabham. 2001. Conversations among writers in author circles. *The Reading Teacher* 54: 494–497. Explores conversations with students involved in Author's Chair.

Dialogue Journals

Purpose

Dialogue Journals, as originally described by Staton (1980), are intended to provide students an opportunity to share privately in writing their reactions, questions, and concerns about school experiences (and sometimes personal matters) with the teacher without any threat of reprisal or evaluation. It affords the teacher an opportunity to learn what each individual child is doing and thinking, and then to offer counsel.

Rationale

Although the term *Dialogue Journal* has a rather recent history, the use of journals per se has a long history dating back to when individuals began using writing as a means of record keeping and of reflecting upon their lot in life. In school situations, journal writing has often assumed a life of its own as English teachers, and sometimes science teachers, have introduced it into the daily or weekly life of their students. Often journals were used to encourage diarylike entries of what took place in the way of progress on a project; sometimes they were used to give students the opportunity to respond freely to what took place at school or home, or to respond to a book or some other form of literature. The negative side of journals is that they can become tedious or, with some students, never take hold. Some students don't enjoy the experience and find the task boring; some may be very withdrawn or are not sufficiently introspective to talk "to themselves." Also, if journal writing becomes a preoccupation, then both the students and the teacher will likely find the experience a chore. On the positive side, and what accounts for the widespread advocacy of journal writing, are testimonies of the benefits. As Kirby and Liner (1981) suggest:

> Simply stated, the journal is the most consistently effective tool for establishing fluency that I have found. True believers swear that the journal works on some mystical principle

> because some nonfluent, nontalking, and apparent nonthinking students have blossomed so dramatically through journal writing. (p. 45)

Other testimonies attest to further advantages: (1) the opportunity that journal writing provides for more open responses to classroom assignments; (2) the vehicle that it provides for teacher feedback, counseling, and response; and (3) the chance that it gives for dealing with each student individually.

The notion of Dialogue Journals is a partial refinement of journal writing. The major characteristic that distinguishes Dialogue Journals from other forms is the importance given to communications between the student and the teacher. Dialogue Journals are more like a daily letter or memo to the teacher. While the teacher might not respond to every entry, the intent of Dialogue Journals is to have students write to the teacher and to have the teacher write a genuine response to the student. Often the Dialogue Journal is quite open-ended and the student includes letters on all sorts of matters, from diets to schoolwork to sporting events. Sometimes students have journals that are intended to record reactions and concerns to specific experiences, such as reading and writing. If the latter is the case, the teacher might ask the students to include, either occasionally or on a regular basis, specific types of information in their journals. In all of these situations, the child writes and the teacher responds. The advantage is that the teacher and student can share, on a one-to-one basis, matters for which most classroom situations do not allow sufficient time in the course of the day.

Intended Audience

Dialogue Journals can be used with students at any age level.

Description of the Procedures

To illustrate the procedures for Dialogue Journals, the following examples (Figures 9.1 and 9.2) are taken from a third-grade classroom in which the teacher provided time every day for students to write entries in two journals: a reading journal and a writing journal. The original entries have been rewritten, and the names of the student and teacher changed to ensure their privacy. Otherwise they are reproduced exactly.

The four journal entries represent some of the different types of comments that students might be prompted to make in their journals. They include examples of comments by the students about what they have been reading and writing and their experiences in doing so. They include reflections about peer relationships, and responses to and inquiries directed at the teacher.

The teacher's entry represents a rich assortment of reflections in response to what the student has shared and an attempt to extend the child's thinking. One of the comments offered by the teacher discusses how the student's experiences were similar to her own (I also picture in my head as I read); at the same time the teacher's comments reflect an attempt to extend these ideas (it is a sign of good writing) and offer some advice (tell the author). It is interesting to note the teacher's written comments following one student's lengthy discussion of a classmate with whom there is some enmity. The teacher does not evaluate the student's comments as either right or wrong. The student's feelings are accepted as legitimate,

OCT. 20, Sailing
I could really see and hear and feel the waves That really was neat. I like the part when Billy and the kids race and the boat tips over! The picturs were neat to! They did a excellent job.

Sara,
I sometimes can see, hear, and feel things that I am reading about too. It's usually when the writing is good, when the author makes every thing come alive!
You describe their writing and congratulate them as one author would to another. I think that's neat!
Thank You,
L. Rietveld

April 13
Today I am writing on Indian Art with Brenda. We done a lot so far but we are kind of having trouble because we have to interview Mrs. Johnson and she wasn't there when we went. Any way we'll try again.

Sara,
I must congratulate you on your Carnival story. You included so many interesting details!
As for interviewing Mrs. Johnson perhaps you could put a note asking for an appointment in her box. Have you and Brenda written down the questions you wish to ask her? Would you like to borrow a tape recorder?
L. Rietveld.

FIGURE 9.1 Examples of Dialogue Journal Entries

Dear Miss Rietveld
Do We have to Do It. !!!!

Feb, 10
Today I will write about Kara. SHE A JERK!!! She writes on my desk and she wrote me a note and asked me If I liked Sam. I didn't think she is funny. Kara Stinks!!!
The End

Angie,
You sound very angry. Maybe, you, Kara, and I could meet to discuss this problem. Or maybe you could show her this part of your journal?
What do you think you should do?
L. Rietveld

FIGURE 9.2 Examples of Dialogue Journal Entries

and the teacher offers a couple of suggestions as to how she might deal with her feelings. What is important to note is the teacher's respect for the privacy of the journal as well as the nonjudgmental and nonprescriptive nature of the teacher's reaction. Decisions to be made are left up to the student.

Getting Started. Nancy Atwell has discussed beginning Dialogue Journals in her eighth grade classroom (Atwell, 1984). She described how she initiated the journals:

> This folder is a place for you and me to talk about books, reading, authors, and writing. You're to write letters to me, and I'll write letters back to you.
>
> In your letters to me, talk with me about what you've read. Tell me what you thought and felt and why. Tell me what you liked and didn't like and why. Tell me what these books meant to you and said to you. Ask me questions or for help, and write back to me about my ideas, feelings, and questions.

While there are other ways to begin Dialogue Journals and other types of journals, Atwell's comments describe for students the purpose of the journal and give a very open-ended sense of what might be included. Once initiated, it is important that the journal writing not be shortchanged in terms of time allocation. Unless uninterrupted time is put aside during the school day for everybody to write in his/her journal, the possibility of obtaining meaningful journal entries diminishes.

Responding to Journals. In many ways suggestions for responding to journals should be rather obvious, yet there are guidelines to keep in mind when responding. Apart from recommending that journal responses by a teacher be sincere, thoughtful, and regular, the following represents a compilation of commonsense suggestions based upon Kirby and Liner (1981).

1. Protect the privacy of the journal. Don't ever read aloud journal entries or share journal entries without the permission of the author.

2. Be an active reader and sincere respondent. Write general remarks, share your ideas, make specific suggestions, and react rather than correct.

3. Be honest with students. In those situations where students tell you more than what you want to know or include language you would not care to read, tell them to cut it out.

4. Look for something good. Don't give up on students; rather, encourage them and avoid sarcasm.

5. Make journal writing special and interesting. Don't let it become a chore; respond eagerly and with interest. Take a break from journal writing if necessary.

6. Be aware that you cannot be expected to respond every day to each student's journal entry. Don't make promises to the students about the frequency with which you might respond.

Staton (1987) also provides some guidelines for the content of teachers' responses:

- acknowledge the students' topics and encourage them to elaborate on their interests;
- affirm and support each student: the private dialogue is a great place for compliments about appearance, behavior;
- add new, relevant information about topics, so that *your* response is interesting to read;
- don't write (much) more than the students do;
- avoid glib comments like "good idea" or "very interesting." These cut off rather than promote dialogue.
- ask very few questions. The goal is to get students to ask *you* questions, and make your writing so interesting that they will want to know more (p. 62). [italics original]

Hallberg (1987) points out some possible ethical problems in teachers' responses to students' journals. Although he is discussing journals in the college classroom, his concerns may be equally important for younger students. Further, while he discusses intensive journal writing, the issues he raises may be of concern in Dialogue Journals as well:

> There are some ethical problems involved in using such intensely personal and emotional materials in a college classroom. There may be some psychological hazards as well. Does the assignment of "Intensive Journal" work invade a student's right to privacy? And does the emotional intensity of the work involve classroom instructors in activities best left in the hands of trained psychotherapists? (p. 296)

Finally, Lewis (1993) describes a moment in her own teaching in which she failed to recognize the legitimacy of a child's interpretation of a story; her own economic class values prevented her from seeing that the child had found a way of understanding a text that was based on his experience and the text itself but which was different from the "standard" reading of the text. Although this moment occurred during a "think-aloud" interaction between teacher and student, the point may be well taken for Dialogue Journals. The advantage of the Dialogue Journal is that it provides individualized contact between teacher and student. The disadvantage may be the same—if the teacher cannot engage with the multiple possibilities for reading that result from ethnic and economic diversity in the classroom.

Cautions and Comments

The description of journal writing that has been offered is quite condensed. The present discussion is restricted to Dialogue Journals that were used by elementary students for purposes of responding to reading and writing. Journals can easily be used in other ways—with projects, such as a group investigation of a problem or topic, with field trips, or with any special activity. For example, Gordon and Macinnis (1993) report on the use of Dialogue Journals in mathematics; the journals helped teachers to understand children's mathematical misconceptions and to address their instruction accordingly. Beach and Anson (1993) describe a variation of the Dialogue Journal in which peers respond to each other and Funkhouser (1991), as well as Finnegan (1997), reports on having parents respond in a Dialogue Journal to their children's writing. Taylor (1991) used a variation of the Dialogue Journal, "literature letters," to have children respond to each other about their own writing—as a form of peer feedback. There are no age restrictions on the use of journals; some educators have even successfully used them with preschoolers. For example, Elliott, Nowasad, and Samuels (1981) have reported involving parents in helping their preschoolers with the transcription. There are also numerous examples of its use with indigenous populations as well as with students from a range of backgrounds and special abilities (e.g., Cathro, 1987; Kirk, 1989; Mlynarczyk, 1998; Mudgett-DeCaro and Hurwitz, 1997).

Finally, Bruce (1991) points out that one function of computers is as a form of communication. With networks between classroom computers, across schools, and via electronic mail across the world, the Dialogue Journal can begin to provide students with a chance to enter written book discussions with other readers from all over.

What is the value of journal writing? There have been very few traditional research studies in which the worth of any type of journal writing has been explored. In terms of evidence of their worth, most of the support comes in statements from educators who have been involved in the experience. Staton (1980), for example, has commented on the value that was derived from using Dialogue Journals by a teacher, Leslee Reed:

> . . . the openness of the journal as a forum for personal problems as well as for academic ones captures the natural function of language as intentional communication about what matters most to the person. An attitude of trust and interest in everything the writer says characterizes Leslee Reed's attitude toward her students and what they write in their journals. "I learn something new everyday about each one of them. They are fascinating and exciting to get to know." It is no wonder that their willingness to express their own ideas, feelings and experiences in written language improves and creates in them a confidence about writing in general that too few people their age or any age enjoy." (p. 518)

Or, as Nancy Atwell (1984) commented when describing how Dialogue Journals and other factors worked together in her classrooms, "It's a dining room table with seventy chairs around it" (p. 251).

REFERENCES

Atwell, N. 1984. Writing and reading literature from the inside out. *Language Arts* 61: 240–252. Describes the use of Dialogue Journals for reading and writing in an eighth grade classroom.

Beach, R., and C. M. Anson. 1993. Using peer-dialogue journals to foster response. In G. E. Newell and R. K. Durst (Eds.), *Exploring Texts: The role of discussion and writing in the teaching and learning of literature.* Norwood, MA: Christopher-Gordon Publishers.

Bruce, B. 1991. Roles for computers in teaching the English language arts. In J. Flood, J. M. Jensen, D. Lapp, and J. R. Squire (Eds.), *Handbook of research on teaching the English language arts.* New York: Macmillan. Describes roles for the computer in the language arts classroom and related research.

Cathro, L. 1987. Dialogue Journals. *Canadian Journal of Native Education* 14(2): 54–59. Discusses the use with indigeneous populations.

Davis, F. A. 1984. "Why you call me Emigrant?": Dialogue Journal writing with migrant youth. *Childhood Education* (November–December). Describes the use of Dialogue Journals in a migrant education project by New Jersey teachers.

Elliott, S., J. Nowasad, and P. Samuels. 1981. "Me at School," "Me at Home": Using journals with preschoolers. *Language Arts* 58: 688–691. Describes the use of journal writing in a preschool where the teacher and the parents were involved in transcribing entries.

Finnegan, E. M. 1997. Teaching reading. *The Reading Teacher* 51 (3): 268–272. Describes the use of Dialogue Journals as a way of supporting parents.

Funkhouser, L. L. 1991. Gifted students respond to their reading. In J. T. Feeley, D. S. Strickland, and S. B. Wepner (Eds.), *Process reading and writing: A literature-based approach.* New York: Teachers College Press. Describes using Dialogue Journals (between teacher and child and between parent and child) in a classroom for gifted students.

Gordon, J. C., and D. Macinnis. 1993. Using journals as a window on students' thinking in mathematics. *Language Arts* 70: 37–43. Dialogue Journals can help teachers understand how their students are thinking about mathematical concepts.

Hallberg, F. 1987. Journal writing as person making. In T. Fulwiler (Ed.), *The journal book.* Portsmouth, NH: Heinemann. Discusses personal journals in the classroom and ways of keeping these from becoming problematic experiences for students.

Harste, J. C., K. G. Short, and C. Burke. 1988. *Creating classrooms for authors.* Portsmouth, NH: Heinemann. Provides suggestions for using Dialogue Journals as well as related activities such as written conversations.

Kirby, D., and T. Liner. 1981. *Inside out.* New York: Boynton-Cook. Presents an overview, guidelines, and suggestions for journal writing.

———. 1988. *Inside out* (2d ed.). Portsmouth, NH: Heinemann. Updates the previous edition with a fuller discussion of practices and their theoretical underpinnings.

Kirk, B. V. 1989. Dialogue Journals: A technique to strengthen ethnic pride and achievement. *Journal of American Indian Education* 29(1): 19–25. Explores Dialogue Journals use with indigenous populations.

Kreeft, J. 1984. Dialogue writing—Bridge from talk to essay writing. *Language Arts* 61: 141–150. Addresses the question of how Dialogue Journals help students' writing skills, with examples to highlight teacher strategies and student growth.

Lewis, C. 1993. "Give people a chance": Acknowledging social differences in reading. *Language Arts* 70: 454–461. Analysis of a think-aloud in which a child offered a reading of a text that was significantly different from that of the teacher.

Markman, M. 1985. *Teacher-student dialogue writing in a college composition course: Effects upon writing performance and attitude.* Unpublished doctoral diss., University of Missouri. Researches the effectiveness of Dialogue Journals with college students.

Mlynarczyk, R. W. 1998. *Conversations of the mind: The uses of journal writing for second-language learners.* Mahwah, NJ: Erlbaum. Explores use of Dialogue Journals with second language learners.

Mudgett-DeCaro, P., and T. A. Hurwitz. 1997. Classroom dialogues and deaf identities. *Annals of the Deaf* 142(2): 96–99. Explores Dialogue Journals use with hearing impaired students.

Newkirk, T. 1982. Young writers as critical readers. In T. Newkirk and N. Atwell (Eds.), *Understanding writing.* Chelmsford, MA: Northeast Regional Exchange. Describes the notion of bringing students inside written language as critics, enthusiasts, and participants.

Peyton, J. K., and J. Staton (Eds.). 1996. *Writing our lives: Reflections on dialogue journal writing with adults learning English.* McHenry, IL: Delta Systems, Inc.

Purves, A. C., L. Papa, and S. Jordan (Eds.). 1994. *Encyclopedia of English studies and language arts.* New York: National Council of Teachers of English. This encyclopedia has more than 800 annotated entries/topics that succinctly address this topic and related areas.

Reid, L. 1997. Exploring the ways that dialogue journaling affects how and why students write: An action research project. *Teaching and Change* 5(1): 50–57. Explores Dialogue Journals use in conjunction with writing development.

Reyes, M. de la L. 1991. A process approach to literacy using dialogue journals and literature logs with second language learners. *Research in the Teaching of English* 25(3): 291–313. Explores the use of Dialogue Journals in conjunction with other literature based activities.

Staton, J. 1980. Writing and counseling: Using a Dialogue Journal. *Language Arts* 57: 514–518. Describes the use of Dialogue Journals and their value.

———. 1984a. Thinking together: The role of language interaction in children's reasoning. In C. Thaiss and C. Suhor (Eds.), *Speaking and writing, K–12.* Describes the rationale, purposes, and benefits of Dialogue Journals.

———. 1984b. *The interactional acquisition of practical reasoning in early adolescence: A study of Dialogue Journals.* Unpublished doctoral diss., University of California at Los Angeles. A research study of the use of Dialogue Journals.

———. 1987. The power of responding in Dialogue Journals. In T. Fulwiler (Ed.), *The journal book.* Portsmouth, NH: Heinemann. Describes several aspects of Dialogue Journals (as reading events, communication, and place for response) and provides guidelines for their implementation.

Staton, J., J. Kreeft, and L. Gutstein (Eds.). *Dialogue.* Washington, DC: Center for Applied Linguistics. *Dialogue* is a newsletter about the uses, benefits, and theory of Dialogue Journals. It is available through the Center for Applied Linguistics, 3520 Prospect Street, N.W., Washington, DC 20007.

Staton, J., R. Shuy, and J. Kreeft. 1982. *Analysis of Dialogue Journal writing as a communicative event.* Washington, DC: National Institute of Education Grant No. G-80-0122, Center for Applied Linguistics. A two-volume description of the use of Dialogue Journals, including purposes, structure, and benefits.

Staton, J., R. W. Shuy, J. K. Peyton, and L. Reed. 1988. *Dialogue Journal communication: Classroom, linguistic, social and cognitive views.* Norwood, NJ: Ablex. Represents the original extended study of Dialogue Journals.

Talburt, S. 1995. Dialogue journals in adult ESL: Exploring and creating possibilities. *College ESL* 5(2): 67–82. Explores use of Dialogue Journals with adults learning English.

Taylor, D. F. 1991. Literature letters and narrative response: Seventh and eighth graders write about their reading. In J. T. Feeley, D. S. Strickland, and. S. B. Wepner (Eds.), *Process reading and writing: A literature-based approach.* New York: Teachers College Press. Describes using a Dialogue Journal approach in which students write about each other's writings.

Thomas, S., and P. Oldfather. 1995. Enhancing student and teacher engagement in literacy learning: A shared inquiry approach. *The Reading Teacher* 49(3): 192–202. Details a method of shared inquiry with Dialogue Journals.

Wollman-Bonilla, J. E., and B. Werchadlo. 1995. Literature response journals in a first-grade classroom. *Language Arts* 72: 562–570. Describes the use of response journals to express literature responses.

Style Study

Purpose

Style Study has two purposes: (1) to engage students in critically reading their own writing and the writings of others (classmates as well as professional authors); and (2) to enhance students' appreciation of stylistic options, including their sensitivity to the styles of different authors.

Rationale

Caplan developed Style Study in conjunction with her teaching experiences in high school literature classrooms. All of the activities involved in Style Study revolve around using student writing as a springboard for developing an appreciation of rhetorical options. Students write paragraphs and essays on selected themes, share these texts with each other, and compare their renditions with those developed by professional authors. One of the goals is to have the students consider what makes different paragraphs effective. As Caplan (1987) states, "Students learn new composing strategies from each other as they notice how different writers tackle the same idea with varying approaches" (pp. 10–11). Caplan suggests that such comparisons are not intended to establish that the novelist's version is better than the students' or that the students should be writing like the novelist, but to help the students notice alternatives while preparing them for an author's style. It is Caplan's claim that when students parallel and later evaluate distinguishing styles of major authors, not only may they come to appreciate the talent and craft of the writer—develop "a feel" for a writer that enables them to appreciate how style contributes to the story—but they may also learn new rhetorical devices for delivering ideas. It should be noted that Caplan's activities extend beyond writing that is so directly tied to reading; many of her activities center upon having students pull together their own ideas in response to a story.

Intended Audience

Although Caplan's activities were developed for use with high school students in literature classrooms, they can be adapted for use with students at the elementary level.

Description of the Procedures

Style Study activities tend to fall into the following categories: (1) "showing" and "telling" writing activities; (2) parallel writing; and (3) extended writing activities using reading selections as resources.

1. Showing and Telling Writing Exercises. Showing writing involves having students elaborate on a general statement using specifics. The goal of showing writing is to challenge a writer to convince a reader of an idea without directly "telling" the idea. To this end, Caplan suggests steering students away from topic sentences toward developing an idea in much the same way that one pursues the game of charades: that is, dramatizing an idea without giving the whole thing away. In order to demonstrate what a showing paragraph is, she begins by presenting students with the following two paragraphs and discussing their differences.

> ***A Telling Paragraph***
> Each morning I ride the bus to school. I wait along with the other people who ride my bus. Sometimes the bus is late and we get angry. Some guys start fights and stuff just to have something to do. I'm always glad when the bus finally comes.
>
> ***A Showing Paragraph***
> A bus arrived. It discharged its passengers, closed its doors with a hiss and disappeared over the crest of a hill. Not one of the people waiting at the bus stop had attempted to board. One

> woman wore a sweater that was too small, a long skirt, white sweater socks, and house slippers. One man was in his undershirt. Another man wore shoes with the toes cut out, a soiled blue serge jacket and brown pants. There was something wrong with these people. They made faces. A mouth smiled at nothing and unsmiled, smiled and unsmiled. A head shook in vehement denial. Most of them carried brown paper bags rolled tight against their stomachs.
>
> (E. L. Doctorow, *The Book of Daniel,* New York: Random House, Signet Edition, 1971, 15)

Then she presents them a thesis statement for which they are expected to develop a paragraph. Examples of these statements are presented in Figure 9.3.

What is crucial is that once these writings are developed, they are shared and critiqued. Caplan emphasizes that it is important to have students go beyond saying, "It was really good!" to "What was good about it? How did he show . . . ?"

These exercises are often tied directly to reading selections. After the first chapter of *Call of the Wild,* for example, students might be assigned the sentence "Buck is an intelligent dog" or, after reading the first two chapters of Hemingway's *The Sun Also Rises,* students might be assigned the sentence "Jake disapproves of Robert Cohn." The students' task is to prove the claims using evidence from the chapters. Sometimes the writing activity may precede the reading of a selection. For example, prior to reading a segment from *The Great*

FIGURE 9.3 Thesis Statements

The room was vacant.
She has a fantastic personality.
The party was great.
I was very embarrassed.
My room is a mess.
The concert was disappointing.
My mother bugs me.
The math test was a killer.
The food at the party was incredible.
Those girls are snobs.
The jocks think they're cool.
He looked guilty.
He eats like a pig.
The weather made me nostalgic.
The relationship changed.
The drive in the car was uncomfortable.
School is boring.
Teenagers should not have curfews.
My friend was steaming mad.
This school has great school spirit.
The pizza tasted good.
The loss was devastating.
The living room was a warm, inviting place.
She acted older than her age.
People make or break a party.
Advertisements can be misleading.
The F grade should be abolished.
Camping is a rewarding experience.
My parents are great people.
Reality set in.
She changed.
The weather was perfect.
A student's life is hard.
The streets were crowded.
The puppy was a terror.
He is artistic.
She is creative.
The afternoon was a romantic one.
The principal was effective.
The game was a close one.
The book was intriguing.
Haste makes waste.
They lived happily ever after.
The climb was exhausting.
The roller coaster was the scariest ride at the fair.
The crossword puzzle was tricky.
The new student was lonely.
The fire drill went miserably.
The substitute teacher was strange.
The speaker got everyone's attention.

Gatsby, students might develop paragraphs from the statement "The living room was romantic." As students share and compare their paragraphs, they consider features of style and various rhetorical options. Then, as they move on to reading the Fitzgerald excerpt from *The Great Gatsby,* they have the opportunity to discuss this work in the same spirit as they discussed each other's. At the same time that they can look back to appreciate their style, they become attuned to the subtleties of Fitzgerald.

A final variation of these writing exercises involves the reverse—moving from showing paragraphs to telling sentences. For example, students might be given the task of generating a statement that provides meaning to or explains the significance of all the collected facts for a paragraph from Mark Twain.

> The house was a double log one, with a spacious floor (roofed in) connecting it with the kitchen. In the summer the table was set in the middle of that shady and breezy floor, and the sumptuous meals—well, it makes me cry to think of them. Fried chicken, roast pig; wild and tame turkeys, ducks and geese; venison just killed; squirrels, rabbits, pheasants, partridges, prairie chickens; biscuits, hot batter cakes, hot buckwheat cakes, hot "wheat bread," hot rolls, hot corn pone; fresh corn boiled on the ear, succotash, butter-beans, string-beans, tomatoes, peas, Irish potatoes, sweet potatoes, buttermilk, sweet milk, "clabber"; watermelons, muskmelons, cantaloupes—all fresh from the garden; apple pie, peach pie, pumpkin pie, apple dumplings, peach cobbler—I can't remember the rest. The way that the things were cooked was perhaps the main splendor—particularly a certain few of the dishes. For instance the corn bread, the hot biscuits and wheat bread and the fried chicken.
>
> (Samuel Langhorne Clemens, *The Autobiography of Mark Twain,* ed. by Charles Neider, 1959. New York: Harper and Row Publishers, Inc., 4)

2. Parallel Writing. Caplan also advocates having students try to parallel the writer's style. As she states, "If possible, I want them to match his structures part-of-speech for part-of-speech, supplying their own fictional scenes for narration." She suggests beginning with a simple sentence, "The men paraded by the stand," which might become "The leaves fluttered by the monument," then graduating to inventing parallel versions of several paragraphs. After they have practiced paralleling a number of author's passages, she then suggests going one step further and experimenting with versions of simple stories (e.g., Cinderella) in the style of Hemingway, Fitzgerald, or others.

For example, Caplan's students took simple stories and mimicked Fitzgerald and Salinger.

Peter Peter Pumpkin-Eater
by Jennifer

Peter Peter Pumpkin-Eater
Had a wife and couldn't keep her
He put her in a pumpkin shell
And there he kept her very well.

The Great Pumpkin-Eater: F. Scott Fitzgerald

About halfway between Peter's cottage and his barn was a mammoth pumpkin. This was where Peter kept his wife—in a giant hollowed out squash, with a door and a window carved out of the thick orange skin, and a chimney where the prickly stem should be, a thin wisp of smoke always trailing its way to the crystal-blue sky.

The fact that he kept his wife in a pumpkin was known by virtually everyone. His neighbors resented having such an eyesore on their street, ruining the appearance of the other glittering, fashionable houses; they were shocked that his wife actually resided there, amid slimy walls and large seeds that peppered the squishy floor.

Though I was curious to see the girl who allowed her husband to keep her in a pumpkin I had no desire to actually set foot in an overgrown vegetable—but I did. I met Peter on his way home from work one day, and when we stopped by his gate he stared hard at me and, taking hold of my elbow, literally forced me up the graveled path.

"Come along," he insisted. "I want you to meet my wife."

I followed him to the door of the pumpkin, aware that a pair of eyes watched our approach through filmy white curtains.

It was then that I realized that I could never go inside that pumpkin. I mumbled an apology and, wheeling around, I hurried back out onto the street, thoughts massing like turbulent clouds in my head.

I went to the park and sat there brooding on Peter's odd habit of keeping his wife in the shell of a pumpkin. Peter believed in it, though, and if his wife was content to reside in a squash, then maybe one morning we would come to understand them.

The Wife in the Pumpkin: J. D. Salinger

I had nothing to do in my damn crummy hotel room except think. I remembered a story a friend had told me once. Well, not really a friend. I had only met him once, at a party. I remember. Anyway, this guy told me about some bastard named Peter. Peter Pumpkin-Eater is what all his neighbors called him. They really did. That killed me. At first, I thought it meant he actually ate pumpkins. Raw or something. But damn if he doesn't keep his wife in this great big hollowed out one. A pumpkin, I mean. I wonder how they got all that crap out of it. You know, the damn pumpkin guts and all. And what did they do with all the seeds? Did they just throw them away or did they plant them? Maybe there's a farm full of overgrown pumpkins somewhere.

Well, old Peter, he keeps his wife in there because he can't pay the lousy mortgage on his house. So he doesn't own the house anymore and they've got nowhere to stay. Then old Peter, he comes up with this swell idea of living in a squash. I guess his wife didn't mind. She could have left the bastard. I wonder what her name was. I forgot to ask. Anyway, my friend says that Peter keeps her very well. He must or else he has a very dumb wife. I don't know why he got the name "Pumpkin-Eater" though. I would have called him old "Peter Peter Pumpkin-Dweller" or something. But that damn story kills me every time I think of it anyway.

3. Extended Writing Activities Using Reading Selections as Resources. Caplan's suggestions for activities extends beyond preparing students to deal with an author's stylistic idiosyncrasies to having students pull together their own ideas. For example, when students have read *The Great Gatsby,* Caplan suggests that they might be asked to compare Gatsby's quest for Daisy Buchanan with the quest for the American Dream. In conjunction with being introduced to investigative reporting (including the use of field notes, interviews, and other research techniques), students were asked to examine certain books (e.g., Tom Wolfe's *The Right Stuff*) and articles for purposes of seeing examples of reporting style.

In addition to these activities, Caplan has developed procedures for introducing students to research reports, compare-contrast papers, and persuasive essays. These are reported at length in *Writers in Training* (1984).

Cautions and Comments

Caplan's suggestions for developing writing in conjunction with teaching literature distinguish themselves from other strategies in that her approach is quite structured. In particular, for most activities, all of the students are expected to respond to the same topic in a similar fashion either showing, telling, or developing parallel versions. Furthermore, most of the suggestions tie writing to reading in a rather deliberate fashion. Students are expected to fine-tune their ability to read their own texts evaluatively at the same time that a great deal of emphasis is placed upon fine-tuning their appreciation of stylistic alternatives.

Although detailed research studies of this approach are lacking, Caplan and Keech (1980) and Caplan (1987) have pursued analyses of students' writings, and have interviewed graduates in hopes of attaining an understanding of the strengths and weaknesses of the approach. The outcomes of their analyses of these data support Caplan's claims at the same time that they highlight some of the potential limitations. For example, one of the students who had been involved in the program made the following comment: "It's a way of growing, expanding oneself through voicing one's thoughts (writing) and listening to others' thoughts (reading)" (Caplan, 1987, 29). In contrast, other students were reported to be less favorably inclined. As Caplan (1987) commented:

> When I asked my students what they considered to be the value of parallel writing, one student commented: "It gives you a little confidence to think, hey man, I can do that; I can sound like F. Scott Fitzgerald." Another student confessed that she really didn't like doing the writing but that "It worked out after awhile. You just kept working at it, and your writing sounded neat—definitely neat. It didn't sound as though a high school student had written it." (p. 29)

In accordance with this student's comments, several questions remain regarding the effects of the activities: Do students feel empowered or overwhelmed by the styles of others? Do they lose their own voice as they parallel the style of others? In what ways do comparisons of their responses with those of professional authors fuel their own stylistic development?

Caplan is the first to admit to the possible limitations of her approach. As she stated:

> For some students I expect the practices related to Style Study might have been burdensome, and the question remains whether or not some students might have felt deflated—even disempowered—by having to do the parallel writings and mimickings. (1987, 31)

What she is quite adamant about is that examining stylistic alternatives should be used with the view of celebrating achievements. She endorses neither the lock-step use of these activities nor a predetermined set of stylistic preferences.

REFERENCES

Alexander, P. A., and T. L Jetton. 2000. Structural aspects of constructing meaning from text. In M. L. Kamil, P. B. Mosenthal, P. D. Pearson, and R. Barr (Eds.), *Handbook of reading research,* Vol. III. Mahwah, NJ: Erlbaum, 311–336. Explores issues around the impact of genre on reading.

Caplan, R. 1984. *Writers in training: A guide to developing a composition program for language arts teachers.* Palo Alto, CA: Dale Seymour. A comprehensive explanation of the activities, rationale, and outcomes of Style Study.

———. 1987. Style Study. *The Quarterly* 9: 10–14, 29–30, 31. Describes those aspects of Style Study involving the integration of reading and writing with reflections on interview comments of poor students.

Caplan, R., and P. Keech. 1980. *Show-writing: A training program to help students be specific.* Berkeley, CA: Bay Area Writing Project. Discusses the use of showing writing and earlier thinking of Caplan. Includes analyses of the effects upon student writing.

Farnan, N., and K. Dahl. 2000. Children's writing: Research and practice. In J. Flood, J. Jensen, D. Lapp, and J. R. Squire (Eds.), *Handbook of research on teaching the language arts,* Vol. II. New York: Macmillan, 993–1007. Explores the role of writing in terms of preparing students to read and write different genre.

Goldman, S. R., and J. A. Rakestraw, Jr. 2000. Learning from text: A multidimensional and developmental perspective. In M. L. Kamil, P. B. Mosenthal, P. D. Pearson, and R. Barr (Eds.), *Handbook of reading research,* Vol. III. Mahwah, NJ: Erlbaum, 285–310. Explores a range of issues concerning text genre, including hypertext.

Johns, A. (Ed.). 2002. *Genre in the classroom: Multiple perspectives.* Mahwah, NJ: Erlbaum. Explores the genre approach especially as developed in Australia with key chapters by Michael Halliday and others.

Killgallon, D. 1997. *Sentence composing for middle school: A worktext on sentence variety and maturity.* Portsmouth, NH: Heinemann. Offers exercises to engage students in imitating the styles of professional authors.

Myers, M. 2000. Issues in teacher preparation and staff development in English Language Arts. In J. Flood, J. Jensen, D. Lapp, and J. R. Squire (Eds.), *Handbook of research on teaching the language arts,* Vol. II. New York: Macmillan, 459–477. Explores teacher-based research of instructional possibilities, including the work of Barthomolae, Caplan, and others on text genre.

Purves, A. C., L. Papa, and S. Jordan (Eds.). 1994. *Encyclopedia of English studies and language arts.* New York: National Council of Teachers of English. This encyclopedia has more than 800 annotated entries/topics that succinctly address this topic and related areas.

Tierney, R. J., R. Caplan, L. Ehri, M. K. Healy, and M. Hurdlow. 1989. Writing and reading working together. In A. H. Dyson (Ed.), *Writing and reading: Collaboration in the classroom?* Urbana, IL: National Council of Teachers of English. Describes Caplan's Style Study in the context of research on and practical applications of the writing and reading relationship.

Wade, S., and E. B. Moje. 2000. The role of text in classroom learning. In M. L. Kamil, P. B. Mosenthal, P. D. Pearson, and R. Barr (Eds.), *Handbook of reading research,* Vol. III, Mahwah, NJ: Erlbaum, 285–310. Explores a range of issues concerning text and its role in reading and writing.

Story Impressions

Purpose

Story Impressions was developed by McGinley and Denner (1987) as a way to help students realize that reading involves actively thinking about ideas. The developers of the procedure consider the use of Story Impressions akin to doing the first draft of a composition.

Rationale

Story Impressions is a prereading writing activity that differs from most kinds of prereading activities in that it involves students' using key concepts from a story to develop their own story or impression of how these key concepts might fit together. McGinley and Denner (1987) developed the procedure based upon the belief that a major goal of a prereading activity should be to have the reader build anticipatory models or blueprints that are confirmed or modified as the reader encounters the actual text. They claim that the technique is "wholly consistent with and directly derivable from current model based views of the reading process" (1987, 239), which they suggest supports the following view of readers:

> To comprehend, the reader must use the clues supplied by the author to activate appropriate prior knowledge structures, usually called schemata. Once active, the schemata can serve as a basis for making predictions.
>
> The proficient reader then tests his or her schema based predictions by evaluating them for goodness of fit with the subsequent information (clues) supplied by the author. (1987, 248)

They point out that the technique varies in two important ways from the directed reading-thinking activity (DRTA). First, clues are systematically sampled from the top-level structure of the story. Second, with Story Impressions the students develop a story based on the clues they are provided.

Intended Audience

McGinley and Denner (1987) suggest that the approach can be used with students of all ages. They claim that they have had teachers use the approach successfully with grades two and above.

Description of the Procedures

Story Impressions are key concepts in the form of clue words and phrases that the student is expected to fit together into an impression or draft of a story. Figure 9.4, for example, lists key concepts selected from Edgar Allen Poe's "The Tell-Tale Heart" and a story developed by an eighth grader.

Introduction of Story Impressions. To introduce Story Impressions to students, McGinley and Denner suggest the following steps:

- Step 1. Provide a general introduction, e.g., "Today we're going to make up what we think this story could be about."
- Step 2. Direct students to the list of key concepts by saying, "Here are some clues about the story we're going to read. We're going to use these clues to write our own version of the story. After that, we'll read the story together to see if the author had ideas similar to ours."
- Step 3. After students read through the list of clues, they are encouraged to brainstorm how the ideas might connect. The teacher might jot down possibilities on an overhead or the chalkboard.
- Step 4. Using the brainstormed ideas, a class story is developed (on the board or transparency) that ties together the clues.
- Step 5. The students read the author's actual story and discuss how their story compares. McGinley and Denner stress that a match with the author's story is not important. Instead, what is important is to compare how the clues were woven together similarly or differently.
- Step 6. Either in small groups or as individuals, the students develop their own stories based upon clues from another story.

FIGURE 9.4 Story Impressions (Prereading) Activity Based on Poe's "The Tell-Tale Heart"

Story impressions given to a class	An eighth grader's story written from the story impressions
house ↓ old man ↓ young man ↓ hatred ↓ ugly eye ↓ death ↓ tub, blood, knife ↓ buried ↓ floor ↓ police ↓ heartbeat ↓ guilt ↓ crazy ↓ confession	There was a young man and his father, an old man. They lived in a house on a hill out in the bouniey's. The old man hated his son because he had an ugly eye. The young man was asleep in his bedroom when he was awakened by screaming. He went to the bedroom and saw his father laying in the tub. There was blood everywhere and a knife through him. The young man found a tape recording hidden behind the door on the floor. He turned it on there was screaming on the tape. The young man started to call the police, but then he stopped and remembered what his mother had told him. She had told him that he had a split personality. So he called the police and confessed to being crazy and killing his father. His heartbeat was heavy as he called.

Guidelines for Developing a Set of Story Impressions. McGinley and Denner have established guidelines for developing a set of Story Impressions:

1. Include key words and phrases (preferably from the text with a maximum of three words per clue) that represent the character, setting, and key elements from the plot.

2. Restrict the number of key words or phrases to ten or fifteen for a short story or fifteen to twenty for a young adult novel.

3. Arrange the clues vertically with arrows or lines to indicate their order.

Suggestions for Variations on the Use of Story Impressions. McGinley and Denner (1987) offer various suggestions of ways that Story Impression clues can be used for other purposes. For example, they suggest that Story Impressions might also be used as guideposts from which students offer their own questions prior to reading or as aids to having students develop reports, as well as make notes. In addition, they suggest that Story Impressions could be used to develop or reinforce selected skills (e.g., how ideas interrelate and are sequenced).

Cautions and Comments

The authors have reported the results of several studies that substantiate the positive contribution that Story Impressions makes to comprehension (Denner, 1989; Denner, Rickards, and Albanese, 2003; McGinley and Denner, 1985). What seems to be missing from their studies, however, is a comparison with other prereading activities and an examination of on-line measures to assess the impact of Story Impressions on the thought processes of students as they read. Also, it would be interesting to learn how students compare their renditions with those of the author (e.g., what features they note in common or at variance).

As a vehicle for integrating reading and writing, Story Impressions seems to have definite potential. The technique affords the students the opportunity to relate their experiences to key concepts. In other words, it allows the students to establish their frameworks and themselves as authors prior to being introduced to a text developed by a professional author. The procedure, as presently described by McGinley and Denner, tends to fall short in offering suggestions for how the students' versions might be shared, discussed, and compared en route to validating the students' drafts. Likewise, their research needs to consider the impact upon the students' view of themselves as authors, their appreciation of their craft and the craft of others, and their development as writers.

REFERENCES

Alexander, P. A., and T. L Jetton. 2000. Structural aspects of constructing meaning from text. In M. L. Kamil, P. B. Mosenthal, P. D. Pearson, and R. Barr (Eds.), *Handbook of reading research,* Vol. III. Mahwah, NJ: Erlbaum, 311–336. Explores issues dealing with the impact of genre on reading.

Denner, P. R. 1989. *The effects of providing story impressions as prereading/writing activity on the story comprehension and oral reading miscues of second grade readers.* Research report, Idaho State University. Presents a study exploring the use of Story Impressions with second graders.

Denner, P. R., and W. J. McGinley. 1986. The effects of story-impressions as a prereading/writing activity on story comprehension. *Journal of Educational Research* 82(6): 320–326. Presents a study of the effects of Story Impressions upon eighth graders' comprehension.

Denner, P. R., J. P. Rickards, and A. J. Albanese. 2003. The effect of story impression preview on learning from narrative text. *The Journal of Experimental Education* 71(4): 313–332. Reports the findings of a research study on the use of story impressions.

Farnan, N., and Dahl, K. 2000. Children's writing: Research and practice. In J. Flood, J. Jensen, D. Lapp, and J. R. Squire (Eds.), *Handbook of research on teaching the language arts,* Vol. II. New York: Macmillan, 993–1007. Explores the role of writing in terms of preparing students to read and write different genres.

Goldman, S. R., and J. A. Rakestraw, Jr. 2000. Learning from text: A multidimensional and developmental perspective. In M. L. Kamil, P. B. Mosenthal, P. D. Pearson, and R. Barr (Eds.), *Handbook of reading research,* Vol. III. Mahwah, NJ: Erlbaum, 285–310. Explores a range of issues concerning text genre, including hypertext.

McGinley, W. J., and P. R. Denner. 1985. *The use of semantic impressions as a previewing activity for providing clues to a story's episodic structure.* Paper presented at the Northern Rocky Mountains Educational Research Association Annual Meeting, Jackson, WY. Describes the use of Story Impressions as a previewing activity.

———. 1987. Story impressions: A prereading/writing activity. *Journal of Reading* 31:248–253. Presents a detailed description of the use of Story Impressions.

Myers, M. 2000. Issues in teacher preparation and staff development in English Language Arts. In J. Flood, J. Jensen, D. Lapp, and J. R. Squire (Eds.),

Handbook of research on teaching the language arts, Vol. II. New York: Macmillan, 459–477. Explores teacher-based research of instructional possibilities, including the work of Barthomolae, Caplan, and others on text genre.

Purves, A. C., L. Papa, and S. Jordan (Eds.). 1994. *Encyclopedia of English studies and language arts.* New York: National Council of Teachers of English. This encyclopedia has more than 800 annotated entries/topics that succinctly address this topic and related areas.

Wade, S., and E. B. Moje. 2000. The role of text in classroom learning. In M. L. Kamil, P. B. Mosenthal, P. D. Pearson, and R. Barr (Eds.), *Handbook of reading research,* Vol. III. Mahwah, NJ: Erlbaum, 285–310. Explores a range of issues concerning text and its role in reading and writing.

Expository Reading-Writing Think-Sheets

Purpose

Expository Reading-Writing Think-Sheets is the label we have given to the expository writing program and, more recently, the cognitive strategy instruction in writing developed by Raphael and others. Expository Reading-Writing Think-Sheets are intended to guide the development of expository reading and writing skills in conjunction with teacher-student, student-student, and student-self interactions through the various phases (planning, drafting, and revising) of writing.

Rationale

Raphael, Englert, and Kirschner (e.g., Raphael, Englert, and Kirschner, 1986, 1989; Raphael and Kirschner, 1985) developed Expository Reading-Writing guides in an attempt to teach upper elementary students expository reading and writing skills. As they argue:

> when children reach the upper grades of elementary school, where there is a greater emphasis on learning content, their progress in writing often declines. . . . One reason for this decline may be that children are not being taught how to read and learn from informational or content area texts. (1989, 262)

With this in mind, Raphael, Englert, and Kirschner have pursued a program of research exploring the viability of guiding the development of expository reading/writing skills. Several areas of research serve as the basis for their approach: studies of the influence of text structure (especially mapping) on comprehension and composition; the role of different social contexts (especially peer response groups) upon student learning; and tenets emerging from teacher-researcher collaborations and explicit teaching. Essentially the approach of these authors involves extensive use of what they refer to as Think-Sheets:

> to prompt teachers to model and think aloud as they teach writing, to encourage teacher-student dialogue about strategies appropriate to each phase, to prompt appropriate student-student dialogue during peer editing and to encourage useful student-self dialogue as students write independently. (Raphael, Englert, and Kirschner, 1989, 774)

Over time, Raphael, Englert, and Kirschner hope that the Think-Sheets serve more as reminders (rather than guides) as students internalize the hints.

Intended Audience

The strategy was intended for use with upper elementary students but also seems appropriate for use with older students.

Description of the Procedures

Raphael, Englert, and Kirschner (1986) have emphasized that their approach has been subjected to a great deal of refinement and will likely be subjected to further refinement in conjunction with additional research and development. In its current form, the use of Think-Sheets and the changing teacher role is central to the approach.

Seven Think-Sheets constitute their current approach. They are Think-Sheets intended as guides for:

Planning
Organizing
First draft
Thinking about first draft
Editing
Revision
Final draft

The Planning Think-Sheet is intended to guide a consideration of the topic, purposes, and audience. The Think-Sheet for planning (Figure 9.5) merely prompts the reader to consider these items.

The Organizing Think-Sheet involves the selection and use of a mapped pattern guide (See Unit 12 for a description of mapping). The pattern guides offer students a way of framing their ideas in accordance with whether the predominant text structure is compare/contrast, problem solution, explanation, or narrative. Figure 9.6 is an example of a Think-Sheet for a compare/contrast guide.

The First Draft Think-Sheet is merely a blank sheet of lined colored paper. The use of color is to denote that the paper is a first draft—that is, a work in progress.

In hopes of prompting students to reflect upon their first draft, a Think-Sheet is directed to thinking about the first draft. The questions on this sheet represent a self-check directed at having students consider how interesting, clear, and organized their first draft is. In addition, it is intended to prepare students for the possibility of an editing conference. Figure 9.7 includes a copy of a Thinking about the First Draft Think-Sheet.

The fifth Think-Sheet is for editing. To this end, Raphael and associates have developed five versions—one for each of the four text structures taught as well as a generic version. They state that the generic version "is used when students begin to combine the different structures as they write more complex papers" (Raphael et al., 1989, 277). The Editing Think-Sheet is intended for use in conjunction with having a student author share his or her piece with a peer editor. The author reads the piece to the editor and then asks him/her to respond to several questions ranging from what the piece is about, its clarity, its interestingness, how well the piece is organized, and, for purposes of revision

Author's name ______________________ Date ________

TOPIC: ______________________

WHO: Who am I writing for?

WHY: Why am I writing this?

WHAT: What do I already know about my topic? (Brainstorm)

1. ______________________
2. ______________________
3. ______________________
4. ______________________

HOW: How do I group my ideas?

FIGURE 9.5 Think-Sheet for Planning

What is being compared/contrasted?	
On what?	
Alike?	Different?
On what?	
Alike?	Different?
On what?	
Alike?	Different?

FIGURE 9.6 Think-Sheet for Organizing: Comparison/Contrast

Author's Name ______________________________

Read to check information.

What is my paper mainly about?

What do I like best? Put a * next to the best part and explain why.

What parts are not clear? Put a ? next to the unclear parts, and tell why they are not clear.

Is the paper interesting? Tell why or why not here:

Question yourself to check organization.

Did I:			
Tell what two things are compared and contrasted?	Yes	Sort of	No
Tell things they are being compared and contrasted on?	Yes	Sort of	No
Tell how they are alike?	Yes	Sort of	No
Tell how they are different?	Yes	Sort of	No
Use keywords clearly?	Yes	Sort of	No

Plan for editing conference.

What parts do I want to change? (For anything marked "Sort of" or "No," add to, take out, reorder?)

1. ______________________________

2. ______________________________

What questions do I want to ask my editor?

____

____

FIGURE 9.7 Think-Sheet for Thinking about the First Draft: Comparison/Contrast

suggestions for change. A copy of the Editing Think-Sheet for compare/contrast texts is shown in Figure 9.8.

The Revision Think-Sheet is then used to help the student author decide what suggestions will be heeded. As they state, "The Revision Think-Sheet . . . is designed to promote author's consideration of their editor's comments but still give them control of their papers" (Raphael et al., 1989, 278). To this end, students are expected to list all of the suggestions and then decide on those they plan to address. A copy of the Revision Think-Sheet is shown in Figure 9.9.

After revising their draft, the students then move to the Final Think-Sheet, which is their final draft. The format of this Think-Sheet is simply blank, white, lined paper.

Teacher's Role. Raphael and associates emphasize that the Think-Sheets are intended to provide a structure to guide and model different aspects of writing at the same time that students acquire shared understandings and vocabulary for discussing what they are doing. They hope that the students will become more self-initiating and self-regulating as they internalize the strategies and notions about writing made explicit via the Think-Sheet. As they state:

> As students gradually internalize the questions on the Think-Sheets and take ownership of the writing process themselves, they begin to work independently of the teacher. When they

Author's Name ______________________ Editor's Name ______________________

Read to check information. (Authors: Read your paper aloud to your editor.)

What is the paper mainly about?

What do you like best? Put a * next to the part you liked best and tell why you like it here:

What parts are not clear? Put a ? next to the unclear parts, and tell what made the part unclear to you:

Is the paper interesting? Tell why or why not here:

Question yourself to check organization.

Did I:

Tell what two things are compared and contrasted?	Yes	Sort of	No
Tell things they are being compared and contrasted on?	Yes	Sort of	No
Tell how they are alike?	Yes	Sort of	No
Tell how they are different?	Yes	Sort of	No
Use keywords clearly?	Yes	Sort of	No

Plan revision.

What two parts do you think should be changed or revised? (For anything marked "Sort of" or "No," should the author add to, take out, reorder?)

1. ____

____

2. ____

____

What could help make the paper more interesting?

Talk.

Talk to the author of the paper. Talk about your comments on this editing think-sheet. Share ideas for revising the paper.

FIGURE 9.8 Think-Sheet for Editing: Comparison-Contrast

reach the level of self-regulation, they will no longer need external support, either from the Think-Sheets or the teacher. (Raphael et al., 1989, 281)

Cautions and Comments

Expository Reading-Writing Think-Sheets represent one of a number of different strategies for guiding the development of an expository report. For example, Cunningham and Cunningham (1987) have suggested the use of a feature matrix to show teachers how to help students extract and organize ideas in conjunction with reading and writing.

Several features distinguish Raphael and associates' Think-Sheets. The set of Think-Sheets is tied to a program of research and development, and, as a result, has been subjected to a great deal of refinement and revision. The Think-Sheets are relatively comprehensive. As guides to writing different texts, they represent an amalgamation of procedures intended to help students generate, organize, reflect upon, frame (using different text structures), share, enlist feedback on, and revise ideas. Finally, suggestions for using the Think-Sheets are tied to an attempt to support self-regulated learning.

Author's Name ______________________

List suggestions from your Editor.

List all the suggestions your editor has given you:

a. ______________________

b. ______________________

c. ______________________

d. ______________________

e. ______________________

Decide on the suggestions to use.

Put a * next to all suggestions that you will use in revising your paper.

Think about making your paper more interesting.

List ideas for making your paper more interesting to your reader.

____

____

____

Return to your first draft.

On your first draft, make all changes that you think will improve your paper.
Use ideas from the list you have made on this think-sheet.

FIGURE 9.9 Think-Sheet for Revision

In terms of shortcomings, Raphael and associates (1988) have discussed the possibility that Think-Sheets may become an end unto themselves rather than a springboard for students' self-regulated and flexible thinking. They have reported, for example, that some students may treat the Think-Sheets as distinct from one another and pay "little attention to the purpose of the Think-Sheet or to the general goal of sharing information on a given topic, making the paper as interesting and informative as possible" (Raphael et al., 1988, 794).

REFERENCES

Alexander, P. A., and T. L Jetton. 2000. Structural aspects of constructing meaning from text. In M. L. Kamil, P. B. Mosenthal, P. D. Pearson, and R. Barr (Eds.), *Handbook of reading research,* Vol. III. Mahwah, NJ: Erlbaum, 311–336. Explores issues concerning the impact of genre on reading.

Brock, C. H., and T. E. Raphael. 2003. Guiding three middle school students in learning written academic discourse. *Elementary School Journal* 103(5): 481–502. Describes a two-year collaborative writing project of sixth and seventh graders designed to help students learn academic discourse for the purpose of writing a chapter in an edited volume.

Camp, D. 2000. It takes two: Teaching with twin texts of fact and fiction. *The Reading Teacher* 53: 400. Explores the development of expository sense in conjunction with bridging reading and writing.

Cudd, E. T., and L. Roberts. 1989. Using writing to enhance content area learning in the primary grades. *The Reading Teacher* 42: 392–405. Uses paragraph frames as a means of guiding expository writing and reading.

Cunningham, P. M., and J. W. Cunningham. 1987. Content area reading-writing lessons. *The Reading Teacher* 40: 506–512. Explores the use of feature matrix and other devices to show teachers how to help students extract and organize critical information.

Donovan, C. A. 2002. Children's genre knowledge: An examination of K–5 students' performance on multiple tasks providing differing levels of scaffolding. *Reading Research Quarterly* 37(4): 428–465. Article examines the issue of scaffolding in children's writing.

Donovan, C. A., and L. B. Smolkin. 2002. Considering genre, content, and visual features in the selection of trade books for science instruction. *The Reading Teacher* 55(6): 502–520. Discusses how analyses of different aspects of stories and informational books can help teachers make informed decisions to enhance science instruction.

Farnan, N., and K. Dahl. 2000. Children's writing: research and practice. In J. Flood, J. Jensen, D. Lapp, and J. R. Squire (Eds.), *Handbook of research on teaching the language arts,* Vol. II. New York: Macmillan, 993–1007. Explores the role of writing in terms of preparing students to read and write different genres.

Furr, Derek. 2003. Struggling readers get hooked on writing. *The Reading Teacher 56:* 518–525. Presents a brief description of an expository writing lesson taught in the context of a modified writing workshop and includes a sample of the development of a web for a report.

Goldman, S. R., and J. A. Rakestraw, Jr. 2000. Learning from text: a multidimensional and developmental perspective. In M. L. Kamil, P. B. Mosenthal, P. D. Pearson, and R. Barr (Eds.), *Handbook of reading research,* Vol. III. Mahwah, NJ: Erlbaum, 285–310. Explores a range of issues dealing with text genre, including hypertext.

Harvey, S. 2002. Nonfiction inquiry: Using real reading and writing to explore the world. *Language Arts* 80(1): 12–23. Explores nonfiction writing in conjunction with projects.

Johns, A. (Ed.). 2002. *Genre in the classroom: Multiple perspectives.* Mahwah, NJ: Erlbaum. Explores the genre approach, especially as developed in Australia, with key chapters by Michael Halliday and others.

Purves, A. C., L. Papa, and S. Jordan (Eds.). 1994. *Encyclopedia of English studies and language arts.* New York: National Council of Teachers of English. This encyclopedia has more than 800 annotated entries/topics that succinctly address this topic and related areas.

Raphael, T. E., and B. W. Kirschner. 1985. *The effects of instruction in comparison/contrast text structure on sixth-grade students' reading comprehension and writing products* (Research Series No. 161). East Lansing: Michigan State University, Institute for Research on Teaching. Discusses research related to the use of Think-Sheets.

Raphael, T. E., C. S. Englert, and B. W. Kirschner. 1986. *The impact of text structure instruction and social context on students' comprehension and production of expository text* (Research Series No. 177). East Lansing: Michigan State University, Institute for Research on Teaching. Reports research related to the use of Think-Sheets.

———. 1986. *Students' metacognitive knowledge about writing* (Research Series No. 176). East Lansing: Michigan State University, Institute for Research on Teaching. Discusses the students' awareness of the writing process and structures.

Raphael, T. E., B. W. Kirschner, and C. S. Englert. 1986. *Text structure instruction within process-writing classrooms: A manual for instruction* (Occasional Paper No. 104). East Lansing: Michigan State University, Institute for Research on Teaching. Provides samples of materials and lessons for implementing the Expository Writing Program.

———. 1988. Expository writing program: Making connections between reading and writing. *The Reading Teacher* 41: 790–795. Discusses the use of Expository Reading-Writing Think-Sheets with less able students.

———. 1989. Acquisition of expository writing skills. In J. Mason (Ed.), *Reading and writing connections.* Boston: Allyn and Bacon. Represents a comprehensive description of the strategy and research program.

Wade, S., and E. B. Moje. 2000. The role of text in classroom learning. In M. L. Kamil, P. B. Mosenthal, P. D. Pearson, and R. Barr (Eds.), *Handbook of reading research,* Vol. III. Mahwah, NJ: Erlbaum, 285–310. Explores a range of issues concerning text and its role in reading and writing.

UNIT 10

Response to Literature and Drama

UNIT OVERVIEW

One can read and write with a reverence for the authority of text and with a desire to recall, memorize, and to know exactly what someone intended them to learn or understand. While some may view such goals as the mainstay of reading and writing, many literacy educators would suggest that reading and writing should be approached quite differently—namely, as a means of achieving perspectives on oneself and others. They would suggest that literacy should be enlisted as a way to explore the human experience and to pursue various forms of inquiry, as well as for communication and negotiation. Some of us have used the metaphor of criss-crossing one's exploration of a topic or the notion of applying multiple lenses to explore one's world and achieve various perspectives. Others, such as Boal (1979), advocate these modes (e.g., drama) as a means of social problem solving and as a precursor to activism.

In some respects, the present unit has links to various other units (especially Units 2 and 9), but the primary focus of this unit relates to practice that offers different ways to criss-cross topics and issues in conjunction with achieving multiple perspectives. These ways of knowing include drama as well as sketches and other forms of response. As ways of knowing they appear to engage learners in ways that differ from each other, especially in terms of the nature of the engagement they prompt as well as the lens/perspective they afford. They afford an opportunity for readers to engage in what some might consider different virtual worlds as a way of seeing anew or differently. In Unit 2, Short, Harste, and Burke discussed the role of such engagements as essential to enriching ways of knowing by what is termed *transmediation.*

We expect that such engagements will increase in the future—especially as we move into an age where video explorations will be as easy to pursue as paper and pencil possibilities. We would hope that such ways of knowing propel multiple perspective-taking and reflection versus non-examination consideration of ideas. Will they help improve reading and writing? Studies suggest that they do contribute to improvements in reading and writing. But we would stress their role in supporting the development of complex understandings and multiple meanings, including meanings informed by alternative perspectives.

Five strategies and practices are included in this unit. Two of the strategies enlist the use of drama; two involve a mix of writing, reading, and discussion; one involves sketching. The majority are oriented toward activating thinking and facilitating new perspectives and reexamination.

Process Drama. Process Drama represents the use of drama in the classroom in a manner that is not theatrical, but generative, provocative, and spontaneous. Process Drama is based upon the ideas of a pioneer in education, Dorothy Heathcote.

Point, Counterpoint. Point, Counterpoint represents an attempt to empower students' interpretative repertoire by affording a forum for having them discuss various interpretations of the same story.

Response Heuristic. The Response Heuristic represents a procedure by which students are given a structured procedure for responding to text, and then interacting with others about their response.

Sketch to Stretch. Sketch to Stretch affords students the opportunity to develop a sketch of what a text meant to them and to use this text as a springboard for interacting with others about the interpretation of a text.

Readers Theatre. Readers Theatre involves having students develop their own adaptations and interpretations of stories, poems, and other text for presentation to peer groups.

REFERENCES

Alejandro, A. 1994. Like happy dreams—Integrating visual arts, writing, and reading. *Language Arts* 71: 12–21.

Berghoff, B. 1998. Multiple sign systems and reading. *The Reading Teacher* 51: 520–523.

Boal, A. *Theater of the oppressed.* New York: Vrizan Books.

Edmiston, B., and P. Enciso. 2003. Reflections and refractions of meaning: Dialogical approaches to classroom drama and reading. In J. Flood, J. Jensen, D. Lapp, and J. R. Squire (Eds.), *Handbook of research on teaching the language arts,* Vol. II. New York: Macmillan.

Ernst, K. 1994. Writing pictures, painting words: Writing in an artist's workshop. *Language Arts* 71: 44–52.

Labbo, L. D. 1996. A semiotic analysis of young children's symbol making in a classroom computer center. *Reading Research Quarterly* 31: 356–385.

Marshall, J. 2000. Research on response to literature. In M. L. Kamil, P. B. Mosenthal, P. D. Pearson, and R. Barr (Eds.), *Handbook of reading research,* Vol. III. Mahwah, NJ: Erlbaum, 381–402.

McMaster, J. C. 1998. "Doing" literature: Using drama to build literacy. *The Reading Teacher* 51: 574–584.

Moss, B. 1995. Nurturing artistic images in student reading and writing. *The Reading Teacher* 48: 532–608.

Olshansky, B. 1997. Picturing story: An irresistible pathway into literacy. *The Reading Teacher* 50: 612–613.

Rowe, D. W. 1998. The literate potentials of book-related dramatic play. *Reading Research Quarterly* 33: 10–35.

Smagorinsky, P., and J. Coppock. 1996. Exploring artistic response to literature. In C. K. Kinzer and D. J. Leu (Eds.), *Multidimensional aspects of literacy research, theory, and practice.* Chicago: National Reading Conference, 335–341.

Stephens, D. 1994. Learning what art means. *Language Arts* 71: 34–37.

Wagner, B. J. 2003. Imaginative expression. In J. Flood, J. Jensen, D. Lapp, and J. R. Squire (Eds.), *Handbook of research on teaching the language arts,* Vol. II. New York: Macmillan, 1008–1025.

Wolf, S. A. 1998. The flight of reading: Shifts in instruction, orchestration, and attitudes through classroom theatre. *Reading Research Quarterly* 33: 382–415.

Wolf, S. A., and P. E. Enciso. 1996. Multiple selves in literary interpretation: Engagement and the language of drama. In C. K. Kinzer and D. J. Leu (Eds.), *Multidimensional aspects of literacy research, theory, and practice.* Chicago: National Reading Conference, 351–360.

Process Drama

Purpose

The term *Process Drama* has been adopted by us to refer to educational drama practices advocated by Dorothy Heathcote and others (e.g., O'Neill, Bolton, Booth). The aim of Process Drama is to build on past experience of pupils and to facilitate a deeper understanding of oneself and others and society in its present, past, and future.

Rationale

Use of Process Drama in the classroom has changed enormously during the last twenty-five years in England and more recently in other countries. As Johnson and O'Neill (1984) stated:

> There has been a shift in direction from an interest in personal development of the individual pupil, through the acquiring of theatrical and improvisational skills to the recognition of drama as a precise teaching instrument, which works best when it is part of the learning process. Drama is no longer considered simply as another branch of art education, but as a unique teaching tool, vital for language development and invaluable as a method in the exploration of other subject areas. (1984, 42)

Dorothy Heathcote has been to a large extent responsible for an increased interest in using drama as a tool for self-exploration and learning. Through her writings, talks, and work with children, she has done a great deal to move drama from a performance upon a stage to a dynamic means of exploring issues within the classroom. At the heart of Heathcote's drama activities is a frame or dramatic context that the teacher establishes for students to explore "in role" as they engage in a form of improvisation that requires their ongoing involvement in issues that emerge from the frame. What distinguishes Process Drama from regular improvisation is the teacher's involvement and the tensions, self-reflections, and engagements that he or she creates to move the drama. What is key is the relationship between involvement and reflection. As O'Neill has contended:

> reflection is a crucial element. In drama we experience an "as if" world and at the same time create the means of reflecting on existence. A conscious and reflective attitude is likely to develop in drama because of the dynamic relationship between reality and pretense. (1985, 160)

Process Drama can be used in various ways with reading material as a stimulus for reading certain materials in a role, as a follow-up to a drama, or as a basis for the drama.

Process Drama provides a strong context for articulating a complex response to literature. The second world, created in the context of drama, takes the first world of the literary text as a starting point. Rogers and O'Neill (1993) state:

> [The parallel drama world] will share some significant features with the world of the text but may expand some and overlook others. The characters that inhabit this world may not appear in the original text, and the events and encounters that occur may have no exact parallel. But

> the drama world will illuminate the original and, above all, give students access to it. The keys that unlock the doors of this second [drama] world are buried in the original and can be discovered through a number of active and transferable strategies. (1993, 75)

The drama world features new characters, often characters who investigate or explain events—e.g., reporters, lawyers, or detectives—as well as characters who might have witnessed or participated in significant events—e.g., neighbors and friends. As Edmiston (1993) points out, this allows all the children in the class to take part in the experience. The drama world is based not on the external features of the text (e.g., having the same characters); instead, it brings to light the drama of the text—the motivations that drive the plot—through the students' adoption of various roles. Finally, because students may adopt several different roles in a process drama, students have an opportunity to explore the same plot events from several perspectives.

Intended Audience

Process Drama is appropriate for use with students at any level.

Description of the Procedures

Creating the Drama Context or Frame. The teacher's first task in Process Drama is to consider his/her objectives for a topic or a selection. For example, a teacher might consider what issues or themes she/he wishes to have students address or think about related to a selection. Perhaps the teacher just wants the students to consider possibilities surrounding a certain event, character, or setting more fully. With this purpose in mind, the teacher's goal is to create a drama context that has the following features: it helps students get "inside" the story; it is open-ended in that the context is not overly prescribed so that participants in this framed drama can contribute to the story or world that is created; it has certain tensions or an unpredictability associated with the drama.

To illustrate some possibilities, O'Neill, Lambert, Linnell, and Wain-Wood (1976) developed *Drama Guidelines.* One of their examples intended for use with first and second graders follows.

> *DETECTIVES*
>
> Preparation
>
> At the beginning of the lesson, the teacher brings a number of objects into the drama room, such as: a necklace; a pill bottle; a large photograph of a teenage girl; an alarm clock. On the blackboard she scrawls the word 'Boathouse—'.
>
> *1. The Disappearance*
>
> *Whole Group*
> The teacher introduces herself as coming from Scotland Yard. She has been given to understand that the pupils are all competent detectives. She needs their help. They have been called in to assist her in solving what is a rather baffling case.
>
> On the previous night, a young girl disappeared from her home. Her name was Anne Robinson and she was 16. She was last seen when the housekeeper said goodnight to her at

10 p.m. When the housekeeper went to Anne's room at 8 a.m. the following morning, she had disappeared. Her bed had not been slept in, and there were some signs of a struggle. The alarm clock had been found on the floor, and had stopped at 11 p.m. Robbery did not appear to have been a factor in her disappearance, since a valuable necklace given to Anne by her father was still on her dressing-table. The pill bottle was open and empty. The message on the blackboard was what had been found scrawled on the dressing-table mirror in lipstick. What questions would the group like to ask?

The rest of this session consists entirely of the group questioning the teacher very closely and listening carefully to the answers which are given. In response to their questioning, it emerges that Anne's parents were recently divorced, that her father was a distinguished scientist who was attending a conference abroad at the time of her disappearance, and that she had been alone in the house with the housekeeper. The 'clues' are passed around the class and examined closely. Many searching questions are asked about the room, the possibilities of outsiders gaining entrance to the house, the various clues, particularly the pill bottle, the kind of girl Anne was, her friends, her relationship with the housekeeper, the existence of a boathouse nearby.

2. Solutions

The pupils begin to form hypotheses which include all the known clues.

The lesson ended with the class having formed a number of different opinions about the case. The teacher had succeeded in her objective of gaining the group's commitment and interest, and the pupils had listened intently throughout the lesson, both to the teacher and to each other.

In later lessons, developing this theme, the teacher's objectives were to encourage pupils to adopt different roles, and to begin to take responsibility for their own work. They interviewed various people connected with the case, with some of the pupils taking on these roles. In this case they eventually decided that the girl had been taken hostage by international terrorists. In the final sessions on this topic, they planned and carried out the rescue of the girl.

3. Further Developments

Interviews with the girl's friends, teachers, parents, neighbors.
Reenacting the possible events of the night she disappeared.
Examining the house and grounds for further evidence.
Formally presenting this evidence and its implications to the police.
An item on the girl's disappearance to be included in the 10 o'clock news.
Holding a press conference about the case.
Breaking the news of her disappearance to her parents.
Going back in time to examine the motives, plans, and purposes of Anne's captors.
A list of the terrorists' demands for the press.
As her captors, explaining to Anne why she has been taken hostage.
Planning and carrying out the rescue attempt.
Helping the hostage adjust to normal life after the rescue.

In this example, the students define the mystery, including the elements and new relationship to one another. The enlistment in the drama frame ensures that they assume a vital role in the unfolding drama. It is as if the drama affords them a "safe place," allowing them to share perspectives and reactions without fear of evaluation. It is as if students can adopt what Heathcote terms "the mantle of an expert"—that is, where they can function as experts. But one should not diminish the responsibilities and commitment expected of the students. In any framed drama, students are expected: (1) to pretend; (2) to adopt/create a role; (3) to maintain and build upon the dramatic context; and (4) to cooperate/transact with others in the context of the drama.

In terms of the teacher, it is important to recognize the multifaceted nature of their responsibilities. The teacher creates the initial frame and manages the evolution of the drama, including being sensitive to the roles assumed by students and the issues being explored. Adeptly, the teacher in the previously described Process Drama: (1) moved the students quickly and economically into the drama context; (2) presented a challenge that focused the children's thinking and contributed to their being more concerned; (3) offered not only encouragement and support but also respected each student's contributions.

Two aspects of the teacher's involvement in the drama were central to the drama's success. First, the teacher assumed a role in the drama that afforded him or her the place or power to direct the drama. That is, the drama was structured from the inside. (Some dramas can be structured from the outside; others can be structured from both inside and outside.) Second, the teacher (in role) created the tension necessary to move the drama along and fuel development as well as involvement. As Heathcote (Johnson and O'Neill, 1984) has stated: "Tension of some kind must be present in the drama" (p. 95). While the task of creating tension is key, the means of doing so may not be straightforward. As Heathcote stated:

> The simple factor in making tension work is that something must be left to chance, but not more than one thing at a time. So long as there is that one factor and no one in the room knows precisely when that thing will occur (though everything has been set up so that it must occur), we have tension.
>
> Subtle tensions are useless in a class that will only respond to cruder ones. An example of such tension might be waiting in the dark for an intruder to enter a room. Or a less crude one, demanding more patience, awaiting one's turn to be interrogated, knowing that one of the group will be found guilty. The pressure must come from within the situation, not from the teacher/role insisting that it be done right. (Johnson and O'Neill, 1984, 95)

O'Neill and Lambert (1982), in their book *Drama Structures,* offer an extended discussion of Process Drama that includes guidelines for teachers. The following set of questions, guidelines, and considerations are taken from their book to illustrate some of the issues that need to be addressed in planning and orchestrating a Process Drama. When using a role, teachers should ask themselves:

- What kind of role will be appropriate?
- Should the teacher be in a position of authority?
- Could the class cope with the teacher being in a position that is humble?
- What kinds of interactions is the role required to promote?
- With what challenges can I confront the participants within my role?
- What actions can I employ (in role) to heighten surprise, contrast, or tension?
- What aids are needed that might establish the pupil's belief in the drama (a document, a photo, keys)?
- Are the tasks that are asked of pupils through the role consistent with that role?
- What steps should be taken to ensure the pupils know when the teacher is in or out of the drama or adopting a different role?
- What questions can the teacher ask that will help create, develop, and focus the drama?

Examples of questions that might be useful:

- To set the scene:
  What are you doing looking in that drawer?
  How long have you been waiting?
- To seek information:
  When did this happen?
  Who was involved?
  How shall we get ready for the arrival?
- To locate group in space and time:
  I'm calling you to check if everything is okay—what's happening?
  Is this the corner where the incident occurred?
- To stimulate research:
  How long will it take us to get across country?
  What weapons can we obtain?
- To provide information:
  Are you ready to have your automobile inspected?
  How many people will be present?
- To give control:
  What can we do to make a decision?
  Are you ready to sign up?

Reflection and Discussion. Previously it was stated that the key to the drama lies in the reflection. As teachers strive to immerse students in the drama, they also must consider ways to prompt reflection. Reflection can occur in two places—inside the context of the drama or outside the Process Drama. Several drama educators contend that reflection during the drama is apt to be more powerful than after the drama. As Booth (1987) contends, drama educators want "children to stumble upon authenticity in the work" and to both experience and reflect at the same time. This kind of reflection might include having participants in the drama develop a log, discover a diary, negotiate a treaty, and so on. It might entail introducing a role (a news reporter, scientist, police officer) designed solely to engage the students in reflective thought.

While reflection within the drama may be invaluable, its role after the drama should not be ignored. After the drama, reflection affords students opportunities to revisit and rethink their thoughts and observations. By using journals, sketches, or discussion, the students might, as Booth contends:

> begin to explain the motives and behavior evidenced during the drama, finding reasons and implications for assumptions and decisions they had made. . . . They reflect on the implications and consequences of their actions as the teacher questions and deepens their ideas. The children have the opportunity to make explicit the learning that occurred. (Booth, 1987, 19)

Evaluation and Assessment. O'Neill and Lambert (1982) encourage teachers to examine the quality of the drama experience—in particular, to assess their own work and that of their pupils. As they state, "Without feedback provided by effective assessment it will be difficult for either teachers or pupils to make progress."

In assessing the drama experience, they suggest that teachers should judge the effectiveness of the strategies being used, the engagement of the pupils with the developing meaning of the work, and whether the objectives were relevant or realistic. As they stated:

> The atmosphere in the room, the level of commitment to the work, the ways in which pupils reflect on the experience, both within and outside it, their capacity to draw parallels between the dramatic situation and the real world, and their transformation of the drama experience into other expressive modes, will all be measures of the significance of the experience. (O'Neill and Lambert, 1982, 145)

Cautions and Comments

In *Drama Words,* David Booth offers an extended discussion in which he speculates about the benefits that Process Drama offers for reading and developing meaning. His summary list of the benefits is as follows:

Drama can:

- Broaden the child's experiences, both active and symbolic, before he or she reads the text
- Motivate the child's need or desire to read the text
- Prepare the child for what is to be read
- Intervene in what is being read, so that new understanding can be brought to the text
- Examine what has been read in a new light, with a view toward building new expanded meanings in a collaborative, interactive mode
- Make immediate and vital narrative that seems at first to be without contemporary application
- Help children discover the story—its challenge, its beauty, its caring, its healing, its joy, its power of revelation
- Help children develop the skills of oral interpretation. While in role, they can read aloud poems, songs, dialogue, and excerpts from novels and stories. While reflecting about the drama experience, they can share poems and journal writings
- Give children opportunities to reveal their private comprehensions in role so that through interaction these personal meanings can be expanded, adapted, clarified, and altered
- Build curriculum connections, since drama and story are the stuff of learning
- Motivate children to do both parallel reading and further reading, using other genres, reference materials, and related writings
- Stimulate children to write their own text, in role, as reflection or in appraisal. Children can do research and background writing as planning and preparation for the drama, or to find new directions as the drama develops
- Build a sense of story—words, shapes, syntax, style, structures, and author's voice
- Find or restore voice to the text

Booth (1987) is not alone in his view that Process Drama offers numerous advantages. Bolton (1985) offered the following comments about the unique learnings accrued through Process Drama. As he stated:

> Learning in drama is essentially reframing. What knowledge a pupil has is placed in a new perspective. To take on a role is to detach oneself from what is implicitly understood and to blur the edges of a given world. It invites modification, adjustment, reshaping and realignment of concepts already held. Through detachment from experiencing we can look at one's experiencing anew. (1985, 156)

The research examining the effects of drama upon reading tends to provide general support for drama and role-playing activities, but offers limited information on the extent to which ongoing reflection, perspective taking, and other features of Process Drama (e.g., tension) prompt the degree of generative learning suggested by the affidavits of drama educators. These range from an impact on the engagement of students to their critical exploration of ideas to overall reading and writing development. For example, Jasinski-Schneider and Jackson (2000) demonstrated the impact of process drama activities on fifth graders' writing and students' engagement in reading and writing.

Heathcote's work, and the efforts of those who have extended it (e.g., O'Neill, Booth, Bolton), represent a major attempt to bring drama back to the classroom and redefine its nature and function. It would be a mistake to view the approach as simply improvisation or role play; Process Drama represents an attempt to thoughtfully create a learning dynamic in the classroom that engages students in first-hand experience and paces as well as adjusts the experience to afford reflection and perspective taking. Unmistakably the approach places a great deal of responsibility on the teacher. As Heathcote (1978) stated:

> The teacher must make this time slow enough for inquiry, interesting enough for loitering along the way, rigorous enough for being buffeted in the matrix of the ideas, but with sufficient signposts seen for respite, planning, and regathering of energy to fare forward on the way. Arrivals are those moments of being able to demonstrate our knowing, and the wandering is the time of learning. The teacher must delay arrivals, so that time is made for trying on, turning around, testing this way and that; to preserve interest and concern so that in each new examination there is chance for more understanding to take place; to press and pummel during the journey in such a way that all elements come to light, and the traveler feels the journey to be there; to illuminate the parts as they come clear, and guide to the next dark patch. The teacher encourages the patience to delay, curiosity to seek out, relationships to matter, people and ideas to be explored. We must make the task worth the doing, and as the artist pressures himself into fighting for the only creation form to bring to fruition the ideas he struggles to make clear.

Process Drama uses as its material the conflicts that drive literature—ultimately the conflicts that are of major concern to all human beings. It is interesting to note that several recent examples in the literature on drama frames involve teachers using children's literature on conflicts between groups of people—for example, the internment of the Japanese Americans during World War II (Edmiston, 1993), race relations in a Southern town (Purves, Rogers, and Soter, 1990), and relations between Native Americans and European

Americans (Rogers and O'Neill, 1993). These dramatic situations offer children opportunities to consider both literary texts and the history that literature represents. They also offer children opportunities to experience multiple perspectives and to problem-solve in response to human conflict. When used with multicultural literature, Process Drama may help students learn how to negotiate with each other by having first-hand access to different perspectives.

Process drama has some important parallels to the efforts of political activitist Augusto Boal and the Theater of the Oppressed—especially some of the techniques used in conjunction with the Forum. In particular, his dramas encourage multiple paths and solutions as a form of social problem solving in conjunction with spectators' becoming participants in dramas and a designated "jocker" assessing the power of the solutions explored. Theater of the Oppressed has been explored in a range of school, agency, and other public settings as an actual precursor to empowerment and action (Boal, 1979, 1995; Cohen-Cruz and Schutzman, 1994).

REFERENCES

Boal, A. 1979. *Theater of the oppressed.* New York: Urizen Books. The primary sources for a discussion of Theater of the Oppressed.

Boal, A. 1995. *The rainbow of desire: The Boal Method of theatre and therapy.* New York: Routledge. Extends the discussion of Boal Method procedures, especially in the context of a therapeutic model.

Bolton, G. 1979. *Towards a theory of drama in education.* London: Longman. Discusses the learning that takes place in conjunction with Drama Frames.

———. 1985. Changes in thinking about drama. In *Theory into Practice* 24: 151–157. Columbus: The Ohio State University. Traces the history of drama in schools, with special attention given to Heathcote's work.

Booth, D. 1985. Imaginary gardens with real roads. In *Theory into Practice* 24: 193–198. Columbus: The Ohio State University. Explores the relationship between drama and reading.

———. 1987. *Drama words.* Toronto: Language Study Center, Toronto Board of Education. Explores the significance of his work with drama in schools.

Carroll, J. 1980. *The treatment of Dr. Lister: A language functions approach to drama in education.* Bathurst, Australia: Mitchell College of Advanced Education. Explores the language functions served when students are involved in Process Drama.

Cohen-Cruz, J., and M. Schutzman. 1994. *Playing Boal: Theater, therapy and activism.* New York: Routledge. Explores Boal's notions of theater as a basis for exploring problems, especially oppression.

Edmiston, B. 1993. Going up the beanstalk: Discovering giant possibilities for responding to literature through drama. In K. E. Holland, R. A. Hungerford, and S. B. Ernst (Eds.), *Journeying: Children responding to literature.* Portsmouth, NH: Heinemann. Using examples of drama in the classroom, this article explores the ways in which drama frames extend texts, allow children to enter the world of the story, and help children make active responses to the text.

Edmiston, B., and P. Enciso. 2003. Reflections and refractions of meaning: Dialogical approaches to classroom drama and reading. In J. Flood, J. Jensen, D. Lapp, and J. R. Squire (Eds.), *Handbook of research on teaching the language arts,* Vol. II. New York: Macmillan. Excellent survey of work on drama and reading and their role in meaning making.

Flynn, R. M., and G. A. Carr. 1994. Exploring classroom literature through drama: A specialist and a teacher collaborate. *Language Arts* 71: 38–43. Describes the nature and techniques for using process drama.

Heathcote, D. 1978. Of these seeds becoming. In R. Shuman (Ed.), *Educational drama for today's schools.* Metuchen, NJ: The Scarecrow Press, 1–400. Explores her notions of drama and their impact.

———. 1983. Learning, knowing and language in drama. *Language Arts,* 60: 695–701. Relates drama frames to language use and learning.

Heathcote, D., and G. Bolton. 1995. *Drama for learning: Dorothy Heathcote's Mantle of the Expert approach to education.* Portsmouth, NH: Heinemann. Explores the *Mantle of the Expert* as a learning tool in classrooms.

Heathcote, D., and P. Herbert. 1985. A drama of learning: Mantle of the Expert. *Theory into Practice*

24: 151–157. Discusses the notion of Mantle of the Expert.

Henderson, L. C., and J. L. Shanker. 1978. The use of interpretative dramatics versus basal reader workbooks for developing comprehension. *Reading World* 17: 239–243. Explores the use of interpretative dramatics for enhancing comprehension.

Jasinski, J., S. Schneider, and S. A. W. Jackson. 2000. Process drama: A special space and a place for writing. *The Reading Teacher* 54(1): 38–51. Discusses the use of drama as a tool for instruction and learning to support literacy development while also fostering children's imagination.

Johnson, E., and C. O'Neill. 1984. *Dorothy Heathcote: Collected writings on education and drama.* London: Heinemann. A collection of the articles, lectures, and notes of Heathcote.

Manley, A., and C. O'Neill. 1997. *Dreamseekers: Creative approaches to the African American heritage.* Portsmouth, NH: Heinemann. Various teachers explore the use of process drama to engage students in exploring history, art, and issues.

Miccinati, J. L., and S. Phelps. 1980. Classroom drama from the children's reading: From the page to the stage. *The Reading Teacher* 34: 269–272. Describes the use of classroom drama and role playing in conjunction with children's reading.

O'Neill, C. 1985. Imagined worlds in theatre and drama. *Theory into Practice* 24: 158–165. Discusses the role and nature of drama in the classroom.

O'Neill, C., and A. Lambert. 1982. *Drama structures.* London: Hutchinson. Perhaps the most accessible description of how to initiate Process Drama.

O'Neill, C., A. Lambert, R. Linnell, and J. Wain-Wood. 1976. *Drama guidelines.* Portsmouth, NH: Heinemann. Includes examples of drama frames with commentary.

Purves, A. C., L. Papa, and S. Jordan (Eds.). 1994. *Encyclopedia of English studies and language arts.* New York: National Council of Teachers of English. This encyclopedia has more than 800 annotated entries/topics that succinctly address this topic and related areas.

Purves, A. C., T. Rogers, and A. O. Soter. 1990. *How porcupines make love II: Teaching a response-centered literature curriculum.* New York: Longman. Includes a section on a Process Drama response to *To Kill a Mockingbird.*

Rogers, T., and C. O'Neill. 1993. Creating multiple worlds: Drama, language, and literary response. In G. E. Newell and R. K. Durst (Eds.), *Exploring texts: The role of discussion and writing in the teaching and learning of literature.* Norwood, MA: Christopher-Gordon Publishers. Discusses Process Drama as a way of responding to and extending literature.

Shoop, M. 1986. Inquest: A listening and reading comprehension strategy. *The Reading Teacher* 39: 670–675. Describes the use of the Inquest procedure, including a delineation of the steps.

Taylor, P. 1998. *Redcoats and patriots: Reflective practice in drama and social studies.* Portsmouth, NH: Heinemann. Taylor draws from his narrative reflections and classroom-based research to explore the role of drama in social studies.

Wagner, B. J. 1976. *Dorothy Heathcote: Drama as a learning medium.* Washington, DC: National Education Association. Discusses Heathcote within drama.

———. 1978. The use of role. *Language Arts* 55: 323–327. Explores role taking and its impact on learning.

———. 1983. The expanding circle of informal classroom drama. In B. Busching (Ed.), *Integrating the language arts in the elementary school.* Urbana, IL: National Council of Teachers of English. Describes the nature of informal classroom drama.

———. 1985. Elevating the written word through the spoken. *Theory into Practice* 24: 166–172. Describes the thinking underlying Heathcote's work.

———. 1988. Does classroom drama affect the arts of language? *Language Arts* 65: 46–56. Reviews some of the research examining the effects of drama and role taking upon learning.

———. 2003. Imaginative expression. In J. Flood, J. Jensen, D. Lapp, and J. R. Squire (Eds.), *Handbook of research on teaching the language arts,* Vol. II. New York: Macmillan, 1008–1025. Explores the impact of drama and other forms of imaginative expression on learning, including reading and writing.

Wilhelm, J., and Edmiston, B. (Eds.). 1998. Imagining to learn: Inquiry, ethics and integration through drama. Portsmouth, NH: Heinemann. Edited volumes with a range of excellent contributions exploring drama worlds.

Wolf, S., B. Edmiston, and P. Enciso. 1997. Drama Worlds: Places of the heart, head, voice and hand in dramatic interpretation. In J. Flood, S. B. Heath, and D. Lapp (Eds.), *A handbook for literacy educators: research in teaching the communicative and visual arts.* New York: Macmillan. Discusses how process drama and other drama enactments afford students the opportunity to be active participants in ways that are generative and supportive of collaborative learning from different perspectives and that build upon cultural and linguistic backgrounds.

Point, Counterpoint

Purpose

The Point, Counterpoint response strategy was developed by Rogers (1987, 1990, 1991) as a way of helping students "build a repertoire of interpretative strategies" for dealing with complex stories.

Rationale

Rogers (1990, 1991) contends that students should be encouraged to develop their own interpretations of stories rather than acquiesce to either conventional interpretations or the imposition of a teacher's view of the selection. As she stated:

> during discussions of literature there is a reliance on examining standard elements of the text (e.g., setting and plot) and building toward a conventional interpretation or "class theme" instead of building on the transactions between readers and texts. (1990, p. 278)

According to Rogers (Rogers, 1990; Rogers, Green, and Nussbaum, 1990; Rogers, 1991) students need practice in dealing with the subtleties of complex narrative, drawing upon textual and extra-textual information to derive their own interpretations rather than adopting the singular and sometimes didactic interpretation of a teacher. With this in mind, Rogers (1990, 1991) has explored the viability of carefully guided response-based discussions of literature. In particular, for purposes of alerting students to the variance that may exist across understandings of themes as well as elements (e.g., character traits) which inform various interpretations, she has developed procedures for soliciting interpretations from students, and engaging students in comparisons and contrasts of these interpretations together with interpretations offered by professional critics. As she states:

> The key to the strategy is that the students begin with their own responses and move toward more public and generalized interpretations. Interpretive authority is shared among the teacher, the students and professional critics, but final interpretations rest with individual students. (1990, p. 281)

Intended Audience

Rogers (1990, 1991) developed the strategy for use with advanced high school students engaged in interpreting literature. With some adaptation, the strategy might be suitable for use with students at various levels.

Description of the Procedures

The strategy consists of three stages:

1. Initial written responses to story
2. Discussion of class responses and themes along with the interpretations of professional critics
3. Development of final responses

Stage 1: Initial Written Responses to Story. In the first stages, Rogers (1990) suggests that the students should read the story and jot down any responses that come to mind (e.g., what the story reminds them of, personal reflections, confusions, questions, and so on). Upon completion of students' reading, Rogers (1990) has them develop a preliminary essay relating their interpretation of the story—in particular, discussing themes they feel are significant. To illustrate, Rogers (1990) acquired the following initial responses from students after reading "A Clean Well-Lighted Place" by Ernest Hemingway.

> Think of your home. Everyday you come back to it and you cook and watch T.V. and sleep in it. People are there to talk to you and understand you. This is not the case for the old man in the story. The story centered on the difference between his home and the cafe that was "a clean, well-lighted place."
>
> I think this story is about the difference between young and old. It shows that the younger waiter and the younger generation only care about themselves. The young waiter just wants the old man to go home and even says he wishes his suicide attempt had been successful, which is extremely insensitive. The older waiter sympathizes with the old man and is more sensitive to his wanting to stay in "a clean, well-lighted place."
>
> It is through the waiter's introspection that Hemingway expresses his theme that some people believe that everything is nothing and is worth nothing and how nothing really matters. However, he still believes he should try to make everything as nice as it can be. He is a realist and an idealist at the same time.

Stage 2: Discussion of Responses. The second step in the Point, Counterpoint strategy involves a discussion based on the written responses. The goal of the discussion is to have students elaborate upon their responses and then compare them. The teacher's task is to facilitate the elaboration and comparison of interpretations while maintaining the stance that a variety of interpretations are reasonable. The following is an excerpt from the class discussion of "A Clean Well-Lighted Place" that Rogers (1990) guided. Please take special note of the discussion leader's (T's) role. During the discussion, the leader points out different kinds of strategies that the readers used and contrasts the elements that informed these various interpretations.

> **T:** Quite a few of you wrote about the theme of young vs. old in this story in terms of the younger waiter and the older waiter. Let's see, Bob, do you want to start by telling us why you thought that was an important theme?
>
> **BOB:** I remember putting that as one of two themes. It was basically because of the differences in what the two waiters thought of themselves and other people. The young waiter was very concerned about himself and he just kept saying, I just want to go home and go to bed, and the older waiter feels more concern with the people and the world around him. And he showed that by opening the cafe to people who might need it.
>
> **JOAN:** Well, I think the light versus dark theme is more important. It kind of goes along with the young and old theme because, well, the light imagery goes with the old waiter because he liked the lighted place and that was a bright place. And also the younger waiter liked the dark place, the cafe. Well, that's what I thought.
>
> **T:** Karen, you mentioned the light and dark theme but you saw it a little differently. Can you tell us about that?

KAREN: What I thought about the light and dark theme was that the old waiter is dark and the younger waiter is light because the older waiter and the old man had to go to light places and couldn't sleep until it was light, but the young waiter already had light in his life—a wife and comfort—so he didn't need the light.

T: So he didn't have to seek it out.

KAREN: Yes.

T: So either way, we might say that the contrasting images or themes of lightness and darkness are central to our interpretation of the story.

Rogers (1990) suggests that sometimes the teacher may want to bring in professional critical pieces about a story as a means of illustrating the range of interpretations and interpretative strategies. For example, Rogers used the following critical pieces of "A Clean Well-Lighted Place" as a means of expanding the students' views of the range of possible interpretations viable for that story.

> Though we have reason to believe Hemingway's heart is in the waiter's prayer to nada, we also know that his heart is with the waiter in his desire to provide a clean well-lighted place for all the solitary wanderers who must face the bitterness of nada. Unlike some other of Hemingway's stories, in which the characters are allowed to speak for his values without having earned, as it were, the right to do so, in this story the author's spokesman carries real power. Expressing a mood of bitterness against the darkness combined with a determination to fight the darkness with light—if only the clean, well-lighted place of art itself—the story can accommodate a dramatized spokesperson of a very simple, direct kind. (Booth, 1983).
>
> [Hemingway's] style, with its avoidance of syntactical subordination—the linguistic tool with which we arrange the items of our knowledge to show priorities or relationships of cause and effect—carries a large philosophical implication: the suggestion that life is ultimately meaningless. (Lodge, 1971).

Stage 3: Development of Final Responses. The third stage of the Point, Counterpoint strategy involves the students' revising their initial interpretation. Rogers (1990) suggests directions somewhat similar to the following:

> You now have an opportunity to rewrite your original essay. Feel free to incorporate any of the ideas discussed or any other reflections you may have. But, remember to back up your ideas or explain how you arrived at your ideas.

Ideally, the development of final responses takes the form of a self-assessment, including statements by students that either allude to their uncertainties or attribute a perspective to their viewpoints. Some of Rogers' (1990) examples will illustrate:

> Although even after the class discussion I'm not absolutely sure what the meaning of this story is, I have discovered a few themes, the theme of lightness and darkness and the theme of old versus young. It seems like the young people, such as the young waiter and the couple who walk by in the beginning of the story, somewhat seem to live more and thrive more during the daylight, while the older people, even though they needed light, were more like night people. So the light and dark theme can be incorporated into the young and old theme because the views and tastes of the older people throughout the story are contrasted to those of the young people.

My interpretation of "A Clean Well-Lighted Place" focuses on the older waiter. He desires a clean, well-lighted place because he fears darkness which symbolizes nothing. So he also fears nothing. He fears darkness and nothing because of his lack of confidence: "No, I have never had confidence." Another sentence that parallels this lack of confidence and his preference for light: "In the daytime, the street was dusty, but at night the dew settled the dust." The unsettled dust represents his lack of confidence. Because of his insecurity and fears, the older waiter prefers cleanliness and light.

The old waiter says that light and cleaner is better, while the young waiter thinks and acts as if it is not important. For instance, when he pours the old man a drink he did it very messily. The older waiter, and probably the older man, don't like the dirty bars. The older waiter thinks light is better. These things all show how the old and young theme and light and dark theme are important and intertwined.

Cautions and Comments

The Point, Counterpoint strategy proposed by Rogers (1990) represents an attempt to help students develop a more thoughtful approach to reading and interpreting complex literature. It offers teachers a framework by which they can do the following: (1) expose students to various interpretations; (2) engage students in a comparison of the elements that inform these different interpretations; and (3) encourage students to reflect on and self-assess their own interpretations. A major and worthwhile goal of Point, Counterpoint is helping students attain perspectives on their own interpretations and the procedures for doing so. The self-assessments and reflection, which are apparent in the written response Rogers has offered as illustration, suggest that the Point, Counterpoint achieves this goal. Indeed, Rogers (1991) has acquired some empirical support for this claim in a study involving a detailed analysis of selected students who were involved in using the strategy across a three-week period. Nonetheless, among several key questions remaining to be answered are: What are the characteristics of teachers, students, and curriculum that contribute to or detract from its use? Does the strategy contribute to sustained consideration of Points and Counterpoints by students?

The strategy lends itself to a number of adaptations. For example, the students might be encouraged to respond to the selection with sketches, which are then shared and revised. In this regard, some of the procedures proposed by Harste and associates for Sketch to Stretch (this unit) might be enlisted. The strategy also might be extended to require students to co-author a final essay incorporating or contrasting selected interpretations. Activities akin to televised reviews by opposing critics might be proposed. Finally, some consideration might be given to the possibility of helping students become independent users of the Point, Counterpoint strategy. Perhaps students could be encouraged to initiate dialogues with others and themselves as a means of prompting a consideration of different possible interpretations of stories.

REFERENCES

Booth, W. 1983. *The rhetoric of fiction.* Chicago: University of Chicago Press.

Galda, L., G. E. Ash, and B. E. Cullinan. 2000. Children's literature. In M. L. Kamil, P. B. Mosenthal, P. D. Pearson, and R. Barr (Eds.), *Handbook of reading research,* Vol. III. Mahwah, NJ: Erlbaum, 361–380. Reviews some of the work on response to children's literature, including the impact of strategies akin to those included in this unit.

Lodge, D. 1971. Hemingway's clean, well-lighted puzzling place. *Essays in Criticism* 21(1).

Marshall, J. 2000. Research on response to literature. In M. L. Kamil, P. B. Mosenthal, P. D. Pearson, and R. Barr (Eds.), *Handbook of reading research,* Vol. III. Mahwah, NJ: Erlbaum, 381–402. Reviews work on response to literature, including the impact of strategies akin to those included in this unit.

Martinez, M., and N. Roser. 2003. Children's responses to literature. In J. Flood, J. Jensen, D. Lapp, and J. R. Squire (Eds.), *Handbook of research on teaching the language arts,* Vol. II. New York: Macmillan, 799–813. Explores issues and research concerning response to literature, including classroom-based studies.

Probst, R. E. 2003. Response to literature. In J. Flood, J. Jensen, D. Lapp, and J. R. Squire (Eds.), *Handbook of research on teaching the language arts,* Vol. II. New York: Macmillan, 814–824. Explores issues and research concerning response to literature, including classroom-based studies.

Purves, A., T. Rogers, and A. Soter. 1990. *How porcupines make love II: Teaching a response-centered literature curriculum.* New York: Longman. Includes a description and discussion of point–counterpoint.

Rogers, T. 1987. Exploring a socio-cognitive perspective on the interpretive processes of junior high school students. *English Quarterly* 20(3): 218–230.

———. 1990. A Point, Counterpoint response strategy for complex short stories. *The Journal of Reading* 34: 278–282. Describes the strategy including the rationale, procedures, and use.

Rogers, T. 1991. Students as literary critics: The interpretive experiences, beliefs, and processes of ninth-grade students. *Journal of Reading Behavior* 23(4): 391–423.

Rogers, T., J. Green, and N. Nussbaum. 1990. Asking questions about questions. In S. Hynds and D. Rubin (Eds.), *Perspectives on talk and learning.* Urbana, IL: National Council of Teachers of English. Discusses the role of teacher and student talk in the development of interpretative abilities and attitudes.

Response Heuristic

Purpose

The Response Heuristic (Bleich, 1978) is designed to promote students' response to literature by helping them independently analyze and interpret literary texts.

Rationale

Answering questions after reading is the most frequently used means to get students to respond to text material, literary or otherwise. Unfortunately, questions rarely provide students with sufficient structure to enable them to evaluate ideas as they are encountered. In addition, students may become dependent on external prompts in their efforts to react to literature, i.e., they rely on teacher questions to stimulate their thinking. Thus, students do not gain a structure for their own independent analysis of text and may not be able to react beyond a mere literal parroting of it.

In order to move beyond a literal repetition of text, students need to be able to use their prior knowledge in conjunction with the text information. Thus, comprehension becomes a shared experience between reader and text or, as Petrosky (1982) stated, comprehension occurs "through some kind of structured response that leads to a dialectic which represents the interaction of readers with a text" (p. 21).

A number of reading and language educators (e.g., Tierney and Pearson, 1983) have suggested that reading is a composing process. In other words, comprehending text and composing text are seen as the same process—both are acts of understanding—and language use is viewed holistically rather than as a series of discrete pieces. Writing, therefore, may provide the best means to represent students' understandings of text, if reading is viewed as a composing process and not merely as an act of recall prompted by questions.

One strategy for responding to literature that provides students a structured response format as they interact with text, and that views reading, writing, and responding all as aspects of understanding, is the Response Heuristic (Bleich, 1978). Bleich stated that the only way to show understanding is for readers to become writers who express their understandings of the text in their responses. Comprehension, then, means expressing in writing a response to explain the connections that readers make between their reality (prior knowledge) and the texts they create in light of that reality. Thus, unlike recall models of comprehension, the Response Heuristic provides readers the means to discuss their thoughts and feelings while at the same time making meaning by writing an explanatory response to their reading. Bleich believes this approach to literature response represents comprehension more accurately than the use of questions.

Intended Audience

The Response Heuristic may be used with all students once they have attained the ability to express themselves in writing. Thus, it is probably most appropriate when used with upper elementary and with older students as a means of getting them to respond to literary texts.

Description of the Procedures

The Response Heuristic asks students to react in writing in the following three-part format:

1. Text perceptions
2. Reactions to the text
3. Associations with the text

1. Text Perceptions. Since free response to text has a tendency to lack focus and be sketchy, the Response Heuristic is designed to get students to structure their responses in a more focused manner. The Response Heuristic begins with references to the text read. It is simply a statement of what a reader sees in the text. For instance, if the Response Heuristic were being used in conjunction with "Richard Cory" by E. A. Robinson and popularized by Simon and Garfunkel in song, some references to the text might include the following:

> Richard Cory was a gentleman admired by all. He was polite and rich, and everyone wished they were in his place.

2. Reactions to the Text. Once some references to the text are given, the next step of the heuristic is for students to react to those references by writing how they felt about them. It is at this point in the response that students begin to make some links to their experiences. To continue with our example of the poem "Richard Cory," some reactions might be:

> I can understand how people look at how things appear on the outside, without bothering to look further, without bothering to find out what's going on inside. It's important to me, though, that people go beyond mere appearances.

3. Associations with the Text. The last part of the Response Heuristic is where students write about the associations—their feelings and thoughts—that emanate from their perceptions of the text. It is here that the response is further explained by using examples from the students' prior knowledge and beliefs. Associations that might be formulated using our "Richard Cory" example are:

> When I was younger, I was big for my age. People, my friends, and family—especially my father—told me that I'd make a great football player because of my size. They said I was strong and fast enough to be a great back. But nobody—not a single person—bothered to ask me what I wanted. They just told me what I should do. Sure, I was big enough to play, but what good is size if the desire's not there. Besides, I hated football! People were just responding to how I looked and what I had, just as people did with Richard Cory.

Cautions and Comments

Key to the success of the Response Heuristic, or any other literature response technique, is what happens after students have responded in writing. It is essential that a sharing/discussion of students' individual responses take place. In this way, readers can see how others have interpreted a literary text and can see that a variety of thoughts, feelings, and opinions, and reasons for them, can exist about the same text or topic. Readers can begin to treat their responses as critical statements that need to be examined and discussed. In addition, they can treat their writing as drafts to be refined, revised, and edited. Following such a procedure, students gain experiences in reading, writing about what was read, discussing others' thoughts about reading, critiquing others' writing, and editing and revising.

Another concern in using the Response Heuristic is the teacher's role. If an offshoot of this literature response strategy is to create a community of readers and writers, then teachers cannot remain outside observers. They must become part of the context in which the Response Heuristic is taking place. Teachers also need to read and write and share their unique perspectives with students. If the procedure is to work, it will work best with teachers who are alert to the models that students are being provided and are either finding appropriate peer models or acting as models themselves for students.

The Response Heuristic is one way to approach response to literature. Indeed, the following frameworks for examining responses to literature strategies are recommended as possible alternatives to the Response Heuristic. They represent alternative frameworks by which teachers might structure response activities or reflect upon students' comments. They represent ways by which students might begin to analyze the actions and motives of characters, etc.

1. Transactional analysis structures (Readence and Moore, 1979) based on the experiences that describe all transactions between individuals as set forth by T. A. Harris (e.g., withdrawal, rituals, pastimes, activities, games, and intimacy).

2. Stages of moral reasoning (Readence, Moore, and Moore, 1982) based on Kohlberg's view of the sequence by which Western cultures develop moral standards, for example, in simple terms Kohlberg's stages are punishment/obedience, the marketplace, good boy/nice girl, law and order, social contract, and universal ethics.

3. Stages of confronting death (Moore, Moore, and Readence, 1983) based on individuals' reactions to death as described by E. Kübler-Ross. These stages include denial, anger, bargaining, depression, and acceptance.

REFERENCES

Bleich, D. 1978. *Subjective criticism.* Baltimore: Johns Hopkins University Press. A discussion of the Response Heuristic, as well as a critical examination of responses and texts.

Galda, L., G. E. Ash, and B. E. Cullinan. 2000. Children's literature. In M. L. Kamil, P. B. Mosenthal, P. D. Pearson, and R. Barr (Eds.), *Handbook of reading research,* Vol. III. Mahwah, NJ: Erlbaum, 361–380. Reviews some of the work on response to literature with children's literature, including the impact of strategies akin to those included in this unit.

Marshall, J. 2000. Research on response to literature. In M. L. Kamil, P. B. Mosenthal, P. D. Pearson, and R. Barr (Eds.), *Handbook of reading research,* Vol. III. Mahwah, NJ: Erlbaum, 381–402. Reviews work on response to literature including the impact of strategies akin to those included in this unit.

Martinez, M., and N. Roser. 2003. Children's responses to literature. In J. Flood, J. Jensen, D. Lapp, and J. R. Squire (Eds.), *Handbook of research on teaching the language arts,* Vol. II. New York: Macmillan, 799–813. Explores issues and research concerning response to literature including classroom-based studies.

Moore, D. W., S. A. Moore, and J. E. Readence. 1983. Understanding characters' reactions to death. *Journal of Reading* 26: 540–544. Describes how Kübler-Ross's stages of confronting death can be used as a means to help students respond to death-related literature.

Petrosky, A. R. 1982. From story to essay: Reading and writing. *College Composition and Communication* 33: 19–36. A discussion of the connections between reading, writing, and response to literature, including some examples of the Response Heuristic.

Probst, R. E. 2003. Response to literature. In J. Flood, J. Jensen, D. Lapp, and J. R. Squire (Eds.), *Handbook of research on teaching the language arts,* Vol. II. New York: Macmillan, 814–824. Explores issues and research concerning response to literature, including classroom-based studies.

Purves, A. C., L. Papa, and S. Jordan (Eds.). 1994. *Encyclopedia of English studies and language arts.* New York: National Council of Teachers of English. This encyclopedia has more than 800 annotated entries/topics that succinctly address this topic and related areas.

Readence, J. E., and D. W. Moore. 1979. Responding to literature: An alternative to questioning. *Journal of Reading* 23: 107–111. Examines the use of transactional analysis structures as a strategy for students' independently responding to literature.

Readence, J. E., D. W. Moore, and S. A. Moore. 1982. Kohlberg in the classroom: Responding to literature. *Journal of Reading* 26: 104–108. Delineates the procedures for using the stages of moral development as a technique for literature response.

Tierney, R. J., and P. D. Pearson. 1983. Toward a composing model of reading. *Language Arts* 60: 568–580. Discusses the notion that both reading and writing are composing processes.

Sketch to Stretch

Purpose

Sketch to Stretch is intended to help readers use sketches as a means of exploring, expressing, and sharing interpretations of selections.

Rationale

Sketch to Stretch was originally developed by Jerome Harste, Carolyn Burke, Marjorie Siegel, and Karen Feathers at Indiana University. The rationale for Sketch to Stretch is tied to the notion of transmediation—that is, taking meanings in one communication system and recasting them in terms of another system. It assumes that recasting meanings in a visual medium (sketches) allows for the generation of new meanings and the achievement of insights as a result of shifting media. In addition, it affords the reader a means of capturing meanings in art that may not be able to be captured in verbal responses.

Sketch to Stretch also places a great deal of emphasis on the assumption that it is important for students to realize that different readers generate different interpretations and that even the same reader may have more than one interpretation of a selection. With this in mind, integral to Sketch to Stretch are opportunities for students to have others react to the interpretations as well as share their own, and to revise their interpretations based upon these various inputs.

Intended Audience

Sketch to Stretch is appropriate for use by readers at any age level.

Description of the Procedures

In short, Sketch to Stretch involves having students generate a sketch depicting their interpretations of a text or event and then sharing it with a small group of classmates who offer their interpretations of each other's sketches.

Sketch to Stretch requires that students have a copy of a reading selection plus paper, pencil, and crayons. Harste, Short, and Burke (1988) suggest placing students in groups of four or five. In conjunction with reading a selection, the students are asked to think about the selection and draw a sketch of "what the selection meant to you or what you made of the selection. . . ." (p. 354).

Harste, Short, and Burke (1988) emphasize that it is important to do the following: (1) encourage students to experiment, (2) alert them to the fact that there are many ways of representing meanings, (3) help students focus on interpretation rather than on artistic talents, and (4) provide them ample time so that they are not rushed.

When the sketches are complete, each person in the group shares his or her sketch with other group members. Without the originator of the sketch's telling other group members of his or her interpretation, each group member says what he or she thinks the artist is attempting to say. Once everyone has been given the opportunity to suggest an interpretation, the artist presents his or her interpretation. Sharing continues in this manner until all group members have shared their sketches.

Each group selects one sketch to share with the entire class via the overhead projector if necessary. Again, class members share their interpretations prior to the artist's and the artist's group members' sharing their interpretations.

Figures 10.1, 10.2, and 10.3 represent some examples of sketches in conjunction with work with school-age children. Sometimes, it is useful for students to see examples by others or the teacher so that they have some sense of the possibilities.

Harste, Short, and Burke (1988) point out that some students may need repeated opportunities to try the activity before they begin to experiment with the meanings they are creating.

In conjunction with sharing sketches, Harste, Short, and Burke emphasize that teachers should discuss: (1) why various readers have different interpretations, and (2) that differences represent different interests and backgrounds of readers and should not be viewed as right or wrong.

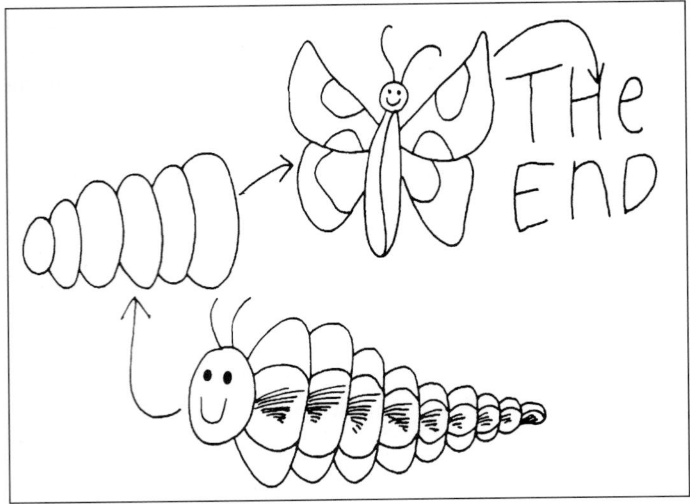

FIGURE 10.1 Sketch for *The Very Hungry Caterpillar* (Carle 1969).
Source: Siegel (1984).

FIGURE 10.2 Sketch for *Ira Sleeps Over* (Waber 1972)
Source: Siegel (1984).

FIGURE 10.3 Sketch for *Nana Upstairs, Nana Downstairs* (De Paola 1972).
Source: Siegel (1984).

Follow-up activities suggested by Harste, Short, and Burke (1988) include:

1. Developing sketches for related texts.

2. Using sketches in conjunction with doing drafts, presenting written texts, or complementing written projects.

3. Compiling sketches for class books, message boards, and the like.
4. Extending Sketch to Stretch to doing videos or animation.

Cautions and Comments

Siegel (1984) argues that the opportunity to explore interpretations through art (or dance, drama, etc.) affords the interpreter ways to access understandings, explore interpretations, and consider alternative interpretations. What is important to recognize is that meanings cast in a visual medium, such as art, are apt to afford possibilities that more verbally oriented procedures (e.g., retellings, answers to questions) might not.

In time past, both researchers and practitioners have restricted themselves to verbal displays of "correct" interpretations rather than multimedia illustrations of a variety of interpretations. The research of Siegel (1984) with fourth graders points to the power of this practice to enhance displays of understandings and motivate interest in interpretation. In her doctoral dissertation "Reading as Signification," Siegel provides a theoretically rich justification for "Sketch to Stretch" and, from working with fourth graders, substantive evidence of its worth. In a similar vein, the work of Dyson (1988a, 1988b) suggests that transmediation offers learners important scaffoldings as well as vehicles for building and sharing meanings.

As Paula Whitin (2000) noted, "The sketches are metaphorical by nature, so it is impossible to have literal retellings. . . . [T]his strategy [is] effective in encouraging a diversity of perspectives about a story, and in using it, many potential at-risk readers as well as stronger students become valued literary interpreters" (p. 53).

REFERENCES

Alejandro, A. 1994. Like happy dreams—Integrating visual arts, writing, and reading. *Language Arts* 71: 12–21. Explores art as a meaning-making tool and as a way of enhancing the language arts program.

Berghoff, B. 1998. Multiple sign systems and reading. *The Reading Teacher* 51(6): 520–523. Discusses incorporating multiple sign systems into the classroom.

Dyson, A. H. 1988a. *Drawing, talking, and writing: Rethinking writing development.* Center for the Study of Writing, Occasional Paper No. 3, University of California, Berkeley. Discusses changes in children's imaginative texts as supported by drawing and talking with peers.

———. 1988b. Negotiations among multiple worlds. The space/time dimensions of young children's composing. *Research in the Teaching of English* 22: 355–390. Discusses the interrelationships between the children's creation of written, imaginative worlds and their use of symbolic media (drawing talk).

———. 1989. *Multiple worlds of child writers: Friends learning to write.* New York: Teachers College Press. Longitudinal study of children using reading, writing, drawing, and talk in their acquisition of literacy.

Ernst, K. 1994. Writing pictures, painting words: Writing in an artist's workshop. *Language Arts* 71: 44–52. Discusses the integration of art as a meaning-making tool.

Harste, J., C. Short, and C. Burke. 1988. *Creating classrooms for authors.* Portsmouth, NH: Heinemann. Presents a brief description of the use of Sketch to Stretch.

Labbo, L. D. 1996. A semiotic analysis of young children's symbol making in a classroom computer center. *Reading Research Quarterly* 31(4): 356–385. An ethnographic study of computer generated symbols by kindergartners.

Moss, B. 1995. Nurturing artistic images in student reading and writing. *The Reading Teacher* 48(6): 532–608. Explores different ways art can be used to explore images in concert with reading and writing.

Olshansky, B. 1997. Picturing story: An irresistible pathway into literacy. *The Reading Teacher* 50(7): 612–613. Uses picture making and collages as a way of enhancing reading and writing stories.

Purves, A. C., L. Papa, and S. Jordan (Eds.). 1994. *Encyclopedia of English studies and language arts.* New York: National Council of Teachers of English. This encyclopedia has more than 800 annotated entries/topics that succinctly address this topic and related areas.

Purves, A. C., T. Rogers, and A. O. Soter. 1991. *How porcupines make love II: Teaching a response-centered literature curriculum.* New York: Longman. Includes visual responses to literature with adolescents.

Short, K., J. Harste, and C. Burke. 1996. *Creating classrooms for authors and inquirers.* Portsmouth, NH: Heinemann. Explores the use of Sketch to Stretch in various settings and discusses the relationship of such pursuits for meaning making.

Short, K., G. Kauffman, and L. Kahn. 2000. "I just need to draw": Responding to literature across multiple sign systems. *The Reading Teacher* 54: 160–171. Discusses the role of Sketch to Stretch as a means of enhancing response to literature.

Siegel, M. 1984. *Reading as signification.* Doctoral diss., Indiana University, Bloomington. Presents an extensive discussion of the theoretical underpinnings and describes a study with fourth graders involved in Sketch to Stretch.

Smagorinsky, P., and J. Coppock. 1996. Exploring artistic response to literature. In C. K. Kinzer and D. J. Leu (Eds.), *Multidimensional aspects of literacy research, theory, and practice.* Chicago: National Reading Conference, 335–341. Pursues a case study of a 16-year-old using art in response to literature.

Stephens, D. 1994. Learning what art means. *Language Arts* 71: 34–37. Discusses the use of art to make meaning.

Whitin, P. 1994. Opening potential: Visual response to literature. *Language Arts* 71: 101–107. Describes the use of Sketch to Stretch with middle grades.

———. 1996. *Sketching stories, stretching minds.* Portsmouth, NH: Heinemann. Provides a rich array of classroom based examples of the use of Sketch to Stretch.

———. 2000. Inventing metaphors to understand the genre of poetry. *Journal of the Association for Expanded Perspectives on Learning* 6: 52–63. Explores Sketch to Stretch as a vehicle for understanding poetry.

———. 2002. Leading into literature: Circles through the Sketch to Stretch strategy. *The Reading Teacher* 55(5): 444–450. Discusses Sketch to Stretch as an aid to engagement with students of varying abilities.

Readers Theatre

Purpose

Readers Theatre is a procedure for integrating the language arts and advancing a student's motivation to read. In addition, it focuses on improving students' oral reading and interpretation, as well as their composition and comprehension abilities.

Rationale

In a book on Readers Theatre, Sloyer (1982) described it in these terms:

> Readers Theatre is an interpretative reading activity for all the children in the classroom. Readers bring characters to life through their voices and gestures. Listeners are captivated by the vitalized stories and complete the activity by imagining the details of scene and action. . . . Used in the classroom, Readers Theatre becomes an integrated language event centering upon oral interpretation of literature. The children adapt and present the material of their choice. A story, a poem, a scene from a play, even a song lyric, provide the ingredients for the script. As a thinking, reading, writing, speaking and listening experience, Readers Theatre makes a unique contribution to our language arts curriculum. (p. 3)

Unlike many of the strategies described in this book, Readers Theatre has emerged largely from the hands of teachers as they have crafted its use in the classroom. The rationale for using it stems largely from the enthusiasm with which students are drawn to it.

Reading material that was drab and unappealing in normal classroom circumstances becomes alive, exciting, and interpretable when done in conjunction with Readers Theatre. Apart from its motivational value, what contributes to the worth of the procedure are the reading, writing, and listening skills that are refined in conjunction with the development and redevelopment of a script and its performance. What drives Readers Theatre is the performance, rather than some arbitrary determination of what is satisfactory by the teacher.

Intended Audience

Readers Theatre can be used with students at all age levels regardless of their abilities.

Description of the Procedures

Readers Theatre involves students in the process from start to finish. Students select their own material, adapt it for presentation to the class, and portray the characters in performances to classmates and others. The steps that might be used in guiding the process are described below. With slight variation these steps are based upon those offered by Sloyer (1982).

1. Selecting Material. A great deal of care needs to go into the selection of materials. Certainly teachers must judge for themselves the interests of their students. But what seems desirable are tight plots with clear endings and suspense, interesting characters, lively dialogue, and appealing themes. Other than the dramatization of stories, poems, popular songs, advertisements, and other types of text lend themselves to use in Readers Theatre. For variation, sometimes the dramatization can be done in the form of a musical, a TV newscast, or a documentary.

2. Getting Started. A classroom discussion about theater or a movie is a natural springboard for Readers Theatre. The discussion should be both open-ended and focused on what it would take to change a book into a movie.

3. A Sample to See and Read. Once students have brainstormed about play- or moviemaking, they should be introduced to an example of a short story for which a script exists. The students should be given an opportunity to read both versions and discuss the types of adjustments that were made in changing the text from a story to a play and other issues that need to be considered if the play is to be performed.

4. Plan for an Adaptation. Using the story for which there already is a script as a model, the students are encouraged to choose another story from their readers or some other source for them to adapt. A short story or a single scene from a story that students will not find difficult to make into a play is recommended. Before any adaptation takes place, students should read or reread the story and discuss elements of story that are key to its dramatization. These include the characters and their attributes, the plot, the theme, and the setting.

5. Adapt the Story. For purposes of adapting the story, use larger poster paper, an overhead, or the chalkboard. Place the title as well as the time, setting, and list of characters on the poster. Then discuss the adaptation.

a. Depending on the story, the students might discuss:

The characters in the story and what each says

The role of the characters and the narrator (sometimes a character can act as narrator; at other times, an observer who is not part of the action may). In order to give more students an opportunity to participate, the students may decide on two or more narrators;

The events, descriptions of feelings or observations and how they might be included in the play as action, sound effects, dialogue, or the narrator's remarks.

b. Following some discussion, write the names of the characters, including the narrator, in bold letters in the margin of the poster. Write the lines assigned to each character next to his or her name. Once the skeleton has begun to develop, encourage the students to make the language more interesting and realistic. If there are characters with no or very few lines, have them suggest revisions so that they have more to say.

c. Once the script is completed, reproduce it for performance. The fable "The Shepherd's Boy and the Wolf" and an adaptation are shown in Figures 10.4 and 10.5.

6. Preparing for Theatrical Production. In preparing for the theatrical production, students need to be introduced to some aspects of stage craft, including working out the positions and actions of the readers on the stage. For this purpose, students can be introduced to the different areas on the stages where action might occur and characters might stand or move. Props and body movements can be discussed and notes made by the students as they discuss what should occur in their play. To assist the students, time might be provided for warm-up exercises in which students experiment with expressing themselves with body actions.

Likewise, students should be given an opportunity to discuss and experiment with their lines. Again warm-up exercises might be used as a means of exploring different voices (angry, friendly, frightened), as well as appropriate pauses and pacing.

FIGURE 10.4 The Shepherd's Boy and the Wolf

A Shepherd's Boy was tending his flock near a village, and thought it would be great fun to hoax the villagers by pretending that a Wolf was attacking the sheep: so he shouted out, "Wolf! Wolf!" and when the people came running up he laughed at them for their pains. He did this more than once, and every time the villagers found they had been hoaxed, for there was no Wolf at all. At last a Wolf really did come, and the Boy cried, "Wolf! Wolf!" as loud as he could. But the people were so used to hearing him call that they took no notice of his cries for help. And so the Wolf had it all his own way, and killed off sheep after sheep at his leisure.

You cannot believe a liar
even when he tells the truth.

FIGURE 10.5 Adaptation

"The Shepherd's Boy and the Wolf"

NARRATOR I: A shepherd's boy was tending his flock near a village, and thought it would be great fun to hoax the villagers by pretending that a wolf was attacking the sheep: so he shouted

BOY: Wolf!

NARRATOR II: And when the villagers came running up . . .

VILLAGERS: Wolf? Where?!

NARRATOR I: he laughed at them for their pains:

BOY: Ha ha . . . I had you fooled!

NARRATOR I: He did this more than once, and every time the villagers found they had been hoaxed, for there was no Wolf at all.

BOY: Ha ha . . .

VILLAGERS: (grumbling) That boy! He's fooled us again. Look at him laugh.

NARRATOR II: At last a wolf really did come . . .

WOLF: Yum yum! Look at those tasty lamb chops!

NARRATOR II: and the Boy cried . . .

BOY: Wolf! Wolf!

NARRATOR II: as loud as he could.

NARRATOR I: But the people were so used to hearing him call that they took no notice of his cries for help.

VILLAGERS: Ignore him. He only wants to laugh at us. He's a liar.

NARRATOR II: Meanwhile, the wolf had it his own way, and killed off sheep after sheep at his leisure.

ALL: But no one ever came to help, for you cannot believe a liar even when he tells the truth.

Source: V. S. Verson Jones, *Aesop's Fables* (New York: Avenel Books, 1912), p. 41.

With large groups of students, the teacher may wish to organize different casts and production teams. A production team might include a director, a lighting engineer, a sound effects engineer, and a stage manager.

Once the students and teacher feel satisfied with issues of staging, students should be given an opportunity to rehearse with their cast. It should be noted that in Readers Theatre students read their lines. Memorization of a script is not pursued.

7. Performing the Play and Follow-Up. A language event does not end with the performance of the play. Once students perform, the teacher and class discuss how the different characters were portrayed and other aspects of how the play was staged. These discussions serve a variety of functions. Not only do they give the students feedback, they also introduce students to the possibility of revision and further refinement of a play as well as techniques and procedures that might be used in subsequent productions.

8. Preparing a Full-Length Program. Now that the students have worked through the process of adapting and performing a short story, they are ready to go on to longer productions, adapting other types of text, experimenting with different types of scripts, and trying out variations in how a play is staged. For this purpose, a number of different teams might be organized. During adaptation of the story, different segments might be parceled out to different work groups. During the planning of the performance, different groups can be involved in directing, performing, or being theater critics or reviewers.

Cautions and Comments

For over two decades, Readers Theatre has been used in classrooms by teachers who have reported the benefits of the approach with enthusiasm. In an age of musical videotapes and young moviegoers, students not only enjoy being actors and members of an audience, they also are attracted to moviemaking and playmaking. Readers Theatre provides students an opportunity to learn about plot, characterization, and some of the less tangible features of stories such as theme, voice, and mood. Students can also explore a variety of subject matters through Readers Theatre, as Young and Vardell (1993) point out. Furthermore, this learning involves participating rather than observing, is child-centered rather than teacher-directed, and is goal-directed rather than arbitrarily required. Certainly it is impossible to incorporate Readers Theatre into a classroom and not enjoy these types of capabilities.

Technology, in the form of word processing, may be beneficial to Readers Theatre activities, particularly during the process of developing the script. Additionally, there are special word processing programs just for producing drama script format.

Care should be taken not to initiate goals that surpass student capabilities. Sometimes a teacher may try to do too much or have overly high expectations for staging a play. Indeed, one of the advantages and disadvantages of Readers Theatre is the extent to which it formalizes what in many classrooms occurs rather incidentally and spontaneously. The formality of the procedure extends the use of dramatization of a story to the development of more precise reading, writing, and oral interpretation abilities. At the same time, the formality of the procedure may detract from the frequency with which teachers encourage students to project themselves, dramatize story segments, and explore different voices as they read different stories on a more frequent and incidental basis.

Although Readers Theatre is used as a means of adapting literature and for purposes of learning about dramatic form and elements, its uses extend to exploring certain key issues (similar to Process Drama and Theater of the Oppressed described in this unit) and as a means of exploring topics in science and other subjects. Readers Theatre has the potential to bring to the fore complexities, multiple perspectives and multiple voices in a manner that may not be as forthcoming in other modes of presentation or exploration.

REFERENCES

Adams, W. 2003. *Institute book of Readers Theatre: A practical guide for school, theatre, and community.* San Diego: Institute for Readers Theatre. A comprehensive treatment of Reader's Theatre.

Barchers, S. I. 2002. *Classic Readers Theatre for young adults.* Adapted by S. I. Barchers and J. L. Kroll. Greenwood Village, CO: Teacher Ideas Press. Adaptation of over fifteen classics by well-known authors such as Alcott, Cervantes, Maupassant, Dickens, Hawthorne, Kipling, Poe, and Stevenson.

Bauer, C. F. 1987. *Presenting Reader's Theater: Plays and poems to read aloud.* New York: H. W. Wilson. Scripts adapted from a variety of children's authors, plus advice.

Busching, B. A. 1981. Readers Theatre: An education for language and life. *Language Arts* 58: 330–338. Discusses the value of Readers Theatre and offers suggestions for its implementation in the elementary school.

Coger, L. I., and M. R. White. 1982. *Readers Theatre handbook: A dramatic approach to literature.* Glenview, IL: Scott, Foresman. This book presents the rationale, history, and principles underlying Readers Theatre. Several scripts and summaries of presentations are included.

Dixon N., A. Davies, and C. Politano. 1996. *Learning with Readers Theatre.* Winnipeg, Manitoba: Peguis. Presents the background and theory on Readers Theatre and ideas for staging, script writing, and assessment strategies.

Donmoyer, J., and R. Donmoyer. 1991. Readers Theatre: Give us some "for instances." *Literacy Matters* 3: 4–9. Provides examples of Readers Theatre and some steps for getting it started. This entire issue of *Literacy Matters* is devoted to Readers Theatre.

Edmiston, B., and P. Enciso. 2003. Reflections and refractions of meaning: Dialogical approaches to classroom drama and reading. In J. Flood, J. Jensen, D. Lapp, and J. R. Squire (Eds.), *Handbook of research on teaching the language arts,* Vol. II. New York: Macmillan. Excellent survey of work on drama and reading and their role in meaning making.

Feola, M. S. 1996. Using drama to develop college students' transaction with text. *Journal of Adolescent & Adult Literacy* 39(8): 624–628. Describes the impact of having students dramatize texts they read.

Fredericks, A. D. 2002. *Science fiction Readers Theatre.* Westport, CT: Teacher Ideas Press. Offers science fiction possibilities for Readers Theatre, Grades K–2. Provides a collection of quality literature listed under seasonal themes, and provides Reader Theatre activities.

Haven, K. 1996. *Great moments in science: Experiments and Readers Theatre.* Portsmouth, NH: Teacher Ideas Press. Combines scripts about famous scientists with experiments that illustrate the principles they discovered.

Hoyt, L. 1992. Many ways of knowing: Using drama, oral interactions, and the visual arts to enhance reading comprehension. *Reading Teacher* 45: 580–584. Presents Readers Theater as a strategy for improving comprehension.

Jackson, F. R., and L. Kerr-Norflett. 1997. Improving literacy skills through Jamaican-style play building. *Journal of Adolescent & Adult Literacy* 41(2): 98–103. Describes how Jamaican-style play making could be used to help students see multiple perspectives.

Kieff, J. 2002. Voices from the school yard: Responding to school stories through Readers' Theater. *Journal of Children's Literature* 28(1): 80–87. Discusses Readers Theater and its use in schools.

Maclay, J. H. 1971. *Readers Theatre: Toward a grammar of practice.* New York: Random House. Discusses the worth of Readers Theatre and makes suggestions on material selection, casting, directing, and staging.

Post, R. M. 1974. Readers Theatre as a method of teaching literature. *English Journal* 64: 69–72. Discusses the use of Readers Theatre in high school English classes.

Purves, A. C., L. Papa, and S. Jordan (Eds.). 1994. *Encyclopedia of English studies and language arts.* New York: National Council of Teachers of English. This encyclopedia has more than 800 annotated entries/topics that succinctly address this topic and related areas.

Raczuk, H., and M. Smith. 1999. *Early literacy—A seasonal approach.* Winnipeg, Manitoba: Portage and Main Press.

———. 1996. *Invitation to Munsch.* Winnipeg, Manitoba: Portage and Main Press. Grades K–6. A guidebook for using literature in the elementary classroom. Includes Readers Theatre.

———. 1997. *Invitation to Readers Theatre.* Winnipeg, Manitoba: Portage and Main Press. Grades K–6. Contains over two dozen scripts to help celebrate holidays and special events.

———. 2000. *Invitation to Readers Theatre book 2.* Winnipeg, Manitoba: Portage and Main Press. Contains reproducible scripts of folk tales from around the world.

Rinehart, S. D. 2001. Establishing guidelines for using Readers Theater with less-skilled readers. *Reading Horizons* 42(2): 65–75. Explores the use of Readers Theatre in classrooms.

Shepard, A. 1993. *Stories on stage: Scripts for Reader's Theatre.* New York: H. W. Wilson. A collection of Readers Theatre scripts, with adaptations of stories by a variety of authors for a wide range of reading levels, focussed on ages 8 to 15.

———. 1994. From script to stage: Tips for Readers Theatre. *The Reading Teacher* 48(2): 184–188. Provides a rich discussion on Readers Theatre.

Sloyer, S. 1982. *Readers Theatre: Story dramatization in the classroom.* Urbana, IL: National Council of Teachers of English. Presents a comprehensive discussion of Readers Theatre, including suggestions for planning and implementing. Represents a rich resource for locating materials appropriate for scripting.

———. 2003. *From the page to the stage: The educator's complete guide to Readers Theatre.* Portsmouth,

NH: Teacher Ideas Press. Scripts for elementary and middle grades.

Tyler, B., and D. J. Chard. 2000. Using Readers Theatre to foster fluency in struggling readers: A twist on the repeated reading strategy. *Reading and Writing Quarterly* 16: 163–168. Explores Readers Theatre as a support for reading development.

Wagner, B. J. 2003. Imaginative expression. In J. Flood, J. Jensen, D. Lapp, and J. R. Squire (Eds.), *Handbook of research on teaching the language arts,* Vol. II. New York: Macmillan, 1008–1025. Explores the impact of drama and other forms of imaginative expression on learning, including reading and writing.

Wertheimer, A. 1974. Story dramatization in the reading center. *English Journal* 64: 85–87. Discusses the use of Readers Theatre with reluctant readers at the elementary level.

Wolf, S. A. 1993. What's in a name? Labels and literacy in Readers Theatre. *The Reading Teacher* 46: 540–545. Yearlong study of Readers Theatre and remedial readers in a classroom.

Wolf, S., B. Edmiston, and P. Enciso. 1997. Drama worlds: Places of the heart, head, voice and hand in dramatic interpretation. In J. Flood, S. B. Heath, and D. Lapp (Eds.), *A handbook for literacy educators: Research in teaching the communicative and visual arts.* New York: Macmillan. Wolf, Edmiston, and Enciso argue that process drama and other drama enactments afford students the opportunity to be active participants in ways that are generative and supportive of collaborative learning from different perspectives, and that build upon cultural and linguistic backgrounds.

Worthy, J., and K. Prater. 2002. "I thought about it all night": Readers Theatre for reading fluency and motivation. *The Reading Teacher* 56(3): 294–297. Discusses theory, research and benefits of Readers Theatre and includes a short list of books to develop a Readers Theatre library.

Young, T. A., and Vardell, S. 1993. Weaving Readers Theatre and nonfiction into the curriculum. *The Reading Teacher* 46: 396–406. Discusses using Readers Theatre in content area reading.

UNIT 11

Discussion and Cooperative Learning

UNIT OVERVIEW

It should come as no surprise that a number of educators argue for reading instruction that allows students the opportunity to interact with one another about what they read. They lament what appears to be the status quo—namely, teacher control of the floor, limited extended interchanges between students and teachers or among the students themselves, and students' view that the end goal is achieving a single correct response to a text. Further, most literacy theorists and practitioners concede that meanings are socially constructed, whether meanings are shared or informed by and across communities of learners. To be literate involves not only learning from others but also learning to be literate with others (Bloome and Green, 1984; Rogers and Soter, 1997).

In the late eighties, discussion and cooperative learning received an increased amount of attention as educators became interested in the aforementioned issues and adopted a view of meaning making that encompassed the social nature of literacy and the influence of peers on learning. In particular, recent reviews of research (e.g., Morrow and Gambrell, 2000) have indicated that in discussion groups students have shown the ability to construct meaning and evaluate text as well as demonstrate strategic reading behaviors such as interpreting, predicting, and generalizing. Further, the National Reading Panel (2000) emphasized that cooperative learning increases reading comprehension.

The present unit includes a description of a few representative strategies. However, it should be noted that other units include procedures that could be considered cooperative and Drama, and Responding to Reading as Writers and Genre Study, include several strategies incorporating the use of peer interaction and discussion. A somewhat expanded list of references to discussion strategies follows this overview.

The present unit includes four discussion and cooperative learning techniques.

Literature Circles. Literature Circles afford students at various ages opportunity to engage in student-led discussion groups around self-selected readings as a way of making classroom interactions around reading richer, more dynamic, more real, and more collaborative.

Great Books' Shared Inquiry. Shared Inquiry is the discussion procedure suggested by the Great Books Foundation. The discussion procedure features interpretive reading and group discussion of selected works using a rather structured approach to ensure that responses are text-based and that respondents are fully involved.

Conversational Discussion Groups. Conversational Discussion Groups involves creating an environment using a selected stimulus and ground rules for discussion that mimic an "outdoor cafe" conversation in hopes of motivating and enhancing student involvement and comprehension.

Jigsaw. Jigsaw is considered a cooperative learning technique directed at having students develop expertise in certain topic areas and then using this expertise to inform group members.

REFERENCES

Alvermann, D. E., and M. Commeyras. 1994. Inviting multiple perspectives: Creating opportunities for student talk about gender inequalities in texts. *Journal of Reading* 37: 566–571. Presents discussion techniques that are intended to engage students in gender issues around text.

Barnitz, J. G. 1994. Discourse diversity: Principles for authentic talk and literacy instruction. *Journal of Reading* 37: 586–591. Presents principles that contribute to authentic talk in culturally diverse schools.

Bloome, D., and J. Green. 1984. Directions in the sociolinguistic study of reading. In P. D. Pearson, R. Barr, M. L. Kamil, and P. Mosenthal (Eds.), *Handbook of reading research* (Vol. I). New York: Longman, 395–422. Explores social processes of literacy.

Calfee, R. C., K. L. Dunlap, and A. Y. Wat. 1994. Authentic discussion of texts in middle grade schooling: An analytic-narrative approach. *Journal of Reading* 37: 546–556. Discusses analyses of discussions of narrative in middle school classrooms en route to detailing how to improve them.

Dugan, J. 1997. Transactional literature discussions: Engaging students in the appreciation and understanding of literature. *The Reading Teacher* 51: 86–96. Explores a new approach, Transactional Literature Discussion, as a way to guide students' conversations about literature.

Gambrell, L. B., and J. F. Almasi. 1996. *Lively discussion! Fostering engaged reading.* Newark, DE: International Reading Association. Strategies for using discussion to engage students in reading.

Gaskins, I. W., E. Satlow, D. Hyson, J. Ostertag, and L. Six. 1994. Classroom talk about text: Learning in science class. *Journal of Reading* 37: 558–565. Suggests six axioms to foster discussion in middle school science classrooms.

Horowitz, R., and S. H. Freeman. 1995. Robots versus spaceships: The role of discussion in kindergartners' and second graders' preferences for science text. *The Reading Teacher* 49: 30–40. Explores the role of discussion in science with kindergartners and second graders.

Kletzien, S. B., and L. Baloche. 1994. The shifting muffled sound of the pick: Facilitating student-to-student discussion. *Journal of Reading* 37: 540–545. Suggestions for fostering student discussion.

Lehman, B., and P. Scharer. 1996. Reading alone, talking together: The role of discussion in developing literary awareness. *The Reading Teacher* 50: 26–35. Explores the important role discussion can play among children and adults as well as ways for adults to learn about children.

Morrow, L. M., and Gambrell, L. B. 2000. Literature-based reading instruction. In M. L. Kamil, P. B. Mosenthal, P. D. Pearson, and R. Barr (Eds.), *Handbook of reading research,* Vol. III. Mahwah, NJ: Erlbaum, 563–586. Presents the research on discussion groups.

National Reading Panel. 2000. *Teaching children to read: An evidence-based assessment of the scientific research literature on reading and its implications for reading instruction: Report of the subgroups.* (NIH Publication No. 00-4754). Washington, DC: National Institute of Child Health and Human Development. Chapter 4 describes the importance of cooperative learning on comprehension.

Rogers, T., and A. Soter. 1997. *Reading across cultures.* New York: Teachers College Press. Explores how understandings are acquired from cultures across students.

Smith, L. J., and D. L. Smith. 1994. The discussion process: A simulation. *Journal of Reading* 37: 582–585. Presents the use of simulation as a vehicle to enhance discussion.

Worthy, J., and I. L. Beck. 1995. On the road from recitation to discussion in large-group dialogue about literature. In K. A. Hinchman, D. J. Leu, and C. K. Kinzer (Eds.), *Perspectives on literacy research and practice.* Chicago: National Reading Conference, 312–324. Documents one teacher's attempt to shift from teacher-centered recitation to learner-centered discussion.

Literature Circles

Purpose

Literature Circles are intended to afford students at various ages opportunity to engage in student-led discussion groups around self-selected readings as a way of making classroom interactions around reading richer, more dynamic, more real, and more collaborative.

Rationale

Literature Circles appear to have emerged (and continue to emerge) as a practice in conjunction with educators exploring ways of engaging students in meaningful discussions of literature in their classrooms in combination with considering shifts in our thinking about the nature of response, comprehension, and the roles of discussion and collaboration as well as the importance of student engagement and self-monitoring. It may be impossible to detail the various threads that have contributed to the development of Literature Circles. In some ways, Literature Circles represent a practice which teachers developed, modified, extended, adapted, borrowed, explored, revamped, and then further developed as they considered its possibilities, including its marriage to other practices. Across the suggestions for Literature Circles, there are elements which have their roots in other forms of student-led discussions, cooperative learning, learner-centered forms of assessment, author cycle, comprehension development, and other developments. Certainly, the practice is most directly tied to an amalgamation of independent reading and collaboration.

Kathy Short and Gloria Kauffman are credited with coining the term *Literature Circles* in conjunction with their research based upon observations of a teacher and the role and nature of small group discussions of literature. Later, the practice was described in Short, Harste, and Burke's book *Creating Classrooms for Authors.* Harvey Daniels, in collaboration with various teachers, has been responsible for much of the development and articulation of the steps and elements that constitute the approach as well as discussions of its merit and roots. His book *Literature Circles: Voice and Choice in the Student-Centered Classroom* serves as the primary reference for the practice.

While Literature Circles was invented by teachers, its invention or inventors were fueled by developments and notions of reading development that have been foregrounded over the past 20 years. Daniels suggests the following as foundational to Literature Circles:

- Constructivist views of reading comprehension, which emphasize the strategic nature of meaning making prior to, during, and after reading
- Reader response theory, which emphasizes the role of personal responses and the contribution of different responses to each person's emerging interpretations
- The importance of independent reading to improvement in reading ability
- The role of scaffolding by teachers and peers as support for readers and, tied to this scaffolding, the importance of predictability, playfulness, a focus on meaning, role

playing, and role reversal as well as modeling and developing a language for talking about books

- The importance, contribution, nature, and role of successful collaborations, including the power of group dynamics and its essential elements (clear expectations, mutually developed norms, shared leadership and responsibility, open channels of communication, diverse friendship patterns, and conflict resolution mechanisms)
- Detracting from the power of heterogeneous grouping
- The importance of a balanced instructional program

Intended Audience

Literature Circles can be used in most settings with students of various ages.

Description of the Procedures

Harvey Daniels (1994) describes Literature Circles as follows:

> Literature circles are small, temporary discussion groups who have chosen to read the same story, poem, article, or book. While reading each group-determined portion of the text (either in or outside of class), each member prepares to take specific responsibilities in the upcoming discussion, and everyone comes to the discussion with the notes needed to perform that job. The circles have regular meetings, with discussion roles rotating each session. When they finish a book, the circle members plan a way to share the highlights of their reading with the wider community; then they trade members with other finishing groups, select more reading, and move into a new cycle. Once readers can successfully conduct their own wide-ranging, self-sustaining discussions, formal discussion roles may be dropped. (p. 13)

Accordingly, some of the essential elements are:

- Students choose their own reading materials.
- Based upon these choices, small temporary groups are formed.
- These different groups read different books.
- Regular times are scheduled to meet and discuss these books.
- Readers are encouraged to use notes, post-its, or study guides as they read from different perspectives or stances.
- Discussions are student led and are intended to be natural and open, affording digressions, personal connections, and open-ended questions.
- Teachers are facilitators and monitors of the groups, but not participants.
- Students are expected to play rotating roles in the group, including introducing topics, issues, and questions for discussion.
- When books are finished, the readers share with classmates and then new groups are formed.
- Evaluation involves a mix of observations by the teacher, portfolios, other informal procedures, and various forms of student self-evaluation.
- Playfulness and fun are seen as key elements.

Literature Circles will be described using the following: (1) introducing Literature Circles, (2) roles, and (3) monitoring and observations by the teacher.

Introducing Literature Circles. Daniels (1994) suggests that students may need different types of orientation depending upon their sophistication—especially in terms of their history of collaborative experiences. Students more accustomed to group activities might be provided with a range of material from which they are expected to choose and then based upon these choices negotiate for themselves groups of four. Upon forming these groups, they might be introduced to the roles that they are to play as they read and in discussions. They are then assigned to read the text or sections; at the same time they might be presented sheets to guide their reading according to the role that they are assigned or select. When everyone has completed the reading of text, the students are placed in discussion groups for 15–20 minutes with the goal to have a "natural conversation" about the book. The discussion director is expected to moderate, including watching the time as well as inviting all students to participate. The teacher visits with each group but operates strictly as an observer. Following the discussion there is a debriefing, including a discussion of problems, procedures, etc.

For the students who are less accustomed to group discussion or unfamiliar or wary of roles, Harvey suggests a more gradual introduction to the practice. He suggests beginning with a single story and single role for the whole class and a discussion of the nature of Literature Circles as students participate in small groups and then participate in debriefing. Then in subsequent sessions, try other roles prior to using Literature Circles with multiple texts and roles simultaneously. He also recommends having students visit other classrooms or watch videotape where Literature Circles are taking place or using older or more experienced students to teach younger or less experienced ones.

Roles. As Daniels (1994) suggests: "Other than kids and books, the most important ingredient in newly formed Literature Circles is the set of role sheets, which give a different task to each group member—both for the individual reading and for the group discussion" (p. 60). He has identified two sets of roles for students to use: the first is a rather generic set of required roles; the second optional set is keyed for specific kinds of reading.

Required roles

- Discussion director
- Literary luminary/passage master
- Connector
- Illustrator

Optional roles

- Researcher
- Summarizer/essence extractor
- Character captain
- Vocabulary enricher/word master
- Travel tracer/scene setter

Role sheets are seen as almost essential to support the students in these roles as they read and as they discuss. And, while these role sheets per se (see Figures 11.1 through 11.5 for examples) are deemed as important scaffolding, Daniels does indicate that he would hope that they become unnecessary as students become capable of guiding their own reading and discussions within role without these sheets. The sheets do appear to serve as a kind of reminder as well as a way of maintaining focus.

FIGURE 11.1 Discussion Director

Date(s) ______________ Name ______________________

Group name or members ______________ Book ______________________

Started page ______________ Ended page ______________________

Your role of discussion director is to guide group discussions. You might develop a list of questions that lead to discussions, such as:

What if something happened that was different or what if you were:

What if, ______________________

What if, ______________________

What if, ______________________

You might develop questions that have students share their impressions of the story.

How did you feel about ____

What did you like and dislike about ________________________________

You might also ask the students to suggest their own question.

____

____

You might also suggest the students make predictions about what might happen next.

____

____

You might have them suggest other stories that this is like and why.

____

Can you think of something else that you can do?
Remember to encourage everyone to say something.

Daniels also indicates that they had initially included another required role which they have now dropped—called process checker. The process checker was used to monitor and rate members of the group. For a host of reasons (the authority of the role, the potential for the removal of a student from other responsibilities, the policing function that might have occurred), they stopped using this role.

Sharing projects emanating from the discussions is seen as integral to sharing and making connections across groups. At the end of the Literature Circle, each group is expected to determine what they might share and how they might share with the rest of the class. These share meetings may last a couple of days and might also afford teachers the opportunity to review and brainstorm solutions to problems, new possibilities, and issues that arose in groups.

FIGURE 11.2 Literary Luminary/Passage Master

Date(s) ______________ Name ______________________

Group name or members ______________ Book ______________________

Started page ______________ Ended page ____________________

Your role of literary luminary is to select key sections of the book that you think your group would find interesting, exciting, fun, or strange, or there may be other reasons.

You might read it aloud or have someone else do so. Sometimes you can have students create sound effects or images.

Also, have your classmates suggest possibilities.

Location	Reasons for picking	Plan for reading/sharing
1. Page __ Paragraph __	____________	______________
2. Page __ Paragraph __	____________	______________
3. Page __ Paragraph __	____________	______________
4. Page __ Paragraph __	____________	______________

Topics to be continued tomorrow ____

FIGURE 11.3 Connector

Date(s) ______________ Name ______________________

Group name or members ______________ Book ______________________

Started page ______________ Ended page ____________________

Your job is to think of ways the story connects to you and other group members. How does this connect to school, your own lives outside of school, the community, experiences that you have had?

Are the characters like people you know?

Is the book like other stories you have read?

Is the story like stories classmates have written?

Are there things you might do based upon the story?

Some possible connections

____

____

____

____

____

Topics to be continued tomorrow ____

FIGURE 11.4 Illustrator

Date(s) ______________ Name ______________________

Group name or members ______________ Book ______________________

Started page ______________ Ended page ______________________

Your job is to draw some kind of picture or sketch or other kind of diagram (chart, web, cartoon, etc.). You might draw something that you read about or something suggested by what you read.

When the Director asks you to share, you might show the picture, etc. and ask them to comment on what it is about prior to sharing what you were trying to do.

Topics to be continued tomorrow ______________________________________

FIGURE 11.5 Summarizer

Date(s) ______________ Name ______________________

Group name or members ______________ Book ______________________

Started page ______________ Ended page ______________________

Your job is to prepare a brief summary of today's reading and the key points.

Summary

____

____

Key points

1. ____

2. ____

3. ____

Other ____

Topics to be continued tomorrow ______________________________________

While Literature Circles are not viewed as the only element in the reading program, Daniels stresses the need to establish regular daily sessions to pursue Literature Circles rather than try to fit these activities into spare moments that arise. For a single book, he suggests time across several days and sometimes weeks but emphasizes that an ending date needs to be specified. During these scheduled periods, he suggests it may be important to schedule reading time as well as discussion time. However, at times, reading assignments might be pursued outside of the regular class-times.

Monitoring and Observations by the Teacher. Daniels (1994) argues for teacher and student engagement in various forms of classroom-based assessment that engages students, teachers, and others in decision-making tied to the goals for Literature Circles. They suggest including portfolios as well as projects and other artifacts as a way of pursuing a partnership with the students which might entail occasional conferencing with the students about achievements, improvements, and future goals. While not advocating grading, Daniels does offer some suggestions for the elements that might constitute a grade. These are productivity, growth, and quality of reading. Productivity includes quantity of reading as well as preparation for and participation in the conference. Growth includes application of new learnings, variety of books, use of input, and improvement. Quality includes consideration for the range and difficulty of material read as well as the sophistication of projects. Again, key elements in such evaluations are the artifacts and the teacher's observations as well as student portfolios and conferences.

Cautions and Comments

A great deal of the power of Literature Circles may lie in the nature of its ongoing development. Undergirding the practices are years of exploration of its use in different classrooms by teachers with a keen idea to improving their practice with an eye to student engagement and student improvement. At the heart of Literature Circles are teachers encouraged to reflect upon their practice as they reflect upon their students' needs. The suggestions for Literature Circles are more propositions than edicts. Just as Literature Circles are intended to invite students to respond and reflect, advocates of Literature Circles invite others to explore, adapt, and extend what they are doing. As Daniels (1994) states: "every good session of literature circles I've attended departs from the basic definition in some way" (p. 31).

Certainly, Literature Circles spark student engagement. Numerous testimonies by teachers and students serve as evidence of the motivating possibilities of the practice—especially the enjoyment and value students see for the different roles they are expected to assume and the responsibilities they are given. While there appears to be little direct evidence of improvement in overall reading achievement, there is indirect evidence based upon careful study of classrooms that engage in cooperative discussions. Certainly, there is ample evidence of the worth of student-led discussion groups in terms of the ideas that are explored. Daniels and others would argue that Literature Circles can contribute significantly to a change in the level of the students' engagement in reading and an increased interest in both reading and sharing. Also, they would suggest that Literature Circles will likely spur connections across books as well as a more in-depth or far-reaching consideration of themes and the big ideas in what one reads.

In terms of the development of Literature Circles as a practice, Daniels offers suggestions for how different teachers might introduce Literature Circles to their classrooms and addresses several key questions that teachers might confront in their implementation. Perhaps missing from current descriptions or needing further development are the guidelines by which teachers more astutely observe and support students. Teachers may need more guidance, including ways to support students, delve into the text more, examine their arguments, adopt the perspectives or roles that they do, and address long-term developmental goals for Literature Circles. Perhaps more discussion and explorations of connections to other practices such as writing or Process Drama might be explored. A more dynamic enlistment of roles might be pursued—where readers are encouraged to adopt more than one role. At the same time teachers need to be aware when the role may be confounding the reading. For example, some students tend to focus on their role to the detriment of reading the text. Perhaps teachers should look for ways roles might emerge from reading rather than be imposed a priori and perhaps supersede the reading and their emergence.

While Daniels and others address the issue of individual differences and ways to meet the needs of a diverse student body, further discussion and consideration seem in order. Certainly, linguistic diversity needs to be addressed as well as differences in participants' expectations of the norms for participation in such discussions.

Finally, Literature Circles lend themselves to use with technologies. Chat rooms and threaded discussions might be adapted or incorporated with elements of Literature Circles in meaningful ways that afford discussions without need for proximity in either time or place. Chat rooms could invite folks from around the world to discuss a text at the same time; threaded discussions could allow for extended discussions (sometimes over weeks) through the use of e-mail. A powerful characteristic of these discussions might be to have a written record, so that shifts in understanding, perspective, or contributions can be monitored.

REFERENCES

Daniels, H. 1994. *Literature circles: Voice and choice in the student-centered classroom.* New York: Stenhouse. Provides details of the history as well as underlying assumptions of Literature Circles. Also includes loads of examples of their use in different classrooms.

Labbo, L. D. 1996. Beyond storytime: A sociopsychological perspective on young children's opportunities for literacy development during story extension time. *Journal of Literacy Research* 28: 405–428. Investigates different stances young children assumed during storytime reading.

Long, T. W., and M. K. Gove. 2003–2004. How engagement strategies and Literature Circles promote critical response in a fourth-grade urban classroom. *The Reading Teacher* 57: 350–361. Using Literature Circles as a springboard to critical response.

Noll, E. 1994. Social issues and literature circles with adolescents. *Journal of Reading* 38: 88–93. Explores secondary students' involvement in Literature Circles tied to exploring social issues.

Paterson, P. O. 2000. The role of text in peer-led Literature Circles in the secondary classroom. In T. Shanahan and F. V. Rodriguez-Brown (Eds.), *49th yearbook of the National Reading Conference.* Chicago: National Reading Conference, 235–251. Analysis of a Literature Circle in a secondary classroom.

Robertson, J. F., and D. Rane-Szostak. 1996. Using dialogues to develop critical thinking skills: A practical approach. *Journal of Adolescent and Adult Literacy* 39: 552–556. Students evaluate written dialogues for biases, dialogues, interpretations, and errors, and then take part in discussions involving role play.

Short, K. 1986. *Literature as a collaborative experience.* Unpublished doctoral dissertation, Indiana University, Bloomington. Details her observations of Literature Circles and the types of learnings that were occurring across time for students.

Short, K. G., J. C. Harste, and C. Burke. 1996. *Creating classrooms for authors and inquirers* (2d ed.). Portsmouth, NH: Heinemann. Offers a description of Literature Circles and many other strategies.

Short, K. G., and G. Kauffman. 1995. So what do I do? The role of the teacher in literature circles. In N. L. Roser and M. G. Martinez (Eds.), *Book talk and beyond: Children and teachers response to literature.* Newark, DE: International Reading Association. Describes in detail the nature of the teacher's role in Literature Circles, including learning to facilitate discussions and observe students.

Simpson, A. 1994. Not the class novel: A different reading program. *Journal of Reading* 38: 290–294. Details a version of Literature Circles used in some Australian secondary schools.

Great Books' Shared Inquiry

Purpose

Shared Inquiry is the discussion procedure suggested by the Great Books Foundation. The Great Books Foundation claims that the procedure achieves a number of goals, including flexibility, critical analysis skills, reading comprehension, a deeper understanding of self and others, as well as the motivation and desire to be lifelong learners.

Rationale

Founded in 1947, the Great Books Foundation (GBF) aims to foster the education of children and adults through reading and group discussion of books carefully selected for their richness, complexity, literary merit, meaningfulness, appeal, and length. The book selection includes a set of paperbound Great Books and Junior Great Books, as well as reader aids and a handbook on reading and discussion.

The discussion procedure features interpretive reading and group discussion based upon what might be considered a rather text-based view of literary interpretation. As the Foundation has stated:

> Reading serious literature is a collaboration—a meeting of minds—between author and reader. The author provides the complete work, but doesn't tell the reader what to think about it: the reader must strive to understand, to interpret, what the author is saying. It is this interpretative process that is the focus of shared inquiry. (Great Books Foundation, 1987, v)

The Great Books Foundation suggests that questions addressing "specific problems about the meaning of a work" are at the heart of Shared Inquiry. At the start of the discussion, the group leader poses an interpretive issue derived from his/her own reading of the work and for which he/she has not yet developed a satisfactory answer. The group leader probes the responses of participants with follow-up questions to guide their scrutiny of the text, to tie together ideas from the group, and eventually to derive a resolution. The leader may challenge and probe but must not provide answers. Although the goal is helping readers understand the work, a number of secondary purposes are supposedly achieved. As has been stated:

> By trying out ideas and exchanging and examining opinions, they (participants) build their own answers to the interpretive question under discussion, and they develop their own ways of understanding the work . . . participants gain experience in communicating complex ideas, and in supporting, testing, and expanding their own thoughts . . . participants develop the habit of reflective thinking . . . participants learn to give full consideration to the ideas of others, to weigh the merits of opposing arguments, and to modify their initial opinions if the evidence demands it. (Great Books Foundation, 1987, v–vi)

A key assumption underlying their approach to integrating a work is tied to an assumption verging upon the belief that comprehension proceeds from literal to interpretive to evaluative and that the reader's task is to unravel the author's meaning. As the GBF states:

> Comprehension and appreciation of the facts of a work lay the foundation for the next level of reading: interpretation. To interpret a story or essay is to construct explanations of what the author wants us to think about. (1987, 2)

The Great Books Foundation recognizes that both leaders and participants may need time and practice to achieve much in the way of success with Shared Inquiry. It also should be noted that the Great Books Foundation requires group leaders to make a commitment to the Great Books program by using their materials and being trained to lead discussion groups.

Intended Audience

Shared Inquiry is designed for students from the second through the twelfth grade. With adaptation, it could be used with younger students.

Description of the Procedures

The following description of Shared Inquiry includes:

1. Guidelines for leaders preparing for discussion
2. Guidelines for leading a discussion
3. Other features

1. Guidelines for Leaders Preparing for Discussion. The Great Books Foundation suggests that group leaders follow a number of steps prior to initiating Shared Inquiry. They include:

1. Reading the selection twice and taking notes addressing insights, questions, interesting issues, and important points.

2. Identifying genuine issues of meaning: issues that are puzzling and that lend themselves to alternative interpretations, and from these issues, writing just as many interpretive questions. Suggestions are offered regarding possible sources for interpretive questions. They include: character motives, striking or unusual use of language, prominent details, words, phrases, or sentences that can be understood in more than one way or connections between parts of the text.

3. Sorting questions by issue and for each issue trying to identify the basic questions and cluster of questions.

4. If possible, prediscussing the issue with a colleague to ensure that your questions are clear, interesting, and truly interpretive.

5. Selecting one of your clusters to discuss first, reserving others for use after your initial interpretive issue is addressed.

2. Guidelines for Leading a Discussion

a. Rules governing discussion. There are four rules that govern Shared Inquiry. They are:

- Only those who have read the selection may take part in discussion.
- Discussion is restricted to the selection that everyone has read.
- All opinions should be supportable with evidence from the selection.
- Leaders may only ask questions—they may not answer them.

b. Opening the discussion. Participants are expected to prepare as the group leader did. That is, they are expected to read the selection twice and take notes. In the case of initiating Shared Inquiry for the first time, Great Books Foundation suggests that the group leader might emphasize the following:

- Selections have been chosen for their literary merit.
- Shared Inquiry involves participants learning from one another.
- Discussion will focus on a question that seems key to understanding the story.
- Four rules (previously mentioned) apply for various reasons (which the leader should explain).

In introducing notetaking, the Foundation suggests that the leader should: (1) encourage the participants to mark anything that interests them or puzzles them, or anything they want to remember for discussion; (2) share their own notes and/or have participants show their notes.

For the discussion to begin the teacher poses a question (e.g., Why does Jack climb the beanstalk the third time?). The participants write down the question and record their initial answers. Then, after every question is read, the teacher asks one of the participants, by name, to give his or her response. The teacher uses a seat chart to keep track of the participants' ideas and to note contributors' names and what they said.

c. Conducting discussion. The Great Books Foundation offers several guidelines for leading discussions. They include:

- Lead slowly so that answers can be clarified and explored.
- Listen carefully to participants' ideas, looking for subtle differences or ways to relate comments.
- Use seating charts (see Figure 11.6) to keep track of ideas, who said what, and as a way to follow-up on discussion. (Also, charts might be shared with participants.)
- Encourage participants to talk with one another, asking each other questions and answering each other directly.
- Strive for clarification of ideas.
- Help participants relate ideas to each other and to the basic questions.
- Have participants turn to the text frequently to support and check ideas.
- Encourage participants to challenge any assumptions in the leader's questions.
- Make sure everyone has an opportunity to contribute.
- Ask follow-up questions often (to clarify comments, to substantiate opinions, to solicit additional opinions, to develop an idea by pursuing its implications, to test whether an idea is consistent with the facts, to select a line of inquiry).

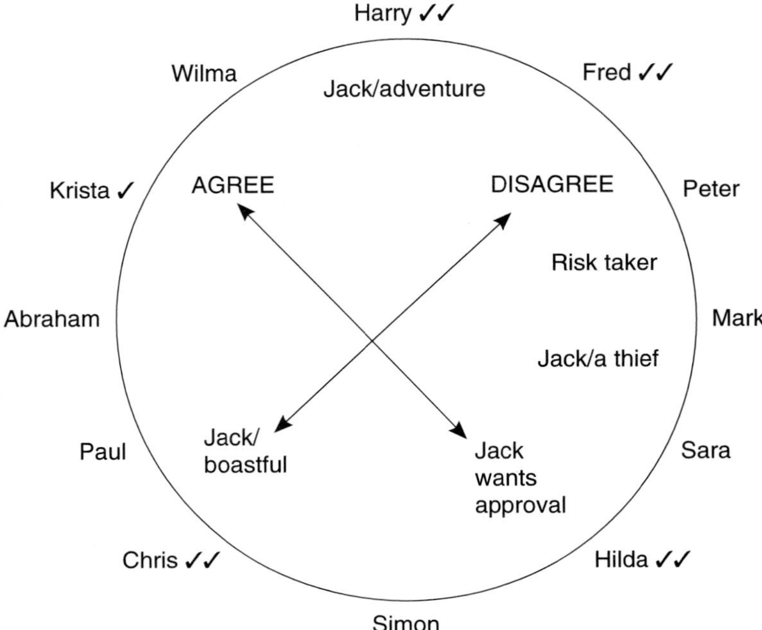

FIGURE 11.6 Example of a Seating Chart

d. Reaching a resolution. Once the leader considers that the interpretive issue has been thoroughly discussed and that further discussion is not likely to be productive (e.g., ideas are being repeated, digressions are occurring), the leader is expected to: (1) repeat the basic question; (2) give the opportunity for input to anyone who did not have an answer addressed; and (3) compose a final answer taking into account the ideas offered by the group. After participants have had a chance to formulate their response, the leader asks if anyone arrived at a response that differs substantially from his/her previous response and has those students share how their ideas were influenced.

e. Post-discussion activities/new line of inquiry. Following the resolution phase, a line of inquiry might be launched with a different basic question. Post-discussion activities such as writing projects can also be suggested.

3. Other Features. The Great Books Foundation offers guidelines for helping leaders deal with difficulties that might emerge (e.g., digressions, inattentiveness, failure to respond to the question, nervousness, vocabulary) and proposes a text analysis procedure for looking at a passage in a story or essay closely en route to achieving a foothold. "In textual analysis, a group discusses a single passage line by line and sometimes word by word, raising questions about its meaning" (Great Books Foundation, 1987, 48).

Cautions and Comments

Shared Inquiry has been well received. In 1987, the Great Books Foundation claimed to be training over 18,000 leaders every year.

As a procedure for guiding discussion, Shared Inquiry offers discussion leaders a systematic approach for preparing for discussion, mobilizing student interactions, and reading resolutions. At the same time, the procedure includes carefully developed guidelines by which group leaders might monitor the success of discussions and initial strategies to improve them. In this regard, some of the guidelines are worth reviewing for purposes of any type of discussion—that is, whether a Shared Inquiry approach is adopted or Great Books are used.

Some assumptions upon which the Shared Inquiry is based may be questionable. First, the mandate to use a selected list of books may appear to be somewhat suggestive of having a canon. Second, the approach places a great deal of emphasis on the text and appears to discount a reader's background of experience and any connections that a reader might make from that to other works. This seems rather problematic, given what we know about how the reader's active involvement, including intertextual ties, is crucial to comprehension. Third, there is the stated assumption that reading proceeds from literal to interpretive to evaluative. Current views of reading comprehension suggest a more dynamic view in which comprehension is never purely literal and is apt to proceed from the evaluative to interpretive to literal as in reverse. Fourth, the approach is teacher-directed in that basic questions stem from the teacher rather than the child. While the approach sponsors participant input and interrogation of one another, it seems that a worthwhile next step would be to have participants develop their own basic questions and clusters.

The claims offered by the Great Books Foundation pertaining to the benefit accrued from such an approach warrant careful study. Although several studies report that the approach has a generally positive impact, the precise claims suggested in their handbook have not been studied.

REFERENCES

Davis, J. A. 1961. *Great Books and small groups.* New York: Gephard Press. Describes the use of the Great Books discussion procedures.

Feiertag, J., and L. Chernoff. 1987. Inferential thinking and self-esteem: Through the junior Great Books program. *Childhood Education* 63(4): 252–254. Explores the development of thinking abilities and self-esteem with the use of the Great Books program, including discussion procedures.

Fitzpatrick, E. A. 1952. *Great Books: Panacea or what?* Milwaukee: Bruce Publishing. Discusses some of the strengths and weaknesses of the Great Books program.

Great Books Foundation. 1987. *An introduction to shared inquiry.* Chicago: Great Books Foundation. The primary source for information on how to plan and implement Shared Inquiry.

Conversational Discussion Groups

Purpose

The purpose of Conversational Discussion Groups is to create an environment for the discussion of reading selections that facilitates sharing and a balance between peer interaction and expert guidance—and enhances exploration, transmission, and construction of meanings.

Rationale

Conversational Discussion Groups was developed by O'Flahavan (O'Flahavan and Huxtable, 1987; O'Flahavan, 1989) in response to the question "What if classroom discussions were more like conversations, more like the sorts of discussion people have over coffee, after seeing a movie—a common text—together?" As O'Flahavan stated:

> The goal as we conceived it was fashioned after an "outdoor cafe" metaphor, where a group of people come together after seeing a movie and discuss what it meant to them. The group process . . . was relinquished to the students, as was the on-line negotiation of meaning during discussion.

O'Flahavan (1989) sees the procedure as a first step toward openness and student participation in classroom situations where the teacher's control of the floor and lines of thinking predominate. While the approach spells out a specific procedure, it is intended to be more of an abstract way of thinking rather than formulaic. Instructionally, the approach aspires to build upon the Vygotskian notion of the role of social learning, principles drawn from studies examining parent-child interactions, and metacognitive notions associated with attempts to prime student independence. Accordingly, O'Flahavan claims the approach has the following characteristics: immersion in a meaningful problem; equal access to monitoring and regulation of relevant group processes for all participants; group as scaffold for the individual; and reflection about group and individual process.

Intended Audience

The strategy can be used with students at any level.

Description of the Procedures

There are three stages to Conversational Discussion Groups:

1. Introduce/review rules
2. Lines of thought
3. Debriefing

O'Flahavan (1989) suggests that, prior to initiating how a Conversational Discussion Group might be orchestrated for use in a classroom, consideration should be given to the students' ability to participate in groups. To this end, he suggests that a teacher might try out a story discussion. Specifically, he suggests the following:

- Establish a heterogeneous group (six to eight students) who can work together.
- Direct the students to read a thought-provoking story.
- Construct a thematic question (e.g., with *Stone Soup,* "Is it okay to use tricks to get what you want?") that is presented to the students. Begin the discussion, but leave for a few minutes and observe from a distance how the group participates. Note group processes and how the students use the text to support their ideas. Return and finish the discussion.

Based on such tryouts, O'Flahavan proposes that the teacher can develop the group process rules and problem-solving heuristics to help the students develop their interpretations as they are involved in the Conversational Discussion Groups. With this as a basis, the teacher moves to introduce students to the rules for the subsequent discussion.

1. Introduce/Review Rules. The teacher introduces/reviews the rules and strategies with the group and discusses with the group others that might be added or might substitute for those on the list. Examples of rules for the discussion and heuristic strategies for negotiating are presented in Table 11.1.

O'Flahavan suggests that the rules should be visible to the group members as reminders of strategies they might use. With this in mind, he suggests that they be placed on large cards and attached to a wall, and so on, so that group members can evoke them from time to time.

2. Lines of Thought. After reading the story selection, the teacher presents to the group the first of three questions. Each question is presented on a sheet of paper large enough for all members of the group to review. The teacher does not return to the group until asked to do so by the group or when they perceive an opportune moment. O'Flahavan (1989) proposes that teachers adhere to the following code of conduct as the students discuss:

> I begin the discussion with one of my predetermined questions, and do not ask another until the students let me know it is time;
> I monitor their discussions from afar;
> I look for possible opportunities for intervention and make plans to address them later;
> I am a resource to the students when they need me;
> I speak only when spoken to.

Upon returning to the group, the teacher has the freedom to initiate, instruct, monitor, give feedback or praise, and the like. For instance, when the teacher returns (usually upon the

TABLE 11.1 Examples of Discussion Rules and Heuristic Strategies for Negotiating Meanings

Discussion Rules

One at a time
If you say yes/no, state why
Stay on the subject
Ask each other questions when someone is quiet
Don't hog the floor
Let other people talk
When you are ready, ask me (the teacher) to return

Heuristic Strategies

Back up your ideas with the story
Back up your ideas with your own experience

request of the group), the group's response or responses are presented, and, at this point, the teacher might model a key strategy, comment, provide feedback, challenge, and so on, prior to presenting the next question.

The three question types that O'Flahavan suggests might be left with the group are:

a. Background knowledge question. The intent of this question is to have the students discuss how their experiences relate to the selection. For example, the first question in a line of thought for the story "The Hare and the Tortoise" might be "How do you feel about someone who is always bragging?"

b. Transition to the text question. The intent of this question is to have the students consider the ideas gleaned from the text. For example, the second question in a line of thought for the story "The Hare and the Tortoise" might be "Did the hare's bragging affect the tortoise and did the tortoise's attitude affect the hare?"

c. Beyond the text question. The intent of the third question is to have the students pull together an interpretation based on the text and their personal reactions. A question that might serve this purpose is "What can we learn from this story?"

3. Debriefing. A debriefing serves the purpose of having students reflect on what they have achieved and learned, which might help them next time. To this end, O'Flahavan (1989) suggests that the teacher should return to the group and have them discuss three questions:

- How did we go about getting our answers today?
- How did we do?
- What can we do to improve next time?

Another device for helping students reflect on their contribution is the use of pieces of a pie as a means of getting students to talk about their contribution to the discussion. For example, O'Flahavan suggests presenting students with a model of a pie with different-colored wedges representing different shares of the whole pie. As he stated: "If discussion were like a pie and each person could carve out a slice for him/herself, how big would the shares of pie be?"

Cautions and Comments

O'Flahavan (1989) has stressed that the Conversational Discussion Group should be viewed as a framework for enabling students to achieve equal participation with teachers as they put forth "theories, conjectures, queries, conclusions, challenges, and rebuttals while talking about texts." Recognizing that different groups of students and teachers may be more or less capable of taking control of elicitation right away, O'Flahavan suggests that the teacher may want to initiate the Conversational Discussions with varying degrees of teacher responsibility. Teachers, O'Flahavan suggests, should begin with the question "What can we do to get better talking about literature?"

To date, a limited amount of research on the procedure has been pursued. In one study, second graders were involved in Conversational Discussion Groups for sixteen weeks (O'Flahavan, 1988). Their responses were compared to students in regular teacher-directed discussions of stories. The data collected consisted of student observations as well as student perceptions of the group, themselves, and measures of reading comprehension. The procedure tended to have the most effect on the students' perception of the group itself and the worth of the process; the impact on comprehension seemed negligible.

In a second study with fourth graders, using a variation of Conversational Discussion Groups over an eleven-week period, Almasi (1995) found that peer-led groups enabled students to express themselves more fully than students in teacher-led groups. Additionally, peer-led groups allowed students to explore more topics of interest, resolve episodes of conflict better, and have richer and more complex discussions.

What remains unanswered are the following questions: Do this and other forms of discussion prompt students to consider more ideas (text-based and reader-based) and connect as well as evaluate these ideas? To what extent do students need some support in developing interpretations that compare each other's responses and build on such analyses? To what extent do teachers need some support in understanding the nature of interpretation and ways to expand the repertoire of their students' skills and strategies?

REFERENCES

Almasi, J. F. 1995. The nature of fourth graders' sociocognitive conflicts in peer-led and teacher-led discussions of literature. *Reading Research Quarterly* 30: 314–351. Study using Conversational Discussion Groups which revealed that students become more fully engaged and have richer, more complex discussions.

Goldenberg, C. 1992–1993. Instructional conversations: Promoting comprehension through discussion. *The Reading Teacher* 46: 316–326. Describes another strategy on which the premise is that discussion should be more like a conversation.

O'Flahavan, J. 1988, December. *Conversational discussion groups: A study of second graders leading their own discussions.* Paper presented at the National Reading Conference, Tucson, AZ. An examination of the effects of Conversational Discussion Groups on student perceptions and other variables.

———. 1989. *An exploration of the effects of participant structure upon literacy development in reading group discussion.* Doctoral diss., University of Illinois-Champaign. Extended study comparing the effects of Conversational Discussion Groups (teacher-led and student-led) with traditional practice.

O'Flahavan, J., and J. Huxtable. 1987, December. *A case for teacher/researcher collaboration: Commitment to change.* Paper presented at the National Reading Conference, St. Petersburg, FL. Describes the evolution of the strategy along with a discussion of teacher change.

Wieneck, J. and J. F. O'Flahavan. 1994. From teacher-led to peer discussions about literature. Suggestions for making the shift. *Language Arts* 71: 489–498. Using Conversational Discussion Groups as a framework, this article offers suggestions for changing to peer-led discussions.

Jigsaw

Purpose

The purpose of Jigsaw (Aronson, Stephan, Sikes, Blaney, and Snapp, 1978; Slavin, 1986) is to help students cooperatively learn new material using a team learning approach. Students are responsible for becoming an "expert" on one part of a lesson and then teaching it to other members of their team.

Rationale

Jigsaw was originally developed as a means to promote positive race relations in public school classrooms (Aronson et al., 1978) but was also found to have beneficial effects on learning. The basic premise behind the strategy is that giving students the opportunity to share what they have learned, to hear what others have to say, and to teach and be taught by their peers is essential in the lifelong process of learning and socialization. Johnson, Maruyama, Johnson, Nelson, and Skon (1981) have found that instruction that was based on cooperation and collaboration resulted in significant gains in achievement, social development, and self-esteem.

As such, Jigsaw embodies the concept of peer tutoring in its efforts to help students read and learn from text. It is designed to increase students' sense of responsibility for their own learning and that of others. Not only must students learn their assigned material, but they must also be prepared to share and teach that material to other members of their team. Thus, students are dependent on one another and must cooperatively work together in order to learn the material.

Intended Audience

Jigsaw seems most appropriate for middle and secondary students in subjects such as social studies, literature, and some parts of science, and in other areas where concepts rather than rote learning are the goal of instruction. Radebaugh and Kazemak (1989) also recommend the use of cooperative learning in college and study skills classes.

Description of the Procedures

Slavin (1986) discussed the use of Jigsaw in two parts: teacher preparation and classroom use. Teacher preparation consists of materials development and preparation, and assignment of students to teams. Classroom use consists of introducing the strategy to the class, facilitating the use of teams and expert groups, and giving the quiz.

1. Teacher Preparation. Select a unit of study that you would like to cover in a two-day to three-day period and that can be broken down into four sections. If students are to read the material in class, the sections should not require more than 30 minutes to read; if the material is to be assigned for homework, sections may be longer. For instance, if the unit of study is Andrew Jackson, the material might be broken down into his early life, his war exploits, the presidency, and his later life.

a. Expert sheet. For each section of the material, design an "expert sheet" that tells students what material they are to read, gives them purpose-setting questions, and tells them which expert group they will work with. Thus, students will be provided the pages to be read and what they must gain expertise in and teach to their team members.

b. Quiz. Make a two-question quiz for each section of the unit. Quiz questions should be challenging since students will have the time necessary to read and discuss the material.

Multiple-choice questions should be used for ease of scoring. There will be 10 possible points for the quiz, as students will get double credit for the questions for which they become an expert.

c. Team assignment. Students should be assigned to teams to represent a cross-section of the class. In other words, students should be assigned by achievement, sex, and if appropriate, race. In this way, all teams will be heterogeneously balanced, and no team will have an advantage over another. In addition, students will not be able to self-select themselves into teams with their friends.

2. Classroom Use. Plan to introduce Jigsaw and have the students begin reading on Day 1. On Day 2 they can finish reading and work in their expert groups. Finally, on Day 3 students report to their assigned teams and take the quiz. This schedule can be adjusted depending on the difficulty of the material and whether the reading assignment is given for homework.

Day 1. Introduce the idea of Jigsaw in the following manner:

> You are going to work in learning teams to study the unit on _________. Each of you will have a special topic to learn about. You will read the material and discuss it with members of other teams. Then you will return to your team as an expert to teach your teammates about your topic. Finally, everyone will be quizzed on all topics. You must work with one another so that the whole team can do well on the quiz. Your team's score will be totaled and compared with other teams' scores.

Next, students are grouped into their preselected teams, and the expert sheets are handed out randomly to individual team members. Students are directed to read their sheets so that they know the topic about which they will be learning and what questions they need to answer. Finally, tell students to begin reading their assignments. Teachers will need to decide if students will read only their assigned pages or will read the whole assignment and concentrate on the assigned pages. Even more of a premium is placed on cooperative learning if students each possess a unique set of learnings.

Day 2. Have students finish their reading and introduce the expert groups as follows:

> Now you will have a chance to discuss your topic with others who have the same topic. In these groups you will decide what are the most important ideas about your topic. You will each share your information with one another. Take notes on important ideas. Try to think of what questions will be asked on the quiz. You will then go back to your team to report your findings.

Students should work in their expert groups for approximately 20 minutes.

Day 3. Have students return to their respective teams and report on what they have learned from their expert groups. Main points should be emphasized, and attention should be paid to what they think might be on the quiz. Team reports should take approximately 20 minutes. If deemed necessary, a class discussion may follow the team reports that should focus on input from the "experts." At the conclusion of the reports and discussion, the quiz should be given. Once the quizzes are scored, team members can add their point totals together to get their team score.

Cautions and Comments

A tremendous amount of research has been conducted concerning cooperative learning (see Johnson et al., 1981; Slavin, 1983, for reviews), the basis of Jigsaw. The research consistently indicates that students engaged in such learning achieve more, have better attitudes toward learning, and feel more positive about themselves. In particular, Slavin (1983, 1986) indicated that cooperative learning works best when groups are given a goal that can be attained only through cooperation and are held individually accountable for achieving the group goal.

However, it is still not surprising that Jigsaw and other cooperative learning techniques are used infrequently. The lecture method is still the predominant means of instruction in the classroom, and teachers, by and large, feel uncomfortable using small groups. As such, teachers who feel that chaos will result if small groups are used will probably not use this strategy.

Other concerns about Jigsaw need to be mentioned. Absences can cause problems, since teams rely on their members to learn and score well on quizzes. Sometimes, no matter how well teams are planned, team members may not get along. Indeed, Battistich, Solomon, and Delucchi (1993) found that the quality of the group interaction was directly related to the friendliness of the group members and their desire to work collaboratively. Constant reassignment of team members will cause problems. A predominance of slow learners in one classroom may cause problems with the student balance teachers are trying to achieve across teams. It may be that a slow learner has to be paired with a higher achiever so that individual and team learning can be more effective. Finally, existing materials sometimes do not easily lend themselves to be divided into four sections. Sections of text may not always stand by themselves.

REFERENCES

Aronson, E., C. Stephan, J. Sikes, N. Blaney, and M. Snapp. 1978. *The Jigsaw classroom.* Beverly Hills: Sage. Describes the use of Jigsaw as a means to deal with integration.

Battistich, V., D. Solomon, and K. Delucchi. 1993. Interaction processes and student outcomes in cooperative learning groups. *The Elementary School Journal* 94: 19–32. A study that examined cooperative learning in relation to various academic and social outcomes in elementary schools.

Johnson, D. W., G. Maruyama, R. T. Johnson, D. Nelson, and L. Skon. 1981. Effects of cooperative, competitive, and individualistic goal structures on achievement: A meta-analysis. *Psychological Bulletin* 89: 47–62. A synthesis of research on cooperative learning attesting to its effectiveness in increasing student achievement and self-esteem.

Mattingly, R. M., and R. L. Vansickle. 1991. Cooperative learning and achievement in social studies: Jigsaw II. *Social Education* 55: 392–395. Research showing the effectiveness of a version of Jigsaw with ninth-grade students in geography.

Radebaugh, M. R., and F. E. Kazemak. 1989. Cooperative learning in college reading and study skills classes.

Journal of Reading 32: 414–418. Description of the use of cooperative learning in college developmental reading/study classes.

Ragains, P. 1995. Four variations on Drueke's active learning paradigm. *Research Strategies* 13(1): 40–50. Description of how Jigsaw can be used for library research learning strategies.

Slavin, R. E. 1983. *Cooperative learning.* New York: Longman. Another review of research on cooperative learning.

———. 1986. *Using student team learning* (3rd ed.). Baltimore: Johns Hopkins University, Center for Research on Elementary and Middle Schools. Instruction manual for using Jigsaw and other team learning strategies.

UNIT 12

Content Area Literacy

UNIT OVERVIEW

Whereas content literacy scholars are beginning to focus their attention on how students use literacy in real settings, the focus of content area literacy has tended to remain on helping students read and write single texts—usually for information. Accordingly, attention continues to be given to how information is presented in narrative and expository text (Kamil, Mosenthal, Pearson, & Barr, 2000). Researchers have invested considerable effort and devised elaborate systems for analyzing how different texts are structured and whether there are certain text features that regularly cause students difficulty. As these characteristics of text have been described, educators have devised strategies and lesson frameworks to prepare students to deal with text features.

The present unit describes seven strategies, which range from procedures for preparing students to read a selection by presenting key concepts, to training students to research a topic for a class assignment, to teaching students about complex text structures (for purposes of dealing with content area textbooks).

Graphic Organizers. The Graphic Organizer can be used as a preteaching or post-teaching strategy for purposes of introducing or reinforcing the key concepts in a text and how they might be structured.

Study Guides. The backbone of the instructional framework is the Study Guide, which students use in dealing with the content. Study Guides can guide students through their content area textbook reading by focusing their attention on the major ideas presented.

Selective Reading Guide. The Selective Reading Guide provides the content teacher with an opportunity to guide the students to the relevant information within the content unit.

Idea Mapping. Idea Mapping is a method of spatially representing the overall structure of expository text. It provides students with a framework for carefully reading expository text, and it provides teachers a tool for examining the nature of text prior to classroom use.

Text Structure Strategy. The Text Structure Strategy is based on the premise that if students are taught different prototypical expository structures, they can use an understanding of these structures as an aid in comprehending texts that have similar structures.

Story Grammars and Story Maps. Story Grammars and Story Maps include a description of two different strategies that are based on the theoretical notions of the structure of stories. Story Maps present guidelines to generate questions that accompany short narratives found in basal readers. Story Grammars provide students with a framework for identifying the plot structure and other key elements of a story.

I-Search Paper. The I-Search Paper is a technique designed to help students research a topic by capitalizing on their need to investigate that topic. It incorporates a discussion of what is known about a topic, a story of the investigation of the topic, and what was learned about it.

REFERENCES

Barry, A. L. 2000. Reading strategies teachers say they use. *Journal of Adolescent & Adult Literacy* 46: 132–141. Bibliography of content strategies teachers say they use in the classroom.

Kamil, M. L., P. B. Mosenthal, P. D. Pearson, and R. Barr (Eds.). 2000. *Handbook of reading research,* Vol. III. Mahwah, NJ: Erlbaum. Chapters by Bean (pp. 629–644) and Wade and Moje (pp. 609–627) discuss the research on reading and writing in the content areas.

National Reading Panel. 2000. *Teaching children to read: An evidence-based assessment of the scientific research literature on reading and its implications for reading instruction: Report of the subgroups.* (NIH Publication No. 00-4754). Washington, DC: National Institute of Child Health and Human Development. Chapter 4 discusses the research on text comprehension.

O'Brien, D. G., R. A. Stewart, and E. B. Moje. 1995. Why content literacy is difficult to infuse into the secondary school: Complexities of curriculum, pedagogy, and school culture. *Reading Research Quarterly* 30: 442–463. Critiques teaching practices for helping students deal with content literacy.

Spor, M. W., and B. K. Schneider. 1999. Content reading strategies: What teachers know, use, and want to learn. *Reading Research and Instruction* 38: 221–231. Discussion of the strategies K–12 teachers use in the content areas.

Graphic Organizers

Purpose

The Graphic Organizer (Barron, 1969), originally called the Structured Overview, is designed to: (1) provide a logical means of preteaching the technical vocabulary of a content chapter, (2) present the students an idea framework designed to show important conceptual relationships between content vocabulary, and (3) help content teachers clarify teaching goals.

Rationale

The technical vocabulary of a content subject often proves quite difficult for students. It is Barron's argument that content teachers must be ever mindful of this fact and should seek ways of making the task less complicated for the students. The Graphic Organizer provides a systematic approach for doing just that. The subject matter instructor presents a picture, or schematic diagram, of the important words in the chapter and discusses with the students how these words relate to one another. Barron (1969) stated that "words assume the form of 'advance organizers' and provide the students with the cues to the 'structure' of subjects" (p. 29). Thus, the organizer serves as a point of reference as the students begin reading and studying the text in more detail.

Intended Audience

Earle (1969) reports the use of the Graphic Organizer with students in grades seven and above. It is further suggested that teachers in the elementary grades could profit from the use of the technique. On occasion, the procedure might be used by the teacher alone in the preparation of a particularly difficult unit.

Description of the Procedures

In order to describe the use of the Graphic Organizer by the content teacher, the following three stages will be discussed:

1. Preparation
2. Presentation
3. Follow-up

1. Preparation. Perhaps the most critical stage in the development and use of Graphic Organizer is this first step. It is at this point that the instructor, by working through this rather simple process, makes some key decisions regarding the major ideas to be stressed during the unit. Four components of the preparation stage summarize the desired sequence.

a. Select words. Rather than moving through the chapter in search of difficult words, the teacher proceeds in a more systematic manner. The first step in this preparation stage, then, is for the instructor to select the major concepts or understandings that are important for the students to know at the conclusion of their study of the topic. By working through the chapter in this manner, the teacher is actually establishing instructional objectives for that particular chapter.

Word selection logically follows selection of major concepts. The teacher can now deal with one major idea at a time and ask the question "What important words in this text help to describe, explain, or communicate this idea?" By asking this question for each of the major concepts, the content teacher has identified those technical terms that the student will need to know. Often a number of difficult words within the text are eliminated because they do not tie in directly to the major concepts.

To give an example, a social studies teacher may be introducing a text on organization of the United States government. The concepts chosen for instruction are: (1) the United States government consists of three governing branches; and (2) a system of checks and balances maintains the powers of each branch of government. The words that might be selected by the teacher as important for understanding these concepts are *checks and balances, Senate, legislative, United States government, executive, judicial, House of Representatives, president, veto override,* and *judicial review.*

b. Arrange words. The task now is to arrange these words into a diagram form that helps students see the terms and how they interrelate. There is not necessarily a right or a wrong diagram for a given set of terms, but it would appear that some arrangements are better than others. With several pieces of scratch paper available, the teacher might try out several possibilities, then select the one that appears to be the most appropriate. Continuing the example of the words chosen by the social studies teacher, the words might be arranged in numerous ways. Figure 12.1 gives one example.

Graphic Organizers may be designed for the total text chapter. For longer, more complicated chapters, the subject matter instructor may design several organizers, each tied to a major concept. Whatever the decision, the overriding question to be answered is "Will this organizer assist students to better understand the major concepts and major words of the text?" If the answer is "yes," then the teacher has developed a valuable teaching tool.

c. Add previously learned key words and ideas. Learning new information is generally easier for students if they can relate the new ideas to previously learned information; therefore, the content instructor is advised to select several important words that the students mastered in previous units and insert them in this new organizer. By completing this step, the teacher is saying to the students that the subject is more than a set of isolated units with little or no relationship to each other. In the example of the words dealing with the United States government, the teacher may decide to add previously learned vocabulary, if that would enhance understanding of the Graphic Organizer.

d. Evaluate organizer. Content instructors, by their very training, interest, and experience, are experts in their chosen fields; therefore, they may have forgotten what it was like

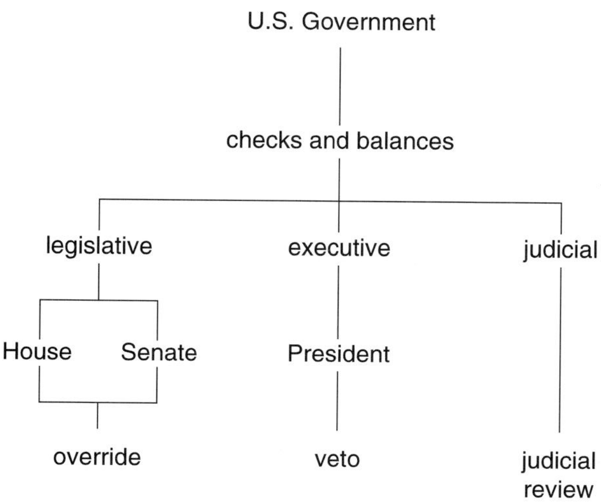

FIGURE 12.1 An Example Graphic Organizer

when they first began to pursue information in their major subject. A Graphic Organizer may be easily interpretable by the content specialist but still be too difficult for a group of students. This final step in the preparation stage, therefore, is critical. It is advisable to try out the organizer on someone who is not an expert in the field. One could do this with a student or with a fellow teacher in another discipline. Explain the organizer and then ask appropriate questions that tell you whether the person grasps the relationships among the terms used in it. Often people will answer questions in such a manner that they provide the kind of information necessary to suggest some minor revisions that result in a more appropriately constructed design. Once satisfied with the appropriateness of the organizer, the teacher should use it in the context of a total lesson in a regular classroom.

2. Presentation. As a preteaching tool, the organizer is presented on the chalkboard or with an overhead transparency. The instructor actually talks the students through the organizer and adds new pieces to it. Students are encouraged to participate. They may add information with which they are already familiar or ask questions regarding the organizer. The teacher may pose questions to check the students' understanding of it. The important thing is that the teacher and the students use the language of the subject matter and simultaneously explore the relationships of these words to each other. It is important to remember that one should not anticipate mastery of terms and relationships at this time.

The entire procedure may take from five to ten minutes, depending on the ability and achievement level of the students and on the complexity of the organizer. At the conclusion of this segment of the preparation stage, the students should have an idea framework that should make more detailed learning easier.

3. Follow-Up. The Graphic Organizer may also be used as the students move further into the text itself. A student's reaction to an especially difficult idea encountered in the reading might result in the teacher's responding, "Do you remember how this idea tied to . . . ?" as a portion of the organizer is created on the chalkboard. Thus, the organizer becomes a major point of reference throughout the teaching of a particular text. New information may be added when the instructor suggests, "Let's see how this new information fits into the organizer that we have been using." For some classes, the organizer might be placed on a large piece of poster paper and put on the bulletin board. In this way, students may refer to it at any time.

Cautions and Comments

The Graphic Organizer alone may not teach the technical vocabulary of a chapter as thoroughly as the content instructor may desire. A support system designed to teach the language of the subject more thoroughly is suggested. Earle and Barron (1973) outline a strategy that includes three components: (1) Graphic Organizer, (2) skills teaching, and (3) extension activities. Graphic Organizers are designed and utilized in the manner just described. The skills teaching phase of the strategy occurs in the preparation stage of the lesson and involves the detailed teaching of several of the more important terms used in the organizer. Extension activities give students opportunities to use the words during or following the reading of the text. Extension activities are generally paper-and-pencil exercises designed to reinforce the students' understandings of the terms. Matching exercises, word puzzles, and categorizing activities may be used for this purpose. Small-group and whole-class discussion may follow the completion of the activities.

Several studies cited in the reference section indicate the value of this procedure (e.g., National Reading Panel, 2000). However, one wonders whether a strategy that imposes upon students a structure for thinking and reading would be as beneficial as a strategy that might activate students' own ideas. To this end, an organizer might be developed from the student's own ideas prior to, during, or after reading. In this way, the organizer may become more personalized and less abstract.

Barron (1979) has suggested that Graphic Organizers can be used as a means of postreading reinforcement and review if students are given the task of constructing their own organizers. Multiple copies of each word to be used in the organizer are made, using index cards, and passed out to students in small groups. Students are given the task of arranging the words in a diagram to show how they are related. Blank index cards are also provided if students wish to add their own vocabulary terms. The teacher's responsibility in this postreading Graphic Organizer strategy is to circulate among the groups, providing support and feedback. The culminating activity is for the class to develop a single Graphic Organizer under the teacher's direction. By using organizers in this manner, students become more actively involved in their learning.

For students who may have trouble initially in constructing their own Graphic Organizers, an interim step between teacher-constructed and student-generated organizers may serve as an effective transition. The same diagram that was presented to students in the prereading portion of a lesson can be used to help students recall the assigned reading material after reading. Words are deleted from the original organizer and replaced with blanks. Deleted words are listed below the incomplete Graphic Organizer in random order. The students' task is to complete the diagram using the deleted words, either from recall or by using the text. Individual ditto sheets would be advantageous in this activity.

Finally, in reviews of Graphic Organizer research, Moore and Readence (1984) and Dunston (1992) found that students exposed to postreading Graphic Organizers learned more than those students exposed to prereading Graphic Organizers, particularly when vocabulary was the criterion variable. They also found that one of the advantages for using prereading organizers was that the teachers involved in the studies felt that they were better prepared to teach their lessons after having constructed a Graphic Organizer.

REFERENCES

Alvermann, D. E., and P. R. Boothby. 1986. Children's transfer of graphic organizer instruction. *Reading Psychology* 7: 87–100. Research study finding that postreading Graphic Organizers enabled fourth graders to transfer the effects of that instruction to their ability to recall novel text.

Barron, R. F. 1969. The use of vocabulary as an advance organizer. In H. L. Herber and P. L. Sanders (Eds.), *Research in reading in the content areas: First year report.* Syracuse, NY: Syracuse University Reading and Language Arts Center, 29–39. Presents the basis for the use of Graphic Organizers within the content classroom. Describes how Graphic Organizers may be used in relation to a total vocabulary teaching strategy utilizing preteaching and extension activities.

———. 1979. Research for classroom teachers: Recent developments on the use of the structured overview as an advance organizer. In H. L. Herber and J. D. Riley (Eds.), *Research in reading in the content areas: Fourth report.* Syracuse, NY: Syracuse University Reading and Language Arts Center, 171–176. Describes the evolution of the Graphic Organizer strategy and its application in postreading.

Dunston, P. J. 1992. A critique of Graphic Organizer research. *Reading Research and Instruction* 31: 57–65. Updated review on the effectiveness of Graphic Organizers.

Earle, R. A. 1969. Use of the structured overview in mathematics classes. In H. L. Herber and P. L. Sanders (Eds.), *Research in reading in the content areas: First year report.* Syracuse, NY: Syracuse University Reading and Language Arts Center, 49–58. Describes a study in which Graphic Organizers were used in both seventh- and ninth-grade mathematics classes. Significant differences in favor of the use of Graphic Organizers versus no preteaching were observed when a delayed-relationship test was administered.

Earle, R. A., and R. F. Barron. 1973. An approach for testing vocabulary in content subjects. In H. L. Herber and R. F. Barron (Eds.), *Research in reading in the content areas: Second year report.* Syracuse, NY: Syracuse University Reading and Language Arts Center, 84–100. Describes a total vocabulary teaching strategy designed for content teachers. Strategy components include (1) Graphic Organizers, (2) skills teaching, and (3) extension activities.

Egan, M. 1999. Reflections on effective use of Graphic Organizers. *Journal of Adolescent and Adult Literacy* 42: 641–645. Provides instructional suggestions for using Graphic Organizers.

Griffin, C. C., L. D. Malone, and E. J. Kameenui. 1995. Effects of Graphic Organizer instruction on fifth-grade students. *The Journal of Educational Research* 89: 98–107. Students who received instruction in using Graphic Organizers, in combination with explicit instruction, performed better on transfer measures in social studies than those students receiving basal instruction.

Merkley, D. M., and D. Jefferies. 2000–2001. Guidelines for implementing a Graphic Organizer. *The Reading Teacher* 54: 350–357. Using Graphic Organizers at the elementary level.

Moore, D. W., and J. E. Readence. 1984. A quantitative and qualitative review of Graphic Organizer research. *Journal of Educational Research* 78: 11–17. A synthesis of the research examining the effectiveness of the Graphic Organizer as a classroom strategy.

National Reading Panel. 2000. *Teaching children to read: An evidence-based assessment of the scientific research literature on reading and its implications for reading instruction: Report of the subgroups.* (NIH Publication No. 00-4754). Washington, DC: National Institute of Child Health and Human Development. Chapter 4 points out the effectiveness of graphic organizers on text comprehension.

Robinson, D. H. 1998. Graphic Organizers as aids to text learning. *Reading Research and Instruction* 37: 85–105. A discussion of how best to construct Graphic Organizers for the classroom.

Study Guides

Purpose

Study Guides (Earle, 1969; Herber, 1978) are designed to (1) guide a student through reading assignments in content area textbooks, and (2) focus a reader's attention on the major ideas presented in a text.

Rationale

Reading in a content area textbook may demand a relatively high level of skill development. This kind of reading entails the student's acquiring an awareness of levels of comprehension and of how to function at each level. Then, once secure in these levels, the student should acquire the ability to consider and deal with the organizational patterns of the different reading materials. Toward this end, Study Guides can be useful in developing the ability of students to learn how to read. Specifically, Study Guides purport to develop the student's understanding of, and ability to deal with, levels of comprehension, the organizational patterns of different texts, and the specific skills these might require. Study Guides do this by structuring and guiding the reading of text material or students' postreading reasoning.

Intended Audience

Study Guides are used mainly in conjunction with content area subjects. They may be used in both individual and group instructional situations and can be adapted to aid students regardless of the students' ability level in reading.

Description of the Procedures

Discussion of Study Guides as an integral part of a well-planned lesson will include the following three components: (1) development of Study Guides, (2) construction of Study Guides, and (3) use of Study Guides.

1. Development of Study Guides. Before they can construct a Study Guide for use with their students, teachers must analyze the content material to be read by the students for both content and process (Earle, 1969). By analyzing the materials, teachers are assured that the Study Guide material used by students will be in keeping with the content objectives teachers have in mind.

In analyzing the material for both content and process, teachers themselves should first thoroughly read the material they plan to assign to students. Teachers are then better able to select the content to be emphasized during the lesson. In this way, portions of the assigned material that fit the overall objectives of the subject will be emphasized, and those portions not doing so can be deleted, thus leaving students the opportunity to concentrate on the portions deemed important.

For example, with a reading assignment from a social studies course involving "the Black Revolution," a teacher might decide that the concepts *black nationalism, nonviolence, black power, separatism,* and the advocates of these courses of action are important for students to master.

Once the content to be emphasized has been decided, teachers must then decide the processes (skills) that students must use in acquiring that content. Earle (1969) suggested that the decisions made regarding the skills to be used in mastering the material concern an understanding of levels of comprehension and patterns of organization.

Three levels of comprehension are described: literal, interpretive, and applied. Literal understanding involves identifying factual material and knowing what the author said. Interpretive understanding involves inferring relationships among the details and knowing what the author meant. Finally, applied understanding involves developing generalizations that extend beyond the assigned material. With the content to be emphasized, the teacher must decide what levels of understanding students will need.

Earle (1969) described four patterns of organization in which textual information is frequently found: cause and effect, comparison and contrast, sequence or time order, and simple listing. Dealing with the particular way in which information is organized in a text aids students in mastering the content. Therefore, the teacher must ascertain the pattern of organization for the information in a given text. Together with levels of comprehension, the identification of patterns of organization provides students with the necessary structure to study the assigned material.

Continuing with our example of the Black Revolution, the teacher might determine that all three levels of understanding are necessary to deal successfully with the portions of the text to be emphasized. In addition, the comparison-and-contrast pattern of organization may be found to be used by the text authors in organizing their information.

One last step must be accomplished before the Study Guide is constructed. The teacher must consider the students' abilities in relation to the content and processes to be emphasized. By doing this, the teacher can provide differing amounts of assistance to ensure that all students complete the assignment successfully.

In this step the teacher must consider two points: the students' competencies and the difficulty of the material itself (Earle, 1969). Keeping these two factors in mind, the teacher decides how much structure should be provided for each student to address the content. For instance, the teacher can provide aids to locate the desired material in the form of page and/or paragraph numbers. Also, the teacher must decide whether guides should be constructed for only a single level of comprehension or for differential levels, so particular students may be assigned only to deal with those levels commensurate with their abilities. Teachers, knowing the individual needs and abilities of their students, will have to make these kinds of judgments and vary the structure of Study Guides to ensure the success of their students.

2. Construction of Study Guides. Once decisions have been made regarding the content and process and the types of assistance to be provided, teachers are ready to construct their Study Guides. Although there is no standard form that a Study Guide must take, Earle (1969) recommends the following guidelines:

a. Avoid overcrowding print on the Study Guide, as overcrowding may overwhelm some students.

b. Make the guide interesting enough so students will be motivated to deal with the information.

c. Be sure the guide reflects the instructional decisions made with regard to content and process.

Continuing with our previous example, Study Guides can be constructed to aid students in mastering the concepts and in acquiring the skills needed to do so. Here are two examples of Study Guides, one concerning levels of comprehension and the other involving the comparison-and-contrast pattern of organization.*

Study Guide #1: Levels of Comprehension

*Literal level
**Interpretive level
***Applied level

* 1. What are the basic steps of a nonviolent campaign? (p. 634, par. 4)
*** 2. Why did the political leaders of Birmingham refuse to engage in good faith?

(continued)

*From Dishner and Readence (1977). Copyright © 1977 by the College Reading Association. Reprinted by permission of the College Reading Association, J. E. Readence, and E. K. Dishner. Based on material from M. Sandler, E. Rozwenc, and E. Martin. "Strategies of the 'Black' Revolution," in *The People Make a Nation.* Boston: Allyn and Bacon, 1971, 634–644.

** 3. Why does Stokely Carmichael think "integration is a joke"? (p. 636)
*** 4. Why do you think the authors say that the SNCC has become more militant since the early 1960s?
** 5. Why did SNCC choose the black panther as its symbol? (p. 637)
* 6. What is black nationalism? (p. 639, par. 1)
** 7. Why did the man in the tavern say the extremists would end up in concentration camps? (p. 640)
*** 8. Why do so many people think the racial problem has to be solved in our generation? (p. 640)
* 9. What does the term "black Jim Crow" mean? (p. 641, par. 4),
*10. Who is Thurgood Marshall? (p. 642, par. 3),
**11. Why does Thurgood Marshall fear the black militants? (p. 643, par. 2),
***12. Why do black people think black studies programs are essential?

Study Guide #2:
Patterns of Organization

Directions: **1.** Match the name of a black leader in Column A with his strategy in Column B. Put the number of that name in the blank provided in Column B.
2. Match the name of a black leader in Column A with the ideas in Column C. Put the number in the blank provided in Column C.

A. Names	***B. Strategies***
1. Martin Luther King	______ black nationalism
2. Stokely Carmichael	______ anti-separatism
3. Roy Innes	______ nonviolence
4. Roy Wilkins	______ leadership through education
5. Thurgood Marshall	______ black power

C. Ideas

______ Our philosophy is one of self-determination.
______ White power has been scaring black people for 400 years.
______ Direct action is the only way to force the issue. (p. 635)
______ You can't use color for an excuse for not doing what you should be doing. (p. 643)
______ Current black studies programs represent another form of segregated education. (p. 641)
______ Nothing will be settled with guns or rocks.
______ You must be able to accept blows without retaliation.
______ We must rehabilitate blacks as people. (p. 639)
______ Black history is significant only if taught in the context of world history.
______ Our idea is to put people in office who will work for the people they represent. (p. 638)

It should be noted that these sample guides have been constructed with varying amounts of assistance (page and paragraph numbers) and level of comprehension designated. Teachers may decide to use only one or all of the levels, depending on what decisions have been made with regard to individual students.

3. Use of Study Guides. Study Guides should be used in the context of a well-planned lesson. Students should be prepared for the reading assignment through background development and a purpose-setting discussion. A follow-up discussion also might be provided after the guides have been used. The Scaffolded Reading Experience or the Directed Reading Activity (both described in Unit 1) may provide the lesson framework needed to incorporate the Study Guides as one element in that lesson.

When first using Study Guides, teachers may need to walk students through a portion of a guide so that they will become acquainted with the procedure and will be better able to use the guides. Specifically, this step may aid students in seeing how the relationship between content and process can be fostered.

Groups of students can work on Study Guides cooperatively in lieu of using them individually. In this way, students can collaboratively arrive at responses to the guide. The activity promotes students' active involvement in the reading/learning process.

Finally, as students develop sensitivity to Study Guides and begin to transfer their new learning to other situations, the varying structure included in the initial guides may be progressively withdrawn. In this way, students are encouraged toward independence in their reading.

Cautions and Comments

Study Guides can provide a means of encouraging students to become active participants in the learning process rather than passive observers. In addition, Study Guides aid teachers in ensuring that the important concepts present in text material are communicated to students. Particularly in group situations, Study Guides represent a unique opportunity to explore ideas; they do not tie students directly to recall-type learning.

Study Guides are versatile, and their judicious use may provide the kind of instructional environment necessary to develop students' independence in reading and thinking. As such, various studies have provided substantial support for the efficacy of Study Guides (see Herber and Barron, 1973; Herber and Vacca, 1977; Herber and Riley, 1979).

However, two cautions should be mentioned concerning Study Guides. First, it does take time and effort on the part of the teacher to develop, construct, and use them effectively. This caution, however, should be put into perspective alongside the benefits to students' understanding and the possibility that teachers might work cooperatively on their development.

Second, although Study Guides are designed to move readers toward eventual independence, they are essentially teacher-directed activities. Teachers, not readers, decide what is important in reading the texts. Decision making, therefore, in this learning situation rests almost entirely with teachers. Those educators concerned with creating a learning environment that involves students as much as possible must bear this factor in mind when using Study Guides.

REFERENCES

Armstrong, D. P., J. Patberg, and P. Dewitz. 1988. Reading guides—Helping students understand. *Journal of Reading* 31: 532–541. Reports the successful use of Study Guides with narrative material in high school.

Bean, T. W., D. Searles, H. Singer, and S. Cowen. 1990. Learning concepts from biology text through pictorial analogies and an analogical Study Guide. *Journal of Educational Research* 83: 233–237. Study demonstrating the effectiveness of Study

Guides when coupled with pictorial analogies for high school biology students.

Dishner, E. K., and J. E. Readence. 1977. Getting started: Using the textbook diagnostically. *Reading World* 17: 36–49. Recommends the use of Study Guides as diagnostic tools for the content area teacher.

Earle, R. A. 1969. Developing and using Study Guides. In H. L. Herber and P. L. Sanders (Eds.), *Research in reading in the content areas: First year report.* Syracuse, NY: Syracuse University Reading and Language Arts Center, 71–92. Provides directions for the content area teacher in how to develop and use Study Guides as an instructional tool.

Herber, H. L., and R. F. Barron (Eds.). 1973. *Research in reading in the content areas: Second year report.* Syracuse, NY: Syracuse University Reading and Language Arts Center. Includes studies exploring the effectiveness of Study Guides.

Herber, H. L., and R. Vacca (Eds.). 1977. *Research in reading in the content areas: The third report.* Syracuse, NY: Syracuse University Reading and Language Arts Center. Includes studies that examined the use of Study Guides.

Herber, H. L., and J. D. Riley (Eds.). 1979. *Research in reading in the content areas: The fourth report.* Syracuse, NY: Syracuse University Reading and Language Arts Center. Features additional studies that examined the use of Study Guides.

Miller, K. K., and J. E. George. 1992. Expository passage organizers: Models for reading and writing. *Journal of Reading* 35: 372–377. Study that revealed positive effects in reading and writing for sixth graders using Study Guides highlighting the structure of textbooks.

Wood, K. D., D. Lapp, and J. Flood. 1992. *Guiding readers through text: A review of study guides.* Newark, DE: International Reading Association. A practical guide to the use of Study Guides, with numerous examples.

Selective Reading Guide

Purpose

The major objectives of the Selective Reading Guide (also called Selective Reading Guide-o-Rama) (Cunningham and Shablak, 1975) are: (1) to lead students to the major ideas and supporting details within a content text selection, and (2) to teach students flexibility in their reading.

Rationale

The Selective Reading Guide assumes that since most students are not experts in the subject, they are not able to select with ease the important textual information. That is, it assumes most students read the material as if everything within the text were of equal importance. The subject matter instructor is in a position to guide students through the reading assignment by providing them with clues as to which information is important and which can be skimmed lightly.

Intended Audience

The Selective Reading Guide can be used with students in grades six and above. It would appear to be better suited for use with those students who need additional guidance in their reading.

Description of the Procedures

Before an instructor can design any type of guidance tool for students, several important decisions must be made during the planning stage of the lesson. Of primary importance is the identification of the major concepts and understanding to be derived from the text. Subject matter instructors should ask themselves the following questions:

1. What should students know when they finish this text?
   a. What are the major concepts that the students should understand?
   b. What supporting information or details should they remember on a long-term basis?
2. What should students be able *to do* when they finish the text?
   a. What background information is essential to perform the required tasks?

By making a brief list of the answers to the above questions, content teachers can identify the essential information within the text that they want their students to understand. The next step is to move through the text and identify portions of it that provide students with the previously identified important information. After lightly noting in the margins of their teacher's edition the letters *M* for main ideas and *D* for important details, content instructors are ready to design the Selective Reading Guide.

Perhaps the easiest way to approach this task is to imagine a group of three or four students. It is assumed that content teachers have already completed the preparation stage of the lesson. Students will have their texts open to the first page of the text to be studied and are now ready to read. What information should the teacher provide so that the students will key in on the important ideas that have been identified? The response to this question is the type of information that will be written down in guide form.

Several examples might be in order to illustrate the preceding discussion. The teacher might note important information in the following manner:

- Page 93, paragraphs 3–6. Pay special attention to this section. Why do you think Hunter acted in this manner? We will discuss your ideas later in class.
- Page 94, subtopic in boldface print at top of page. See if you can rewrite the topic to form a question. Now read the information under the subtopic just to answer the question. You should pick up the five ideas very quickly. Jot down your answers in the space provided below.
- Page 94, picture. What appears to be the reaction of the crowd? Now read the fifth paragraph on this page to find out why they are reacting as they are.
- Page 95, paragraphs 5–8. Read this section very carefully. The order of the events is very important and you will want to remember this information for our quiz.

The same approach is used when noting information within the text that, based upon the content teacher's analysis, is of little or no importance. The following example illustrates this situation:

- P. 179, all of column 1. The author has provided us with some interesting information here, but it is not important for us to remember. You may want just to skim over it and move on to the second column.
- Pp. 180–181. These pages describe a fictitious family who lived during the Civil War. You may skip this section because we will learn about the lifestyles of the time through films, other readings, and class discussions.
- Pp. 221–222. Recent discoveries in science have improved the information contained on these pages. I will discuss this information with you in class. Now move on to page 223.

By pointing out unimportant information as well as important ideas in the text, content teachers are purported to be effectively communicating to their students that they must be flexible in their reading. Teachers may even wish to communicate literally to their students the notion that all words in print are not necessarily of equal value for the reader who is attempting to ascertain the author's important ideas.

The completed guide should appear in a logical order and should move the student from the beginning of the text through the end of the unit. Thus, through the use of the Selective Reading Guide, content teachers are saying to the youngsters: (1) pay close attention to this, (2) skim over this material, (3) read this section carefully, and (4) you can read this section rather quickly, but see if you can find out why, and so on.

Cautions and Comments

As with most guidance tools, this strategy should be used sensitively. The Selective Reading Guide might work best with those students who need the assistance and who could profit from structured approaches to developing selected skills. A conscious effort should be made by the teacher to remove this assistance as the students learn the mechanics of reading and studying text material. This weaning process might begin following the use of the Selective Reading Guide for a two- or three-month period. The students should be told when this is taking place and occasionally reminded that, for example, they should continue to pay particular attention to the pictorial information within the unit.

For those students who have difficulty handling the written version of a Selective Reading Guide, the instructor can just as easily design a tape version. Oral direction will now lead the students through the selection. The instructor might advise the student to ". . . turn off the recorder now and read very carefully these first two paragraphs on page 96. When you have finished, turn the recorder on again and I will discuss the material you read." By providing approximately five seconds of dead space on the tape, the student is allowed sufficient time to handle the mechanics of turning off and on a tape recorder. Of course, the student will have all the time necessary to read and study once the recorder is off.

REFERENCES

Cunningham, D., and S. L. Shablak. 1975. Selective Reading Guide-o-Rama: The content teacher's best friend. *Journal of Reading* 18: 380–382. Introduces the concept of the Selective Reading Guide and provides examples for its construction.

Davey, B. 1986. Using textbook activity guides to help students learn from textbooks. *Journal of Reading* 29: 489–494. Discusses the advantages of using a form of the Selective Reading Guide and suggests how it can be implemented in content classrooms.

Idea Mapping

Purpose

Idea Mapping (Armbruster and Anderson, 1982) was developed for purposes of spatially representing the overall structure of expository text. It is purported to have several instructional uses: (1) to afford teachers a tool for examining the nature of a text prior to classroom use; (2) to direct students to appreciate the structure characteristics of different text; and (3) to provide teachers and students with a framework for carefully reading expository text.

Rationale

Based upon the work of Hanf (1971), Merritt, Prior, and Grugeon (1977), and, most notably, Armbruster and Anderson (1982), mapping has emerged as one of the more popular tools for analyzing text. The mapping technique incorporates the visual-spatial conventions for diagramming ideas and the nature of relationships between ideas: concept and example, concept and properties, concept and definition, temporal succession, cause and effect, conditional, and comparison. These relationships and their mapping scheme are depicted in Figure 12.2. If extended to a whole text, as depicted in Figure 12.3, the overall pattern provides a spatial representation across the whole text. Armbruster and Anderson (1982) suggest that a variety of basic text structures are forthcoming from these overall analyses of text. If the question is asked, "Why or how was the text written?" then the following description of text types usually emerges: (1) description—a listing of properties, characteristics, or attributes; (2) compare/contrast—a description of similarities and differences between two or more things; (3) temporal sequence—relationship between ideas that is largely sequential; (4) explanation—an interaction between at least two ideas or events that is causal or conditional; and (5) definitional/examples—a definition of a concept and examples of the concept. In conjunction with these overall text patterns, Armbruster and Anderson (1982) suggest that there are two types of frameworks or frames of text: static and dynamic. Static refers to text that is largely descriptive or definitional in character; dynamic refers to text that is more explanatory in nature.

Instructionally, Armbruster and Anderson (1982) argue that mapping is a tool by which teachers and students can build a coherent model of the meaning of the text. It serves to involve students with the meaning of the text; it focuses their attention on text structure; and it provides for the transformation of prose into a diagrammatic or visual representation. However, in one research study in which the worth of mapping was examined, training in the use of mapping did not sustain long-term gains in comprehension (Armbruster and Anderson, 1980).

Intended Audience

Mapping has been used extensively with high school students and college-level students as an aid to improving their comprehension of expository text. Simplifications of the procedure (see Cautions and Comments) might be appropriate to use with students at the elementary level.

Description of the Procedures

Mapping can have countless uses, ranging from simply revealing the map of a text to students prior to having them read the text, to having students (or the teacher) create detailed analyses of a text. The present description of mapping is restricted to proposals by Armbruster and Anderson (1982) in which students respond to maps generated by the teacher. In particular, they have pursued the use of maps in two different ways: (1) top-down, or starting with the overall framework for a text and refining it or filling in the text, and (2) bottom-up, or generalizing from some given details to higher order structures.

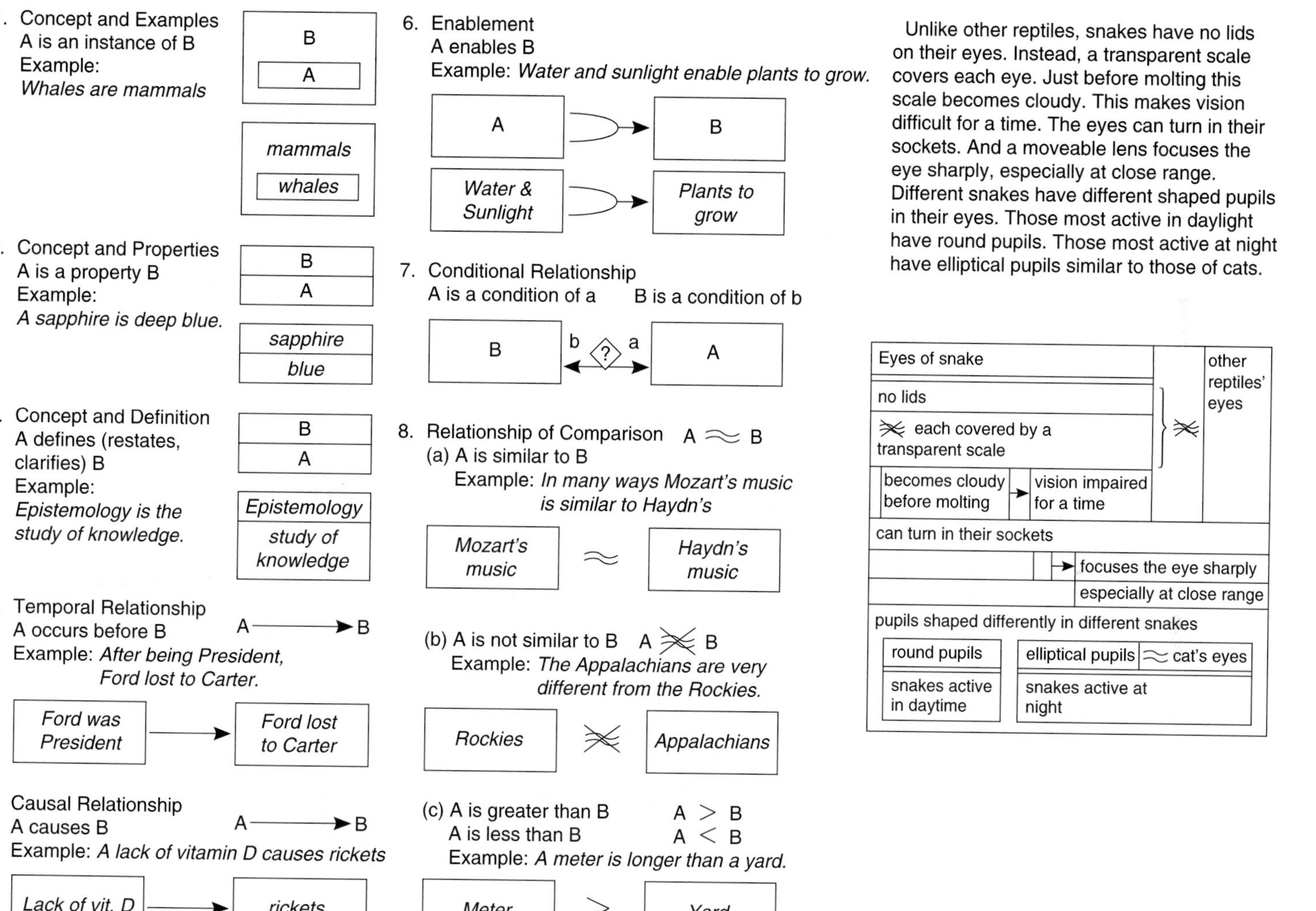

FIGURE 12.2 Types of Mapped Relationships

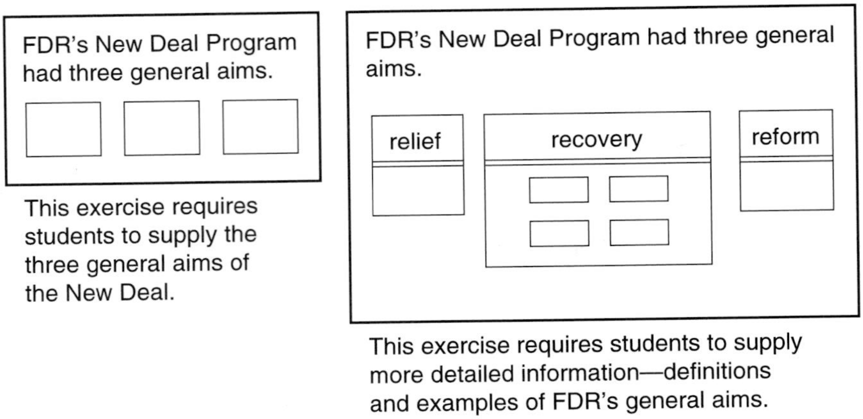

FDR's New Deal Program had three general aims.

This exercise requires students to supply the three general aims of the New Deal.

FDR's New Deal Program had three general aims.

relief | recovery | reform

This exercise requires students to supply more detailed information—definitions and examples of FDR's general aims.

FIGURE 12.3 Sample of Top-Down Exercise

Using Maps Top-Down. The goal for top-down use of maps is to have students generate higher order structures or the main idea and to use this top-level structure to complete written map exercises. For example, a teacher about to assign a text on the establishment and growth of cities might begin by giving students a map similar to Figure 12.3.

This frame or map represents the higher order ideas that readers could use to guide their reading of the text. As a written exercise and as a form of evaluation, students could fill out the details of the map. To constrain the task further, the teacher could use the specialized mapping symbols to indicate the exact type of information the reader would be expected to insert. For example, in the map given in Figure 12.4, the form of the map tells the students whether they are to provide definitions, examples, attributes, and so on.

Sometimes a text is especially difficult to understand. Say the purpose for which the text was written or for which you wish to have your students read it is not congruent with the structure of the text. In these types of situations, it might be useful to introduce the students to the general principle that is overriding. This might be done in the form of introducing students to an additional map that complements, but does not match, the texts assigned to be read.

Using Maps Bottom-Up. Using maps bottom-up involves helping students derive higher order structures by guiding the students to generate principles, supraordinate concepts, or main ideas. For example, a bottom-up exercise might have students infer the label for slots from a definition for some attributes. In Figure 12.5 several examples of this type of activity are given. As Armbruster and Anderson (1982) indicate, in many respects these activities represent merely "the converse of the top-down" (p. 16).

Other variations of a bottom-up approach might entail presenting the students with a listing of the ideas from a text that they are to organize into a map based on a reading of the text. Figure 12.6 includes such an exercise.

Obviously there are a variety of different ways in which students can be involved in moving from the details of a map or text to representing that text coherently. Of course, teachers need to have examined the text carefully prior to being able to develop such activities. They need to have developed their own map of the text and considered what they deem

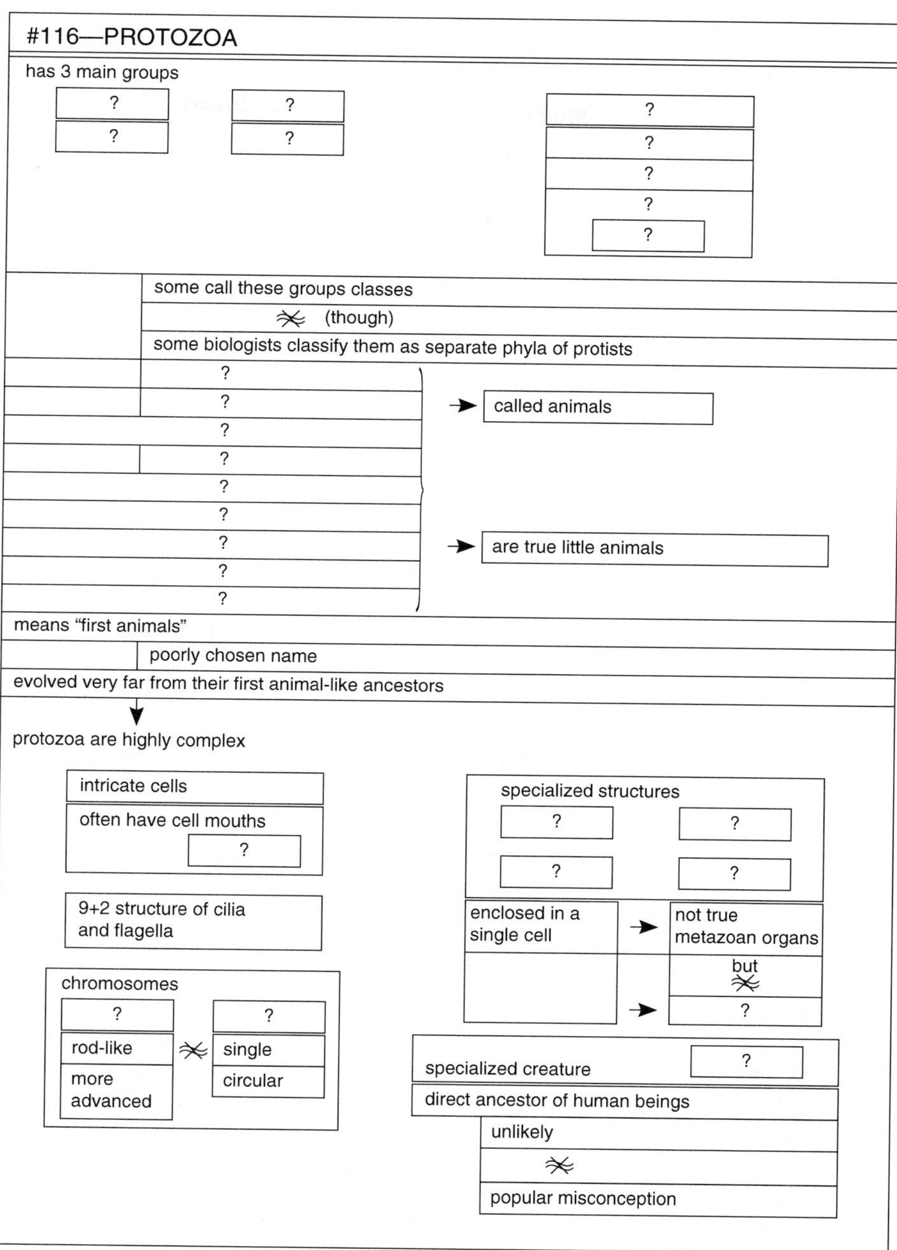

FIGURE 12.4 Sample of Top-Down Map

as desirable learning outcomes for their students. In choosing mapping as a tool, whether mapping be used in a bottom-up or top-down fashion, they need to consider just what content they want their students to address, as well as how they would like them to approach the

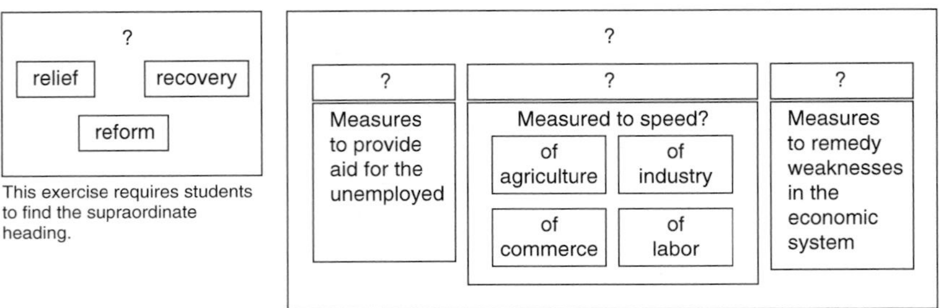

FIGURE 12.5 Samples of Bottom-Up Exercises

texts. Mapping is not just a vehicle for examining ideas from a text; it is intended to alert students to text features. Indeed, in order to engage in the different activities that have been suggested, students need to be familiar with mapping procedures. They need to know the symbols used to represent different relationships in text, the basic text structures, and the fact that information is presented in different variations of these standard forms.

Cautions and Comments

Mapping is not the only form of text analysis, nor is it the only one that provides for the diagrammatic representation of texts and that has been applied to classrooms. Two other such approaches have been developed and adapted for use as instructional tools: networking (Dansereau, 1979) and flowcharting (Geva, 1983). Networking and flowcharting, like mapping, involve having students diagram or use diagrams to chart the ideas and relationships represented within the text. Studies by Bartlett (1978), Dansereau, Holley, and Collins (1980), Geva (1983), Margolis (1982), and Armbruster and Anderson (1980) tend to offer rather mixed results about the benefits of using such techniques. These studies have suggested that most students find that the procedures offer very little, and have no obvious or immediate payoff for the investment in time and effort to learn such systems. In all cases, the researchers appear to have been forced to streamline their presentation of the system to students, have gone to great pains to make it interesting, and have tended to avoid making students repeatedly do detailed analyses of texts. As is the case with mapping, most researchers tend to support the use of text analytic procedures by teachers for purposes of creating instructional activities based upon diagrammatic depictions of text and to appreciate the information represented by a text.

Instead of detailed analyses of text, some educators have proposed simplified procedures for interconnecting ideas (see Davidson, 1982; Bulgren and Scanlan, 1997–1998). Apart from mentioning these developments, there are some other issues. One of the major drawbacks to mapping and these other text analysis procedures is the extent to which they make readers accountable to another author's text. As students read, they should be pursuing their own goals and composing their own text. As presently used, text analysis, specifically mapping, ties the readers to the text they are assigned to read when perhaps it would be more worthwhile to have students generate maps of what they glean from a text and what

Directions to students:

Make an idea map using the following terms from the chapter on muscle structure.

striations
muscle fibers
striated muscles
elongated cells
sarcolemna
40% of body weight
highly specialized cells

Possible Student Response:

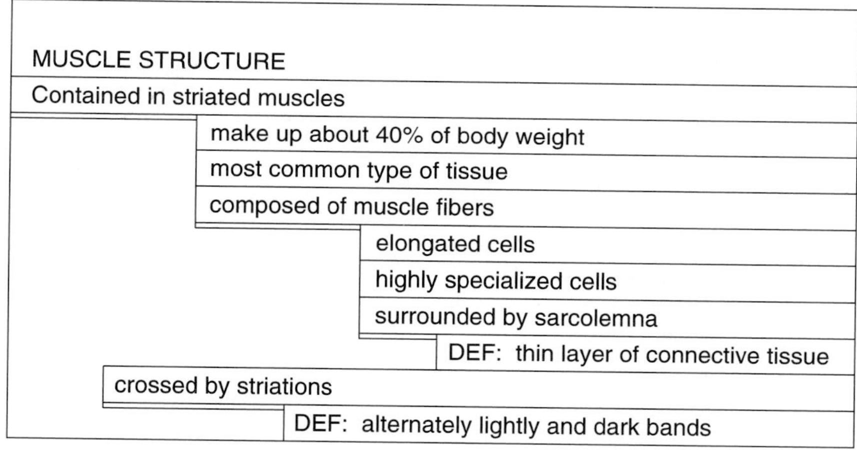

FIGURE 12.6 Sample of Bottom-Up Map

they might write for themselves. A second drawback to mapping and other text analytic procedures is the extent to which learning how to use a system requires learning the terminology and symbols of that system. Perhaps it would be more appropriate to let students develop their own systems initially and leave the adoption of standardized procedures to later and more extensive uses of the procedure.

REFERENCES

Armbruster, B. B., and T. H. Anderson. 1980. *The effect of mapping on the free recall of expository text* (Tech. Rep. No. 160). Urbana: University of Illinois, Center for the Study of Reading. Presents a research study in which college-age students were trained in the use of mapping.

———. 1982. *Idea Mapping: The technique and its use in the classroom* (Reading Education Report No. 36). Urbana: University of Illinois, Center for the Study of Reading. Presents various guidelines and examples of how Idea Mapping might be used in the classroom.

Bartlett, B. J. 1978. *Top-level structure as an organizational strategy for recall of classroom text.* Unpublished doctoral diss., Arizona State University, Tempe. Presents a thorough research study that examines the benefits of teaching text structures.

Bulgren, J., and D. Scanlon. 1997–1998. Instructional routines and learning strategies that promote understanding of content area concepts. *Journal of*

Adolescent and Adult Literacy 41(4): 292–302. Presents a dynamic variation of Idea Mapping with middle and secondary students.

Dansereau, D. F. 1979. Development and evaluation of a learning strategy training program. *Journal of Educational Psychology* 71: 64–73. Discusses the use of networking with college-level structures.

Dansereau, D. F., C. D. Holley, and K. W. Collins. 1980. *Effects of learning strategy training on text processing.* Paper presented at the annual meeting of the American Educational Research Association, Boston. Presents the findings of a research study in which networking was taught to college-level students.

Davidson, J. L. 1982. The group mapping activity for instruction in reading and thinking. *Journal of Reading* 26: 52–56. Describes a simplified version of Idea Mapping.

Geva, E. 1983. Facilitating reading comprehension through flow-charting. *Reading Research Quarterly* 18: 384–405. Presents the findings of a research study in which flowcharting was used to help students deal with expository text.

Hanf, M. B. 1971. Mapping: A technique for translating reading into thinking. *Journal of Reading* 14: 225–230. Presents a simplified version of mapping for use by high school students.

Holley, C. D., and D. F. Dansereau (Eds.). 1984. *Spatial learning strategies: Techniques, applications, and other issues.* Orlando, FL: Academic Press. Includes several articles describing the use of mapping and other spatial learning strategies.

Lambiotte, J. G. 1992. Effects of knowledge maps and prior knowledge on recall of science lecture content. *Journal of Experimental Education* 60: 181–201. Study demonstrating positive effects for maps when used with students who have lower prior knowledge in biology.

Margolis, K. 1982. *An instructional study of helping readers identify the gist in expository text.* Unpublished diss., University of Illinois, Urbana-Champaign. Presents a research study in which high school students were involved in topically defining expository text.

Merritt, J., D. Prior, and D. Grugeon. 1977. *Developing independence in reading.* Milton Keynes, England: Open University Press. Describes the use of mapping and how it might be applied to text.

Miccinati, J. L. 1988. Mapping the terrain: Connecting reading and academic writing. *Journal of Reading* 31: 542–551. Explores the use of maps and their influence on reading and writing.

Piccolo, J. A. 1987. Expository text structure: Teaching and learning strategies. *The Reading Teacher* 40: 838–847. Explores the uses of mapping with reading and writing of selected topics.

Tierney, R. J., and J. Mosenthal. 1982. Discourse comprehension and production: Analyzing text structure and cohesion. In J. Langer and M. Smith-Burke (Eds.), *Reader meets author/bridging the gap.* Newark, DE: International Reading Association. Presents an overview of six different text analysis techniques, including mapping, together with implications for classroom use.

Wood, J. K., and S. L. Petz. 1997. Using Idea Mapping to aid comprehension of hearing-impaired students. *Journal of Adolescent and Adult Literacy* 40: 644–645. Presents a discussion of using Idea Mapping with hearing-impaired high school students.

Text Structure Strategy

Purpose

The Text Structure Strategy is designed to help students recognize and use expository text structures in order to better understand and recall informational-type texts.

Rationale

The ability to perceive the organization of text material has long been viewed as a valuable reading strategy (Niles, 1974). For example, it has been suggested that knowledge of how the ideas in a text can be bound together to form a logical whole enables students to understand, and later recall, that material better than if the text is perceived as a series of discrete entities. Indeed, research (e.g., McGee, 1982) has shown that readers who are knowledgeable about text structure have an advantage in comprehension and recall over readers who aren't aware of the organization of text.

There are roughly two types of text material encountered by students in schools: (1) narrative, or story-type, texts such as those found in much of the content of basal readers and literature anthologies; and (2) expository, or informational-type, texts such as those found in science or social studies books. Not surprisingly, students are more familiar with narrative text than expository text. One of the reasons for this is simply that students have more exposure to story-type material both before they start school and in the primary grades, where it predominates instruction.

A second reason is that narrative texts have a consistent structure (setting, initiating event, internal response, attempt, consequence, and reaction), while expository texts may take a variety of structures. Meyer and Freedle (1984) list five different types of expository text structures: (1) description, (2) collection, (3) causation, (4) problem/solution, and (5) comparison. In addition, they found that text structures that are better organized (causation, problem/solution, comparison) are more easily recalled than text structures that display less organization (description, collection). The following teaching strategy focuses primarily on the first three types of expository text structures.

Intended Audience

Expository text structure is mainly encountered in content area textbooks that are usually associated with middle and secondary schools. However, content area texts are frequently used in the primary grades, and samples of expository passages are increasingly finding their way into basal readers. Therefore, teaching students to use expository text structure is appropriate for students at all grade levels.

Description of the Procedures

Prerequisite to any strategy to teach text structure successfully are three factors suggested by McGee and Richgels (1986). First, teachers must be knowledgeable about structure, i.e., they have thoroughly analyzed text so they can focus students' attention on the specific aspects that let one recognize and use text structure. Second, the passages used for instruction are well organized and consist of a predominant structure. Third, the students must become actively involved in using the strategy while they read and afterward.

Before we present a teaching strategy for expository text structure, the three main text structures mentioned earlier will be defined. A causative text structure is one in which a relationship is specified between reasons and results in a time sequence. A problem/solution structure is similar to a causative structure except that solution is added to the structure that is designed to break the causative link. Finally, a comparative structure organizes elements on the basis of their similarities and differences and implies no causality or time sequence. (For an in-depth examination of text structure in general, see Pearson and Camperell, 1985.)

The following general strategy for teaching expository structure is recommended by Readence, Bean, and Baldwin (2004) and consists of (1) modeling, (2) recognition, and (3) production.

1. Modeling. Before expecting students to use text structure, it is necessary to demonstrate what it is. This can be done by having teachers model their thought processes for students as they (the teachers) use text structure. In essence, teachers think aloud for students. Passages that students will encounter in their reading should be used, since those are most relevant for students. During modeling, it is essential to show students a particular text structure and point out *why* it is a certain type and *how* that structure type is organized. Furthermore it is necessary to point out any words that signal, or cue, the reader into what the text structure is. It has been found that signal words such as *however, because,* and *therefore* assist students in becoming aware of text structure and improving their recall (Meyer, Brandt, and Bluth, 1980).

2. Recognition. This part of the teaching sequence amounts to walking students through a particular text structure. This can be accomplished by asking judicious questions that focus students' attention on selected aspects of the structure. Teachers may wish to start the recognition step on a listening level first. By listening, students can attend directly to the structure, particularly when a difficult text might cause students to divide their attention between reading the text and perceiving the structure. In addition, teachers may also choose to begin with sentences or paragraphs before moving on to lengthier passages. The essential part of this step, however, is that the students verbalize the why and how of the text structure. In this way teachers begin to shift responsibility for learning text structure from themselves to the students. As a guide to helping students recognize text structure, Bartlett (1978) offers the accompanying checklist.

Sample Checklist for Teaching Text Patterns

1. Did you pick out the organization as *problem-solution*?
If so, _________ great!
If not, _________ did you ask the two questions before reading?
or,
_________ Did you find the main idea? ("The problem is . . . sugar and starch?")
_________ Did you find how this main idea was organized? (one part about a *problem,* another part about a *solution*)

2. Did you write the name of the top-level organization at the top of the recall page?
If so, _________ so far, so good!
If not, _________ mmmmm!

3. Did you write down the main idea as the first sentence?
If so, _________ keep it up!
If not, _________ oh no!

4. Did you have *two* parts in arranging your sentences?
If so, _________ not far to go now!
If not, _________ tut tut!

5. Were there *two* parts: one for the problem, one for the solution?
If so, _________ I bet you remembered a lot!
If not, _________ oh cripes!

6. Did you check?
If so, _________ double halo!
If not, _________ don't be overconfident!

*3. **Production.*** Once students have gained some facility in perceiving text structure, they should now be ready to produce a text structure on their own. Just as recognition precedes production, a logical extension of perceiving text structure through reading is producing it through writing. Using a Graphic Organizer (this unit) or some other form of skeletal outline based upon a text passage, students are directed to compose their own version of the passage. They are told to write using a particular text structure and whatever signal words are appropriate to cue that structure. Writing is thus used as a means to reinforce students' knowledge of text structure; and writing with a particular structure in mind should also reinforce the logical organization necessary in effectively communicating through writing.

Cautions and Comments

Attempts to teach text structure have yielded mixed results. Taylor and Beach (1984) were able to be successful at improving the reading comprehension abilities of middle graders by instruction in certain text structures. Other studies have yielded fewer gains. We would question whether text structure can or should be taught isolated from content and purpose. Teaching text structure by itself, without any emphasis on what is being written and why, would seem likely to detract from meaningful negotiations between authors and readers.

Another problem relates to reality. It is cautioned that not all text that students encounter will be well organized. In reality, often text is not organized in a straightforward manner. To cope with this dilemma, Alvermann (1981) has suggested that the text be reorganized into more useful relationships by employing a Graphic Organizer, which places the important ideas in a format that depicts a well-organized text structure. By doing so, she found that both the quantity and quality of recall by students was facilitated.

McGee and Richgels (1986) go one step further in their suggestions for dealing with poorly formed text. They recommend that, instead of Graphic Organizers, a discussion should take place of the text in comparison to what an idealized, or well-organized, text on that topic would look like. Following that, the text should be revised, creating a well-formed piece with an apparent structure and explicit links. Thus, writing is again used as a means to reinforce students' knowledge of text structure. Along this line of reasoning, Harrison (1982) has had a great deal of success in having high school students rewrite their text material for each other.

REFERENCES

Alvermann, D. E. 1981. The compensatory effect of graphic organizers on descriptive text. *Journal of Educational Research* 75: 44–48. Research study showing positive effects on comprehension for the use of Graphic Organizers with poorly organized text.

Armbruster, B. B., T. H. Anderson, and J. Ostertag. 1989. Teaching text structure to improve reading and writing. *The Reading Teacher* 43: 130–137. Describes a strategy for teaching text structure to fifth graders that enhances reading comprehension and summary writing.

Bartlett, B. J. 1978. *Top-level structure as an organizational strategy for recall of classroom text.* Unpublished doctoral diss., Arizona State University, Tempe. A study that yielded very positive results due to the teaching of four commonly found structures to ninth graders.

Harrison, C. 1982. *The nature and effect of children's rewriting school textbook prose.* Paper presented at the Ninth World Congress of Reading, Dublin. Describes a study in which high school students rewrote texts and their rewritten versions were compared with the original texts for comprehensibility.

McGee, L. M. 1982. Awareness of text structure: Effects on children's recall of expository text. *Reading Research Quarterly* 17: 581–590. Study that found that those students who were aware of text structure comprehended better than those who were not aware of structure.

McGee, L. M., and D. J. Richgels. 1986. Attending to text structure: A comprehension strategy. In E. K. Dishner, T. W. Bean, J. E. Readence, and D. W. Moore (Eds.), *Reading in the content areas: Improving classroom instruction* (2d ed.). Dubuque, IA: Kendall/Hunt, 234–245. Discusses the use of writing as a means to teach text structure.

———. 1992. Text structure strategies. In E. K. Dishner, T. W. Bean, J. E. Readence, and D. W. Moore (Eds.), *Reading in the content areas: Improving classroom instruction* (3d ed.). Dubuque, IA: Kendall/Hunt, 234–247. An update of their 1986 discussion.

Meyer, B. J. F., and R. O. Freedle. 1984. Effects of discourse type on recall. *American Educational Research Journal* 21: 121–143. Study that found that certain types of expository text were comprehended better than others.

Meyer, B. J. F., D. Brandt, and G. J. Bluth. 1980. Use of top-level structure in text: Key for reading comprehension of ninth-grade students. *Reading Research Quarterly* 16: 72–103. Study that found an advantage for using signal words to assist students in perceiving text structure and improving recall.

Moore, S. R. 1995. Questions for research into reading-writing relationships and text structure knowledge. *Language Arts* 72: 598–606. A discussion of the issues surrounding text structure and how reading and writing activities can help students learn to use it.

Niles, O. S. 1974. Organization perceived. In H. L. Herber (Ed.), *Perspectives in reading: Developing study skills in secondary schools.* Newark, DE: International Reading Association. Emphasizes the practical aspects of teaching text structure.

Pearson, P. D., and K. Camperell. 1985. Comprehension of text structures. In H. Singer and R. B. Ruddell (Eds.), *Theoretical models and processes of reading* (3d ed.). Newark, DE: International Reading Association, 323–342. Review of research on text structure with recommendations for research and instruction.

Readence, J. E., T. W. Bean, and R. S. Baldwin. 2004. *Content area reading: An integrated approach* (8th ed.). Dubuque, IA: Kendall/Hunt. Describes a variety of strategies for teaching text structure.

Richgels, D. J. 2002. Informational texts in kindergarten. *The Reading Teacher* 55: 586–595. Discusses the case for using the reading and writing of informational texts in kindergarten.

Slater, W. H. 1985. Teaching expository text structure with structural organizers. *Journal of Reading* 28: 712–718. Study in which ninth grade students were taught to use text structure through highly structured practice and application.

Taylor, B., and R. W. Beach. 1984. The effects of text structure instruction on middle grade students' comprehension and production of expository text. *Reading Research Quarterly* 19: 134–146. Describes a research study in which the authors evaluated the effects on comprehension of writing texts with structures.

Story Grammars and Story Maps

Purpose

Story Grammars and Story Maps aid readers in their development and use of a sense of story. During reading comprehension, they direct the questions that teachers use in conjunction with the guided reading of a story.

Rationale

In 1947, Gates advocated the importance of a sense of story in the reader's comprehension of narrative. Now several decades later, a number of educators are proponents of procedures for developing in readers a sense of story and ensuring that the guidance they receive is true to the story line. What has spurred this interest in stories is the propagation of a number of different procedures for analyzing stories—for defining what some researchers have labeled as a grammar for stories. In this vein, the efforts of Kintsch (1977), Mandler and Johnson (1977), Rumelhart (1975), Stein and Glenn (1979), Thorndyke (1977), and Warren, Nicholas, and Trabasso (1979) are most notable. One of the major theses in this work is that stories have a somewhat predictable grammar that readers can sense and use in comprehending them. Consider the following story and its depiction in Figure 12.7.

Although there are various ways a story might be depicted graphically, this figure illustrates some features of attempts to define what constitutes a story in terms of these grammars. As the figure suggests, a story can be organized into several categories of events, such as setting and event sequences, which in turn can be broken down into subseries of initiating events, reactions (internal and external responses), and resolutions.

With these methods, educators have generated two types of strategies for improving readers' comprehension of stories. Beck and McKeown (1981) developed the notion of a Story Map for use in preparing the questions to guide a reader through a narrative selection. Cunningham and Foster (1978) and Dreher and Singer (1980) generated guidelines for developing in students a sense of story, which the students themselves can apply to narratives.

Intended Audience

For purposes of generating questions for a story, the Story Map procedures can be applied to any story—whether it be a narrative intended for adults or for very young children. If

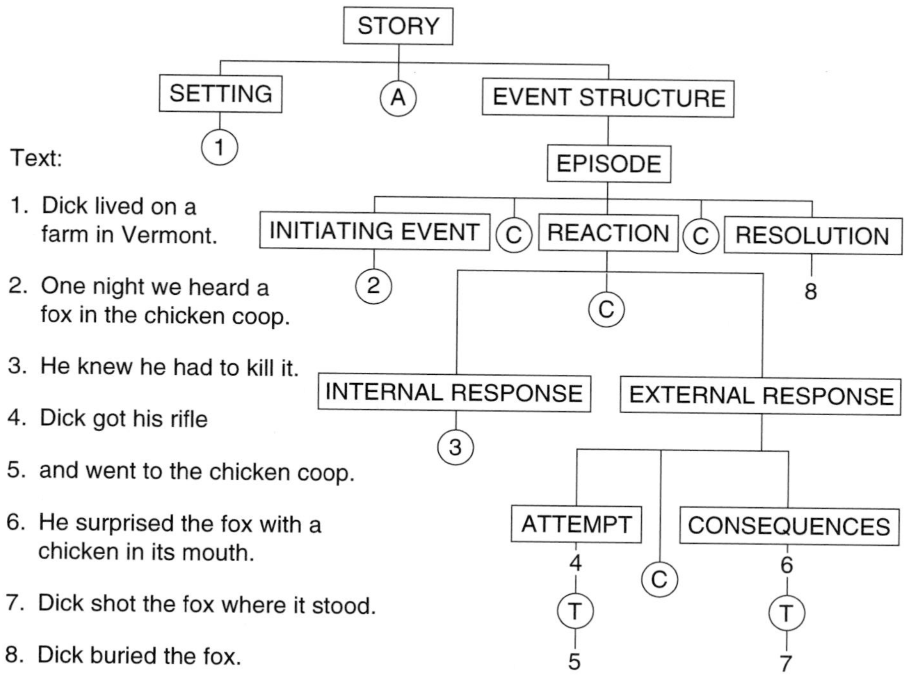

FIGURE 12.7 Example of a Story Grammar Analysis of a Simple Text

developing a sense of stories by using a Story Grammar framework is your goal, most students beyond the sixth grade have such a sense. Some researchers have suggested that even at the fourth grade level, most children have a sense of story.

Description of the Procedures

Both the use of a Story Grammar (Cunningham and Foster, 1978; Dreher and Singer, 1980) and the use of Story Maps (Beck and McKeown, 1981; Pearson, 1982) will be described.

Story Grammars. Apart from their use in text analysis research, Story Grammars have been used in instructional settings for purposes of heightening student awareness of the structure of stories. Cunningham and Foster (1978) describe procedures they developed and used with sixth-grade students. Their intent was to generate a guide framework that they might be able to use with not just one but most of the stories the students are assigned. The framework that was developed is presented in Figure 12.8.

What follows is a description of what occurred as the procedure was introduced to the class:

> Ms. Foster noted the group's resistance to something new, then told them that it would be clearer once she gave them an example. She proceeded to tell them a story of the knight rescuing the lady and filled in the diagram on the board as she went along. Several students commented that they understood a little better, and Ms. Foster proceeded to do the first story in the short story book. All of the students read along silently as Ms. Foster read the story aloud. As she read a page, she filled in the diagram on the board.

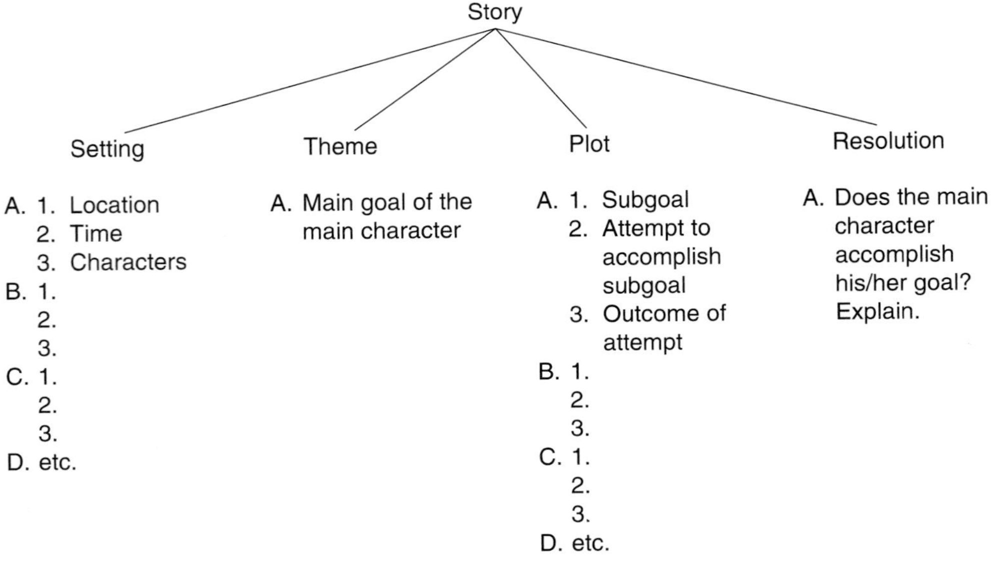

FIGURE 12.8 Simplified Diagram of a Story's Structure

Source: Cunningham and Foster (1978).

> By the time she reached the third page of the first story, some students were joining her in choosing answers. She then shifted the procedure by saying, "Okay, who are the characters in this part of the story? . . . "Has the location changed?" (p. 368)

The lesson continued in this fashion throughout the remainder of the story. Once the story was complete the teacher explained that the diagram, when completed, included the important parts of the story.

In a similar attempt, Dreher and Singer (1980) had students fill out the chart given in Figure 12.9. The first step in their procedure was to explain the chart and its components, and then distribute a story and copies of the chart for the students to complete with the help of the teacher. After discussing the chart with students and the reasons for responding as they did, a second story and chart were distributed for them to complete in groups of three. This was followed with a third story and chart, which were to be completed independently by each student.

Story Maps. Story Maps are used to generate questions for the guided reading of any narrative. The design of questions around a Story Map involves a rather simple procedure. Based upon an intuitive sense of what the premise or starting point of a story is, the teacher lists major events and ideas that make up the story. This list includes explicit and implicit events, as well as any links between these events. This framework serves as the basis for generating questions for the story. It ensures questions that, as Beck and McKeown (1981, 915) point out, "match the progression of ideas and events in the story." They feel it is more appropriate to keep to addressing a story's progression in terms of events and ideas, before dealing with ideas out of sequence or extending the reader's interpretation of the story. As they stated, "The extension of text ideas can enhance comprehension if a map of the story has already been developed" (p. 915).

Figure 12.10 is an example of a Story Map generated for a story and the questions derived from the map. The last few questions deal with the resolution and, although there is no fixed number of questions that might be asked, the key is to have addressed the main story elements based on the story map. Other questions that might be more provocative (If you were. . . .?) or allow for more interpretive responses (What might the ring symbolize. . . .?) might be introduced at this time.

Cautions and Comments

The use of Story Grammars as a tool to sensitize students to stories, and the application of Story Maps for the purpose of developing questions to guide the treatment of story selections, represent sincere attempts to apply research to practice. What is debatable is whether they have taken all factors into consideration. For instance, Cunningham and Foster (1978) report that the bottom students liked reading stories using Story Grammar frameworks, and they believed these students improved in their ability to comprehend stories. In contrast, in a similar study Dreher and Singer (1980) were not as impressive with the results they got with fourth graders. Subsequently, they criticized Cunningham and Foster (1978) for their claims and argued that students did not appear to need Story Grammar instruction because they already have a well-developed sense of story. A later study by Fitzgerald and Spiegel (1983) seems to have, at least, temporarily put an end to the disagreement. In their study,

Fill in the sentences from the story that fit each part of this chart.

1. Setting
Where does the story take place?
Who are the main characters of the story?
When does the story take place?

____

____

Is there any other information that helps us get the picture of what things are like at the beginning of the story?

____

____

2. Goal
What is the main *goal* or purpose of the main character?

____

____

Is there any other information about the main character's goal?
Maybe the story explains the reason the main character wants the goal.

____

____

____

3. Plot
How does the main character try to get the goal?

A. First try
Something happens.

____

____

What does the main character do?

____

____

How did it turn out?

____

Is there any other information about the *first try?*

____

____

B. Second try
Main character makes a new plan to get the goal.

____

____

Main charcter tries new plan.

____

____

How did it turn out?

____

Is there any other information about the *second try?*

____

____

4. Ending

Did the main character get the goal?

____

Is there any other information about the way the story ended?

____

FIGURE 12.9 Story Structure Chart

Source: Dreher and Singer (1980).

FIGURE 12.10 Story and Story Map

Ring Story (By Julia De Voss)

"You'd better not lose this ring, Pam" Pam's sister advised as Pam slid the shining ring onto her middle finger. "It's my favorite ring and I'm letting you wear it only because of the dance."

Pam looked at the golden ring glittering in the sun. The tiny red stone shone like a light and sent an oblong red shadow across Pam's hands. Tonight was the dance and now everything was perfect—her dress, her shoes, and the ring.

Putting the finishing touches on her dress, Pam heard her father's voice. "Let's go, Pam," he called, "it's time go to the dance!" Pam ran excitedly down the stairs, glancing at her image reflected in the hall mirror. All was in place . . . everything except the ring. Pam stared at her empty finger in disbelief. Where had it gone?

Quickly Pam raced back upstairs. In a panic she looked everywhere she had been since she placed the precious ring on her finger. She tore through her dresser drawers, through her closet, back through the hallway. Her eyes scanned every inch of the floor. There was no ring.

"Daddy!" Pam yelled downstairs, "Wait a minute more, I'm coming!" Pam ran into the bathroom. She had just washed her hands. Perhaps the ring had slipped off her finger and had fallen into the sink. Pam stared down into the empty bowl. The ring was gone. Slowly she raised her eyes to her face now streaked with tears.

"I'll tell Daddy I can't go to the dance until I find the ring," she said to herself.

Sadly Pam raised her hands to wipe her eyes—and there on her finger twinkled the golden ring. It had been there all the time, on her other hand.

"Next time," Pam said as she smiled at her reflection, "I'll stop and think before I look so hard for something that isn't lost!"

STORY MAP

THE SETTING

Character(s): Pam, Pam's sister and father

Place: Pam's home

↓

THE PROBLEM

Pam cannot find her sister's ring.

↓

THE GOAL

Pam must find the ring.

→ Event 1 Pam looks everywhere she had been in her bedroom.

→ Event 2 Pam looks in the bathroom sink.

→ Event 3 Pam looks at her hands.

↓

THE RESOLUTION

Pam finds the ring on her own hand.

Question 1. Where and when did the story occur? (The first question always deals with the setting. Leave the question out only if it does not seem important to the story.)

Question 2. Who is the hero or heroine? (Usually a question about the protagonists will follow.)

Question 3. What is Pam's problem? What did Pam need? Why is Pam in trouble? (This question can take various forms, but it deals with the protagonist's problem and leads into the next question, which is a goal question.)

(continued)

FIGURE 12.10 Continued

Question 4. What does Pam need to do? (This is the first of a series of questions that follow the events of the story.)
Question 5. What was the first thing Pam tried to do to get out of her predicament?
Question 6. What did she do when that didn't work?
Question 7. Why did she become depressed?
Question 8. How did Pam finally solve her problem?
Question 9. What lesson did she learn?

20 fourth graders who were identified as lacking a keen sense of story profited from instruction directed at developing their sense of stories. The fact that they were able to identify such students and that these students showed gains due to instruction supports the use of such frameworks with selected students.

What about Story Maps? Are Beck and McKeown's claims reasonable? Beck and McKeown (1981) claim that an integrated and sequential line of questioning will lead to better story understanding than either a random barrage of questions or a mix of provocative questions, opportunities for interpretative response, and story line questions. Intuitively, a well-ordered set of questions would seem to be better than a random set, but less intuitively reasonable is the suggestion that provocative questions and interpretative probes may detract from story understanding. Often such probes may be what engages the reader; indeed, they may fuel the reader's interest to read more thoughtfully and diligently. Speculation aside, the review of studies using Story Maps by the National Reading Panel (2000) found them to be an effective tool for improving text comprehension.

There are some issues that cut across the use of both Story Maps and Grammars. As Brewer and Lichtenstein (1982) argued, a Story Grammar framework does not make a story a story. In fact, their research points to the fact that what distinguishes a story are more aesthetic aspects of a reader's response, such as suspense. Perhaps an argument can be made for facilitating emotional response to a story over or in conjunction with dealing with the story elements. Maybe readers should be encouraged to enjoy rather than dissect a story.

REFERENCES

Beck, I., and M. G. McKeown. 1981. Developing questions that promote comprehension: The story map. *Language Arts* 58: 913–918. Provides an overview of the Story Map and reasons for its use.

Beck, I., M. G. McKeown, E. S. McCaslin, and A. M. Burke. 1979. *Instructional dimensions that may affect comprehension.* Pittsburgh: University of Pittsburgh Learning, Research and Development Center. Presents the notion of Story Map and compares it with strengths and weaknesses of the guided reading in basals.

Brewer, W. F., and E. H. Lichtenstein. 1982. *Stories are to entertain: A structural-affect theory of stories* (Tech. Rep. No. 265). Urbana-Champaign: University of Illinois, Center for the Study of Reading. Presents an argument against the value of Story Grammars and for the role of suspense in story understanding.

Cudd, E. T., and L. L. Robert. 1987. Using story frame to develop reading comprehension in a first grade classroom. *The Reading Teacher* 41: 74–81. Offers suggestions for having students respond in writing to story frames for selections.

Cunningham, J., and E. O. Foster. 1978. The ivory tower connection: A case study. *The Reading Teacher* 31: 365–369. Discusses a teacher's attempt to use

Story Grammars as a way of sensitizing sixth graders to story structures.

Davis, Z. T., and M. D. McPherson. 1989. Story Map instruction: A road map for reading comprehension. *The Reading Teacher* 43: 232–240. A practical discussion of the use of Story Maps to promote elementary students' comprehension.

Dreher, M. J., and H. Singer. 1980. Story Grammar instruction is unnecessary for intermediate grade students. *The Reading Teacher* 34: 261–268. In conjunction with a partial replication of the Cunningham and Foster (1978) study, this article questions whether Story Grammar instruction is necessary.

Emery, D. W. 1996. Helping readers comprehend stories from the characters' perspectives. *The Reading Teacher* 49: 534–541. Describes the addition of characters' perspectives to Story Maps to aid elementary students' comprehension.

Fitzgerald, J., and D. L. Spiegel. 1983. Enhancing children's reading comprehension through instruction in narrative structure. *Journal of Reading Behavior* 15: 1–17. Reports a research study involving training 20 students who were found lacking in story structure awareness.

Gates, A. I. 1947. *The improvement of reading* (3d ed.). New York: Macmillan. A classic among college texts with some discussion of the importance of developing a sense of story.

Gurney, D., R. Gersten, J. Dimino, and D. Carnine. 1990. Story Grammar: Effective literature instruction for high school students with learning disabilities. *Journal of Learning Disabilities* 23: 335–342. Study showing the effectiveness of Story Grammar with learning disabled students in high school literature classes.

Kintsch, W. 1977. On comprehending stories. In M. Just and P. Carpenter (Eds.), *Cognitive processes in comprehension.* Hillsdale, NJ: Erlbaum. Offers a description of the processes involved in story comprehension.

Mandler, J. M., and N. S. Johnson. 1977. Remembrance of things parsed: Story structure and recall. *Cognitive Psychology* 9: 111–151. Presents justification for the use of Story Grammars.

National Reading Panel. 2000. *Teaching children to read: An evidence-based assessment of the scientific research literature on reading and its implications for reading instruction: Report of the subgroups.* (NIH Publication No. 00-4754). Washington, DC: National Institute of Child Health and Human Development. Chapter 4 points out the effectiveness of graphic organizers on text comprehension.

Pearson, P. D. 1982. *Asking questions about stories.* Boston: Ginn. Discusses and demonstrates the use of Story Maps with basal story selections.

Pincus, A. R. H., E. B. Geller, and E. M. Stover. 1986. A technique for using the story schema as a transition to understanding event-based magazine articles. *Journal of Reading* 30: 152–159. Explores the use of story analysis together with cloze and summary writing to guide the reading of expository text.

Rumelhart, D. E. 1975. Notes on a schema for stories. In D. G. Bobrow and A. M. Collins (Eds.), *Representation and understanding: Studies in cognitive science.* New York: Academic Press. Presents one of the seminal theoretical discussions of Story Grammars.

Spiegel, D. L., and J. Fitzgerald. 1986. Improving reading comprehension through instruction about story parts. *The Reading Teacher* 39: 676–685. Discusses the impact on comprehension of teaching story elements.

Staal, L. A. 2000. The story face: An adaptation of Story Mapping that incorporates visualization and discovery learning to enhance reading and writing. *The Reading Teacher* 54: 26–31. Describes an adaptation of story maps for use with elementary students.

Stein, N. L., and C. G. Glenn. 1979. An analysis of story comprehension in elementary school children. In R. O. Freedle (Ed.), *New directions in discourse processing.* Norwood, NJ: Ablex. Discusses Story Grammars and the research pertaining to children's story understanding.

Thorndyke, P. W. 1977. Cognitive structures in comprehension and memory of narrative discourse. *Cognitive Psychology* 9: 77–110. Presents research and theory related to Story Grammars.

Warren, W. H., D. W. Nicholas, and T. Trabasso. 1979. Event chains and inferences in understanding narratives. In R. O. Freedle (Eds), *New directions in discourse processing.* Norwood, NJ: Ablex. Presents a method for analyzing stories based upon event chains that can be applied to all stories and used as a basis for generating questions.

I-Search Paper

Purpose

The purpose of the I-Search Paper (Macrorie, 1980; 1988) is to provide an alternative to the traditional research, or term, paper that is frequently used as a class assignment. With the I-Search Paper students are asked to investigate a topic of their choosing, interview people and visit places associated with the topic, and tell the story of their search.

Rationale

Macrorie conceives of the traditional term paper assignment as dull and unimaginative. It forces students to report on a topic, possibly not of their choosing, by reading, synthesizing, and rewriting the works of others. Although the intent of the assignment is to help students learn to use the library and to write research reports, in the process Macrorie fears the term paper might actually destroy students' natural curiosity for books, for reading, and for writing.

The I-Search Paper, on the other hand, is designed to inspire students to capitalize on their innate curiosity and experience in a hands-on fashion the topic of their investigation. Students choose their own topic and interview people who have something to do with it. They visit places to observe people engaged in activities related to the topic. They read outside sources to give them the information to enhance their knowledge of the topic and help them to interpret what they observe. Students' papers become the story of their search and of what they learned, or didn't learn. Because they have chosen topics of interest they care about and devised their own means of investigation, Macrorie believes students will want to write their papers.

Intended Audience

The I-Search Paper can be used in any classroom where term papers might regularly be given as assignments to students. With modification for age or ability levels, the I-Search Paper could be used across the curriculum with a variety of grade levels.

Description of the Procedures

Although there seems to be no set procedure for doing the I-Search Paper, students become engaged in the following stages in formulating the paper:

1. Choosing a topic
2. The search
3. Writing the paper

1. Choosing a Topic. For the I-Search assignment to be effective, students must select a topic that will engage them, or sustain their interest over a period of time. The topic must be something students truly want to know about. It should be something that will fulfill a need in the student's life rather than a teacher's idea of what would be good for the student to pursue. In other words, the topic must be something to satisfy the student and not just something that seems appropriate for school. Macrorie suggests, therefore, that there is no limit to what the topic for the I-Search Paper becomes.

2. The Search. Once the topic is decided upon, the experience of the investigation begins. Macrorie provides the following suggestions:

a. The topic should be shared with the class, or an assigned small group of students, for feedback. Reasons for pursuing the topic should be shared, and any offers of help should be given. This might include leads to follow, names, addresses, phone numbers, and so forth. If the chosen topic were "hot-air ballooning," the name of someone who's taken a hot-air balloon ride would be useful, as would the phone number of a local company.

b. Students should consult with experts or authorities about where to find pertinent information about their topic. Students need to know what are the most important books, magazines, newspapers, and other sources on the topic. In our example, telephoning an experienced balloon rider might turn up all kinds of useful information. This information should be tracked down, and notes made of what might be useful.

c. Before students interview an expert on a topic, they should discuss how best to approach that individual. They need to decide if they can approach the individual directly, through someone who knows the person, or by telephone, and when the best time to do it would be. In our hot-air balloon example, it would not be wise to approach an expert when that person is getting ready to take off in a balloon; making an appointment at the person's convenience would probably be most appropriate.

d. Students should know something about their topic before they interview an expert. People who are experts are busy because they are experts; but, they usually enjoy helping others because it gives them a chance to talk about what they know best. On the other hand, they usually don't like to waste time. Therefore, it is best to be informed before the interview. In our example it would be best to read about hot-air balloons, the chase crews, and the kinds of competition that a balloonist might enter before encountering the expert.

e. Once an interview is completed, students should test the information gained from the expert against that of other experts. Students need to find out how the expert's peers rate the information. Does it hold up against other people's comments? How do the peers rate the reputation of the expert?

f. Students need to be sure to consult with both primary as well as secondary sources. Primary sources are those individuals who can talk to you about what they're doing, or events or objects you can observe on your own; secondary sources are the people, newspapers, or books that can tell you what others have done.

3. Writing the Paper. Macrorie points out that a good way to organize the I-Search Paper is for the student to write the story of what was done in the search, in the order in which the events occurred. Not everything that was said or done needs to be reported; however, anything important in the search or that caused the student to make a decision during the search should be reported. He suggests that the paper be written in four parts:

a. What the student knew—or didn't know when the topic was selected.
b. Why the student is writing the paper. The need for pursuing the topic should be made evident; students should discuss the potential difference the search may make in their lives.
c. The search.
d. What the student learned—or didn't learn, and what was gained from the experience.

Macrorie suggests that the I-Search Paper conclude with documentation in the form of a list of sources and experts that were consulted during the search. In this way the reader is provided an overview of the information sources and can also assess the reliability of the search itself.

Cautions and Comments

The I-Search Paper seems to be a strategy that teachers can use with students of any age or ability level. Because of the experiential basis of the strategy, it seems particularly appropriate for at-risk students in multicultural settings where the relevancy of what is being taught can take on greater meaning. In fact, Alejandro (1989) describes a unit on cultural values and behavior with which students could use the concept of the I-Search. Arnold (1989) also shows how I-Search could be adapted for remedial students.

I-Search lends itself to cooperative learning (see Unit 11). Instead of individual I-Search topics, a small group of students might decide to collaborate to investigate a mutually agreed-upon topic. In this way, the reading of secondary source material, the interviewing and/or observation of primary sources, and the writing of the paper all could be done cooperatively.

Finally, Caplan (1984) suggests that students might need to engage in some preparatory exercises which would help them rehearse for the writing of the paper before it actually has to be written. For instance, he suggests that students should read an effective piece of personal journalism from a known author before attempting such writing on their own, or participate in an exercise that teaches them how to describe an environment before they initiate a search in which such a task is required.

REFERENCES

Alejandro, A. 1989. Cars: A culturally integrated "I-Search" module. *English Journal* 78: 41–44. Describes a unit on culture using I-Search techniques.

Arnold, L. K. 1989. A new approach to I-Search for remedial students. *English Journal* 78: 44–45. Describes a means to adapt the I-Search procedures to remedial students.

Caplan, R. 1984. *Writers in training: A guide to developing a composition program for language arts teachers.* Palo Alto, CA: Dale Seymour. Chapter 8 of this text discusses the I-Search Paper.

Dellinger, D. G. 1989. Alternatives to clip and stitch: Real research and writing in the classroom. *English Journal* 78: 31–38. Discusses the I-Search Paper as an alternative to the traditional research paper.

Kaszyca, M., and A. M. Krueger. 1994. Collaborative voices: Reflections on the I-Search project. *English Journal* 83: 62–65. Shows how an English teacher developed an I-Search project for high school students that integrated literacy research with peer support to create a community of writers.

Macrorie, K. 1980. *Searching writing.* Rochelle Park, NJ: Hayden. Original source of the I-Search Paper.

———. 1988. *The I-Search Paper.* Portsmouth, NH: Heinemann. Revised and updated edition of the original text.

Zorfass, J., and H. Copel. 1995. The I-Search: Guiding students toward relevant research. *Educational Leadership* 53: 48-51. Describes the use of the I-Search Paper with seventh graders immersed in a motivating theme.

UNIT 13

Studying

UNIT OVERVIEW

Some view studying as a special form of reading. Study-type reading is an attempt to enlist and organize material from texts in such a way as to enhance thinking as well as later attempts to review and retain it. Thus, students need to have access to strategies that will develop their thinking as they focus their attention on selected aspects of text, and teachers need to be aware of what these strategies are and the value of them (Jackson and Cunningham, 1994). Such strategies should include techniques that enable students to deal with information gleaned from various sources: textbooks, oral presentations, media, and so on.

Additionally, studying involves the awareness of and the ability to control one's own learning, or metacognition. Metacognition is knowing what you know and knowing how you know what to do. Individuals with good metacognitive abilities can actively control their learning from text.

The five strategies discussed in this unit present various ways to help students study and retain text and text-related information. They range from a strategy that teaches students to take notes, to one that helps students independently set their purpose for reading, to one that employs the Internet to acquire information.

Survey Technique. Designed as a spinoff of the SQ3R method of study, the Survey Technique offers the teacher and students an opportunity to walk through the chapter together. Most useful with students who might find the material especially difficult, the Survey Technique also furnishes the teacher an opportunity to show the students a model of good study behavior.

PORPE. Based on the use of writing and a model of what effective readers do when reading text, PORPE (*P*redict, *O*rganize, *R*ehearse, *P*ractice, *E*valuate) is a study strategy designed to help students prepare for essay exams.

Notetaking System for Learning. Much of what students learn in secondary classrooms comes from the instructor via the lecture method. Effective notetaking procedures can do much to aid students in learning and retaining a vast amount of information. The Notetaking System for Learning provides a systematic means to organize and review class notes.

PLAE. PLAE (*P*replan, *L*ist, *A*ctivate, *E*valuate) involves students in planning activities before undertaking studying, monitoring those strategies as they learn, and checking and evaluating their effectiveness after learning.

Internet Workshop. This procedure consists of independent reading about a topic on the Internet, followed by a workshop session for sharing and exchanging ideas and strategies discovered by students during their work on the Internet.

REFERENCES

Applegate, M. D., K. B. Quinn, and A. J. Applegate. 1994. Using metacognitive strategies to enhance achievement for at-risk liberal arts college students. *Journal of Reading* 38: 32–40. Compares various study strategies.

Jackson, F. R., and J. W. Cunningham. 1994. Investigating secondary content teachers' and preservice teachers' conceptions of study strategy instruction. *Reading Research and Instruction* 34: 111–135. Study revealing that teachers lack a knowledge of, and do not see the value in, study strategies.

National Reading Panel. 2000. *Teaching children to read: An evidence-based assessment of the scientific research literature on reading and its implications for reading instruction: Report of the subgroups.* (NIH Publication No. 00-4754). Washington, DC: National Institute of Child Health and Human Development. Chapter 4 on text comprehension and Chapter 6 on computer technology are pertinent to studying.

Nist, S. L, and M. L. Simpson. 2000. College studying. In M. L. Kamil, P. B. Mosenthal, P. D. Pearson, and R. Barr (Eds.), *Handbook of reading research,* Vol. III. Mahwah, NJ: Erlbaum, 645–666. Though this review deals with college studying, there are many applications to secondary school studying.

Survey Technique

Purpose

The Survey Technique (Aukerman, 1972) is intended to: (1) provide the students with a systematic approach for previewing a content chapter and (2) provide the classroom teacher with an additional approach to use in preparing students to read the text.

Rationale

The acquisition of effective study skills is recognized as one of the major goals of upper-level reading instruction. The Survey Technique described by Aukerman (1972) provides the content teacher with a systematic means of walking the students through the first step of Robinson's (1961) SQ3R method of study. Specifically, the Survey Technique is designed to prepare the students for the reading of a text by arranging a whole-class overview of the text material. By using the technique on numerous occasions throughout the school year, the teacher attempts to lead the student to understand the importance of previewing prior to reading.

Intended Audience

Although probably more useful at the secondary level, the Survey Technique may also be used at the upper elementary level. It could certainly be useful at this level when the students are scheduled to tackle an especially difficult chapter. As with most highly structured procedures, the technique would appear most valuable for students who have difficulty with the text material.

Description of the Procedures

The Survey Technique serves as a substitute for the readiness stage of the Directed Reading Activity or the prereading stage of the Scaffolded Reading Experience (both Unit 1). The objective is to prepare the students for the actual reading of the text by arranging a whole-class overview procedure that results in an understanding of the total chapter content.

As with other instructional strategies discussed in this book, decisions must be made by the teacher as to what particular information to emphasize. By identifying the major understandings the students are to acquire in a given chapter, the content instructor becomes aware of portions of the chapter that need to be emphasized during the class survey.

Aukerman (1972) outlined a six-step procedure that can be used with any traditionally designed content textbook. The technique follows easily when the text chapter contains the following format: chapter title, introduction, main headings with subtopics, summary, review questions, and exercises.

With that format in mind, the teacher can adapt Aukerman's six-step procedure in this way.

1. Analysis of Chapter Title. After reading the title with the students, the instructor might ask questions such as, "What do you think this chapter is going to be about?" "What do you already know about this topic?" "How do you see this chapter relating to the unit we just completed?" Regardless of reading ability, all students can participate in this type of activity.

2. Analysis of Subtitles. The teacher will note each of the subtitles so that each student will understand the overall outline for the chapter topic. This preview may also involve the second step in Robinson's (1961) SQ3R method—the question step. Students could be asked to turn each of the headings into a question. The resulting questions provide the students with specific purposes for reading the text under each of the headings. For example, the subtitle "Advantages of Cotton Production" results in the question, "What were the advantages of cotton production?"

Questions can be developed by the class as a whole and placed on the chalkboard or on an overhead projector. After using the Survey Technique on several occasions, the content instructor might request that each student develop his or her own set of questions. Whether as a whole-class or as an individual activity, the development of questions results in a student-produced guide that should be extremely valuable when students are later asked to read and study the chapter in more detail.

3. Analysis of Visuals. Often some of the most important information in a chapter can be found in the visuals of the chapter. Many students ignore these aids, while others may not possess the necessary skills to interpret the pictorial information. This third step in the Survey Technique gives the content teacher an opportunity to stress the importance of these visual aids and, if necessary, to teach the students how to obtain information from them. The following bar graph example, Figure 13.1, might appear in a seventh-grade geography book.

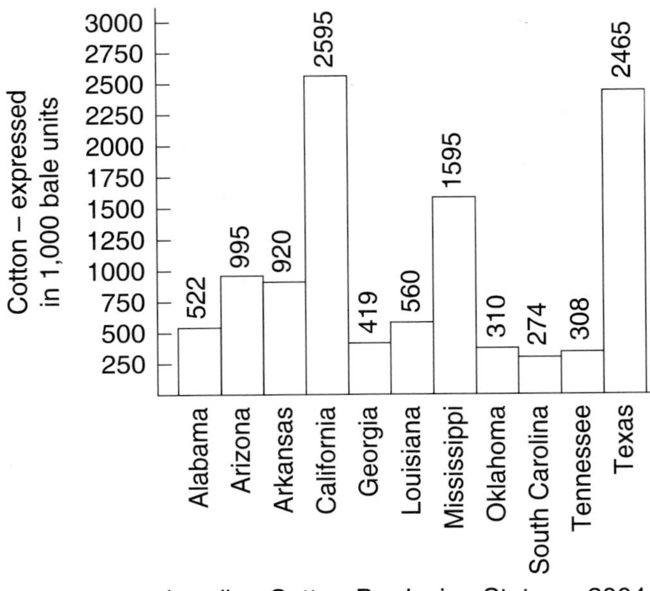

FIGURE 13.1 Example of a Bar Graph

The teacher would ask questions to determine if the students were able to glean information from the bar graph. Two questions might be: "What is the major cotton producing state in the United States?" "What do you suppose the authors of our text meant by the term 'Expressed in 1,000-Bale Units?' " If the students have difficulty with these two questions, the teacher could take a brief period of time to describe the major features of a bar graph and to show students how much information can be obtained from such a simple figure. With the graph shown in the particular example, it would probably be necessary to explain the numerical system so that students would understand that they would need to multiply the number of units depicted on the graph times 1,000 to determine the actual number of bales produced by each state; i.e., in 2004, California actually produced 1,000 × 2,595 = 2,595,000 bales of cotton. Other questions might include the following: "Where are the majority of the leading cotton-producing states located?" "Why do you think Kentucky is not one of the major cotton-producing states?"

4. Introductory Paragraph(s). Many textbook authors use one or more introductory paragraphs to set forth the important ideas within the chapter. Students might be asked to read this information silently. The discussion that follows should concentrate on how the information in the introduction fits with the information discovered in the first three steps of the procedure. A question like the following might be used: "Now that we have read this introductory material, can you see how this information supports some of the things we discovered as we surveyed the chapter?"

5. Concluding Paragraph(s). Generally, the final paragraphs of a content text chapter provide a summary of the chapter content. By reading the summary before reading the total chapter in detail, students receive additional confirmation of what they discovered in all the previous steps of their survey.

6. Deriving the Main Idea. Aukerman suggests that out of Steps 4 and 5, reading and discussing the introductory and concluding paragraphs, the class as a whole should develop a concise statement that could stand as the main idea of the chapter. The statement should be written out on the board or put on a transparency for all to see. Students should now be ready to pursue a more detailed study of the chapter content.

Cautions and Comments

The Survey Technique appears to be worthwhile in its own right as well as serving as an excellent means of introducing students to the initial phases of the SQ3R method of study and of demonstrating the value of this technique for studying content material. In addition, as instructors observe students using the Survey Technique more effectively, instructors could gradually withdraw this structure, thus allowing the students to take more responsibility for their own learning.

A minor shortcoming of the procedure is the exclusion of review questions at the end of a chapter. Assuming they are worthwhile, they could be used as a check of the efficacy of surveying other facets of a chapter prior to reading the text. For example, one effective way of using end-of-chapter questions within Aukerman's Survey Technique would be to deal with these questions immediately after a discussion of the chapter title. The teacher or a student could read aloud each question to the class and ask the students to note briefly what they think the answer to that question might be. If students have no idea of the answer to a particular question, they are advised to leave it blank. After each question has been considered individually by each student, and possibly after a small group discussion, the instructor can deal with the questions in a whole-class discussion. By using the chapter questions in this manner, the teacher is saying to the students, "Let's find out what the author thinks is important in this chapter and let's see how much of this information we already know." Thus, students have an opportunity to review their previous knowledge of the topic before they move on to more detailed study of the unit.

Following this procedure, the remaining five steps of the Survey Technique could be used to gain further information on the topic. After the main idea has been derived, the class could return to the questions at the end of the chapter to discover how many new answers resulted from the survey procedure. It is not unusual for students to answer correctly 20 to 30 percent of the questions during their initial attempt at them and answer another 20 to 30 percent after surveying the chapter.

REFERENCES

Aukerman, R. C. 1972. *Reading in the secondary school classroom.* New York: McGraw-Hill, 47–62. Presents a detailed discussion of how the Survey Technique might be used by the content teacher.

Robinson, F. P. 1961. *Effective study* (rev. ed.). New York: Harper & Row. Provides a detailed description of the SQ3R method of study.

PORPE

Purpose

PORPE (*P*redict, *O*rganize, *R*ehearse, *P*ractice, *E*valuate) is a study strategy developed by Simpson (1986, 1992) designed to help students in: (1) actively planning, monitoring, and evaluating their learning of content; (2) learning the processes involved in preparing for essay examinations; and (3) using the process of writing as a means for learning content area material.

Rationale

Simpson has stated that PORPE evolved in response to: (1) her desire to see if writing could be used as an independent learning strategy for any content area and (2) students' anxieties and lack of knowledge about preparing for and taking essay examinations.

PORPE is based upon the work of Baker and Brown (1984), Emig (1977), and Palincsar and Brown (1984). Baker and Brown (1984) described effective readers as individuals who possess the following metacognitive skills:

1. Clarify their purposes for reading by understanding the explicit and implicit demands of the task
2. Identify the important aspects of a message
3. Focus attention on the major content and not the trivia
4. Monitor their ongoing activities to ascertain whether comprehension is occurring
5. Engage in self-questioning to determine if their purpose is being achieved
6. Take corrective action when failures in comprehension are identified

Emig (1977) advocated that students be required to put into writing the concepts they are reading about to be able to more fully understand and evaluate their learning. Finally, Palincsar and Brown (1984) found that when students are given the specific steps in performing a comprehension task, receive extensive teacher modeling and repeated practice in relevant contexts, and are told why the steps are important in their learning, they can learn to behave as effective readers.

Intended Audience

PORPE was developed for use with college students who lacked a comprehensive study system. As such, it can be used with high school students for the same purpose.

Description of the Procedures

PORPE consists of the following five steps: (1) predict, (2) organize, (3) rehearse, (4) practice, and (5) evaluate.

1. Predict. This first step is designed to have students predict potential essay questions to guide their subsequent study after they have finished an initial reading of the text. In doing so, students are expected to clarify their purposes for future reading, identify crucial aspects of the text, and focus on the major content. In addition, the predicted essay questions must cause the students to synthesize and evaluate the material, since lower-level, text-explicit thinking would not be helpful to them.

Because of the difficulty of this step and its importance to the rest of the strategy, Simpson has broken it down into four phases. In the first phase students should be introduced to the language used in essay construction. Words such as *explain, compare, contrast,* and *criticize* should be defined and discussed for them. In the second phase the teacher should model for students the processes involved in predicting essay questions from a text assignment. These should be recorded and discussed so that students understand how and why the questions were formed. In this way students can be made to see that such questions originate from important aspects of the reading.

Once many sessions of modeling are completed, the third phase begins: provide students stems for potential essay questions on a specific topic. Ask them to complete the questions, cueing the students into the use of the words used for constructing essays introduced earlier. For instance, the words *compare* and *contrast* should be used in writing an essay question about causes of the War Between the States from the perspectives of the North and the South. After much practice in a variety of content areas, students can enter the fourth phase in which they will independently develop their own questions. These predicted questions should be shared with the class, working in small groups. The questions should be discussed and evaluated to identify the most plausible ones.

2. Organize. In this step students organize the key information that will answer the predicted essay questions. They summarize and synthesize the material in an effort to sense the overall structure of the unit. Then, for each predicted question, students are to outline their answers in their own words or create a map, chart, or graphic organizer depicting the answer.

Simpson suggests that teachers can facilitate this process in a number of ways. Initially, teachers should share their own outlines or maps of the predicted essay questions and explain their construction. Students can then use these as models and rehearse and practice for the test. However, since it is the intent of PORPE to have students work through this process independently, teachers should quickly move them into small groups where they can generate their own organization. The results of each small group should be shared with the class and discussed.

Teachers may also find it useful to provide the students with examples of several different student maps or outlines for their critique. It would be profitable to include a bad example—one in which the question is ignored, key examples are overlooked, and/or the organization is lacking or completely missing. The final part of this step occurs when students work on their own organization with written teacher feedback. Although the actual format is left up to each student, the teacher needs to check for accuracy, completeness, and use of examples. The importance of the selective rereading and thinking that precedes the construction of a map or outline also should be stressed at this point.

3. Rehearse. During this step of PORPE, students are to place key ideas, examples, and overall organization into their long-term memory for later recall during the essay examination. The notion of recall versus recognition should be discussed as well as the processes of memorization, in particular the ideas of recitation and self-testing. The following guidelines might prove helpful:

a. Have students begin rehearsal by reciting aloud the organization they have generated. They are expected to test themselves by repeating the structure orally or in writing from memory.

b. Once this is mastered, students are expected to gradually add key ideas and examples from the outline, a section at a time. They should test themselves and, if correct, add a new section.

c. Once the overall structure, ideas, and examples are committed to memory, students are expected to test themselves several times over a period of days to ensure that the information stays in long-term memory. It should be emphasized that rehearsal is a slow, continual process, not one that is conducted overnight.

4. Practice. In the practice step, students validate their learning by writing out in detail what they recited in the rehearsal step. Simpson suggests that many students may need the teacher to model the processes involved in writing effective essay answers. In doing so, the teacher should stress the following to the students:

a. Sketch an outline of the answer to the question before writing actually begins.

b. Make sure the opening statement of the answer rephrases the question or takes a position.

c. Use transitional words such as *first* or *on the other hand* to ensure that the structure of the answer is obvious.

d. Include examples for each major point made.

e. When the writing is finished, check the outline to see if it matches the written answer. Finally, read the written answer to be sure it makes sense.

5. Evaluate. The final step of PORPE requires that students evaluate the quality of their practice essay answers. Students are expected to learn to evaluate their answers as a teacher would; in this way they will learn to monitor whether they need to return to the organizing or rehearsal step of the strategy or are really ready for the actual examination. To facilitate this evaluation, it is suggested that students might rate themselves on their answers to the following questions:

a. Is the question answered directly?

b. Is there an introductory sentence that rephrased the question or took a position on the question?

c. Is the essay organized with major points made obvious to the reader?

d. Were examples used to prove and clarify each point?

e. Were transitions used to cue the reader?

f. Did the content make sense?

The guiding questions can be used in several ways. The teacher may collect the practice essays and judge the quality of the essays themselves. The teacher can also provide sample essays and ask students to rank order them from best to worst. Students should be prepared to justify their decisions in a group discussion. Because of the difficulty of the step, teachers may need to organize several sessions where students read, discuss, and evaluate the quality of various essays. Once they become accustomed to judging the merits of essay answers, they can begin to work independently at this task.

Cautions and Comments

PORPE capitalizes on an integrated language arts approach to content area learning as well as the principles behind the Explicit Teaching of Reading Comprehension (see Unit 7) in the development and use of the strategy. According to Simpson, it has been tried successfully for a number of years with college developmental students. Furthermore, Simpson (Hayes, Simpson, and Stahl, 1994; Simpson, Hayes, Stahl, Connor, and Weaver, 1988; Simpson, Stahl, and Hayes, 1989) conducted research validations of the strategy in which she found that students trained in using PORPE outperformed students using traditional methods on recognition and recall measures. In addition, PORPE students wrote better essays.

By the author's own admission, PORPE "not only takes a while to master, but also takes a lot of study time" (Simpson, 1986, 412). Moreover, she points to the fact that steps one and five are difficult for students; therefore, teachers will need to organize their time and instruction and plan accordingly. Thus, it seems that students will have to persevere in order to see positive effects with the strategy; students needing more immediate feedback may give up on the strategy. The length of time that students persevere may also be dependent on the amount of time teachers give to the strategy and the quality of instruction they provide. This criticism may not be unique to PORPE; it may be true of any study system that students are taught.

REFERENCES

Baker, L., and A. L. Brown. 1984. Metacognitive skills and reading. In P. D. Pearson, R. Barr, M. L. Kamil, and P. Mosenthal (Eds.), *Handbook of reading research.* New York: Longman. Review of the research on metacognition as it relates to comprehension and study.

Emig, J. 1977. Writing as a mode of learning. *College Composition and Communication* 28: 122–129. Examines the role of writing in the process of learning.

Hayes, C. G., M. L. Simpson, and N. A. Stahl. 1994. The effects of extended writing on students' understanding of content-area concepts. *Research and Teaching in Developmental Education* 10: 13–34. Research study showing that PORPE increased at-risk college students' performance on immediate and delayed essay tests.

Palincsar, A., and A. L. Brown. 1984. Reciprocal teaching of comprehension-fostering and comprehension-monitoring activities. *Cognition and Instruction* 1: 117–175. Research showing that poor readers can become effective readers with proper comprehension training.

Simpson, M. L. 1986. PORPE: A writing strategy for studying and learning in the content areas. *Journal of Reading* 29: 407–414. The introduction and description of the strategy.

———. 1992. PORPE: A study strategy for learning in the content areas. In E. K. Dishner, T. W. Bean, J. E. Readence, and D. W. Moore (Eds.), *Reading in the content areas: Improving classroom instruction* (3d ed.). Dubuque, IA: Kendall/Hunt. 340–348. Updated discussion of the strategy.

Simpson, M. L., C. G. Hayes, N. Stahl, R. T. Connor, and D. Weaver. 1988. An initial validation of a study strategy system. *Journal of Reading Behavior* 20: 149–180. Research study pointing to the effectiveness of PORPE.

Simpson, M. L., N. A. Stahl, and C. G. Hayes. 1989. PORPE: A research validation. *Journal of Reading* 33: 22–28. Research studies that substantiated the claims for the effectiveness of PORPE.

Notetaking System for Learning

Purpose

The Notetaking System for Learning (Palmatier 1973) is designed to: (1) provide students with a systematic means of organizing class notes, and (2) provide a sound means for reviewing content information.

Rationale

Although there are certainly exceptions, many content classrooms at the secondary and college levels are structured around class lectures, supplemented by textbook assignments. Most traditional notetaking techniques consider only one portion of the class at a time; i.e., they deal with taking notes in lectures or with notetaking procedures for specific reading assignments. Palmatier's Notetaking System for Learning (NSL) is a flexible system that encourages the student to combine the two approaches.

Intended Audience

Although it is believed that some simplified notetaking procedures should be taught at an earlier point, the Notetaking System for Learning appears best suited for students in the ninth grade through college. It also would seem appropriate for above-average students in grades seven and eight.

Description of the Procedures

Obviously, in order for students to use any type of notetaking procedure, they need to have available the basic notetaking materials—paper and pencils. As many classroom teachers know, this is the point at which many notetaking strategies can and do break down.

It is suggested that students use only one side of 8 1/2 × 11-inch loose-leaf notebook paper with a three-inch margin on the left side of the page. If this legal-line paper cannot be purchased, students can add their own margins to standard notebook paper. The following discussion of the procedure will focus on these three major components of the system: (1) recording, (2) organizing, and (3) studying.

1. Recording. Notes generally are first recorded from the lecture, with reading notes added at a later time. The lecture notes are placed to the right of the three-inch marginal line. The specific format is best left to the individual student, but Palmatier (1973) does suggest the use of a format that utilizes both (a) subordination—a modified outlining procedure—and (b) space. Space will vary depending upon the degree of change between items presented. If the lecture information appears to flow easily from one idea to another, then little space is left between the noted ideas; however, at the point when the topic obviously changes course or when there is some confusion as to how the ideas tie together, the student would be advised to leave a larger space so that more information may be added later.

Again, the student should not use the back of the notebook paper. This will only cause confusion when the student later tries to organize or study the notes. The completed note-taking procedure should result in a format similar to the one shown in Figure 13.2. Note that each page should be numbered as the notes are recorded. This will avoid some confusion during the study portion of the procedure.

2. Organizing. If time is available, immediately following the lecture session the student should organize his or her notes while the ideas and details are fresh. The student has two tasks during this portion of the NSL procedure:

a. *Labeling.* By examining separately each informational unit within the recorded notes, the student should be able to provide labels that briefly describe the information presented. Labels should be placed to the left side of the marginal line and directly in line with the appropriate recorded notes.

b. *Adding.* Following the labeling process, Palmatier (1973) suggests that the student now insert important information from the text directly into the lecture notes. If adequate space has been provided between important ideas, the reading notes may be easily added to the lecture note page; if more space is needed, the back of the notebook paper can now be used in this integration process. Following the above procedure, a page of notes now could resemble the example in Figure 13.3.

3. Studying. The Notetaking System for Learning provides not only a simple means for recording ideas but also a systematic approach to the study of the notes. Since both lecture and reading notes are recorded within the system, the student will have no need to return to the text material or to shuffle back and forth between two sets of notes.

For study purposes, the notes are removed from the loose-leaf binder and spread out so that only the left-hand margin of each page is visible. The labels now become the focal point for the study session.

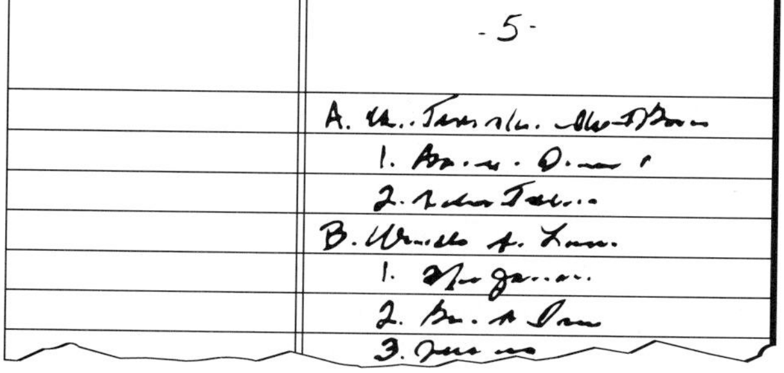

FIGURE 13.2 Example Notetaking Format

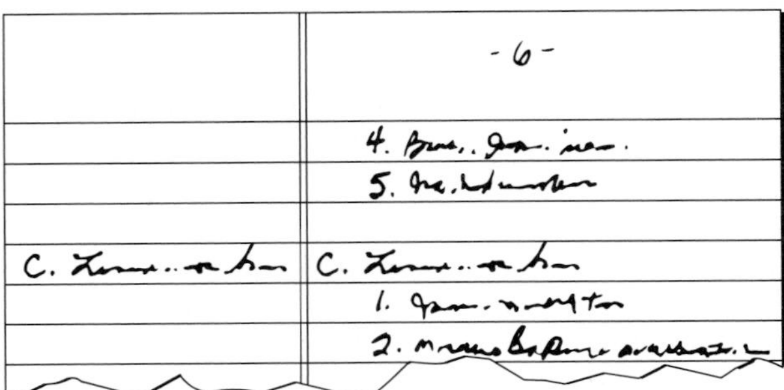

FIGURE 13.3 Example Notes Page

The type of exam for which the student is studying can dictate the manner in which the notes are approached. For an objective test, the student might approach the labels at random, thus approximating the multiple choice, true-false, and matching questions on this type of exam. For an essay test, the student might approach the study task in a more organized manner, usually starting at the beginning of the notes and moving through them in the order in which they were presented. The labels in the left hand margin become the question stems for the purpose of study. A label is transformed into a question, which the student proceeds to answer. Verification is obtained by lifting the next page of notes and reading the information written to the right of the label. This procedure is followed throughout the study period. As the information on a page is learned, it can be returned to the loose-leaf notebook. Study concludes when all the pages are back in their proper place in the notebook.

Cautions and Comments

Secondary teachers and college professors often complain about the inability of their students to take adequate notes. Yet it is rare indeed to find the word notetaking in a secondary text or in a school district's curriculum guide. Very simply, the skill is not taught; rather, it is assumed the student will develop it.

Teachers at the secondary level who rely heavily upon the lecture method may want to spend a portion of their instructional time teaching the students how to take notes efficiently. The time investment should pay off in students' more complete understanding of the subject. Teachers will also be developing an important survival skill that their students will be sure to need in other course work.

In teaching a strategy such as the Notetaking System for Learning, it is important that it be presented early in the school year. To determine if the class as a whole needs such instruction, the teacher might conclude a presentation near the beginning of the first unit by asking the students to turn in their day's notes for the purpose of an informal evaluation. As Anderson and Armbruster (1984) have cautioned, for any notetaking strategy to be viewed as effective, attention focusing and purposeful information processing should be apparent.

REFERENCES

Anderson, T. H., and B. B. Armbruster. 1984. Studying. In P. D. Pearson (Ed.), *Handbook of reading research.* New York: Longman. Discusses the efficacy of notetaking as a study strategy.

Grant, R. 1994. Comprehension strategy instruction: Basic considerations for instructing at-risk college students. *Journal of Reading* 38(1): 42–48. Details a combination of variations on strategies (e.g., SCROL, LETME, textmarking) and how they might work together.

Malda, P. 1995. Reading and note-taking prior to instruction. *The Mathematics Teacher* 88: 470–473. Suggests that students' understanding of text may be enhanced by taking notes prior to class discussion of new concepts.

Palmatier, R. A. 1971. Comparison of four notetaking procedures. *Journal of Reading* 14: 235–240, 258. Compares four notetaking procedures for relative effectiveness and efficiency.

———. 1973. A notetaking system for learning. *Journal of Reading* 17: 36–39. Presents a detailed explanation for a notetaking procedure that has proved useful to secondary and college students.

Tierney, R. J., J. E. Readence, and E. K. Dishner. 1990. *Reading strategies and practices: A compendium* (3d ed.). Boston: Allyn and Bacon. Discusses the Herringbone Technique (pp. 312–316), another notetaking technique that capitalizes on asking six basic questions of text: Who? What? When? Where? How? and Why?

PLAE

Purpose

The purpose of PLAE (*P*replan, *L*ist, *A*ctivate, and *E*valuate) is to provide students with a study system to monitor and control their learning. Simpson and Nist (1984) conceptualized PLAE as a means to help students become independent learners through developing their metacognitive awareness during studying.

Rationale

Success in studying seems to revolve around both the awareness and knowledge about strategies to use and the ability to regulate them. Strategy regulation amounts to planning activities prior to undertaking a task, monitoring those activities during learning, and evaluating their effectiveness after task completion. Because many students lack the metacognitive ability to regulate their study strategies, their chances of academic success are limited.

As a consequence, Simpson and Nist developed PLAE based upon a model of learning developed by Bransford (1979). In this model Bransford stated that, if learning is to occur, the following factors must be considered: (1) the nature of the materials, e.g., how they are structured, the difficulty level; (2) learner characteristics, e.g., skills, attitudes, knowledge; (3) the learning activities, e.g., attention, rehearsal, elaboration; and, (4) the evaluative tasks, e.g., recognition, recall, problem solving. Using this framework, PLAE takes into consideration five operations necessary for student-directed strategy control and regulation (Nist and Simpson, 1989):

1. Students must learn how to establish goals, allocate resources, and make a plan of action that will incorporate the appropriate strategies and distribute practice over time.
2. Students must have a repertoire of strategies for the many tasks and texts they will encounter, since there is no one superior or generic method of study.

3. Students must learn how to select the most appropriate strategies based upon the characteristics of the text, the task, and their own learning preferences.
4. Students must learn how to activate and monitor a plan of action and make appropriate changes, when necessary.
5. Students must learn how to evaluate their plan's success or failure in terms of goals and the task in order to plan for future situations. (p. 183)

Intended Audience

PLAE was originally developed with at-risk college students in mind. However, it seems logical that the strategy could also be used with high school as well as upper-level junior high students.

Description of the Procedures

Four stages describe the implementation of PLAE: (1) Preplanning, (2) Listing, (3) Activating, and (4) Evaluating.

1. Preplanning. In this stage of the strategy students are asked to define the study task assigned. Simpson and Nist (1984) suggest that students ask themselves a series of questions to get a clear idea of the task and complete this initial stage of PLAE:

a. When will the test be? What other tasks need I complete during the time before the test?
b. What will the test cover? Will it cover just the assigned reading? Class lectures? Outside reading?
c. How many questions will be on the test? What kind of questions will they be? What kind of thinking will be required?
d. What will the format of the test be?
e. How much will this test count in the total grade?
f. What kind of grade do I want on this test?
g. How much time will I need to spend in studying and reviewing for the test?
h. How will studying for this test change my regular schedule?

2. Listing. In this stage of PLAE students must decide how to deal with the task outlined in preplanning and develop a plan for studying. In essence, they must decide which of the study strategies that they have at their disposal is most appropriate for the demands of the studying task. Then they must decide how to implement the selected strategies. Simpson and Nist suggest that students record the strategies, why they think the strategies are appropriate, and how they will complete their study plan.

For instance, if students decide that PORPE (described earlier in this unit) is an appropriate study strategy for the assignment they have been given, they should record that strategy and why they decided to use it. In this case it might be to give themselves preparation for an essay test. In completing their plan of study they will record that they plan to predict some essay questions and write answers to them. Further, they should record when and where they will do their studying and how long it will take them. In this case they might say, "Tomorrow at home in my room for 90 minutes."

3. Activating. Here students implement their plan of study and monitor its effectiveness in accomplishing the task. They should question whether the selected strategies are getting them ready for the test to come or whether they should decide to change their plan. Simpson and Nist suggest students use the following questions as a guide during plan activation:

a. Am I following my proposed plan?
b. If not, why? What seems to be causing me trouble? Did I schedule something else I didn't take into account?
c. Can I make changes without sacrificing the goals I set in preplanning?
d. Am I comprehending and retaining the ideas I want to? If not, why?
e. Should I choose another study strategy or reallocate my study time?

4. Evaluating. In the final stage of PLAE students check what they gained from this studying session against their performance on the test. If they followed carefully the previous stages of the strategy, students should feel confident about what they know and how well they are prepared for the test. In evaluating their test performance, they are giving themselves feedback on how well PLAE worked. Simpson and Nist argue that students should do a question-by-question evaluation for each item missed so that modifications can be made before the next cycle of PLAE occurs. Since the PLAE procedure is cyclical rather than linear, this step is important for success in future tests. Simpson and Nist offer the following questions for students to ask in guiding the evaluation of their test performance:

a. Why did I miss this question? Did I misunderstand it? Did I not read it correctly? Or did I just not know the answer?
b. If I didn't know the answer, from where did the question originate? Assigned reading? Class lectures?
c. What type of question was it?
d. Is there any pattern to my mistakes?
e. Did I select the most appropriate strategies for the assigned task? If not, what strategies should I use next time a similar task occurs?

Cautions and Comments

PLAE attempts to get students to experience the metacognitive processes necessary for independent learning by guiding them in how to define their learning tasks, select the most appropriate study strategies, and activate/evaluate the effectiveness of their plan of action. Indeed, in empirical studies by Nist and Simpson (1989, 1990) and Nist, Simpson, Olejnik, and Mealey (1991), students who used PLAE not only improved their test performance but also their metacognitive abilities.

These research studies do make PLAE unique among most instructional strategies in that there is evidence of its effectiveness in multiple experiments. However, further exploration of the long-term effects of PLAE is needed as well as investigating qualitatively what is going on when students apply PLAE techniques in studying situations. Most importantly, however, would be to investigate the applicability of PLAE with other than college-level subjects. Studies using younger students would be most appropriate.

REFERENCES

Bransford, J. D. 1979. *Human cognition: Learning, understanding, and remembering.* Belmont, CA: Wadsworth. A very readable text on cognitive psychology.

Nist, S. L., and M. L. Simpson. 1989. PLAE, a validated strategy. *Journal of Reading* 33: 182–186. The initial empirical validation of the strategy.

———. 1990. The effects of PLAE upon students' test performance and metacognitive awareness. In J. Zutell and S. McCormick (Eds.), *Literacy theory and research: Analyses from multiple paradigms.* Thirty-ninth Yearbook of the National Reading Conference. Chicago: National Reading Conference, 321–327. The second of three studies on PLAE that found that the strategy was successful in improving test performance and metacognitive abilities.

Nist, S. L., M. L. Simpson, S. Olejnik, and D. L. Mealey. 1991. The relation between self-selected study processes and test performance. *American Educational Research Journal* 28: 849–874. Results of this study corroborate those previously conducted on PLAE.

Simpson, M. L., and S. L. Nist. 1984. PLAE: A model for planning successful independent learning. *Journal of Reading* 28: 218–223. The original source of PLAE.

Internet Workshop

Purpose

The purpose of Internet Workshop (Leu and Leu, 2000) is to provide an instructional framework that incorporates new technology, in this case the Internet; is easy to implement; and does not take away from the time a teacher needs to devote to other aspects of the instructional day. It is designed to provide an additional vehicle for teachers to use in implementing their curriculum.

Rationale

There is no doubt that technology, including the Internet, is changing the nature of literacy and literacy learning (Leu, 2000, 2002b; National Reading Panel, 2000) as well as the nature of our society. Internet Workshop is designed around three themes. First, literacy is deictic (Leu, 2000); that is, new kinds of literacies emerge from new kinds of technologies, so what it means to read and write is regularly changing. Second, as multiple literacies emerge from our changing technologies, literacy becomes more and more social. As rapidly as new technologies for reading and writing emerge, no one can be expected to be literate in all of them. Thus, what becomes important is being able to acquire that information from other, more knowledgeable individuals when needed and to share information and strategies with them about the new literacies. Finally, learning how to learn continuously the new literacies as they emerge becomes critical. It is not that we just want students to know how to read and write; we also want them to be able to apply this knowledge to learn the new skills and strategies required by the emergent literacies.

Intended Audience

Internet Workshop seems appropriate for students at all grade levels.

Description of the Procedures

Internet Workshop consists of independent reading on the Internet about a topic and a location initially chosen by the teacher. This is followed by a workshop session for sharing and exchanging ideas and strategies discovered by students during their work on the Internet, permitting them to learn socially about content information, the Internet, and critical literacy skills. Leu and Leu (2000) view the Internet Workshop as one of the easiest approaches to use with the Internet because it should be familiar to any teacher who has previously used a workshop approach in reading or writing instruction. Internet Workshop generally can be implemented using the following procedures: (1) locate an Internet site, (2) design an activity for the site, (3) complete the research activity, and (4) have students share their work.

1. Locate an Internet Site. Teachers prepare for using Internet Workshop by locating an Internet site that relates to the unit under study and contains information appropriate for the age and ability level of the students. When the site has been selected, a bookmark is set so random exploration of Internet sites unrelated to the unit is limited. Internet sites are most quickly found by using one of the many available search engines (e.g., Yahoo, Ask Jeeves, Netscape) or, for younger students, a directory organized for teachers and children that screens out inappropriate sites for children (e.g., Yahooligans [www.yahooligans.com], Ask Jeeves for Kids [www.ajkids.com]). As teachers explore the Internet, they will become more proficient at locating sites and will discover their own favorite sites of information.

2. Design an Activity for the Site. Using the bookmarked site, teachers should design an activity that will meet the learning goals you have established for the unit. The activity may be designed for any of the following purposes (Leu and Leu, 2000): (1) to introduce students to the site you plan to use in your unit of instruction, (2) to expand background knowledge for the next instructional unit, (3) to help develop Internet navigation strategies, and (4) to build students' critical literacies for use on the Internet. An activity page can be developed and handed out, or the activity can be written where everyone can see it.

Most important to remember in designing the activity is to make sure it is open-ended and not merely fact-based. Students need to have some choice in the kind of information they bring to share in the workshop portion of this framework. Choice will eliminate students' bringing back identical information, stimulate their curiosity, and encourage discussion when they share. This is the heart of the Internet Workshop framework. Having students think about how the website is constructed and who did the construction in the activity also opens the door to building their critical literacy skills.

3. Complete the Research Activity. Give students sufficient time to complete the activity. Depending on whether you can use a computer lab or work in a self-contained classroom with a few computers, teachers might consider pairing up students so they can learn from each other as they gain information from the Internet.

4. Have Students Share Their Work. The framework concludes with a short workshop session in which students share their information, compare what they have found, discuss their strategies of discovery, and generate new questions to be explored and answered. Among the discoveries that should be discussed is what the students found out about who developed the website, usually found in a link labeled "About This Site." This type of information helps students understand the authors' motivation in presenting the information on the site in the way they did. Each workshop session can add to students' developing critical literacy abilities in this way. Internet Workshop can be concluded with research questions to explore in the next session as the instructional cycle begins anew. As students become more familiar with the framework, they may also begin their inquiry projects on their own or in small groups.

Cautions and Comments

Internet Workshop is extremely flexible and has many variations to the normal directed learning experience. Its use is only limited by the creativity of the teacher. It can become a simulation or a center activity, or it can be coupled with other instructional practices you currently use to introduce or close a unit. For instance, Internet Workshop could become the framework for a simulation about the Lincoln-Douglas debates. Students could be assigned the roles of Lincoln, Douglas, members of Congress, concerned citizens representing opposing viewpoints, and so on. Such an experience could serve as an engaging way to review the unit.

Internet Workshop can also be used as the basis for a center activity. In math it might be used to research math problems. In English and language arts it might be used to study children's literature on a specific topic, or it might be used to study an important author. Certainly, almost any subject area could provide a multitude of topics to use with this framework. Internet Workshop can become the ongoing vehicle to discover how to use the features of a new search engine, to investigate other websites that can provide additional information on particular topics, to find an online expert to assist students in data collection, and to find out what other classrooms in their school as well as around the world might be doing in the area under study.

Finally, a word of caution about the instructional use of the Internet is appropriate. Computer technology is a relatively new field, and the number of research studies published in this area is small. Those that are published, report positive results (National Reading Panel, 2000). However, in the specific area of research in Internet applications the research is next to absent. Nevertheless, the possibilities about using the Internet for instruction are unimaginable. Certainly, a strategy such as the Internet Workshop can provide a relatively simple forum for discovery and can prepare students in important ways for the world of tomorrow.

REFERENCES

Labbo, L. D., and D. Reinking. 1999. Negotiating the multiple realities of technology in literacy research and instruction. *Reading Research Quarterly* 34: 478–492. Considers the relationship between literacy research and practice as it applies to new technologies.

Leu, D. J. 2000. Literacy and technology: Deictic consequences for literacy education in an information age. In M. L. Kamil, P. B. Mosenthal, P. D. Pearson, and R. Barr (Eds.), *Handbook of reading research,* Vol. III. Mahwah, NJ: Erlbaum, 743–770. Review of the literature on technology and its impact on literacy.

———. 2002a. Internet Workshop: Making time for literacy. *The Reading Teacher* 55: 466–472. Discussion of the Internet Workshop framework for enhancing the changing nature of literacy.

———. 2002b. The new literacies: Research on reading instruction with the Internet. In S. J. Samuels and A. Farstrup (Eds.), *What research has to say about reading instruction.* Newark, DE: International Reading Association, 310–336. Discussion of Internet research and its implications for reading instruction.

Leu, D. J., and D. D. Leu. 2000. *Teaching with the Internet: Lessons from the classroom* (3d ed.). Norwood, MA: Christopher-Gordon. Thorough discussion, with multiple examples, of the Internet Workshop framework.

National Reading Panel. 2000. *Teaching children to read: An evidence-based assessment of the scientific research literature on reading and its implications for reading instruction: Report of the subgroups.* (NIH Publication No. 00-4754). Washington, DC: National Institute of Child Health and Human Development. Chapter 6 discusses the research on computer technology and reading instruction.

Ryder, R. J., and M. F. Graves. 1996. Using the Internet to enhance students' reading, writing, and information-gathering skills. *Journal of Adolescent and Adult Literacy* 40: 244–254. Explanation and use of the Internet in secondary classrooms.

Reinking, D., M. McKenna, L. Labbo, and R. Kiefer (Eds.). *Handbook of literacy and technology: Transformations in a post-typographic world.* Mahwah, NJ: Erlbaum. Text examining technology and literacy.

UNIT 14

Assessment Strategies for Classrooms, Teachers, and Students

UNIT OVERVIEW

Assessment strategies for classrooms, teachers, and students represent a departure from the types of strategies and practices we have included in other sections of this volume. Some readers may consider this shift to be problematic, since the book has always focused on teaching, not assessment.

It is our belief that assessment should work in partnership with teaching and learning. Teachers are expected to learn to use a repertoire of assessment strategies in conjunction with their teaching; indeed, these assessment strategies are integrated into the teaching and learning within the classroom.

So how did we choose strategies to include in the present unit? A key criterion was that the assessment strategies selected for presentation were those clearly integrated within the fabric of teaching and learning.

Although some of the strategies that we present are not altogether new, most (not all) represent a major shift away from the domination of standardized tests toward redefining assessment in terms of the following:

1. A definition of assessment that is connected with what is going on in the classroom in terms of teaching, learning, the social negotiations of authority, meaning making, and so on.

2. A view of literacy achievement that is upgraded to fit with current views of literacy, current teaching practices, and respect for the complexities and nuances of literacy development.

3. An orientation to assessment practices that is relativistic, intersubjective, jointly negotiated, and context-specific.

4. An orientation to assessment that is driven by concerns for student and teacher empowerment.

5. An orientation to assessment that is concerned with the relevance, meaningfulness, or authenticity of what is assessed.

6. A concern for the teacher's roles (as observer, decision maker, student advocate, educator, interpreter) in ongoing assessment activity in the classroom.

7. A concern for the student as the learner and partner in the assessment activities within the classroom.

Several terms have been suggested to capture some of the goals of some of these kinds of assessment: *authentic, learner-based assessment; performance assessment; context-responsive assessment,* and so on.

In essence these kinds of assessments strive to interconnect teaching, ongoing learning, and student development. Sometimes the interweaving of assessment and teaching and learning may appear invisible; at other times it will be more apparent but not detached, anomalous, disruptive, or overshadowing.

A quick perusal of our listing will indicate that we have not exhausted the possibilities. Indeed, there are a number of other strategies that we might have added ranging from think-aloud and introspective techniques to self-rating scales to logs, rubrics, conferences, questionnaires, interviews, and so on. We apologize for all of these omissions and recognize that what we have done should be viewed as a start and tied to what we deem as a significant shift toward the teacher as observer, "kidwatcher," assessor, collaborator, documenter, and so on.

The strategies:

Performance Assessment. The first practice that is described is perhaps the most encompassing, for Performance Assessment includes a host of possible practices including Portfolios. The purpose of Performance Assessment is to develop assessment tools that are more closely aligned with the goals of the curriculum—an attempt to assess students using activities that are more tied to the nature of the learning with which students are involved rather than traditional assessment formats that may not be considered authentic.

Portfolios. Portfolios have the possibility of serving a multitude of purposes: to engage students in a form of self-assessment of their improvement, efforts, and achievement across a range of activities; to engage students, often in partnership with teachers and parents, in periodical evaluations and goal setting; and to serve as a vehicle whereby teachers or other interested parties can pursue a process for collecting, analyzing, and developing plans or interpretations from a range of primary artifacts of students' work and explorations. We would suggest that Portfolios have the potential of introducing teachers to the power of classroom-based assessment systems that are student-centered, engaging, and empowering.

Anecdotal Records. As teachers assume more responsibility for the assessment and decision making pertaining to their students, they need to learn ways to document student achievement, behavior, and learning as it occurs. To achieve these ends, teachers need to learn ways to observe and document their observations without compromising their ongoing interactions with students. Anecdotal Records provide the mechanisms for such documentation. They represent a way of recording information about a child's literacy as they do literacy in classrooms or other settings. They usually represent information that is collected "on the run" by a teacher or observer.

Rubrics. Rubrics are developed as a means of analyzing literacy processes and outcomes arising from performance based assessments as well as other open-ended responses such as retellings, written compositions, and portfolios.

Running Records. Whereas Anecdotal Records might include a wide array of observations by teachers, Running Records are a means of pursuing a more focused analysis of selected reading behaviors for purposes of monitoring student progress and needs. The Running Records offer teachers procedures for collecting reading behaviors tied to oral reading and ways to analyze these behaviors.

Retelling. Retelling offers an alternative way of observing reading behavior tied to the students' ability to recall what they have read. No approach will ever afford a complete depiction of a student's reading, but these different lenses afford the basis for making some tentative judgments of reading comprehension behaviors and outcomes.

Cloze. Whereas the Cloze procedure has been criticized as a method of assessing comprehension, some have argued that it can only be a useful tool for assessing some facets of reading. Since it is still used extensively by teachers, the present description of Cloze as a testing and teaching tool is described along with several caveats.

Parent-Teacher and Student-Led Conferencing. Assessment conferences with parents and students are intended to support ongoing engagements of students and parents in decision making around teaching and learning in conjunction with reviewing via portfolios, dossiers, and other artifacts of student learning.

Performance Assessment

Purpose

The purpose of Performance Assessment is to develop assessment tools that are more closely aligned with the goals of the curriculum. It represents an attempt to assess students using activities that are more tied to the nature of the learning with which students are involved rather than traditional assessment formats that may not be considered authentic.

Rationale

The development of authentic assessment procedures has its roots in the negative criticisms that have been leveled at traditional means of assessing reading and writing. These criticisms include: concern that multiple-choice items or other forms of "closed" assessment may be inconsistent with constructivist views of reading; questions that the passages used on most standardized tests are unique to those tests; concern that the prepackaged and standardized assessment procedures effect a form of collecting information that is disconcerting for many students and inconsistent with the culture of the classroom; and disagreement with the methods used to measure progress, as well as a growing realization that what is taught may or may not be measured on these tests. As was espoused by the Office of Technology Assessment in their summary "Testing in America: Asking the right questions":

> The move toward new methods of student testing has been motivated by new understandings of how students learn as well as changing views of curriculum. These views of learning, which challenge traditional concepts of curricula and teaching, also challenge existing methods of evaluating student competence. For example, it is argued that if instruction ought to be individualized, adaptive, and interactive, then assessment should share these characteristics. In general, educators who advocate performance assessment believe assessment can be made an integral and effective part of teaching. (1992, 16)

Furthermore, as more legislatures (state and federal) and districts use tests as motivations for improving curriculum or as ways to monitor progress toward their goals, we would hope that the search for assessment tools tied to these goals would increase.

In general, Performance Assessment is tied to the goal that assessment should be clearly linked to the goals of education, meaningful classroom activities, and the nature of the learning itself. In other words, Performance Assessment is woven into the fabric of classroom life. As such, Performance Assessment strives for methods consistent with the nature of behavior and outcomes to which teachers and students are aspiring.

Performance Assessment may cover a broad and diverse range of activities. It may include: observations that students do of their own reading or writing, logs that they keep of their reading and writing, webs generated prior to or after reading and writing, open-ended responses, the actual performance of a task, and so on. The key is that the activities are clearly linked to goals and meaningful activities connected to these goals; furthermore that teachers assess behaviors as directly as possible using criteria grounded in the activities themselves and the goals represented by these activities. These assessments, therefore, may range from the simplest student-constructed response to comprehensive demonstrations or collections of large bodies of work over time (e.g., Portfolios).

As the Office of Technology Assessment, in their summary "Testing in America: Asking the right questions," suggested:

> . . . response to these testing tasks can reveal to the teacher more than just what facts they have learned; they reveal how well the student can put knowledge in context. *Well-crafted classroom performance tasks are useful diagnostic tools that can reveal where a student may be having a problem with the material.* They can also help the teacher gauge the pacing and level of instruction to student responses. At their best, these tasks can be exciting learning experiences in themselves, as when a student, required to create a product or answer that puts knowledge into context, is blessed with that flash inspiration, "Aha! I see how it all comes together now!" In addition, these tests can signal to students what skills and content they should learn, help teachers adjust instruction, and give students clear feedback. (1992, 18)

Intended Audience

Performance Assessment tasks are appropriate for students regardless of age in any setting.

Description of the Procedures

Performance Assessment should have the feel and look of worthwhile teaching and learning activities. Therefore, while Performance Assessment activities may look familiar, recognition or formalization of their use in assessment may be less so. Certainly, teachers are constantly assessing students as they are teaching, and making adjustments or noting performance. Performance Assessment makes the nature of these assessments more visible, perhaps more systematic, and certainly more influential. Above all it creates a relationship between teaching and assessment that is more natural, ongoing, and constructive.

Understandably, the form and complexity of Performance Assessment may vary considerably. For example, it might entail activities such as the following:

> Imagine yourself drafting a letter of appeal to the Vietnamese regarding the release of POWs.
>
> Describe the irony in E. B. White's *Charlotte's Web* and what this made you feel about the different characters and the author.
>
> Draw a map of the town, including locations, for Virginia Hamilton's "Zeeley."
>
> Dramatize the discussions among town folk in response to what they discussed the next day in "Tuesday."
>
> Look back over your journal entries in response to the stories you've read. What do you focus upon? Why? How do your journal entries change over time, and why?
>
> Using your notes, webs, jottings, etc., what steps did you follow in the development of your project? What do you think are the strengths of what you did? What things would you like to do the same or different with other projects?

Sometimes teachers may choose to develop their own sets of activities. These might represent miniteaching activities as a way of exploring with students across a range of different kinds of activities akin to what might be pursued in the class or viewed as a goal.

Such tryouts may take the form of miniprojects. For example,

> a teacher watches how a student pulls together ideas from various sources (different content books) as a way of judging research skills (ability to focus, set purposes, take notes, synthesize material, etc.) en route to preparing for an extended unit of work.
>
> a teacher explores the students' self-questioning and predictions as she or he reads several different kinds of selections.
>
> a teacher debriefs a student in a conference in terms of how he or she selects books to read for pleasure and his or her reading behavior across a number of these books.

Vignettes of Performance Assessment during regular classroom activities:

In the context of a Shared Book Experience, the teacher was noting how different children responded: the types of questions that they asked, their predictions, as well as the comments and responses that were offered among the group. What was particularly noteworthy was the extent to which Nigel offered some of his own ideas and recounted experiences that he had that paralleled the story. This was one of the few times that Nigel had responded in this fashion and the teacher viewed it as significant. As a follow-up, the teacher decided to pull together some books on similar themes and to interact with Nigel and some of his friends around the topic. As a further check she also brought along a couple of selections that dealt with different themes. The teacher was able to note differences across these different materials. For those texts for which Nigel had had some similar experiences, he self-questioned, made predictions, and embellished. For those for which he had a limited number of related experiences from which to draw, his responses faltered and his self-questioning and predicting were minimal.

Sherry, Michael, and Tony were 16-year-old ninth graders who were having difficulty pulling together ideas for themselves from their reading. The teacher decided to take a closer look at their approach and behaviors as they read. She wanted to get a sense of why they were reading and some of their behaviors as they read—i.e., (1) self-questioning, purpose setting (predictive) capabilities, and subsequent modification/confirmation of predictions; (2) developing understandings; (3) use of experiential background; (4) ongoing goals and use of these materials.

In the context of their working on a project on climate, she decided to sit beside them and observe their reading of a passage on weather forecasting excerpted from a science text. At various points the teacher noted what they were doing and asked them to talk about their thinking as they proceeded. She looked to see what they were noting and thinking about and how they planned to incorporate and use those ideas.

The teacher became aware that the students did not approach the text with any of their own questions or a sense of how they might incorporate those ideas into their project. Instead, they read the material as if they were going to be required to answer questions about memorized sections.

Some Advice about Judging, Using, and Scoring Performance Assessment Responses. In scoring Performance Assessment, the approach that seems to have the most integrity may require a shift away from scores to trying to see patterns in response and asking yourself, "What does this mean for teaching and learning and ongoing record keeping?" To these ends, an integral part of the scoring or judging might involve student participation in these analyses. Students might be encouraged to suggest how they would judge their responses en route to suggesting ongoing learning goals. It is recommended that you keep your analyses and the responses together so that you can return to the responses either for a second look or a different use. Finally, the goals of the assessment should be kept in mind. Often the analyses of student responses go beyond the needs of the teacher or may not be usable. Teachers and students should ask themselves whether the nature of the return befits the analyses being pursued.

Cautions and Comments

There are many reasons for supporting Performance Assessment. Performance Assessment brings assessment closer to the classroom in which the learning is occurring and instructional decisions are being made. It increases the professionalism of teachers, as well as the value placed upon the teacher's place, including powers of observation and responsibilities in terms of decision making. It also brings to the fore the student's role in assessment—namely, the importance of shifting assessment toward a more learner-based orientation (similar to client-centered).

When the impact upon students and teachers is considered, the value of Performance Assessment is most apparent. Namely, teachers and students are more enthusiastic and more informed from these kinds of assessments. Furthermore, when selected forms of

Performance Assessment have been compared with more traditional forms of assessment (multiple-choice items, short-answer questions), the results are different. In particular, students appear to perform differently depending upon the method of assessment. It is noteworthy that the Performance Assessment responses are apt to correspond more closely to teacher judgments of student learning and also apt to be sensitive to differences in curriculum. Whereas traditional forms of assessment may not show any differences in students engaged in dramatically different curricula, Performance Assessment indices will. (See Shavelson, Baxter, and Pine, 1992.)

Criticisms directed at Performance Assessment tend to focus on issues of feasibility. In this regard, the Office of Technology Assessment, in their summary "Testing in America: Asking the right questions," suggested the following:

> It is important to recall that the basic concept of direct assessments of student performance is not new. American schools traditionally used oral and written examinations to monitor performance. It was the pressure to standardize those efforts, coupled with the perceived need to test large numbers of children, that led eventually to the invention of multiple-choice format as a proxy for genuine performance. Evidence that these proxies were more efficient in informing administrative decisions rapidly boosted their popularity, despite their less obvious relevance to classroom learning. The modern performance assessment movement is based on the proposition that new testing technologies can be more direct, open ended, and educationally relevant than conventional testing, and also reliable, valid, and efficient. (1992, 21)

Nonetheless, there are growing concerns over a number of complex issues:

1. The additional workload that such assessments might demand from teachers
2. The need to improve the capabilities of teachers for developing and interpreting such assessments
3. The development of ways to manage these assessments without detracting from teaching and learning
4. The problems with developing methods of interpreting the responses of students to these tasks
5. The tension between qualitative analyses (which seem more appropriate for such data) and the desire to quantify and simplify these data
6. The possibility that these tests may not be highly correlated with other measures
7. The costs associated with the use of these techniques for large-scale assessment purposes

Could they be used for high-stakes decision-making? They could serve as a form of due process or as a way of cross checking, but to be accepted as a sole alternative one might be advised to examine the laws that apply to educational testing and decision-making and align what one does with what would be accepted practice. For example, in the United States this might entail the following:

- Provide advance notice to parents and others of the intention to use classroom-derived performance measures.
- Establish a review procedure by constituencies.

- Document relationship to learning objectives.
- Define what will be deemed acceptable performance-based measures.
- Review material for bias—especially tied to language, cultural biases.
- Pursue consensus on evaluative criteria and develop procedures for dual evaluation.
- Ensure adequate sampling of the student's performance.

REFERENCES

Allington, R., A. Butler, and R. J. Tierney. 1993. *Teacher's guide to evaluation: Assessment handbook.* Celebrate Reading series. Glenview, IL: Scott, Foresman. This handbook contains performance assessment materials for the reading program specifically but also some general assessment ideas.

Anthony, R. J., T. D. Johnson, N. I. Mickelson, and A. Preece. 1991. *Evaluating literacy: A perspective for change.* Portsmouth, NH: Heinemann. Brings together information about assessment and new assessment practices. Provides forms that can be used in the classroom.

Blum, R. E., and J. A. Arter 1996. *A handbook for student performance assessment in an era of restructuring.* Alexandria, VA: ASCD. Provides guidelines for the development of rigorous performance assessments.

Cambourne, B., and J. Turbill (Eds.). 1994. *Responsive evaluation.* Portsmouth, NH: Heinemann. Presents various articles exploring learner-centered and performance-based assessments in schools.

Clay, M. M. 1990. Research currents: What is and what might be in evaluation. *Language Arts* 67: 288–298. A review of current practices in New Zealand elementary schools documents how teachers have developed informal measures that go beyond the standardized tests to evaluate student growth and change. Clay calls for the development of measures at all levels of education that evaluate process and product, and reminds us that such methods empower teachers as well as learners.

DeLain, M. T. 1995. Equity and performance-based assessment: An insider's view. *The Reading Teacher* 48(5): 440–442. Discusses the possibilities with Performance Assessment.

Education Department of South Australia. 1991. *Literacy assessment in practice: R-7 language arts.* Adelaide: Education Department of South Australia. Provides a framework for assessment that is being used in Australian schools. Includes samples of forms and children's work.

Farr, R., and B. Tone. 1994. *Portfolio and performance assessment: Helping students evaluate their progress as readers and writers.* Fort Worth: Harcourt Brace College Publishers. Detailed background and guidelines for using portfolios for a range of performance-based goals.

Johnston, P. 1987. Teachers as evaluation experts. *The Reading Teacher* 40: 744–748. Johnston discusses how teachers can most effectively evaluate the process of literacy development by suggesting they become experts at "detecting patterns, knowing classroom procedures, and by listening." He further suggests that such individualized process-centered evaluation not only serves instruction but also allows students and teachers to collaborate in the learning process.

Linn, R. L., E. L. Baker, and S. B. Dunbar. 1991. Complex performance assessment: Expectations and validation criteria. *Educational Researcher* 20: 15–21. Discusses issues related to the problems with the validity of Performance Assessment from a traditional testing perspective.

Mehrens, W. A., and I. J. Lehman. 1984. *Measurement and evaluation in education and psychology* (3rd ed.). New York: Holt, Rinehart and Winston. Contains numerous evaluation tools for use by teachers.

Nystrand, M., and J. V. Knapp. 1987. *Review of selected national tests of writing and reading.* Report for Office of Educational Research and Improvement (Grant No. OERI-6008690007). Presents problems with standardized writing assessment.

Oakley, Karla. 1998. The performance assessment system: A portfolio assessment model for beginning teachers. *Journal of Personal Evaluation in Education* 11(4): 323–341. Explores the use of portfolios as a means of assessing beginning teachers.

Office of Technology Assessment. 1992. *Testing in America: Asking the right questions.* Congress of the United States, Office of Technology Assessment. Provides a detailed discussion of Performance Assessment and the bases for renewed interest.

Perrone, V. (Ed.). 1991. *Expanding student assessment.* Alexandria, VA: Association for Supervision and Curriculum Development. This volume includes a range of articles addressing issues and procedures of authentic assessment. These articles raise an array of provocative practical, political, and theoretical issues.

Popham, W. J. 1999. *Classroom assessment: What teachers need to know* (2d ed.). Boston: Allyn and Bacon. Provides guidelines for rigorous classroom-based assessments.

Rhodes, L. K., and N. Shanklin. 1993. *Windows into literacy: Assessing learners K–8.* Portsmouth, NH: Heinemann. Contains many forms of authentic assessment for literacy teachers. Includes sample forms and articles by teachers who actually use them.

Shavelson, R., G. P. Baxter, and J. Pine. 1992. Performance Assessment: Political rhetoric and measurement reality. *Educational Researcher* 21: 22–27. Presents a study detailing the advantages of Performance Assessment over traditional means of assessment as well as the problems associated with their implementation on a large scale.

Shepard, L. A. 1989. Why we need better assessments. *Educational Leadership* 46: 4–9. The large-scale use and limitations of standardized tests are discussed, and the separation of such accountability measures from those that inform instruction is suggested. Problems facing the construction of such accountability tests are noted, and the resulting practices of teaching to the test are discussed. It is suggested that better instructional assessment needs to be developed, which allows assessment to resemble learning tasks and involves the development of portfolios that contain samples of students' work.

Smith, L. M., T. M. Kuhs, and J. M. Ryan. 1993. *Assessment of student learning in early childhood education.* South Carolina Center for Excellence in the Assessment of Student Learning. ERIC Document 358–163. Provides information on several alternatives to testing in the assessment of young children.

Stiggins, R., and N. F. Conklin. 1992. *In teachers' hands: Investigating the practices of classroom assessment.* Albany: SUNY. This book represents several years of exploration of issues of assessment in schools and the shift to legitimizing alternative forms of assessment.

Tierney, R. J. 1993. *Classroom-based assessment systems for literacy.* Glenview, IL: Scott Foresman. Provides a brief discussion of a range of classroom-based assessment procedures from on-the-run assessments to periodical assessments of students using Portfolios and other procedures.

Valencia, S., E. Hiebert, and P. Afflerbach (Eds.). 1993. *Authentic reading assessment.* Newark, DE: International Reading Association. This volume includes nine case studies representing a range of assessment initiatives from the innovative to the more traditional. The editors provide provocative commentary on some of the issues involved in Portfolios and other authentic assessment practices.

Valencia, S., and P. D. Pearson. 1987. Reading Assessment: Time for a change. *The Reading Teacher* 40: 726–732. In this article Valencia and Pearson claim that the current view of reading that emphasizes the active role of readers as they construct meaning with a text is not reflected in our present practices.

Valencia, S. W., W. McGinley, and P. D. Pearson. 1990. Assessing reading and writing. In G. G. Duffy (Ed.), *Reading in the Middle School.* International Reading Association, 124–153. The authors advocate a move to contextualized assessment that views assessment as "continuous, multidimensional, grounded in knowledge and authentic."

Wiggins, G. 1989. Teaching to the (authentic) test. *Educational Leadership* 46: 41–47. In this article, Wiggins argues that authentic tests should be truly representative of performance in the field, tied to criteria that make sense, related to student self-assessment, and so on.

Wolf, K., and Y. Siu-Runyan. 1996. Portfolio purposes and possibilities. *Journal of Adolescent and Adult Literacy* 40(1): 30–37. Describes the use of the portfolio for various purposes.

Portfolios

Purpose

Portfolios have the possibility of serving a multitude of purposes: to engage students in a form of self-assessment of their improvement, efforts, and achievement across a range of activities; to engage students, often in partnership with teachers and parents, in periodical evaluations and goal setting; to serve as a vehicle whereby teachers or other interested parties can pursue a process for collecting, analyzing, and developing plans or interpretations from a range of primary artifacts of students' work and explorations; to serve as a vehicle for screening students or prospective employees on the basis of a dossier of what they have done.

Rationale

Portfolios have their roots in various professions (e.g., art, journalism, architecture, etc.) in which traditional assessment procedures were obviously unable to adequately represent performance. In their most recent manifestation, portfolio assessment has emerged in response to the criticisms being leveled at traditional assessment procedures, such as standardized tests, and the desire to realign assessment with teaching and learning. In this regard, the rationale undergirding portfolio assessment is that assessment should not be viewed as detached from learning and teaching but inextricably tied to them.

A view of teaching and learning	Some goals for assessment
Dynamic and ongoing	Dynamic and ongoing
Child-centered	Child-centered or client-centered
Interactive	Interactive
Jointly constructed meanings	Jointly constructed assessment
Collaborative	Collaborative
Multifaceted	Multifaceted
Personalized	Personalized
Generative	Generative
Involving taking risks and experimentation	Involving taking risks and experimentation
Nurturing and facilitative	Nurturing and facilitative
Experiential	Experiential
Context-supported	Context-supported
Based on real texts and meaningful activities	Based on real texts and meaningful activities
Supports multiple literacies	Supports multiple literacies
Encourages self-improvement and ownership	Encourages self-improvement and ownership

Essentially, the portfolio represents some major shifts in some basic tenets of assessment. In conjunction with a shift in views of science away from positivism to constructivism, there has been a movement from absolutism to relativism, as well as an acceptance of subjectivity over objectivity, interpretability over reliability, thickness of description over sampling, collaboration over imposition, emerging over a priori, ongoing over summative, and so on. A discussion of traditional versus portfolio classrooms follows.

With traditional assessment students are assessed by some outside person or using what is touted as an "objective" measure. In a portfolio classroom the students are involved in assessing themselves and establishing their own learning goals. To do so, they may work with their peers, teachers, and parents in reviewing their efforts, selecting representative pieces, keeping logs, and developing self-assessments. Admittedly, portfolios may be assessed "subjectively," but fairly—especially considering that the goal is to enhance learning and teaching.

In portfolio classrooms, sameness gives way to diversity. Whereas standardized tests involve the same test's being given at the same time to all students, each student's portfolio provides a unique and multifaceted portrait of a student. Reading-writing portfolios provide a portrait of the range of literacy experiences with which each student has been engaged over time. A portfolio might include a collection of each student's "Sunday best": drafts, pivotal pieces, different kinds of working documents, as well as records and reflections of their efforts, achievements, processes, improvement, and future learning goals. As students using portfolios will say, they provide "a portrait of me, who I am and how I have changed."

Whereas traditional assessment may yield a single score or grade, portfolios yield profiles, tentative goal statements, and interpretative reports or narratives. These profiles, goal statements, and reports serve as the basis for evaluative and planning conferences with the students and the parents of the child. Moreover, they serve as the springboard for the students' negotiations of goals for themselves.

Furthermore, the portfolios represent a form of grounded assessment versus secondary assessment. As a result a portfolio allows a form of assessment that allows the evaluator to return to the actual experiences or data from which evaluations/interpretations are made. In other words, just as historians might return to journals written at the time by participants in an event, so portfolios allow the evaluator to return to the primary sources.

Perhaps the way to begin thinking about assessment is to take a step back and ask yourself, "What do I want in terms of assessment in my classroom?" Be careful not to define yourself in terms of how assessment currently takes place. Think about what it is that you would prefer. So, before jumping to conclusions about the validity of such an approach to assessment or dismissing the use of Portfolios as too radical a departure, ask yourself whether your current assessment practices are serving your purposes. Just how do the assessment practices in your classroom measure up?

Do your assessment practices empower your students' self-understanding and allow them to pursue their own meaningful learning goals? Do they provide you information that you can use in your teaching and to mobilize appropriate support services for each student? Do your assessment practices enhance learning and teaching in your classroom? Is assessment well integrated into your instruction? Do your assessment practices have a relationship with teaching and learning that is ongoing, dynamic, and not disruptive? Do your assessment practices reflect what we know about learning and development? Above all, do your assessment practices empower teachers, students, and parents?

Intended Audience

Portfolio assessment is appropriate for students regardless of age in any setting.

Description of the Procedures

We will provide you a quick glimpse of the Portfolio process and some of the steps involved in implementing portfolio assessment in your classroom. Essentially, students are encouraged to review and examine their current efforts and begin to define their future learning goals. Teachers and students begin by maintaining a file of their work including working drafts, lists of ideas, finished work, notes, logs, and journals. Then they periodically peruse these efforts to check and reflect upon their improvements, the range of experiences, their breakthroughs, new learnings, and future goals.

Is it as simple as it sounds? It is simple, but it is also a major leap in faith. It requires teachers to simultaneously assume a new measure of professionalism and adopt an approach to assessment that is student-centered and classroom-based. The list below offers an overview of the procedure:

PORTFOLIOS Step by Step

1. GETTING STARTED
   - Introduce parents to your plans
   - Share personal portfolio
   - Parent/professional share portfolio, e.g., artist, architect, journalist
   - Develop a class portfolio
   - Brainstorm with students about purposes and possibilities

2. COLLECT AND TAG
   - Develop collections: process, product, seminal pieces, representative pieces, best
   - Be sure to tag each item (e.g., date, significance, pertinent details)
   - Consider home-school connections
   - Ongoing sections: logs, journals, self-appraisals, favorite works, etc.

3. SELECT, SORT, SAVOR
   - Organize to organize
   - Establish possible/tentative guidelines
   - Consider possible samples to include in portfolio
   - Refrain from making final selection until obtaining feedback/input from others
   - Model decision making
   - Conference
   - Adjust or add tags bases for selection

4. SHARE, REFLECT, AND PLAN
   - Conference with peer, parent, teacher, and student
   - Develop overall analysis/narrative, etc.

5. THEN
   - COLLECT AND TAG, then
   - SELECT, SAVOR, AND SHARE, then
   - SHARE AND PLAN, etc.

What do you include in portfolios? Students are usually encouraged to include a range of their writings as well as drafts or other seminal items that may not always look like their best work but may reflect important discoveries or breakthroughs. Students might include what might be labeled as reader response entries. These can run the gamut from time lines to sketches of characters to book reports or journal entries. In addition, students might include logs of their readings, writings, and projects, as well as notes describing their assessments of their progress and future goals. Finally, students might include projects that they work on at home, with or without their parents.

But, then, how does a teacher start?

Several Portfolio advocates encourage teachers to develop their own portfolios. They would encourage teachers to pull together a portfolio of their own reading, writing, and other interests en route to sharing it with someone else or their students. If teachers are hesitant to pull together their own portfolios, there are other ways to introduce the concept to students. Some teachers have enlisted the help of other teachers, parents, or members of the community who maintain portfolios in the course of their profession. For example, some teachers have had art students share their portfolio with their classes. Others have introduced the concept of Portfolio to students by bringing in material representing the range of work of famous individuals such as Leonardo da Vinci. Sometimes teachers have just described what portfolios are and then discussed possible guidelines for students' gathering and selecting materials for their own portfolios. Teachers and their students need to realize that they have access to a great deal of material that can be used as a basis for starting to decide what they might include. In some classes, the teachers and students prescribe a number of particular kinds of material to be included; in other classrooms the material will vary across students. Usually, the students are encouraged to include material other than their Sunday best. For example, students might include thought pieces, breakthrough moments, jot lists, webs, or pivotal pieces.

As students ponder and peruse possible entries, teachers and other students are encouraged to offer support, whether they serve as sounding boards or as facilitators. In addition, students might jot down the basis for their selection of individual pieces by using captions or 3 × 5 cards and including an extended narrative, Venn diagrams, or profiles describing the whole portfolio. Teachers typically put time aside to have students deliberate over future directions for themselves, and to share their portfolios and plans with the class.

The issue of evaluation of the portfolio is a matter for which there exists a certain amount of disagreement in the field. In the everyday use of Portfolios in classrooms, Tierney, Carter, and Desai (1991) prefer that any assessment of the portfolios be done either by the student or collaboratively between teachers and students. With some exceptions, student self-assessment is a new venture for teachers. It is important to be willing to support students in their own self-assessments and to value their efforts at so doing. Portfolios may not prove beneficial if teachers assume total control of them and are unwilling to enter into the kind of partnership that their use calls for. Accordingly, Tierney, Carter, and Desai strongly encourage having the students discuss their portfolios on their own terms. Although the authors might encourage the teachers to help the students group the material in their portfolios, they prefer that teachers encourage the students to generate their own criteria for judging pieces.

At the risk of being repetitive, Tierney, Carter, and Desai emphasize that the student should be viewed as the client and that the portfolio should be viewed as their property. In several districts, they see portfolios being given to teachers or district personnel by students for use by the district, school, or teacher. They strongly urge schools and districts intent on reviewing student portfolios to either return them or to start up their own portfolios or dossiers especially for those purposes and in partnership with the students. If the portfolios are to be used to assess, the authors would emphasize that portfolios be judged in the spirit with which they were developed. That is, a goal of assessment with portfolios should be to support the students' assessment of their own work, not to supplant their assessment with that of a teacher or an outsider.

In terms of using portfolio assessment for accountability mandates, Tierney, Carter, and Desai would emphasize that we should be careful to respect the integrity of the portfolio and the possibilities that might be forthcoming. Sometimes portfolios are assessed in ways that are not consistent with the complexity they represent. Sometimes rubrics are developed that are imposed upon Portfolios rather than emerging from them. We have found that Portfolios tell us a lot more useful information than an overall achievement level or how well the student performs in specific skill areas. Portfolios provide information on the extent to which students pursue learning activities for a variety of purposes, the nature of the collaborations with which they have been engaged, their investment in different activities, the learning outcomes, and the relevance that they see in these activities, as well as the strategies that they employed. To ignore these multiple facets of learning is to artificially simplify what we know about learning.

In turn, Portfolios are apt to have an impact upon the methods of reporting student performance—especially, report cards and parent-teacher-student conferences. Portfolios lend themselves to jointly constructed narrative descriptions of performance rather than grades. The various dimensions of Portfolios can be portrayed in words much better than in grades. Portfolios have prompted many to question whether the report card (especially those resorting to grades) can ever do justice to the student's achievements, improvement, efforts, and idiosyncrasies. Indeed, they often prompt teachers to move toward the development of interpretative summaries and goal statements in collaboration with students and parents.

Cautions and Comments

The effectiveness of the portfolios as a tool for evaluation is tied partially to how the portfolio process is implemented and the students' developing abilities to pursue self-analyses and trace their development; Portfolios tend to be product-oriented. Portfolio approaches vary significantly along a host of dimensions, especially the extent to which they are prescribed or emerging, for outsiders or for teachers and students. In other words, the label *portfolio* may mean different things in different settings.

Certainly, portfolios have other attributes that other forms of assessment do not. Comparisons that have been made of portfolio assessment and traditional assessment (such as standardized tests and other assessment practices in operation in classrooms) favor Portfolios. Portfolios consistently provide more and better information about student learning. Teachers and parents appear to achieve a fuller understanding of student abilities, interests, and development. Students achieve a fuller and more positive view of themselves and become more invested in their ongoing development.

Student ownership and independence appear to be outgrowths, because they place students in the position of learning to assess themselves, share who they are with others, and set their own learning goals. It has been reported by several authors that students from preschool to adulthood gain immensely from being able to assess themselves and set their own learning goals. They not only learn about their progress as learners, but also how their views on life and social issues have shifted.

Portfolios also help reestablish the students and those in closest contact with the students as primarily responsible for assessment. Assuming that they are defined by students and teachers within classrooms, portfolios ensure that the professionalism of teaching remains intact, and that those most directly involved with the students' learning are recognized. As assessment practices are increasingly removed from the classroom and from the control of students and teachers, the likelihood of mismatches between what should be assessed and what is assessed increases.

Portfolios afford teachers the opportunity to assess students' various activities, strategies, attitudes, interests, and abilities in the context of their work. Whereas standardized tests provide information on students' strategies and abilities on items students meet just once and in rather contrived circumstances, Portfolios enable teachers to see these same features and others as students use them in different and meaningful situations. Sometimes standardized testing descends upon the classroom and, like an unwelcome house guest, requires your making special preparations, involves a great deal of disruption to your life, and often you are glad when it is over.

Portfolios appear to fit into today's classrooms—in fact, Portfolios seem a natural extension of the various learning activities with which students are engaged. Portfolios appear to help teachers and students keep track of, reflect upon, and plan their extended reading and writing projects and activities such as conferencing, journals, and shared book experiences. They also provide an umbrella for the integration of learning. Students are apt to include in their portfolios material from across subject areas as well as activities related to their interests outside of school.

Portfolios appear to: (1) afford students ownership and goal setting; (2) empower students, teachers, parents, and administrators; (3) bring to the fore rather than simplify the complexities of literacies and literacy development; and, (4) enhance the ability of students, teachers, and other interested parties to make effective decisions. In addition, portfolios encourage teachers (1) to be responsive to the nuances of each student's literacy development; (2) encompass rather than retreat from the range of experiences with which students might be engaged; (3) embrace rather than ignore the diverse nature of students' literacies, their approaches, experiences, goals, and interests; and, (4) rethink methods of reporting progress and setting goals with the students and their parents.

At the same time, Portfolios may represent different things to different groups. Indeed, Wile and Tierney (1994) argue that some portfolio assessment practices have a number of pitfalls. They include: (1) imposed versus emerging portfolios; (2) overly rigid and overly prescriptive guidelines for portfolios; (3) formalizing self-assessment; (4) imposed and standardized criteria to guide student evaluations; (5) viewing the portfolio as the end rather than a means of engaging students in reflection, self-assessment, and ongoing goal setting; (6) district and teacher takeover of students' portfolios; (7) methods for evaluation that are not befitting the portfolio purposes, process, elements, and contexts; and (8) prepackaged portfolios. Portfolios are not without their constraints. Specifically, Portfolios should be viewed in terms of what they represent. In this regard, it is important to recognize that Portfolios represent the students' experiences and their perceptions of those experiences; knowledge of context and the interplay of other factors is usually important in assessing student progress via Portfolios; Portfolios trace development but they may not afford a full and in-depth picture.

Tierney and Clark (1998) provide an in-depth discussion of portfolios, including a comparison of portfolios with traditional measures used for high-stakes assessment. We do suspect that portfolios could serve multiple purposes including being used for making high-stakes decisions—especially, as a form of due process or as a way of cross checking. But, to be accepted as the basis for such decisions, one might be advised to examine the laws that apply to educational testing and decision-making and align what one does with what would be accepted practice. For example, in the United States this might entail establishing development procedures that involve opportunities for input and review by all parties in conjunction with ensuring procedures for collecting, reviewing, and evaluating materials, are deemed acceptable.

Ideally, any high stakes decision is never based upon any single performance measure or apart from lengthy deliberation with all stakeholders. If a portfolio is enlisted to assist with such decisions, one should be careful that the integrity of the portfolio is not undermined, especially if it is aligned with approaches to assessment that are non-collaborative and more arbitrary.

REFERENCES

Belanoff, P., and M. Dickson. 1991. *Portfolios: Process and product.* Portsmouth, NH: Heinemann. This edited volume provides descriptions by several contributors of the use of portfolios in higher education.

Bergeron, B. S., S. Wermuth, and R. C. Hammar. 1997. Initiating portfolios through shared learning: Three perspectives. *The Reading Teacher* 50(7): 552–562. Describes the use of portfolios in conjunction with the professional development of teachers.

Berryman, L., and D. R. Russell. 2001. Portfolios across the curriculum: Whole school assessment in Kentucky. *English Journal* 90(6): 76–83. Discusses the use of portfolios across a school in the context of the school reform efforts in Kentucky.

Carter, M., and R. J. Tierney. 1988. *Reading and writing growth: Using portfolios in assessment.* Paper presented at National Reading Conference, Tucson. Describes the impact of Portfolios upon teachers and students in different classrooms. Specifically, Carter and Tierney present the findings of a study that examines how teachers' awareness of students, teaching practices, and students' views of themselves as readers and writers shifted in conjunction with their use of portfolios for reading and writing.

Chen, Y., and M. A. Martin. 2000. Using performance assessment and portfolio assessment together in the elementary classroom. *Reading Improvement* 37(1): 32–38.

Clay, M. M. 1990. Research currents: What is and what might be in evaluation. *Language Arts* 67: 288–298. A review of current practices in New Zealand elementary schools documents how teachers have developed informal measures that go beyond the standardized tests to evaluate student growth and change. Clay calls for the development of measures at all levels of education that evaluate process and product, and reminds us that such methods empower teachers as well as learners.

Clemmons, J. L., L. Cooper, D. Aregaldo, and N. Dill, 1993. *Portfolios in the classroom: A teacher's sourcebook.* New York: Scholastic. This publication represents the efforts of a team of educators in Virginia who have amassed a wealth of material and practical suggestions on the implementation of portfolios.

Courtney, A. M., and T. L. Abodeeb. 1999. Diagnostic-reflective portfolios. *The Reading Teacher* 52 (7): 708–715. Explores use of portfolios for diagnostic purposes.

Courts, P. L., and K. H. McInerney. 1993. *Assessment in higher education: Politics, pedagogy and Portfolios.* Westport, CT: Praeger. This volume examines critically aspects of assessment in higher education and the possibilities that portfolios offer.

Flood, J., and D. Lapp. 1989. Reporting reading progress: A comparison portfolio for parents. *The Reading Teacher* 42: 508–514. Flood and Lapp describe the portfolio as a tool to be used in parent conferences to document student change across time.

Gillespie, C. S., K. L. Ford, R. D. Gillespie, and A. G. Leavell. 1996. Portfolio assessment: Some questions, some answers, some recommendations. *Journal of Adolescent and Adult Literacy* 39(6): 480–491. Discusses the use of Portfolios at the secondary and post secondary levels.

Goodman, K. S., Y. M. Goodman, and W. J. Hood. 1989. *The whole language evaluation book.* Portsmouth, NH: Heinemann. Describes various attempts by teachers to develop assessment procedures in line with classroom practices. Among those discussed are portfolios.

Graves, D., and B. Sunstein (Eds.). 1992. *Portfolio portraits.* Portsmouth, NH: Heinemann. This edited volume captures the intimate and personal descriptions of different teachers' adventures with Portfolios.

Hall, B. W., and C. M. Hewitt-Gervais. 2000. The application of student portfolios in primary-intermediate and self-contained multiage team classroom environments: Implications for instruction, learning, and assessment. *Applied Measurement in Education* 13(2): 209–228. Reports a research study on the use of student portfolios.

Hebert, E. A. 2001. *The power of Portfolios: What children can teach us about learning and assessment.* San Francisco: Jossey-Bass. Discusses what is learned from student portfolios for teaching and assessment.

Helm, J. H., S. Beneke, and K. Steinheimer. 1998. *Windows on learning: Documenting young children's work.* New York: Teachers College Press. Explores ways of assessing students in a fashion that is classroom based.

Hewitt, G. 2001. The writing portfolio: Assessment starts with A. *Clearing House* 74(4): 187–190. Emanating from his work in Vermont, Hewitt explores the use of portfolios.

Hoffman, J. L. 1995. The family portfolio: Using authentic assessment in family literacy programs. *The Reading Teacher* 48(7): 594–597. Details a collaborative form of portfolios involving families.

Levi, R. 1990. Assessment and educational vision: Engaging learners and parents. *Language Arts* 67: 269–273. Using the work of his students, and the words of the students' parents, Levi documents how portfolios involve students, parents, and teachers as collaborators in the assessment process.

Mathews, J. K. 1990. From computer management to portfolio assessment. *The Reading Teacher* 43(b): 420–421. In this article Mathews details the steps taken and challenges faced as the district begins to move its elementary schools to a portfolio approach to literacy assessment.

Mills, R. P. 1989. Portfolios capture rich array of student performance. *The School Administrator,* December: 8–11. As Vermont's Commissioner of Education, Mills provides an overview of Vermont's struggle to develop a statewide measure of educational performance.

Mitchell, J. P., T. V. Abernathy, and L. P. Gowans. 1998. Making sense of literacy portfolios: A four-step plan. *Journal of Adolescent and Adult Literacy* 41(5): 384–389. Offers a plan for using portfolios including an evaluation scheme.

Moni, K., S. Dwyer, and C. Kleindinst. 1994. Involving students in assessing their reading: The winter count. *The Reading Teacher* 48(1): 80–83. Explores the use of a mural dealing with a winter count of growth as a learner.

Murphy, S., and M. A. Smith. 1992. *Writing portfolios: A bridge from teaching to assessment.* Markham, Ont.: Pippin. Presents a rich and powerful discussion and description of student involvement in writing portfolios.

———. 1990. Talking about portfolios. *The Quarterly* 12. Believing that portfolios can take many forms and that there is no one right way to develop a portfolio, Murphy and Smith suggest that teachers' decisions regarding expectations of the portfolios will have a profound effect on the resulting format and implementation.

Murphy, S., and T. Underwood. 2000. *Portfolio practices: Lessons from schools, districts and states.* Norwood, MA: Christopher-Gordon. Explores lessons with portfolios at various levels—classroom, school, and state.

Reif, L. 1990. Finding the value in evaluation: Self-assessment in a middle school classroom. *Educational Leadership* 47: 24–29. Reif presents a portrait of how portfolios are used in her seventh- and eighth-grade middle school classes in Durham, NH, by highlighting the portfolio of one of her students.

Salinger, T., and E. Chittenden. 1994. Analysis of an early Literacy Portfolio: Consequences for instruction. *Language Arts* 71: 446–452. Describes portfolios and their impact upon instruction in a school district's elementary school.

Sarroub, L. K., P. D. Pearson, C. Dykema, and R. Lloyd. 1997. When portfolios become part of the grading process: A case study in a junior high setting. In C. K. Kinzer, K. A. Hinchman, and D. J. Leu (Eds.), *Inquiries in literacy theory and practice.* Chicago: National Reading Conference, 101–113. Explores the evolution of portfolios and issues of their grading.

Shepard, L. A. 1989. Why we need better assessments. *Educational Leadership* 46: 4–9. The large-scale use and limitations of standardized tests are discussed, and the separation of such accountability measures from those that inform instruction is suggested. Problems facing the construction of such accountability tests are noted, and the resulting practices of teaching to the test are discussed. It is suggested that better instructional assessment needs to be developed, which allows assessment to resemble learning tasks and involves the development of portfolios that contain samples of students' work.

Simmons, J. 1990. Portfolios as large-scale assessment. *Language Arts* 67: 262–267. Based on the work done by his research team in Durham, NH, Simmons discusses a field test of a large-scale model of portfolio assessment involving portfolios collected randomly to represent the district's entire fifth grade. Unlike a one-shot test, portfolios produced profiles of student writers. They also found that while timed tests and portfolio assessments produced the same rank ordering of students, the portfolios more accurately represented the true abilities of all students.

Stowell, L. P., R. J. Tierney, and L. E. Desai. 1995. Portfolios in the classroom: What happens when teachers and students negotiate assessment? In R. Allington and S. Walmsley (Eds.), *No quick fix: Rethinking literacy lessons in America's elementary schools.* New York: Teachers College Press. Discusses issues of teacher implementation regarding portfolios. Explores the difficulties and transitions that occur as students and teachers explore portfolio assessment.

Taylor, D. 1990. Teaching without testing. *English Education* 22: 4–74. Taylor presents the essence of a project intent on developing biographic literacy profiles from the perspective of the child. She provides a rich description of the features and methods associated with the various objectives of the project: learning to observe children's literacy behaviors; learning to develop note-taking procedures to record observations of children reading and writing; learning to write descriptive biographic literacy profiles; and learning to increase our awareness of the multiple layers of interpretation that we are incorporating into the children's biographic literacy profiles.

Tierney, R. J. 2000. Learner-based assessment: Turning assessment upside down and inside out to make evaluation the right way up and to fit with teaching and learning. In L. Morrow (Ed.), *Language arts in 2000.* Boston: Allyn and Bacon. A practical summary that can serve as an introductory guide to portfolio implementation.

Tierney, R. J., M. Carter, and L. Desai. 1991. *Portfolio assessment in the reading writing classroom.* Norwood, MA: Christopher Gordon. The first book devoted to a description of the use of portfolios in literacy classrooms. Provides an extensive discussion of the rationale for and issues related to the implementation of portfolios. Includes a survey of different portfolio approaches.

Tierney, R. J. and C. Clark. (with L. Fenner, R. J. Herter, C. Staunton Simpson, and B. Wiser). 1998. Portfolios: assumptions, tensions and possibilities. *Reading Research Quarterly* 33(4): 474–486. A comprehensive review of portfolio research, practices, and issues.

Tierney, R. J., T. Crumpler, C. Bertelsen, and E. Bond. 2003. *Interactive assessment: Teachers, parents and students as partners.* Norwood: Christopher Gordon. Explores portfolios (including digital Portfolios) and dossiers as tools in conjunction with developing assessment partnerships with parents, teachers, and students.

Tierney, R. J., J. Wile, A. G. Moss, E. W. Reed, J. P. Ribar, and A. Zilversmit. 1993. *Portfolio evaluation as history: Evaluation of the history academy for Ohio teachers.* National Council of History Education, Inc. Occasional paper. Reports a study dealing with the use of portfolios to pursue project evaluation. Affords a glimpse at pursuing detailed case studies with portfolios combined with profiles and quantitative analyses.

Valencia, S. 1990. A portfolio approach to classroom reading assessment: The whys, whats, and hows. *The Reading Teacher* 43: 338–340. This article highlights the research and instructional practices that make portfolios a viable form of assessment.

Valencia, S. W. 1998. *Literacy portfolios in action.* Fort Worth: Harcourt Brace College Publishers. Details teachers' explorations of portfolios in various classrooms.

Valencia, S., E. Hiebert, and P. Afflerbach (Eds.). 1993. *Authentic reading assessment.* Newark, DE: International Reading Association. This volume includes nine case studies representing a range of assessment initiatives from the innovative to the more traditional. The editors provide provocative commentary on some of the issues involved in portfolios and other authentic assessment practices.

Vavrus, L. 1990. Put portfolios to the test. *Instructor* 100: 48–53. Vavrus introduces the concept of portfolios and outlines several ideas for teachers to consider, including selection of work to go into portfolios, evaluation, and passing portfolios on to other teachers. However, the article neglects the importance of developing portfolio processes in conjunction with students.

Wagner, C. L., D. R. Brock, and A. T. Agnew. 1994. Developing literacy portfolios in teacher education courses. *Journal of Reading* 37(8): 668–674. Describes the use of Portfolios in teacher education.

Wile, J., and R. J. Tierney. 1993. *Analyzing complexity with Portfolio techniques: Exploring the schisms between positivistic and constructivistic perspectives.* Paper presented at the annual meeting of the National Reading Conference, Charleston. Paper raises various concerns regarding the analysis procedures being espoused for use with portfolios and explores issues of their validity, comparability, and reliability.

Wolf, D. P. 1989. Portfolio assessment: Sampling student work. *Educational Leadership* 46: 35–39. In this article Wolf discusses in greater detail the development of propel portfolios as a tool that accomplishes this goal. The article highlights the characteristics of portfolios that enable a student to reflect on the process involved in the development of a wide range of his or her own written work, and discusses the impact this form of evaluation has had on teacher abilities to assess their students and themselves.

Yancey, K. B. (Ed.). 1992. *Portfolios in the writing classroom: An introduction.* Urbana, IL: NCTE. The contributors to this volume describe a range of portfolio efforts. The volume also includes an examination of some pitfalls and limitations pertaining to portfolios.

Young, J. P., S. R. Mathews, A. M. Kietzmann, and T. Westerfield. 1997. Getting disenchanted adolescents to participate in school literacy activities: Portfolio conferences. *Journal of Adolescent and Adult Literacy* 40(5): 348–360. Discusses high schoolers' involvement in portfolio conferences.

Anecdotal Records

Purpose

As a form of assessment, Anecdotal Records are a way of recording information about a child's literacy as they do literacy in classrooms or other settings. They usually represent information that is collected "on the run" by a teacher or observer.

Rationale

Historically, Anecdotal Records have been used to record behaviors of children in the classroom, often for the purpose of making a diagnosis of a problem. Mehrens and Lehman (1984) suggest that they are used to record "social adjustment" (p. 229), while Locke and Ciechalski (1985) suggest that they are useful for collecting information about children who are being referred for special services.

With the advent of Whole-Language, and particularly, the notion of "kidwatching," the Anecdotal Record has become a way of recording and assessing children's literacy development. Unlike checklists, miscue analyses, and so forth, the Anecdotal Record can be made without anticipating the ways in which children engage with various events in school. Thus, the Anecdotal Record allows the teacher not only to engage in "kidwatching," but it also allows teachers to consider their observations and to use those observations in their future interactions with children and their parents.

Anecdotal Records require three roles of teachers:

1. The teacher's ability to draw upon her or his understandings of the child against understandings about literacy development.

2. Recognition of significant events. It is neither possible nor desirable to record every event in the process of a child's acquisition of literacy; the teacher uses the aforementioned knowledge to select events for recording.

3. Instructional practice. The teacher records the event in an appropriate manner, uses the event in a process of analysis and interpretation, and, finally, allows that analysis/interpretation to inform his/her interactions with and about the child.

These three roles for the teacher reflect and enact an ongoing cycle of assessment:

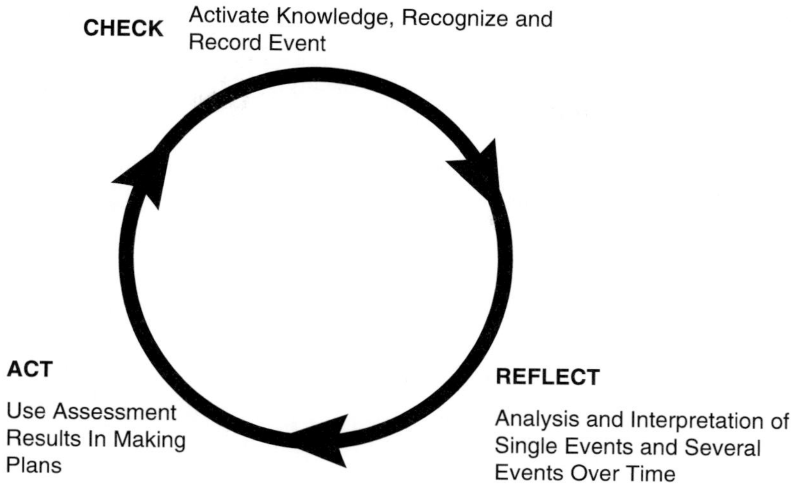

Thus, a set of Anecdotal Records provides the teacher with information that can be used in the classroom, leading ultimately to action and then their collecting more information as events unfold. Assessment is cyclical in nature.

Intended Audience

Anecdotal Records can be used with students of any age.

Description of the Procedures

Anecdotal Records allow the teacher to bring together knowledge of literacy development and the history of a particular child in a process of recognizing events that are significant to that child's development of literacy. In turn, this information leads the teacher to a process of analysis that leads to instructional planning and the generating of new questions for assessment. Figure 14.1 shows the process of making Anecdotal Records and the roles of the teacher in this assessment procedure. Each aspect of this process is discussed below.

Development of Literacy. Since literacy development is a lifelong process that changes significantly from moment to moment in a person's life, it cannot be easily or briefly summed up. Still, a framework such as that of the Education Department of South Australia (1991) provides a list of aspects of both reading and writing that are part of literacy development. They consider five types of information, under the acronym CAASR:

Concepts about literacy
Attitudes to writing and reading
Aspects of written products and comprehension
Strategies for writing and reading
Range of writing and reading (p. 7)

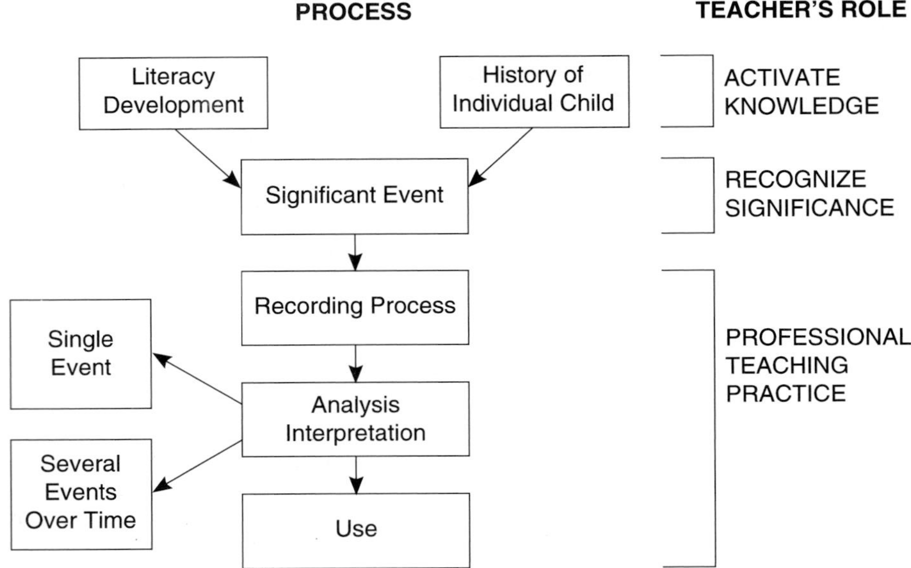

FIGURE 14.1 Anecdotal Records: Process and Teacher's Role

They then provide an overview of these types of information in relation to both reading and writing, as can be seen below:

CAASR: Reading and Writing Overview

CONCEPTS ABOUT LITERACY

Uses for written language
Kinds of written products
The possible range of audiences
The appropriate use of written language
The similarities and differences between speech and writing
The processes readers and writers use

ATTITUDES TO READING AND WRITING

Self-concept
Commitment

ASPECTS OF WRITTEN PRODUCTS

Ideas/Information
- Topic knowledge
- Knowledge of the world
- Presentation of ideas

ASPECTS OF READING COMPREHENSION

Ideas/Information
- Topic knowledge

ASPECTS OF WRITTEN PRODUCTS *(continued)*

Organization
- Kinds of writing
- Focus
- Parts
- Sequences
- Links
- Readers' needs

Language
- Vocabulary
- Sentence
- Style

Mechanics
- Handwriting
- Spelling
- Punctuation
- Layout
- Using word processors

ASPECTS OF READING COMPREHENSION *(continued)*

Organization
- Fiction texts
- Nonfiction texts
- Focus and sequence

Language
- Syntax
- Word meanings
- Style

Mechanics
- Letter-sound relationships
- Directional and positional conventions
- Devices for showing emphasis or importance
- Layout conventions

STRATEGIES FOR WRITING

Prewriting
- Considering possibilities
- Collecting and connecting
- Making plans and rehearsing parts

Writing
- Drafting
- Revising

Postwriting
- Preparing for publishing
- Presenting to the audience and reflecting on responses

STRATEGIES FOR READING

Basic strategies
- Predict
- Confirm and check
- Self-correct

Monitoring for congruence
Creating worlds
Coping strategies

RANGE OF STUDENTS' READING AND WRITING

- Fiction
- Nonfiction
- Multiple literacies
- Informational literacies
- Other

Adapted from Education Department of South Australia, pp. 37–38.

History of Individual Child. Along with the numerous aspects of reading and writing to consider, the teacher must consider the individual child. Anecdotal Records can be used in the process of getting to know the child and his/her literacy development. They can also be used to record unusual events, as Cartwright and Cartwright (1984) point out: "Children behave spontaneously in many ways that often are not anticipated or expected, and the anecdotal record provides a method of recording the observations of these spontaneous behaviors" (p. 114). Obviously, one must either have a sense of a child's history or be interested in working toward that type of understanding in order to know if a behavior is anticipated or not.

Significant Event. What constitutes a significant event? Anthony, Johnson, Mickelson, and Preece (1991) suggest:

> There is usually so much happening in a class that teachers must be highly selective about what to record. Observations can be gathered in two ways: planned or spontaneous. Planned observations should be focused on a predetermined area of learning, and this can be signaled by the use of a key word. . . . Where do the key words come from? Simply put, they come from the teacher. What do I want to know about the processes of student learning? What will the other stakeholders in the child's education want to know? (p. 73)

Thus, Anecdotal Records can be used in a planned fashion to track literacy acquisition; they can also capture for later consideration spontaneous moments of struggle—or epiphany.

Watson (1985) offers a series of questions about the individual child in relation to literacy development (Figure 14.2); Rhodes and Nathenson-Mejia (1992) provide a teacher-generated observation guide (Figure 14.3).

Rhodes and Nathenson-Mejia (1992) suggest that teachers keep a list of this sort available in their classrooms to remind them of the types of things that might be observed.

Recording Process. There are numerous suggestions for both guidelines for making Anecdotal Records and the actual forms that might be used. Figure 14.4 brings together guidelines from two sources.

Texts on anecdotal record keeping written before the invention of sticky notes encourage teachers to use index cards for Anecdotal Records; more current sources suggest that sticky notes can be carried around on a clipboard and then transferred to a notebook that has ongoing records for each student. With the advent of laptops and hand-held computers with handwriting-recognition software, teachers may soon find laptops, handheld devices, or other tools to be a viable way of making Anecdotal Records.

Regardless of the recording system, it is important to provide a sufficient amount of detail so that someone else reading the record will have a sense of what happened. Rhodes and Nathenson-Mejia (1992) suggest that detailed descriptions with examples are more helpful in the long run than general descriptions. At a minimum, each obsevation should be dated and should include key features such as identifiers of students and the assignments themselves.

Analysis/Interpretation

Most sources on anecdotal record keeping suggest recording the event in the most value-free language possible, keeping interpretive or analytical comments separate from the record of the event. Cartwright and Cartwright (1984) suggest dividing the record form in half—one half for reporting the incident. Rhodes and Nathenson-Mejia (1992) provide examples in which teachers record the event first and make interpretive comments at the end of the record.

FIGURE 14.2 Considerations to Guide Observations

Concepts about Print and Print Settings

1. To what extent does the student attend to print? For example, does the student focus on the print as someone else is reading?
2. How does the student handle books? For example, does the student hold the book right side up, turn pages one at a time, and point to the place where one should begin reading?
3. Does the student expect the print to make sense and have personal meaning? For example, does the student seek out text that will satisfy his/her need for information about feeding hamsters?
4. How does the student use information from the print setting, i.e., where the print is found, its format, who asked that it be read, why it is being read?

Use of Background Knowledge

1. How does the reader bring background knowledge and linguistic information to the reading situation?
2. How does the reader approach text? Is there an effort made to appreciate and live the written experiences by relating the text to his/her own life?
3. How does the reader use memory as a reading aid? For example, when asked to read a familiar song, riddle, or self-authored story, does the reader use memory (i.e., familiarity with the material) as a basis for predicting and making inferences?

Use of Strategies

1. How does the student handle the information-giving systems of language? Does the reader use a flexible strategy that encompasses all language cues (e.g., semantic, grammatical, sound/symbol) to construct meaning or does the reader rely on a single cuing system (e.g., symbol/sound)?
2. Does the reader proficiently sample, predict, and construct meaning from text?
3. Does the student monitor his/her reading by asking, "Am I making sense of what I am reading?"
4. Does the reader self-correct when the flow of language and meaning are interrupted?
5. Is there a dialect or first language influence on the student's reading and how does the student handle this influence?
6. What strategies does the reader use to approach suitable but unfamiliar text?

View of Self as Reader

1. What does the student think of himself/herself as a reader?
2. In what circumstances and how often does the student make the decision to read?
3. What risks are taken by the student as he/she reads?
4. How realistic is the student's judgment of his/her knowledge of concepts and discourse forms needed to read various texts (e.g., science or history materials, poems or drama)?

Source: Watson, 1985, pp. 119–121.

However analytical or interpretive comments are made, there are three aspects of Anecdotal Records to consider: (1) the significance of the single event; (2) the significance of the event in relation to other observed events; and (3) how the information will inform teaching. Anecdotal Records can be analyzed with respect to the three.

FIGURE 14.3 Teacher-Generated Observation Guide: Some Areas for Consideration

- Functions served in reading/writing
- Engagement in reading/writing
- What appears to impact engagement in reading/writing
- What aspects of text student attends to
- Interactions with others over reading/writing
- Interactions with materials
- Insightful or interesting things students say
- Hypotheses students are trying out in reading/writing
- Misconceptions students have
- Miscues students make while reading
- Changes students make in writing
- How students use text before, during, and after reading
- How a lesson affects students' reading/writing
- Comparisons between what student say and what they do
- Plans students make and whether/how plans are amended
- How, where, and with whom students work
- What students are interested in
- What students say they want to work on in their reading/writing
- What students say about reading/writing done outside of school
- How students generate and solve problems in reading/writing
- Ideas for reading/writing lessons and materials
- How students "symbol weave" (use multiple symbolic forms)
- How students theorize or talk about reading/writing
- How one reading/writing event relates to another
- How students use a variety of resources in reading/writing

Source: Rhodes and Nathenson-Mejia (1992, 505).

FIGURE 14.4 Guidelines for Anecdotal Records

- Describe a specific event or product
- Report rather than evaluate or interpret
- Relate the material to other facts that are known about the child (Thorndike and Hagen as cited in Rhodes and Nathenson-Mejia, 1992)
- Observe children within a variety of settings and at different times in the school day
- Record observations as soon as possible
- Choose a workable recording system
- Protect confidentiality

Source: Grace and Shores, as cited in Smith, Kuhs, and Ryan, 1993.

Single Event. Figure 14.5 shows an example of an Anecdotal Record Process adapted from Rhodes and Nathenson-Mejia (1992). In this example, the teacher drew on her background knowledge of literacy development and her knowledge of the individual child. The fact that this child began to use letter/sound relationships in her writing was significant, so

PROCESS

Literacy Development

Importance of sound/letter relationships to literacy development.
Importance of understanding word boundaries for literacy development.

History of Individual Child

E. has not demonstrated an understanding of letter/sound relationships in the past.

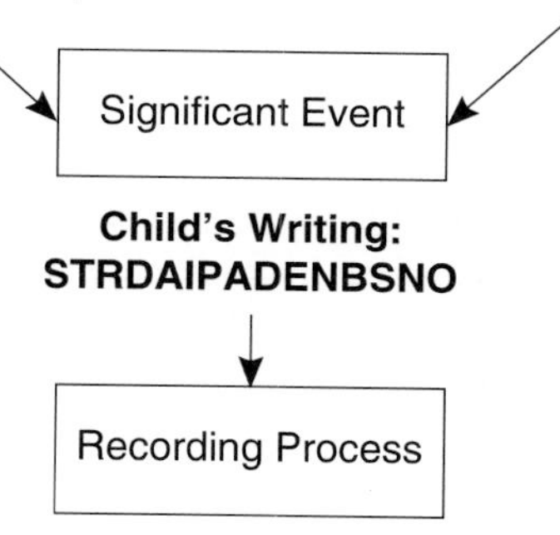

STRDA = yesterday
I = I
PAD = played
EN = in
B = the (said "du" and thought she was writing "D")
SNO = snow

Showed her how to stretch her words out like a rubber band – doing it almost on own by SNO. Asked her at end – what she did in writing today that she hadn't done in previous writing. She said, "I listened to sounds." Told her to do it in her writing again tomorrow.

Analysis Interpretation

E. does have a fairly good grasp of sound/letter relationships. However, has a hard time isolating words and tracking words in sentences in her mind.

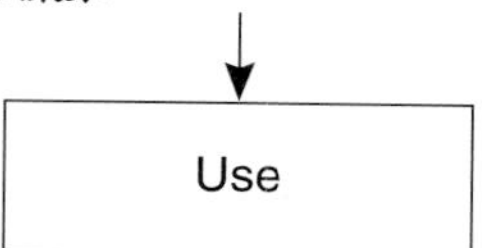

Invitations to continue to practice letter/sound relationships. Look for teachable moments for word boundaries.

FIGURE 14.5 An Example of an Anecdotal Record Process

the teacher chose to record this moment. The teacher recorded the child's actual writing and a translation that would allow her (or others) to read that writing in the future. She also recorded her intervention process (showing child how to "stretch the words" and asking the child what she did that was different).

In the process of analyzing this particular record, the teacher draws on her knowledge of literacy development to remark about what the child is capable of doing as of this observation, and some possible next steps for this child. In analyzing an event, the teacher might consider the factors that make the event significant as well as the implications of the event for the future.

Several Events Over Time. If the teacher in the example in Figure 14.5 made several Anecdotal Records over time for this particular student, the teacher might find that E. is gaining facility with letter/sound relationships or that E. has a problem with a particular set of letter/sound relationships. She might be able to record the moment when E. starts to understand about word boundaries. In conference with E.'s parents, she will be able to show some rich data about E.'s literacy development.

Rhodes and Nathenson-Mejia (1992) suggest three types of analysis that are possible with Anecdotal Records:

- Making inferences
- Identifying patterns
- Identifying strengths and weaknesses

In addition to tracking the progress of a single child over a period of time, Anecdotal Records can help the teacher improve assessment practices, as Maureen Holland (in Rhodes and Shanklin, 1993) points out:

> While sharing my anecdotal notebook with some colleagues, I discovered that for some students I had copious notes and comments, while for others I had only a few. I had unconsciously collected more notes for those students who were behavior problems and those who were struggling academically. My method of gathering notes had been too haphazard. I determined that a more systematic collection was needed. (p. 39)

She chose a different six students each day to focus on in order to ensure that she didn't leave students out.

Use

The information from Anecdotal Records has several possible uses, as Rhodes and Nathenson-Mejia (1992) point out:

- Instructional planning . . . Anecdotal records on children's social behaviors and responses to written language can help teachers plan stimulating situations for the reluctant as well as the enthusiastic reader/writer. . . .
- Informing. In addition to using anecdotal records for planning ongoing instruction, teachers also may use them to periodically inform others, including the students themselves, about students' strengths, weaknesses, and progress . . .

- Generating new questions. Analyzing anecdotal records and using them to plan instruction encourages teachers to generate new questions that lead full circle to further assessment of students and of teaching itself. (pp. 507–508)

Cautions and Comments

Anecdotal Records are potentially a very important part of authentic assessment procedures because they create a picture of a child's engagement within a natural setting or settings, rather than the artificial setting of a test. Further, although traditional sources on assessment state that a disadvantage to Anecdotal Records is that they are time-consuming to produce, they can be done within the context of children's engaging with the activities of the school. In other words, Anecdotal Records do not interrupt the child's work for the process of assessment; they are integral to the child's work.

Finally, Anecdotal Records are a form of assessment that acknowledges—and depends on—the teacher's understanding of children and ability to work constructively with them. Unlike behavior checklists (which limit the process of observation) and even Portfolios (which belong to students), Anecdotal Records allow wise teachers who have a great deal of insight into children's behavior and progress to bring all their skills and information to bear in the process of assessment. For this reason, Anecdotal Records can be a strong part of an assessment program—the part that depends mostly on the teacher. They also can be used in concert with many of the assessment tools described in this unit as well as the analysis procedures (such as rubrics) and reporting mechanisms (such as conferencing).

As with any powerful tool, Anecdotal Records have a potential to be harmful. Judgmental language or other implicit judgments in the process of recording can be detrimental to children, particularly if these records become a part of the child's school record. Further, although the teacher may be a wise person, he or she may not have observed the whole event. There may be another side to the story that is missing from the Anecdotal Record, but one that readers of Anecdotal Records may not look for, since it is so easy to assume that the teacher recorded the event accurately. In the case of Anecdotal Records about problematic events, teachers may want to invite children to record their observations and perceptions and to store the children's records with their own records.

The teachers' Anecdotal Records also depend upon the teachers' understandings of literacy and the nature of literacy development. Oftentimes checklists are used to guide Anecdotal Records and may lead to some practices that are problematic. For example, teachers need to try to describe how the skills and strategies work together in the context of reading and writing. It is not adequate to define the use of a single skill or fail to mention the context within which the skills are used.

Teachers need to be aware that the students' use of skills and strategies are apt to vary from one setting to the next including across story selections. In defining a students' ability, they are apt to find differences from one assignment to the next in terms of the following:

Nature of engagement (active, curious, passive, etc.)

Strategies (planning, predicting, self-questioning, visualizing, connecting ideas, troubleshooting)

Self-monitoring

Outcomes

Across assignments, they might look for patterns in terms of the following:

Values and habits

Flexible use of strategies

Self-assessment of needs, goals, achievement

Range of reading and writing pursued

It is key to realize that differences across settings should be expected, but that a pattern might emerge. In a similar vein, Goodman (1985) suggests that kidwatching (and by extension, anecdotal record keeping) can be beneficial to children whose linguistic backgrounds differ from that of the school:

> There are many issues concerning language differences in the areas of both dialect and second language learning which teachers must consider. Too many children have been hurt in the past because of lack of knowledge about language differences. . . . Attitudes such as "these children have no language" or "bilingualism confuses children" are still too prevalent. Kidwatching can help teachers be aware of how such statements are damaging to language growth . . . By observing the language of children in a wide variety of settings such as role playing, retelling of picture books, or playing games during recess or physical education, teachers gain many kinds of information that help to dispel myths about language and language learning.
>
> For example, Sorita, age 6, would use the following types of construction often in oral conversations with other children or during sharing sessions:
>
> "Lots of my friends was at my house. . . ."
>
> "We was going to the store. . . ."
>
> However, during her narration of "The Three Billy Goats Gruff" which accompanied the acting out of the story by some of her classmates, her teacher heard, "There were three billy goats. . . ." Sorita used this more formal construction throughout the narration. (p. 12)

In this instance, the teacher used her knowledge of an individual child in order to ensure that the child is using both school and home dialect.

Finally, it is very important for teachers to keep this information confidential. Anecdotal Records allow teachers an opportunity to reflect at a very significant level about a child's whole development. Once such records are shared with others; however, the observer may be legally entitled to examine what was shared.

REFERENCES

Allington, R., A. Butler, and R. J. Tierney. 1993. *Teacher's guide to evaluation: Assessment handbook.* Celebrate Reading Series. Glenview, IL: Scott, Foresman. This handbook contains evaluation materials for the reading program specifically but also some general assessment ideas.

Anthony, R. J., T. D. Johnson, N. I. Mickelson, and A. Preece. 1991. *Evaluating literacy: A perspective for change.* Portsmouth, NH: Heinemann. Brings together information about assessment and new assessment practices. Provides forms that can be used in the classroom.

Atwell, N. Making the grade. In T. Newkirk and N. Atwell (Eds.), *Understanding writing: Ways of observing, learning, and teaching* (2d ed.). Portsmouth, NH: Heinemann, 236–244. In this article, Atwell discusses the use of conferences to evaluate students' writing.

Barrs, M. 1990. The primary language record: Reflection of issues in evaluation. *Language Arts* 67: 244–253.

This article discusses the benefits of the Primary Language Record (PLR), an assessment tool developed by the Inner London Education Authority. Barrs briefly discusses several of the strategies incorporated into the observation-based record, including structured observation, samples, error analysis, conferencing, teacher judgment scales, and cumulative records.

Barrs, M., S. Ellis, H. Hester, and A. Thomas. 1988. *The primary language record.* Portsmouth, NH: Heinemann. Developed and piloted as part of an initiative for the Center of Language in primary education, this publication is one of the best sources available for implementable ideas related to analyzing reading and writing.

Cambourne, B., and J. Turbill (Eds.). 1994. *Responsive evaluation.* Portsmouth, NH: Heinemann. Presents various articles exploring learner-centered and performance-based assessments in schools.

Cartwright, C. A., and G. P. Cartwright. 1984. *Developing observation skills* (2d ed.). New York: McGraw-Hill. Provides teachers with numerous traditional forms of "kidwatching."

Crafton, L. 1994. *Challenges of holistic teaching: Answering the tough questions.* Norwood, MA: Christopher-Gordon. Provides rationale and possibilities for anecdotal records.

Drummond, M. J. 1994. *Learning to see: Assessment through observation.* Portland, ME: Stenhouse. Offers classroom advice for teachers in conjunction with the use of observational techniques.

Education Department of South Australia. 1991. *Literacy assessment in practice: R-7 language arts.* Adelaide: Education Department of South Australia. Provides a framework for assessment that is being used in Australian schools. Includes samples of forms and children's work.

Goodman, Y. 1985. Kidwatching. In A. Jaggar and M. T. Smith-Burke (Eds.), *Observing the language learner.* Newark, DE: International Reading Association. Introduces the concept of kidwatching. Provides examples and connects the process of observation with the understanding of children's development.

Jett-Simpson, M., V. Dauer, N. Dussault, B. Gaulke, L. Gerhar, L. Leslie, L. Ruell McClain, J. Pinlott, W. Prentice, and R. Telfer. 1990. *Toward an ecological assessment of reading.* Madison: Wisconsin State Reading Association. This monograph provides a thoughtful discussion of the problems of traditional assessment; suggests guidelines; and describes a host of practices (book selection, observation, response journals, Think-Alouds, interviews, Portfolios) that might be used by classroom teachers.

Johnston, P. 1987. Teachers as evaluation experts. *The Reading Teacher* 40: 744–748. Johnston discusses how teachers can most effectively evaluate the process of literacy development by suggesting they become experts at "detecting patterns, knowing classroom procedures, and by listening." He further suggests that such individualized process-centered evaluation not only serves instruction but also allows students and teachers to collaborate in the learning process.

Locke, D.C., and J. C. Ciechalski. 1985. *Psychological techniques for teachers.* Muncie, IN: Accelerated Development. ERIC Document 344–147. Provides several techniques that are based in psychological practice for teachers to use in the classroom, including information on anecdotal records.

Mehrens, W. A., and I. J. Lehman. 1984. *Measurement and evaluation in education and psychology* (3d ed.). New York: Holt, Rinehart and Winston. Contains numerous evaluation tools for use by teachers.

Parker, E. L., R. Armengol, L. B. Brooke, K. R. Carper, S. M. Cronin, A. C. Denman, P. Irwin, J. McGunnigle, T. Pardini, and N. P. Kurtz, 1995. Teachers' choices in classroom assessment. *The Reading Teacher* 48(7): 622–624. Provides an overview of various assessment tools (concepts about print, running records, self-assessment/goal-setting interviews, rubrics, etc.).

Power, B. M. (1996) *Taking note: Improving your observational notetaking.* York, ME: Sternhouse. Practical guide to notetaking.

Rhodes, L. K., and S. Nathenson-Mejia. 1992. Anecdotal records: A powerful tool for ongoing literacy assessment. *The Reading Teacher* 45: 502–509. Describes using Anecdotal Records. Provides examples of records and their analysis.

Rhodes, L. K., and N. Shanklin. 1993. *Windows into literacy: Assessing learners K–8.* Portsmouth, NH: Heinemann. Contains many forms of authentic assessment for literacy teachers. Includes sample forms and articles by teachers who actually use them.

Sharp, Q. Q. 1989. *Evaluation: Whole language checklists for evaluating your children.* New York: Scholastic. Presents an array of charts that teachers might be able to use in conjunction with observations of readers and writers.

Smith, L. M., T. M. Kuhs, and J. M. Ryan. 1993. *Assessment of student learning in early childhood education.* South Carolina Center for Excellence in the Assessment of Student Learning. ERIC Document 358–163. Provides information on several alternatives to testing in the assessment of young children.

Stiggins, R., and N. F. Conklin. 1992. *In teachers' hands: Investigating the practices of classroom assessment.*

Albany: SUNY. This book represents several years of exploration of issues of assessment in schools and the shift to legitimizing alternative forms of assessment.

Taylor, D. 1990. Teaching without testing. *English Education* 22: 4–74. Taylor presents the essence of a project intent on developing biographic literacy profiles from the perspective of the child.

Tierney, R. J. 1993. *Classroom-based assessment systems for literacy.* Glenview, IL: Scott, Foresman. Provides a brief discussion of a range of classroom-based assessment procedures from on-the-run assessments to periodical assessments of students using Portfolios and other procedures.

Tierney, R. J., L. E. Desai, and L. P. Stowell. 1992. *Dynamic Assessment.* Report prepared for Apple Computer, Inc. Explores the nature of dynamic assessment by teachers in conjunction with the ebb and flow of instruction as well as instructional planning.

Vukelich, C. 1997. Assessing young children's literacy: Documenting growth and informing practice. *The Reading Teacher* 50(5): 430–434. Discusses various techniques (including Anecdotal Records) to assess young children's growth.

Watson, D. 1985. *Watching and listening to children read.* In A. Jaggar and M. T. Smith-Burke (Eds.), *Observing the language learner.* Newark, DE: International Reading Association. Connects the concept of "kidwatching" with the process of reading. Suggests several types of "kidwatching" and various things to watch for as children engage with print.

Rubrics

Purpose

Rubrics are developed as a means of analyzing literacy processes and outcomes arising from performance-based assessments as well as other open-ended responses such as Retellings, written compositions, and Portfolios.

Rationale

The nature and use of rubrics have emerged in conjunction with the following:

1. An increased emphasis on open-ended responses generated by performance-based assessment and direct observation of performance
2. Qualitative analyses of data that involve the exploration of emergent categories as ways of describing complex phenomenon
3. A desire to make statements of complex performance across individuals and sites in a manner that is descriptive, developmental, and distinctive, and that also allows comparisons across individuals
4. Assessments that are more directly tied to learning goals and possible teaching activities
5. An increased emphasis on students to examining their own performance

Most rubrics have instructional goals (e.g., understandings, strategies) that are examined in terms of various dimensions. Models of literacy processes and outcomes, especially developmental models, inform the dimensions of a rubric. For example, research that explores models of reading comprehension through examinations of the strategies used by expert and novice readers might inform a rubric of reading comprehension strategy use. An analysis system could then be used to develop a continuum or scale for each of the dimensions.

A reading strategies rubric, for instance, would be based on an analysis of ways students can flexibly and consciously use strategies across a range of reading situations.

Observations of performance also help define the dimensions and continuum or scales of a rubric. For example, a rubric for comprehension strategies might be based on the actual performance of the students and may vary from one group of students to another, especially if age levels and tasks are different.

In terms of use, Rubrics can be used in an ongoing and dynamic fashion or for more formal purposes.

Ongoing and Dynamic. In these circumstances, the development and use of the rubrics may be woven into the fabric of everyday teaching and learning as a means of facilitating reflection. This reflection might include self-assessment by the student, especially as a lens through which progress and possible next steps are determined. If used in this dynamic fashion, rubrics may be constantly changing rather than static; different students might even develop different rubrics by which to assess themselves and think about their progress and future directions. Used in this fashion, rubrics are seen as a way of provoking conversations and ongoing educational decision-making rather than being used as a form of summative or periodic means of checking progress.

Formal Uses of Rubrics. Alternatively, rubrics can serve more formal purposes, such as to track the progress of students over time, and to make comparisons across students and across classrooms and schools. Sometimes the same rubrics can be used in multiple settings including across large numbers of students for school districtwide or even national assessment purposes. In these circumstances, the rubrics need to meet standards consistent with those needed for assessment tools used for such purposes. For example, the rubric should be used with an adequate sample of student performance and there should be reliability checks on the types of the judgments that are made across students, classrooms, and schools.

Intended Audience

Rubrics can be used at all age levels in any circumstance. They are ideal in situations in which there is a desire to use classroom-based or performance assessment, or when there is an emphasis on self-assessment.

Description of the Procedures

Informal and dynamic use of rubrics supports conversations among students and teachers about performance. The steps involved in developing classroom-based rubrics are similar to steps involved in developing even more formal rubrics.

1. Discuss the dimensions of the area that you are assessing.
2. Gather samples of work—either within or across an individual, depending on the purpose.
3. Look at the examples of student work and reexamine the dimensions.
4. Refine your list of dimensions and discuss their characteristics.

5. Develop a continuum (scale) for describing the range of products and performances on each of the dimensions.
6. Alternatively, instead of a set of rating scales, you may choose to develop a holistic scale or a checklist on which you will record the presence or absence of the attributes of a product or performance. Try out your rubric and have others try it out and compare results.

In the context of using the rubric for classroom purposes, it is key to remember that more emphasis should be placed on the conversations that the development and use of the rubric provoke than on the refinement of the rubric or the rate of agreement on scores. Indeed, the discussions may be invaluable in terms of helping students glean their own criteria and refine their own self-assessment strategies. Linda Fenner (1995) detailed how she explored students' use of rubrics in conjunction with their discussions of portfolios. Fenner had students develop their own rubrics for looking at their own and other students' work. The rubric-based analyses were used then as conversation starters about student work. Interestingly, the rubric is not where the conversation ends, but where it begins. Furthermore, Fenner always ended with a conversation about how well the rubric worked. Indeed, in other activities in Fenner's classroom some of the richest conversations occurred around what should count as criteria. To inform the parents, Fenner often sent the different rubrics home and encouraged parents to look at their children's work in terms of different features on the rubric. Fenner tried to avoid oversubscribing to a single fixed rubric or a rubric that fit all students across all projects.

There exists a large number of rubrics (or profiles) from which school district might select or adapt for their own circumstances, and many of these are used for more formal purposes, such as measuring student growth. For example, one such set of rubrics is the Primary Language Record, which was developed in the United Kingdom. The overall goal of the Primary Language Record is to help teachers and parents engage in conversations around the use of various profiles and records that are gathered on each student. The developers emphasize that the continuum is not infallible and should be shared with a discussion of the caveats to avoid the possibility that parents or teachers might overemphasize analyses using such profiles. Table 14.1 includes their profile together with the notes that the authors of the profile recommend.

It is noteworthy that the authors of the Primary Language Record emphasize some of the limitations of their own profiles. As they stated:

> We encourage our teaching faculty to be descriptive rather than judgmental in their assessments of children's development because it helps them to be more focused on their teaching. However, the detailed knowledge that the teachers have of their students can be very time-consuming to write down, and possibly more than some parents might want to know. To be efficient, we have developed some categories as shorthand for describing students' literacy development. These categories are *early, emergent, maturing,* and *expanding.* Reducing children's development to these single words means trading detailed documentation for ease of reporting, which opens the possibility of misinterpretation.

Sometimes rubrics are more focused on specific elements. For example, in conjunction with her work in Vancouver, B.C., Schools, Theresa Rogers and her colleagues (Rogers,

TABLE 14.1 Primary Language Records: Reading Development in the Primary Grades

Beginning	Early	Emergent	Maturing	Expanding
■ Participates in story reading activities ■ Is curious about print ■ Has memory for book language ■ Retells story to match the illustrations ■ Knows how books work but not how words work ■ Recognizes own name ■ Relies on being read to	■ Has favorite books ■ Consistently recognizes 5 or 6 words ■ Independently engages with books for around 5 minutes at a time ■ Makes connections with other books and experiences ■ Views self as a reader ■ Tries to match each spoken word to a written one in familiar books with one sentence per page, and tries again if the numbers don't match	■ Consistently recognizes 20 or more words out of context ■ Initiates independent reading of favorite books ■ Chooses books of appropriate difficulty ■ Makes connections with own writing ■ Uses initial letters along with meaning and other cues to figure out words and correct errors ■ Still needs some support with unfamiliar texts ■ Is beginning to understand what reading can do for self ■ Is beginning to recognize different authors' styles	■ Is familiar with a range of genres ■ Attempts challenging books ■ Thinks critically, speculating on why the author used particular words, characters, etc. ■ Reads for learning and entertainment ■ Mostly reads silently ■ Beginning to use reference texts ■ Is comfortable using all letters and some analogies to figure out words ■ Initiates conversation with others about books	■ Can think about own response to reading and speculate about others' responses ■ Expects texts to have more than one meaning and notices subtleties ■ Reads independently for at least 45 minutes and cannot be easily distracted when reading a good book ■ Uses library independently ■ Is self-motivated, confident reader ■ Figures out most new words

Source: Barrs, Hester, and Thomas, 1988.

Bryan, and Winters, 2003) use a rubric entitled IRIS (Informal Reading Inventory of Strategies) to assess writing as well as a rubric to assess reading comprehension strategies. The students are asked a range of comprehension strategy questions with an information text and their answers are scored with the rubric. The assessment tool and rubrics are used across schools both to assess student progress and evaluate the project. They collaboratively devised their dimensions or categories with teachers and districtwide consultants, based on past research, goals of the project, classroom observations, and piloting the assessment. The rubric has made visible to all project members the underlying goals of the project: moving children toward sophisticated and flexible use of comprehension strategies across their curriculum. Table 14.2 is a sample of their rubric applied to two of their six comprehension strategies:

Similar rubrics have been developed by other researchers and teachers for particular curriculum areas. For example, Michael Beeth and his teacher colleagues (Beeth, Cross,

TABLE 14.2 IRIS Scoring Rubric for Written Responses and Oral Responses

	1	2	3	4
Making connections (Questions 1 and 2)	No connections or unrelated connections between background knowledge and experiences and the text in terms of purposes for reading or text ideas, genre or writer's craft	Makes some minimally related connections between background knowledge and experiences and the text in terms of purposes for reading, text ideas, genre, or writer's craft to support comprehension	Makes appropriate connections between background knowledge and experiences and the text in terms of purposes for reading, text ideas, genre, or writer's craft that seem to support comprehension	Makes rich connections between background knowledge and experiences and the text in terms of purposes for reading, ideas, genre, or writer's craft, including some that extend beyond the scope of the text
Active meaning construction (Question 3)	No questioning, hypothesizing, or predicting; no connecting of ideas or inferencing, or use of text structure cues to support comprehension	Does some minimally related questioning, hypothesizing, or predicting; minimal connecting of ideas and inferencing; use of text structure cues to support comprehension	Appropriate use of questioning, hypothesizing, or predicting; appropriate connecting of ideas and inferencing; use of text structure cues to support comprehension	Rich use of questioning, hypothesizing, or predicting; appropriate connecting of ideas and inferencing; use of text structure cues, including some that extend beyond the scope of the text

Source: Rogers, Bryan, and Winters, 2003.

Pearl, Pirro, Yagnesak, and Kennedy, 2001) developed a continuum for assessing science learning (Table 14.3).

Cautions and Comments

Over the past 20 years, we have seen an increased use of rubrics, profiles, and other scales as vehicles for placing students developmentally. There are obvious dangers in using rubrics in an overly fixed fashion, as the dimensions have the potential to assume more power than might be warranted. For example, there is a danger that these continua assume a hierarchy of skills to be developed, which may not fit with the distinctive developmental characteristic of the student. Tierney, Crumpler, Bertelsen, and Bond (2003) suggest that "while profiles and scope and sequences provide interesting ways to inform assessments and are better than a score, they should be viewed as menus of possibilities that inform rather than considered a rigid checklist for how students are ranked, classified or forced to proceed" (p. 28). Likewise, in her book, *Making Classroom Assessment Work,* Ann Davies stresses:

TABLE 14.3 Sample Items from Continuum for Science Learning

Beginning View	Developing View	Advancing View	Consolidating View
■ Describes objects ■ Observes how an object interacts with its environment ■ Asks questions about objects and phenomena	■ Gives fuller descriptions ■ Collects and organizes data ■ Details procedures for what is done ■ Relates explanations to observations ■ Suggests different possibilities	■ Predicts how an object will behave if conditions change ■ Locates and uses reference books and extracts information ■ Links events into a chain or sequence ■ Details an outcome ■ Suggests data that might be collected to answer questions	■ Gives causal explanation ■ Suggests further questions

> Making classroom assessment work means reframing the conversation from one about the ranking and sorting students to one about assessing learning in the context of our students' futures. It means talking with and listening to learners, their parents, and the community about learning and assessment. It means involving students and parents, giving choices, and sharing control. When it comes to classroom assessment, solutions can only be found in thoughtful, informed conversation as we work together on behalf of students and their learning. (Davies, 2000, pp. 78–79)

Underlying the use of rubrics is the need for flexibility and recognition that as a tool, the rubric may be fallible unless viewed as intended—to provoke conversations. As Carini (1994) noted, Portfolios help bring to the surface an awareness of the volatility of assessment results or their dialectical nature, as Fenner (1995) discovered in her classroom when her fifth graders discussed each other's work in terms of the criteria from rubrics that they wrestled with applying to their writings and projects. It was a space where students were learning about learning in more and more expansive ways; but it was not straightforward—it was argumentative.

There are numerous websites that include suggestions for rubrics for adoption or adaptation as well as frameworks by which you can develop your own rubrics (e.g., http://rubistar.4teachers.org/index.php).

REFERENCES

Ainsworth, L., and J. Christinson. 1998. *Student-generated rubrics: An assessment model to help all students succeed.* Orangeburg, NY: Dale Seymour. Presents ways to engage students in the generation of their own rubrics.

Arter, J., and J. McTighe. 2001. *Scoring rubrics in the classroom: Using performance criteria for assessing and improving student performance.* Thousand Oaks, CA: Corwin. Discusses use of rubrics in the classroom and their role in improving learning.

Barrs, M., S. Ellis, H. Hester, and A. Thomas. 1988. *The primary language record.* Portsmouth, NH: Heinemann. An excellent source for observational guides for literacy assessment with rubrics to assist with the profiling of students.

Beeth, M. E., L. Cross, K. Pearl, J. Pirro, K. Yagnesak, and J. Kennedy. 2001. A continuum for assessing science process knowledge in grades K–6. *Electronic Journal of Science Education.* Available at http://unr.edu/homepage/crowther/ejse/beethetal.html. Presents a rubric for examining students' science engagement.

Carini, P. F. 1994. Dear Sister Bess: An essay on standards, judgement, and writing. *Assessing Writing* 1(1): 29–65. Discusses the use of criteria for judging student portfolios.

Davies, A. 2000. *Making classroom assessment work.* Merville, BC: Connections. Provides a range of classroom-based assessment suggestions

Fenner, L. 1995. *Student portfolios: A view from inside the classroom.* Unpublished doctoral dissertation, The Ohio State University. A teacher–researcher's exploration of her students' discussions related to the use of a rubric applied to portfolios.

Fine, J. C., and S. W. Kossack. 2002. The effect of using rubric-embedded cognitive coaching strategies to initiate learning conversations. *Journal of Reading Education,* 27(2): 31–37. Uses a rubric as a means of providing strategy development support.

Goodrich, H. 1996–1997. Understanding Rubrics. *Educational Leadership* 54(4): 14–17. Explores the nature and role of rubrics in schools.

Griffen, P., P. Smith, and L. Burrill. 1995. *The American literacy profile scales.* Portsmouth, NH: Heinemann. Provides extensive profiles, akin to expanded rubrics, based on work initially pursued in Australian schools.

Guba, E. G., and Y. S. Lincoln. 1989. *Fourth generation evaluation.* Newbury Park, CA: Sage. Provides a qualitative basis for assessment, including emerging patterns and the tenets of assessment from a constructivist perspective.

Johnston, P. 1987. *Knowing literacy: Constructive literacy assessment.* York, ME: Sternhouse. A comprehensive discussion of assessment issues, including the use of rubrics and other analysis schemes.

Moss, P. 1996. Enlarging the dialogue in educational measurement: Voices from interpretive research traditions. *Educational Researcher* 25(1): 20–28. Explores issues of interpretation in the context of assessment.

Rickards, D., and E. Cheek. 1998. *Designing Rubrics for K–6 classrooms.* Norwood, MA: Christopher Gordon.

Rogers, T., G. Bryan, and K. Winters. 2003. *Developing the IRIS: Toward situated and valid assessment measures in collaborative professional development and school reform in literacy.* Paper presented at the National Reading Conference, Scottsdale, AZ. Discusses the development and use of a rubric in the context of a school district literacy project.

Schirmer, B. R., and A. Schirmer Lockman. 2001. How do I find a book to read? Middle and high school students use a rubric for self-selecting material for independent reading. *Teaching Exceptional Children* 34(1): 36–42. Discusses engaging students in the use of rubrics to help guide their selection of books.

Skillings, M. J., and R. Ferrell. 2000. Student-generated rubrics: Bringing students into the assessment process. *The Reading Teacher* 53(6): 452–455. Explores students' engagement in the development of rubrics.

Taggart, G. L., S. J. Phifer, J. A. Nixon, and M. Wood. 1998. *Rubrics: A handbook for construction and use.* Basel, Switzerland: Technomic. Provides guidelines for developing rubrics.

Tierney, R. J., T. Crumpler, C. Bertelsen, and E. Bond 2003. *Interactive assessment: Teachers, parents and students as partners.* Norwood, MA: Christopher Gordon. Explores issues such as rubrics and other forms of benchmarking and assessing students from the perspective of a partnership with parents, teachers, and students.

Tomlinson, C. A. 2001. Grading for success. *Educational Leadership* 58(6): 12–15. Using rubrics to assess writing of second language students.

Whittaker, C. R., J. Salend, and D. Duhaney. 2001. Creating instructional rubrics for inclusive classrooms. *Teaching Exceptional Children* 34(2): 8–13. Discusses use of rubrics in educating the exceptional child.

Running Records

Purpose

The purpose of Running Records is to "provide an ongoing assessment of the reading strategies being used and developed" (Lyons et al., 1993, 11) as a way of teachers' monitoring a student's reading progress and needs.

Rationale

Advocates for alternative assessment practices proclaim that teachers need to become active constructors of curriculum development and assessment and evaluation programs (e.g., Goodman et al., 1989; Anthony et al., 1991). Through these alternative measures, teachers can "look at individual progress while providing specific information on individual pupils' instructional needs and growth" (Routman, 1988, 204). Weaver (1990) asserts that alternative assessment must "evolve from classroom learning and teaching instead of being imposed or supplied from without; they are not prepackaged or immutable" (p. 211), and that these measures "must be selected and developed to suit the needs of themselves and their students" (p. 212). Routman (1991) concurs by stating that "these techniques must focus on meaningful communication in the language process—listening, speaking, reading, and writing—and the individual's day to day progress. As a result, careful teacher observation and teacher judgement becomes crucial; implying there is trust in teachers as professionals" (p. 204).

Running Records is an an alternative assessment technique that purports to contribute to effective instructional planning, ongoing teacher observation of reading behaviors, and other decision making. The Running Record, a form of miscue analysis, was developed by New Zealand educator Marie Clay as an "easy, but precise, way to observe, record, and carefully analyze reading behaviors" (Lyons et al., 1993, 92; Routman, 1988, 205). This technique provides teachers with

> . . . helpful insights about the strategies a child is using to reconstruct meaning while identifying what needs to be learned next. (New Zealand Board of Education, 1985, 121–122)

It is important that students have opportunities to read familiar as well as unfamiliar texts when being assessed through the Running Record.

> Familiar texts reveal whether the difficulty level of the material the child is using is suitable and in what ways the child is making use of the strategies that have been taught. Unfamiliar texts reveal the child's willingness to take risks, and indicates the ability to use and integrate strategies independently. (New Zealand Board of Education, 1985, 121–122)

In addition, this technique serves the following instructional purposes:

- Ongoing assessment by:
  - identifying gradient level of difficulty
  - capturing student strategic processing
  - providing opportunities for observation and detection of "in the head" strategies being developed
- Record keeping by recording:
  - book levels
  - problem-solving strategies
  - student progress over time
  - evidence of fluent reading in easy or familiar books
- Decision making by:
  - setting the direction for instruction
  - grouping students by strategic processing rather than by ability

- identifying important strategies to praise, reinforce, or reteach in order to gain control/internalize
- developing flexibility in reading
- providing opportunities for students to work within their own Zone of Proximal Development (Vygotsky)
- ultimately accelerating the reader

Another technique that is closely related to Running Records is the miscue analysis (Goodman et al., 1987), which is "a tool that has contributed to the development of a comprehensive theory and model of reading; it can be used to reveal the strengths and weaknesses of pupils and the extent to which they are efficient and effective readers" (Goodman, 1973, 4). Differences between these two techniques are illustrated below:

Miscue Analysis	Running Record
lengthy	"on the run"
response sheets	paper, pencil
comprehending	hypothesizing
contrived setting	authentic setting
tape recorded	live/in person
photocopy of unfamiliar text for student	familiar book for student use
hands-on training with manual	hands-on training with practice

Intended Audience

Running Records can be used with students at any grade level. Adaptations to meet individual needs and classroom purposes may be necessary.

Description of the Procedures

Clay (1993) and Lyons et al. (1993) outline the procedures below when administering, recording, and analyzing a running record. An example of a child's running record (i.e., Cory) and its analysis is found in Figure 14.6.

Administration

The teacher and student sit side by side in a comfortable setting. The teacher holds the paper and pencil for recording what occurs during the oral reading session and maintains a neutral observer role. The student holds and controls the book while reading. The reading session is not tape recorded, but the teacher records the entire reading session by looking into the student's copy of the book while marking correct responses with ticks or checkmarks and any miscues (insertions, omissions, repetitions, and substitutions) with a specific symbol notation as described below.

One or two instructional teaching points are identified immediately following the oral reading. These teaching points can be in the form of verbal comments or praise, which signify the presence and use of particular reading strategies that may not yet be internalized, or can be in the form of a direct instruction lesson in which the particular reading behaviors or strategies not being exhibited can

Cory's Running Record

Text: On a Cold Cold Day — Text Level 3

Scores: Running Words / Error 33/10 — Error Rate 1:3 — ACC. 66% — SC Rate 1:4

Page	Title and level: On a cold cold day	E	SC	Cues used E	Cues used SC
2	✓/On ✓/a ✓/cold ✓/cold ✓/day; ↓[✓/A ✓/rat] R ✓/wears ✓/a ✓/hat				
3	↓[On|sc/A a|sc/fox cold|sc/wears cold|sc/socks] R		4	M Ⓢ V M Ⓢ V M Ⓢ V M Ⓢ V	Ⓜ S Ⓥ Ⓜ Ⓢ V Ⓜ Ⓢ V Ⓜ Ⓢ V
4	✓/A ✓/giraffe ✓/wears ✓/a Coat/scarf	1		M Ⓢ V	
5	A/– goat/goats ✓/wear ✓/coats	2		M Ⓢ V Ⓜ Ⓢ Ⓥ	
6	Kangaroo/Kangaroos ✓/wear ✓/shoes	1		Ⓜ Ⓢ Ⓥ	
7	A/– Cat/Kittens ✓/wear ✓/mittens	2		M Ⓢ V Ⓜ Ⓢ Ⓥ	
8	↓[✓/And –/Paul ✓/wears all/them of/all them/–] R Ⓦ	4		M Ⓢ V M Ⓢ V M Ⓢ V M Ⓢ V	

Analysis: Cory's dominant cuing system is structure. Those neglected are meaning and visual. Meaning is cross checked against structure resulting in self correction. (Cold/SC / Socks)

FIGURE 14.6 Cory's Running Record of Analysis of Strategies

be developed through explicit teaching and demonstration (Clay, 1993, 39). The purpose for teaching is to have students arrive at "an end point in instruction where they have developed a self-extending system which is a set of operations just adequate for reading slightly more difficult text for the precise words and meanings of the author" (Clay, 1993, 39). It is during this time that the teacher wants to build on the strategies already under control while praising and reinforcing those reading strategies that are developing and eventually will become internalized and automatic.

Coding the Running Record

The following notations are used when recording reading behavior on a Running Record. (Clay, 1993, 27–29)

1. Correct words are marked with a checkmark
2. All responses deemed wrong are underlined and written above the word
3. Multiple responses are valued and an MSV coding analysis is required
4. Other codes that will appear on the running record include
   - SC = self-correction
   - — = a hyphen above line omission
   - T = Told
   - R = Repetition
   - — = a hyphen below line insertion
   - A = student appeals for help
   - W = wait (or hesitation, pause)
5. Other guidelines to attend to when counting up errors
   - proper names repeatedly missed is counted as 1 error
   - lowest score for any page read is 0
   - if line or sentence is omitted, count each word as error; if entire page is omitted, deduct number of pages from total score

Using the Running Record to analyze strategies (Clay, 1993)

1. **Searching for cues:** When analyzing errors, the following questions need to be addressed regarding the assumptions of what was going on inside the child's head.
   - Does the child use meaning (M)? Is the student applying his knowledge of the world to his reading?
   - Does the child use structure (S)? Does the student elicit a word that sounds right? What language structure does the child bring to the learning environment?
   - Does the child use visual cues (V)? Does what the student says look visually correct? What part of the word was the child attending to—the beginning, middle, or end? (pp. 41–42)
2. **Self Correction:** Clay (1993) claims that self-correction reflects that "the student will exhibit reading behaviors such as monitoring, searching by using the three cuing systems, cross-checking using different cues, and will attend to and self-correct miscues. Asking open ended questions like 'How did you know it was _______?' invites students to examine reading behaviors after completing a reading operation successfully" (p. 43).
3. **Cross-Checking Information:** According to Clay (1993), the student, when not satisfied with a response, will exhibit overt behaviors that signal to the observer that something does not make sense and that meaning is lost. Such behaviors include "making another attempt, looking back to previous print, rethinking what was already said, or complaints that a necessary letter is missing" (p. 41). When this occurs, the student is encouraged to cross-check (i.e., visual cues, meaning cues, or structural cues) or use two sources of information—checking one against the other" (p. 41).
4. **Using Running Records to monitor and adjust instructional material:** After taking the Running Record, it is important for the teacher to select appropriate instructional material that will challenge and support the learner. In this regard, a teacher tries to challenge the child with material for which he achieves a 90–94% fluency. As Clay (1993) states,

> The goal of teaching is to assist the child to produce effective strategies for working on text, not to accumulate items of knowledge. It is necessary to develop opportunities for the child to problem solve, predict and accommodate new knowledge. In a literate setting, the most important thing that the child can do when reading is to notice that something is wrong and use his own resources for working on a solution. (p. 15)

Beyond 95 percent, the material is viewed as not sufficiently challenging. According to Clay, if a child's instructional program is designed to foster the child's independent level (95–100%), the child most likely will not participate in enough stimulating and challenging opportunities that would encourage, expand, and strengthen his current strategies. There will be little or no authentic opportunities for problem solving, investigating, and taking the initiative to probe and explore.

The opposite will be true for a student with whom instructional learning activities will continually fall within the hard or difficult range (50–89%). If this should occur, the opportunities for the child to utilize, experiment, and risk the few strategies he may have control over will be almost nonexistent. This child needs to be absorbed in authentic, language-rich experiences that will enable him or her to explore what he or she knows while being supported with his or her approximations through scaffolding.

Cory's Running Record results illustrate that he is struggling with reading. Indeed, his teacher might look for material that is not so challenging. Nonetheless, it does appear that he understands what he is reading; however, he relies too much on Meaning (M) and Structure (S) cues without attending to the Visual (V) aspect of words. Although there is evidence he is aware of early reading strategies (directionality, one-to-one matching, searching and monitoring), it appears that Cory has not internalized these strategies enough to initiate them on his own or to utilize these behaviors in a strategic way.

Even though this text (level 3) fell within the hard/difficult range, many positive reading behaviors can be gleaned from this document. For instance, Cory understands storybook language; understands directionality and that words carry the message, not the pictures, but that the pictures are used to assist reading. He is able to locate known words ("here's *a*") but has not yet internalized how this known word can assist him during the reading process; and he understands the functions and forms of language as exhibited in the rhyming of words ("coat/goat and fox/socks match, don't they?").

Cautions and Comments

In the educational arena today, much has been debated regarding the appropriateness and frequency of standardized testing within the school curriculum. Much debate has focused on the aspects of quantitative and qualitative measures. For instance, the standardized test "frequently examines surface behaviors, strategies such as self correction and regressions, which are needed for proficient reading, but are often treated as problematic. Qualitative analysis, on the other hand, evaluates why miscues are made and assumes that they derive from the language and thought that the reader brings to the written material" (Goodman et al., 1987, 4). With the advent of alternative assessment, many teachers have found ways of implementing these techniques that assist them in tailoring their programs to meet "pupils' instructional needs and growth" (Routman, 1988, 204). In addition, teachers began to participate in decision-making processes that could lead to curriculum development and instructional change. For instance, the success classroom teachers have found with Running Records involves useful, immediate, and diagnostic data that are helpful when reporting school progress to parents (Routman, 1988). Another positive attribute of Running Records involves "observation 'on the run' without time spent in preplanning, tape recording, and photocopying text" (Weaver, 1990, 228) as depicted in miscue analysis. Numerous references to Running Records as a means of matching books to readers and tracking progress can be found in discussions of the use of practices such as Guided Reading (see Unit 1) and similar frameworks, especially with at-risk readers.

Running Records are no panacea. They represent a sampling of reading behavior that may or may not give a full or adequate picture. Some students have aversions to oral reading; for others it detracts from their meaning making. Running Records do encourage teachers to be constantly monitoring what students are doing as they are reading en route to making decisions as to appropriate support and materials. Although Running Records may be difficult to manage, as an occasional spot check they afford teachers and the students themselves a teaching tool that is more dynamic than rigid and can be more supportive than intrusive.

REFERENCES

Anthony, R. J., T. D. Johnson, N. I. Mickelson, and A. Preece. 1991. *Evaluating literacy: A perspective for change.* Portsmouth, NH: Heinemann. This is a practical book that focuses on evaluation strategies that could impact classroom, home, and school populations.

Byrd, D., and P. Westfall. 2000. *Guided reading coaching tool.* Portland, ME: Stenhouse. Offers suggestions in conjunction with the use of Running Records.

Clay, M. M. 1993. *An observation survey of early literacy achievement.* Portsmouth, NH: Heinemann. This text was written for teachers and researchers who work with young readers and writers. This text describes the procedures to follow when administering and scoring the six assessment tasks in the Observation Survey and when utilizing a Running Record.

———. 1993. *Reading Recovery: A guidebook for teachers in training.* Portsmouth, NH: Heinemann. This text is used by teachers-in-training. It describes the components and procedures of a Reading Recovery lesson.

Cooper, J. D. 1993. *Literacy: Helping children construct meaning.* Boston: Houghton Mifflin. Provides theoretical and practical techniques in helping teachers guide and facilitate children's literacy development.

Department of Education. 1985. *Reading in junior classes.* Wellington: Author. This handbook offers guidance to teachers while describing the New Zealand way of teaching reading to youngsters.

Fountas, I. C., and G. S. Pinnell. 1999. *Matching books to readers: Using leveled books in Guided Reading, K–3.* Portsmouth, NH: Heinemann. Provides detailed procedures for levelling books and their use in conjunction with Running Records.

Goodman, K. 1973. *Miscue analysis.* Urbana, IL: ERIC Clearinghouse. This text shares several viewpoints on the reading process and miscue analysis and how this procedure can be utilized in classrooms of diversity and grade level.

Goodman, K. S., Y. M. Goodman, and W. J. Hood. 1989. *The whole language evaluation book.* Describes practical and successful alternative evaluation techniques that teachers can utilize in any learning environment.

Goodman, Y. M., D. J. Watson, and C. L. Burke. 1987. *Reading miscue inventory.* New York: Owens. This guidebook describes the steps involved when implementing a miscue analysis. Specific directions, examples, and sample sheets are included.

Lyons, C. A., G. S. Pinnell, and D. E. DeFord. 1993. *Partners in learning: Teachers and children in reading recovery.* New York: Teachers College Press, Columbia University. "This book is written as a text for individuals interested in early or emergent literacy development who want to make a difference in the learning of high-risk children."

Parker, E. L., R. Armengol, L. B. Brooke, K. R. Carper, S. M. Cronin, A. C. Denman, P. Irwin, J. McGunnigle, T. Pardini, and N. P. Kurtz. 1995. Teachers' choices in classroom assessment. *The Reading Teacher* 48(7): 622–624. Provides an overview of various assessment tools (concepts about print, Running Records, self-assessment/goal-setting interviews, Rubrics, and so on).

Routman, R. 1988. *Transitions from literature to literacy.* Portsmouth, NH: Heinemann. Describes how teachers and school personnel can successfully shift from a more traditional setting to one of an integrated, literature-based language arts program.

———. 1991. *Invitations: Changing as teachers and learners K–12.* Portsmouth, NH: Heinemann. An excellent resource to assist teachers when integrating the curriculum and implementing alternative assessments.

Weaver, C. 1988. *The reading process and practice from socio-psycholinguistics to whole language.* Portsmouth, NH: Heinemann. Provides an in-depth study and discussion on the reading process and its relationship to instructional practice.

———. 1991. *Understanding whole language from principles to practice.* Portsmouth, NH: Heinemann. Describes the impact a holistic, integrated, child-centered environment has on literacy learning and the need for authentic means of assessment in relation to literacy learning.

Retelling

Purpose

The purpose of Retelling for classroom assessment is to provide teachers an alternative to asking questions in evaluating students' understanding of what they have read. Using Retelling, students try to recall as much as possible of what they have read, and comprehension performance is judged on the thoroughness of the recall.

Rationale

Critics of the informal reading inventory point out that the question-and-answer format employed by it does not necessarily tap students' understanding of what they read to the fullest extent. Questions, in essence, can function to limit the responses students can make. Retelling, on the other hand, allows students to respond in their own words concerning what they understood from the text. Thus, Retelling can increase both the quantity and the quality of what is comprehended.

Since the procedure involves repetition and rehearsal of what is read, Retelling should add more text information to memory and affect how much is learned. Additionally, the procedure allows for students to make the information gained from the text more personally meaningful than questions and, therefore, should affect the depth of learning.

Intended Audience

Retelling can be used across the curriculum with a variety of grade levels. However, it is most commonly used in elementary level classrooms, particularly those that take a Whole-Language emphasis (see Unit 2).

Description of the Procedures

The procedure for Retelling will be discussed using the following two steps: (1) eliciting the retelling, and (2) scoring the retelling.

1. Eliciting the Retelling. Before Retelling is used as a means to assess students' comprehension, they must be familiar with the procedure. Students will have difficulty doing a retelling if they are unfamiliar with the technique and what is expected of them; therefore, they should have had prior practice doing it.

To begin the retelling, make sure that students understand that they will be asked to retell the story. Since the retelling is not for instructional purposes, the story should not be discussed with the student beforehand, nor should there be any prompts during the procedure. After the story has been read, ask the student to retell it as if it were being told to a friend for the first time who had never heard it before. To ensure the accuracy of the assessment, tape-record the retelling.

2. Scoring the Retelling. Irwin and Mitchell (1983) have developed a holistic system to score a retelling. Because each student's retelling is individualistic with regard to reaction, personality, and depth of understanding, assessment should be done by examining the whole recall and not its component parts. Only by examining the totality can the richness of the reader's understanding be judged.

To assess a retelling, Irwin and Mitchell developed criteria for establishing five levels of richness, from good to poor, to use in judging a student's recall. Figure 14.7 describes the levels of richness of a retelling while Figure 14.8 is a checklist that compares the principal qualities of the five richness levels.

In using this scoring system, teachers will need to make judgments about the quality of a student's retelling by comparing it to the original story and using the criteria to judge its richness. For instance, if a student's retelling shows that the student did not generalize

FIGURE 14.7 Judging Richness of Retellings

Level	Criteria for Establishing Level
5	Student generalizes beyond text; includes thesis (summarizing statement), all major points, and appropriate supporting details; includes relevant supplementations; shows high degree of coherence, completeness, comprehensibility.
4	Student includes thesis (summarizing statement), all major points, and appropriate supporting details; includes relevant supplementations; shows high degree of coherence, completeness, comprehensibility.
3	Student relates major ideas; includes appropriate supporting details and relevant supplementations; shows adequate coherence, completeness, comprehensibility.
2	Student relates a few major ideas and some supporting ideas; includes irrelevant supplementations; shows some degree of coherence; some degree of completeness; the whole is somewhat comprehensible.
1	Student relates details only; irrelevant supplementations or none; low degree of coherence; incomplete; incomprehensible.

Source: From Irwin, P. A., and J. N. Mitchell, 1983. A procedure for assessing the richness of retellings. *Journal of Reading,* 26, 391–396. Reprinted by permission of the International Reading Association.

FIGURE 14.8 Checklist for Judging Richness of Retellings

	5	4	3	2	1
Generalizes beyond text	X				
Thesis (summarizing statement)	X	X	X		
Major points	X	X	X	?	?
Supporting details	X	X	X	X	?
Supplementations	Relevant	Relevant	Relevant	Irrelevant	Irrelevant
Coherence	High	Good	Adequate	Some	Poor
Completeness	High	Good	Adequate	Some	Poor
Comprehensibility	High	Good	Adequate	Some	Poor

Source: From Irwin, P. A., and J. N. Mitchell, 1983. A procedure for assessing the richness of retellings. *Journal of Reading,* 26: 391–396.

beyond the story or provide a summarizing statement, only mentioned some major points and a few supporting details, but did show some signs of story coherence and completeness, then the student's retelling would probably be classified as level 2. This, however, would tell the teacher that the student did not do a very good job of comprehending the story. The teacher may then wish to do some further evaluating, such as a probed recall, to gather additional information. All findings should be added to the student's portfolio to get a more comprehensive look at the student's reading.

Cautions and Comments

Using Retelling enables teachers to get a different look at how students comprehend. A holistic examination helps teachers move away from the small details recalled through questions to look at the richness of a student's retelling and how the student was able to move beyond the story read and how it was related to the student's personal experience. Certainly the global examination of Retelling provides teachers the opportunity to be more consistent in their assessment over time of students' comprehension.

It should be mentioned that the description of the Retelling procedure was based on the student reading a story and orally recalling it. Variations on this procedure allow teachers to accommodate differences in age, reading ability, culture, and so on, by the teacher's reading the story and having the student retell it or even having the student write his retelling.

It is also cautioned that this description of the Retelling was for assessment, not instruction. If teachers were to use the Retelling as a means for comprehension, the procedure would be modified. Prompts could be added to help students embellish their retellings. Brown and Cambourne (1987) suggested that students be asked to make predictions about the story and that those predictions be shared and discussed before it is read. After their retellings students should compare them with one another to examine others' interpretations of the story. In this way the procedure can be adapted to engage students more fully both before and after reading. Peter Johnston (1997) discusses the use of Retellings for assessment purposes, including ways to enhance their authenticity and potential. He also examines other possibilities, such as having students translate text using techniques such as those developed by Patricia Enciso (1990) involving cutouts to represent people and places for assessing engagement.

REFERENCES

Brown, H., and B. Cambourne. 1987. *Read and retell.* Portsmouth, NH: Heinemann. A handbook on the use of Retelling.

Enciso, P. 1990. *The nature of engagement in reading: Case studies of fourth and fifth grade students' engagement strategies and stances.* Unpublished doctoral dissertation, Ohio State University.

Gambrell, L. B., P. S. Koskinen, and B. A. Kapinus. 1991. Retelling and the reading comprehension of proficient and less-proficient readers. *Journal of Educational Research* 84: 356–362. Study showing that practice in Retelling improved the comprehension of both good and poor readers.

Glazer, S. M., and C. S. Brown. 1993. *Portfolios and beyond: Collaborative assessment in reading and writing.* Norwood, MA: Christopher-Gordon. Chapter 6 of this text describes the use of Retelling to assess comprehension.

Irwin, P. A., and Mitchell, J. N. 1983. A procedure for assessing the richness of Retellings. *Journal of Reading* 26: 391–396. Suggestions for assessing a Retelling.

Johnston, P. 1997. *Knowing literacy: Constructive literacy assessment.* York: ME: Stenhouse. Comprehensive and critical examination of a range of assessment practice.

Morrow, L. M. 1988. Retelling stories as a diagnostic tool. In S. M. Glazer, L. W. Searfoss, and L. M. Gentile (Eds.), *Reexamining reading diagnosis: New trends and practices.* Newark, DE: International Reading Association, 128–149. A discussion of procedures for using Retelling for assessment purposes.

Cloze

Purpose

Cloze and variations of Cloze are used to assess reading comprehension. However, research has raised serious questions that suggest that Cloze should be used with an understanding that it measures at best sentence level comprehension—specifically, a reader's ability to align him or herself with the language of an author's text.

Rationale

Taylor (1953) described the Cloze procedure as:

> . . . a method of intercepting a message from a "transmitter" (writer or speaker), mutilating its language patterns by deleting parts, and so administer it to "receivers" (readers and listeners) that their attempts to make the pattern whole again potentially yield a considerable number of cloze units. (p. 416)

Since Taylor made such a statement, Cloze has been widely advocated as a method for assessing whether students can comprehend text and as a procedure for improving reading comprehension. It has come to be widely used in tests such as the Degrees of Reading Power as well as standardized tests and tests tied to instructional material. Unfortunately, recent research is equivocal with regard to what exactly Cloze is measuring, and it should not be assumed to be directly associated with reading comprehension. Notable among these studies is the work of Shanahan, Kamil, and Tobin (1982) and Shanahan and Kamil (1983), showing that Cloze is neither sensitive to intersentential aspects of text nor to prior knowledge. On the other hand, these results have been called into question by Gamarra and Jonz (1987). While further research is conducted to further define what the relationship of Cloze to reading comprehension is, we can say with some certainty that Cloze appears to measure—and maybe heighten—a student's use of the syntax of and information presented with individual sentences.

Intended Audience

The Cloze procedure has been recommended for use with readers at all levels for a variety of purposes, such as instructional placement and an assessment of a student's ability to use context clues and to assess the readability level of certain texts. As an instructional tool, its use has been referenced at the first-grade level (Gove, 1975) through college level (Bloomer, 1962; Friedman, 1964; Guice, 1969).

Description of the Procedures

For those who have used the Cloze procedure as a measure of the comprehensibility of printed material, it would be best to note some differences between the use of the technique in those settings and the use of the strategy as an instructional device. Essential differences are summarized in Table 14.4.

Different forms of Cloze have been developed to achieve different assessment ends. For purposes of assessing students' comprehension or to assess the readability of a text, the most common approach to Cloze requires students to generate exact word replacement for a random selection of deleted words. In this form of Cloze test, every fifth word is deleted,

TABLE 14.4 Cloze Procedure

Characteristic	As a measuring device	As a teaching tool
Length	(1) 250–350-word selections	(1) Initially, may use single sentences. Later, passages of no more than 150 words
Deletions	(2) Delete every *n*th word with approximately 50 for the total word passage	(2) Make deletions selectively and systematically in accordance with proposed use
Evaluation	(3) With this procedure, only exact word replacement is correct. Sometimes a teacher may analyze student responses in terms of their syntactic and semantic characteristics	(3) Synonyms or other replacements are appropriate
Follow-up	(4) Usually none	(4) Student and teacher discussion of the exercise helps comprehension

regardless of the word. Recommended procedures for constructing such a passage are as follows:

1. Select a representative selection from the material to be assessed or that represents the type of material being assigned to children. Look for an intact section of this text (i.e., a section that could stand alone) of approximately 250–350 words. You should avoid material that depends on or is obviously linked to previous material.

2. Keep intact the first and last sentence or sentences depending on the length of the sentence. If the sentence is especially short, you may wish to include more than one sentence.

3. Randomly choose one of the first five words in the second sentence. Beginning with this word, omit every fifth word until 50 words are deleted. Dates would be considered single words, certain hyphenated words may be viewed as single words or two words depending on your rationale.

4. Replace each deleted word by a blank of uniform length.

5. Have students either replace the word in the blank provided or on a separate sheet.

Example Cloze

The Cloze Procedure

The Cloze procedure is based on the psychological notion of closure (hence, Cloze) and the concept of redundancy within the language. The Cloze has been __________ as a procedure for __________ how well a reader __________ comprehending a text. Research __________ suggest that it measures __________-level comprehension not text-__________ comprehension. It will appear __________ assess how well readers __________ align themselves with the __________ choice of words. Another __________ of Cloze has been __________ assess the readability of __________ text. To this end, __________ following criteria have been __________: if readers replace more __________ 60 percent of the __________ words accurately then they __________ can handle the material __________; if readers replace between __________ and 60 percent of __________ words accurately then they __________ need instructional support when __________ the material; if they __________ below 40 percent the __________ may be too frustrating.

__________ constructing a Cloze passage, __________ a passage of around __________ words in length. Type __________ first sentence intact. __________ with the fifth word __________ the second sentence, delete __________ fifth word until you __________ fifty deletions. Replace each __________ with an underlined blank __________ spaces long. Finish the __________ in which the last __________ occurs, then type one __________ sentence intact. . . .

. . . Since the development of the Cloze, variations such as the Maze procedure have emerged.

Intact Passage from Which Sample Cloze Was Developed

The Cloze Procedure

The Cloze procedure is based on the psychological notion of closure (hence, Cloze) and the concept of redundancy within the language. The Cloze has been touted as a procedure for assessing how well a reader is comprehending a text. Research would suggest that it measures sentence-level comprehension, not text-level comprehension. It will appear to assess how well readers can align themselves with the author's choice of words. Another use of Cloze has been to assess the readability of a text. To this end, the following criteria have been used: if readers replace more than 60 percent of the deleted words accurately, then the readers can handle the material independently; if readers replace between 40 and 60 percent of the words accurately, then they may need instructional support when reading the material; if they fall below 40 percent, the material may be too frustrating.

When constructing a Cloze passage, select a passage of around 300 words in length. Type the first sentence intact. Starting with the fifth word in the second sentence, delete every fifth word until you have fifty deletions. Replace each deletion with an underlined blank fifteen spaces long. Finish the sentence in which the last deletion occurs, then type one more sentence intact. . . .

. . . Since the development of the cloze, variations such as the Maze procedure have emerged.

Guthrie and his colleagues (1974) suggest using Maze to monitor comprehension and assess the level of challenge of the material that they are reading. Unlike Cloze, maze requires the reader to choose among three choices: exact word, a word representing the same part of speech, or a word representing a different part of speech. If students are responding to Maze at a level of 90 percent across three or more passages, then the student seems to be able to read these materials independently. If students are responding at between 60 and 69 percent they are operating at optimal instructional level. Below 60 percent they are likely to be frustrated.

Other assessment uses of Cloze tend to represent variations of the aforementioned approaches or uses of Cloze for specific purposes, such as assessing students' ability to use pronominal references or consonant clues, and so on. Such uses involve forms of Cloze created with these specific tasks in mind and parallel the types of Cloze activities described below for using Cloze for instructional purposes.

Cloze Used for Instructional Purposes. Given the questions raised about Cloze, most advocates have shifted away from using Cloze as a method to assess comprehension and instead reserve its use for instructional purposes. Several individuals have attempted to outline systematic procedures for using the Cloze technique as a comprehension-building strategy (Bloomer, 1962; Schell, 1972; Bortnick and Lopardo, 1973; Gove, 1975). The following procedural outline incorporates the thoughts of each of those individuals.

1. Teacher Preparation

a. Selecting materials. Schell (1972) suggests that, in the early stages, materials should be at the students' independent reading level. Teachers can extract written selections from stories and poems in basal readers, from subject matter texts, or from language experience stories the students themselves generate. There are some Cloze-type materials available through several publishers. It is important to note that teachers themselves produce some of the most effective materials.

As we mentioned earlier, passages should be shorter than passages generally used when Cloze is a testing device. For example, teachers may use single sentences initially with first graders, gradually moving to selections in which 10 to 15 deletions have been made (Gove, 1975).

b. Designing the Cloze exercise. There appears to be a logical progression in the format for presenting Cloze exercises. Consider the examples that follow only as a guideline for developing Cloze exercises. We present them in order of difficulty, which the teacher should follow.

1. Sentences in which the teacher deletes one word; a multiple-choice format with two choices. Notice in the following example that the two choices include the correct item and a foil, or an incorrect item that is quite different graphically and is a different part of speech.

1. monkey

"We saw a __________ at the zoo . . .

2. soon

2. The same format as above, but with the foil somewhat graphically similar to the correct item and a different part of speech.

1. mostly

"We saw a __________ at the zoo . . .

2. monkey

3. Two choices, both the same part of speech.

1. monkey

"We saw a __________ at the zoo . . .

2. money

4. Three choices that include the correct item, a word of the same part of speech, and a word that represents a different part of speech.*

"We saw a __________ at the zoo . . .

1. money

2. mostly

3. monkey

*These examples are similar to a testing strategy, the Maze technique, described by Guthrie et al. (1974).

From these highly structured examples, one can move to less structured items. Again, in terms of difficulty, one could progress with exercises of this type:

1. A single graphophonic clue in a sentence where only one word could reasonably fit.
   "I think the square t_________ will look better in the dining room than the round one you considered buying."
2. A single graphophonic clue in a sentence where several choices are possible.
   "We bought a bag of p_________ at the grocery store."

Finally, the teacher could use sentences and passages similar to these, but without the graphophonic rule.*

Again, we suggest this sequence simply to provide a guideline for the development of Cloze activities. Obviously, the teacher must consider the difficulty of the printed materials and the reading sophistication of the students when developing exercises of this type.

The reader may have noticed that each of the examples above contains a noun deletion. Schell (1972) suggests that in the early stages of instruction, the teacher should delete only nouns and verbs. Later, he or she may emphasize categories such as adjectives or adverbs.

2. Instruction. In many kindergarten and first grade classrooms, the instructional program might include oral Cloze activities. The following is an example of one such activity:

> I am going to say some sentences, but I will leave off the last word of each sentence. See if you can tell me what word I left out. Let's try this one: "At Joe's birthday party on Saturday, we had some ice cream and _______." What word(s) make(s) sense there?

Discussion then could center on why students have various answers. Such exercises provide a logical introduction to the use of written Cloze activities.

When initiating written Cloze activities, the teacher might begin with a whole-class activity focused on material presented on an overhead projector. The teacher should direct students to read through the entire sentence or passage before attempting to supply the deleted word(s). A student volunteer could read the material and supply the missing word(s). One other student who has responded differently could read and provide his or her responses. Class discussion would center on such questions as:

> Why did you choose this word? What word or group of words indicate to you "building" should be placed in the blank? How does your word contribute to the meaning of the passage? When your word is in the sentence, what does the sentence (or passage) mean? How does your word contribute to the meaning in a different way? When your word is in the sentence, does the sentence (or passage) have a different meaning? (Gove, 1975, 38)

*These examples are similar to a testing strategy, the Maze technique, described by Guthrie et al. (1974).

Other students could add their suggestions with continued discussion centered on these questions.

Later, the teacher could give the mimeographed Cloze passages to complete individually. In small-group discussions, the teacher asks each student to explain why he or she used a particular word. The small-group discussions would then lead to large-group discussion of some of the more interesting or controversial items.

An exercise such as the following might be used with a group of intermediate level readers. Obviously, the teacher would not type the deleted words on the students' mimeographed copies, but we include the words here for discussion purposes.

> Would you like to find a rich (*gold*) mine? There's one in the Superstition Mountains of Arizona. Jacob Walz, an (*old*) prospector from Germany, was one of the last known persons to (*visit*) the mine. Before Walz died in 1891, he gave (*simple*) directions to the mine. There is also supposed to be a map. But no one has ever been able to find what is now (*called*) "The Lost Dutchman Mine."*

Each of the words in parentheses offers students the opportunity to supply a variety of other words. For example, in place of the word *old,* students might offer replacements such as *elderly, adventurous, interesting, ugly,* or *eccentric.* Discussion then could center on why these choices are feasible, and why words like *young, robust,* and so on are not acceptable.

Jongsma (1980) and others have suggested that this discussion procedure may be the key to the successful use of Cloze as a teaching strategy. There is very little evidence to suggest that Cloze exercises alone will produce better comprehenders.

Cautions and Comments

There appear to be an endless number of ways that teachers can use the Cloze procedure to improve the comprehension skills of readers. For example, Rankin (1959) proposed the use of Cloze exercises to assist readers who have difficulty with text in their content classrooms, and Blachowicz (1977) proposed using the Cloze technique with primary grade students. Furthermore, there seem to be a number of alternative Cloze formats. Two additional Cloze formats have appeared in research studies and may present possibilities for use in teaching. A limited Cloze technique (Cunningham and Cunningham, 1978) employs the traditional deletion pattern of every fifth word with the deleted words randomly ordered and placed in columns on a separate sheet. Another format, the least-major-constituent limited Cloze (Cunningham and Tierney, 1977), deletes every fifth least-major-constituent (syntactic unit sometimes larger than words) and randomly orders them in columns on a separate sheet.

As was suggested in the Rationale, Cloze should not be assumed to be directly associated with comprehension. Indeed, it seems that some people are using Cloze haphazardly. The reader should note that merely completing Cloze activities will not result in students' improved comprehension. Rather, comprehension improvement using Cloze depends on the reader's purpose, the text's demands, and the teacher's follow-up during and after a Cloze activity. To this end, teachers should use Cloze selectively with passages and pur-

*Smith, R. G., and R. J. Tierney, *Fins and Tales,* Scott, Foresman Basics in Reading. (Glenview, IL: Scott, Foresman, 1978) 72.

poses where students' ability to produce replacement words or phrases is a worthwhile activity. For example, Cloze might be inappropriate with text for which a more reader-based understanding is appropriate. Finally, we need to stress the fact that there is very little research that supports the use of Cloze as a procedure either for testing or for developing comprehension (McKenna and Layton, 1990; Shannon, Kamil, and Tobin, 1982).

Johnston (1992) offered a similar view. As he stated:

> There has been considerable debate among researchers about whether the cloze procedure can provide information about a reader's understanding of anything more than a sentence at a time. Some claim that by careful selection of the words to be deleted, the procedure can require the students to know the whole meaning of the text (assuming that only a single meaning can be acceptable). Of course, in order to feel a need to engage in these arguments, you have to feel it is necessary to obtain some numerical indicator of a child's "ability to comprehend." If you do feel such a need, then the cloze procedure remains a useful instructional technique for helping some children attend more to the use of context to figure out unknown words." (p. 123)

REFERENCES

Blachowicz, C. L. Z. 1977. Cloze activities for primary readers. *The Reading Teacher* 31: 300–302. Describes how teachers can use variations of Cloze successfully with primary readers.

Bloomer, R. H. 1962. The Cloze procedure as a remedial reading exercise. *Journal of Developmental Reading* 5: 173–181. Describes the use of the Cloze procedure as a remedial technique for college students.

Bortnick, R., and G. S. Lopardo. 1973. An instructional application of the Cloze procedure. *Journal of Reading* 16: 296–300. Provides specific direction for using Cloze procedure to improve comprehension. Emphasis is placed on the importance of teacher direction.

Carr, E., P. Dewitz, and J. Patberg. 1989. Using Cloze for inference training with expository text. *The Reading Teacher* 42: 380–385. Discusses the use of Cloze procedures intended to enhance inferential comprehension and self-monitoring.

Cunningham, J. W., and P. M. Cunningham. 1978. Validating a Limited-Cloze procedure. *Journal of Reading Behavior* 10: 211–213. Presents a variation of the traditional Cloze format.

Cunningham, J. W., and R. J. Tierney. 1977, December. *Comparative analysis of Cloze and modified Cloze procedures.* Paper presented at National Reading Conference, New Orleans. Provides a comparison of the traditional Cloze format with two modified versions.

Friedman, M. 1964. *The use of the Cloze procedure for improving the reading of foreign students at the University of Florida.* Unpublished doctoral diss., University of Florida. Describes an experimental study in which one group received Cloze passages constructed from McCall-Crabbs Standard Test Lessons in Reading.

Gamarra, A. G., and J. Jonz. 1987. Cloze procedure and the sequence of text. In J. E. Readence and R. S. Baldwin (Eds.), *Research in literacy: Merging perspectives.* Thirty-sixth Yearbook of the National Reading Conference. Rochester, NY: National Reading Conference, 17–24. Calls into question studies that have found Cloze to be unrelated to reading comprehension.

Gove, M. K. 1975. Using the Cloze procedure in a first grade classroom. *The Reading Teacher* 29: 36–38. Describes how the teacher can use Cloze procedure in conjunction with basal readers and with the language experience approach.

Guice, B. M. 1969. The use of the Cloze procedure for improving reading comprehension of college students. *Journal of Reading Behavior* 1: 81–92. Provides a description of four groups of college students who received instruction using Cloze passages.

Guthrie, J. T., N. A. Burnham, R. I. Caplan, and M. Seifert. 1974. The Maze technique to assess, monitor reading comprehension. *The Reading Teacher* 28: 161–168. Presents a multiple-choice-type variation of the Cloze procedure.

Henk, W. 1977–78. A response to Shanahan, Kamil, and Tobin: The case is not yet Clozed. *Reading Research Quarterly* 13: 508–537. Presents a response to the first study of Shanahan, Kamil, and Tobin, which resulted in a second study by them.

Johnston, P. 1992. *Constructive evaluation of literate activity.* New York: Longman. Presents a brief discussion of Cloze in the context of a substantial presentation of literacy assessment issues, theories, and practices.

Johnston, P. 1997. *Knowing literacy: Constructive literacy assessment.* York, ME: Stenhouse. Discusses the use of Cloze along with other comprehension strategies.

Jongsma, E. 1980. *Cloze instruction research: A second look.* Newark, DE: International Reading Association. Presents descriptions of past research that used the Cloze procedure as a teaching tool; offers suggestions for future Cloze research.

McKenna, M., and K. Layton. 1990. Concurrent validity of Cloze as a measure of intersentential comprehension. *Journal of Educational Psychology* 82(2): 372–377. Examines the issue of what Cloze actually measures.

Pikulski, J. J., and A. W. Tobin. 1982. The Cloze procedure as an informal assessment technique. In J. J. Pikulski and T. Shanahan (Eds.), *Approaches to the informal evaluation of reading.* Newark, DE: International Reading Association, 42–62. Provides an extensive discussion of the research and practical uses of Cloze.

Rankin, E. 1959. Uses of the Cloze procedure in the reading clinic. *Proceedings of the International Reading Association* 4: 228–232. Suggests ways of using Cloze procedure to bridge the gap between clinical instruction and instruction in the content classroom.

Sampson, M. R. W., W. J. Valmont, and R. V. Allen. 1982. The effects of instructional Cloze on the comprehension, vocabulary and divergent production of third grade students. *Reading Research Quarterly* 17: 389–399. Presents positive results from a study in which students who received instruction in Cloze with selected deletions outperformed a control group.

Schell, L. M. 1972. Promising possibilities for improving comprehension. *Journal of Reading* 5: 415–424. Presents detailed information on the use of Cloze as a teaching technique.

Shanahan, T., and M. Kamil. 1983. A further investigation of sensitivity of Cloze and recall to passage organization. In J. A. Niles and L. A. Harris (Eds.), *Searches for meaning in reading/language processing and instruction.* Thirty-second Yearbook of the National Reading Conference. Rochester, NY: National Reading Conference. In response to Henk's critique, presents a study that further disputes Cloze as a method of improving comprehension.

Shanahan, T., M. Kamil, and A. Tobin. 1982. Cloze as a measure of intersentential comprehension. *Reading Research Quarterly* 17: 229–255. Presents a research study that raised serious questions about the use of Cloze as a measure of text comprehension.

Taylor, W. L. 1953. Cloze procedure: A new tool for measuring readability. *Journalism Quarterly* 30: 415–453. Provides the first description of the Cloze technique.

Parent-Teacher and Student-Led Conferencing

Purpose

Assessment conferences with parents and students are intended to support ongoing engagements of students and parents in decision making about teaching and learning in conjunction with reviewing via portfolios, dossiers, and other artifacts of student learning.

Rationale

Conferencing among students, teachers, and parents is seen as a means of establishing a partnership in support of student learning that is ethically responsible as well as pedagogically important. In their book *Interactive Assessment: Teachers, Students, and Parents as Partners,* Tierney, Crumpler, Bertlesen, and Bond (2003) suggest:

> In most of our everyday interactions in the world we expect to be involved in joint decision-making. For example, in legal matters, we would seek advice from an attorney who could

> outline options and possible ways to proceed. Or, if we were ill, we would see a doctor who would give advice as to types of medication that might help and whether we need to see a specialist. In each of these brief scenarios, an assessment is made. We are aware of what is at stake and expect to be part of the decision making process, part of a conversation. However there is more going in these situations than might be visible at first glance. On another level, each of these examples outlined above involves inquiry and negotiation. Each conversation involves inquiry into a question about health, or legal options. From there, we may need to negotiate about the necessity of a medical procedure, or the best course to protect one's rights as a citizen. Further, we could pursue other opinions about each of these issues, weigh them against one another, and decide what is best.
>
> In a similar fashion, we might expect schools where assessment is central to a child's future to engage parents or other caregivers and teachers in conversations that lead to joint decision making that is informed by inquiry and negotiation. We further might expect these same schools to cultivate partnerships committed to developing assessments with students that allow these students to demonstrate growth and achievement. (p. 11)

Further, a number of educators would argue that these conferences afford teachers, parents, and students to learn from each other as they engage in ongoing review and reflection of progress, achievement, and expectations. The conferences are an opportunity for a form of "time out" to check on progress and to make plans. Such transactions ensure that there is a give-and-take en route to parents', students', and teachers' being better informed and committed to support ongoing learning goals.

Intended Audience

Conferencing is a means of engaging stakeholders in assessment-related decision making at any age.

Description of the Procedures

Conferencing between students, teachers, and parents may assume a range of forms, from parent-teacher to parent-student-teacher to student-led parent conferencing to peer-to-peer. In other units, we described various forms of peer-to-peer conferencing in conjunction with various holistic and literature-based strategies, especially Book Club and Reading-Writing Workshop. While conferencing can be woven into the everyday fabric of interactions or occur as needed between teachers and parents or teachers and students or among students, the focus in this unit is planned parent-student-teacher conferences. While there are a number of different ways of proceeding with a conferencing, the teacher is responsible for the types of negotiations that might occur, including the venue and ground rules.

Typically, teachers organize conferences in conjunction with open houses, at the end of grading periods, at the end of a major unit, or in conjunction with distributing report narratives, progress reports, or portfolios. They serve as a means of taking stock, celebrating progress, or joint decision making. In preparation for a conference, a teacher might make available the material portfolios, assignments, and so on and review these with the students in preparation for either the teacher's conference with the parents or the student-led conference. For example, as conference time in one class nears, the teacher with some student help gathers stacks of the students' material on a table at the back of the room. Additionally, the students have access to a file where they have stored their ongoing portfolios, as well as past portfolios and other classwork. As the teacher prepares for teacher-parent conferences, she meets with her students one by one at the back table, and together they look through their work from among the stacks. In turn, they do the following: (1) review and discuss their progress, (2) consider needs to be met and recommendations for change, and (3) formulate what they might share with the parents. The teacher asks them to look over their efforts and to suggest features that they notice about their work. She probes each student in terms of what the student might want the teacher to share with her or his parent about her or his progress. The conference with each student's parent is scheduled over a few days and includes sharing of the portfolio selection as well as analyses by the teacher and the student of their progress. For some parents, the teacher is unable to meet face-to-face and instead pursues meetings by phone and e-mail.

In another classroom, the teacher also brainstorms with the students about what they might share with their parents in conjunction with a student-led conference. This includes looking over a reading-writing portfolio to select three different pieces that they have written and like. They are to write why they like their pieces and to choose one that shows improvement. They also look at projects that they and their classmates did as well as a range

TABLE 14.5 Some Steps in Planning and Conducting a Conference

Preparing for Conference

I. Gathering the resources together—teacher-student planning meeting. Students and teachers gather relevant material prior to meeting

II. In-class review of material—teacher-student conference. Classroom-based review with student work in preparation for reports to parents, parent-teacher conferences, parent-student conferences, etc. Student researches efforts and achievements toward organizing for a conference involving discussion of goals, progress, features, achievements, and future goals. This might occur in conjunction with conferences or open houses or via reports to be shared.

Holding Parent-Teacher or Student-Led Conference

I. Review of material. Teacher provides an overview (purpose, format, and ground rules) and then either the teacher or student shares portfolios, classwork, etc., and talks about goals and achievements. Parents review student efforts and are engaged in conversations, especially about achievements and progress to date.

II. Goal setting and planning to meet future needs. The student, teacher, and parents discuss possible future pursuits and talk about goals and needs. They also invite suggestions that might be helpful and plan ways to meet the students needs.

Follow-Up and Ongoing Review

Teacher evaluates the process and ways to improve the student and parent review, assessment, and goal setting. A follow-up report and note of appreciation are sent to the parents and students.

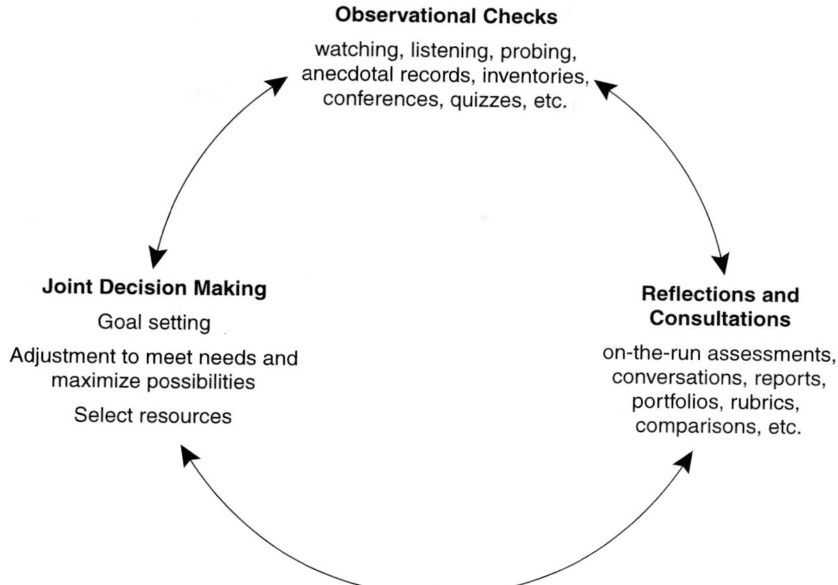

FIGURE 14.9 Cycle of Observational Checks, Reflections, and Decision Making

of other artifacts. Together the students and teacher make a list that serves as the agenda for what the students will share at the student-parent conference, open house, or a sharing meeting at home. The teacher writes notes to the parents to explain the procedure and provide guidelines for the parents' responses. The parents arrive in sets of three at preset times. Each child follows the guidelines and shares with parents their work; at the same time, the parents are invited to offer suggestions as to what they like. The teacher roams the room and sets up separate times to meet with each child's parents if it is requested or needed.

In both classrooms, the teacher orchestrates the review, but the students do the assessment and selection of the work. Also, students organize the material for the conference as well as provide comments on their own work. That is, the review of the material by the teacher and parents is under the direction of the student, regardless of whether the student is present at the conference. However, the teacher and the parents might have the option to hold a separate meeting to discuss some areas. Regardless of the approach, there are a number of steps that undergird decision making, and for each there is likely to be one or more conferences, as outlined in Table 14.5.

Figure 14.9, taken from Tierney et al. (2003), depicts how conferencing might fit into the cycle of classroom-based assessment activities.

A teacher can select from an array of formats for a conference, based on their goals, including how they wish to engage students and teachers around the table. Further, more than one conference format might be enlisted in the course of the schooling.

Tables 14.6 and 14.7 are taken from Tierney, Crumpler, Bertelsen, and Bond's overview of alternative formats for Parent-Teacher and Student-Led Conferencing.

Cautions and Comments

As greater emphasis is placed on accountability and joint decision making with students and parents, school personnel often will enlist conferencing as one of several means of achieving these and other ends. On the one hand, conferencing serves as an invaluable means of affording parents and students an opportunity to engage with one another in review, reflection, and joint decision making. On the other hand, they should not be used as the sole means of interacting with students and parents and in some circumstances may be problematic unless carefully planned and adapted to the needs of specific students and family situations. In particular, for some children and parents, such interactions may need a great deal of support and understanding. Sometimes the student's relationship to his or her parents may require adjustments so that the conference is productive rather than rote, negative, or simply a performance. Sometimes the student's circumstances and those of the parents may make it difficult because the conference times that are planned may conflict with other responsibilities of the parents. There are certainly a host of considerations that may need to be contemplated, and there may be other modes preferable to conferencing.

TABLE 14.6 Parent-Teacher Conference Formats

Type of Conferences	Description	Benefits	Factors to Consider
Format 1: Traditional Parent-Teacher Conference	Parent and teacher meet to discuss student growth and progress. Student is typically not invited to attend.	Open conversations between teacher and parent, sensitive issues can be raised and discussed.	Student not involved in conference, thus input from student. Child may become anxious about what is being said in his/her absence.
Format 2: Parent-Teacher Conference with Child Present	Parent and teacher meet to discuss student growth and progress. Student is invited to attend and listen to what is being discussed.	The student is able to hear the discussion between teacher and parent.	Both teacher and parent are guarded by what is being discussed.
Format 3: Parent-Teacher Conference with Input from the Student	The student begins the conference by sharing work samples that have been selected. Student then leaves the conference so the teacher and parent can continue conference.	Open communication between all stakeholders—student, parent, teacher. Parent can hear how child is doing from child's perspective.	Organization and preplanning of supervised activity for the students after leaving the conference. Some type of transition system in place to minimize distractions to others.

Source: Tierney, Crumpler, Bertelsen, and Bond, 2003.

TABLE 14.7 Student-Led Conference Formats

Type of Conferences	Description	Benefits	Factors to Consider
Format 1: Student leads and teacher prompts	The student leads the conference by discussing the selected pieces. As the child shares the work, the teacher prompts with questions or comments that assist the child in the description.	Child shares the work selected; child leads conference; open conversations between parent, teacher, and child.	Maintain an equal amount of involvement between student and teacher, create a balance between structured and open-ended exchanges, provide more time when planning and implementing this format.
Format 2: Shared conference with specific roles and responsibilities	Both teacher and student have a shared responsibility. The student leads parents through selected work samples. Teacher not present during initial conversations. Parents and student move to another table to set goals and discuss progress with teacher.	Child shares selected work, child leads conference, open conversations between parent and child.	Share conversations with parents during goal setting, emphasize activities with both teacher and students, provide more time when planning and implementing this format.
Format 3: Student leads and teacher floats	Several conferences are going on simultaneously in one room. The child leads the discussion, shares goals, and highlights learning strengths and areas needing improvement. Teacher floats around the room and is available to ask and answer questions.	Child is independent; child shares work selected; child leads conference; open conversation between parent, child, and teacher.	Share conversation with parents while drifting from conference to conference, provide more time when planning and implementing this format.
Format 4: Student as teacher/leader/informant	Conferences are conducted in the absence of teacher. Students share selected work with parents. Students lead parents through written evaluation/summary forms.	Child shares work, child is independent, opportunity for open conversation between parent and child.	Share conversation with parents while drifting from conference to conference, provide more time when planning and implementing this format.
Format 5: Student selects a committee	The committee selection guidelines are established by both students and teacher. The committee membership includes five individuals selected by the student with teacher input. Support and feedback are given by all committee members.	An excellent opportunity for student to showcase work, student selects the persons who will guide and support learning, encourages collaboration and ongoing dialogue between student's support system.	Provide appropriate monitoring and scaffolding of social and academic development, create flexible schedules for conferences, maintain open and continual communication between members.

Source: Adopted from Tierney, Crumpler, Bertelsen, and Bond, 2003.

In terms of learning, conferencing can serve an important role in engaging students in self-assessment and increasing their awareness en route to developing independence through understanding of their achievements and goal setting. In terms of assessment, conferencing ensures that parents, teachers, and students are conversing about issues of teaching, learning, and testing in the interests of the student and in ways that have been underemphasized in many school settings. The necessity of such transactions is key, especially regarding matters of literacy development for purposes of developing shared goals and ways of mutually supporting one another to make better-informed decisions about high-stakes assessment.

REFERENCES

Austin, T. 1994. *Changing the view: Student-led parent conferences.* Portsmouth, NH: Heinemann. Provides classroom-derived practical suggestions for student-led conferencing.

Bailey, J. M., and T. R. Guskey. 2001. *Implementing student-led conferences.* Thousand Oaks, CA: Corwin. Offers suggestions and steps for implementing conferencing.

Barclay, K., and C. Breheny. 1994. Hey, look me over: Assess, evaluate and conference with confidence. *Childhood Education* 70(4): 215–220. Explores the role of conferences in conjunction with student Portfolios and other activities.

Benson, B., and S. Barnett. 1999. *Student-led conferences using showcase Portfolios.* Thousand Oaks, CA: Corwin. Practical suggestions for conferencing in conjunction with student Portfolios.

Borba, J. A., and C. M. Olvera. 2001. Student-led parent-teacher conferences. *Clearing House* 74(6): 333–336. Describes the rationale and use of student-led conferencing.

Cleland, J. V. 1999. We can charts: Building blocks for student-led conferences. *The Reading Teacher* 52(6): 588–595. Explores the use of self-analysis charts in conjunction with student-led conferences.

Crumpler, T. 1996. Exploring a culture of assessment with ninth-grade students: Convergences of meaning within dramas of assessment. Unpublished doctoral dissertation, The Ohio State University, Columbus. Discusses differences in expectations of students as a teacher pursues learner-centered assessments.

Davies, A. 2000. *Making classroom assessments work.* Merville, BC: Connections. Practical suggestions for organizing a class around learner-centered assessment strategies, including conferencing.

Davies, A., C. Cameron, C. Politano, and K. Gregory. 1992. *Together is better: Collaborative assessment, evaluation and reporting.* Winnipeg, Manitoba: Peguis. Drawing on a research set of classroom-based experiences, the book includes guidelines and material to support three-way conferencing and reporting.

Farr, R. C., and B. Tone. 1994. *Portfolio conferences: The key to success in Portfolio and performance assessment: Helping students evaluate their progress as readers and writers.* Fort Worth: Harcourt Brace. Provides a rich description and valuable guidelines for conferencing with Portfolios.

Gregory, K., C. Cameron, and A. Davies. 2001. *Conferencing and reporting.* Merville, BC: Connections. Focuses on practical ways to engage students in their own assessments, including conferencing and reporting.

Kasse, S. 1994. Student–parent conferences: A new generation. *Teaching PreK–8* 25(3): 78–79. Explores practical advice for student–parent conferencing

Kaufman, D. 2000. Hearing Steve's Portfolio: The value of a student's talk. *The Ohio Reading Teacher* 34: 31–37. Discusses a student's self-assessment and its role in learning and assessment.

Le Countryman, L., and M. Schroeder. 1996. When students lead parent–teacher conferences. *Educational Leadership* 53(7): 64–68. Explores some of the issues involved in student-led conferences.

Little, N., and J. Allan. 1988. *Student-led teacher parent conferences.* Toronto: Lugus Productions. Draws on classroom examples to discuss student-led conferencing.

McDonald, J. P., et al. 1993. *Graduation by exhibition: Assessing genuine achievement.* Alexandria, VA: ASCD. Explores the use of exhibitions as a way of students sharing for assessment their achievements.

Monier, J. 1990. *The senior project.* Medford, OR: Far West Edge. Explores the use of a senior project as a way of engaging various parties in assessment.

Rogoff, B., C. G. Rurkanis, and L. Bartlett. 2001. *Learning together: Children and adults in a school community.* Oxford: Oxford University Press. Explores notions of community in teaching and learning theoretically and as part of a collaborative research initiative.

Santa, C. M. 1995. Assessment: Students lead their own parent conferences. *Teaching PreK–8* 25(7): 92–94. Practical advice on student-led conferencing.

Sills-Briegel, T., C. Fisk, and V. Dunlop. 1996–1997. Graduation by exhibition. *Educational Leadership* 54(4): 66–71. Explores the use of exhibitions as a vehicle for interactive assessments.

Tierney, R. J., M. Carter, and L. Desai. 1991. *Portfolio assessment in the reading-writing classroom.* Norwood, MA: Christopher Gordon. Explores conferencing as part of the Portfolio process.

Tierney, R. J., T. Crumpler, C. Bertelsen, and E. Bond 2003. *Interactive assessment: Teachers, parents and students as partners.* Norwood, MA: Christopher Gordon. Explores notions of partnership as well as details of various forms of conferencing.

Woodward, H. 1993. *Negotiated evaluation: Involving children and parents in the process.* Portsmouth, NH: Heinemann. Discusses the role of parents and students in classroom-based assessment, with suggestions for practices including ways to organize, observe, evaluate, and report.

NAME INDEX

SUBJECT INDEX